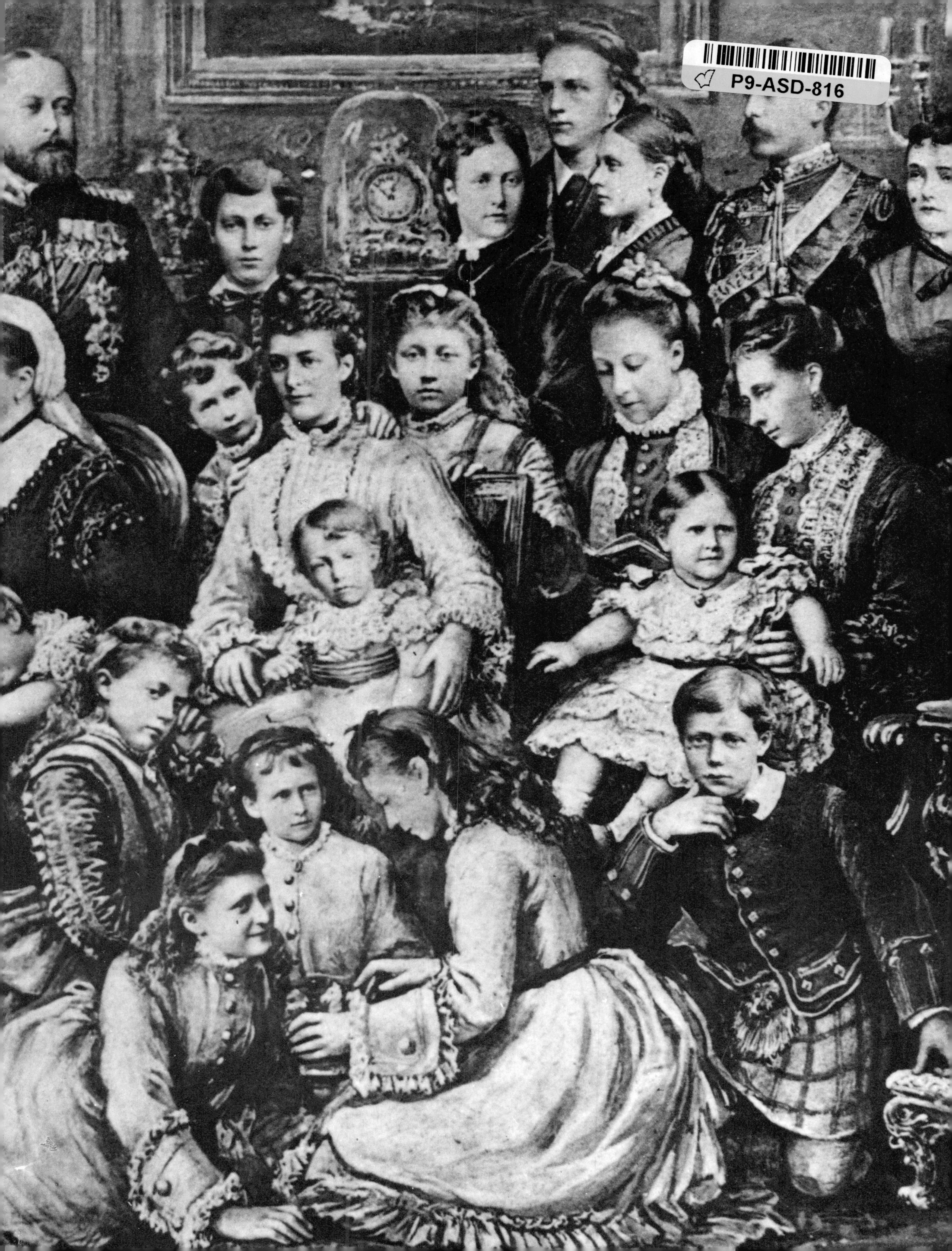

THE VICTORIANS
A WORLD BUILT TO LAST

Designed by Gilvrie Misstear

Published in England under the title *Rule Britannia : The Victorian World*
Copyright © 1974 by Times Newspapers Limited
All rights reserved
Published in 1974 by The Viking Press, Inc., 625 Madison Avenue, New York, N.Y. 10022
Published simultaneously in Canada by
The Macmillan Company of Canada Limited
SBN 670–74599–5
Library of Congress catalog card number : 77–101782
Printed in Great Britain

THE VICTORIANS
A WORLD BUILT TO LAST

Edited by George Perry and Nicholas Mason

The Viking Press

Contents

Acknowledgements

We are grateful to the following people who gave assistance in the preparation and research for this book: Bruce Bernard, Doris Bryen, David Collins, Celestine Dars, Brian Downes, Jeffrey Finestone, Erica Kirtley, Kevin McDonnell, Jane Mason, Margaret Smith, Jasmine Spencer, June Stanier. Thanks are also due to Godfrey Smith, former editor of The Sunday Times Magazine, and to various members of the staff of The Sunday Times and Times Newspapers Ltd.

Aberdeen University Library, 167. Ashmolean Museum, Oxford, 97. Australia News and Information Bureau, 78, 79, 80, 81(2). Baer Collection, 114–5, 116, 117. Mrs. Veronica Bamfield, 154–161(26). B. T. Batsford Ltd., 129, 164, 206–7. Birmingham Art Gallery, 101. British Theatre Museum, 202(2). Cadbury Brothers Ltd., 173. City of Liverpool Museum, 108(2). City of London Police, 219(2). City of Manchester Art Galleries, 102–3, James Coates Collection, 88. Stanley Collins, 21. Thomas Cook, 52. Country Life, 167. Crompton-Parkinson Ltd., 54–5, 58. Gibsons of Penzance, 126–27(12). Greater London Council, 30–1, 166. Greenwich Public Library, 26(2), 27, 28–9, 32(2), 34–5, 38–9. Guildhall Library, London, 100, 214, 217. India Office Library, 72(4). Charles Jerdein Collection, 85, 88. A. F. Kersting, 163. Lady Lever Gallery, Port Sunlight, 86–7, 104. London Electrotype Agency, 191. Lord's Gallery, 249. Mander-Mitchenson Collection, 195, 196, 197, 202(9), 203. Mansell Collection, 16, 26–7, 27(2), 36, 37, 58, 63, 64–5, 68, 69, 70–1, 75–5, 80–1, 106, 106–7, 108, 148–9, 153, 163, 180, 181, 182–3, 186, 187, 188(4), 189(3), 190(3), 191, 204, 211, 224, 225(2), 226. Mary Evans Picture Library, 33, 40(4), 41, 42(4), 43(3), 116, 151, 178, 185, 188, 190(4), 191, 230, 231(3), 232, 247(2), 248(2). Merryweather and Sons, 56. Metropolitan Police, 215(2). Donald McCullin, 170–1. National Army Museum, 73, 134, 137, 138–9, 140–1, 143. National Buildings Record, 22, 23, 24–5, 32, 41, 162(2), 164(2), 165(3), 166(2), 216–7. National Maritime Museum, 146–7, 150. National Monuments Record of Scotland, 165. National Portrait Gallery, 93. Pharmaceutical Society, 205. Walter Pilkington, 112. Popperfoto, 225. Radio Times Hulton Picture Library, 14–15, 16, 44, 45, 46, 47, 48(7), 49(7), 60, 61, 62(4), 63(3), 80(2), 82(4), 83(4), 92(12), 93(11), 107, 108–9, 112(5), 113, 120–1, 123, 124(2), 125, 128, 129(3), 130–1, 136, 142, 172, 185, 192, 197(3), 198–9, 200, 201(4), 206, 209, 210(10), 212(4), 215, 216, 217, 222(4), 223(4), 224(11), 225(9), 230, 231(2), endpapers. Royal Institute of British Architects, 163, 167. Royal National Lifeboat Institution, 124–5. Science Museum, 50–1, Mrs S. Spellman, 193, 195. Sutcliffe Collection, 234–245(15). Tate Gallery, 101. Thomas Photos, Oxford, 208, 210. Times Newspapers Ltd, 7, 8–9, 49, 210. The Times, 122, 123(2). Victoria and Albert Museum, 10–11, 37, 57, 94(2), 95(3), 96, 105, 110–1, 132. Walker Art Gallery, 97, 100. Walker Studios, Scarborough, 163. Young and Marten Ltd, 44, 45.

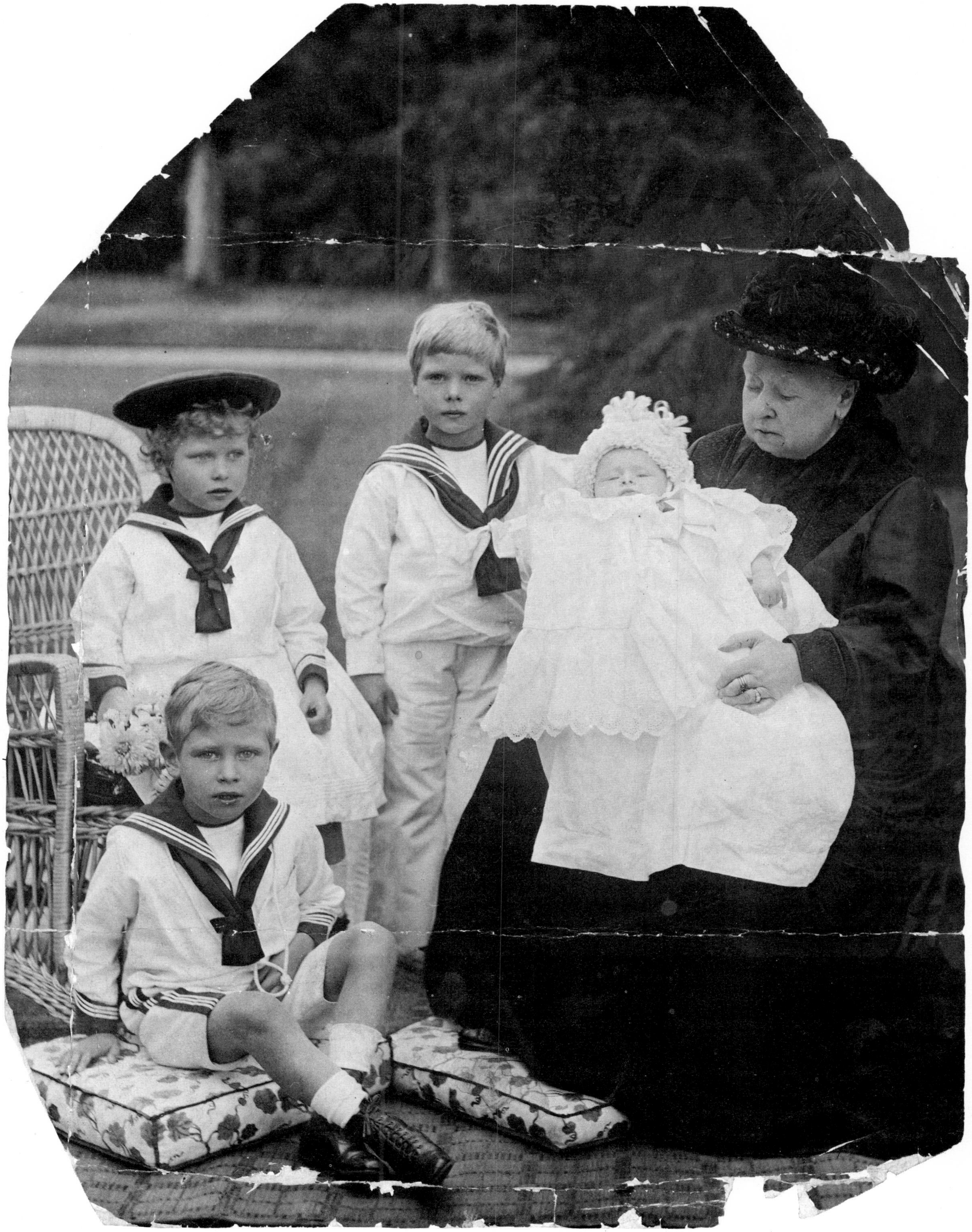

The twilight of an era: the Queen in 1900 with four of her great-grandchildren – from the left, Prince Albert (later George VI), Princess Mary (later the Princess Royal), Prince Edward (later Edward VIII), and the baby Prince Henry (later Duke of Gloucester)

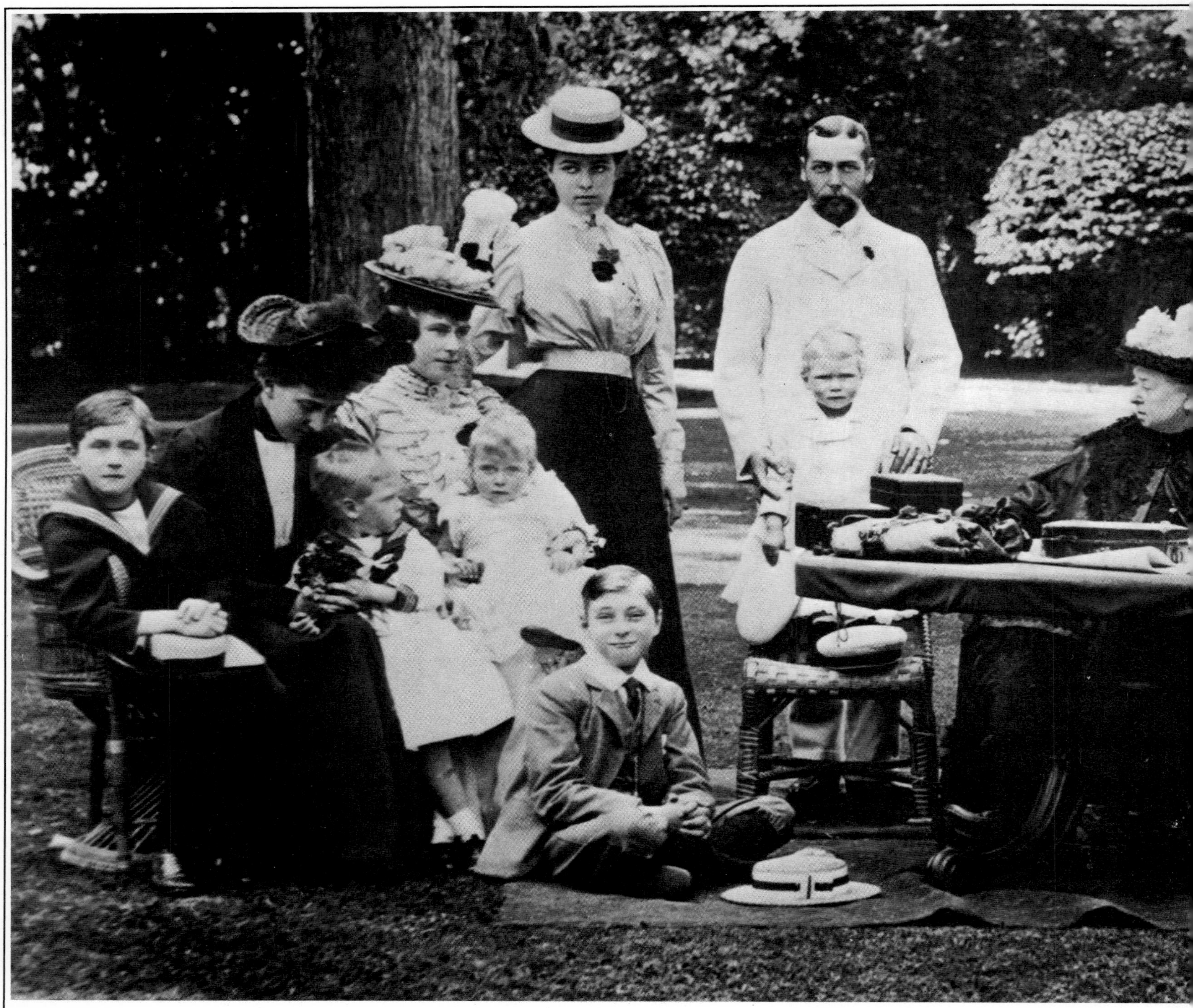

Introduction

To the generations who have witnessed Britain's constantly diminishing world status since the 1945 peace, the age of Queen Victoria seems a wondrous, even unbelievable epoch. Could this same small country only a century ago have been the most powerful nation on earth, its genius for industry, administration and conquest the envy of the world? In a stereotyped way we think of the Victorians as narrow, straitlaced and hypocritical, but in doing so we overlook their magnificent imagination, limitless confidence and passionate strength.

In so many ways that sixty-four-year reign is the apogee of British history. Centuries of mercantile and martial endeavour culminated in the prosperity of high Victorianism. Everything that has followed has inevitably seemed anti-climactic. The great queen survived into the 20th century by a narrow margin, expiring ironically when her Empire had taken its first sharp knock with the reprehensible Boer War. When Victoria ascended her throne in 1837 her England was still a largely agrarian country, its roads muddy and impassable much of the year, its cities dingy choleric slums, its government elected by a tiny elite. When she died it had become a highly industrialised society, and motor cars, telephones, electric power and even rudimentary wireless telephony were forming the beginnings of the modern age.

British society was shaped during the Victorian era. The obsessive Victorian urge for reform constructed the modern parliamentary system, produced the civil service, established the pattern of law and order, and institutionalised the church, education and the popular press in such a way that the marks are still indelibly inscribed today. Great British cities such as Birmingham, Manchester and Leeds are Victorian in conception, dominated by magnificent Baroque or Gothic town halls

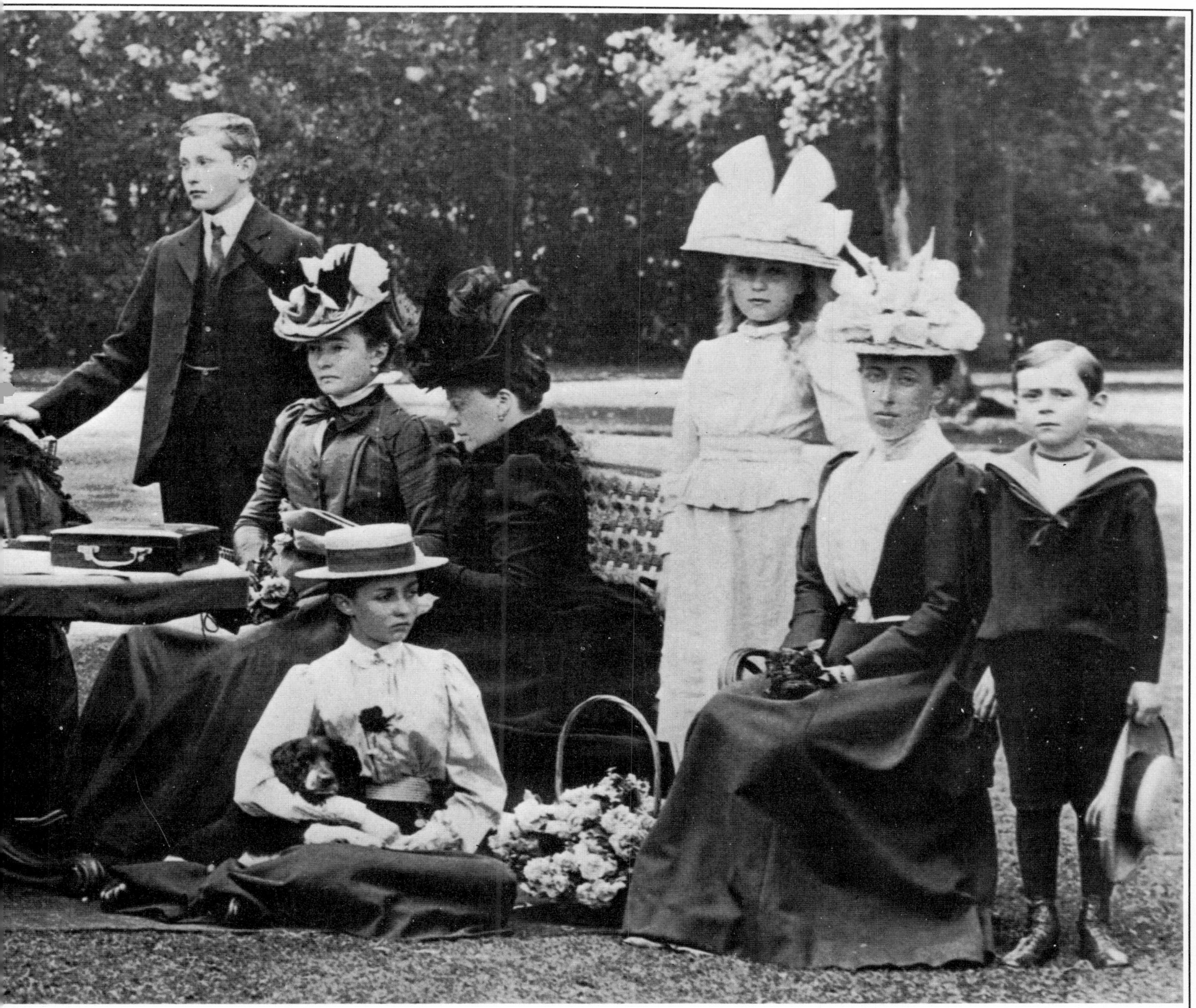

that symbolised the Victorian concept of organised local government. As for London itself the Victorian legacy is immense. From the stucco cliffs of Kensington to the miniature villas of Holloway, the capital was subjected to a building boom like nothing before or since. The Victorians built the suburban railways, giving birth to the commuter and enabling the new lower middle class of clerks to live in the country, yet be at their city desks by a quarter to nine. The parks, the museums, the palaces of entertainment flourished, while beneath the streets the magnificent sewers of Bazalgette ended the threat of typhoid. Outside Britain, the shaping of Australia was solidly Victorian, and in North America the era left its mark on every city and town.

How does Victorian moral rectitude square with the thousands of whores who swarmed throughout London's West End by night, or the canopied *maisons privées* at St John's Wood where a gentleman could install his mistress with perfect discretion? There are many paradoxes in the Victorian character, but of their many qualities a love of excess is very apparent. They were not people to do things by halves. Their booming factories, their garish advertising practices, their bold railways, their cheap newspapers, their devotion to the sabbath, all speak of a people endowed with zealous energy. They were discoverers in every sense, there was a restless need for progress and invention.

The many contributors to this book, with their special fascination for the Victorian period, have often developed new insights into the qualities and the attitudes of those very remarkable people, whose art, industry and social achievements are so fundamental to any understanding of the nineteenth century in the English-speaking world.

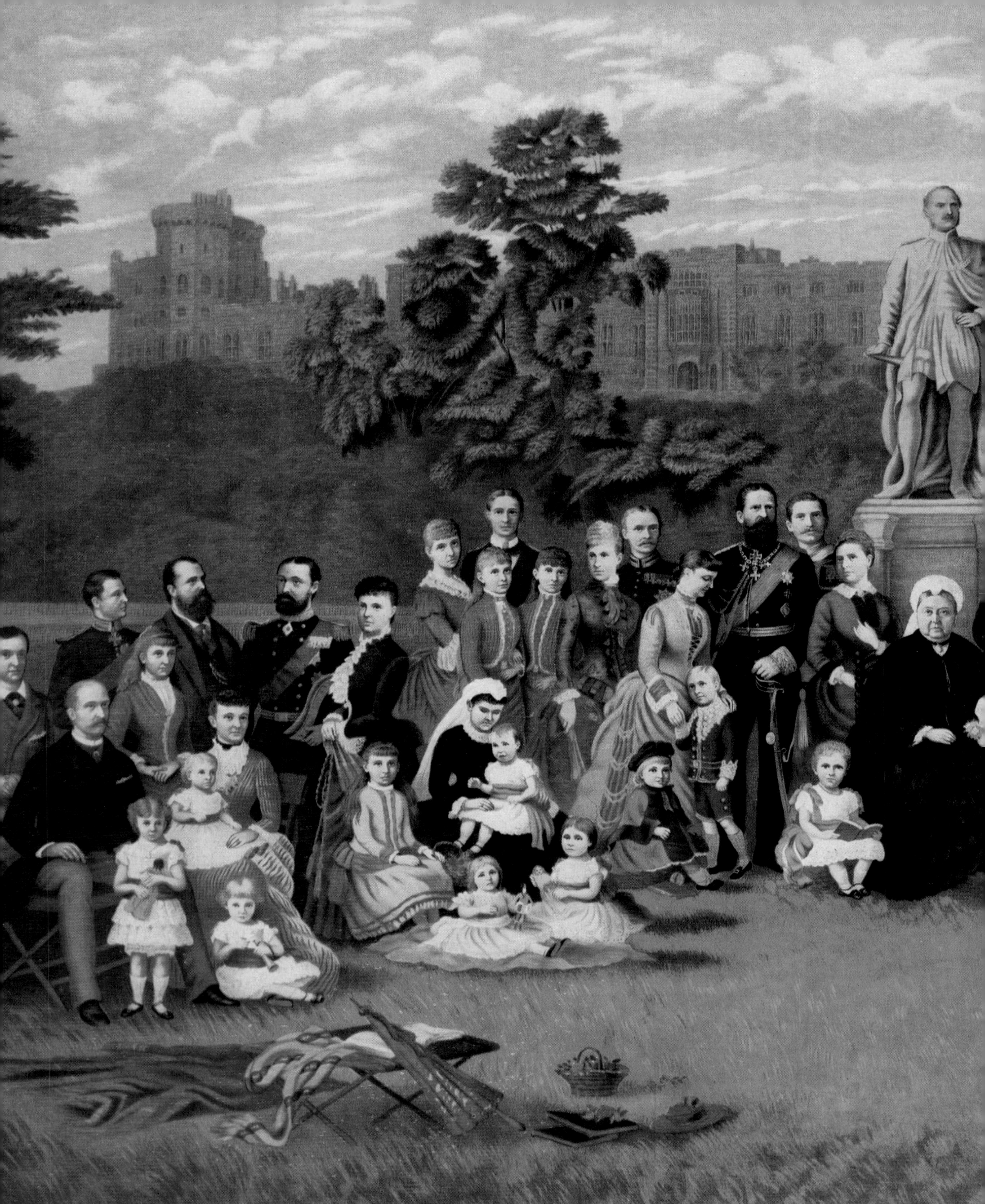

THE NATURE OF VICTORIANISM

By Asa Briggs. By the end of the 19th century (
unprecedented change, during which the word '

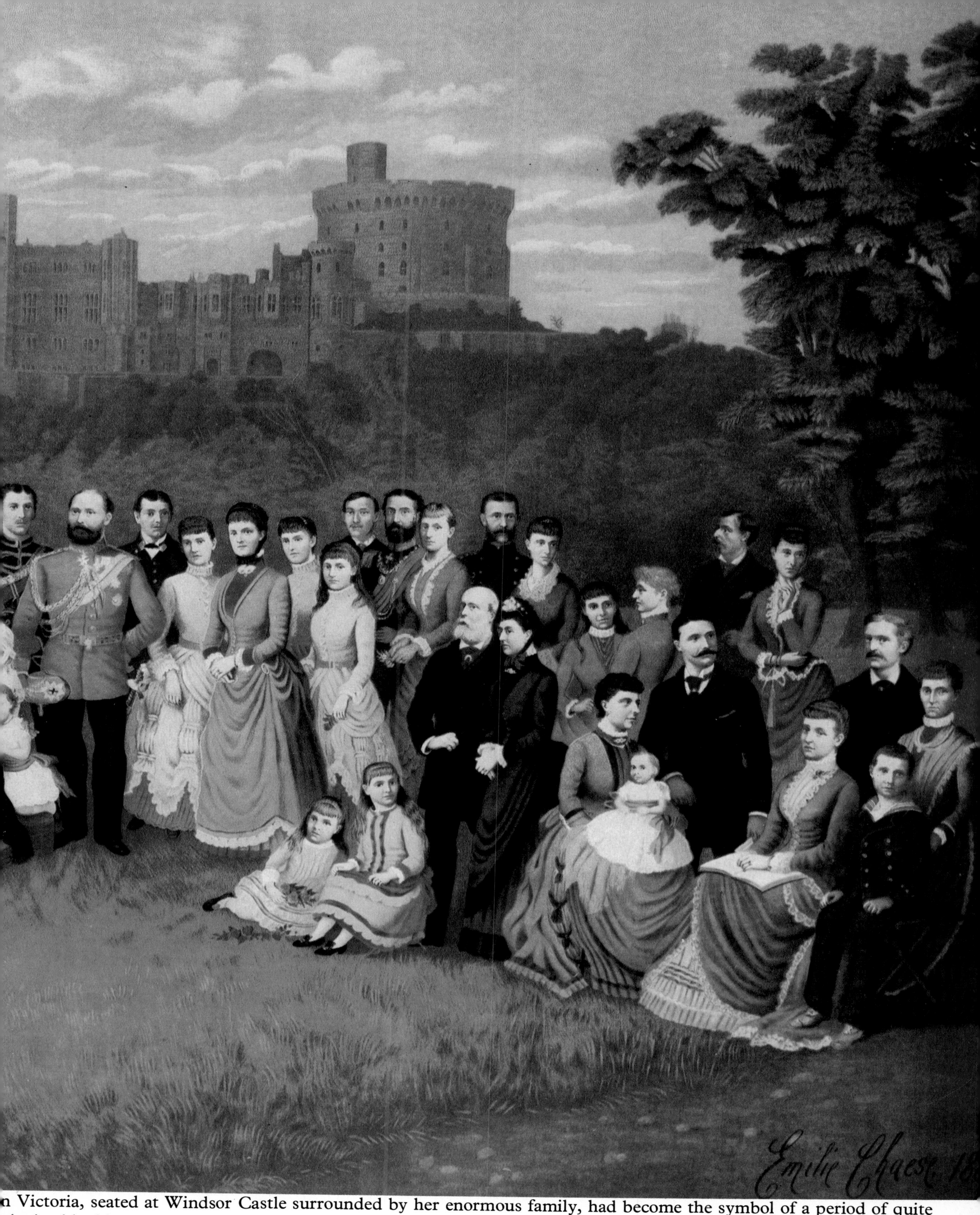
Emilie Chaese

n Victoria, seated at Windsor Castle surrounded by her enormous family, had become the symbol of a period of quite
rianism' had become a generalisation so beset with contradictions that the Victorians themselves had become wary of it

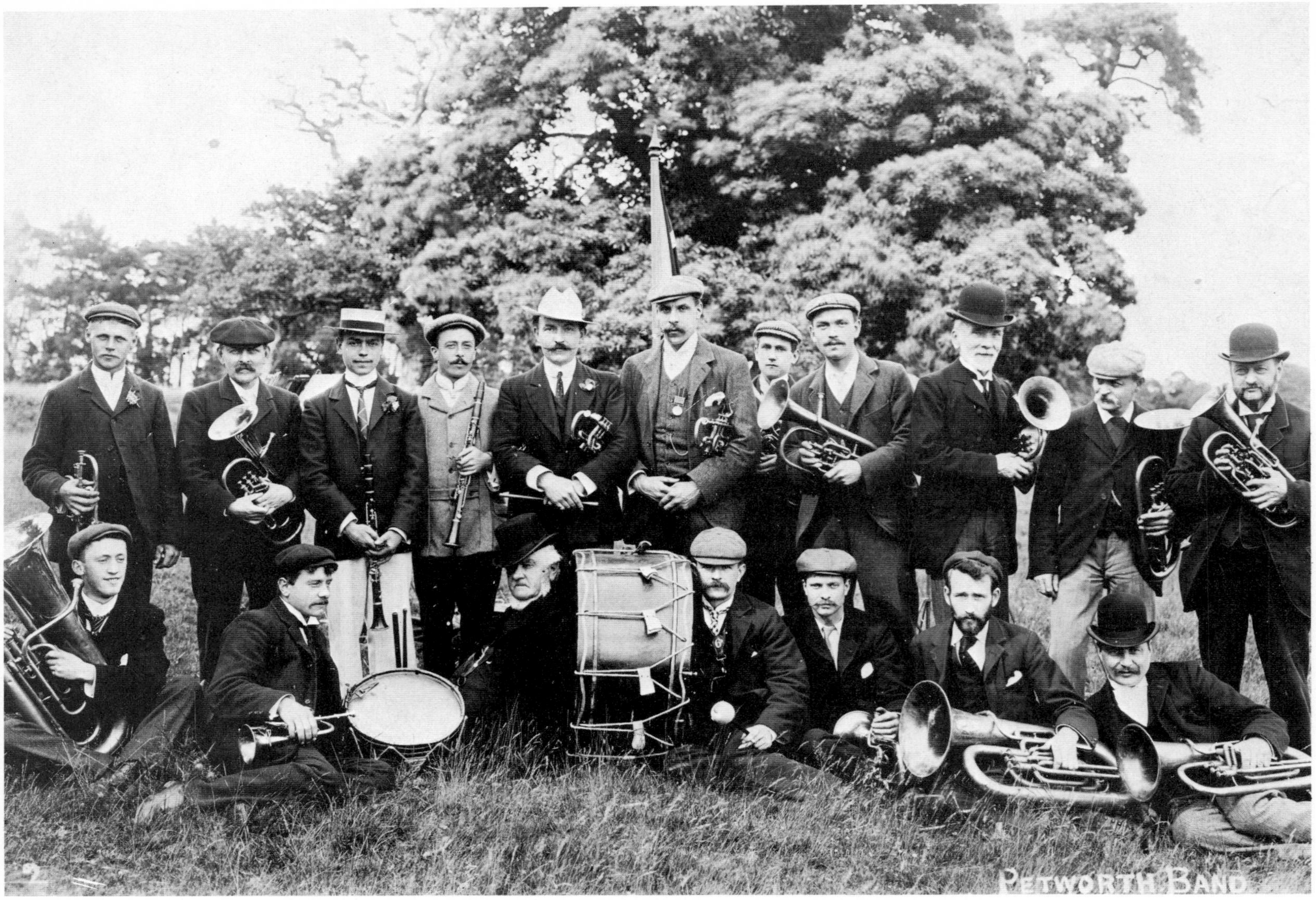
2
PETWORTH BAND

Community pride – the town band of Petworth, Sussex

Queen Victoria, who gave her name not only to an age but to an *ism*, was born in 1819 – the year of the 'Massacre of Peterloo', when the Yeomanry charged a crowd of Lancashire cotton workers – and died in 1901, less than a year after a London Conference had called into existence what soon became the Labour Party. She had reigned since 1837, for so long that in 1901 such was the ignorance of the right procedures to install a new sovereign that Lord Esher wrote in his Diary from the Court that "you would think that the English Monarchy had been buried since the time of Alfred".

Had Victoria not reigned so long, the age to which she gave her name would have been thought of not as one, but as several and the *ism* might never have been formulated at all. There were so many shifts of mood and circumstances between 1837 and 1901 that even the obvious and familiar division of the reign, like Gaul, into three parts – early, middle and late – does not do justice to the elements of discontinuity.

The main theme of the whole period was economic and social change – and the cultural response to it – but different changes took place at different times, at different rates and with different consequences. As for the *ism*, it was formulated not by believers but by late-Victorian rebels, many of whom in retrospect look like good Victorians themselves.

Victoria's death was rightly felt to mark the end of an epoch, carrying with it yet a new "sensation of universal change". Yet at the time of the two Jubilees of 1887 and 1897 and at the end of the old century which the Queen survived, contemporaries had tried to draw up balance sheets of historical achievement and failure. Already, indeed, in 1851, the year of the Great Exhibition, when the adjective 'Victorian' was coined, most of them were counting their "advantages and pleasures" and commenting with pride on what seemed to be a peculiarly British – or English – balance between "movement" and "order", change and continuity.

By 1887 Sir Walter Besant was a little less sure about what was happening and what had happened. The 19th century had 'begun' fifty years before, when the Queen came to the throne. "The steam whistle was already heard across the fields: already in mid-ocean the great steamers were crossing against wind and tide: Privilege, Patronage and the Power of Rank were already beginning to tremble, and were afraid." Yet for all his delight in technical progress, Besant added that "we who have lived in the century, we who are full of its ideas; we who are all swept along the full stream of it – we know not, we cannot see where it is carrying us."

Ten years later there was a great resurgence of pride – this time both of family and of imperial pride – with the large memorial volume *Sixty Years A Queen* providing yet another reappraisal, mainly of the social problems and responsibilities which the nation faced, yet the pride was not unanimous and there were powerful discordant

A country undertaker of 1890 in southern England. His hearse was relatively simple in appearance

voices among the critical minority. Kipling's *Recessional* was published as the days of the Jubilee came to an end: it included a warning against the "wild tongues" of men "drunk with sight of power".

As the century ended, there was no guarantee of future peace, no certainty about either the economic or social prospects of the country. "Who knows what fantastic horrors lie in wait for the world?" George Gissing, the novelist, asked gloomily in 1900. He went on to observe: "It is at least a century and a half since civilisation was in so bad a state."

Later assessments of Victorian England have varied substantially not only according to the mood or predilections of particular writers, but in the light of changing 20th-century experience – the disturbing experience in sequence of war, economic depression, shifts in international power, persisting awareness of predicament and crisis. We are now far enough away, however, from Victorian Britain at least to have disentangled ourselves from the emotional conflicts between fathers and sons or from the intellectual and cultural conflicts between the orthodox Victorians and the dissenters. From our own vantage point, a not very secure one, we can see that the history of the Victorians already has its own history.

Very soon after Victoria died, there was a tendency to forget how much change had taken place in thought and feeling between one part of the reign and another and to ignore the quite remarkable variety of attitudes and responses, hopes and fears, fashions and styles which had characterised 19th-century living. Everything was treated comprehensively as 'Victorian'. Six years before H. G. Wells summarily dismissed Victorian people in 1911 as "restricted and undisciplined, overtaken by power, by possessions and great new freedoms, and unable to make any civilised use of them whatever", A. J. Balfour, the first Conservative prime minister of the 20th century, had reacted sharply against the whole Victorian cultural panorama:

"It is probably due to the natural ingratitude which we are apt to feel towards our immediate predecessors. The middle third of the 19th century reminds me too much of Landseer's pictures and the revival of Gothic. I feel no sentiment of allegiance towards any of the intellectual dynasties which then held sway; neither the thin lucidity of Mill nor the windy prophesyings of Carlyle, neither Comte nor yet Newman, were ever able to arouse in me the enthusiasm of a disciple. I turn with pleasure from the Corn Law squabbles to the great War [the war against Napoleon], from Thackeray and Dickens to Scott and Miss Austen, even from Tennyson and Browning to Keats, Coleridge, Wordsworth and Shelley."

Lytton Strachey's *critique* of the Victorians and of Victorianism was an expression of a trend in thought and feeling which could be discerned long before the publica-

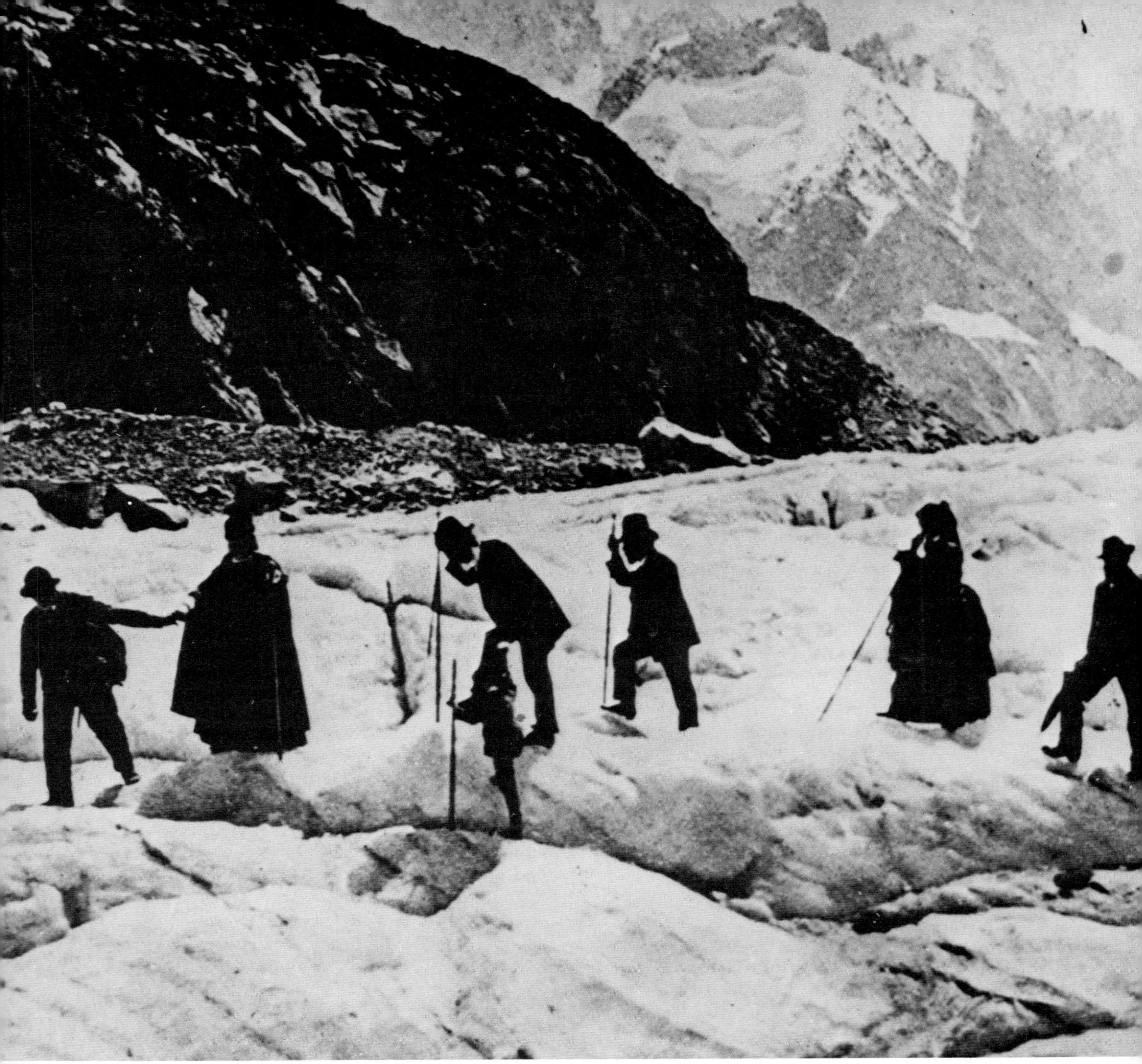

tion of *Eminent Victorians* in 1918 and *Queen Victoria* in 1921.

The counter-trend already has a long history of its own with Harold Nicolson writing in his *Tennyson* as early as 1923 of a "note of wistfulness" mingling with the laughter. "The tide is turning and the reaction is drawing to a close." In this history of changing reactions G. M. Young's brilliant *Victorian England: the Portrait of an Age* (1936) stands out as a landmark. Humphry House, who became interested in the Victorians because he had enjoyed Strachey, not because he was reacting against him, was directly involved in the Victorian 'aftermath'' if only because his first name was Arthur, he had a brother called Lancelot and a sister whose second name was Elaine. His own estimates of Victorian Britain are sensible and balanced, however, as is plain from his essay *Are the Victorians coming back?* which he wrote in 1948 when there were already many signs of a post-war Victorian revival – in history, literature, drama, architecture, the arts and not least in the market for Victoriana and Victorian decorative design.

The Victorians, House pointed out, knew that they were peculiar. They were conscious of belonging to a *parvenu* civilisation. "At one moment they are busy congratulating themselves on their brilliant achievements, at the next they are moaning about their sterility, their lack of spontaneity. In either mood they are agog at being modern, more modern than anyone has ever been before. And in this they were right. They took the brunt of an utterly unique development of human history; the industrialisation and mechanisation of life meant a greater change in human capabilities in the practical sphere than

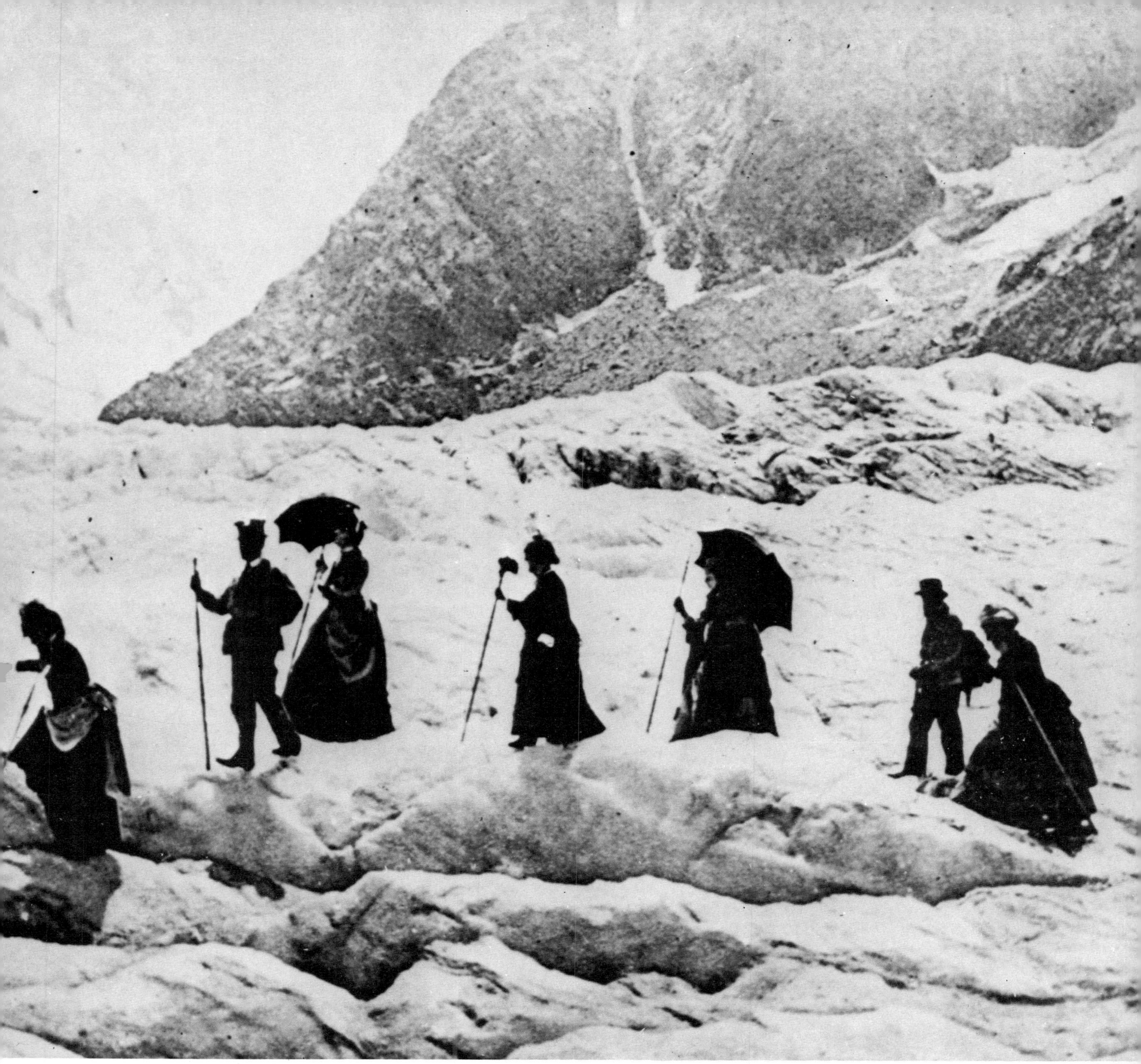

had ever before been possible. The test of assimilating this change meant a total disturbance of the traditional tempo and rhythm of life, an upset of all balance."

Other writers since 1948 have amplified this judgement. Indeed, there has been a burgeoning of Victorian studies on both sides of the Atlantic, with detailed investigations not only of the main trends of Victorian history – economic, social, political and cultural – but of strategic moments of "crisis" and of decision. The "game of selective Victorianism" – picking out particular facets of Victorianism and generalising boldly from them – has been shown to be both easy and dangerous, easy because the documentary materials are so abundant, dangerous because the evidence is contradictory.

The most satisfying way of beginning to understand the Victorians is to return to their own immediate

The Victorians invented group travel and the travel agency. Here English tourists inspect an impressive glacier at Chamonix in 1867

experience and to seek to appreciate and evaluate it directly. There are three difficulties, however, implicit in this approach.

First, much of that experience was "dressed up" in Sunday clothes. The moralising aspects of the *ism* were pervasive: they were expressed in aesthetics as much as in politics. Pictures, like people, for decades were expected to be good. John Ruskin complained feelingly of the painting by Millais *Mariana in the Moated Grange* that "if the painter had painted Mariana at work in an unmoated grange, instead of idle in a moated one, it had been more to the purpose both of art and of life". It is only usually through diaries and letters that we can recapture what Professor W. L. Burn, one of the most sensitive of recent writers on the Victorians, called in an appropriate fashion "moments of perception, cries of delight, the evidence that someone was seeing and living and feeling".

There is a second basic difficulty in the way. Much Victorian experience was not shared. At the beginning of the reign there were such sharp contrasts of experience both in cities and countryside, particularly for the rich and the poor, that those contemporaries who were forced to cross social dividing lines – particularly doctors and clergymen – resorted to the language of international exploration to describe journeys through their own country. "A hovel in one of the suburbs of London which they know least would be as strange to most Londoners as a village in the African forests." In the relatively prosperous middle years of the century Walter Bagehot, whom G. M. Young has described as the most Victorian of the Victorians if not the greatest of them, based his views of government and the need for "deference" and "mystique" on the fact that the Constitution had to satisfy at the same time highly sophisticated men of affairs and unbelievably ignorant Somersetshire labourers. Throughout the century Britain was caught up in the intricacies of a complex class system with two systems of authority conflicting or complementary or interpenetrating – the one derived from the land and its traditional power, the other derived from developing industry. Britain was never either by chance or by design a community of equals. The reign ended, as it had begun, with social exploration, with Charles Booth and others uncovering the cultures of poverty in the metropolis that was London.

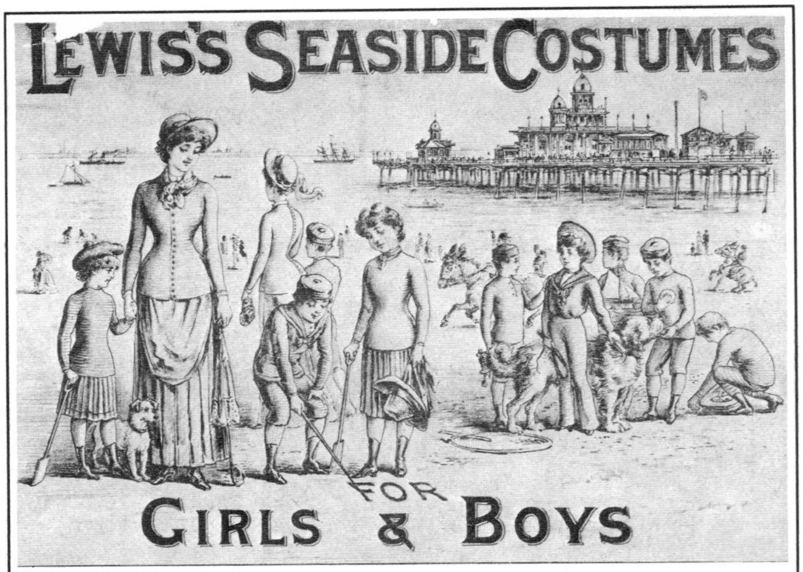
LEWIS'S SEASIDE COSTUMES
FOR
GIRLS & BOYS

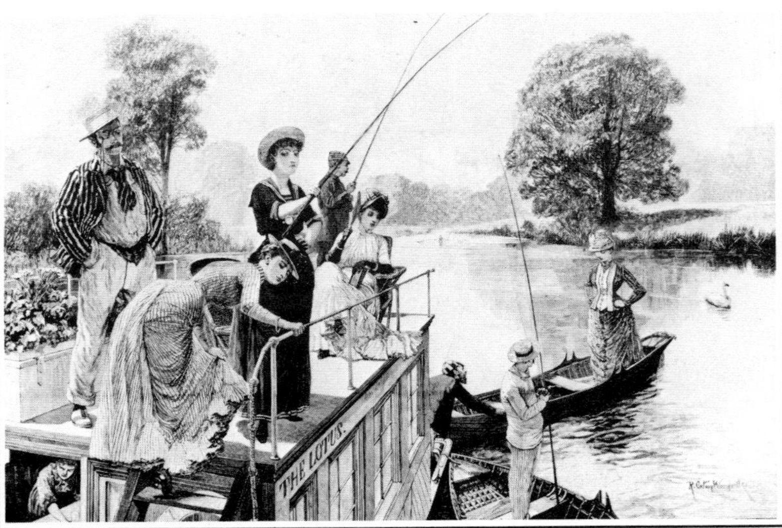
THE LOTUS.

Top: even seaside clothes had a stiff and formal air. Above: fishing from a houseboat could form the pretext of dalliance and flirtation

Sharp contrasts of social experience – and they were vividly expressed in the bleak statistics of life and death as well as of education or living standards – were always accentuated by contrasts of local experience. It was not until the 1880s and 1890s that the diverse provincial cultures began to give ground to London. The unprecedented social phenomenon of the early and mid-Victorian period after the great railway revolution was the large provincial city, and within each city there were distinctive sub-cultures with identifiable ways of life, the direct ancestors of Richard Hoggart's Hunslet. The "middle-class" cultures were as interesting as those of the working-classes. They were dominated by "amateurs" whose industry was as remarkable as their range, men who could turn from geology to philanthropy in the same mood of dedicated commitment. Religious concern could carry with it a cluster of other preoccupations, some leading away from religion itself. Only in the last years of the century did the growth of professionalism begin to change the texture of argument, and it was not by accident that the change was accompanied by the beginnings of the modern mass communications complex. The year 1896 saw the founding of the *Daily Mail*, the granting of wireless patents to Marconi, the first film show in London's West End and the end of the red flag era in motoring. All these instruments of change showed social implications which went further and yet were more difficult to forecast than the railway revolution with which the reign had begun in 1837.

The third difficulty in returning directly to Victorian experience is that it was seldom taken 'straight' even at the time. There were quite different ways of interpreting it. The Victorians were their own best critics – of the 'happy home', for instance, of the 'quiet village'. A periodical like the *Saturday Review* made the most of what was happening commenting, for example, on a murder trial at Aylesbury in 1857: "Fornication and adultery, incest and murder, abortion and poisoning – all the tangled annals of the poor – this is 'Our Village' at work – this is Christian and happy England". The lines of social criticism, not straight lines, from Carlyle to Arnold and Ruskin and from Ruskin to Morris, emphasised both the banality and the injustice of much accepted Unitarian experience.

Questions were asked not only about abstractions like "progress" – there were plenty of these even in 1851 – or about "cant" or about "problems", but about the rhythms of daily life and the sights and sounds of the changing environment. "What was the good of a train taking them quickly from a dismal and illiberal life in Islington to a dismal and illiberal life in Camberwell?" asked Arnold. "Was it all to end in the counting house on the top of a cinder heap," asked Morris, who could never escape questions about long-term direction, "with

Podsnap's drawing room in the offing, and a Whig committee dealing out champagne to the rich and margarine to the poor in such convenient proportions as would make all men contented together, though the pleasure of the eyes was gone from the world, and the place of Homer was to be taken by Huxley?"

During the middle years of the century, there was confidence, generally if not universally shared, that labour and toil could lead to the Elysian fields. No age made more of the gospel of work or of the ideal of the busy, active, outward-looking individual. "The extremely practical character of the English people" was a theme stressed as much by John Stuart Mill as by Samuel Smiles. The new magazine *Engineering* proclaimed boldly in its first leader in 1866 that through the triumphs of industry – still thought of as much as a moral quality of the individual as a segment of economic activity – "a grand plan of civilization" was being worked out. "Fifty years are nothing in the history of mankind – as nothing in relation to time. Yet fifty years have made England a new nation. There is tenfold more practical sense, more genuine Christian feeling – tenfold more natural happiness."

Certain simple values, derived from life not from books, were believed to lay the foundations of character – endeavour, duty, abstinence, thrift were prominent among them – and character was believed to lay the foundations of national strength. "Nothing creditable," Smiles warned his readers, "can be accomplished without application and diligence. The student must not be daunted by difficulties, but must conquer them by patience and perseverance, and above all, he must seek elevation of character without which capacity is worthless."

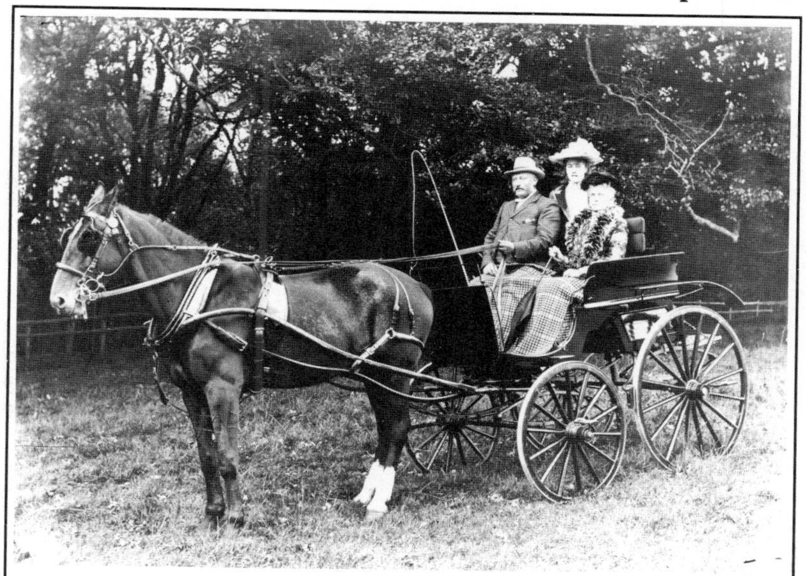

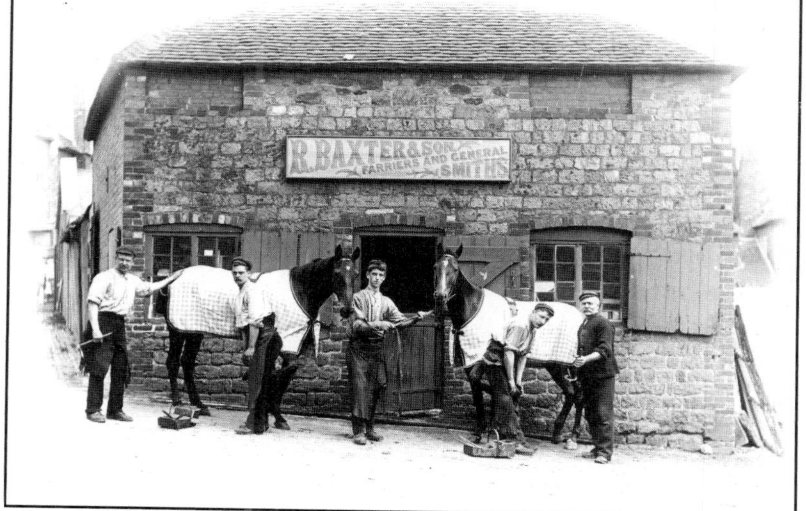
R. BAXTER & SON
FARRIERS AND GENERAL
SMITHS

Top: the dog cart's middle-class respectability. Above: the blacksmith – Victorian service station. Overleaf: country picnic in Sussex

Some Englishmen, even in the middle years of the century, were profoundly uneasy about the limitations of this philosophy. Arnold, for example, extolled the pleasures of standing still and pitted the cultivation of the mind against the restless display of practical energy. Yet foreign visitors were sceptical about both the willingness and the ability of Englishmen to emancipate themselves for the round of toil and the ethics of work which they imposed not only on themselves but on others. Hippolyte Taine in his *Notes on England* remarked on how enthusiastically every after-dinner speaker "trumpeted his own little fanfare in honour of Anglo-Saxon energy, the propagation of British civilization, the future of humanity and the progress of science" to the accompaniment of banging of knives on the table, loud "Hear! Hears!" and a few cheers.

Fortunately, and to the everlasting credit of the Victorians, they argued about themselves at least as passionately as mid-20th-century Americans, with whom they had much in common. Mill complained about their conformity. "The individual or the family do not ask themselves – what do I prefer? or what would suit my character and disposition? They ask themselves what would be suitable to my position? What is usually done by persons of station and circumstances superior to mine?" Dickens, through Pecksniff and Podsnap, complained of hypocrisy, as did George Eliot, through Bulstrode, in the greatest of all Victorian novels, *Middlemarch*. "I don't want to know about it; I don't want to discuss it; I won't admit it" is Podsnap's philosophy as set out in *Our Mutual Friend* in a chapter tellingly entitled 'The Sweat of an Honest Man's Brow'. "A truly refined mind will seem to be ignorant of the existence of everything that is not perfectly proper, placid and pleasant."

We now know enough of the so-called "other Victorians" to realise how murky Victorians could be – how much was left out of the novels or had to be left out; how prostitution was related directly and regularly to the marriage pattern; how pornography coexisted 'naturally' with 'official' writings on sex by William Acton, the Samuel Smiles of continence. We also know how much drudgery was conveniently hidden away from view in statements about the gospel of work. And we also know that it was possible for Arthur Hugh Clough, Arnold's friend, to write at the time in his famous *Decalogue*:

"Thou shalt not steal: an empty feat
When it's so lucrative to cheat.
Thou shalt not covet, but tradition
Approves all forms of competition."

Such criticisms were clearly and openly stated before the late-Victorian rebels created a sense of Victorianism out

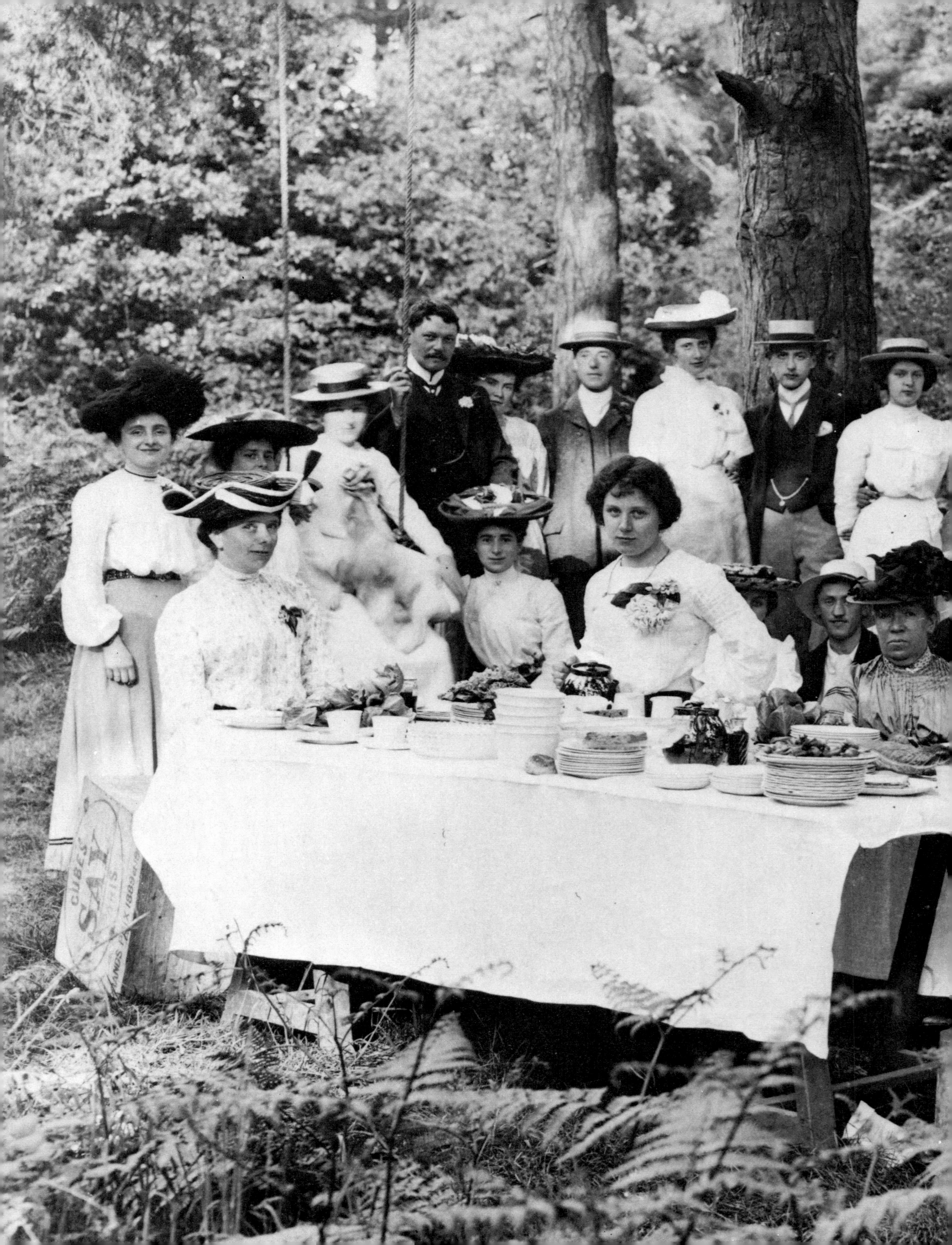
CUBES
SAY
1889

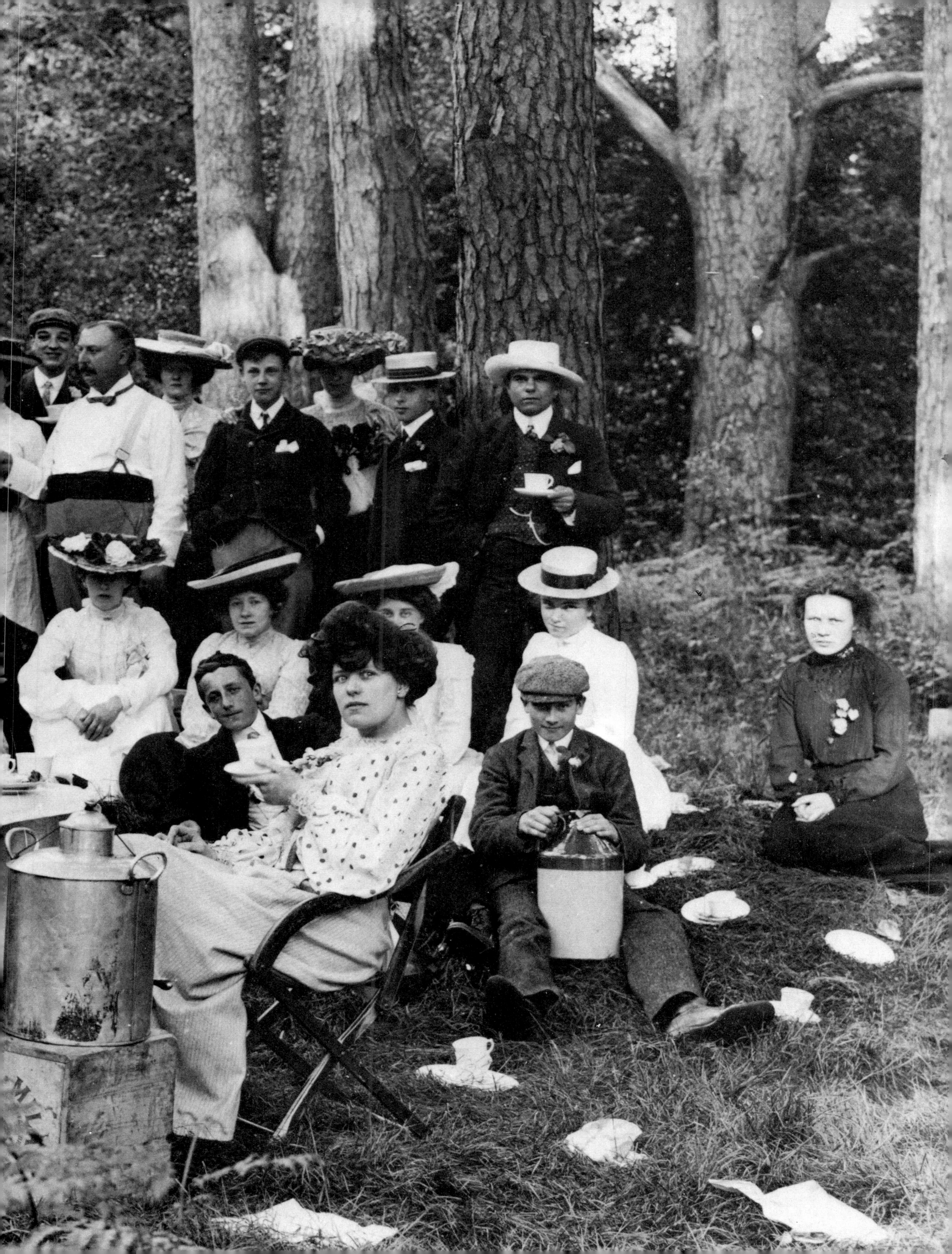

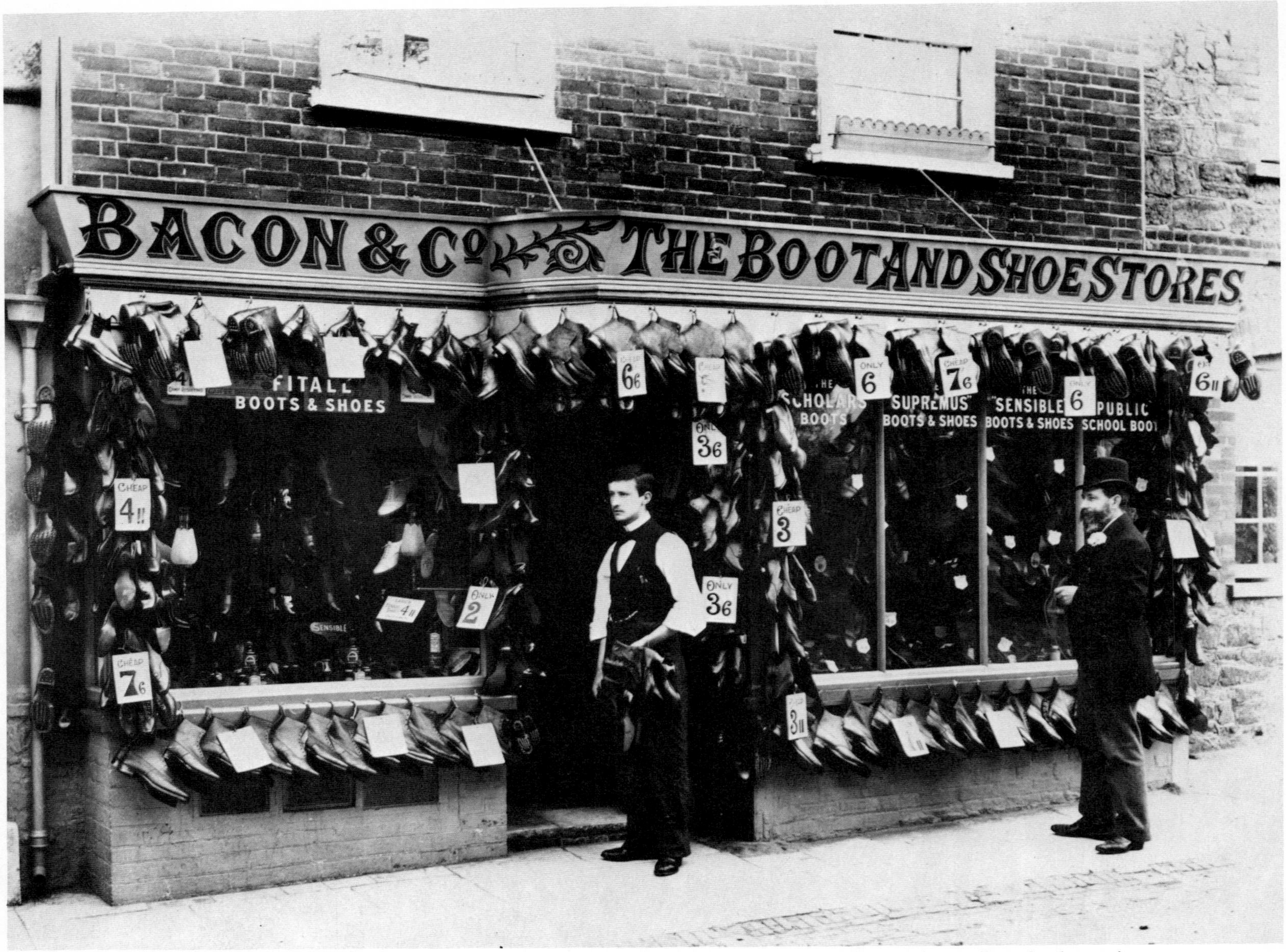
BACON & Co THE BOOT AND SHOE STORES
FITALL BOOTS & SHOES
SUPREMUS BOOTS & SHOES
THE SENSIBLE BOOTS & SHOES
PUBLIC SCHOOL BOOT
Manufacturing transformed the footwear trade and enabled cheap boots and shoes to be marketed at low prices

of a sense of opposition; lampooning earnestness above all else. Ernest Pontifex in Samuel Butler's *Way of All Flesh*, which was not published until 1903, is one symbol of the later attack: *The Importance of Being Earnest* (1896) is another. The sub-title of the latter was "A Trivial Comedy for Serious People: Ernest in Town and Jack in the Country". One of Ernest Pontifex's most memorable remarks is "there are a lot of things which want attacking and yet no one attacks them. It seems to me that I can say things which not another man in England except myself will venture to say, and yet which are crying out to be said."

The late-Victorian rebels stood many things on their heads. Which mid-Victorian could have written as Oscar Wilde did – obviously under the influence of George Bernard Shaw – "The virtues of the poor may be readily admitted, and are much to be regretted. The best among the poor are never grateful. They are ungrateful, discontented, disobedient and rebellious. They are quite right to be so."? Respectability suffered more than any other mid-Victorian virtue, but the attack was general. True individuality, it was maintained, could be asserted only if there were changes in social structures and moral code. For a complete rebel like Edward Carpenter the millennium was not one of "riches nor of mechanical facilities" but of "freedom and joy". In this *milieu*, favourable to Socialism, Shaw was a central figure, poking fun at the mid-Victorian belief in law, proclaiming the will, mocking mid-Victorian tastes, and through his eloquent defence of Ibsen bringing the late-Victorian revolt into line with a general European revolt in which the artist took a prominent place.

Yet the revolt was quelled in the late 1890s – Wilde's trial was something of a turning point – and between the Golden Jubilee and the end of the reign there were more signs of pride and prejudice than of break-through. There were other problems, indeed, in late-Victorian England which are now receiving more attention from historians than the limited cultural revolution. During the last years of the century, the prelude to our own times, foreign competition, along with worries about productivity and industrial relations, led a group of anxious critics to complain that Britain was "slipping" as a great industrial power or at least as a great industrial power with the will and the skill to introduce and to encourage technical innovation. The limitations of the industrial revolution began to be apparent. Britain was no longer the workshop of the world, as the sponsors of the Great Exhibition of 1851 had triumphantly proclaimed. The rate of capital formation lagged far behind

A courting couple from London pay a summer visit to Box Hill, a popular beauty spot near Dorking, in 1877

that of the United States, as did investment expenditure as a proportion of national product, and much of the investment was concentrated in activities which provided no guarantee of future economic growth.

Not surprisingly, much of the social investment on which we continue to rely – schools, hospitals, shopping centres, hotels, places of entertainment – belongs to the last part of the century, and we are often in danger of identifying what looks Victorian in terms of this period. The values, however, had shifted. When Elie Halévy, the great French historian of 19th-century Britain, took up the story again in 1895, having left a great gap in his narrative after the 1850s, he commented shrewdly that "the period between 1895 and 1914 does not belong to the British 19th century, as I understand it. It is at most the epilogue of that century, as it is the prologue of the century which opened with those four years of tremendous upheaval, both military and social." It has rightly been said that there was much Victorianism before Victoria: it may equally properly be said that there was much post-Victorianism before Queen Victoria's death.

The new interest in the late-Victorian years, unlike the immediate post-1945 interest in the mid-Victorian years, is not nostalgic or escapist. It pivots on the question, far too general to be helpful, "Where did the Vic-

torians go wrong?" Was imperialism a deviation? Was the structure of industry too rigid and assured? Was government too smug? Was the new model civil service, which Graham Wallas once described as "the one great political invention in 19th-century England", adequately equipped to deal with a changing society? Was the curiously class-bound society which continued to provide picturesque contrasts of circumstances at the beginning of the new century the kind of society which could expect to transform itself gradually without the country losing drive and momentum? Was G. M. Young right when he observed that "the great Victorian omission" was the failure before 1902 to provide a national secondary school system?

Such questions reveal more about our own preoccupations than they do about the Victorians, though some, at least, of the questions were asked by Victorians themselves. To understand them, we must not forget, as we burrow into the vast store of evidence, statistical, documentary, visual, that they left behind, that they were very different. As Professor Burn has written, "Over and over again, one comes across modes of thought and action so bizarre, so little credible, that the men and women who practised them appear as the inhabitants, not just of another century but of another world."

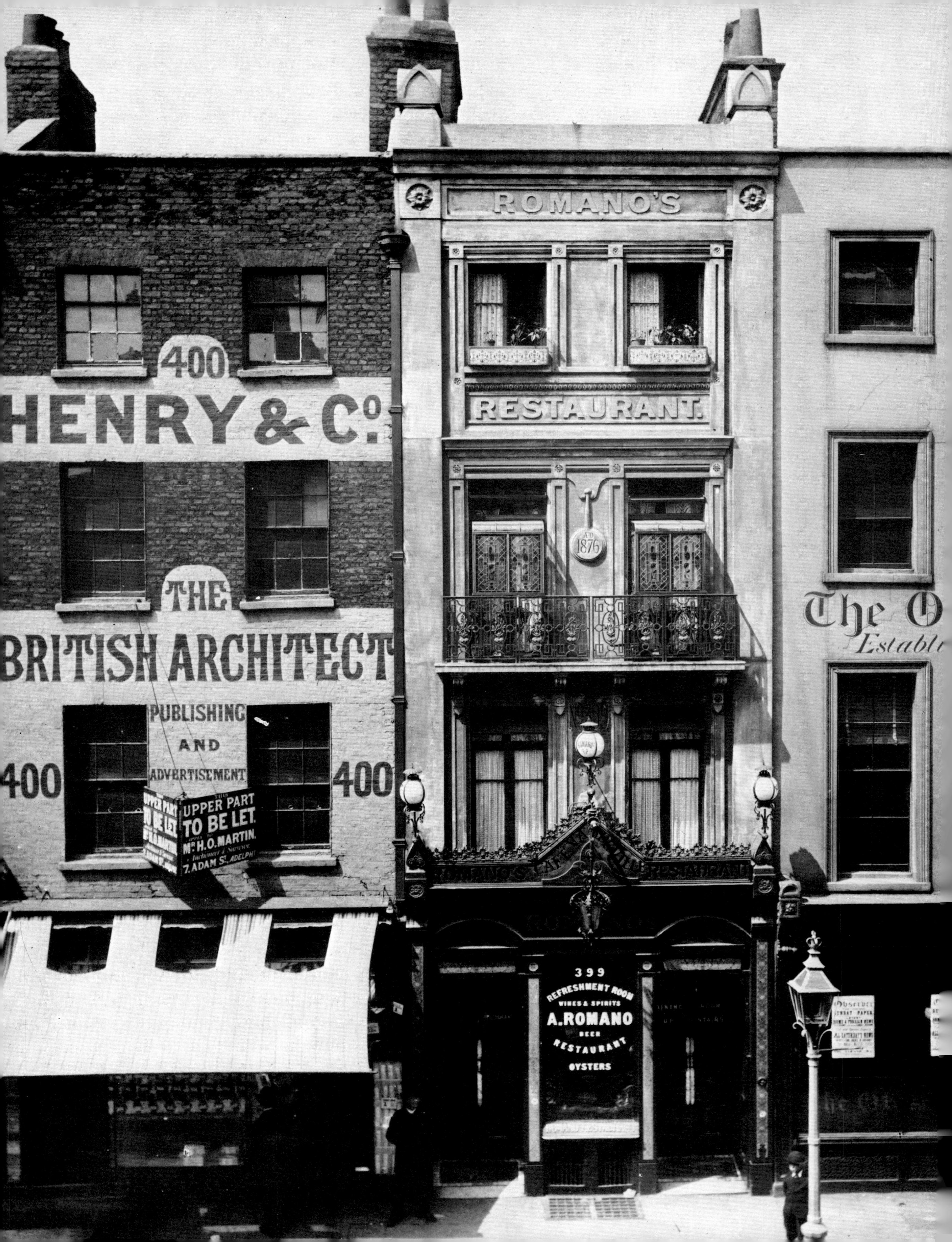
400
HENRY & Co.
THE
BRITISH ARCHITECT
PUBLISHING
AND
ADVERTISEMENT
400
400
THIS UPPER PART TO BE LET.
APPLY TO Mr. H.O. MARTIN.
7. ADAM St. ADELPHI
ROMANO'S
RESTAURANT.
A.D. 1876
ROMANO'S CAFÉ ... RESTAURANT
399
REFRESHMENT ROOM
WINES & SPIRITS
A. ROMANO
BEER
RESTAURANT
OYSTERS
The O
Establi

THE IMPERIAL METROPOLIS

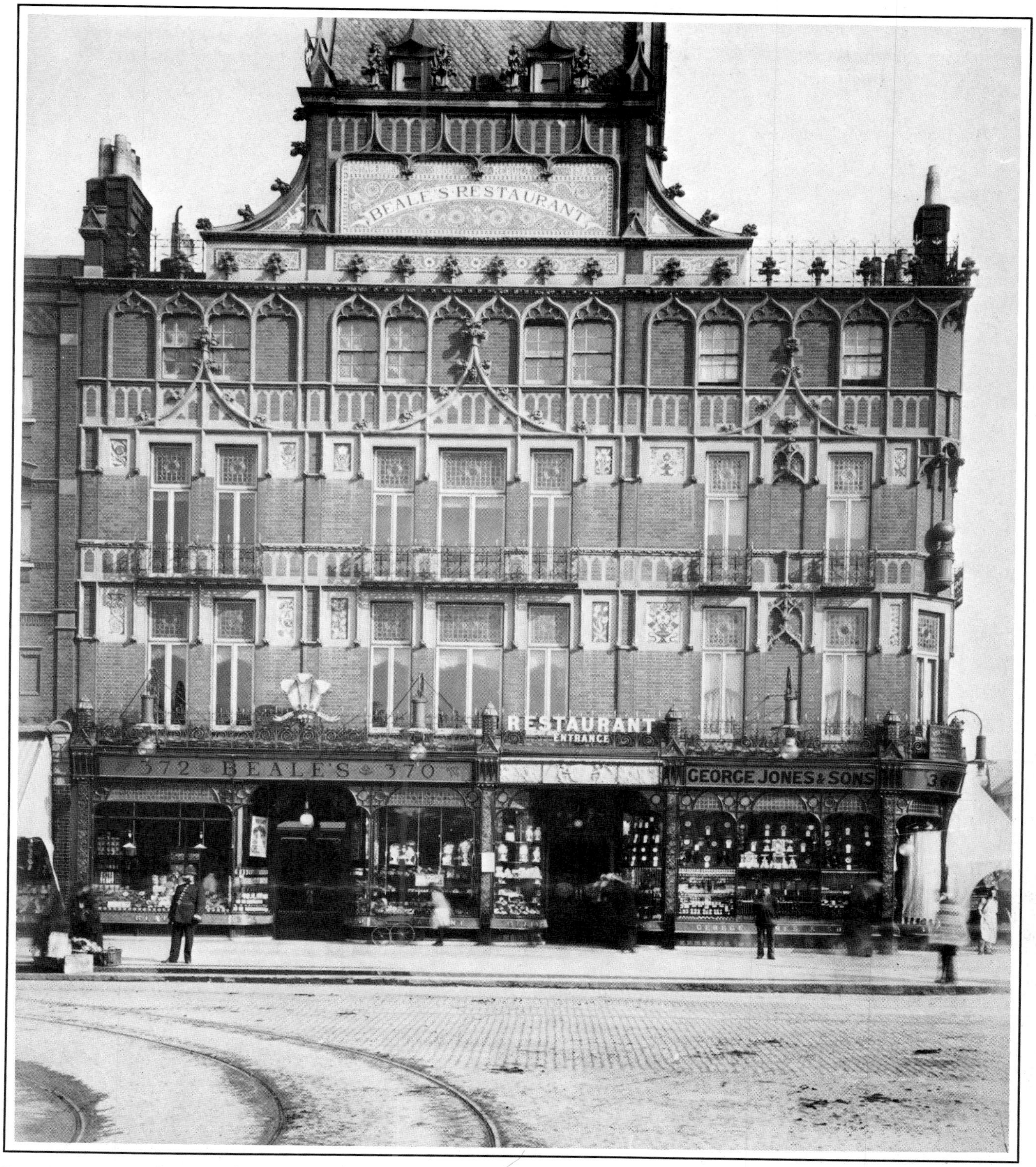
BEALE'S RESTAURANT
RESTAURANT
ENTRANCE
372 BEALE'S 370
GEORGE JONES & SONS

London at the beginning of Queen Victoria's reign was little more than a large country town. Its bridges were clogged with hay carts and sheep were still driven along its streets. But already the first London railway line to Greenwich had been opened. The railways transformed the city. By the end of the 19th century the former villages on the outskirts had been enveloped by a great tide of bricks and mortar and were transformed into dense inner suburbs. The Victorians gave London a transport network of railways, including the first to run underground; horse-buses and trams; a prosperity based on commerce and industry, which was enhanced by the Great Exhibition of 1851; and the finest drainage system in the world. London stood at the centre of a great Empire, a proud capital that was compared to ancient Rome. But it was still a city in which the rich got richer, the new middle class flourished and the poor were left to sink in the stews

Above: This ornate restaurant in Holloway Road had its own grocery store.
Opposite: Romano's in the Strand was for many years a fashionable place for dining out

Piccadilly Circus in the 1890s – the hub of the West End, with the Earl of Shaftesbury's memorial fountain a new London landmark

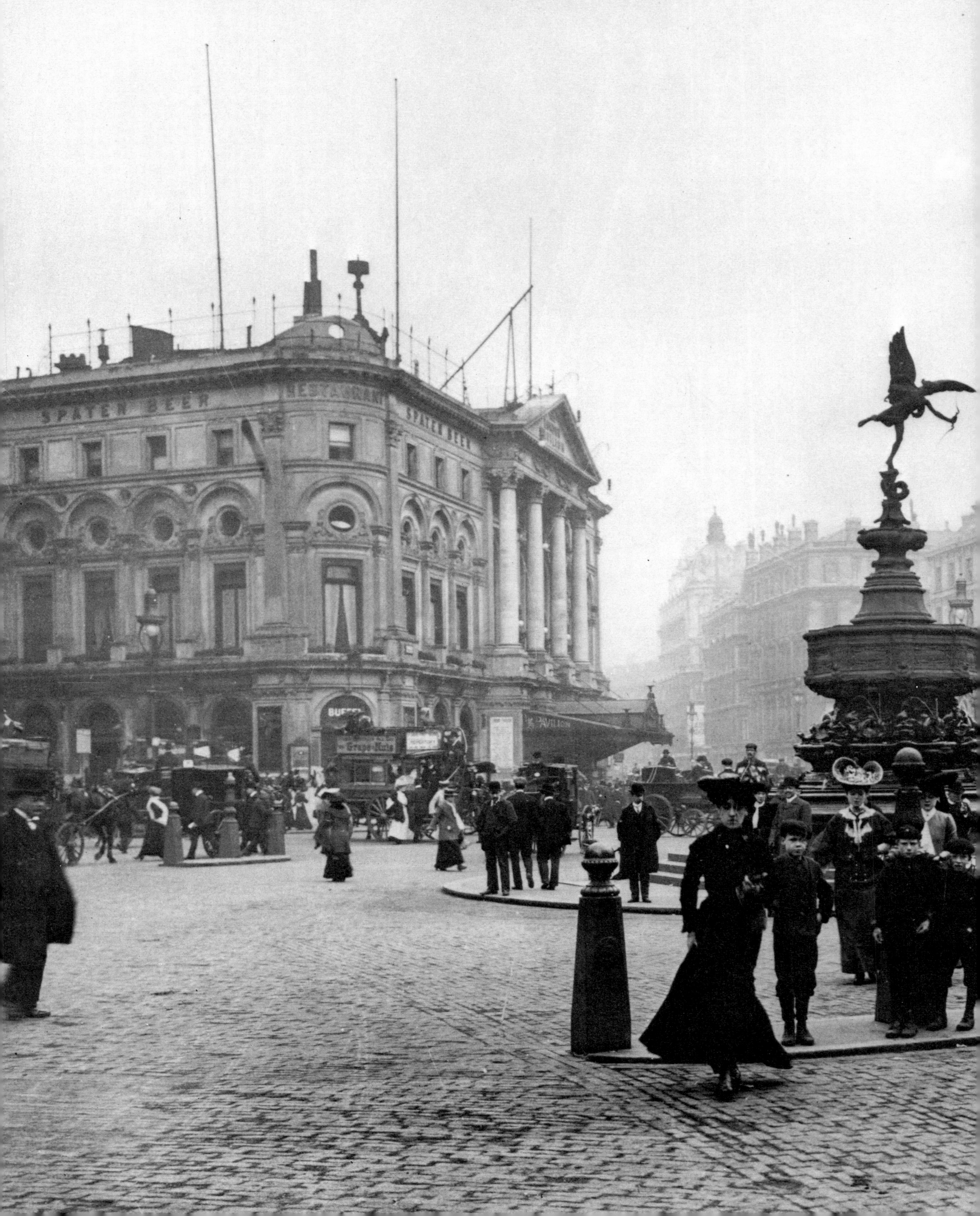
SPATEN BEER
RESTAURANT
SPATEN BEER
BUFFET

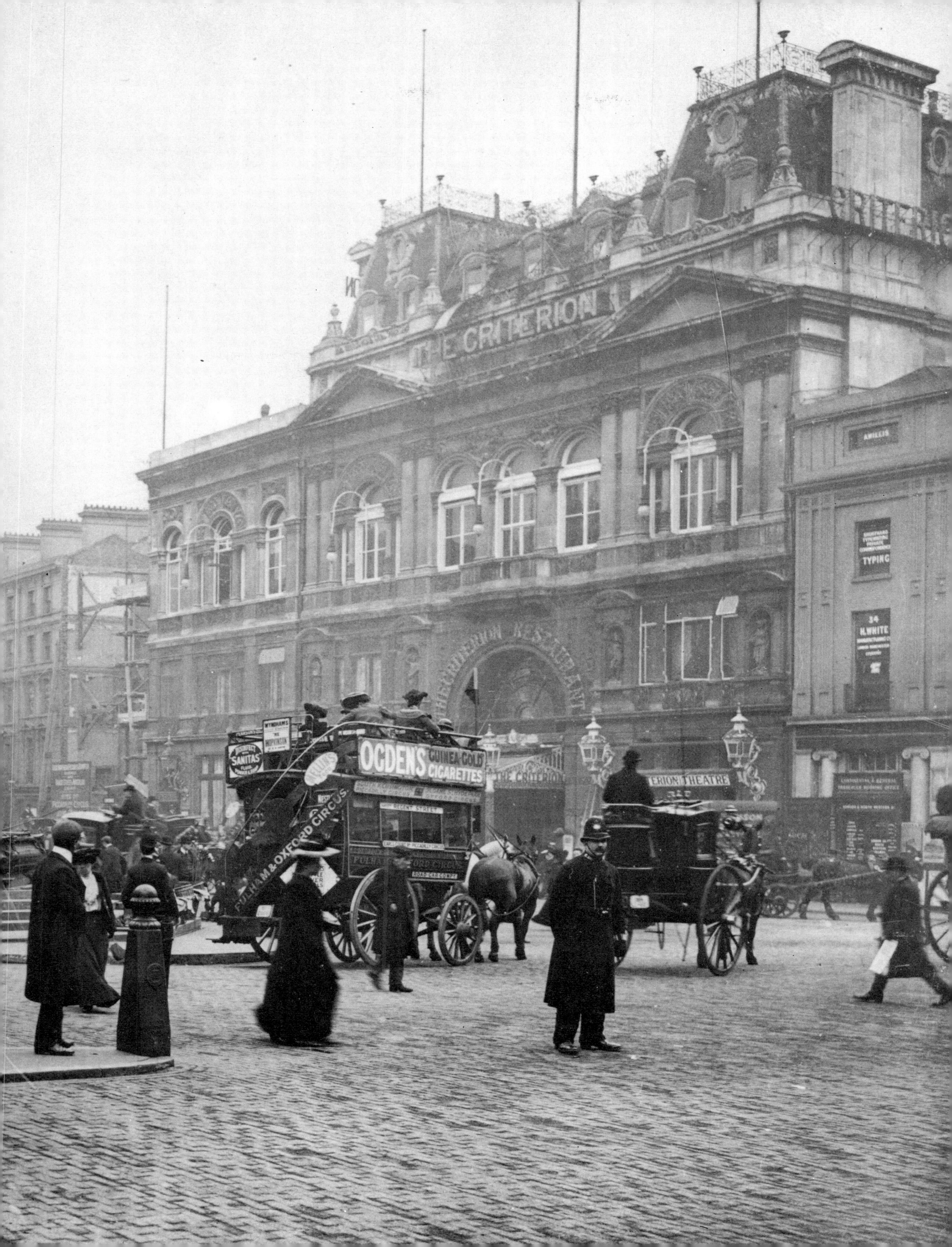
THE CRITERION
OGDEN'S
GUINEA GOLD
CIGARETTES
FULHAM & OXFORD CIRCUS
SANITAS
TYPING

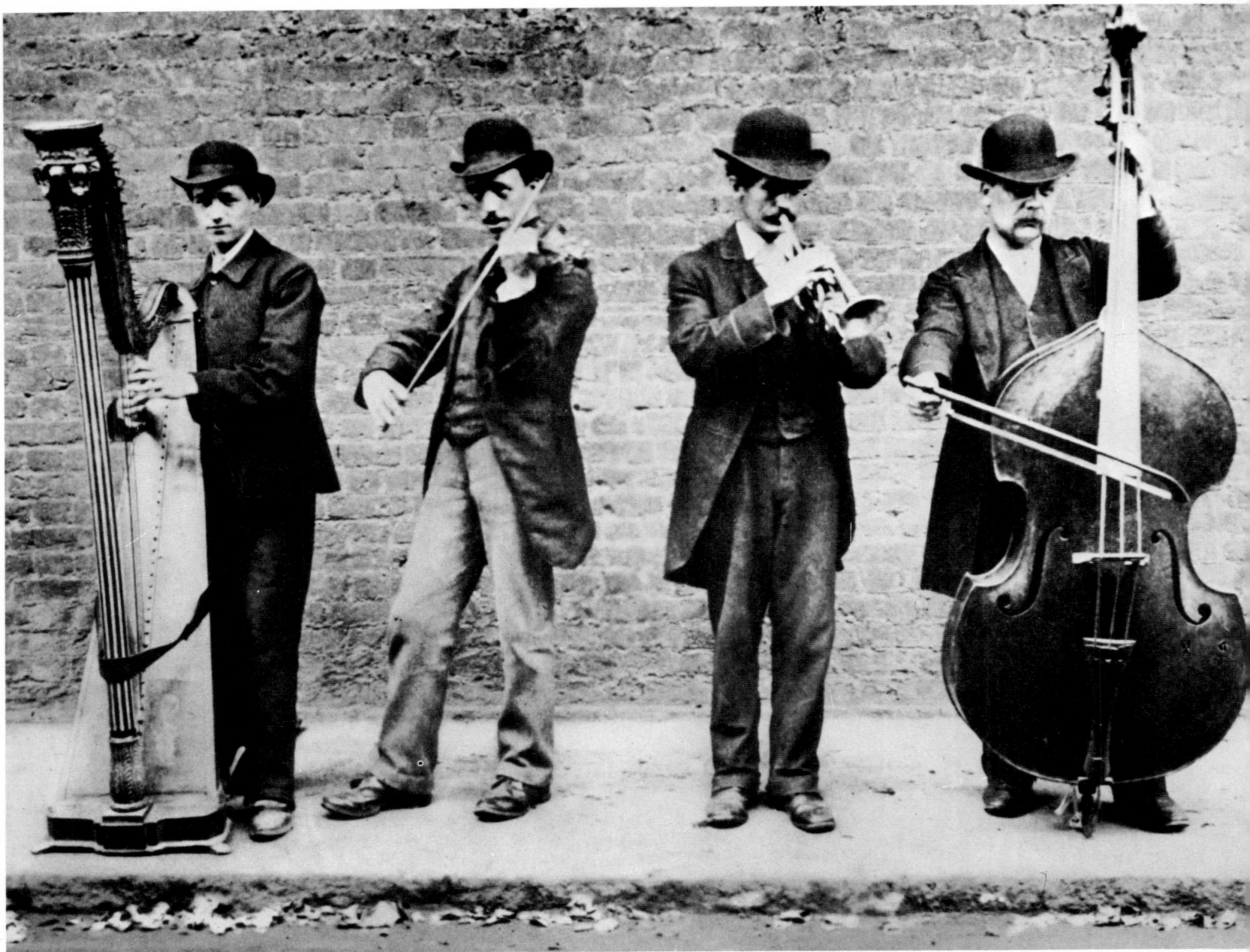

Itinerant street musicians were a common sight on London streets. This string and brass quartet was photographed at Greenwich in 1884

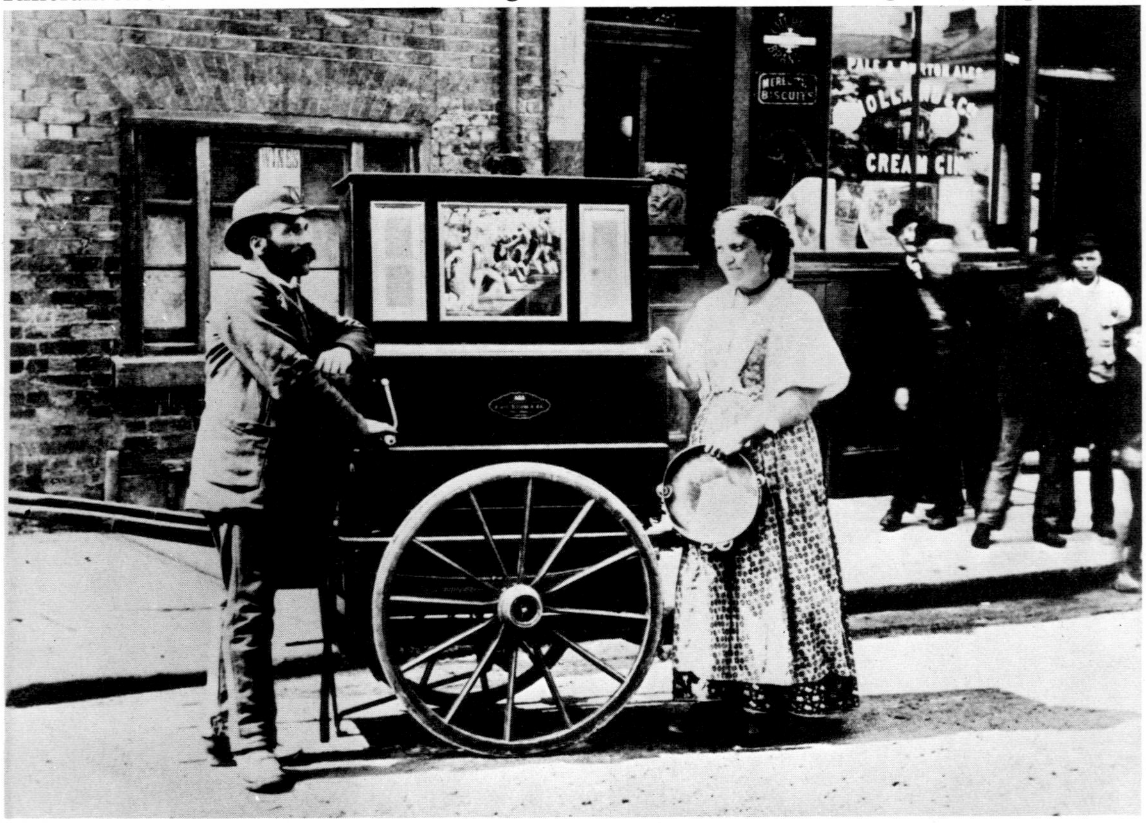
CREAM

The barrel organ – here with tambourine accompaniment – was another popular street attraction

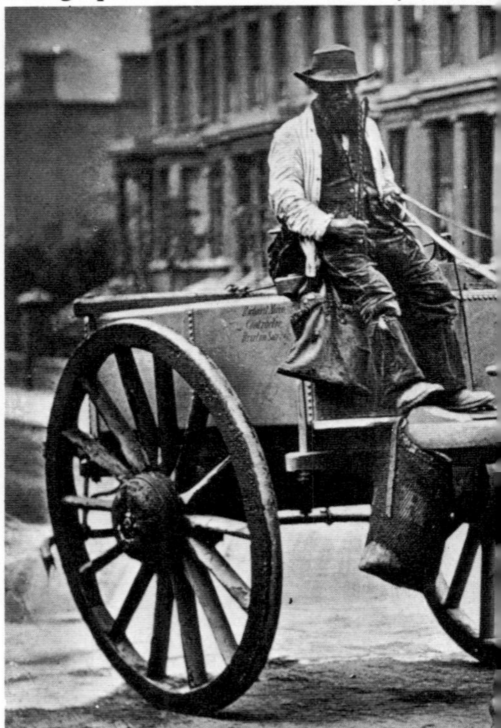

The watercart, carrying a galvanised tank,

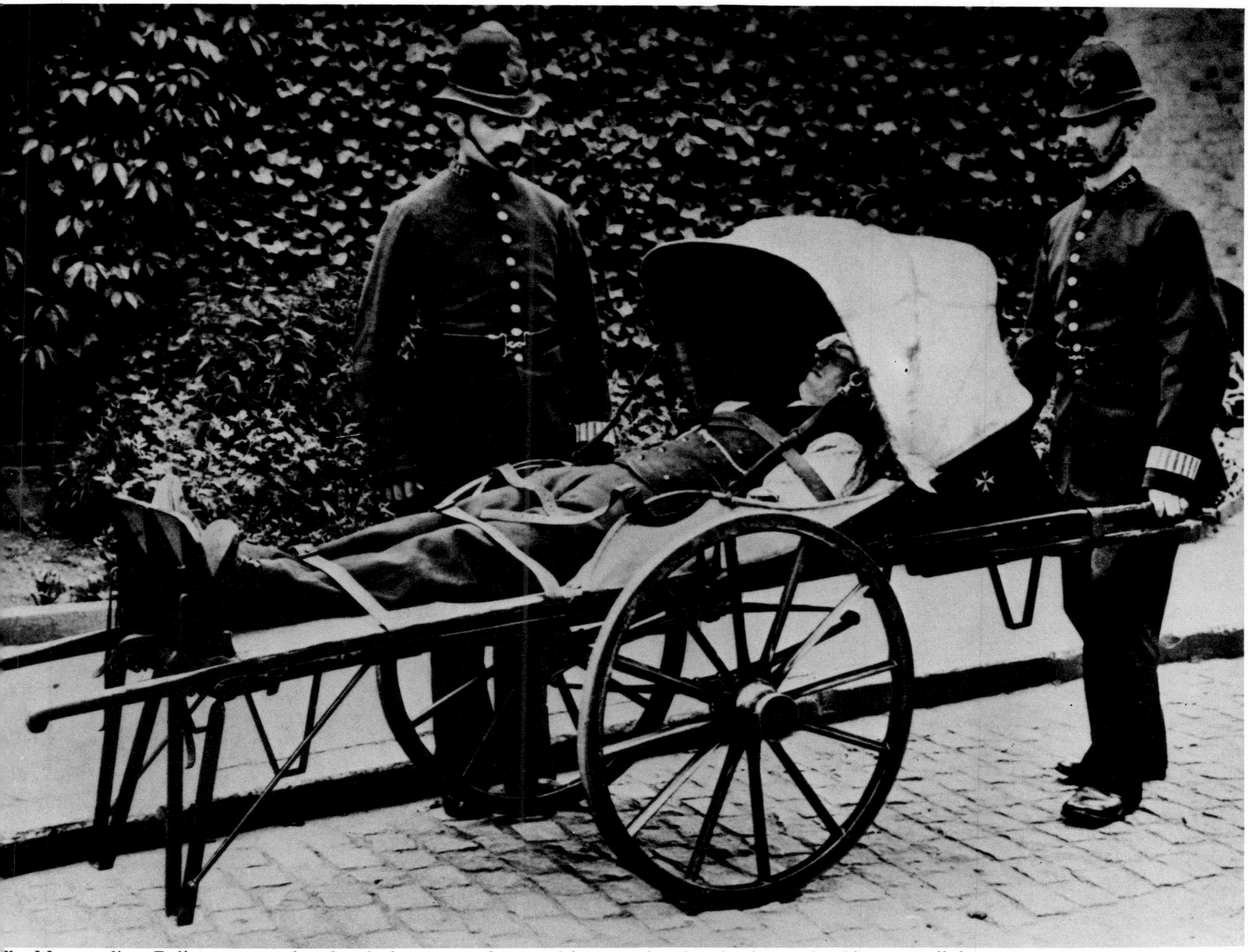

'he Metropolitan Police one-man hand ambulance was often used for arresting drunks; it remained in use until the 1930s

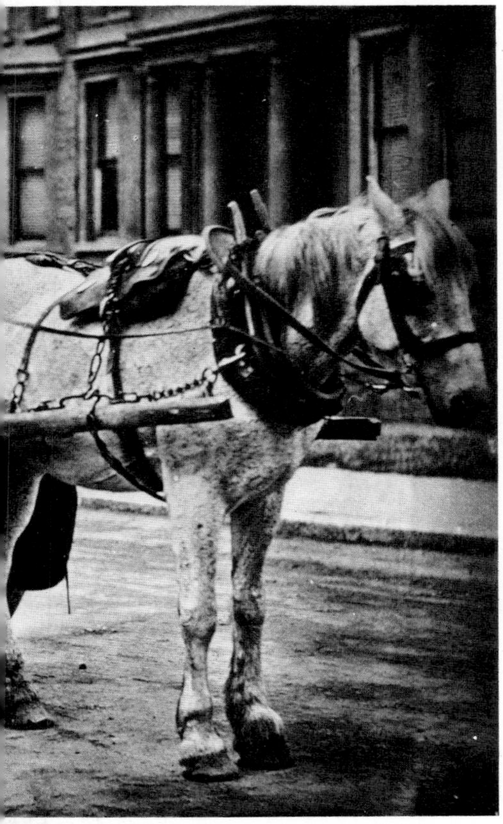

:d households before mains were laid

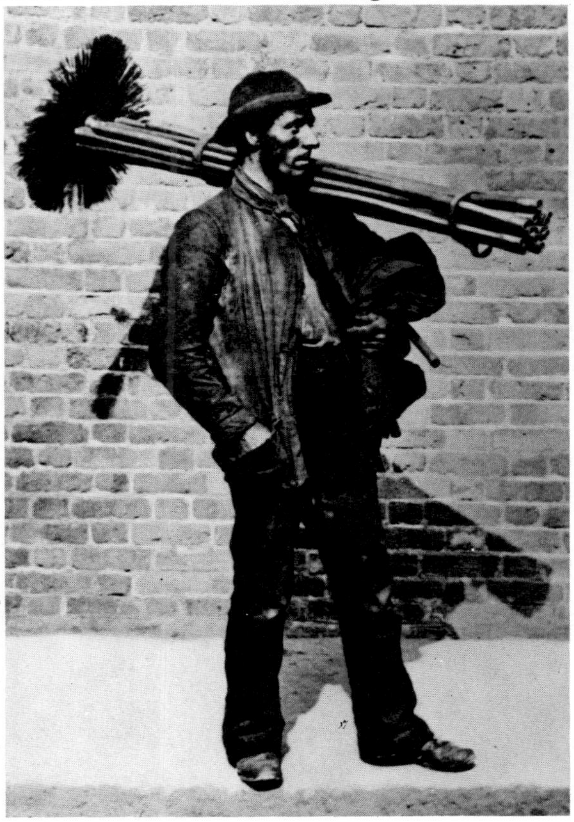

The chimney sweep was kept busy with coal fires

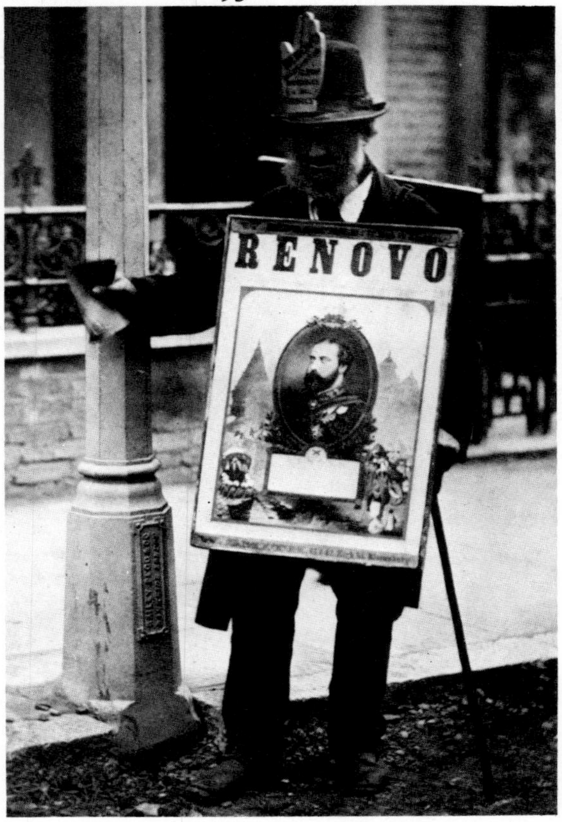

RENOVO

A sandwich-board man could get 1s. 6d. a day

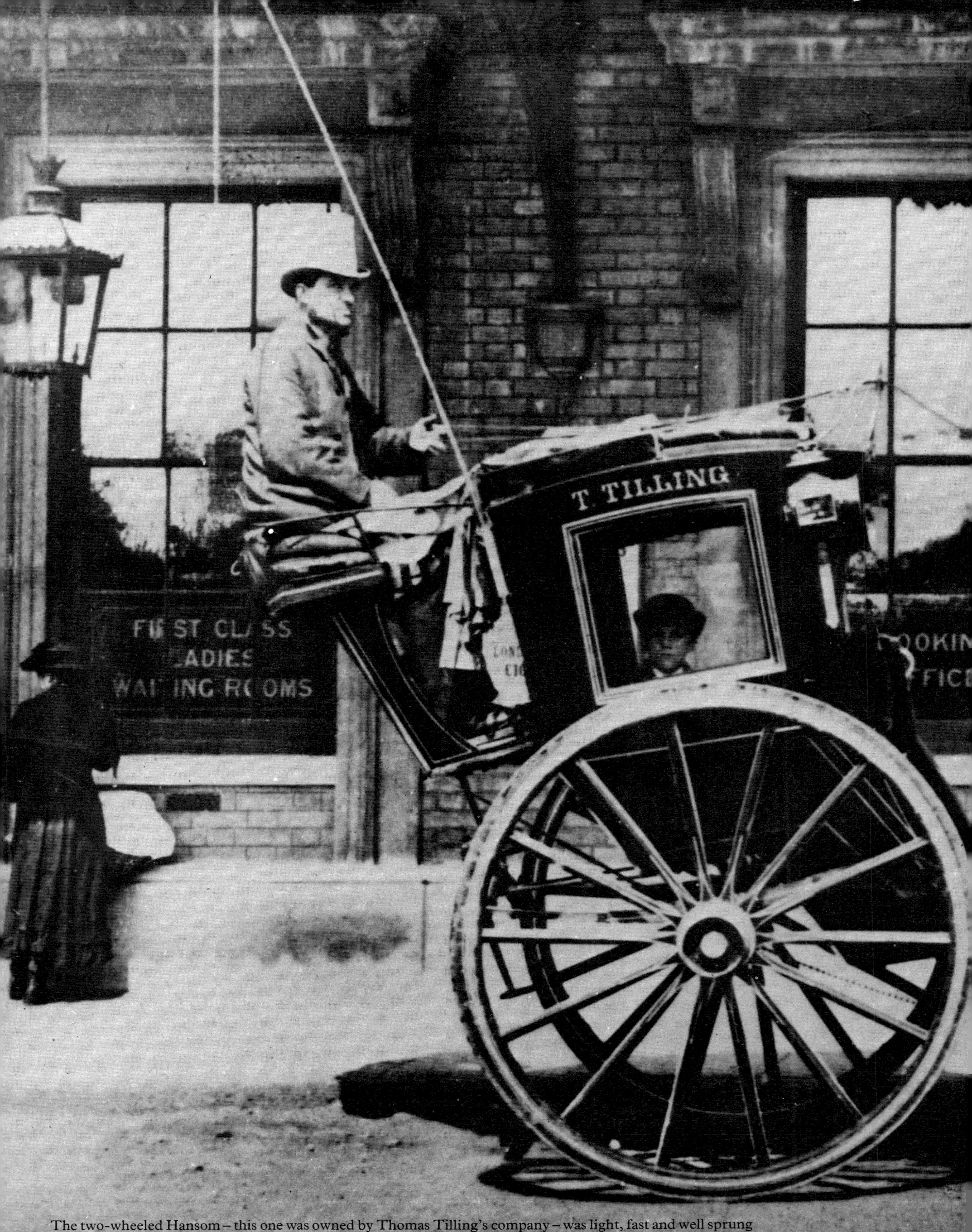
T. TILLING

The two-wheeled Hansom – this one was owned by Thomas Tilling's company – was light, fast and well sprung

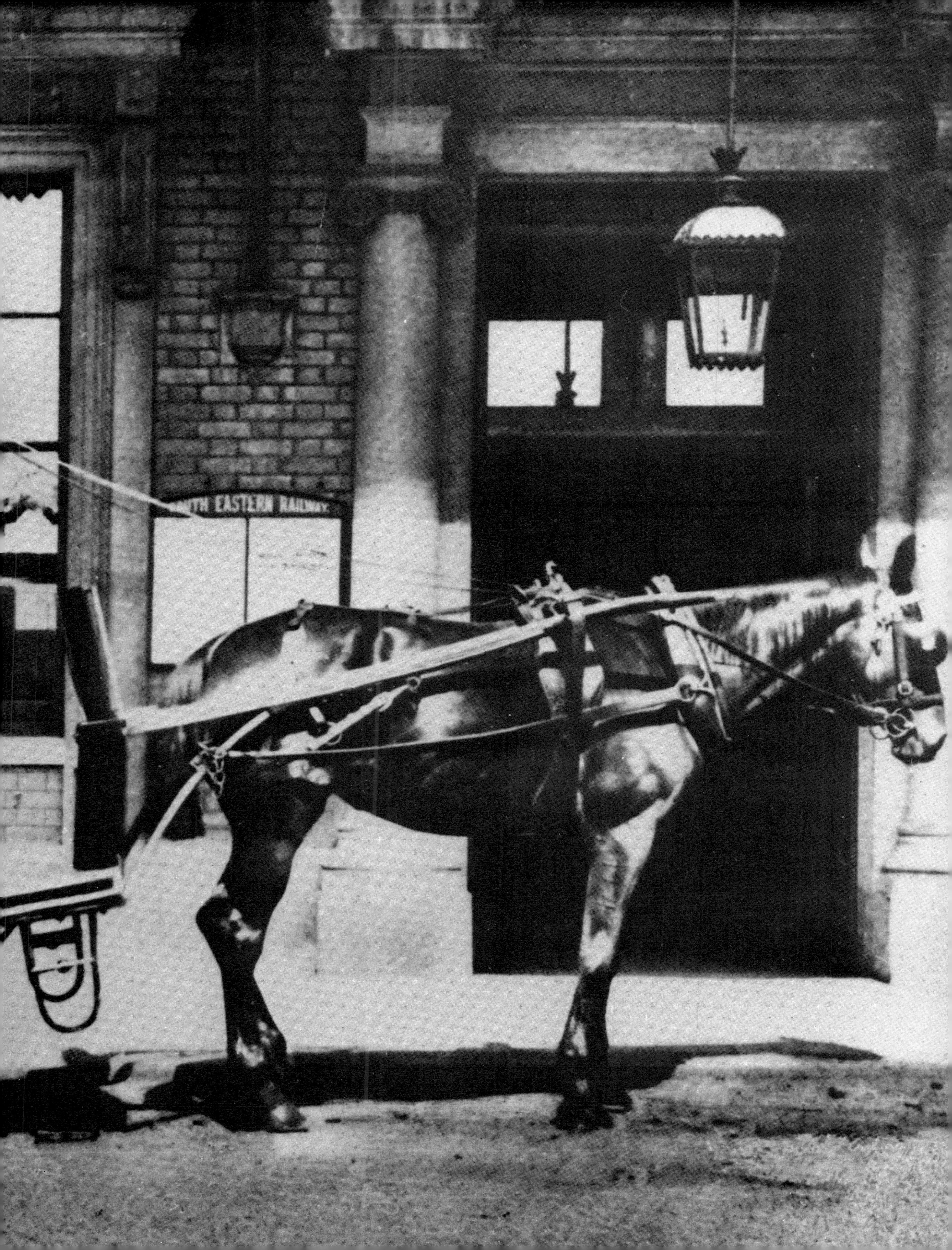
EASTERN RAILWAY.

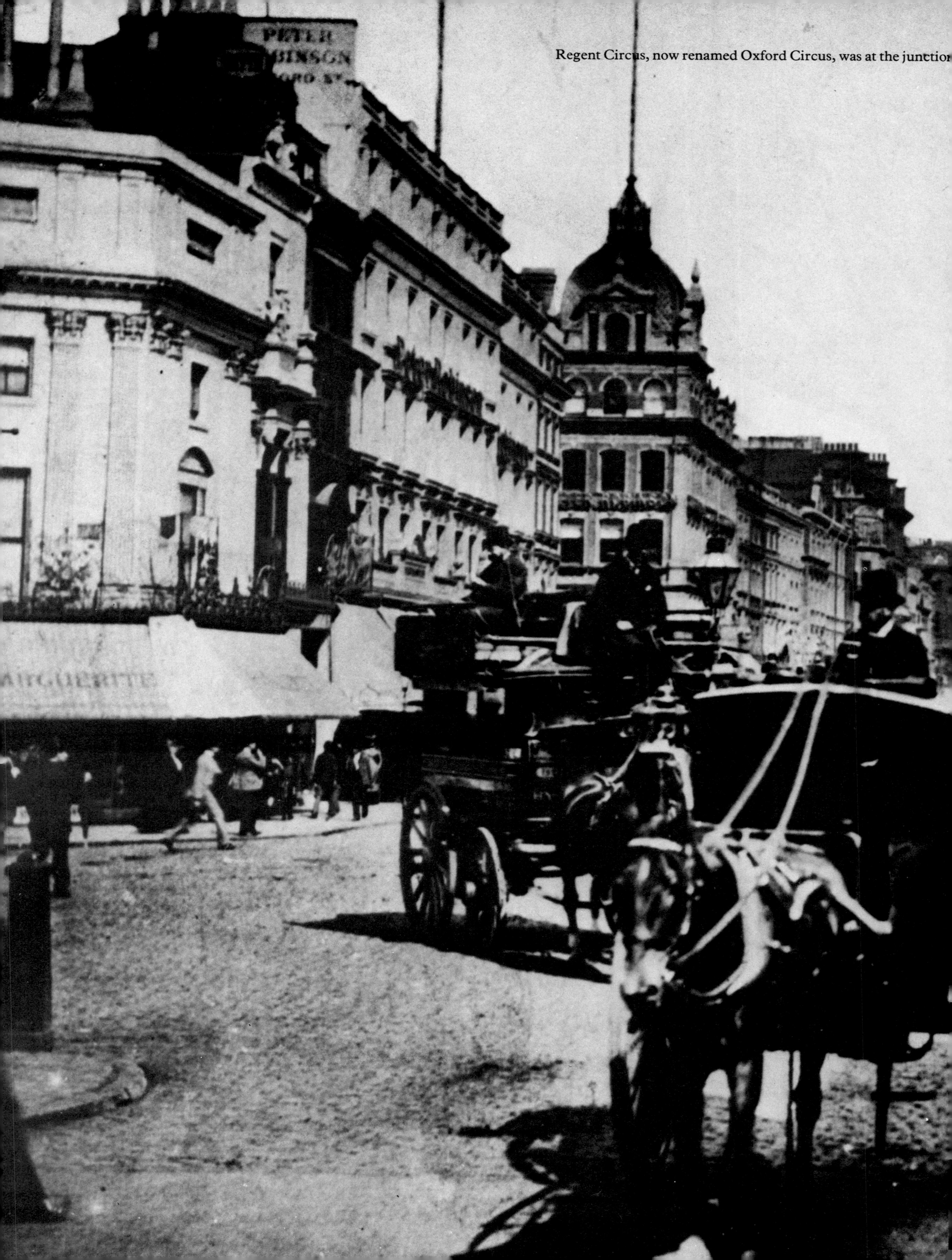
PETER
BINSON
ARGUERITE

Regent Circus, now renamed Oxford Circus, was at the junction ford and Regent Streets in the centre of the shopping district

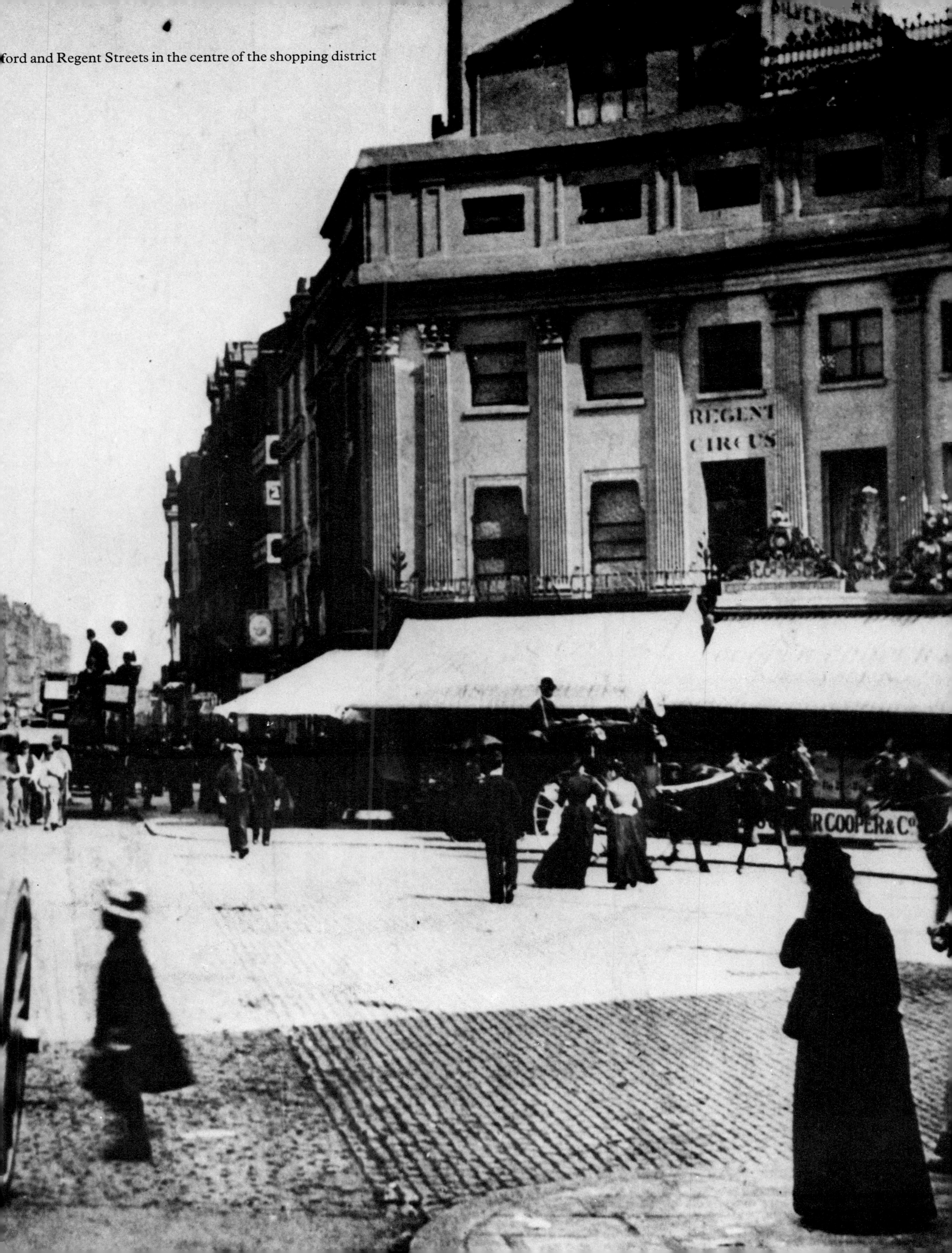
REGENT
CIRCUS
COOPER & Co

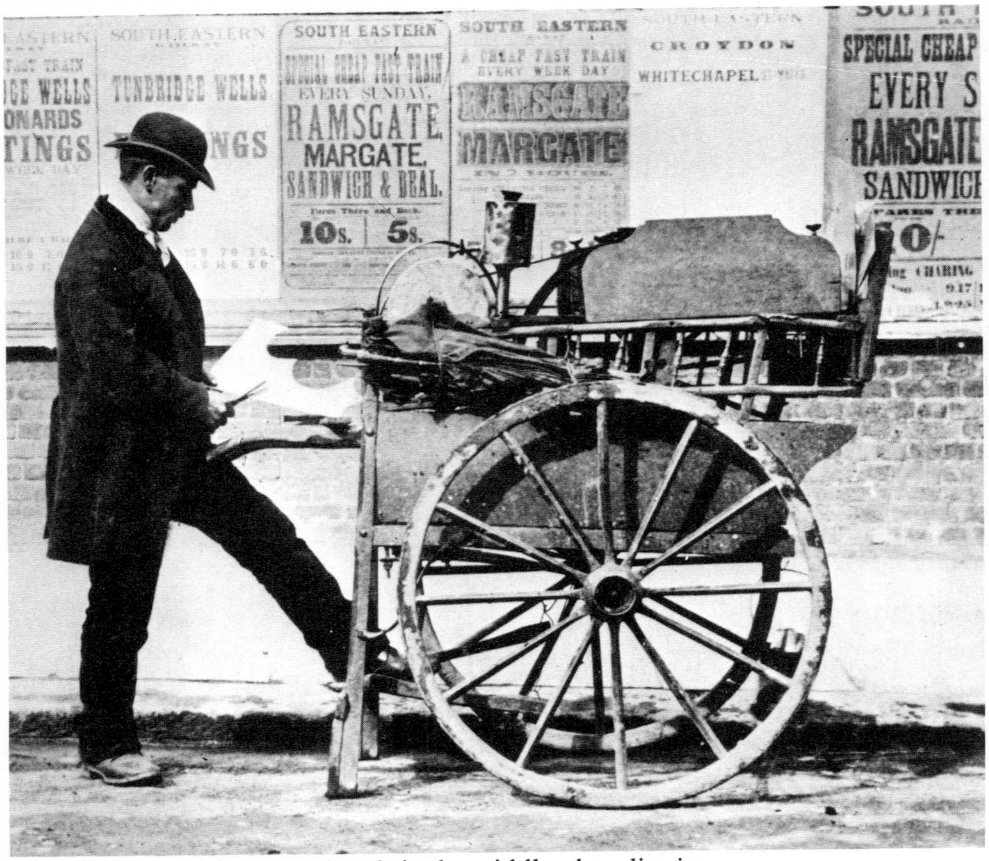
SOUTH EASTERN
TUNBRIDGE WELLS
SOUTH EASTERN
SPECIAL CHEAP FAST TRAIN
EVERY SUNDAY,
RAMSGATE,
MARGATE,
SANDWICH & DEAL.
10s. 5s.
SOUTH EASTERN
A CHEAP FAST TRAIN
EVERY WEEK DAY
RAMSGATE
MARGATE
CROYDON
WHITECHAPEL
SPECIAL CHEAP
RAMSGATE
SANDWICH

Knife grinders found a lot of trade in the middle-class districts

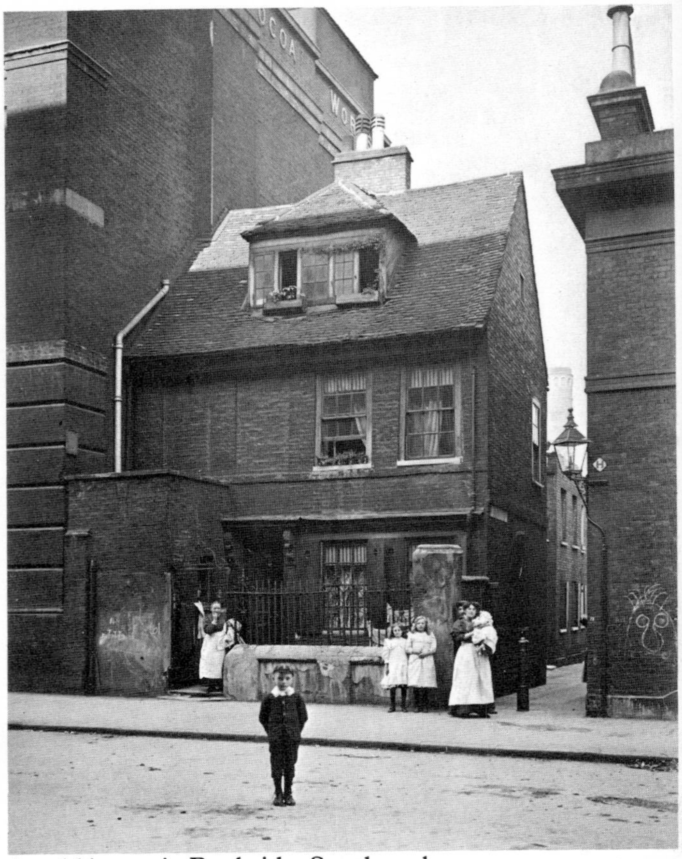

An old house in Bankside, Southwark

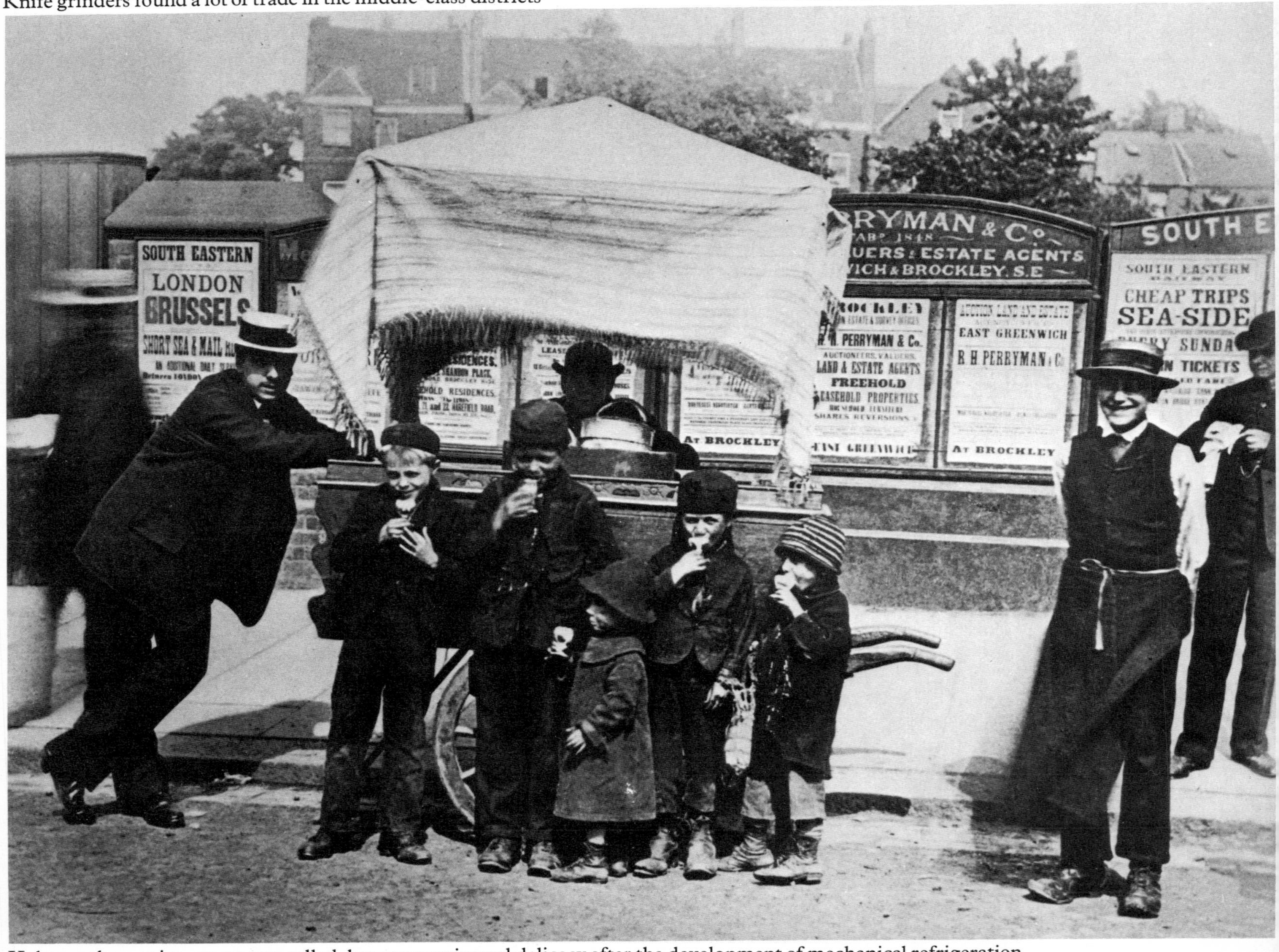
SOUTH EASTERN
LONDON
BRUSSELS
SHORT SEA & MAIL
PERRYMAN & Co.
ESTATE AGENTS
BROCKLEY, S.E.
H. PERRYMAN & Co.
LAND & ESTATE AGENTS
FREEHOLD
AT BROCKLEY
EAST GREENWICH
R H PERRYMAN & Co
AT BROCKLEY
SOUTH EASTERN
CHEAP TRIPS
SEA-SIDE
TICKETS

Hokey-pokey, as ice-cream was called, became a universal delicacy after the development of mechanical refrigeration

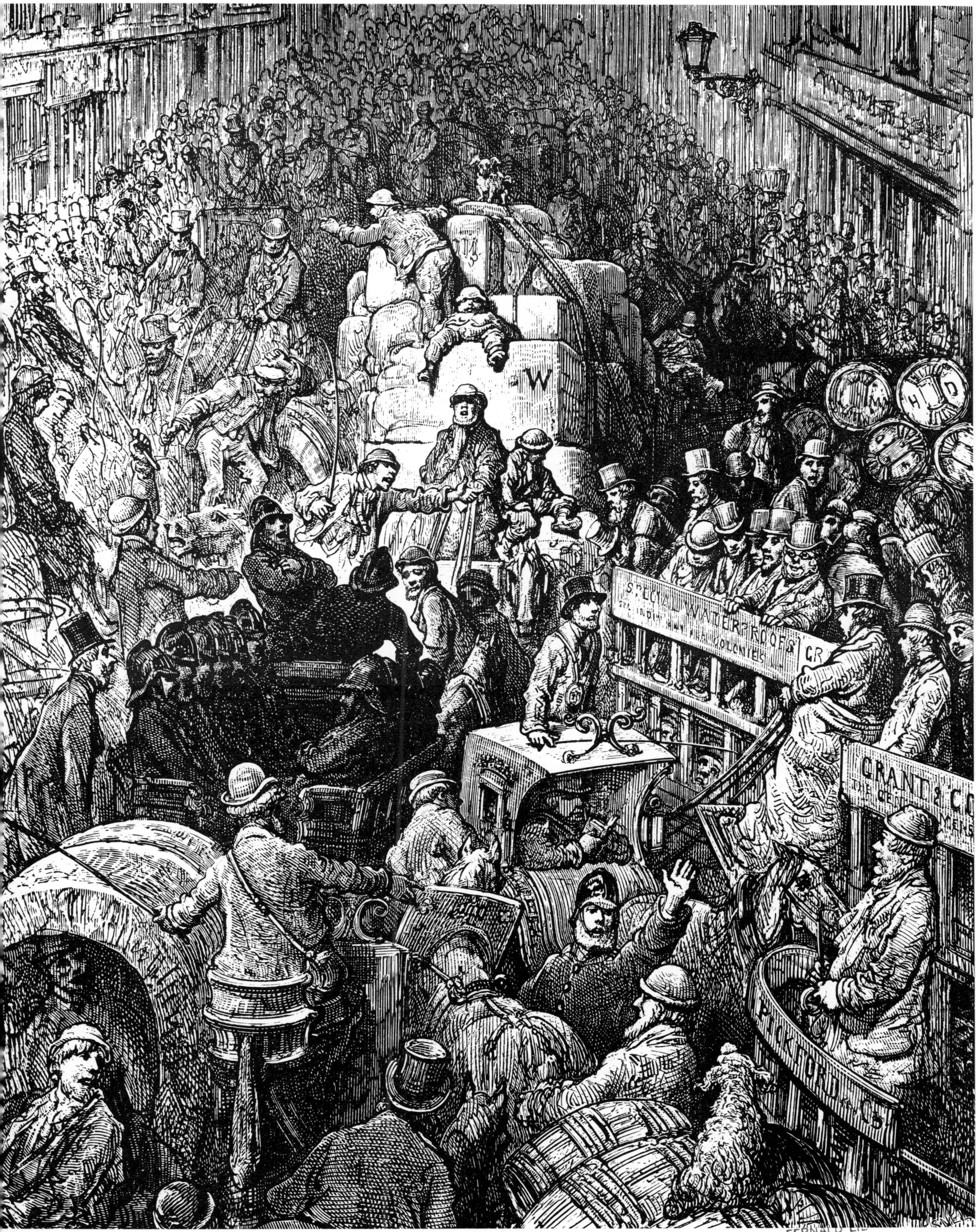
SPECIAL WATERPROOFS
GRANT & CO
PICKFORD

Gustave Doré was impressed by the swarming traffic of Cheapside, and drew this impression of it in 1871

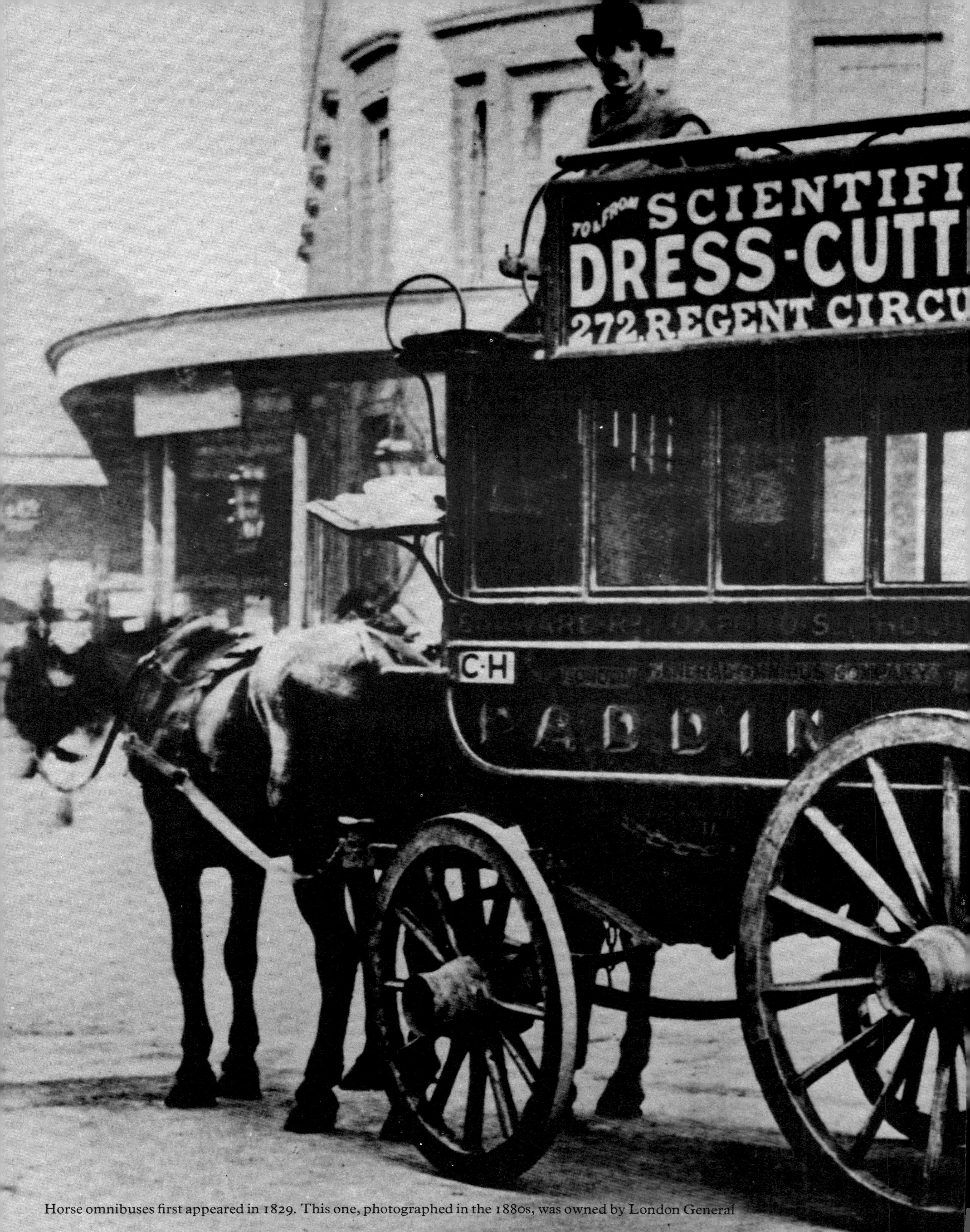
TO & FROM SCIENTIFI
DRESS-CUTT
272 REGENT CIRCU
C·H
PADDIN

Horse omnibuses first appeared in 1829. This one, photographed in the 1880s, was owned by London General

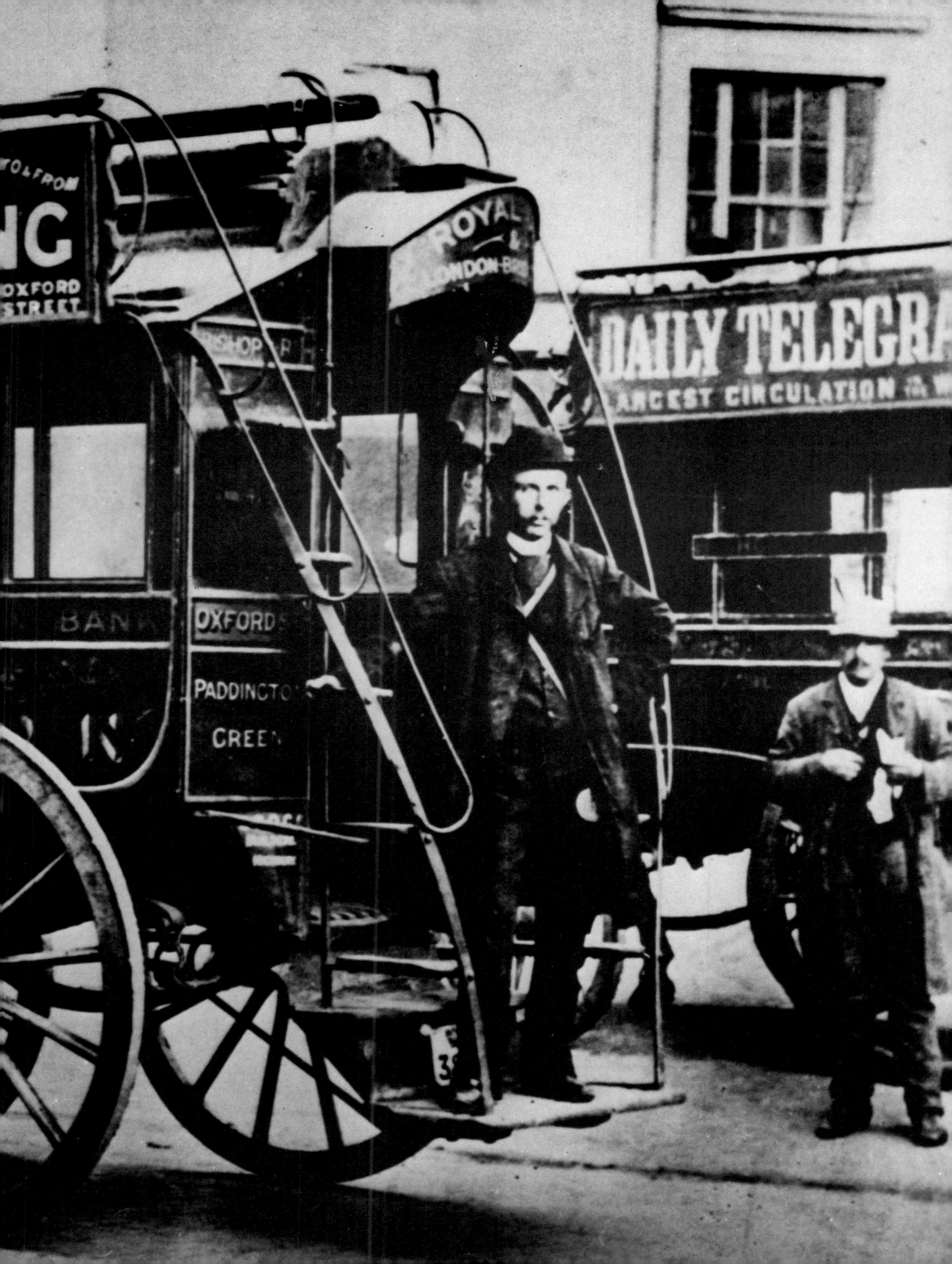

OXFORD
STREET
ROYAL
DAILY TELEGRA
CIRCULATION
OXFORD
PADDINGTON
GREEN

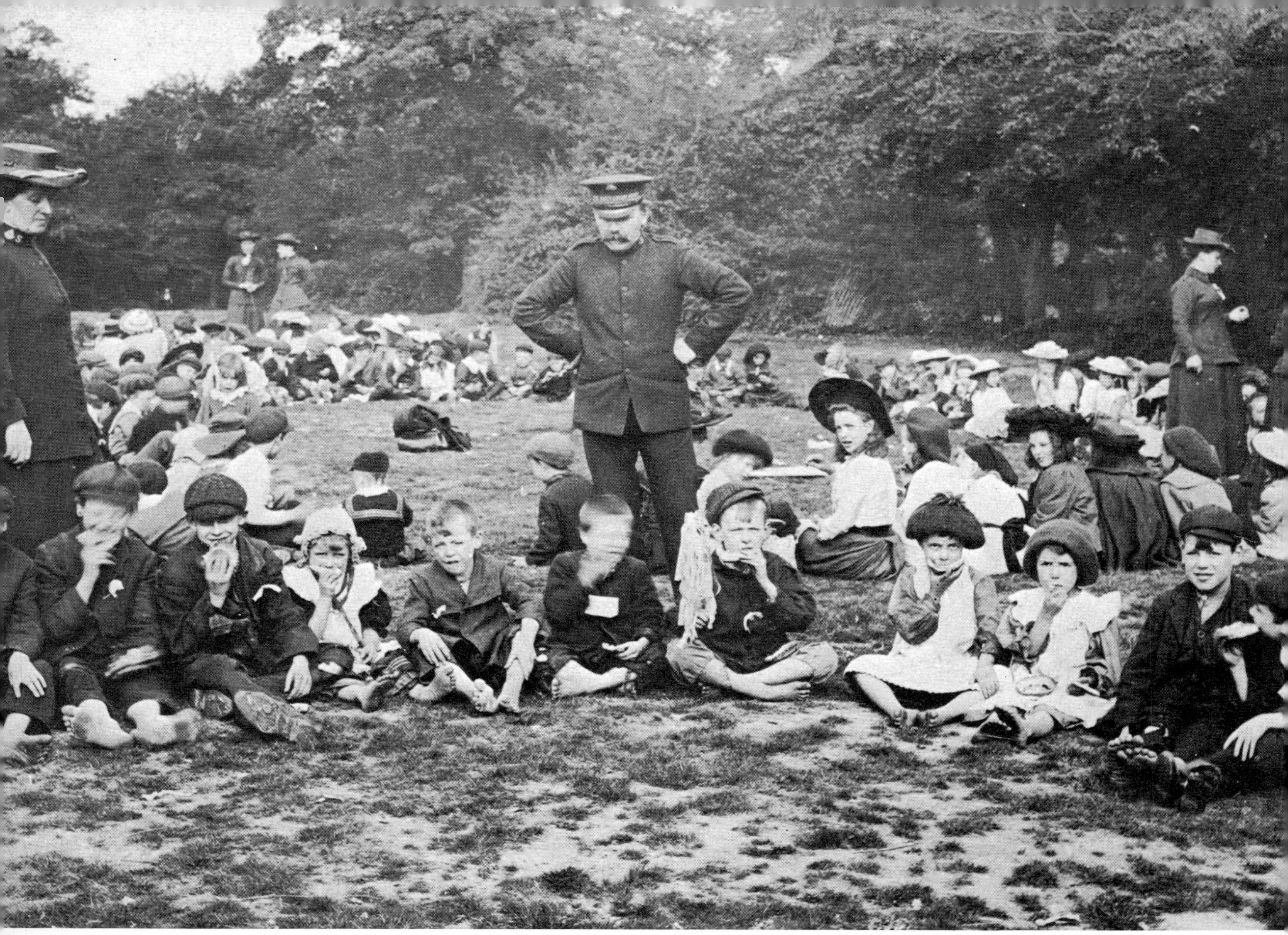

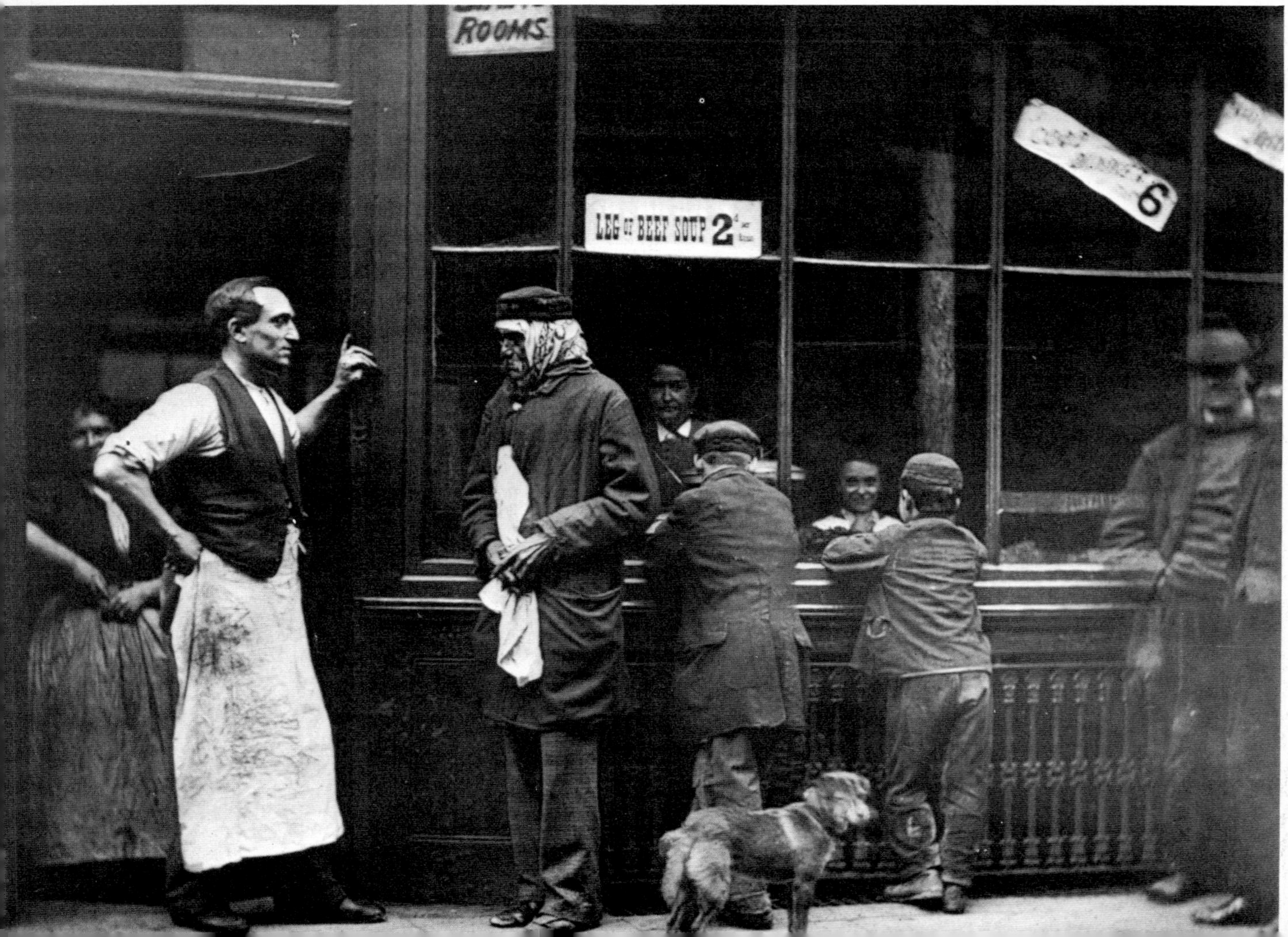
ROOMS
LEG OF BEEF SOUP 2
6

The Victorians believ
that the poor remained t
poor because they knew
better. Philanthropists we
few and dedicated, thou
by the end of the centu
the Salvation Army, whi
General William Booth h
founded in London's Ea
End in the Sixties, h
made its mark on t
slums, combining its robu
Christian evangelism wi
regimented excursions f
children to Epping Fore
(above) and help for t
capital's down-and-ou
The lodging house in Dru
Lane (left) had a cliente
of vagrants and newl
released convicts, but mo
charitable foundations d
little more than hand o
basic nourishment to t
city's ill-fed children (abo
right). The cheap fish sta
in St. Giles's (far righ
might help a family clo
to their starvation budg
Near right: a typical Lan
beth slum in the mid-185

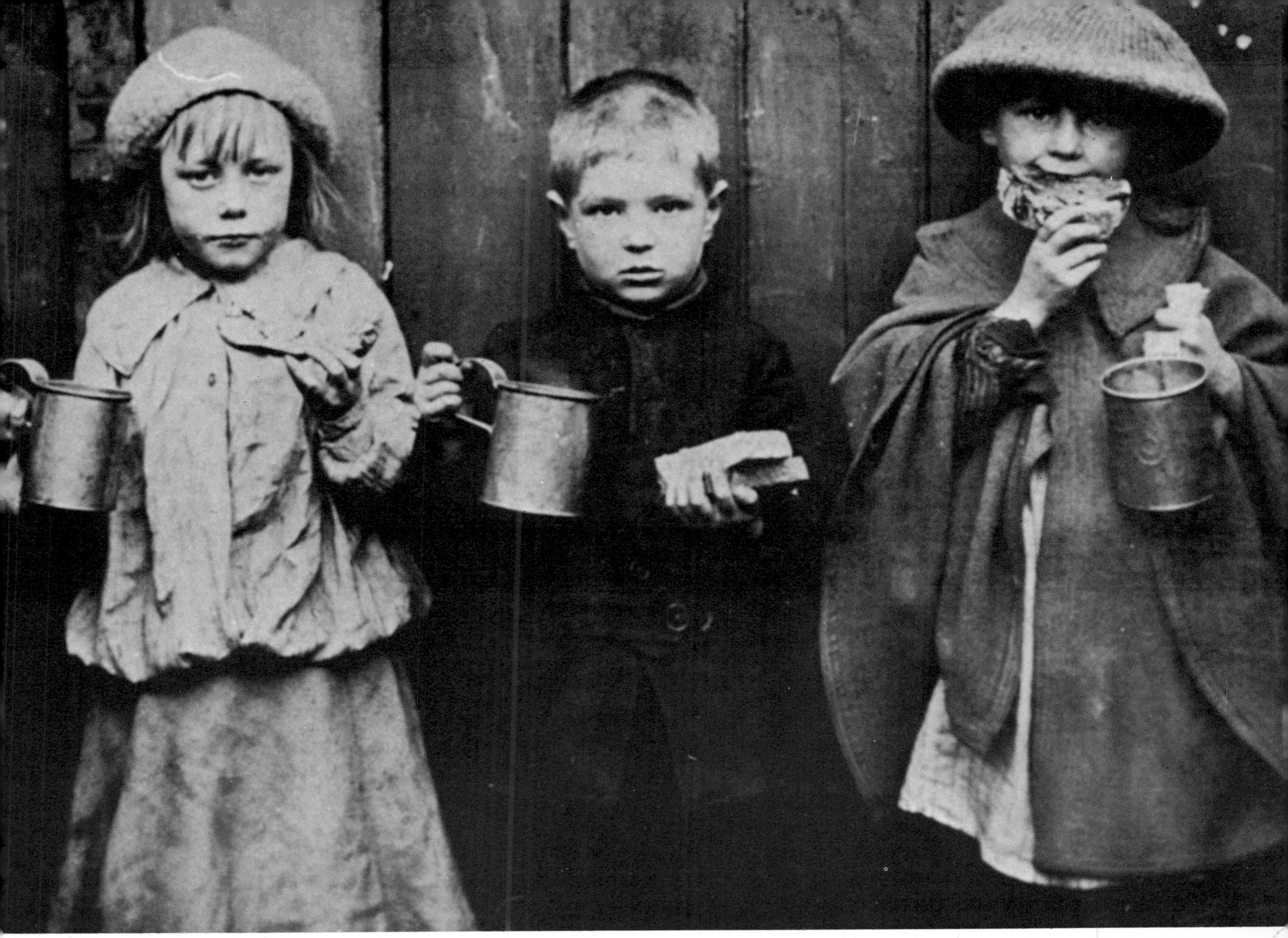

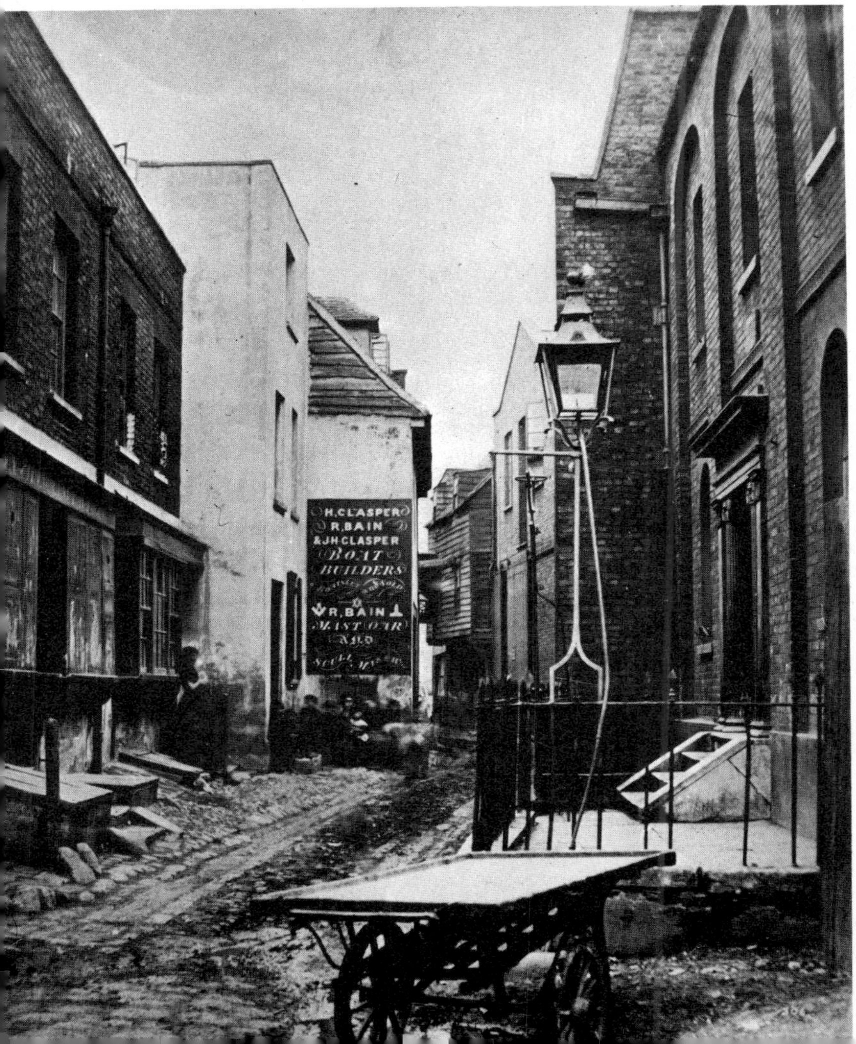
H. CLASPER
R. BAIN
& J.H. CLASPER
BOAT
BUILDERS
R. BAIN
MAST OAR

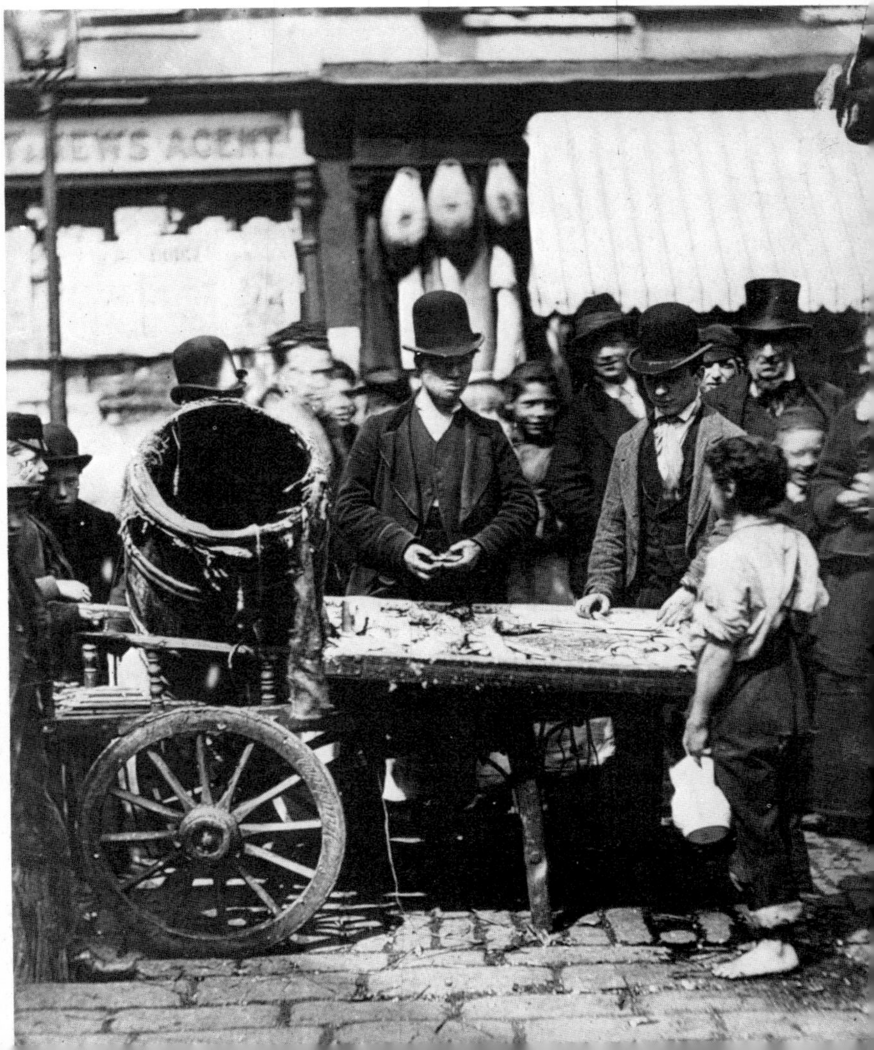
NEWS AGENT

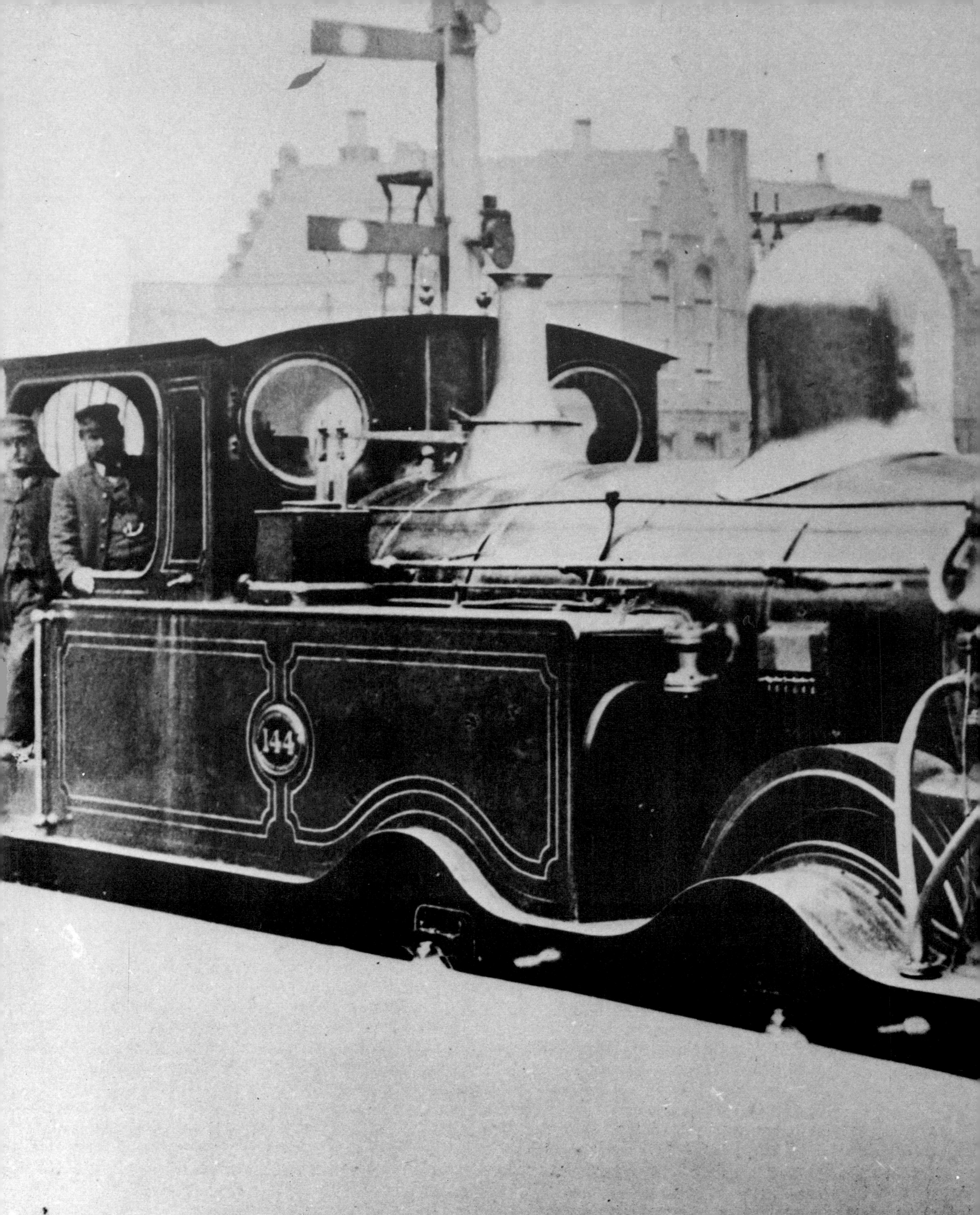
144

The railways made daily travel from the suburbs possible and did more to hasten London's growth than any other single cause. This suburban tra

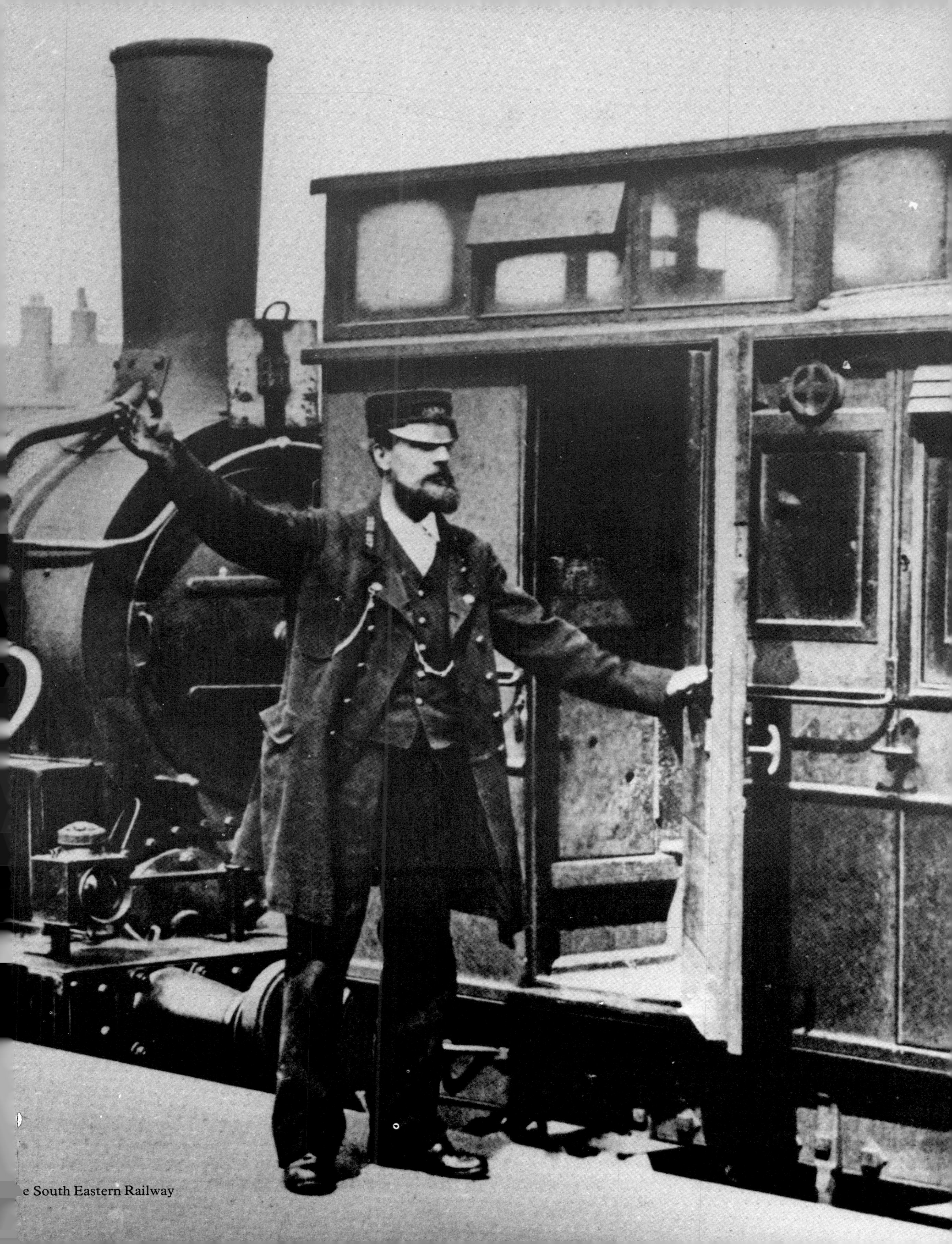

e South Eastern Railway

AN ENGLISHMAN'S HOME

The industrial revolution brought new wealth to new classes and like most rich people they took to conspicuous consumption

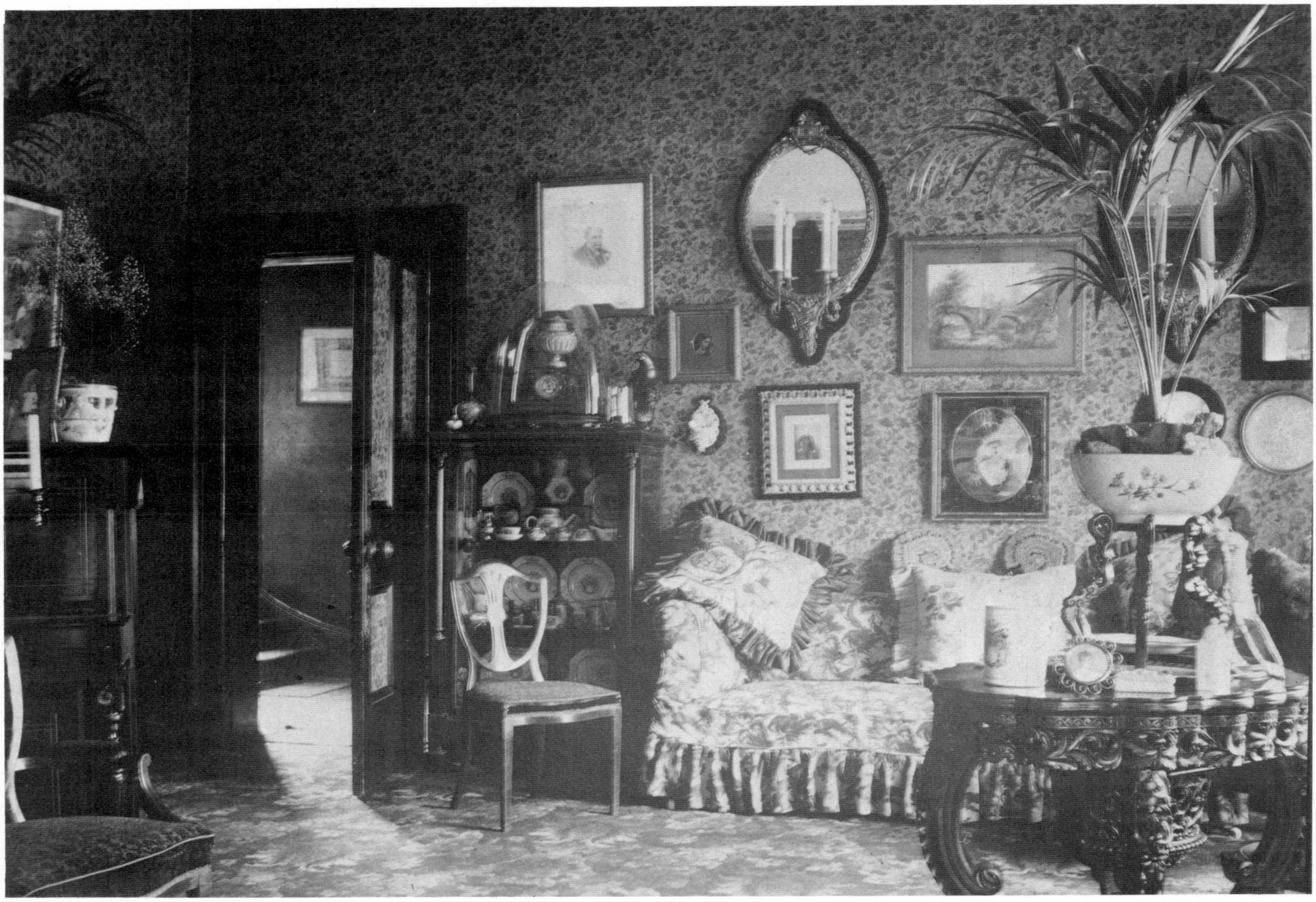

Late Victorian sitting room: family photographs, china in cupboards and on tables, plants, pattern on pattern. A pile-up of confident clutter

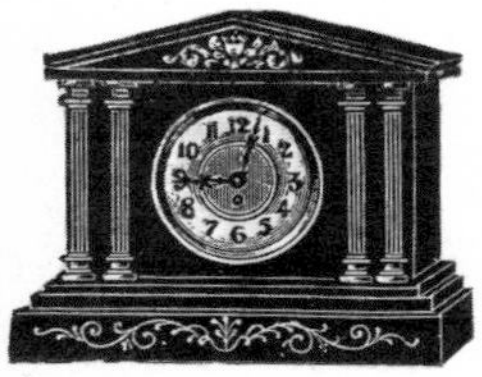

'Madeleine' clock in black marble with bronze columns from Oetzmann's. It cost 32s. 6d.

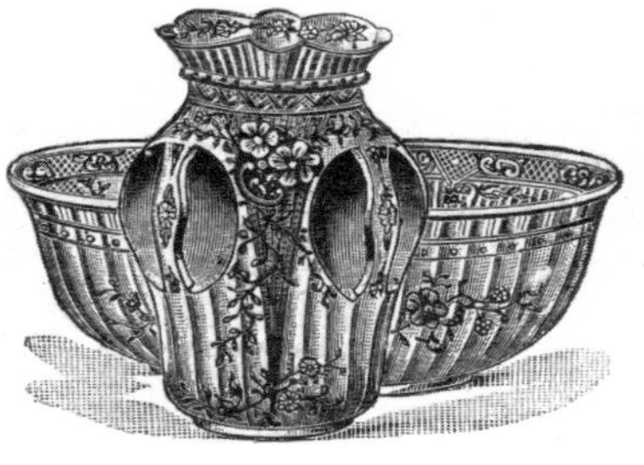

Also from Oetzmann's, in the Hampstead Road, their 'patent toilet service' at 7s. 11d.

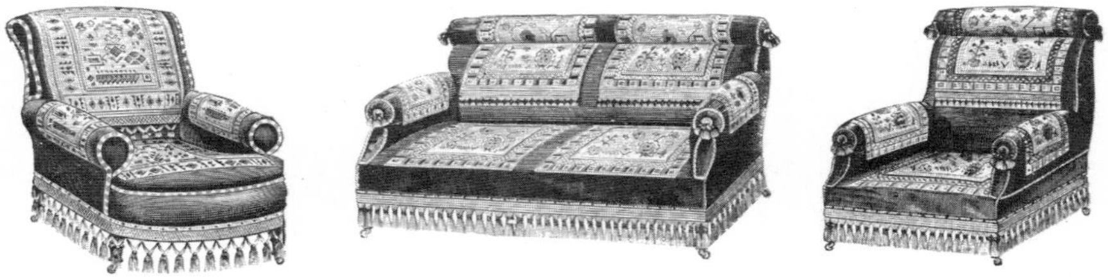

Stuffed furniture was not invented by the Victorians, but they took to it with joy. Left: Maple's Mogadore Gent.'s Easy Chair. Right: the Tavistock Gent.'s Chair and Settee

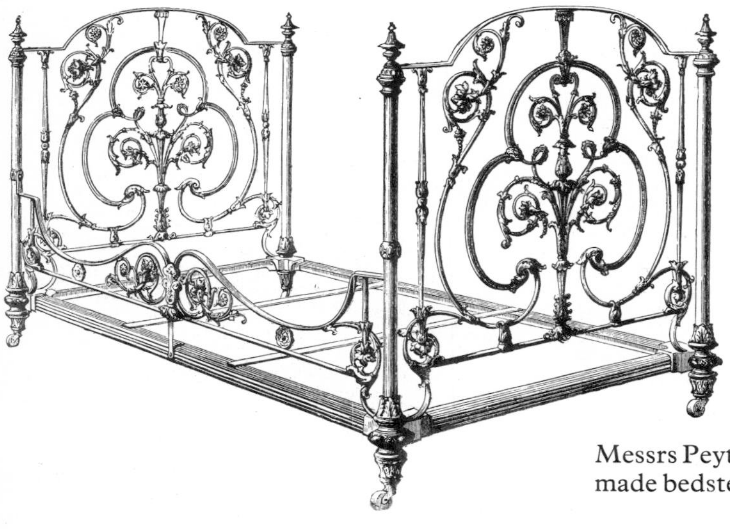

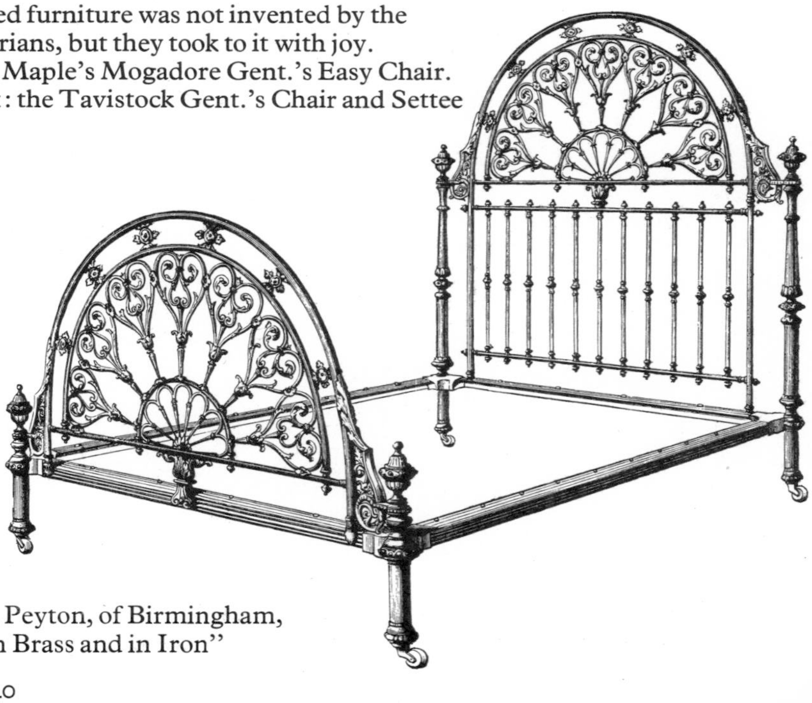

Messrs Peyton and Peyton, of Birmingham, made bedsteads "in Brass and in Iron"

– in buildings, in clothes, in fixtures and furnishings. What they lacked in taste, they made up for in enthusiasm – particularly in a passion for gadgets and novelties, those ubiquitous by-products of the high tide of Victorian invention

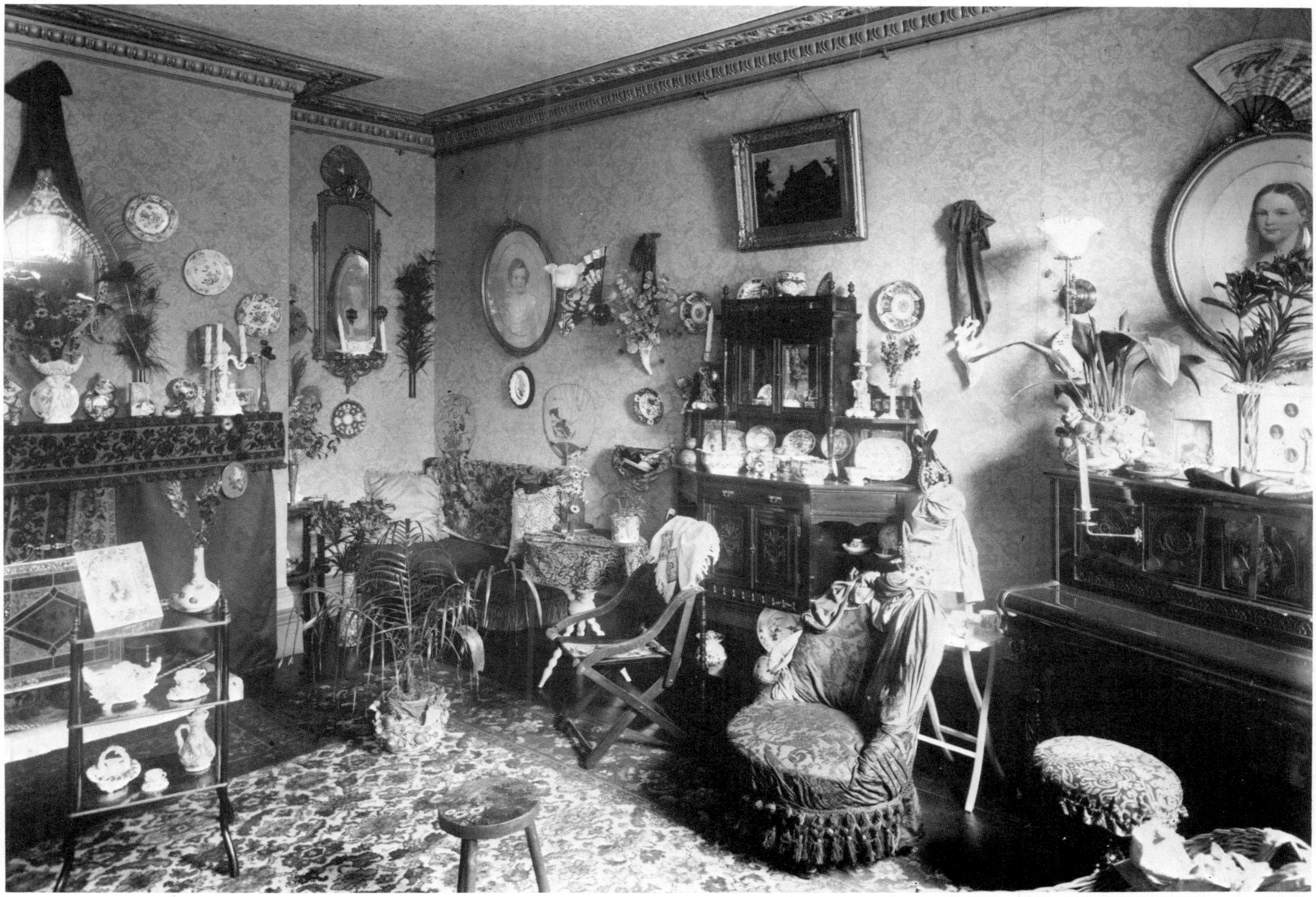

Not only houseplants, but ostrich feathers in vases; not only patterned carpet and wallpaper, but patterned ceiling. Note the 'whatnot', invented to display bric-à-brac; and the fans on the wall; and the upright piano, status symbol of the Victorian middle classes. It all meant a great deal of work for the servants, but then there were a great many of them. Below: the kind of thing that made for much dusting

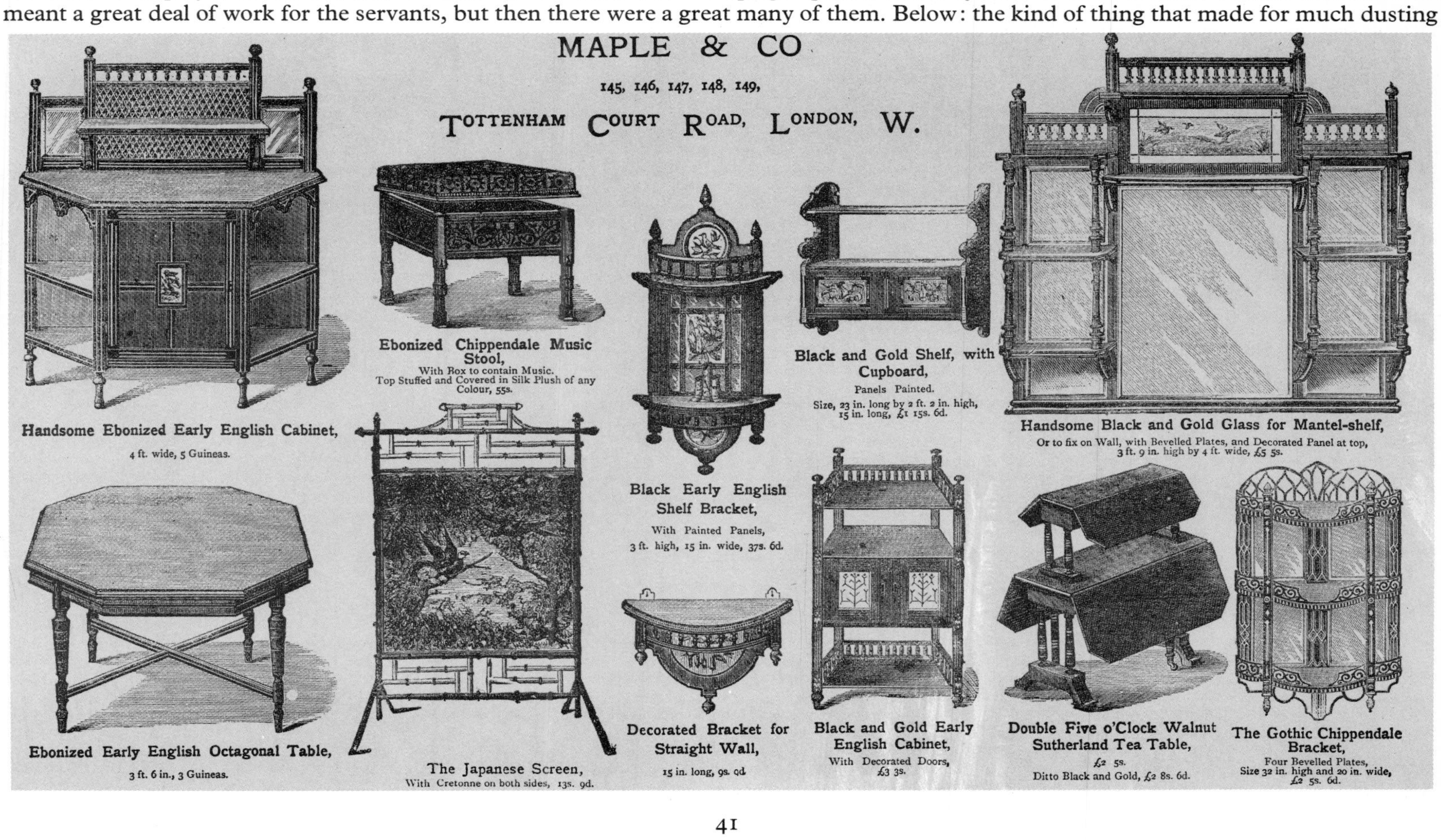

MAPLE & CO
145, 146, 147, 148, 149,
TOTTENHAM COURT ROAD, LONDON, W.
Handsome Ebonized Early English Cabinet,
4 ft. wide, 5 Guineas.
Ebonized Chippendale Music Stool,
With Box to contain Music.
Top Stuffed and Covered in Silk Plush of any Colour, 55s.
Black Early English Shelf Bracket,
With Painted Panels,
3 ft. high, 15 in. wide, 37s. 6d.
Black and Gold Shelf, with Cupboard,
Panels Painted.
Size, 23 in. long by 2 ft. 2 in. high, 15 in. long, £1 15s. 6d.
Handsome Black and Gold Glass for Mantel-shelf,
Or to fix on Wall, with Bevelled Plates, and Decorated Panel at top,
3 ft. 9 in. high by 4 ft. wide, £5 5s.
Ebonized Early English Octagonal Table,
3 ft. 6 in., 3 Guineas.
The Japanese Screen,
With Cretonne on both sides, 13s. 9d.
Decorated Bracket for Straight Wall,
15 in. long, 9s. 9d.
Black and Gold Early English Cabinet,
With Decorated Doors,
£3 3s.
Double Five o'Clock Walnut Sutherland Tea Table,
£2 5s.
Ditto Black and Gold, £2 8s. 6d.
The Gothic Chippendale Bracket,
Four Bevelled Plates,
Size 32 in. high and 20 in. wide,
£2 5s. 6d.

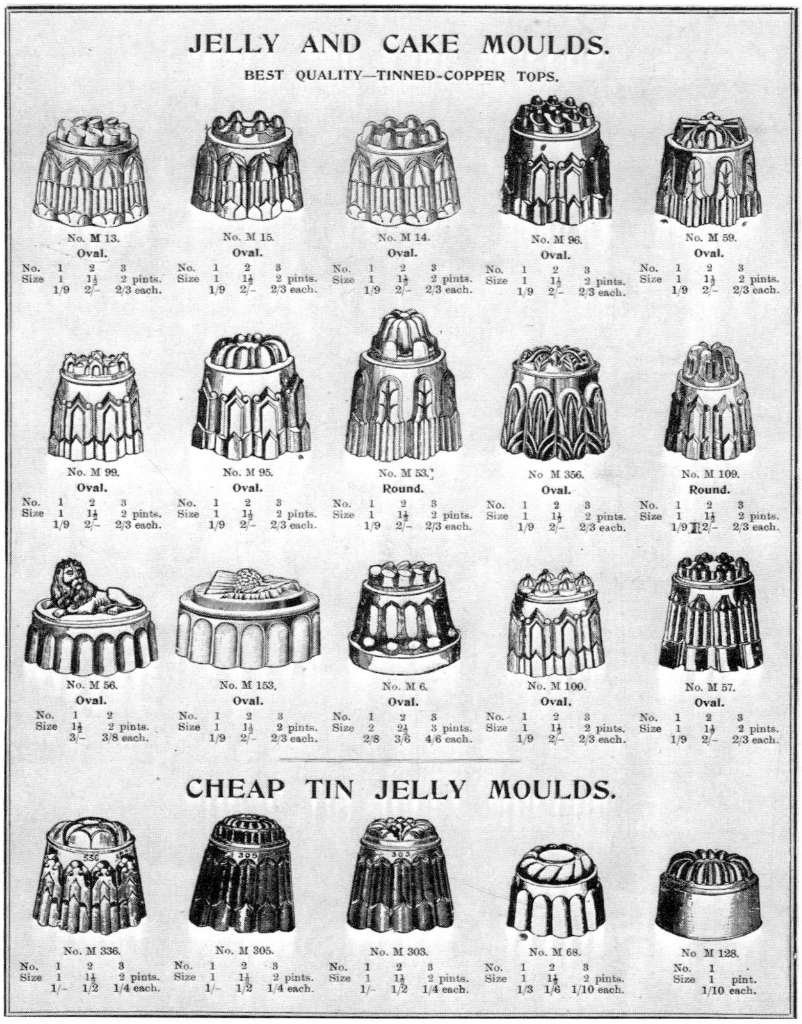
JELLY AND CAKE MOULDS.
BEST QUALITY—TINNED-COPPER TOPS.
No. M 13. Oval. No. 1 2 3 Size 1 1½ 2 pints. 1/9 2/- 2/3 each.
No. M 15. Oval. No. 1 2 3 Size 1 1½ 2 pints. 1/9 2/- 2/3 each.
No. M 14. Oval. No. 1 2 3 Size 1 1½ 2 pints. 1/9 2/- 2/3 each.
No. M 96. Oval. No. 1 2 3 Size 1 1½ 2 pints. 1/9 2/- 2/3 each.
No. M 59. Oval. No. 1 2 3 Size 1 1½ 2 pints. 1/9 2/- 2/3 each.
No. M 99. Oval. No. 1 2 3 Size 1 1½ 2 pints. 1/9 2/- 2/3 each.
No. M 95. Oval. No. 1 2 3 Size 1 1½ 2 pints. 1/9 2/- 2/3 each.
No. M 53. Round. No. 1 2 3 Size 1 1½ 2 pints. 1/9 2/- 2/3 each.
No M 356. Oval. No. 1 2 3 Size 1 1½ 2 pints. 1/9 2/- 2/3 each.
No. M 109. Round. No. 1 2 3 Size 1 1½ 2 pints. 1/9 2/- 2/3 each.
No. M 56. Oval. No. 1 2 Size 1½ 2 pints. 3/- 3/8 each.
No. M 153. Oval. No. 1 2 3 Size 1 1½ 2 pints. 1/9 2/- 2/3 each.
No. M 6. Oval. No. 1 2 3 Size 2 2½ 3 pints. 2/8 3/6 4/6 each.
No. M 100. Oval. No. 1 2 3 Size 1 1½ 2 pints. 1/9 2/- 2/3 each.
No. M 57. Oval. No. 1 2 3 Size 1 1½ 2 pints. 1/9 2/- 2/3 each.
CHEAP TIN JELLY MOULDS.
No. M 336. No. 1 2 3 Size 1 1½ 2 pints. 1/- 1/2 1/4 each.
No. M 305. No. 1 2 3 Size 1 1½ 2 pints. 1/- 1/2 1/4 each.
No. M 303. No. 1 2 3 Size 1 1½ 2 pints. 1/- 1/2 1/4 each.
No. M 68. No. 1 2 3 Size 1 1½ 2 pints. 1/3 1/6 1/10 each.
No. M 128. No. 1 Size 1 pint. 1/10 each.

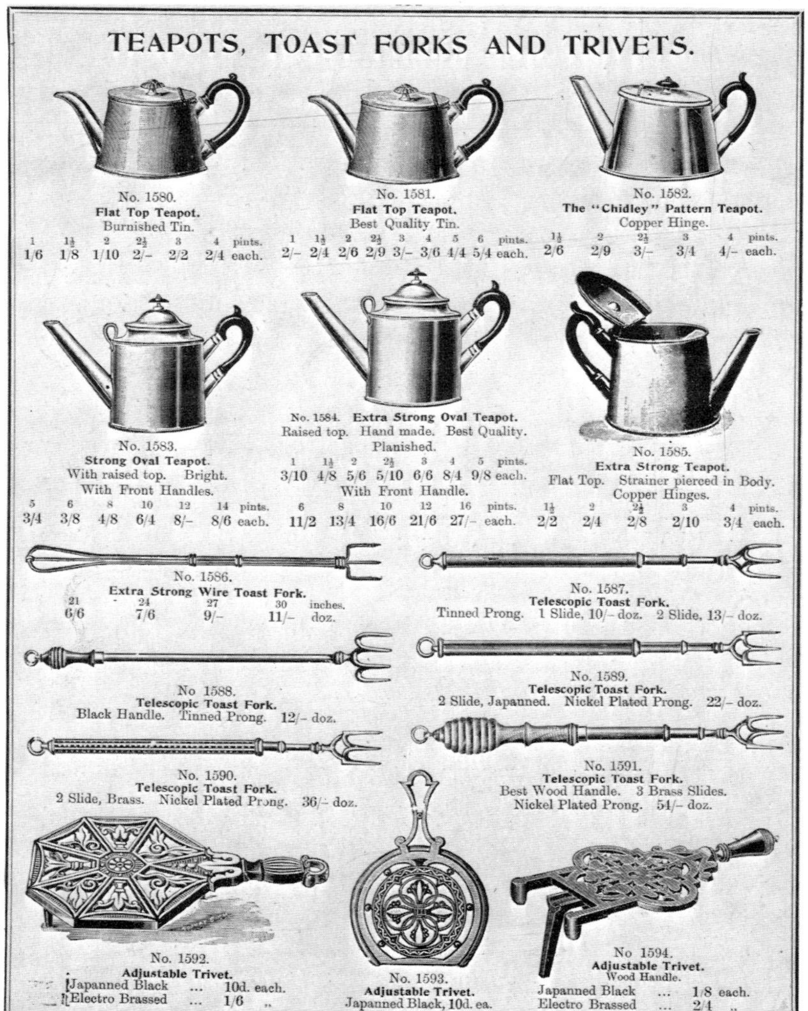
TEAPOTS, TOAST FORKS AND TRIVETS.
No. 1580. Flat Top Teapot. Burnished Tin. 1 1½ 2 2½ 3 4 pints. 1/6 1/8 1/10 2/- 2/2 2/4 each.
No. 1581. Flat Top Teapot. Best Quality Tin. 1 1½ 2 2½ 3 4 5 6 pints. 2/- 2/4 2/6 2/9 3/- 3/6 4/4 5/4 each.
No. 1582. The "Chidley" Pattern Teapot. Copper Hinge. 1½ 2 2½ 3 4 pints. 2/6 2/9 3/- 3/4 4/- each.
No. 1583. Strong Oval Teapot. With raised top. Bright. With Front Handles. 5 6 8 10 12 14 pints. 3/4 3/8 4/8 6/4 8/- 8/6 each.
No. 1584. Extra Strong Oval Teapot. Raised top. Hand made. Best Quality. Planished. 1 1½ 2 2½ 3 4 5 pints. 3/10 4/8 5/6 5/10 6/6 8/4 9/8 each. With Front Handle. 6 8 10 12 16 pints. 11/2 13/4 16/6 21/6 27/- each.
No. 1585. Extra Strong Teapot. Flat Top. Strainer pierced in Body. Copper Hinges. 1½ 2 2½ 3 4 pints. 2/2 2/4 2/8 2/10 3/4 each.
No. 1586. Extra Strong Wire Toast Fork. 21 24 27 30 inches. 6/6 7/6 9/- 11/- doz.
No. 1587. Telescopic Toast Fork. Tinned Prong. 1 Slide, 10/- doz. 2 Slide, 13/- doz.
No 1588. Telescopic Toast Fork. Black Handle. Tinned Prong. 12/- doz.
No. 1589. Telescopic Toast Fork. 2 Slide, Japanned. Nickel Plated Prong. 22/- doz.
No. 1590. Telescopic Toast Fork. 2 Slide, Brass. Nickel Plated Prong. 36/- doz.
No. 1591. Telescopic Toast Fork. Best Wood Handle. 3 Brass Slides. Nickel Plated Prong. 54/- doz.
No. 1592. Adjustable Trivet. Japanned Black ... 10d. each. Electro Brassed ... 1/6 „
No. 1593. Adjustable Trivet. Japanned Black, 10d. ea.
No 1594. Adjustable Trivet. Wood Handle. Japanned Black ... 1/8 each. Electro Brassed ... 2/4 „

Top: jellymoulds for all tastes. Even plain cooking should be made to look complicated. Above: tin teapots and other kitchen equipment

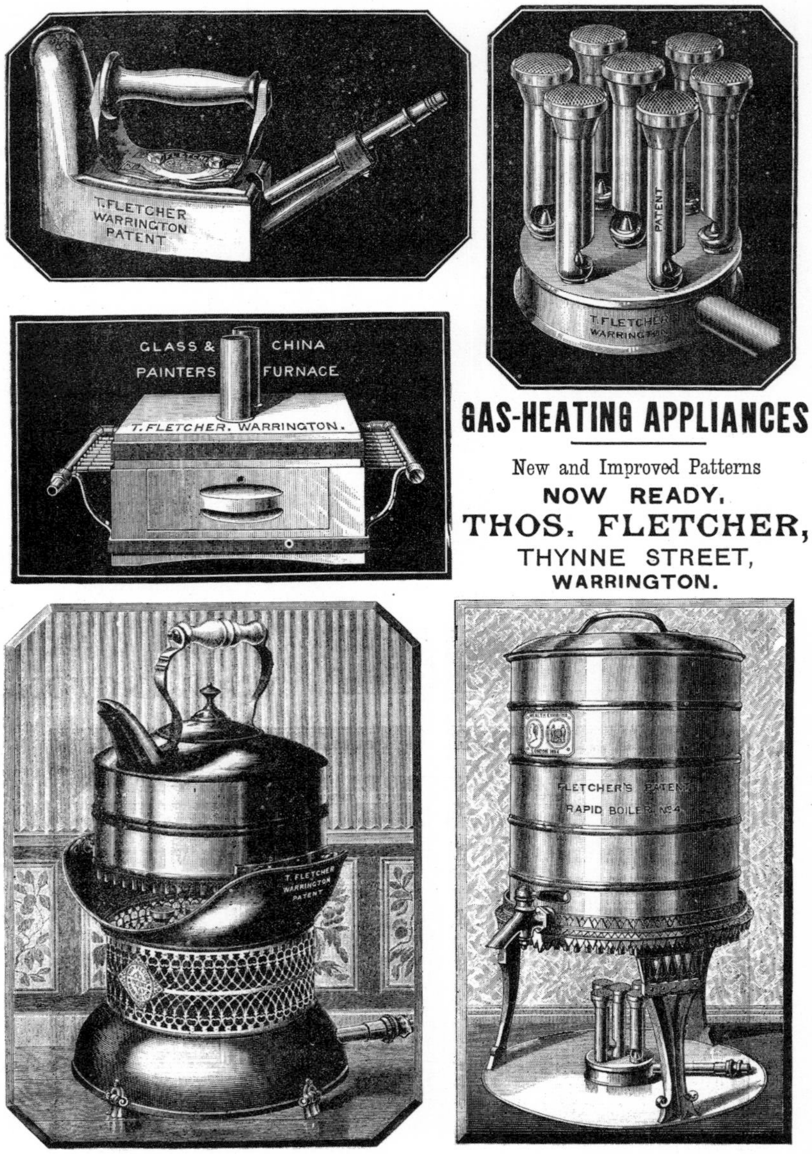
T. FLETCHER WARRINGTON PATENT
GLASS & CHINA PAINTERS FURNACE
T. FLETCHER. WARRINGTON.
T. FLETCHER WARRINGTON
GAS-HEATING APPLIANCES
New and Improved Patterns
NOW READY.
THOS. FLETCHER,
THYNNE STREET,
WARRINGTON.
T. FLETCHER WARRINGTON PATENT
FLETCHER'S PATENT RAPID BOILER No 4

With the arrival of town gas, a whole new class of domestic products was needed. Demand brought supply, and "improved patterns"

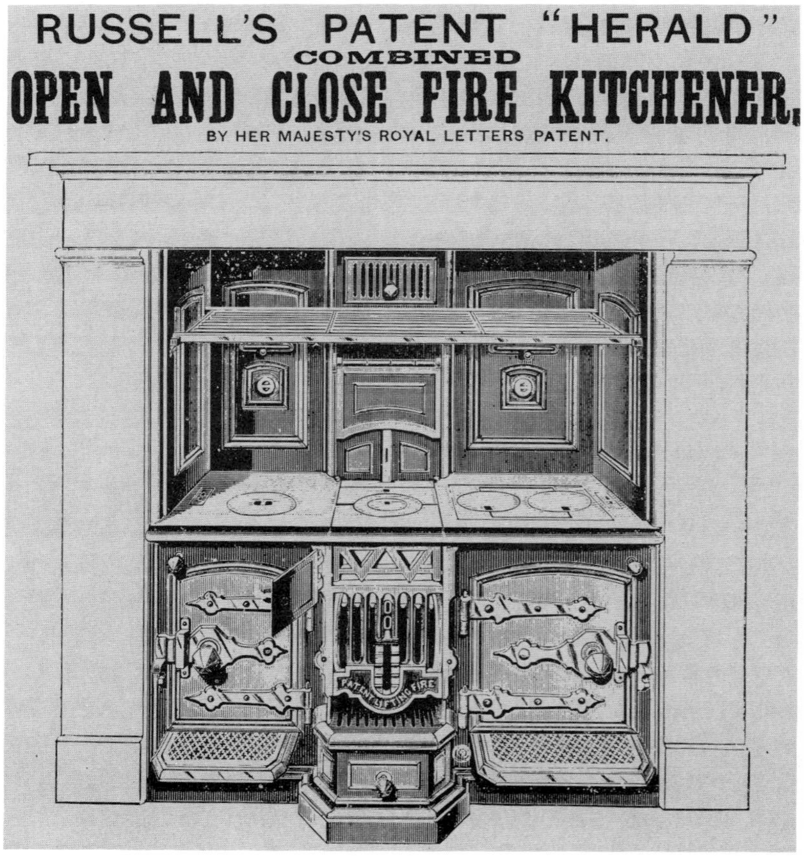
RUSSELL'S PATENT "HERALD"
COMBINED
OPEN AND CLOSE FIRE KITCHENER.
BY HER MAJESTY'S ROYAL LETTERS PATENT.

Coal continued to be the most popular fuel for hearth and home. The kitchen range was one of the best means of cooking ever devised

MAPPIN & WEBB'S ARTISTIC AND USEFUL CHRISTMAS PRESENTS

Registered Design.
Six Solid Silver Afternoon Teaspoons and Tongs, in Rich Morocco Case, lined Silk and Velvet, £2 15s.; Electro Silver, £1 11s. 6d.

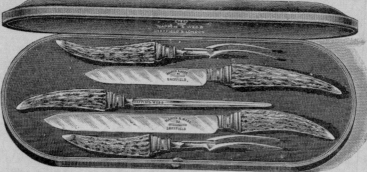

Presentation Carvers, in Morocco Case. 1 Pair each Meat and Game Carvers and Steel, as illustrated, £1 16s.
1 Pair each Meat Carvers and Steel, £1 7s.

Four Chased Solid Silver Salts and Spoons, in Rich Morocco Case, lined Silk, Acorn Design, £3 15s.
Six in Case, £5 15s.

Two Solid Silver Escallop Butter Shells and Two Knives.
In Morocco Case, lined Silk £4 15 0
One Shell and Knife, in Case 2 10 0

Sterling Silver Sweetmeat Dish, £2 5s.

Electro-Silver Teapot, engraved Wild Rose, 2 Pints, £3 10s.; 2½ Pints, £3 15s.

Registered Design. Princess Sugar Bowl and Tongs. Electro Silver, 10s. 6d.; Sterling Silver, £1 15s.

CHRISTMAS LIST, 250 ILLUSTRATIONS, Post-Free.

Four Electro Silver Salt Cellars and Spoons, in Morocco Case, lined Silk and Velvet, £1 1s. Six in Case, £1 10s.

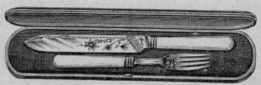

Electro Silver Melon or Cake Carvers, Ivory Handles, Chased Blades, complete in Case, £1 3s.

Richly Chased and Gilt Fruit Spoons and Sifter, in Morocco Case.

	Solid Silver.	Best Electro.
Two Spoons and Sifter	£4 0 0	£1 11 6
Two Spoons only	3 0 0	1 1 0

Sterling Silver Sugar Castor, Richly Chased, 7 inches high, £4.

MAPPIN & WEBB,
18, POULTRY, E.C., & 158, OXFORD-ST., W.,
LONDON.
MANUFACTORIES: SHEFFIELD AND LONDON.

Two Sterling Silver Butter Knives.
In Morocco Case, £1 10s.; Smaller size, £1 1s.

MAPPIN & WEBB'S "Unequalled for hard wear." "Highest attainable quality." SILVER PLATE.

Fruit Spoons in Case, richly Chased, and part Gilt.
Solid Silver, 2 Spoons and Sifter, £4; 2 Spoons, £3. Best Electro, 2 Spoons and Sifter, £1 11s. 6d.; 2 Spoons, £1 1s.

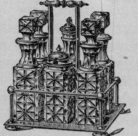

Electro-Silver Dinner-Cruet.
Cut-Glass Bottles, £3 10s.
Plain Cut Bottles, £3.

Electro-Silver on Hard Nickel Breakfast-Dish.
Converts into three Dishes by simply removing the Handle, £3 15s.

Electro-Silver and Cut-Glass Butter-Dish, with XVII. Century Pattern Knife, 10s. 6d.

Registered "Princess" Tea-Service, with Two China Cups and Saucers, Two Spoons and Sugar Tongs.
Complete in Case, Sterling Silver, £11 11s. Best Electro-Silver, £5 5s.

OXFORD-ST., W., 158; & POULTRY, E.C., 18, LONDON.
Manufactory—Royal Plate and Cutlery Works, Sheffield.

CATALOGUES POST-FREE

Crumb Scoop, with Plated Blade and Ivory Handle, 18s. 6d.

Combined Egg-Stand and Toast-Rack.
Best Electro, £1 1s.

The gentry had their tea served in sterling silver – or at the least in silver plate. Cutlery and cruets were also silver; even the crumb scoop

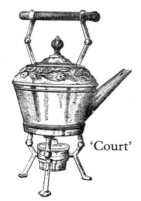

'Court'

'Cambridge'

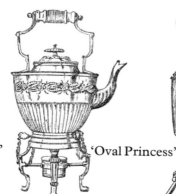

'Oval Princess'

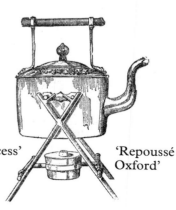

'Repoussé Oxford'

'Gipsy'

43

With the arrival of the penny post in 1840, and the postman's knock, it became necessary to invent, and then provide, the letter-box

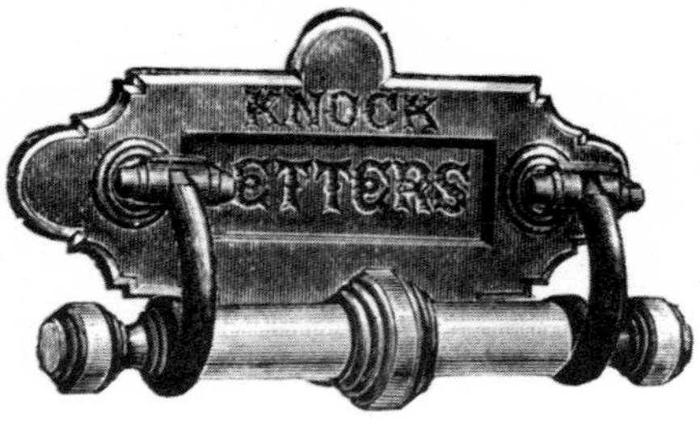
KNOCK
LETTERS

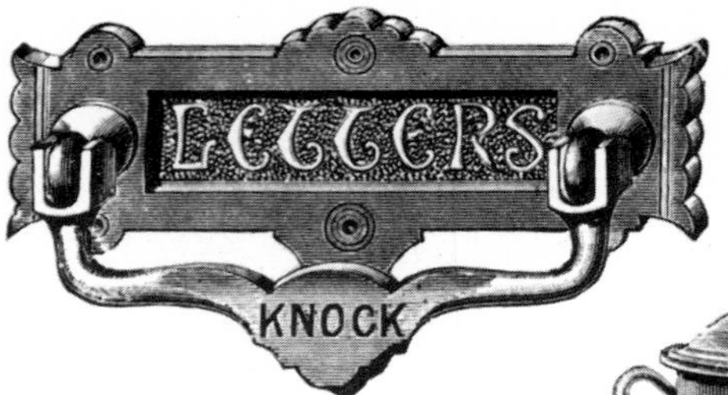
LETTERS
KNOCK

'Combination knockers', "POLISHED BRASS ONLY": more work for someone

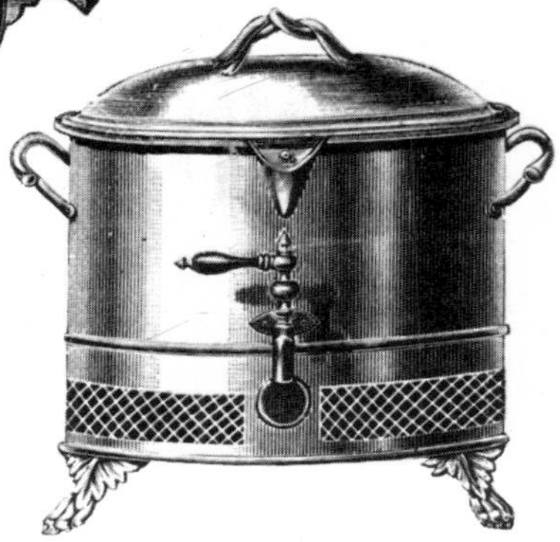

This sausage and potato warmer held 8 quarts. A division down the centre kept the foods apart

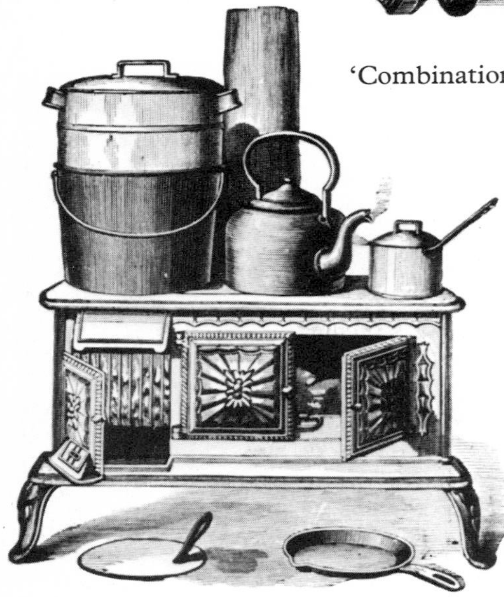

Moulded iron stove: note cabriole legs

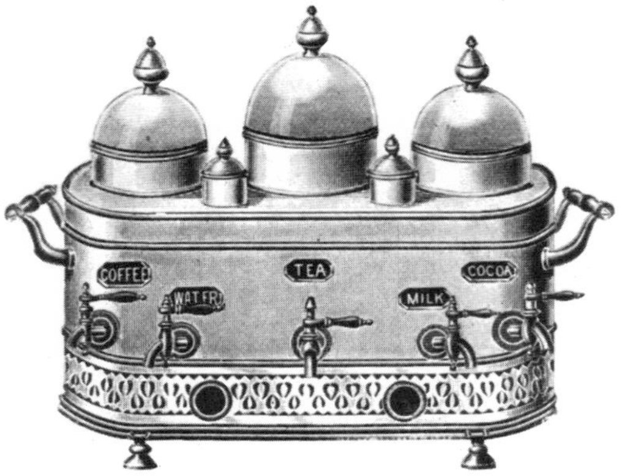
COFFEE
TEA
COCOA
WATER
MILK

A combination urn for the larger household – with "pockets for milk"

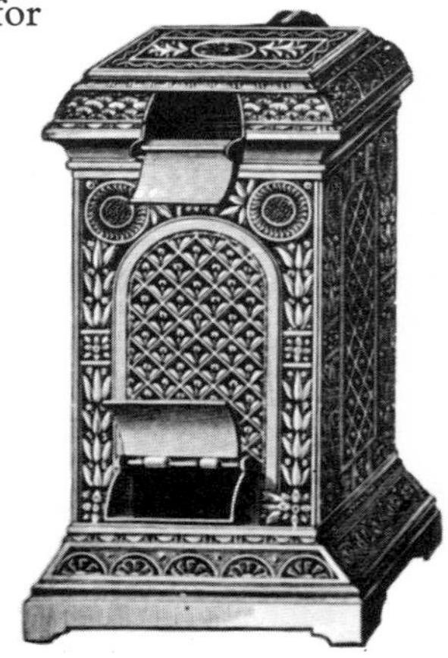

Stove for a hallway

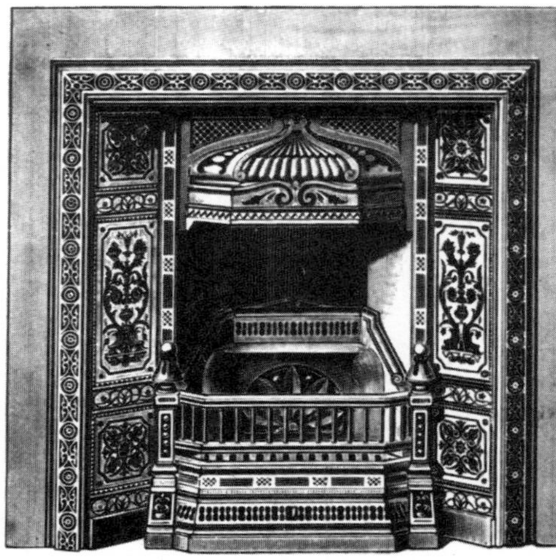

Even a cheap tile grate looked elaborate. This came in 8 sizes, from 23s. 3d. Tiles were extra

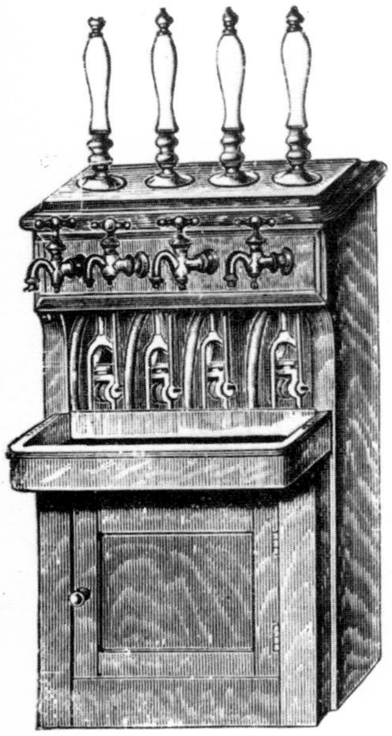

Servants got part of their wages in beer, and a large household might well run to a pub 'beer engine' to dole out the rations

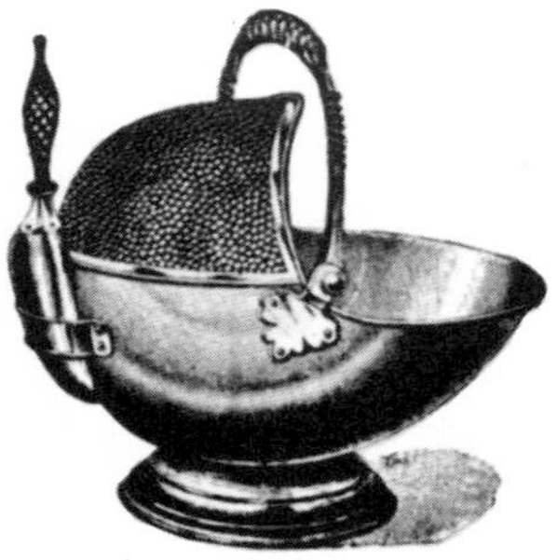

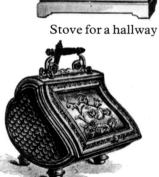

The well-off had fires in every room, and every fire needed a coal scuttle

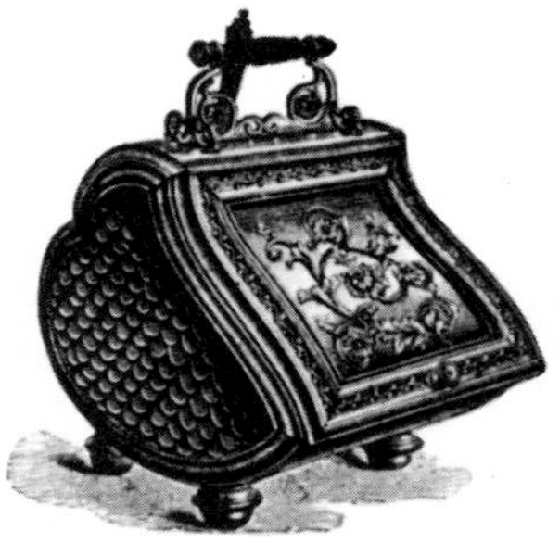

Another scuttle, also with shovel

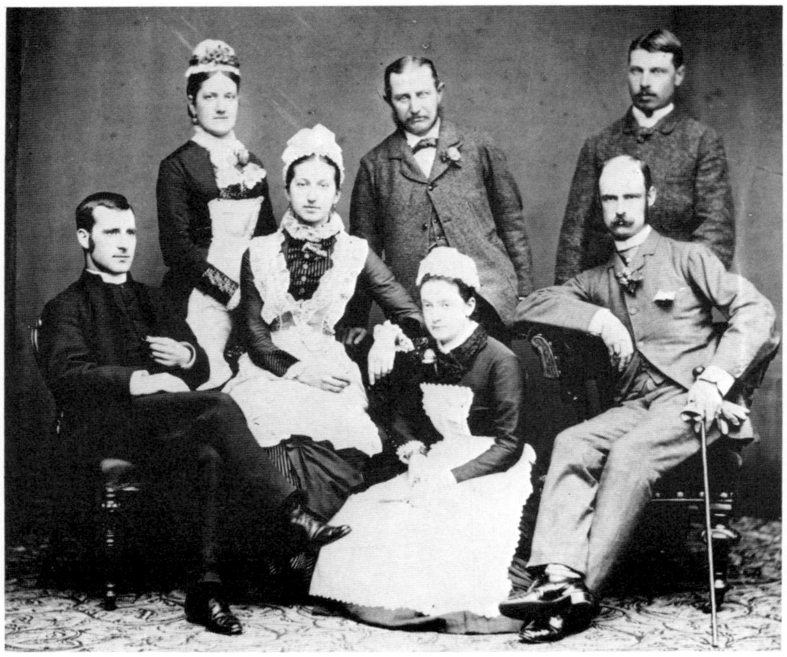

The servants' hall: middle-class families of moderate wealth frequently had six or seven servants – they came cheap. There was plenty of work: coal dust, from the fires in every room, dirtied carpets, furniture, clothes . . . Right: a 'mantel register' with overmantel. Such a dust-trap needed frequent cleaning

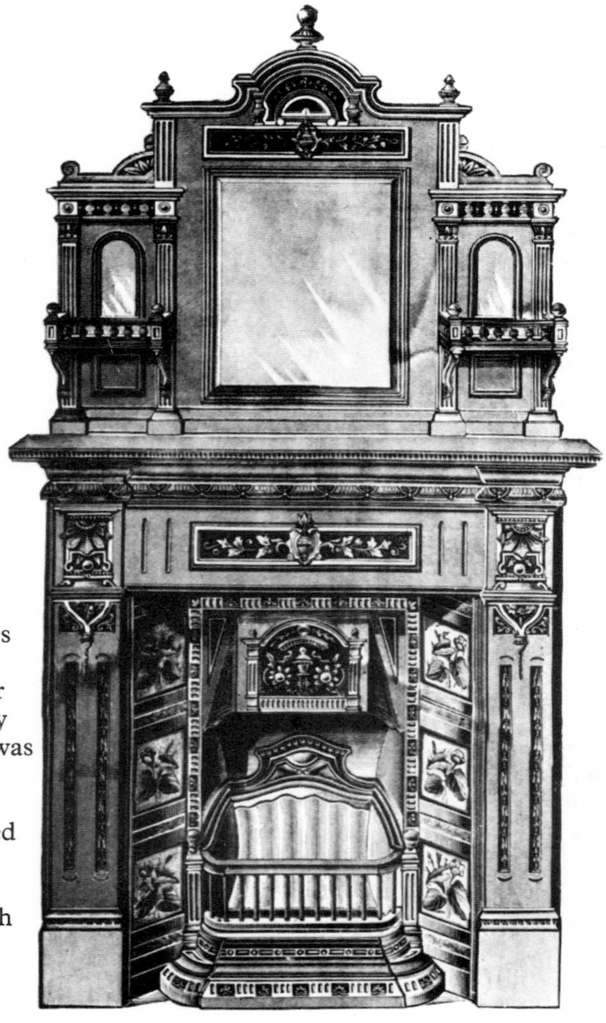

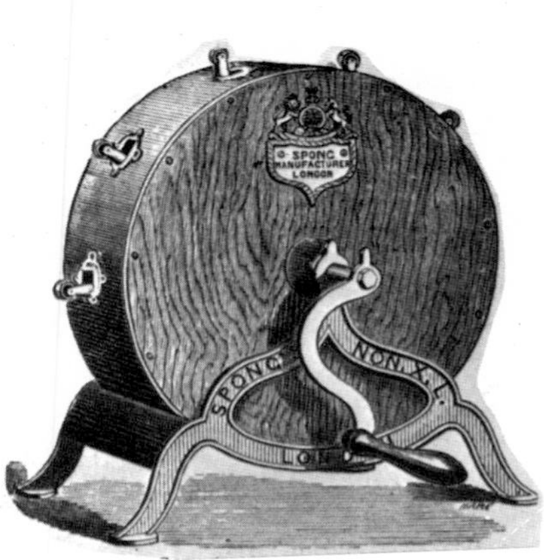
SPONG

In the days before stainless steel, a patent knife-cleaner from Spong was more necessary than it is today

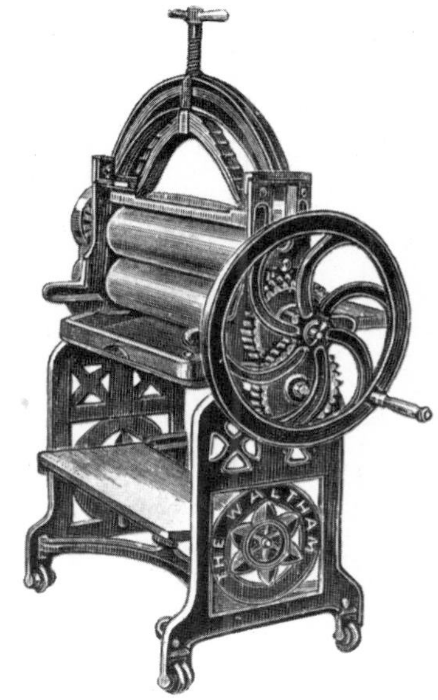

Young & Marten's Special Mangle and Wringer: the beginning of the end of one sort of drudgery

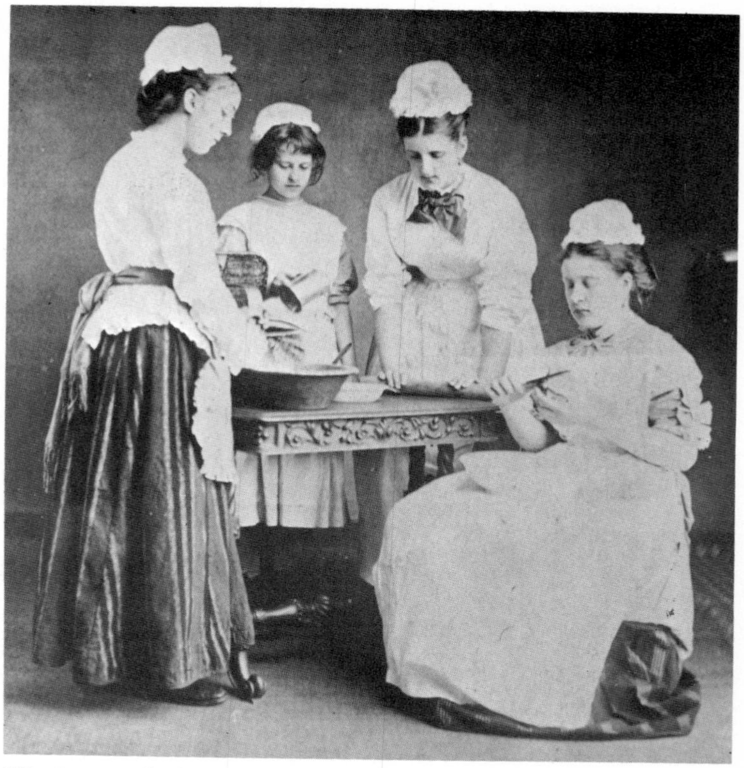

Kitchen staff of a big house near Keswick. Others waited at table

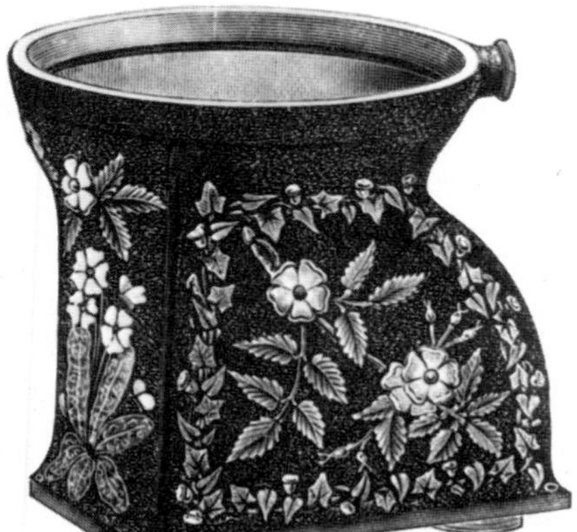

Perhaps what most of us would find most difficult to do without if we were transported back 100 years: decent plumbing. But it was on the way, though so far only for the middle and upper classes. Above: the 'Primrose'

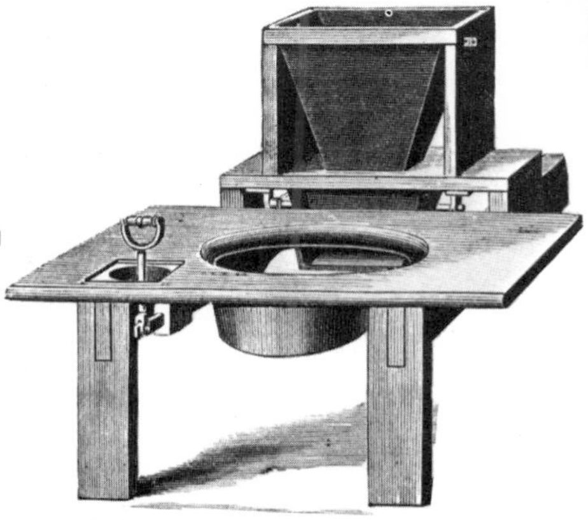

The less affluent might have an earth closet: this threw $1\frac{1}{2}$ pints of earth at each pull

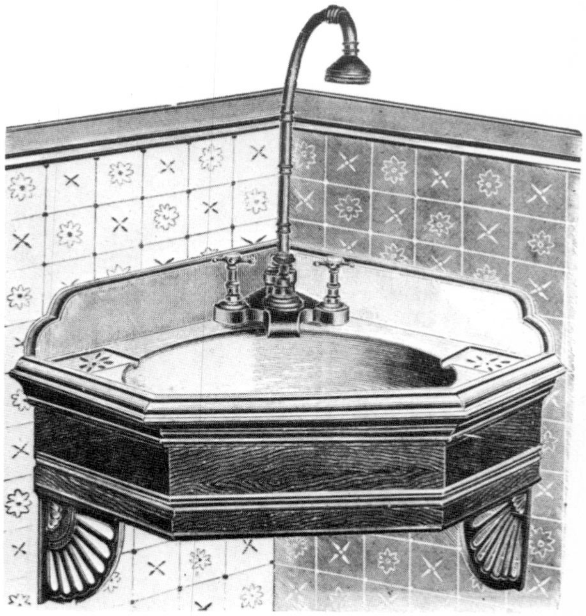

Combined hot and cold taps, as above, were a sensible refinement. This model, which could convert to a shower, came from Young & Marten. It cost 189s. or 228s. complete, according to size

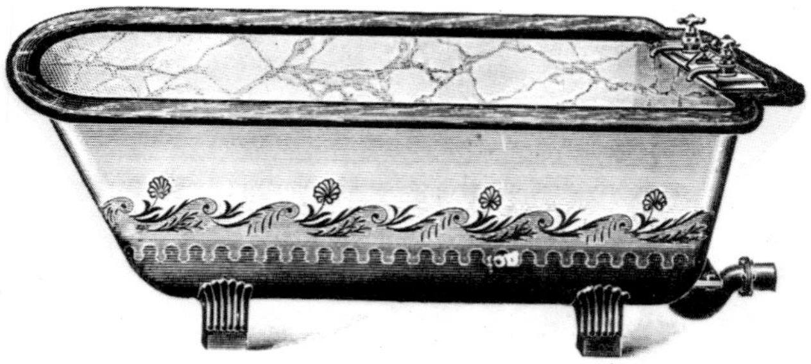

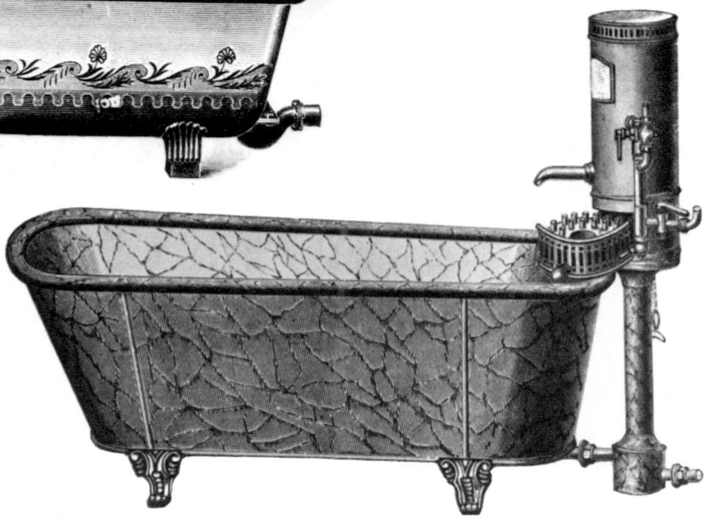

Baths were highly decorative. The gas geyser arrived when town gas was piped to private houses, and has been widely used ever since

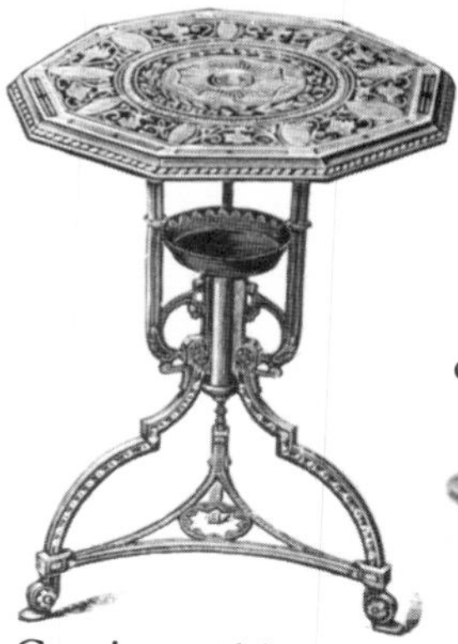

Cast iron table, 9s. 9d.

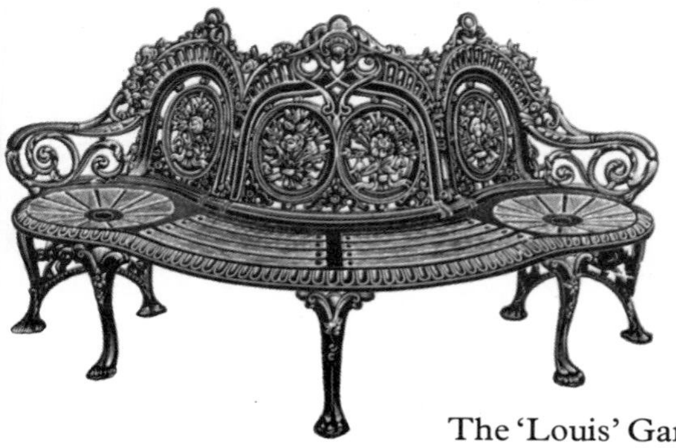

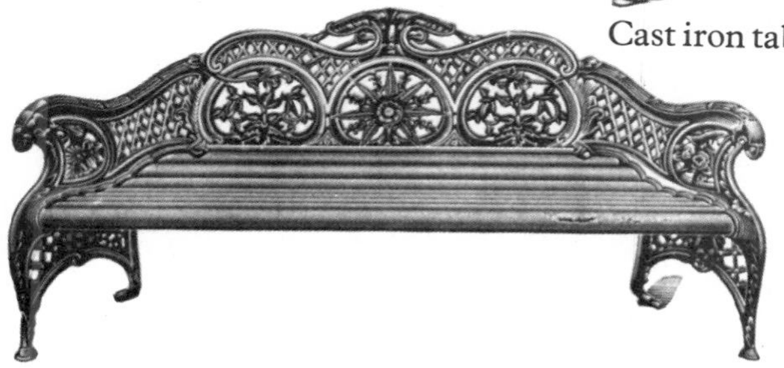

The 'Louis' Garden Chair, Circular or Straight; in chocolate or green

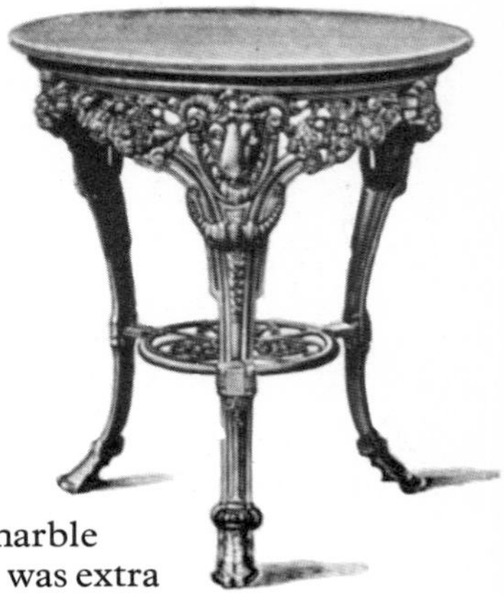

A marble top was extra

THE RISE OF THE PLATFORM

By Bernard Crick

The Queen thought Gladstone a demagogue, Disraeli considered him malicious and hypocritical.
In the see-sawing campaigns of these giants, Britain saw the
emergence of gladiatorial contests dangerously close to the American Presidential system

Gladstone – the 'Grand Old Man'

"To the Queen's satisfaction the ministry was heavily defeated. Gladstone fought his battle with unwearied intrepidity, and was not seriously moved by the Queen's reminder that by persisting in oratorical agitation outside his own constituency he was establishing an undesirable and undignified precedent in ministerial etiquette." Thus wrote even the discreet Sidney Lee facing in 1902, as Editor of the *Dictionary of National Biography*, his most difficult task ever.

Indeed, Gladstone had persisted in "oratorical agitation outside his own constituency". Not merely then in 1886 over Home Rule for Ireland but, the memory was bitter to the Queen, he had done so in 1879 to bring down her favourite, Disraeli, over the Eastern Question and Turkish Atrocities. That autumn in travelling up to Midlothian, his Scottish constituency, he spoke to huge crowds at railway stations wherever the train happened to stop (by prearrangement) – like "a damned American", his opponents said. He intervened in other people's constituencies and tried to turn the simultaneous dissolution of six hundred seats into a truly general election

fought on national issues and dominated by the centre of things – himself.

There was no love lost between the Queen and Mr Gladstone, the "Grand Old Man" as his friends called him, or "the old Fox" and the "Grand Old Meddler" of his opponents. (Disraeli had once called him "a unique mixture of malice, envy, superstition and hypocrisy".)

To the Queen, Gladstone was a demogogue, corrupting and destroying the old political order for Party advantage: stirring up the masses against the social establishment, trying to substitute vulgar passions for respectable reason: the "rule of numbers" rather than the "wisdom of the classes", and even addressing her like a public meeting. But she was wrong to blame Gladstone for the new power of the popular platforms over or – better – in addition to Parliament. She should have blamed the Industrial Revolution. Gladstone, in fact, exploited the medium, but suppressed the message. But for Gladstone's astonishing popularity with the masses, perhaps mainly because he went out to them rather than for what he said or did, the social discontents which resulted in the Reform Bill of 1867 and the consequent new style of politics might have overwhelmed the Old Order, as in America or France. England might, indeed, have become a democracy. If Disraeli claimed to have "dished the Whigs" by his opportunistic acceptance of reform in 1867 (while Gladstone doddered with "fancy franchises"), Gladstone might better claim to have dished the Radicals by accepting "the Platform" as his own.

"The Platform" had been a Wesleyan invention. The revivalist preachers, almost a century before, had been the first to tour, stir and agitate the country – long before the politicians found the need to go "out of doors" from Westminster or had anything to say, beyond their purely local issues, when they did. When political meetings inherited the techniques of the wayside pulpit – in the reform agitations of the 1830s and 1860s, and in Chartism of the Hungry Forties, they took over the very style of oratory. From a High Churchman like Gladstone to an atheist like Aneurin Bevan in our own day, they could all demand that men become "reborn" and search for "the New Jerusalem" – whatever they variously may have meant.

It was 1867 which marked the beginning of mass politics in Britain. After that, the old established Parliamentary leaders had, swallowing their distaste and dignity, to go to the country or to go to the wall. For the first time there was a democratic influence in British politics. The school text-books still have it otherwise: 1832 is the "great Bill". It was, in fact, a rationalisation of the old property-bound order, not the first blast of democratic trumpets. Before 1832, about 5 per cent of the population over 20 years of age had the vote; afterwards, at the next general election, about 7 per cent had it.

Small wonder that the Radicals kept up the agitation, off and on, for over thirty years. After the Act of 1867, 16.4 per cent of the population could vote, and after the Act of 1884 (also by then the secret ballot) 28.5 per cent. If one excludes women (as they were), one can double these figures as the politically effective proportion. But the new constituents could not all be reached on a personal and local basis. Party organisation had to be extended from Westminster to the country, but not expanded in the name of doctrine and creed, but simply to organise the new voters behind the old, overwhelmingly aristocratic parties.

Some of the old parliamentary leaders never accepted the new game. They regarded demands for constant speeches in their own constituencies as quite bad enough, but in other people's as a damned effrontery. But the faster types among their lieutenants saw the point – Joseph Chamberlain and Charles Dilke (until the divorce courts smashed him) among Gladstone's men, Lord Randolph Churchill on the Conservative side, though his concept of "Tory democracy" and his attempt to give the new National Political Union some real power over the Party's Parliamentary chieftains was frustrated.

Gladstone, then, spoke on railway trains out of political necessity, not out of any modernistic or democratic principles, just as he had repealed the newspaper duties to keep the Radicals with the Liberals. But what then were the forces that drove him in this direction; and that drove Disraeli "to shoot Niagara" in 1867?

In Hyde Park on July 23, 1866, though "the respectable leaders" of the Reform League obeyed orders to disperse given by the Home Secretary, "the mob" tore down the railings and proceeded to set up otherwise orderly platforms and pass resolutions. The threat was there all right and was needed. The old Radical game was well played: "What if your stupid obstinacy makes our followers really get out of hand?" *Reynolds' Newspaper* (an endearing mixture, then, of anti-aristocratic salaciousness and

Disraeli – the Queen's favourite

radical politics) rubbed in the salt: "By the exercise of that natural and 'Constitutional' muscular and mental might which God has given them they established their right to enter into their own Park. By a long pull, a strong pull and a push all together, down went the iron railings and the stones in which they are fixed. . . ."

Neither of the great Reform Bills went through because old Whig and Tory gentlemen in Westminster suddenly became convinced that the Radical fellows "had a point". They went through rather because the aristocracy was frightened of the consequences if they did not; because many of them would have been morally unwilling anyway to use the degree of force required to maintain "the old system" (in England, anyway, though Ireland was another matter); and because the old system had become thoroughly discredited – mainly by its flagrant inefficiency in the Crimean War which was, in turn, in part at least a consequence of the narrowness of its base, of its failure to mobilise and integrate the energies and new skills of new men.

Even when the base was broadened, England still did not become a democracy: there was simply a democratic base to which minimal concessions had to be made. The two political Englands still existed side by side. The Marxist Gent., Hyndman, could talk to the elder Disraeli. The basic Liberal slogan was still, ultimately to their ruin, "Masters and Men!". The new Labour movement – the Labour Party was founded in 1900 – could inherit the ruins of the Liberals. But the most remarkable thing was, in the long run, the success of the Conservatives in wooing the masses without, for many many years, in any way diluting the pedigree of their leaders. The "new working-man" appeared all too willing to accept aristocratic and upper-middle-class leadership.

Gladstone lampooned – breaking the Lords

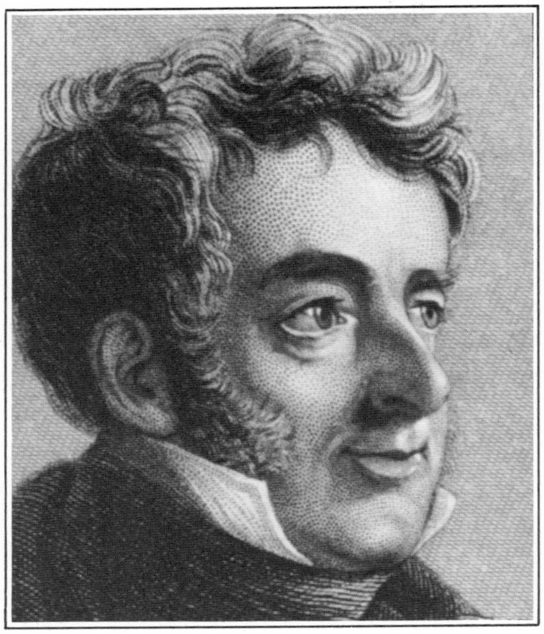

Lord Melbourne (1779–1848)
– mentor to the young Queen

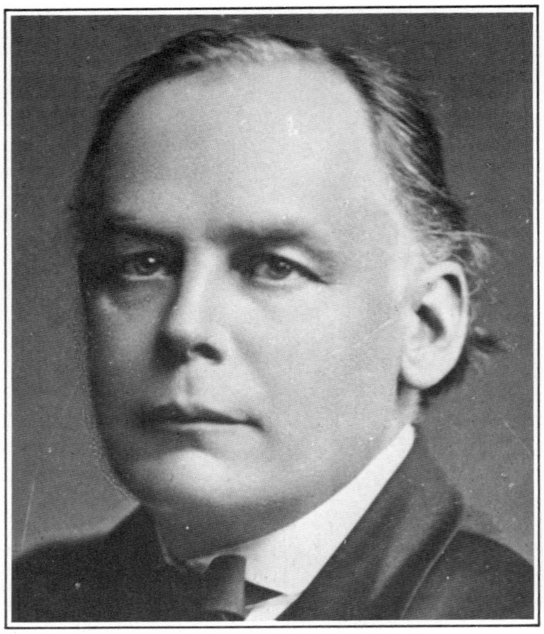

Charles Bradlaugh (1833–1891)
– the first freethinker MP

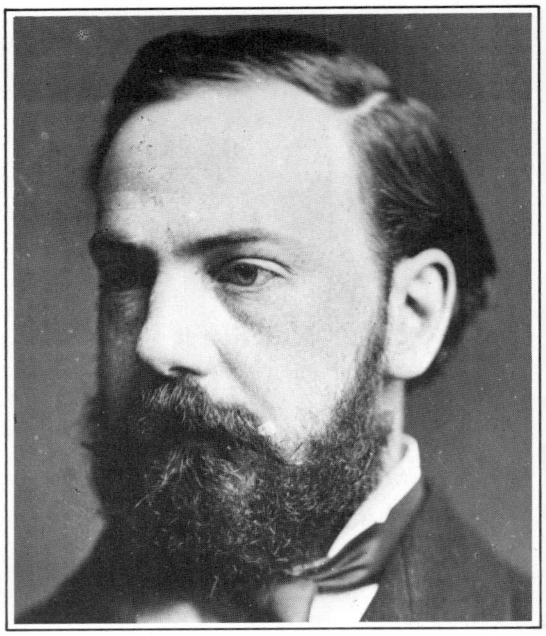

Charles Dilke (1843–1911)
– Republican overthrown by scandal

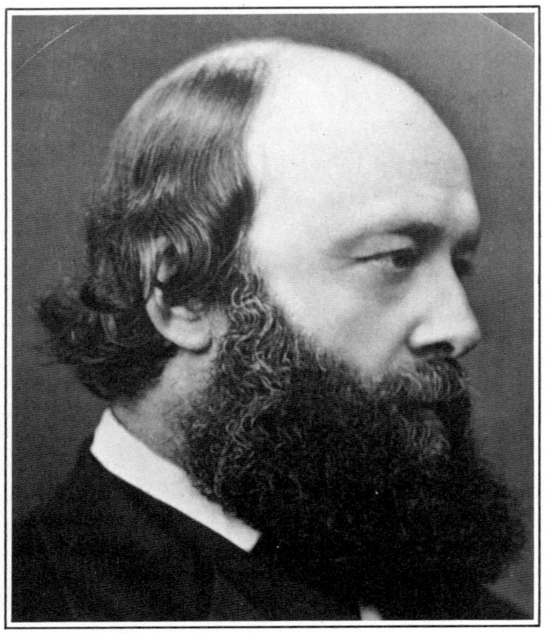

Marquess of Salisbury (1830–1903)
– aristocrat and intellectual

THE QUEEN'S MINISTERS

Encompassing such diverse characters as the Duke of Devonshire and Keir Hardie, even Parliament – Government and back-benchers alike – began to reflect a very much more representative cross-section of the electorate

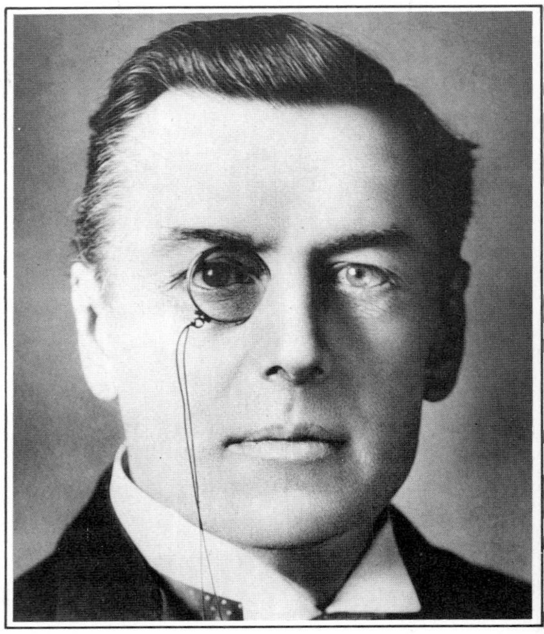

Joseph Chamberlain (1836–1914)
– the first 'machine' politician

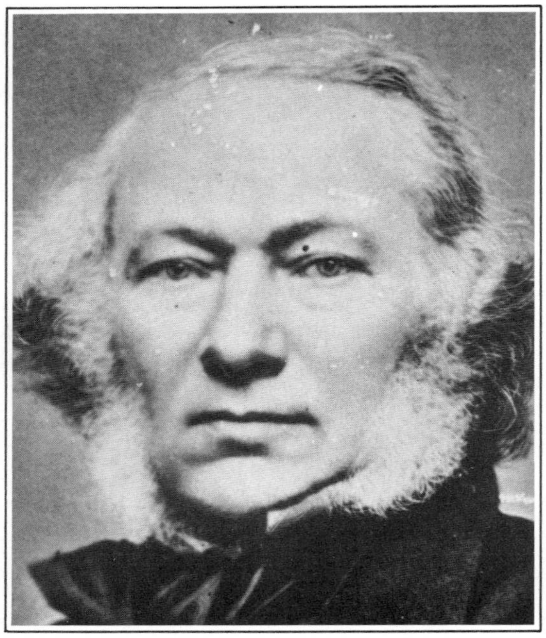

Richard Cobden (1804–1865)
– led Anti-Corn Law League

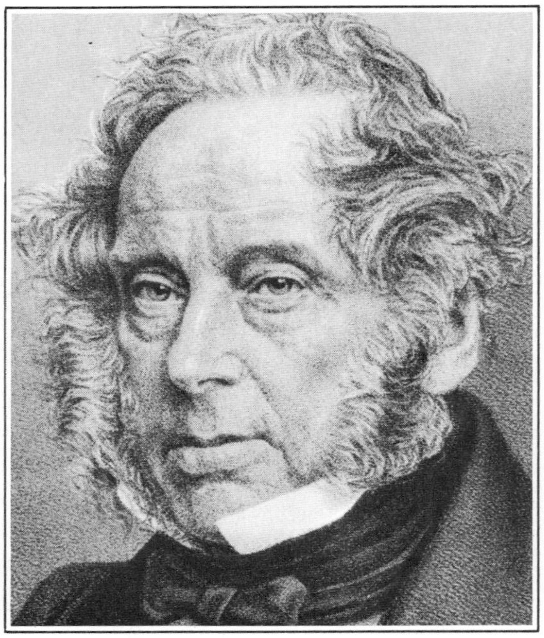

Lord Palmerston (1784–1865)
– staunch advocate of Imperial power

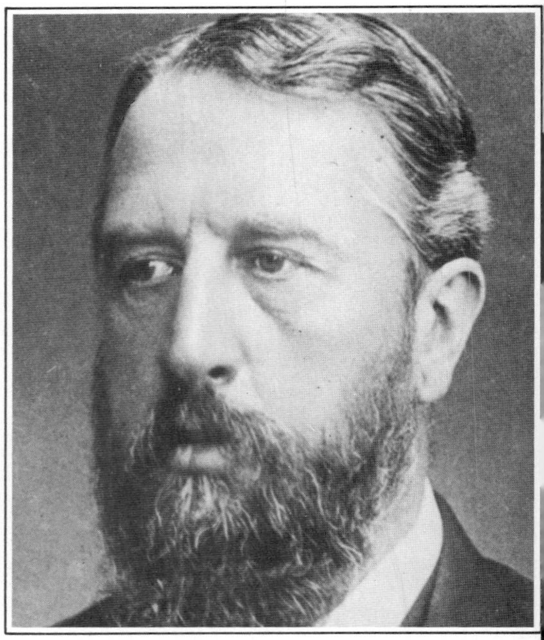

Duke of Devonshire (1833–1908)
– rose to power on his title

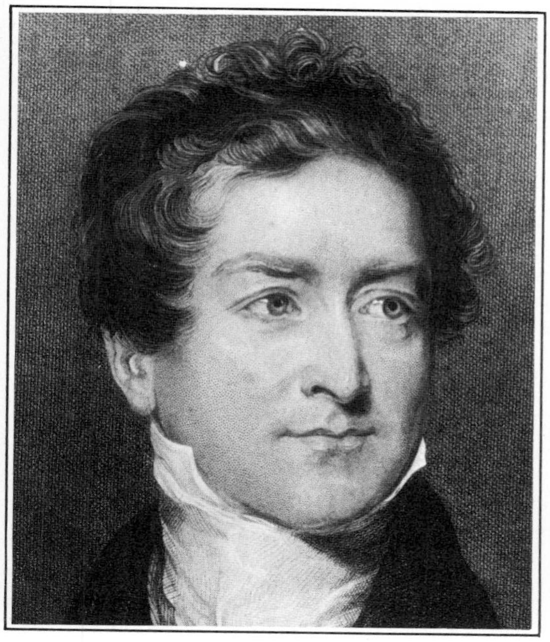

Sir Robert Peel (1788–1850)
– founder of a trained police force

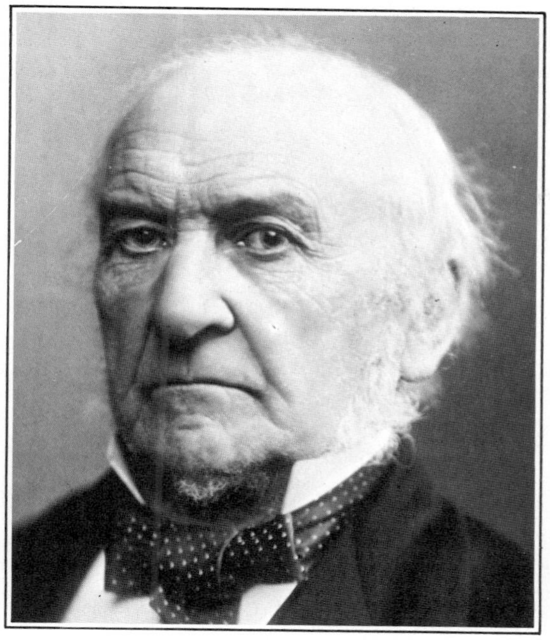

William Ewart Gladstone (1809–1898)
– the Grand Old Man

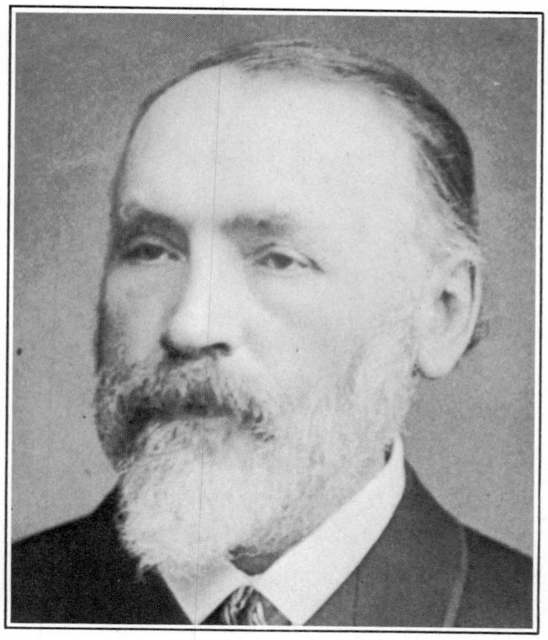

Henry Labouchere (1831–1912)
– MP and radical satirist

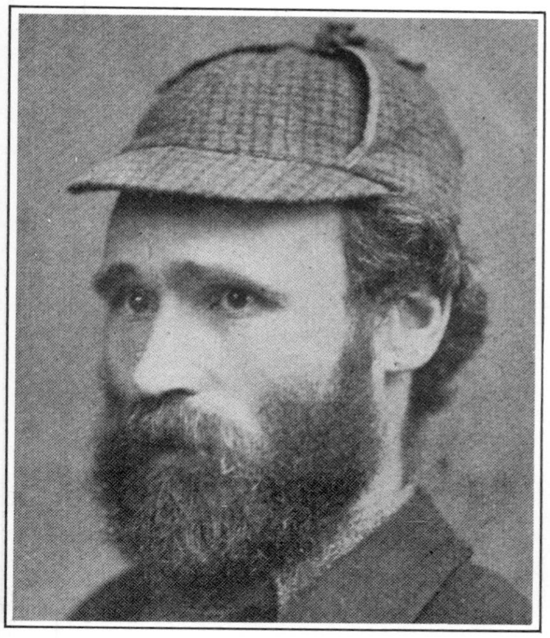

Keir Hardie (1856–1915) – torch-bearer of the Labour movement

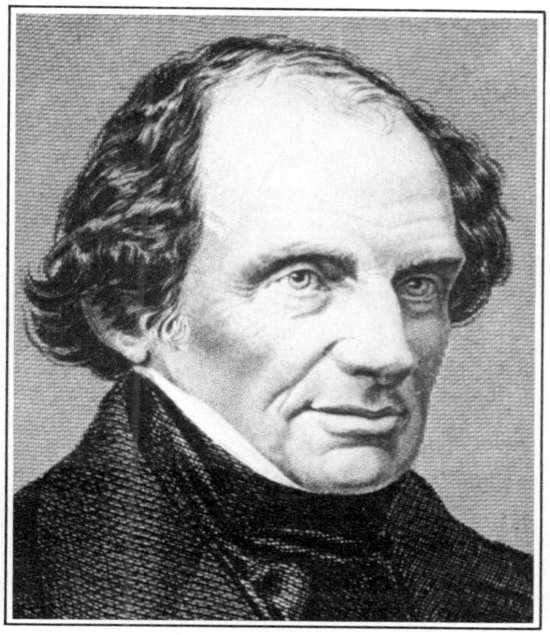

Lord John Russell (1792–1878)
– last of the Whig Premiers

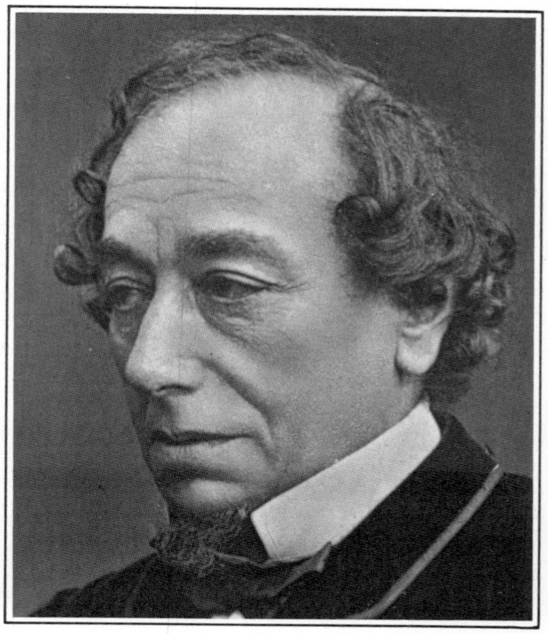

Benjamin Disraeli (1804–1881)
– strong influence over Queen and Tories

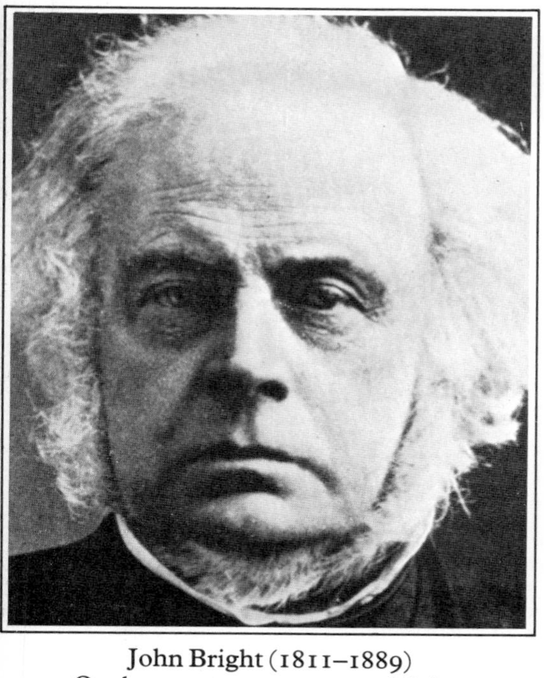

John Bright (1811–1889)
– Quaker, orator, opponent of Crimea

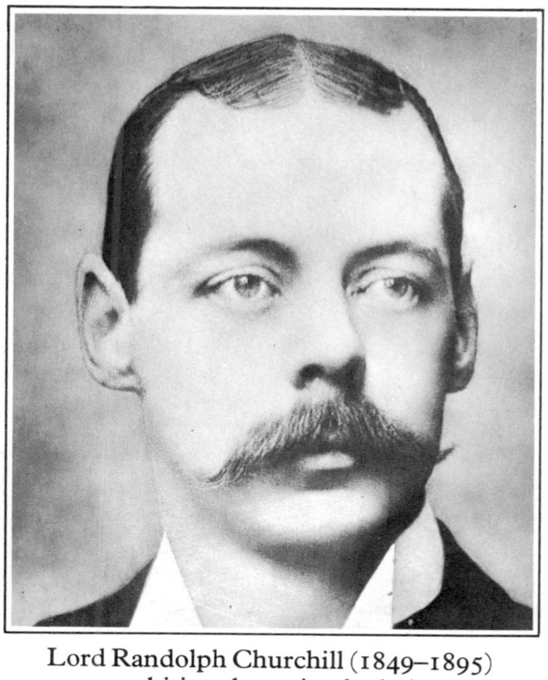

Lord Randolph Churchill (1849–1895)
– ambitious but miscalculating

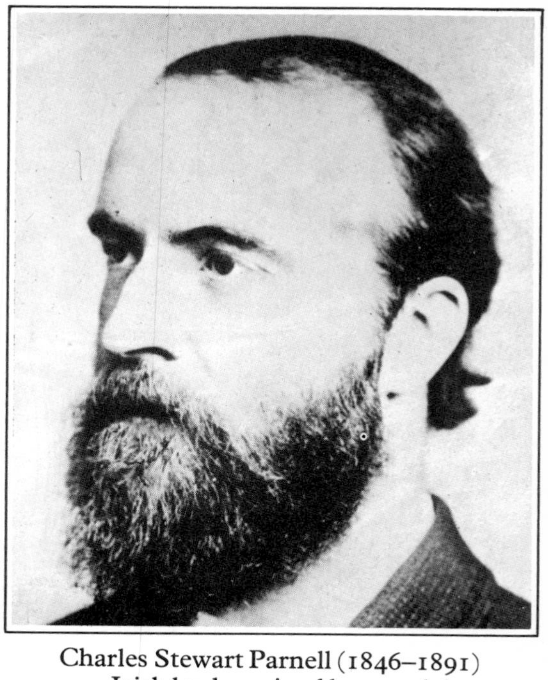

Charles Stewart Parnell (1846–1891)
– Irish leader ruined by scandal

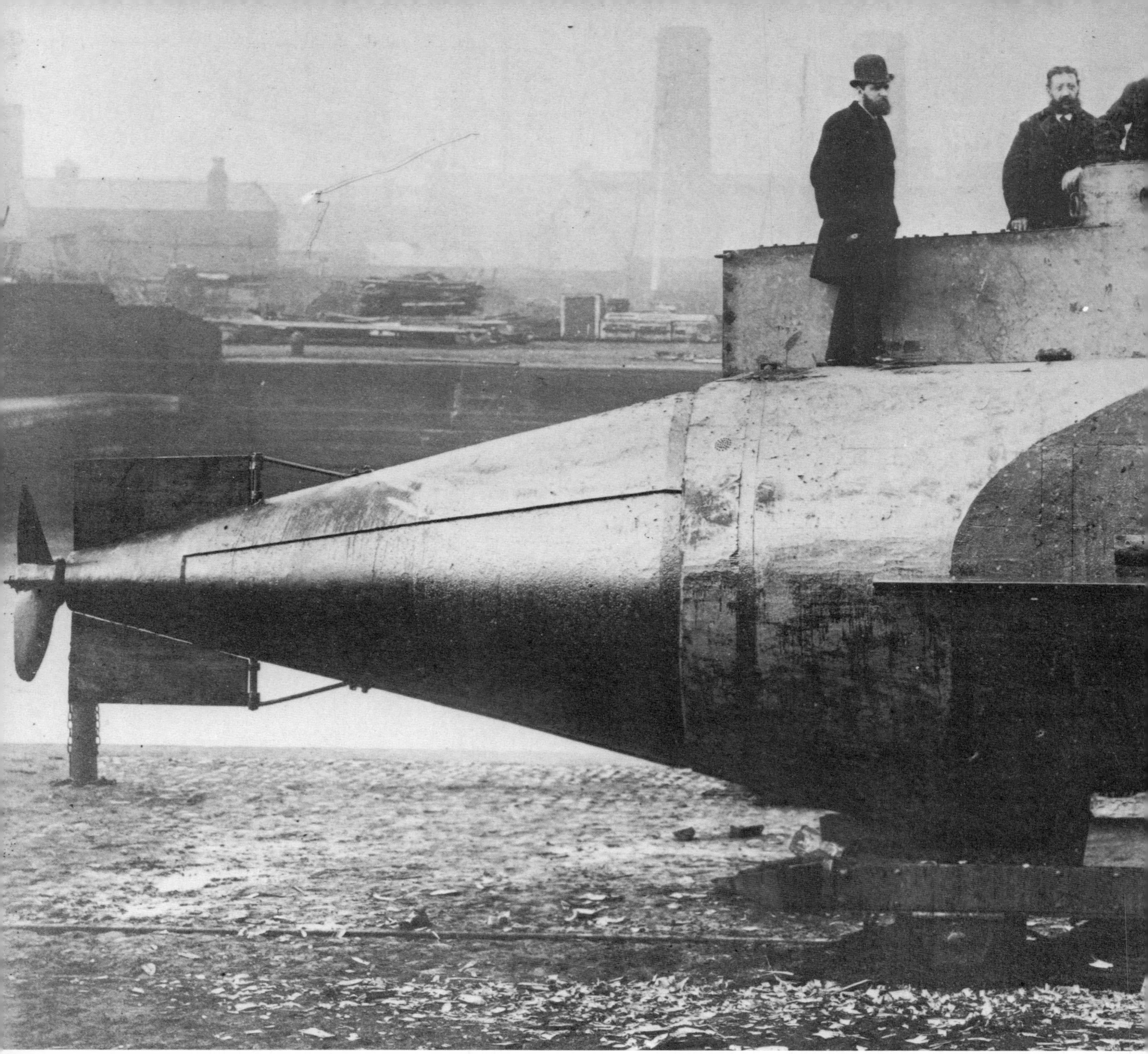

THE TRANSPORT REVOLUTION

By John Pudney

During the years of Victoria's reign, the British became the prime movers in a world revolution of human mobility. In 1840 horse-power meant the power of the horse. By the end of the century steam had multiplied horse-power into public transport capable of speeds up to 100 miles per hour. The remarkable men who fashioned this technological explosion were a unique and exciting breed. Above: Garrett's submersible boat, 1879.

In England, at the outset of Victoria's reign, the masses moved hardly at all. Travel was a luxury for the well-to-do: for the poor it was only undertaken in dire necessity. By the turn of the century, transportation was for all and even the least privileged citizens could contemplate travel for pleasure. There were misgivings about this. The Duke of Wellington had deplored the notion of railways on a national scale as "they would encourage the lower classes to move about". Such dangers were countered, however, only two months after Queen Victoria made her first railroad trip in 1842 when there were strikes and demonstrations in the industrial areas. Northern trade unionists, Chartists and oppressed workers, already feeling the pinch of the Hungry Forties, rioted. The Government, in accordance with tradition, called out the troops – but in a novel and telling way. From Woolwich, Guards and Artillery; from Ports-

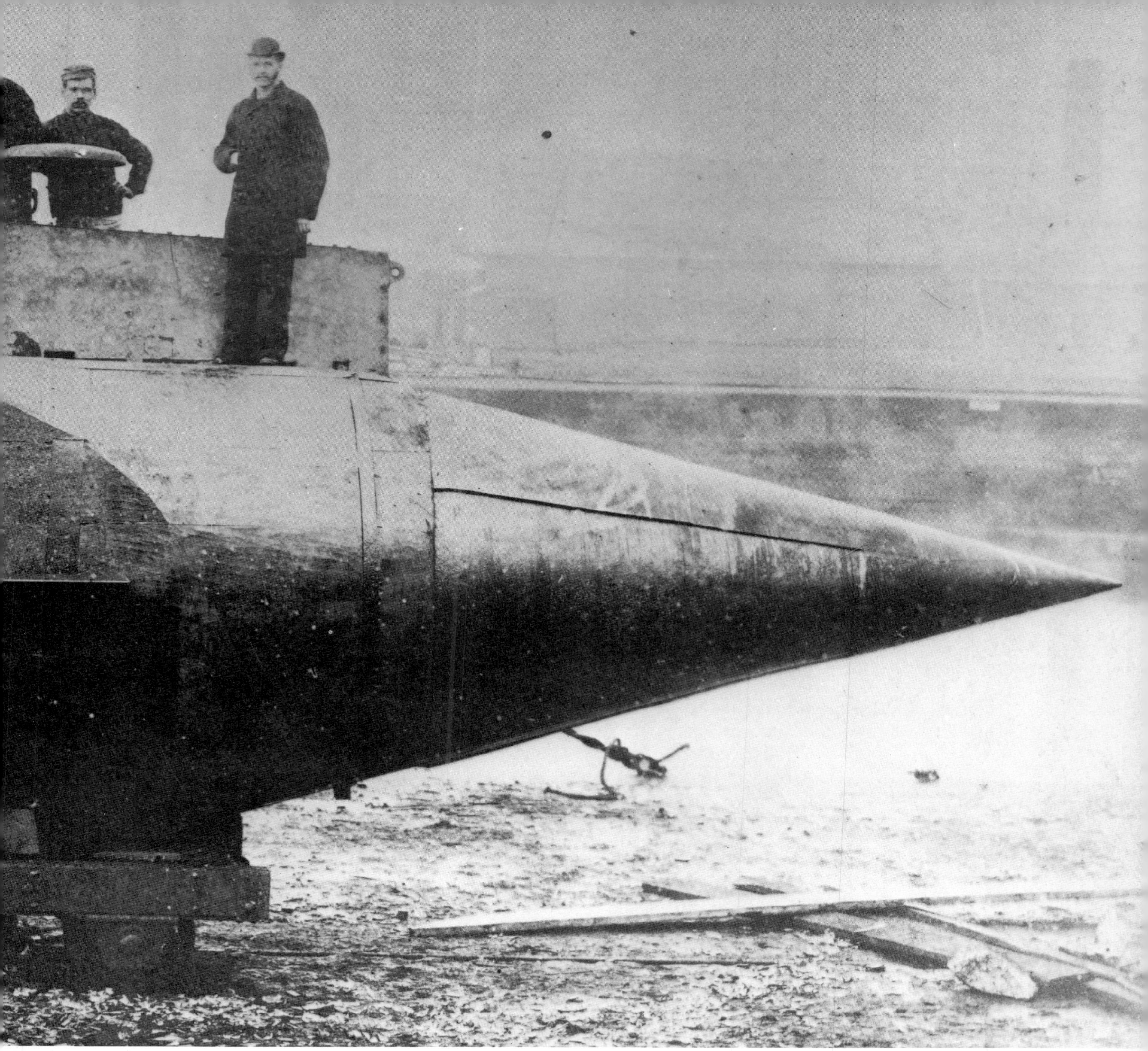

mouth, the 34th Foot; from St George's Barracks, the 3rd battalion of the Grenadiers – who fixed bayonets to march through the menacing crowds, not north on the Queen's highways but to Euston Square station. Manchester was occupied by Royal Dragoons, Bolton by Highlanders. Charles Greville, who had made his own maiden trip by train five years before and had praised the sense of security and the delightful velocity, now wrote: "September 1st, 1842 . . . Parliament was no sooner up, than the riots broke out, sufficiently alarming but for the railroads, which enabled the Government to pour troops into the disturbed districts, and extinguish the conflagration at once . . ." The pathetic embers left by this steam-borne show of force were soon put out by starvation. Not all remained to enjoy even that. From Staffordshire alone, 54 men were transported for life.

While in the 1840s uneasiness about mass mobility still lingered in the minds of the Establishment, a solidly-built 33-year-old carpenter, printer and propagandist, who had only once in his life made a journey by rail, was trudging the 15 miles from Harborough to Leicester on a June day. About halfway – his mind "often reverted to the spot" – he had a vision. "What a glorious thing it would be if the newly-developed powers of railways and locomotives could be made subservient to the promotion of temperance!"

It was: for the name of the man with the vision was Thomas Cook, bent upon good work yet almost fortuitously revolutionising leisure.

You do not come across the name of Thomas Cook very much in the history books: and there are other eminent Victorians, men of enterprise and invention, who are insufficiently acknowledged. For most of us who have not specialised in history, the significance of the

OPENING
OF THE
MELBOURNE RAILWAY
MR. THOMAS COOK
(Formerly of Melbourne)
Respectfully intimates to his old Friends and Fellow Townspeople that, in connection with the visit of his
FIRST EXCURSION PARTY,
FROM LEICESTER,
ON THURSDAY, SEPTEMBER 10th, 1868,
(To arrive at about 4.0 p.m.)
HE WILL GIVE AN
ADDRESS
IN THE ATHENÆUM,
TO INHABITANTS & VISITORS,
Briefly recapitulating some of the events of his EXCURSION and TOURIST LIFE, since leaving Melbourne nearly 40 years ago; and anticipatory of his approaching Trips to
ITALY, EGYPT & PALESTINE.
FREE ADMISSION
AFTER TEA, AT HALF-PAST SEVEN O'CLOCK.

T. COOK, Printer, Granby Street, Leicester.

Thomas Cook invented the tourist industry

Industrial Revolution has been properly stressed, but there never seems to have been adequate emphasis upon the basic revolution in transportation, neither upon the hardware nor upon the men who devoted themselves to it. Their skills, their vision, their acumen, their energies are overshadowed by the potentates, statesmen, generals, legislators who made so much use of their talents in encompassing great events. Yet these men dedicated to the mechanics of transportation, or like Cook to its consolidation, were not guided by precedent or traditional experience. Unlike the more celebrated eminent Victorians they were innovators pioneering areas of activity, power, and force which were unprecedented.

Much of the basic invention had been done when Victoria came to the throne. There was already, so to speak, a certain head of steam. Its power was beginning to be felt. It was a challenge eagerly seized by young men. It was a young man's world. Steam soon had its heroes. They lived in the sort of limelight enjoyed in our times, but more briefly, by film stars, athletes and, sometimes, five-star generals. They were not initiators, not necessarily the inventors of the engines which revolutionised time, space and industry. Their talents lay in the application and promotion of steam. They were practical dreamers, creative technicians, bold and versatile men of vision. We shall never see their like again. Their ardour of uninhibited enquiry and daring individualism is unlikely to be reproduced in a climate of specialisation and controlled team research. Many of them shared a

basic humility, coupled with prodigious self-assurance. There was nothing they could not make steam do. At least, there was nothing they would not try to make it do. Their successes were glorious; so were some of their failures. As professionals, many of them were willing to concede that they had over-reached themselves but few were daunted by this, buoyed up as they may have been by an heroic sense that they were in fact living ahead of their times.

Foremost among such heroes was Isambard Kingdom Brunel who, with Daniel Gooch, drove the locomotive of the train bearing Queen Victoria from Slough to Paddington in 1842. This man, internationally known as the 'Little Giant', was already famous at the age of 20, when he built the first tunnel shaft to be driven beneath a river; and himself came near to perishing in the waters of the Thames in achieving this. He built the Great Western Railway from London to Bristol. When he was 32 he built and launched the Great Western, the first steamship designed for ocean crossings. At 37 he launched the Great Britain, the first iron-built ocean ship and the first to be driven entirely by a propeller. Brunel's vast invention and capacity are summarised by James Dugan in *The Great Iron Ship*:

"The Little Giant built 25 railways in England, Ireland, Italy and India, and the precipitous Taff Vale line in Wales, considered a choice collectors' item by contemporary rail fans. He built eight piers and drydocks, five suspension bridges, and 125 railway bridges. He invented the compartmented freight car, an innovation re-innovated a century later by U.S. railways. He introduced railway telegraphy in 1839. In 1825 he published an argument for a canal through the Isthmus of Panama. During the Crimean War he designed an armoured gunboat which would launch amphibious tanks to attack the Russian forts at Kronstadt. The vehicles were to be powered by jet propulsion. The idea was 90 years too early for the Admiralty. The War Office, however, carried out another Brunel design, a 1500-bed military hospital, prefabricated in England (no part was too heavy for two men to carry) and erected at Renkioi, Turkey, by 18 men in ten weeks. The hospital had excellent plumbing, and pumped 1300 cubic feet of cooled humidified air per minute around each bed. While he was building the Great Eastern, Brunel was also managing the big railway hotel at Paddington Station, 'a very agreeable relaxation from his more important duties,' said his son."

Some idea of the public esteem enjoyed by Brunel, even when he was still the young father of a family, can be drawn from a domestic accident which aroused the concern and interest of the whole nation. He swallowed a gold half-sovereign piece. He was performing one of his favourite parlour tricks in front of his assembled family. The half-sovereign had to pass from his ear to his mouth. It ended up in his right bronchus. When he jerked his head he felt the coin drop towards his glottis. He suffered paroxysms of coughing but had the presence of mind to call in his brother-in-law, Sir Benjamin Brodie, a leading surgeon, to tell him exactly where the coin was and how

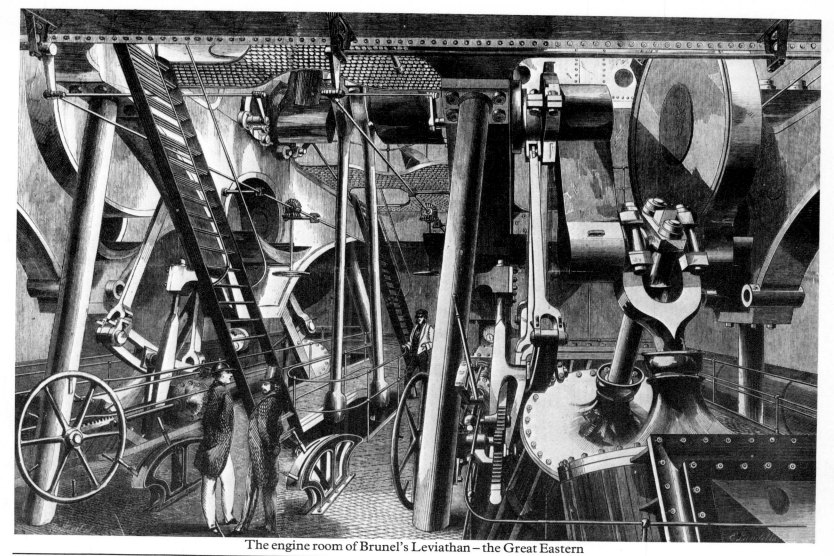

The engine room of Brunel's Leviathan – the Great Eastern

to reach it. This neither Brodie nor a panel of friends and medical experts which soon assembled could even begin to achieve.

Brunel characteristically took matters into his own hands. Invention was called for: and was he not one of the most ingenious men of his age? News of his misfortune was widely reported in the Press. London, and indeed the nation, was soon agog to learn that the Little Giant had designed a frame for himself – and it was an enviable feature of those times that action and construction instantly followed a flight of thought. His was a pivoted contraption not unlike a dressmaker's swing mirror. Upon this he had himself strapped, then turned upside down. In that position he coughed and choked and was continually slapped on the back in the hope that this convulsive torture would eject the coin. Daily bulletins accompanied this treatment, which went on for weeks and was only halted when the medical men insisted that he was in danger of killing himself. They suggested a tracheotomy to which Brunel agreed, but not till he had designed special forceps for the job.

Without the use of any anaesthetic, Brodie made the throat incision. He then used the instrument (still known as Brodie's forceps) but he failed to reach the coin. Another attempt was made on the following day, without success. Then Brunel himself took the initiative gain. On the third day, with the wound still open, he had himself once more strapped upside down to the coughing machine.

After a short convulsion the coin fell back into his mouth, thus resolving one of the strangest domestic dramas of the century, and restoring for a few more years a cherished national figure.

The incident was not without distinguished witnesses. Thomas Babington Macaulay sped from Brunel to the Athenaeum where he cried, "It's out!" In that decorous place where so few, then as now, are given to shouting, everyone knew at once that *It* was the half-sovereign *out* of Isambard Kingdom Brunel.

Like many of the heroes of Steam, Brunel wore himself out and died young. Shorter, less diversified but as intense was the career of John Fowler, the steam agriculturalist. When he died in 1864, aged 38, some 300 of his ploughing machines were at work in various parts of the British Isles and traction engines were being produced by his newly established firm at Leeds at the rate of about six per week – many of them for export. There is no pattern in the early environment of these men who seized upon steam with such creative zest. Fowler's dedication was at first idealistic: he was born in Wiltshire in 1826, the third son of a wealthy Quaker merchant. He might well have lived longer and more comfortably had he followed the business of a corn merchant to which his father articled him. Until he came of age, he dutifully attended this calling, thus gaining experience in farming methods which was particularly useful later when he became a pioneer of mechanised agriculture.

In 1847 he struck out on his own and joined a Middles-

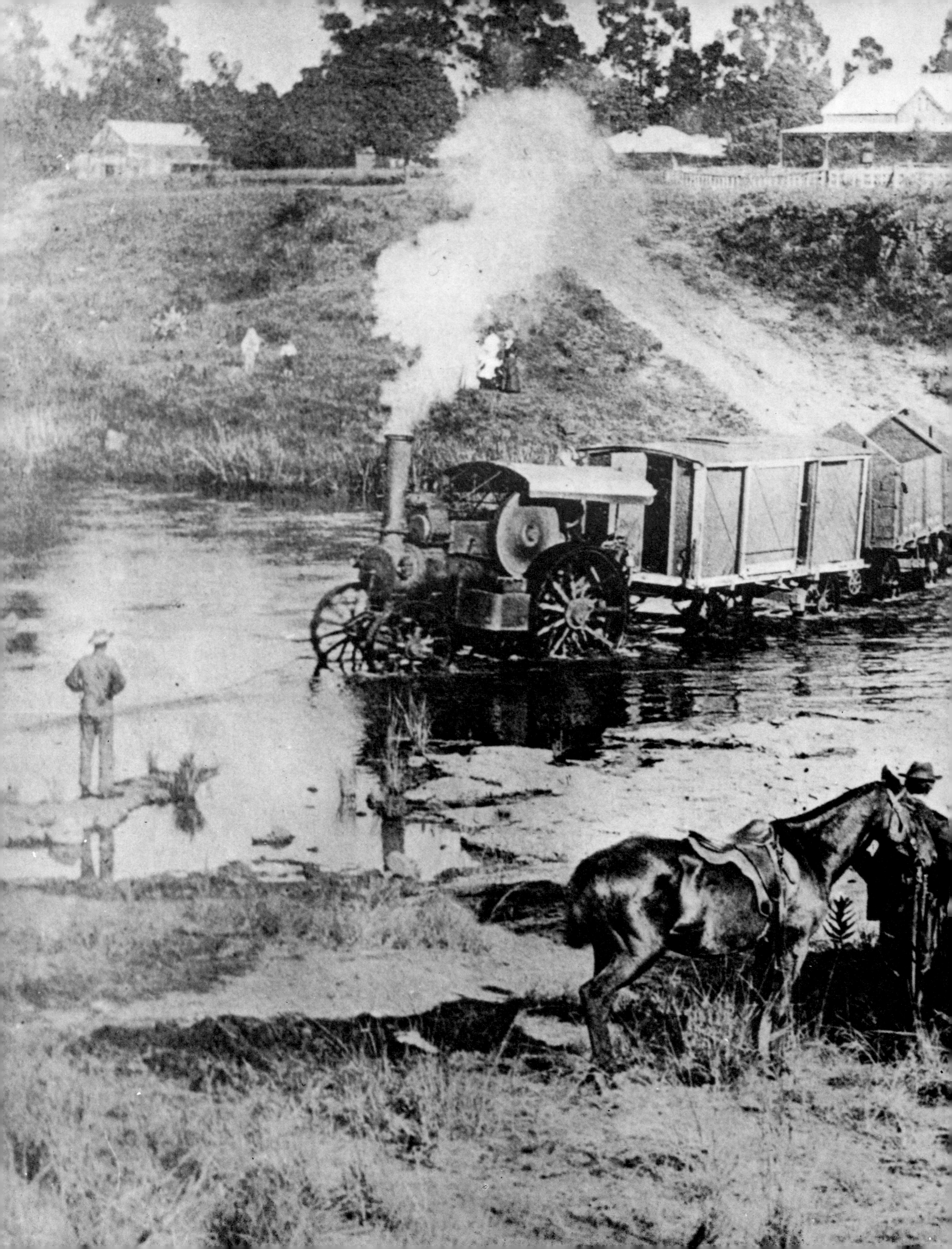

Crompton steam tractors in the service of the War Department during the South African War

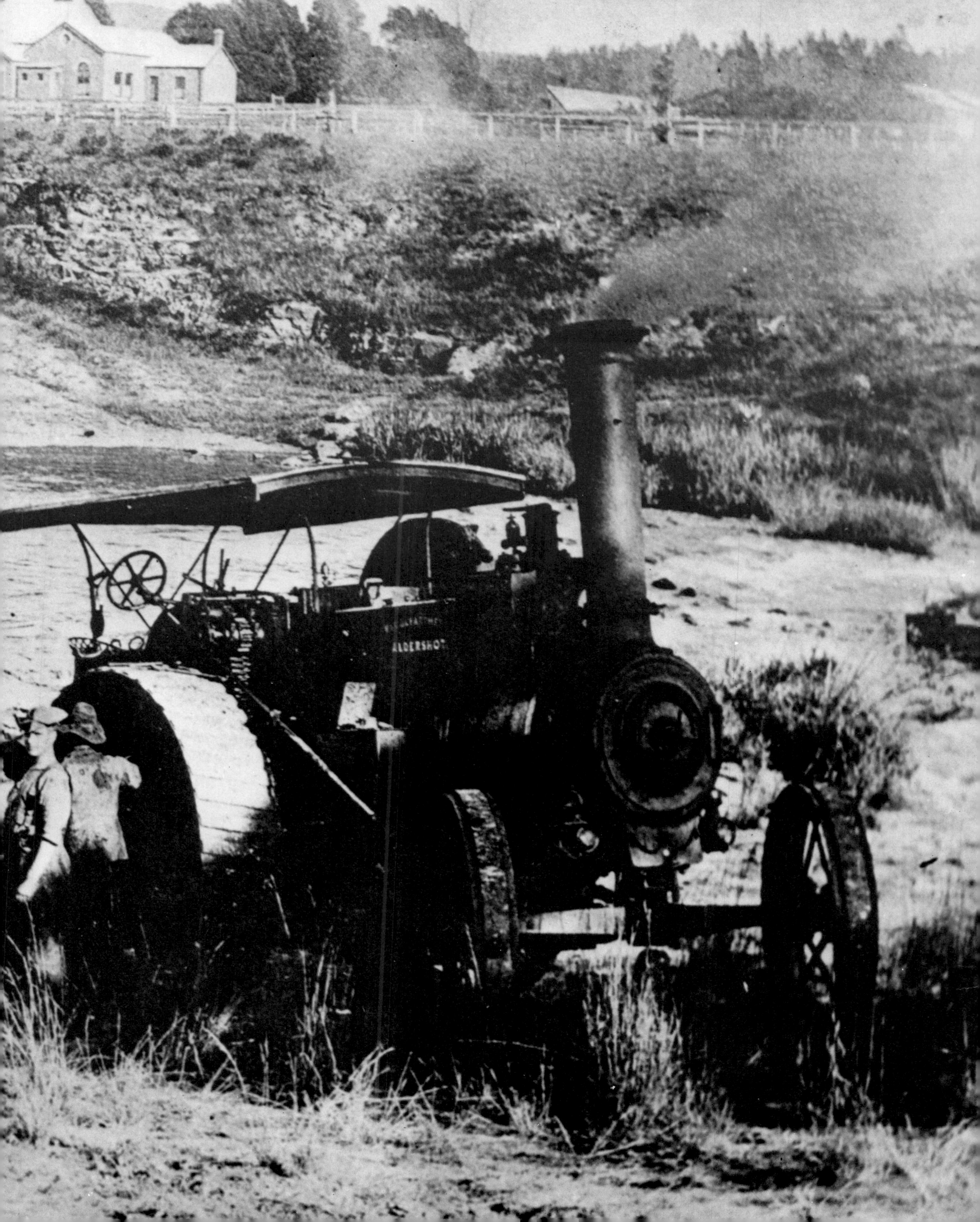

The Merryweather Company are still building fire engines – now under the banner of British Leyland

brough engineering firm manufacturing locomotives, and such items as colliery winding equipment – another useful skill. Again he could have made a good professional living by staying put; but a visit, on the firm's business, to Ireland aroused his Quaker conscience and changed his life.

He witnessed famine and was horrified that a country should be so dependent upon its potato crop while possessing vast areas of unproductive bogland which could be improved by land drainage.

He returned to England and gave up his job, determined on mechanisation of land drainage by steam. The result was his mole-drainage plough shown at the Great Exhibition of 1851 and built for him by Ransomes. The year before he had drained Hainault Forest in Essex with this equipment. It was the beginning of his reputation as a pioneer of steam agriculture. Though his impetus was humanitarian there is no record that his inventions brought any substantial relief to the starving Irish; but they relieved others. Mark Twain praised the use of his steam ploughs working in sugar plantations replacing slave labour freed by the American Civil War.

In 1858 Fowler was awarded the £500 prize offered by the Royal Agricultural Society of England. It was for his balance plough on which he was said to have spent

ten times the amount of the award in experiment. The whole outfit cost £730; 20 sets built by Ransomes were sold in 1858 and Claytons were also building under Fowler's licence; that meant that steam agriculture was well under way. In 1858 Fowler had 40 sets of ploughing tackle at work and was carrying out contract work himself. Stephensons, Claytons and Ransomes built engines for him until the 1860s when he set up in Leeds.

Fowler ploughing engines were still puffing in the Second World War, when they were used in the laying of the pipeline which was run between England and France after the Normandy landings in 1944. Fowler himself died as a result of a hunting accident while still at the height of his powers. His hunting was a case of leisure enforced. He was riding at the command of his doctor, as a supposed cure for overwork.

Other victims of the pace of this age so often blurred by its over-ornate trappings, were the engineers Robert Stephenson and Joseph Locke, both of whom found time to enter Parliament but died in their fifties. Stephenson was 20 when he set up the world's first locomotive building firm. Locke was already a veteran when in his late twenties he became Engineer-in-Chief for the construction of the Grand Junction Railway. Both men exported their talents and engineered impor-

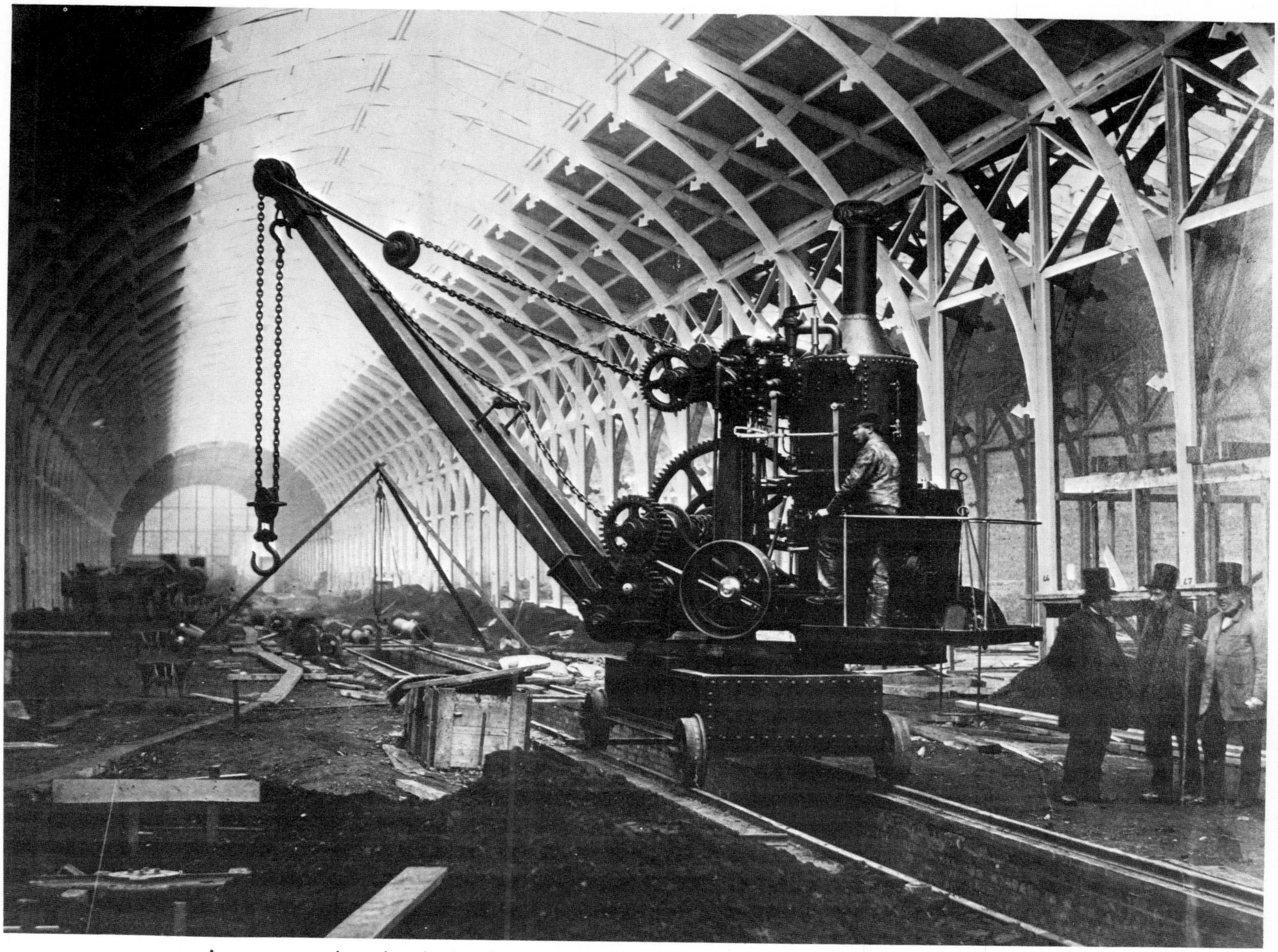

A steam crane in action during the construction of the 1862 International Exhibition in London

tant railways in various parts of the world.

Both were associated with a man of different but equally precocious talent, Thomas Brassey, the railway contractor, a name less known than theirs but one which made a unique impact on the railroad maps of the world. Before he died, prodigiously wealthy, in 1870, he could recall employing 80,000 men at one time on five continents on railway contracts of a total value of £28 million. Between 1835 and 1870 he was responsible for about 150 railway lines great and small; he also built stations, docks, drainage works and other undertakings.

R. E. Crompton began his career as an obsessive steam pioneer before founding the famous electrical firm of Crompton Parkinson. One of Crompton's enterprises was 'Chenab', a road locomotive coupled to a two-wheeled trailer omnibus. This weird pitching vehicle was designed to carry 130 people in its enclosed lower compartment. Its upper deck was canopied and protected by a smoke shield. Its ultimate destination was India where it became known as Govt. Steam Train No. 2. In 1870–71 it was tried out in England and there was a trial run from Ipswich to Wolverhampton where the objective was the Royal Show at which 'Chenab' made its first appearance. The young Mrs Crompton went along as a matter of course. Crompton wrote: "Our party on this journey consisted of myself, my wife and her maid Bremme, the head draughtsman and his wife, one or two pupils, drivers, stokers, a fitter and a boilermaker to carry out road repairs. Our route lay through Stowmarket, Bury St Edmunds, Cambridge, Coventry and Birmingham. As we were passing through Cambridge, a bystander, who had caught sight of my wife

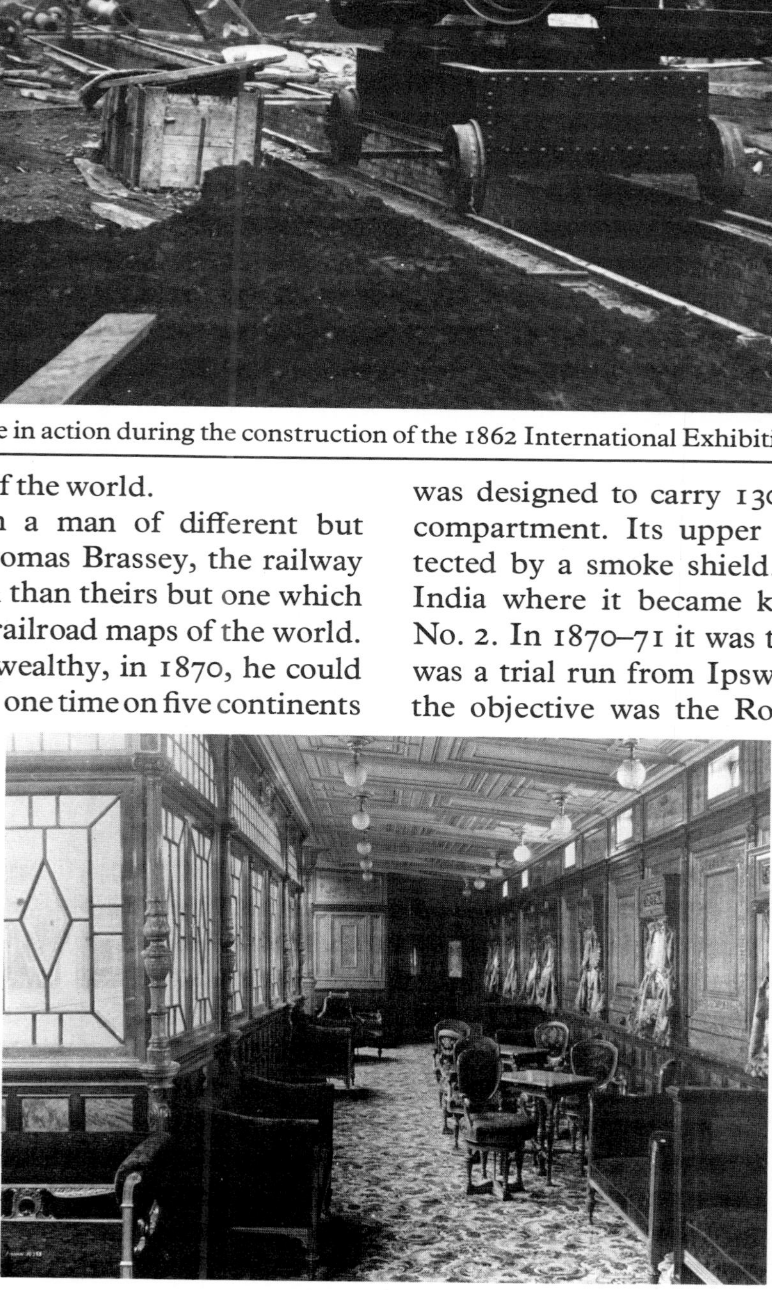

Ocean luxury – the elegant Drawing Room of the liner S.S. Campania, 1894

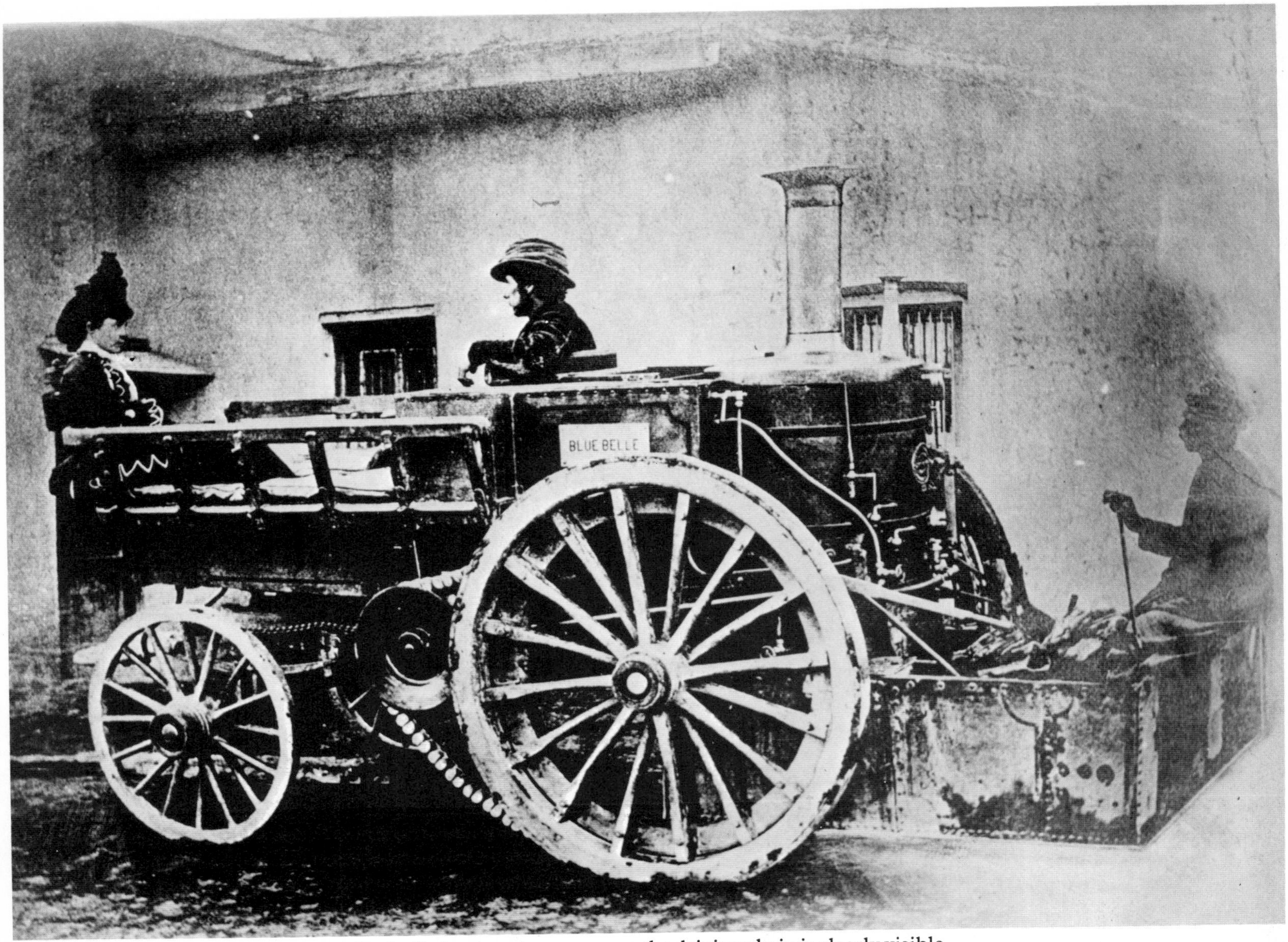
BLUE BELLE
Early Crompton steam wagon; the driving chain is clearly visible

and her maid, was heard to remark that he had never before seen ladies travelling in a threshing machine!"

In spite of such domestic vicissitudes Crompton was happily married for 60 years. This indestructible Victorian spans with his life the significant years of the revolution of mobility – and of warfare. Born in 1845, he was, as a boy, in the trenches before Sebastopol in the Crimean War. He served under Lord Roberts, organising steam transport in the South African War. He was invited by Winston Churchill to develop tanks in the First World War and lived to hear the sirens of 1940. Though dedicated to steam, the triumph of his creative years proved to be electricity. He lit the Vienna Opera House, King's Cross Station, the Crystal Palace and, in 1882, the Law Courts. He provided the first public electricity supply for London in Kensington in 1886.

Though the dream of airborne man was realised and well consolidated in Victoria's lifetime, the revolution in mobility still fell short of complete conquest of the air at the end of the reign. The Victorians had acquired plenty of experience of the uses of balloons and airships for pleasure and for warfare. They were striving for the heavier-than-air machine to give man controlled flight. The know-how eluded them. Even their most creative and versatile innovators failed in this.

A notable failure, who was so successful in everything else he undertook was Sir Hiram Maxim, born an American citizen and naturalised as a Briton who described himself as "a chronic inventor". He was two years old when Queen Victoria made her first journey by train. The First World War was two years old when he died. Apart from his famous weapons of war, his range of invention was prolific, and included a bronchitis inhaler, a mouse trap and much electrical equipment. He also made an attempt to put steam into the air. It cost him at least £20,000 and the main ex-

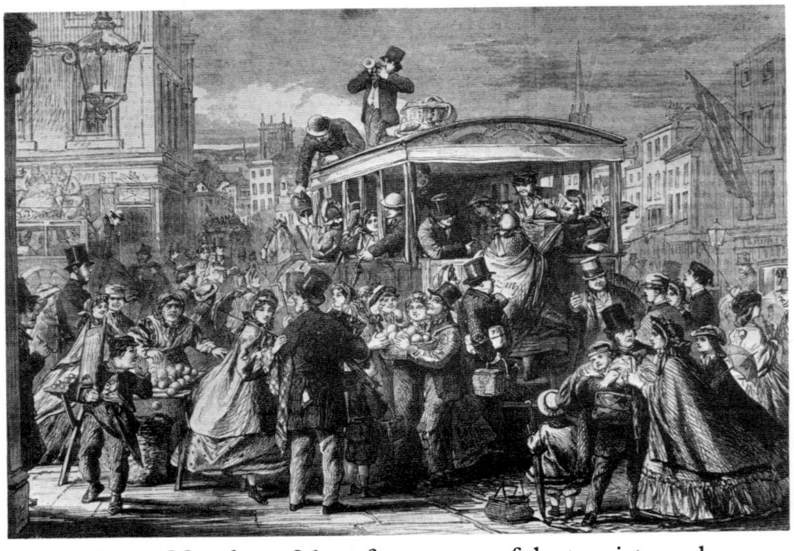
Easter Monday, 1862; a forerunner of the tourist coach

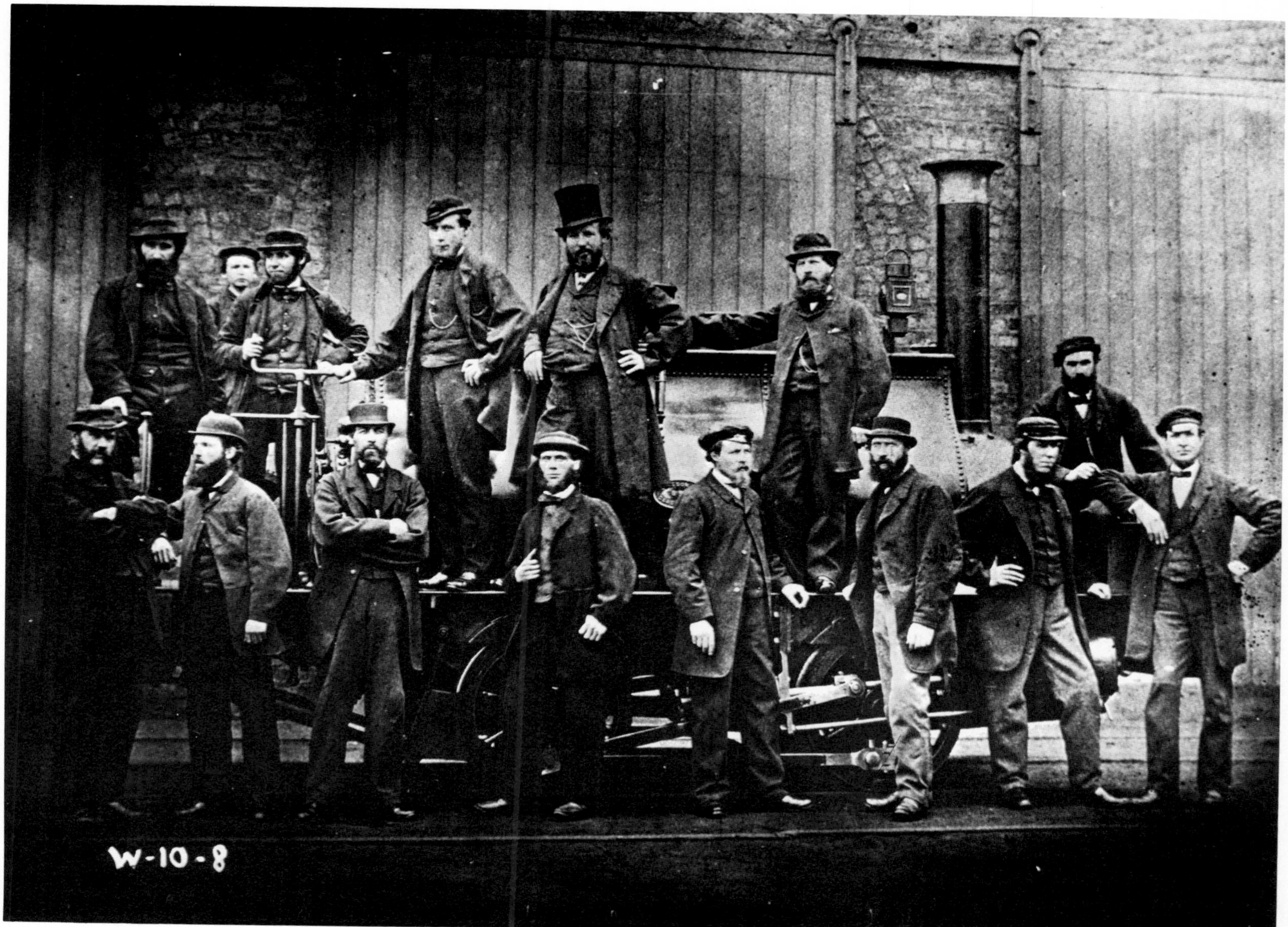
W-10-8
Foremen of the Hyde Park Locomotive works, 1862, with one of the products

periment took place in 1894 in Bexley, Kent. It may seem odd that so late in the century, only nine years before the Wright brothers flew at Kitty Hawk, North Carolina, a man of the stature of Maxim should have been concerned with steam-powered flight. It was not, however, the sudden whim of a wealthy man. He, and he was not alone in this, had been tinkering with the idea of powered flight for much of his life.

For his Bexley experiment Maxim made two steam-engines, each of 180 horse-power driving a propeller some 8 ft in diameter. These were installed in a monstrous bi-plane structure with an overall span of 104 ft, with a dihedral angle to the upper planes, and a total area of 4000 sq ft. Control was by means of two elevators, one fore, the other aft of the wings. This monster was mounted on four wheels on a broad-gauge railway track. On outriggers it carried flanged wheels which could be engaged with wooden guide rails raised about 2 ft above the ground on stilts. Maxim's objective was to become airborne but not to take off altogether. This was achieved but with disastrous results. "When everything was ready, with careful observers stationed on each side of the track," wrote Maxim, "the order was given to let go. The enormous screw thrust started the machine so quickly that it nearly threw the engineers off their feet, and the machine bounded over the track at a great rate. Upon noticing a slight diminution in the steam pressure, I turned on more gas, when almost instantly the steam commenced to blow a steady blast from the small safety valve, showing that the pressure was at least 320 lb in the pipes supplying the engines with steam . . . The first part of the track was up a slight incline, but the machine was lifted clear of the lower rails and all of the top wheels were fully engaged on the upper track when about 600 ft had been covered. The speed rapidly increased, and when 900 ft had been covered, one of the rear axle-trees, which were of 2-in. steel tubing, doubled up and set the rear end of the machine completely free. The pencils ran completely across the cylinders of the dynagraphs and caught on the underneath end. The rear end of the machine being set free, raised considerably above the track and swayed. At about 1000 ft, the left forward wheel also got clear of the upper track and shortly afterwards, the right forward wheel tore up about 100 ft of the upper track. Steam was at once shut off and the machine sank directly to the earth, embedding the wheels in the soft turf without leaving any other marks, showing most conclusively that the machine was completely suspended in the air before it settled to the earth." Nobody was injured. *The Times* reported that the effort was "crowned with success". But Maxim knew when to cut his losses. Air-minded man had to wait till Edwardian times.

'MY GOD, HOW THESE ENGLISH WORK'

By Terry Coleman

Thomas Brassey built railways in five continents and amassed a fortune.
A quintessential Victorian – thrusting
technologist, master of many skills, self-made multi-millionaire –
his name is now barely remembered

For 12 months the bold English navvies had been building a viaduct to take the Paris to Le Havre railway over a valley at Barentin, 12 miles north of Rouen. To watch them had become a new entertainment for the French: "*Mon Dieu, ces anglais, comme ils travaillent.*" The viaduct was 100ft. high and more than a third of a mile long, had 27 arches, and was due to be opened any day. At six in the morning on January 10, 1846, an old man saw bricks falling from the fifth arch on the Rouen side, the arches fell right and left, and in two minutes the whole viaduct had collapsed into the gorge. The French Press set up a joyous howl. The English contractor came up from Rouen and walked over the heaps of red bricks. "I have contracted to make and maintain the road," he said, "and nothing shall prevent Thomas Brassey from being as good as his word." So he rebuilt the viaduct with £20,000 of his own money. It made his name.

In the best sense, Brassey was a Samuel Smiles man. Now Smiles admired railway works, and thought they would be the wonder and admiration of succeeding generations: looking at their gigantic traces, the men of some future age might be found ready to say of the engineer and his workmen that there were giants in those days. But Smiles did not include the railway contractors. Never a profession so notorious as theirs for its numbers of bold, rapacious quacks, and never, you might say, so fitting a name as Brassey's. But he was none of that. He was honest and gentle and much liked, and in spite of this he was the most successful of the entrepreneurs. He was a European power, through whose accounts more flowed in a year than through the treasuries of a dozen duchies and principalities. He built railways in five continents, and died worth at least £5 millions.

He was born in 1805 into a family of Cheshire yeomen who farmed their 300 acres and who had – or so said Brassey's biographer, without giving any evidence for it – come over with William the Conqueror. The boy left grammar school at 16, was apprenticed to a land surveyor, and for a while worked on the Shrewsbury to Holyhead road under the great Telford.

He went into railway work by chance. He owned a quarry and in 1837 had dealings with George Stephenson and his assistant Joseph Locke, who were then engineering the first true public railway in England, the Liverpool & Manchester, and needed stone for the Sankey viaduct. From the start he got on with Locke, who suggested he should try his hand at tendering for a contract here and there. At first his prices were too high, then he got 10 miles of the Stafford and Wolverhampton line which went well, and then in the mid-thirties Locke called him south and gave him 36 miles of the London and Southampton Railway, from Basingstoke to Winchester, where the cuttings are still among the most immense on any railway anywhere.

It was the first of many celebrated lines they were to build together, as engineer and contractor. The engineer designed the line and was responsible to the railway company for seeing it built. But the contractor built it: he supplied the stone and the blasting powder, he got the agents and sub-contractors and gangers and navvies, he took the risk. To the engineer the glory. To the contractor the profit, or the loss.

Now the directors of the London and Southampton had their eyes on France and on a direct line between the two capitals – their railway to Southampton, their ferry to Le Havre, and then, they hoped, their railway to Rouen and Paris. In railways, France was behind. There

The Paris–Le Havre railway – "an immortal work"

had been some horse tramroads for coalmines, and four longer lines had been licensed in 1838 but abandoned. The Englishmen proposed to start with the 82 miles from Paris to Rouen, the French government agreed, and the work began in 1841. Threequarters of the cost of 50 million francs, half the 10,000 navvies, the engineer (Locke of course), and the contractors (Brassey and Mackenzie) came from England. Supervising what he derisively called native labour, the British navvy could point to the earth to be moved, say 'damn' with some emphasis, and stamp his foot. The foreigners generally understood. When they finished the Rouen section, on May 3, 1843, the navvies feasted while the national guard stood by to keep the peace. In a field, a whole ox was roasted and served to 600 navvies.

Next year the "immortal work", as a Paris magazine had dubbed it, pressed on towards Le Havre. The engineering of the whole line is recognisably English, though it is not so much unchanged as, say, an early English line like the London and Birmingham. At Pavilly, by the side of the electrified line, the *tunnel des anglais* stands, but it is disused. But at Barentin the great, curving viaduct still carries the line, making the new bridge which carries the *route nationale 13 bis* across the valley look silly. Underneath the arches is a mudtrack called the Rue De L'Ingénieur Locke, and it is his statue, a copy of the one by Marrochetti at Barnsley, which stands beneath the viaduct. No one, at Barentin or at Rouen, had ever heard of Brassey.

But in 1846 all Europe had. He had built the first main line on the Continent. He went on to complete the Orleans-Bordeaux and Rouen-Dieppe lines, and by 1848 he and his partners had made threequarters of the French railways then existing. At home, in the forties, he had 30 contracts, among them the Lancaster and Carlisle and part of the Great Northern.

These were the great years of the contractors, and Brassey was by now the biggest. Peto, the Baptist, with whom he often collaborated, was a good second. They became financiers as well as contractors. In 1855 Brassey built the direct line from London to Portsmouth on his own, on spec, and then sold it to the highest bidder.

He built the Turin–Novara line, and the Italians called him '*il re degli intraprenditori*'. He hobnobbed with Cavour, advised the Emperor of Austria, and dined with Louis Napoleon. He accepted the Legion of Honour though he never wore it, sending it home saying, "Mrs Brassey will be pleased to possess all these crosses."

The most famous Brassey exploits of all, both in the 1850s, were the Grand Trunk railway of Canada – 539 miles from the Atlantic to the Great Lakes – and the Crimea railway. The first lost him nearly £1 million: for their part in the second, he and his partners became national heroes. By the winter of 1854, 30,000 British soldiers were dug in around Sebastopol, dying of mud, cold, cholera and starvation. From the army, down to the British fleet in the port of Balaclava, there was one impassable road. The casualty lists made it plain that the British army was about to be defeated, if not by the Russians then by the winter. Then Brassey, together with the firm of Peto & Betts, offered to build a supply railway from fleet to army, to ship out materials and men, to engineer the line, and then run it, all at cost, expecting no profit.

On December 2 the contractors advertised for navvies, got twice as many volunteers as they needed, and chose those who had worked on the Grand Trunk and knew how to survive a cold winter. Brassey and his men, said the Press, would go about things in a business-like manner; they were not likely to land their men, as the army had done, without tents or tools, or to fill the hold of a vessel with medical stores and then put tons of shot and shell over them. Throughout December and January the navvies sailed out in 23 ships, and in ten days built their own hutted camp and the first five miles of the line. Captain Henry Clifford wrote home that they looked 'un-

Thomas Brassey – "King of Entrepreneurs"

utterable things', but did more work in a day than a regiment of soldiers did in a week. The engineers had expected to take until the end of April, but three weeks early the main line and its branches, 29 miles in all, were complete, and the army was relieved. The generals were discredited, the contractors were lionised.

Brassey went on to build from Warsaw to Galatz, Bergen to Oslo, Vienna to Trieste, Calcutta to the Ganges; in New South Wales, Queensland, Mauritius, and the Argentine. Often he helped to finance the lines he built, and took payment partly in railway shares and land. He grew richer still, and gave half a million to charities. He talked of a Channel tunnel, and if anyone could have done it, he could. But he was near the end of his life.

In 1868 he had a stroke. He recovered well enough to tour his Moldavian lines next year and covered 6000 miles in three weeks, but in 1870 he was told he had cancer. His men remembered him and many of them came, some from abroad, to see their old master. Some had been his agents on great contracts, others navvies who had followed his works for 30 years.

He died that December and his will was proved at £3,200,000. Apart from this he left a trust fund of £2 millions for his children, who became known as the Brassey grandees. His eldest son, Thomas, at whose wedding there had been 14 bridesmaids and 14 groomsmen, entered Parliament, and became baron, earl, governor of Victoria, and Warden of the Cinque Ports. One of his earliest memories, which he often recounted, was of the dreadful winter of 1843 in Rouen, when as a boy of seven he stood on the boulevards while his father did what he could to relieve the distress of the navvies who had built the line up from Paris and were near starvation while they waited for the spring, and for the line to push on towards Le Havre.

THE NEW PROFESSION

In the Victorian era, the engineer became respectable. A century of amazing technological progress drew its creative talents regardless from every rank of society; yet Royalty smiled on the engineers, politicians cleared

Robert Stephenson built the Rocket locomotive that his father designed, laid the Birmingham-London railway, and built many bridges both in Britain and abroad, including the Menai Strait's bridge and the High Level at Newcastle

James Nasmyth, a Scot, was pre-eminent in the design of power machine tools; when Brunel required a gigantic paddleshaft to drive his steamship Great Britain, Nasmyth designed the great steam-powered hammer for forging it

Sir Henry Bessemer's converter blew impurities out of pig-iron using ordinary air, thereby manufacturing cheaper steel. Another invention was a novel cross-Channel ferry with a free-swinging saloon designed to offset sea-sickness

Robert Napier, Scottish marine engineer, worked under Robert Stephenson before building engines for the early transatlantic paddle-steamers and Cunarders; he subsequently designed the first ironclads for the Royal Navy

their way, the City put its money at their disposal. They invented, designed, organised, contracted and delivered through their own energy and expertise; and few of them failed to achieve honours or riches – or both

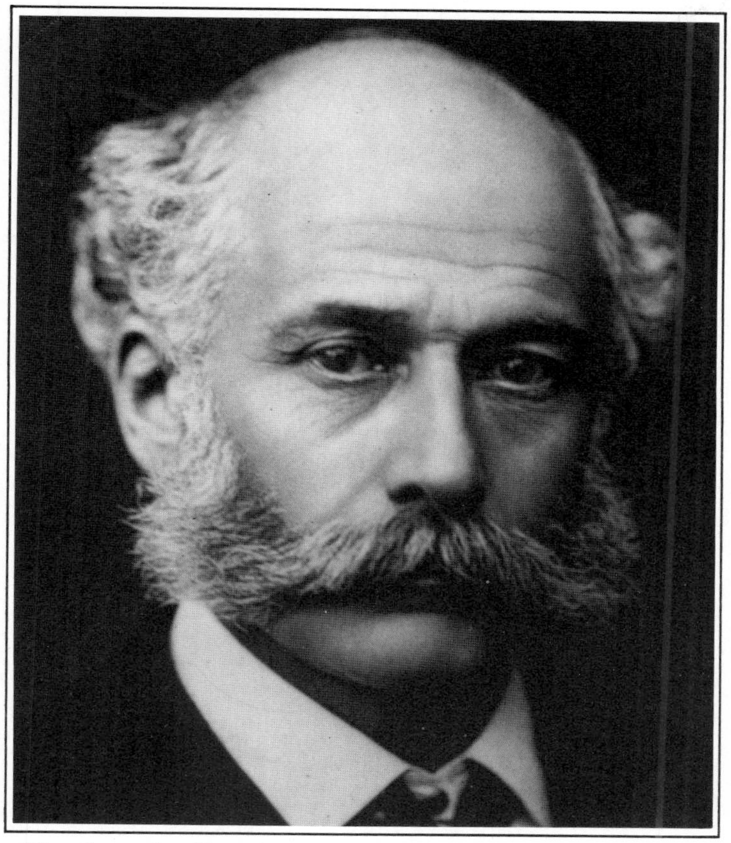

Sir Joseph Bazalgette, of French extraction, was Engineer-in-Chief of London's celebrated sewer system – an incalculable contribution to the public health. He also supervised the construction of the Thames Embankment

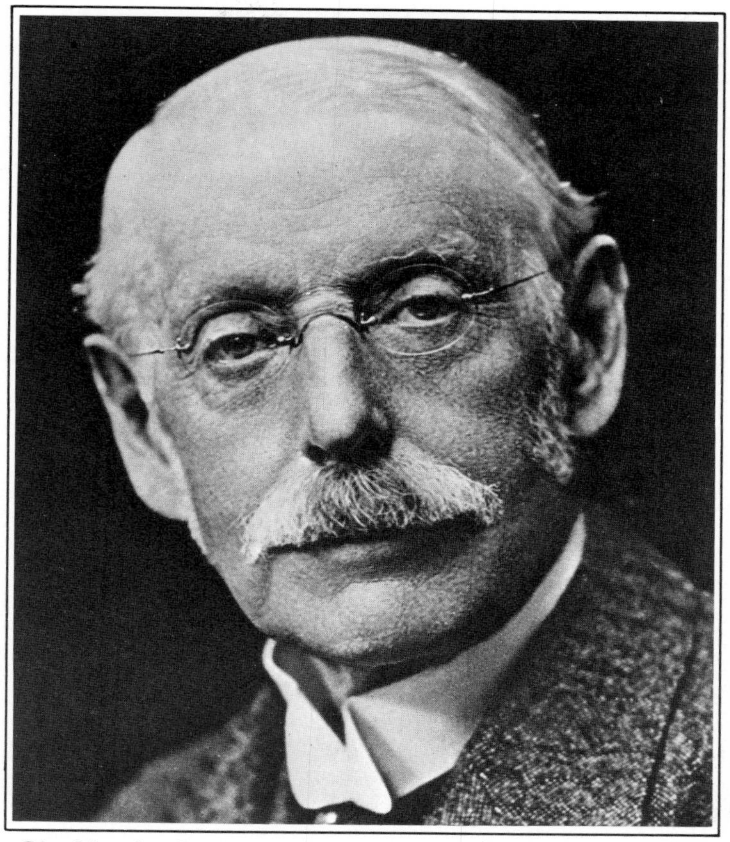

Sir Charles Parsons, the son of an earl, apprenticed himself to the Armstrong factory at Newcastle. He invented the high-speed steam turbine, built the first turbine-driven vessel, and devised turbo-generators for power stations

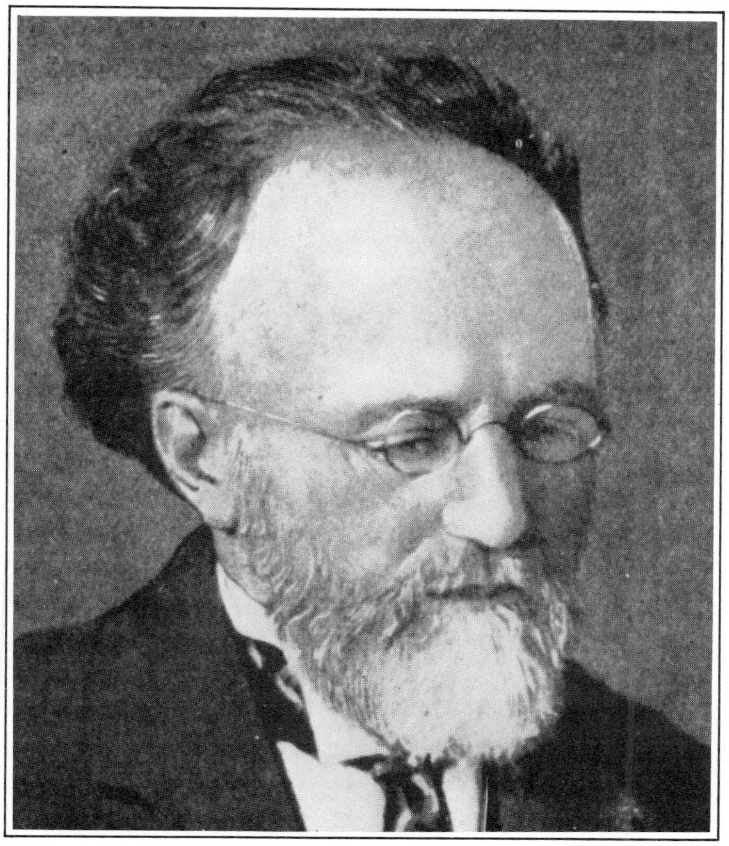

Sir Richard Tangye, the last in a famous succession of Cornish engineer-inventors, migrated to the industrial ambience of Birmingham. His fortune assured when Brunel commissioned his lifting-jacks for the Great Eastern

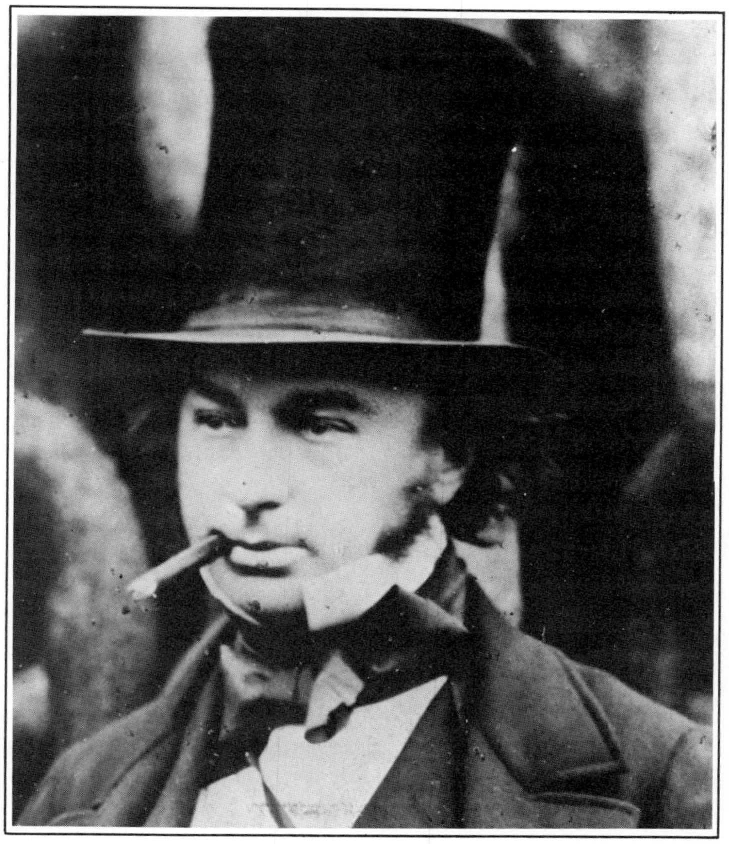

Isambard Kingdom Brunel, flamboyant, archetypal engineering genius of the age; he built greater ships and bridges than had ever been seen before, but perhaps his most striking achievement was the Great Western Railway

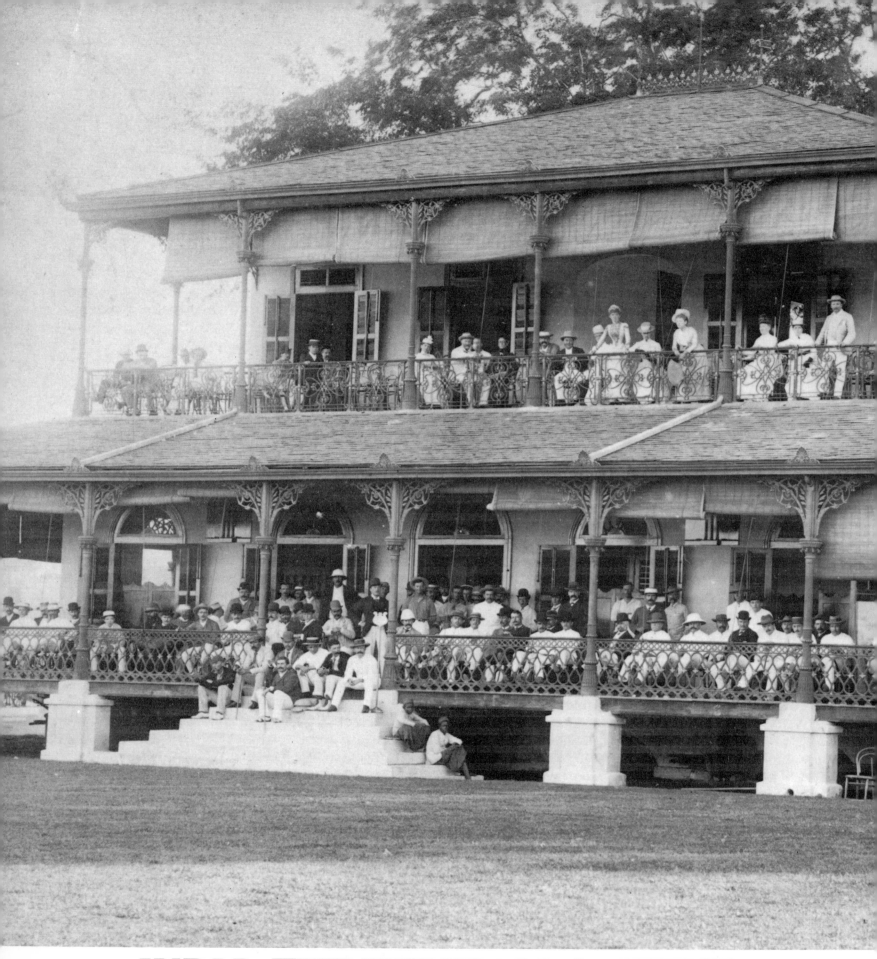

INDIA: THE IMPERIAL SUMMER

By Nicholas Wollaston

No part of the Victorian empire exerted such a strong emotional pull as India – an alien sub-continent wrested from savagery and heathenism by the imposition of British order and values and organised, during the brightest heyday of the Raj, very much like an overseas branch of English suburbia, with bands playing on the lawn to elegant spectators at regimental cricket matches. The age of Victoria leaves a heavy mark on Indian life, institutions and customs

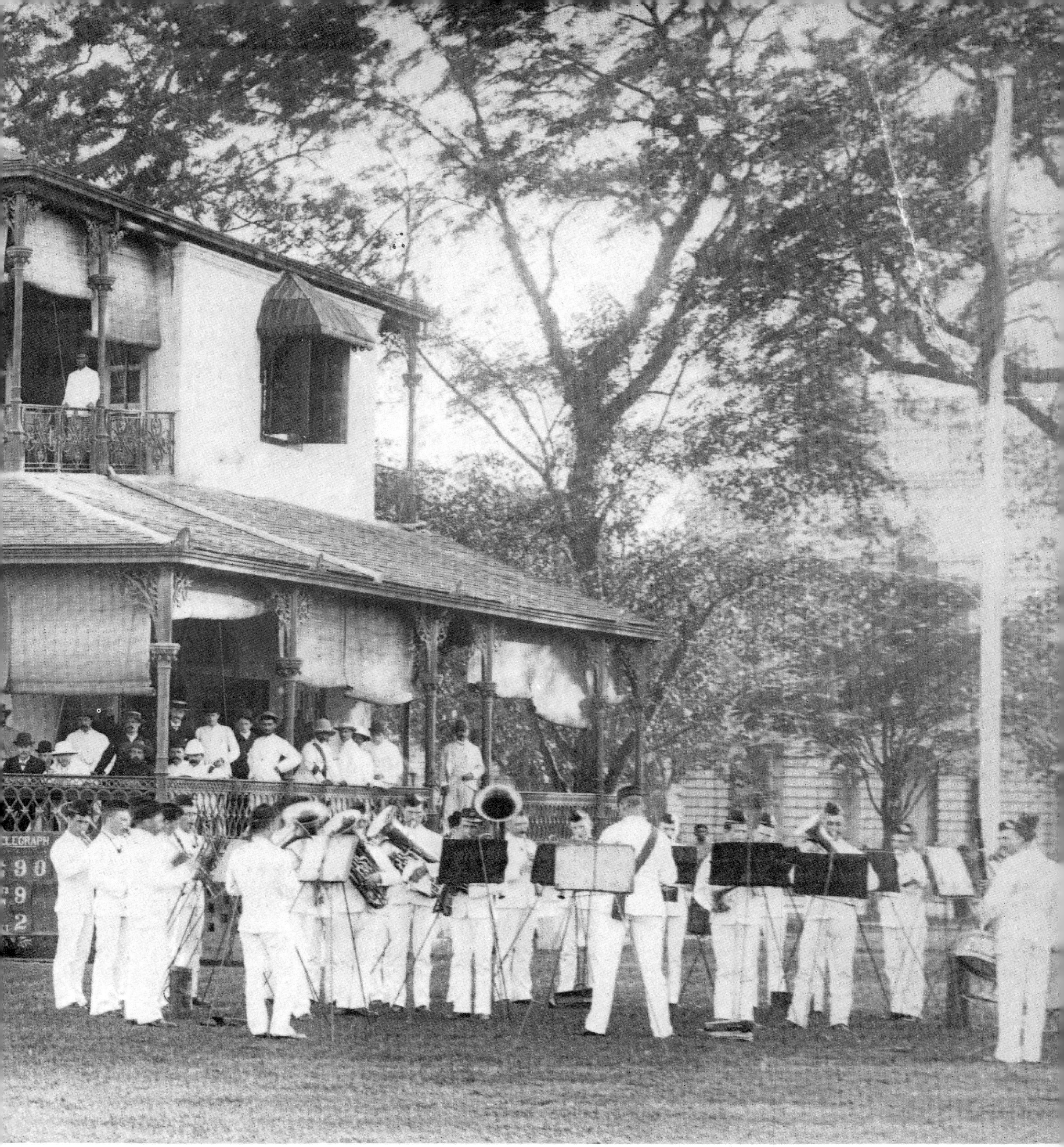
ELEGRAPH

'Kipling' is the first word you think of, at the mention of Victorian India. It seems incredible that that much-adulated, much-reviled poet of the bazaars and barracks, of the forests and plains and hills, actually left India when he was only 24; and except for a few days there two years later, his experience of the country was confined to his very early childhood in Bombay in the 1860s before being sent home to school in England, and his seven years in northern India as a young reporter in the 1880s. *Kim* was written in Sussex more than ten years after leaving India, and the Jungle Books were written in America, based mainly on photographs and descriptions of a district he had never even seen; yet such is Kipling's achievement that his picture of India in the heyday of the empire and his portraits of its people – from Mowgli to Mrs. Hauksbee, from Gunga Din to the Viceroy – have never been improved on; and though it might not surprise the author, much of it is valid even now.

Kipling's India, of course, is partly a vision of that peculiar and golden epoch mid-way between Lord Dalhousie's creation of an empire and Lord Curzon's rearguard defence of it – a sort of Indian summer between the Mutiny and Gandhi; and partly also it is a view of the eternal land, hot and harsh and infinitely variegated, that had existed more or less unchanged for centuries, and still exists today. So Victorian India as it survives now is a confusion of two elements: there are the relics of those alien institutions imported by the conquering English, and there are those inherent Indian characteristics which – because one associates them with the times of the Queen-Empress, because for us they seem to typify the attitudes and atmosphere of her reign, or simply because of Kipling – one also labels generally as 'Victorian'.

The most obvious relics of imported Victoriana in India are the monuments – to justice, to commerce, to warfare, to the Christian faith, to the late Viceroy, to the Queen herself. Bombay, where Kipling was born in 1865, has the best collection, and to read the Bombay pages in *Murray's Handbook* is to be taken on a guided tour of Victorian architecture. The Old Secretariat, one learns, was built in 1874 in Venetian Gothic; and the University Hall, of the same year, is in the French Decorated style of the 15th century, and named in honour of a man who himself epitomises the age – Sir Cowasjee Jehangir Readymoney. It is no surprise to read that the University Library and Clock Tower, in 14th-century Gothic, were designed by Sir Gilbert Scott, architect of St. Pancras Station and the Albert Memorial. The High Court, further down the road and five years younger, is Early English, and the Telegraph Office is Romanesque. The Town Hall, opened four years before Queen Victoria's accession, is Corinthian inside and Doric outside, while the Mint, also not strictly Victorian, has a portico of

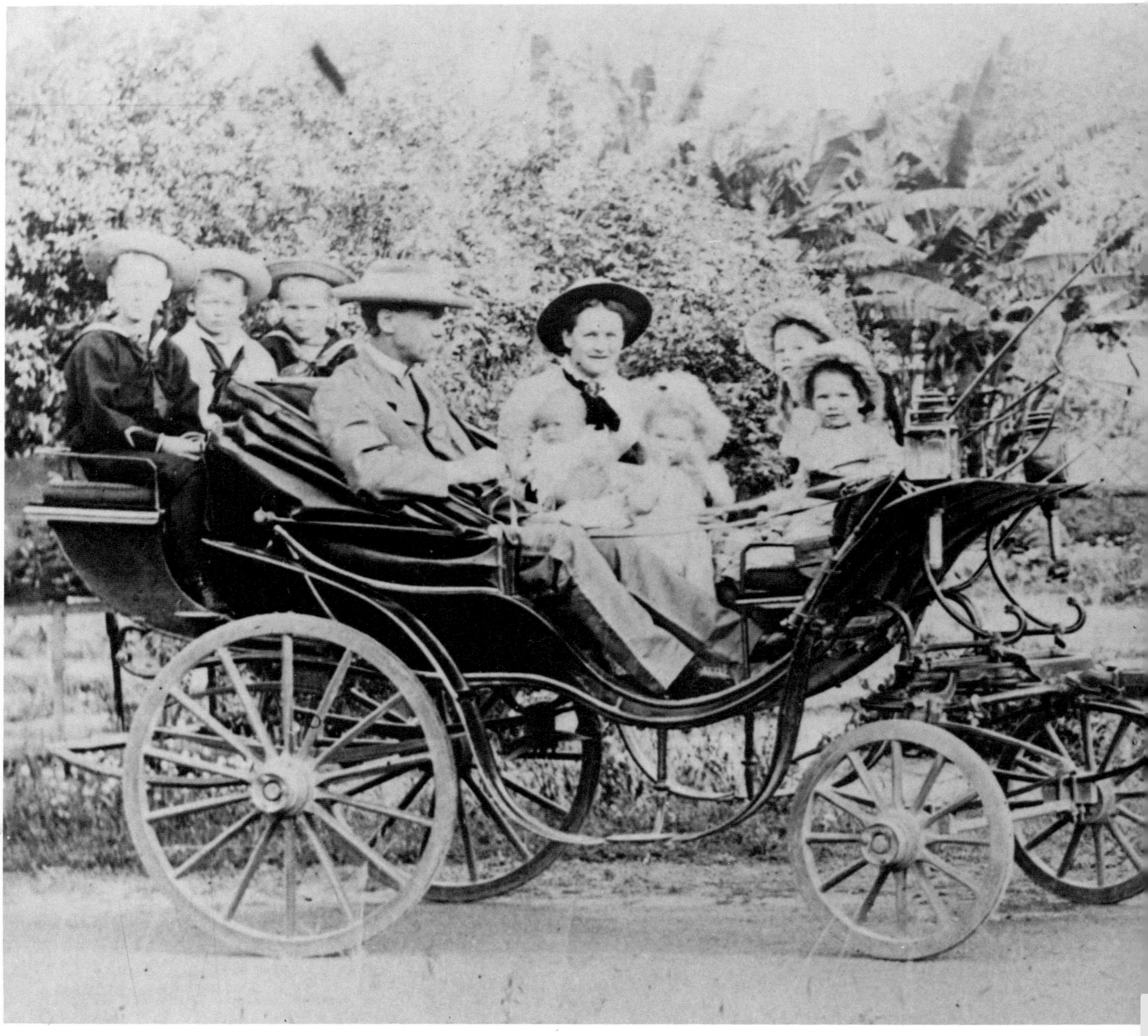

Ionic columns.

Only the Municipality, which was opened in 1893, makes any concession to Hindu or Muslim architecture; the result is a puzzling blend, a meeting of East and West which Kipling would never have condoned. Across the road, however, Bombay's main railway station, Victoria Terminus, is pure imported ingenuity, a fantasy of spikes and pillars full of grime and purple gloom. Arriving there by train and walking out into the street one might be surprised for a moment at not finding oneself in the Euston Road.

But it is not only Bombay. The other old Presidency cities, Calcutta and Madras, as well as the big towns of the northern plains, all contain public buildings, churches, statues, fountains and war memorials that commemorate the pride and confidence of a race of foreign rulers, with no allowance for the social system, let alone the architecture, of their subject people.

What could be a more Victorian transplantation than the Bengal Club in Calcutta? "Most of India's history happened in this building," the secretary told me, gently dismissing everything that happened before Queen Victoria and everything that has happened since; and one morning he showed me round the empty, echoing building.

On the walls were skins, antlers, portraits, prints of old Calcutta – Grecian columns and copies of Classic temples making it the spacious imperial city it never quite became. "The Club will have to go, I suppose, but it's sad. These marble floors – I don't really know what they could be used for." In the reading room there was *Country Life*, *Wisden*, *The Book of the Horse*, and old bound volumes of *Punch*. "These big rooms are all very impressive, I suppose, but they don't make for warmth,

A colonial family makes an outing. Large families were highly regarded; the wife of this settler appears to have had seven children

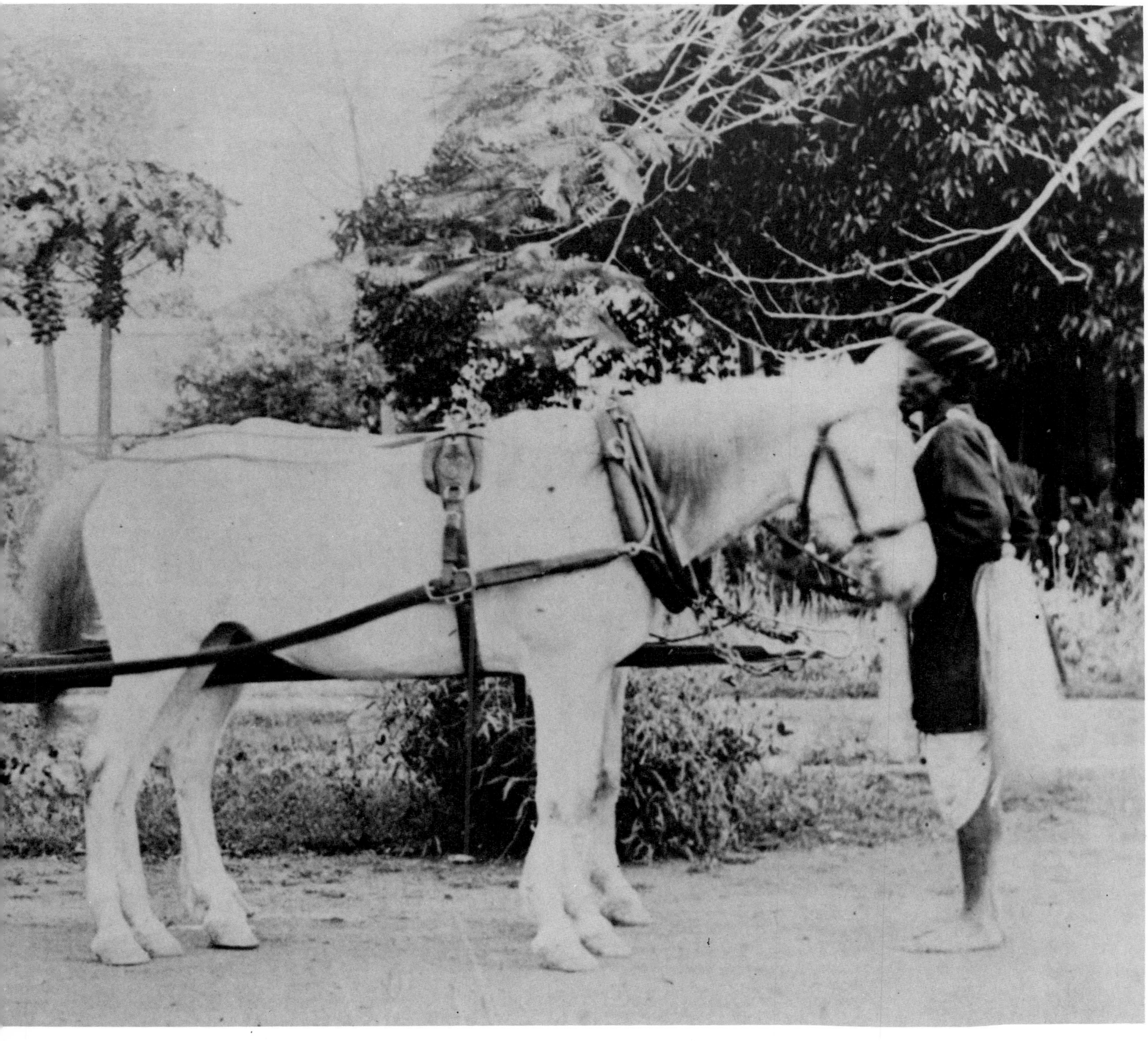

Drawing room of a British family in Calcutta around 1900

friendliness, that sort of thing – which is what people seem to want nowadays."

The membership is down to a little over two hundred, when once it was two thousand. It used to be said that the difference between the Bombay Club and the Bengal Club was that at one they didn't admit dogs or Indians, but at the other they did admit dogs. The legend is not strictly true, for at the Bengal Club there was never a rule against Indians joining; it's just that they were never proposed. They join now – a dozen of them, two dozen – but they hardly ever come. "It's for the prestige, really," said the secretary, "there's nothing else."

On each little table was a silver bell, with an emblem cobra for a handle, but almost nobody to ring and shout for someone to bring another *peg*; one member in a chair on the verandah was flicking through *Blackwood's* magazine. The secretary offered me a drink, and a servant poured out a beer in a presentation tankard, inscribed from some forgotten Englishman; one felt guilty, like drinking in a museum. Downstairs in the entrance hall, on a beautiful Victorian octagonal table, was a book for members to record their subscriptions to the servants' Christmas fund – the names of a few British businessmen, a couple of Bengali civil servants, His Highness the Maharaja of Cooch Behar. "It's very quiet

now," said the secretary, as I left. Outside was the stifling, thronging life of Calcutta.

Most clubs in India, founded in the last century, are still prosperous, having thrown open their doors to what Kipling called the natives; but they have also adapted themselves to the departure of the British in a way that shows a touchingly nostalgic reverence for the Raj. At the bar, if it is in one of the provinces where there is not prohibition, a modernised, republicanised Indian will show that he can swallow beer and Scotch whisky as well as any old imperialistic sahib; and if there is a picture of Gandhi on the wall, as once there was a portrait of the Queen, the chances are that the photographer has caught the Mahatma laughing – the Father of the Nation, as he is called, laughing at his sons.

In the club dining-room, as if to emphasise emancipation, it may be hard to get real Indian food; there was a time when Grilled Ham Steak *à la* Singapore on the menu gave members a sense of participation, reminded them that theirs was not the only outpost in the East, and perhaps provoked a timely anecdote from some old buffer who had knocked about a bit; but now it seems an anachronism in a country where most people are vegetarian by religion, and even among the meat-eaters the majority consider pork unclean; and to call it 'Singapore'

A missionary family poses with Indian friends in the 1880s

hardly makes it more explicable.

In many clubs only for Sunday lunch can you get a decent curry, which was often the rule in British days as well. So Sundays are especially popular, and men turn up in the morning with their wives who parade across the lawns and preen their silks and hiss and sneer as venomously as any Victorians. The 'kala memsahibs' they are called – the black ladies – for they behave much as the white memsahibs used to do, but with even less excuse. And really there is not much difference: adjust a sari slightly, roll down the sleeves, give the lady a big wide hat and a parasol, and young Kipling would recognise her straight away. Even the men: half shut your eyes and those elegant frock coats and narrow trousers are not unfamiliar. They laugh heartily and slap their thighs, and call each other "old chap" and curse "those damn-fool politicians" and use slang that sounds, to an Englishman, oddly archaic.

Murray's Handbook itself is a splendid product of Queen Victoria's reign, apart from being easily the best guide to India. The first edition was published the year after the Mutiny had been quelled, and though it is constantly being revised its pages still have a flavour of more expansive days. On motoring ("a second car for the servants and the baggage is a wise precaution"), on

clothing ("for camp, Jodhpurs should be worn, preferably with canvas spats"), on shooting ("peacocks are sacred, like monkeys"), and on haggling ("one must not forget the maxim *caveat emptor*") Murray is infallible and up to date, but with an old-fashioned courtesy that has survived a hundred years and twenty new editions. Very properly he deplores the obscenities of Khajraho and the licentiousness of Konarak, and of the erotic carvings on the Nepalese temple at Benares he says, "visitors need not see them if the attendant is discouraged from pointing them out"; everywhere, but especially at scenes of British heroism, he is the perfect Victorian gentleman, considerate and knowledgeable and with never a doubt as to what's what.

Travel in India, with or without Murray, is still rather a 19th-century business. It was the railways more than anything else that changed the face of India under British rule, and although some Indians now travel by car and a few even go by aeroplane the railways are significant in a way that they have ceased to be in England. Quite apart from the long distances, a train journey in India has an intrinsic importance, a style about it which the Victorians probably experienced but which we have now forgotten.

Indians, for one thing, travel with an extravagant

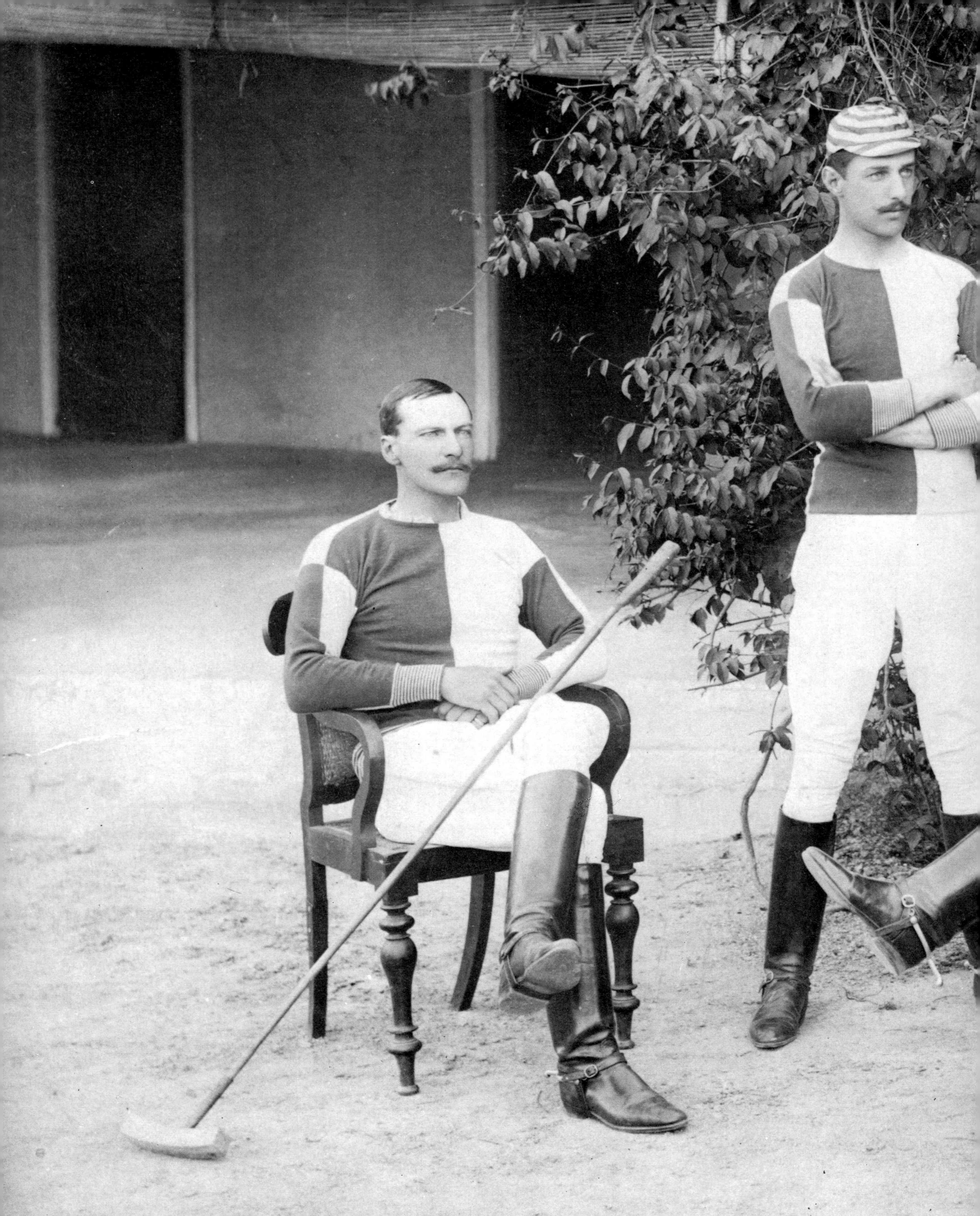

A group of polo-playing British officers. Polo ponies were an almost mandatory part of a subaltern's equipage

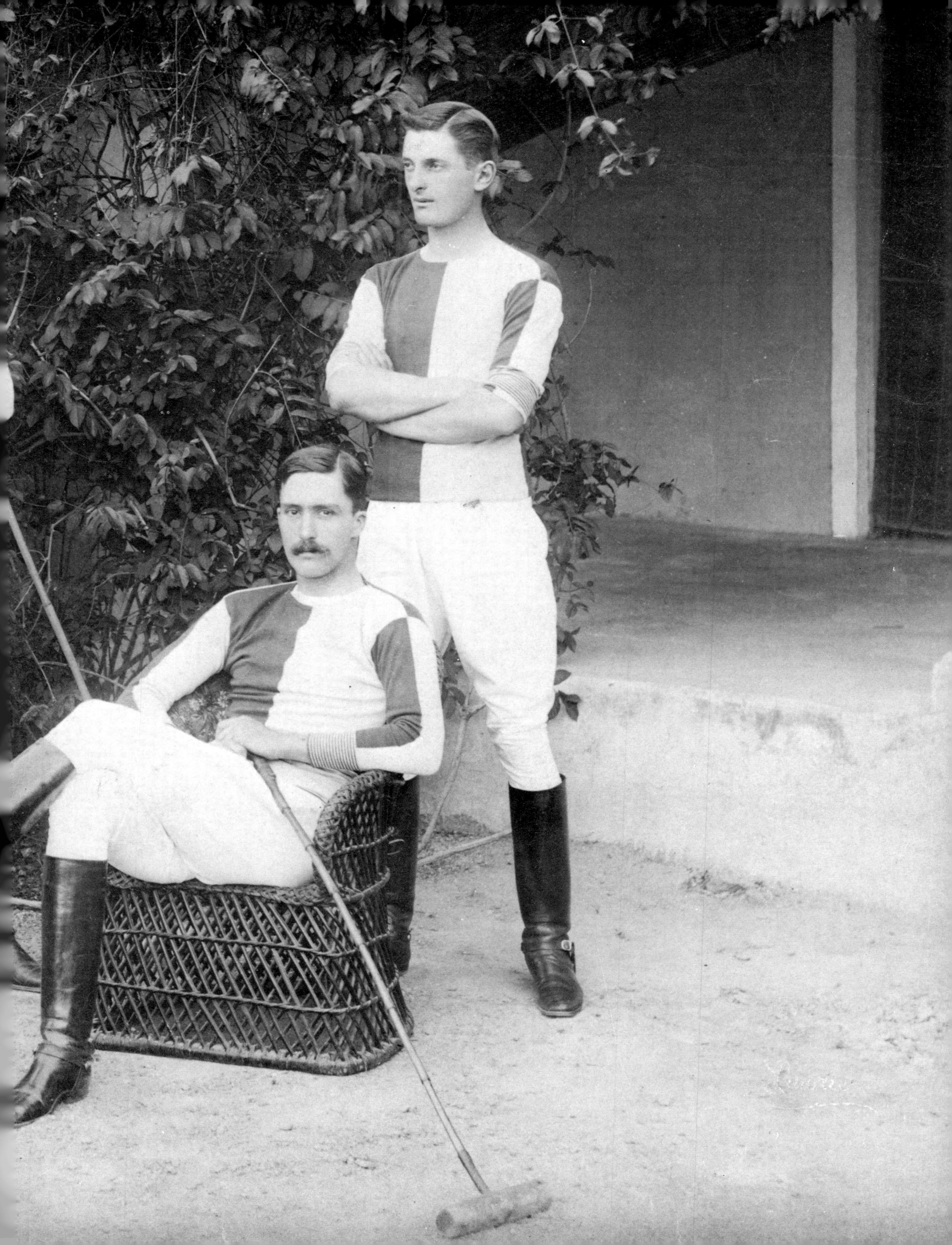

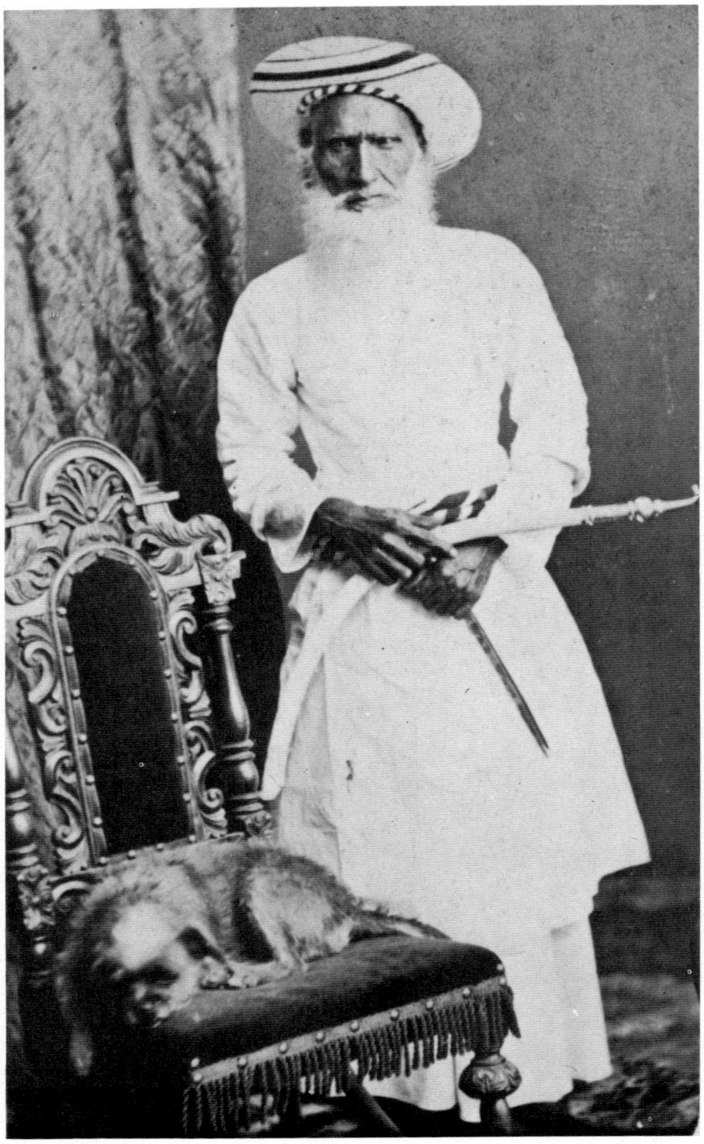
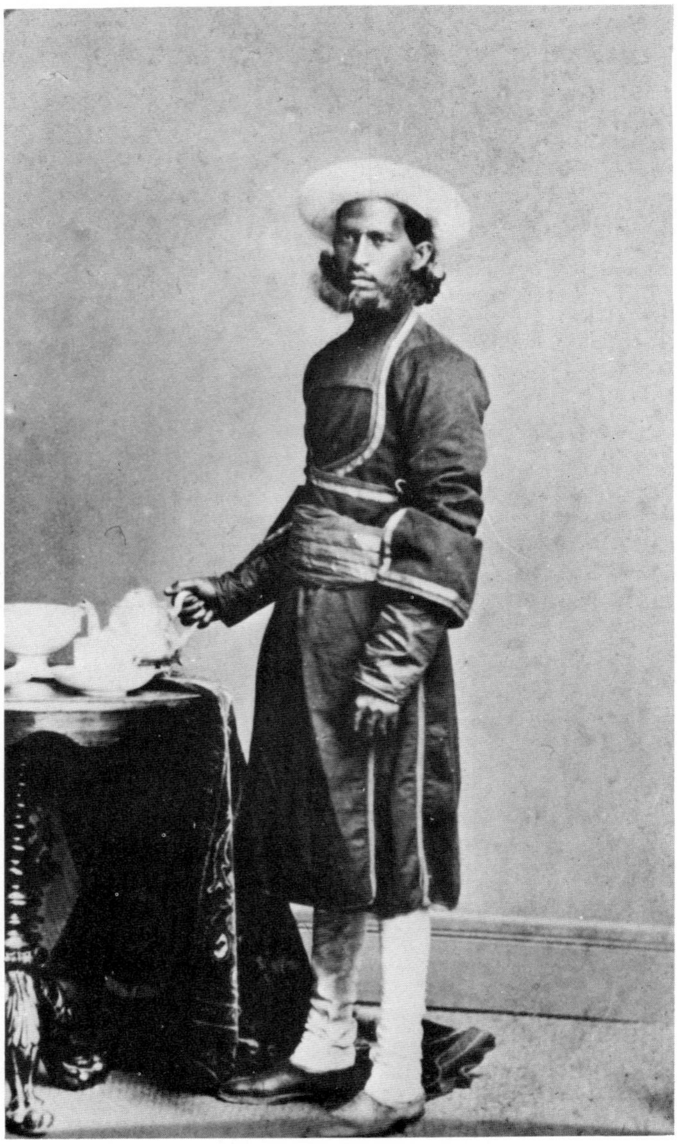
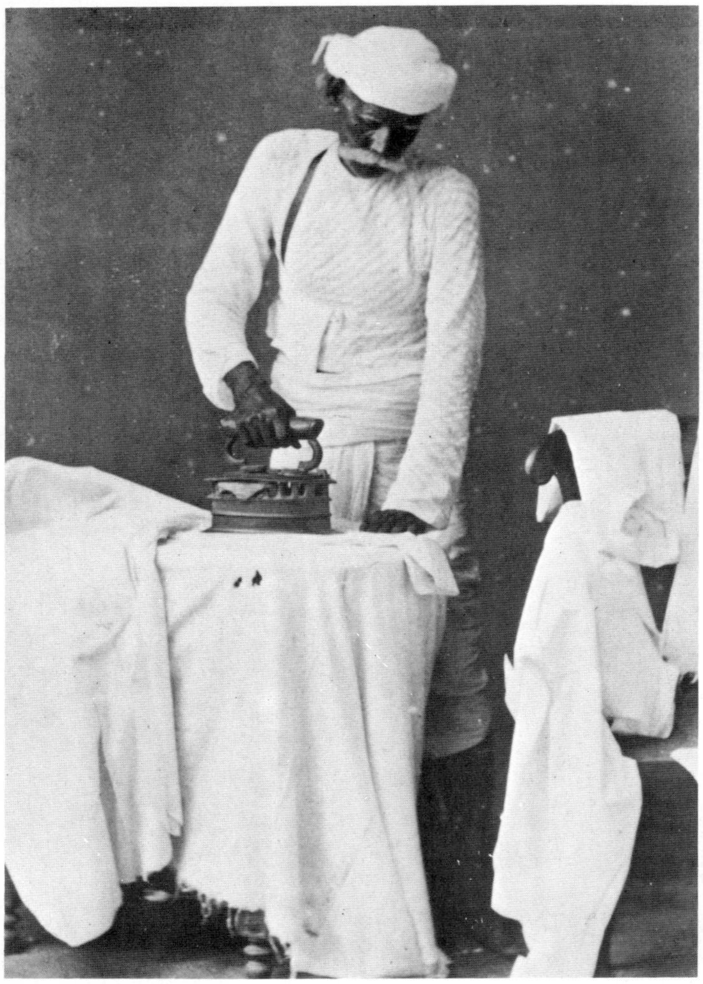
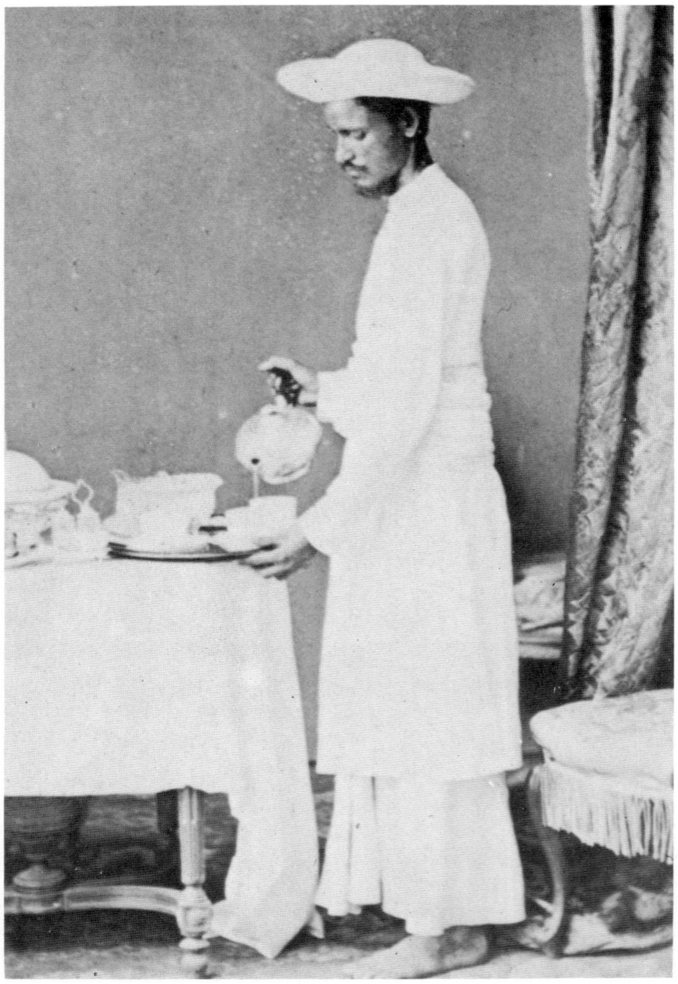

Indian servants were moulded to suit European modes. At top left is a bearer, to his right a butler holds a teapot, while below left a dhobi presses clothes and a table servant pours the tea

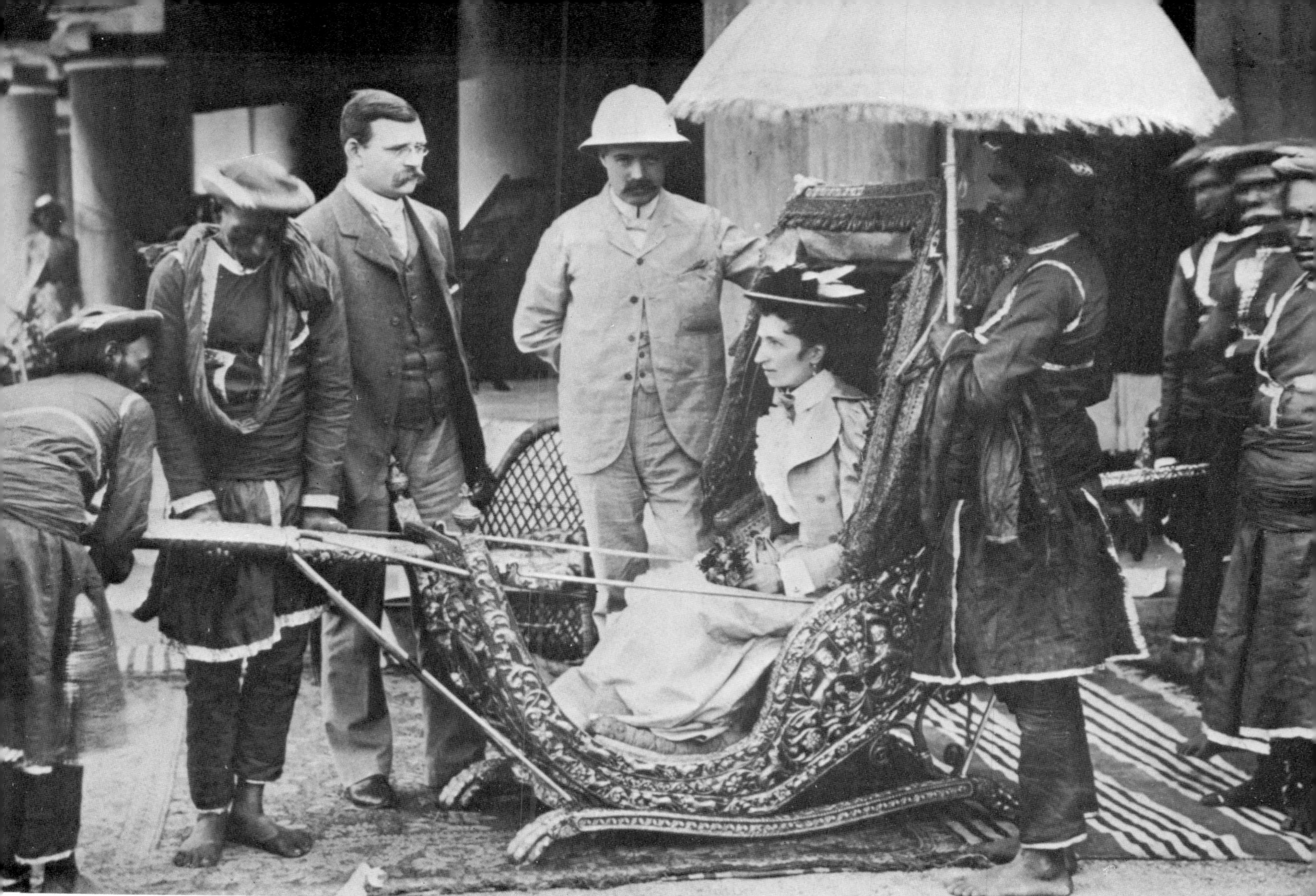

Above: Lady Elgin made her local journeys in style. Below: A day's work in 1864

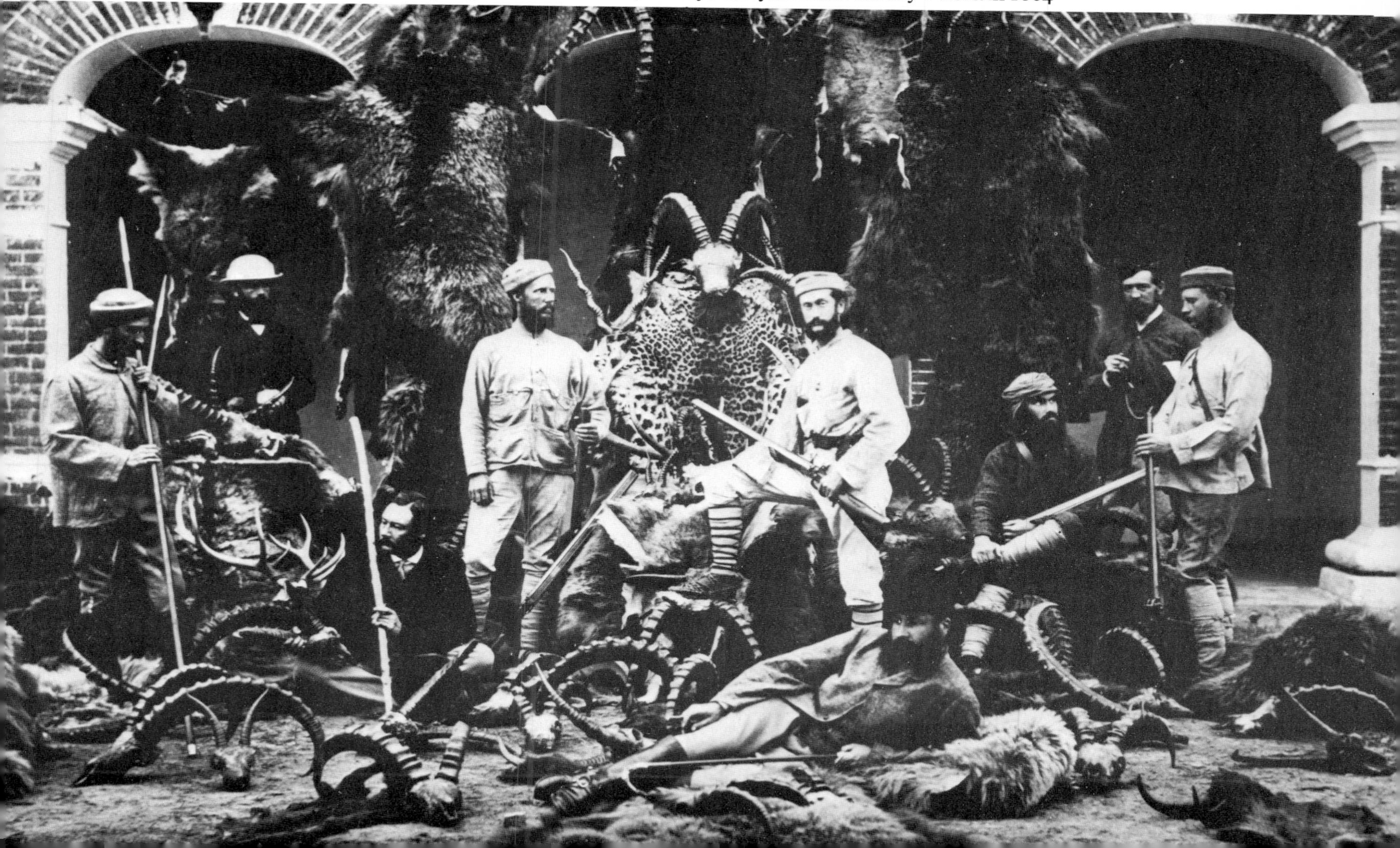

quantity of tin boxes, suitcases, water bottles, tiffin-containers full of curry and chapatis, and hold-alls for their bedding. Some of them take their servants with them, to prepare meals and spread out blankets and provide a target for tempers irritated by the dust and heat. Railway stations still offer a variety of amenities – Retiring Rooms for First Class Gents, Rest Rooms for Officers, mere Waiting Rooms for Second Class Ladies – and in, the restaurants, both Vegetarian and Non-Vegetarian, there are glass-fronted cabinets full of tea-pots and flowery sugar bowls, packets of Nice biscuits and bottles of Worcester sauce. There are boxes provided for your suggestions or complaints, and posters on the wall with moral precepts – "a stitch in time saves nine" or "cleanliness is next to godliness". And even if the boxes are now used for rubbish and nobody noticeably observes the precepts, it is still a wonder that they are there at all.

If the railways have hardly changed since Kipling's day, with engineers sitting under umbrellas on their little inspection trolleys and being pushed along the 'permanent way' by a pair of sweating coolies, other forms of transport are also much the same. There are paddle-steamers, even stern-wheelers, on the Ganges; there are *tongas* pulled by skinny ponies to fetch you from the station, and in parts of India you can still be carried in a palanquin or a sedan chair or a *dholi*, a little stool hanging from a pole carried on the shoulders of two men. And though in most towns the rickshaws are now pedal tricycles, in Calcutta at least they have kept the old two-wheeled kind, with a coolie running between the shafts; some people even own their private rickshaws.

A rickshaw, or rather the ghost of a jilted lady in a phantom rickshaw, was the subject of one of Kipling's best-known stories. It happened in Simla, in the foothills of the Himalayas; and Simla, the former summer capital of Her Majesty's Government in India, is the finest Victorian monument of them all, the queen of all the hill stations. Mussoorie, Darjeeling, Ootacamund, Naini Tal and a dozen others up and down India were the special invention of a temperate race ruling in a tropical and sub-tropical country. There at last they could breathe cool, moist air, walk and ride through the woods and round the lakes, burn log fires at night, dance and flirt and gossip.

They laid out their parks, built their grand hotels and pretty villas, planted English gardens and scattered homely English names. These hill stations are still there, a little tawdry, not quite so smart, but patronised by Indians who like to escape the summer of the plains and who also like, perhaps, to keep up vague appearances. But nowadays the whole Government of India doesn't pack its bags, as it used to at the first suggestion of hot weather, and take the train to Simla.

The modern Government of India, inheriting the legacy of generations of British rulers, is a worthy heir. For the first twenty years of Queen Victoria's reign British India was still governed by the East India Company, but after the unsettling, unexpected explosion of the Mutiny in 1857 responsibility was assumed

directly by the Crown, and the rest of the century is a history of progressive development, justice and welfare. The first three Indian universities were actually founded while the Mutiny was going on, and the next decades saw the Penal Code, the Famine Code and the distant mile-stones, beginning with the first 'native' appointed to the Indian Civil Service in 1864, along the hot road to the almost unimaginable goal of Independence.

But the Mutiny also had the effect of consolidating, on the part of the British rulers, their sense of superiority, and on the part of their Indian subjects, their spirit of humiliation. The remainder of Queen Victoria's reign was the high noon of the Raj, an epoch of paternalism

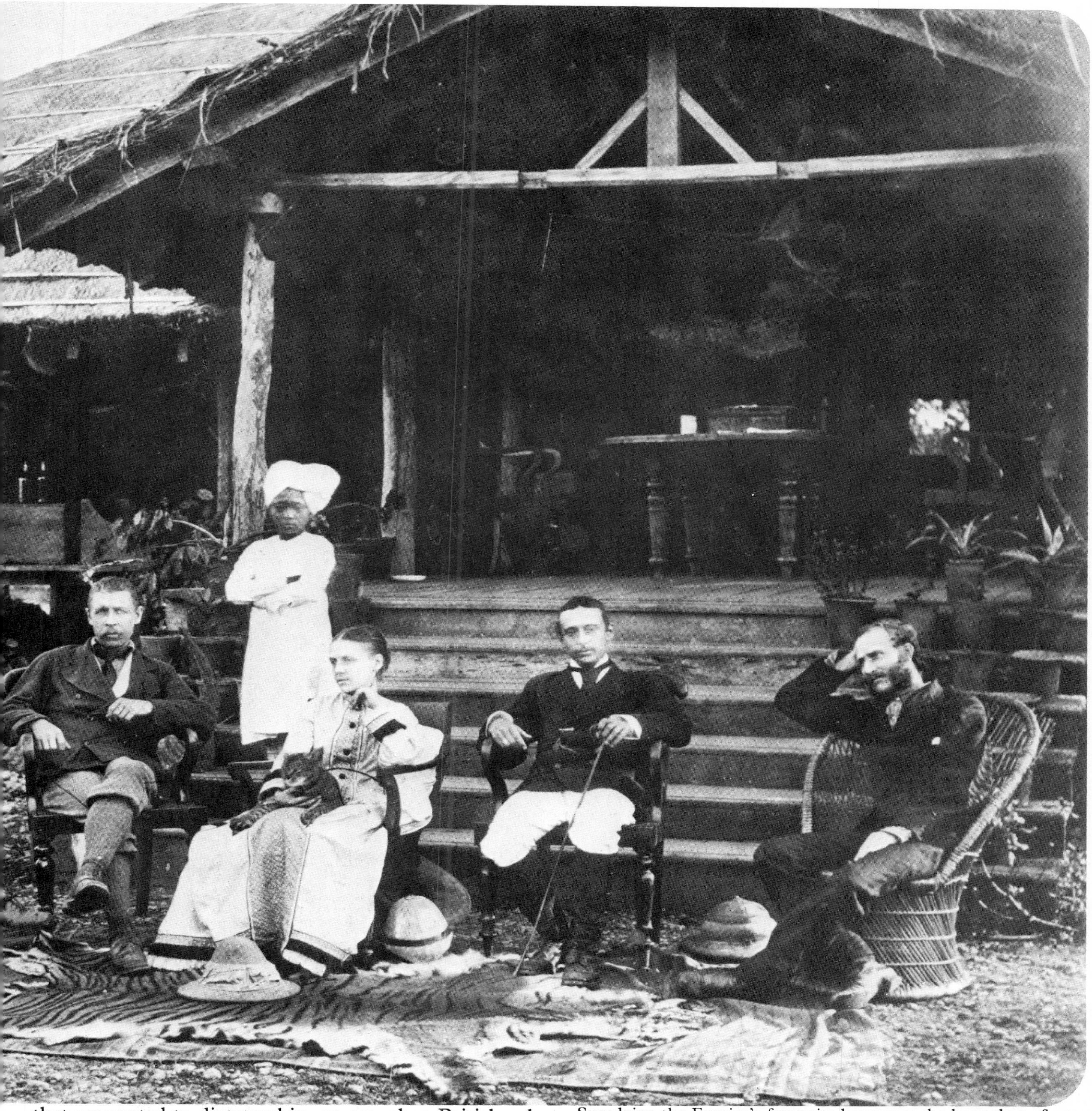

Supplying the Empire's favourite beverage: the bungalow of a tea plantation in 1876. A servant stands by with the ever-ready teacup

that amounted to dictatorship, an era when British rule was hardly questioned and the rulers, aloof and proud, hardly considered the likelihood of it ever ending. It was the age of duty, of service, of the confident belief that westernisation was "good for the natives" even if they sometimes seemed a bit ungrateful, and of that moral obligation which Kipling eloquently pressed on the civilised peoples of the world:

> Take up the White Man's burden,
>   Send forth the best ye breed,
> Go bind your sons to exile
>   To serve your captives' need.

Schools, railways, newspapers, hospitals, irrigation, as well as the army and all the institutions of western government – these were the features of an empire ruled from above by a selected, alien aristocracy which believed profoundly in itself, and that it was acting disinterestedly for the common good. India, which had never in its history been democratic, which had never known the ideal of equal opportunity, which had always been a hierarchy and usually with a priest of some sort at the top, which had never before included within its frontiers so much territory (or has since, for that matter), which had

Primitive scales weigh a bale at a jute processing centre

never been a nation, never a unity, but always split by racial, religious and caste distinctions – India in the last half of the 19th century was the repository for all the materialism that characterised the Victorians; and the results are to be seen everywhere to this day.

It was not entirely a one-way affair, but such interest as there was in England for the native culture was of a patronising kind, like the suite of rooms at Osborne which Queen Victoria had done up in the Indian style, designed, as it happens, by Kipling's father.

The high noon had to pass, of course, and as an old man Kipling had to watch in horror the sun setting on his India. Yet although he might be appalled at many things about the new republic there are others that he might not find so very startling.

He would be pleased, for instance, to see that lawyers on their way to court still wear white collar-tabs as they would in Fleet Street, though he would regret the passing of the judges' ermine. He would like the blazing brass bands that march in gay uniforms through towns and villages, the hawkers and hucksters, the snake-charmers and performing scorpions, the holy men, the side-shows and the smells. He would feel at home in the rare army officers' mess where young subalterns and captains still get drunk on Saturday night, form a rugger scrum among the tables or misbehave with the silver regimental trophies, and have to sober up on Sunday morning with mulligatawny soup for breakfast. He might wince at the

statues everywhere of a spectacled old man in a *dhoti*, but the new figure of Sivaji, the 17th-century hero of the Mahrattas, on his horse behind the Gateway of India in Bombay, Kipling would certainly acknowledge as fine as any of the equestrian Viceroys along the Maidan at Calcutta.

He would recognise the millionaire I know (though he might wish for a moment that the fellow wasn't a native, and a Hindu at that) who lives in a palace where fountains splash in marble courtyards, four-armed goddesses dance over limpid pools, gardeners for ever sprinkle the gaudy melon-flowers, and peacocks do what peacocks do. And he would step aside and doff his hat to the little old dowager who drives through the bazaar, among the veiled Muslim women and the holy Hindu cows, chewing betel in the back of an ancient Rolls-Royce: "D'you know Her Highness Jaipur?" she asked me once, as casually as her grandmother might have turned to Kipling and asked if he knew the Duchess of York.

In searching for Victoriana in the Indian scene it is difficult to pick out authentic pieces from the rest of the bewildering but ageless jumble. You can sit on a verandah in the evening, with a whisky and soda in your hand and your feet up on the long wooden arms of your wicker chair; the coppersmith-bird hidden somewhere in the trees hammers his maddening incessant note, something rattles in the bushes which sounds like a snake

A large Victorian family in India, with servants in attendance

but is only a falling leaf, the mosquitoes suck your blood out through your ankles, and you can think yourself in the garden of Rikki-Tikki-Tavi. But there is really nothing very Victorian about it, except the associations; likewise it is sometimes hard to distinguish between the attitudes and institutions which the Victorians brought with them and which rubbed off on India, and the ones which belonged there anyway or which would have emerged even without the Victorians.

And so it is with Indian society and politics. The barriers are coming down, but slowly and only at the top. Caste, though certainly there are cracks, is still a vast and daunting structure of social precedence; and to be born a Brahmin, a member of the hereditary caste of priests, is to be granted a lifetime of authority which few Hindus would deny. The Victorians, themselves bound by class distinctions even more than we are now, hardly tampered with Indian society; and many of their importations, like boys' boarding schools fashioned exactly on the lines of English public schools, fit comfortably into a social pattern where inherited position, a rigid hierarchy and arranged marriages are the rule.

Victoriana transplanted into India, thriving in a land that found it not so strange and nurtured by a people who are conservative in everything, lingered there when it was already withering where it came from. So India may still be full of all the things – splendid or shameful or ridiculous – that for a post-imperialist Englishman are summed up in the little word 'Poona', but an Indian, steeped in the ways and culture of an earlier English generation, can travel to England and be disappointed with what he finds.

It is the same in politics. The bulk of four hundred million people live in conditions of poverty and starvation very similar to those of a century ago, while the grand old noises of progress, development and industrialisation rumble from the capital. For most people in this vast land the Government of India, cocooned in the imperial splendour of New Delhi, is as remote now as in the days when the ultimate power lay in London.

Though India is now a democracy there is much of the same lofty self-confidence, the same ponderous machinery, the same arrogant and autocratic attitudes as there were when the rulers were a class of Englishmen, bred and educated for the career traditionally followed by the families into which they had been born. And if much of the situation remains the same, one reason is that many of the men in Delhi have hardly altered; it is not irrelevant that Nehru, for all his socialism and secularism, was both a Brahmin and an old Harrovian.

India needs a latter-day Kipling, a native this time, who can show that, though East and West still can't always meet very happily, between them they can turn up some unique surprises.

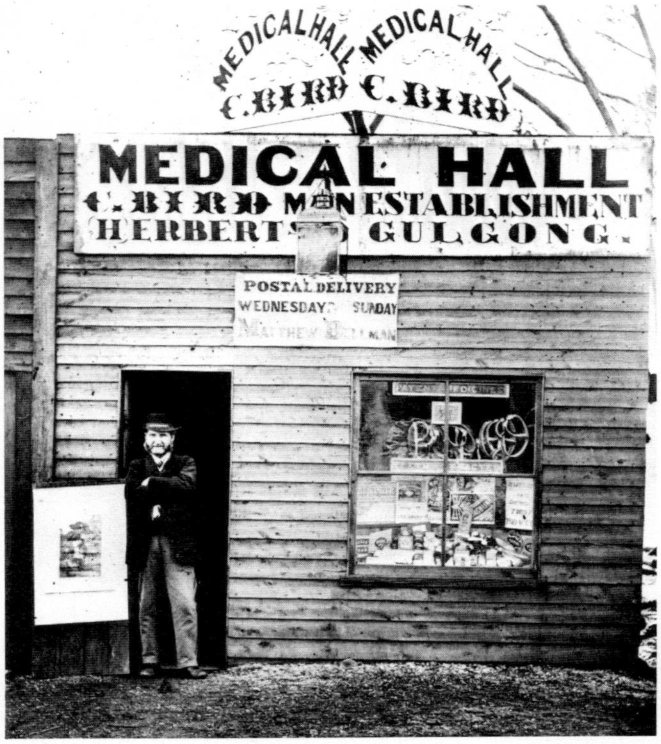
MEDICAL HALL MEDICAL HALL
C. BIRD C. BIRD
MEDICAL HALL
C. BIRD
ESTABLISHMENT
GULGONG
POSTAL DELIVERY
WEDNESDAY
SUNDAY

THE COLONIAL SPIRIT

By W. F. Cater

The shaping of Australia was solidly Victorian; though settlement began 50 years before her reign the years of growth were Victorian years. Settlers, cultural influences and trading partners were Victorian British, and there were more subtle links. Australia could have no pioneers racing American-style across a fertile heartland with towns and cities springing up behind the plough; only an encirclement by sea and, beachheads secured, a pressing into the increasingly unwelcoming interior – for the heartland here was desert. The country was obliged to face the sea and live by trade, a most Victorian life-style.

Yet it was not a slavishly British Victorianism. The land itself and the people determined that. The terrain would no more allow British-style intensive farming that the Australian people would make a curtseying tenantry. Even those fresh out from the homeland would neither bless the squire and his relations nor pray to keep their proper stations; how could a man's station in life be fixed when the gold-rushes began and anyone might dream of riches? It was an egalitarian society; there might be rich men but there was no accepted aristocracy.

All this left a visible mark. Australian cities have fine public buildings and palaces of commerce; there are vast country estates and street after suburban street of comfortable houses; but there are few Stately Homes, and little European-style squalor. This is where the century of the common man began – in Victorian Australia.

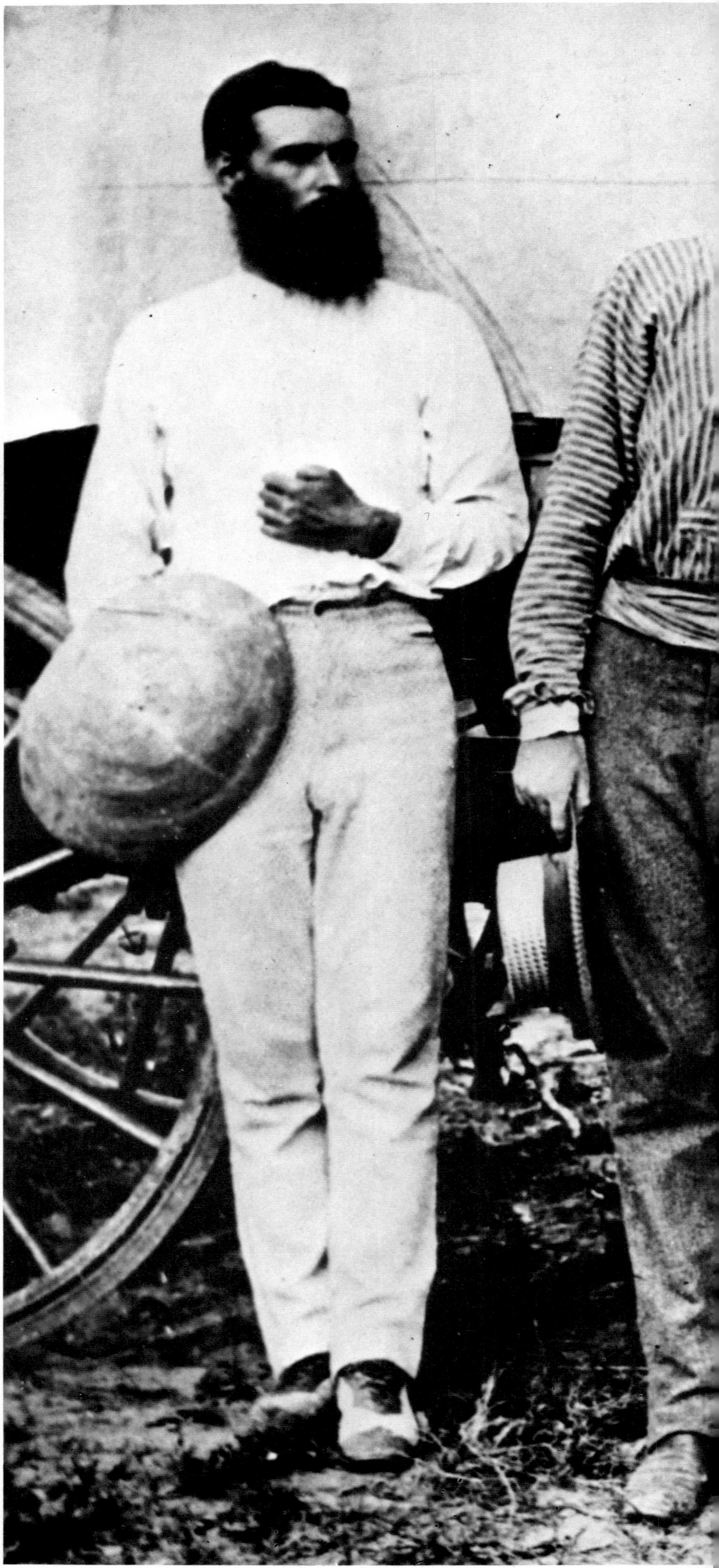

Ending the great explorations and linking their cities with the world, these engineers (including a bespectacled Postmaster-General) strung the telegraph across Australia

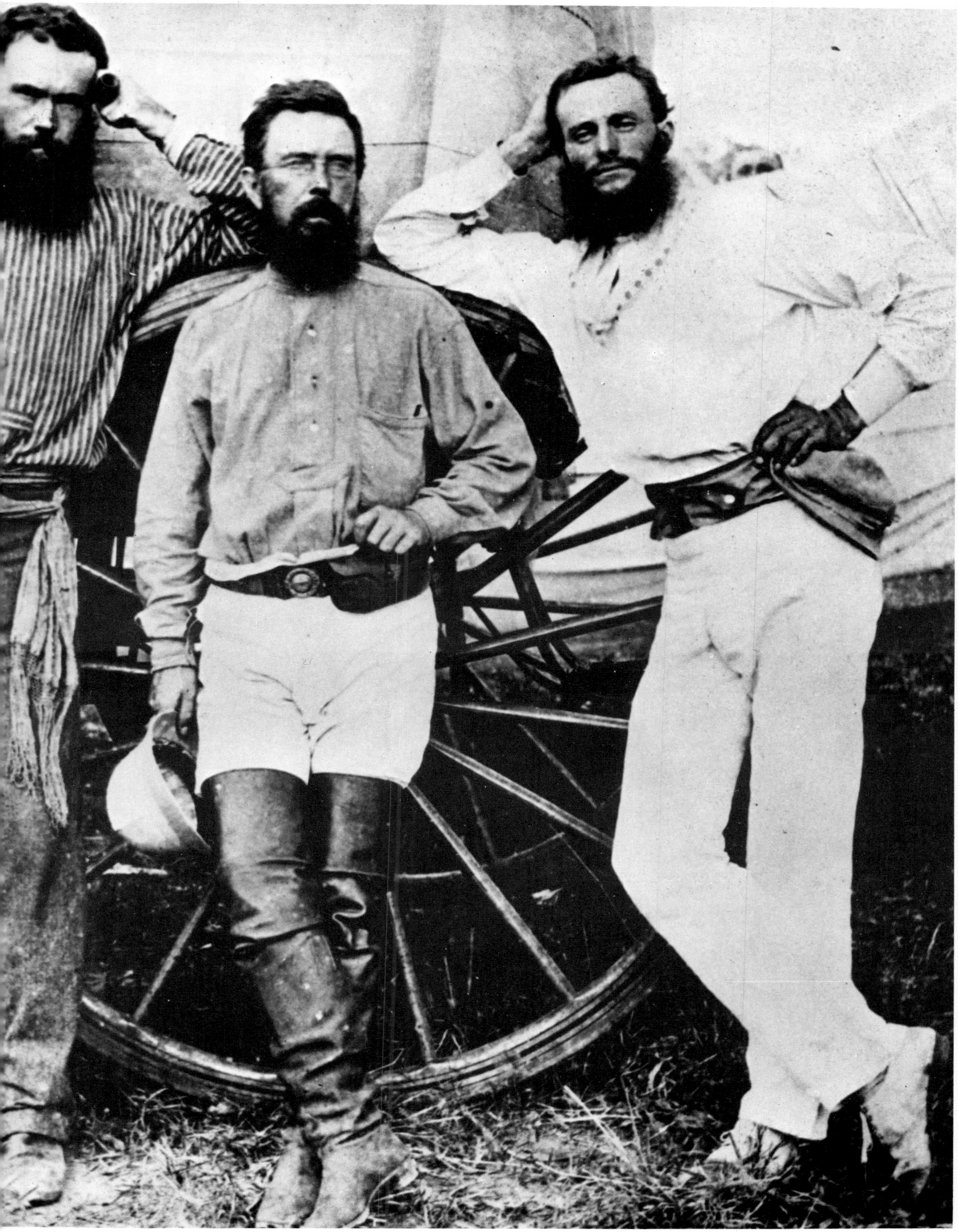

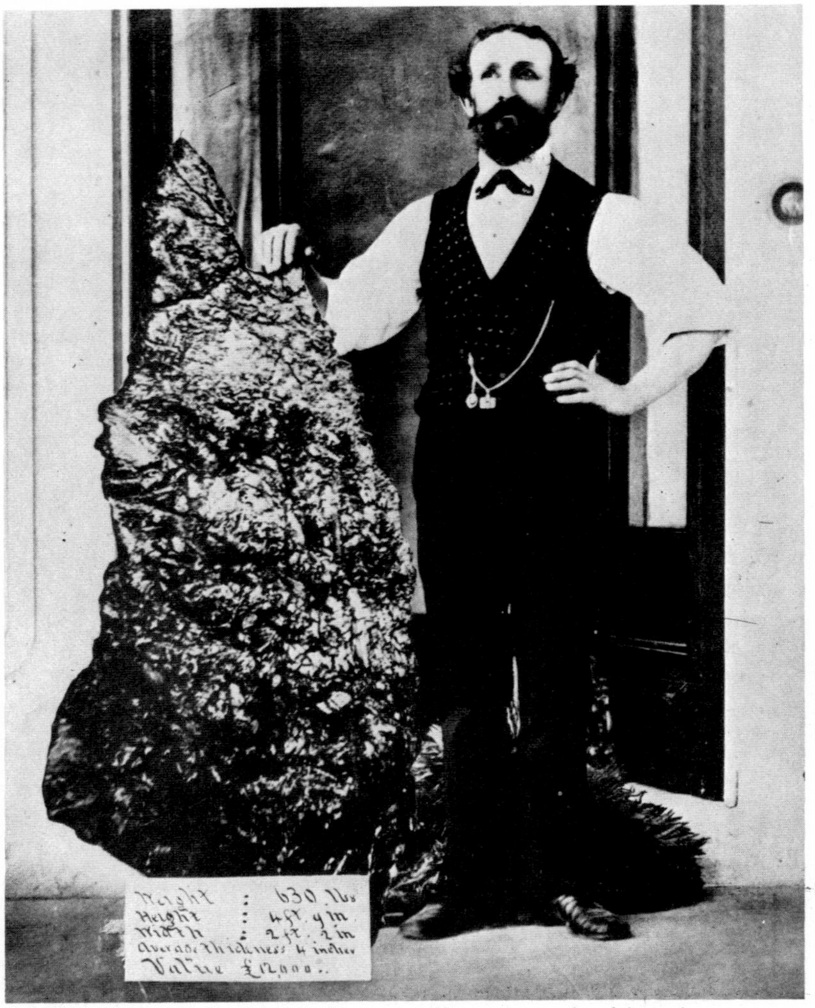
Weight : 630 lbs
Height : 4 ft. 9 in
Width : 2 ft. 2 in
Average thickness 4 inches
Value £12,000

Victorian Australia was built on gold and wool: this mine-owner, Bernhardt Holtermann, posed in 1872 with a chunk of gold-bearing ore then claimed to be largest ever mined: 630 lb, worth £12,000

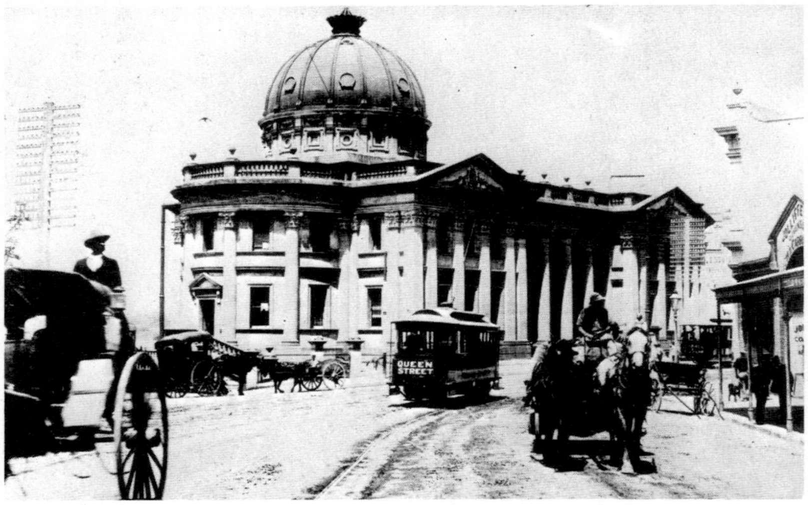
QUEEN STREET

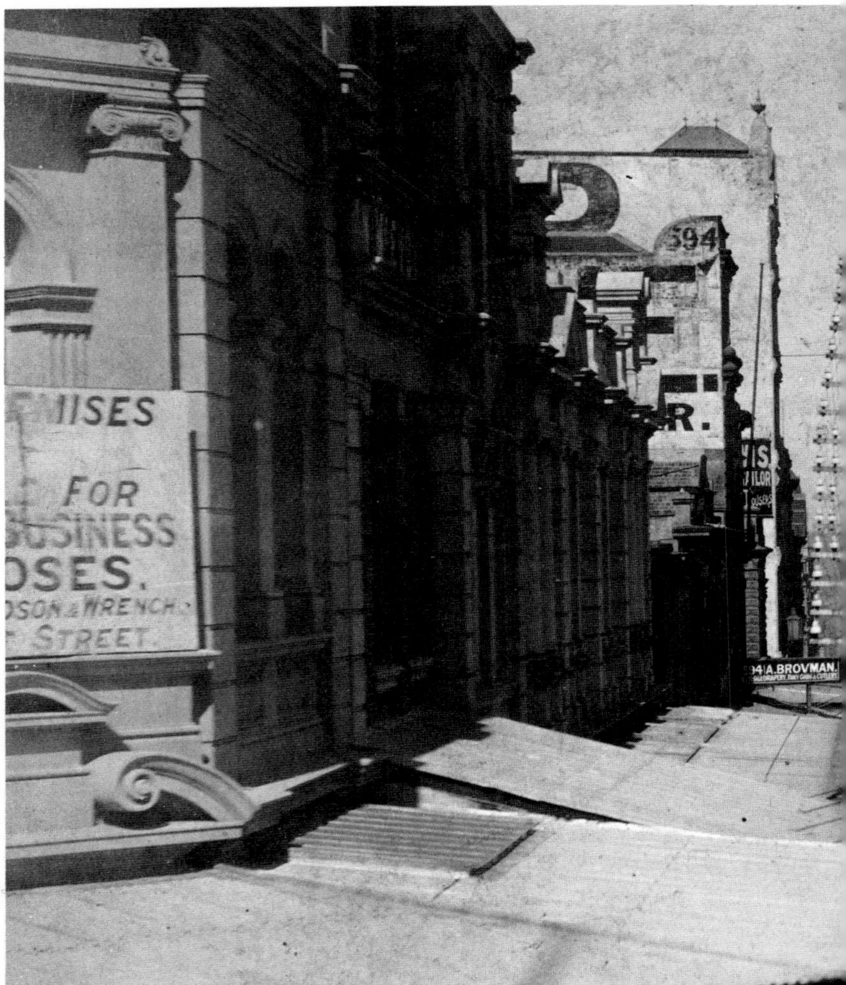
594
FOR
A. BROVMAN.

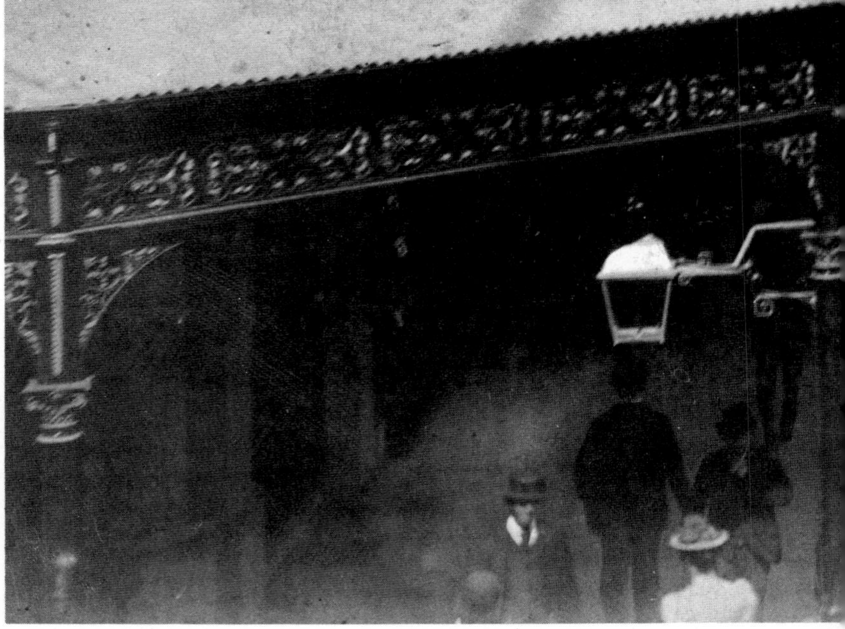

The shearers (below, far right, in 1890 painting) were skilled and fiercely independent men, perpetually on the move about the country from sheep-station to station, perpetually at odds with the pastoralists who hired them, depended on them – and resisted their pay demands. The shearer became an Australian folk-hero – the free man in the wide open spaces, bowing the knee to none but loyal to his group; his struggles also helped found Australia's trade union tradition and its labour movement. It was from the shearing sheds and from the shack towns of the gold-fields (centre, a house at Gulgong in the 1870s) came the wealth which supported public buildings of Victorian grandeur like the Brisbane Customs House (above) and spreading shopping streets (George Street, Sydney, above right). Except for sidewalks covered against a fiercer sun, these cities would not be strange to migrants from Victorian Britain; and if the rural landscape was unfamiliar the sea beckoned (right, a Sydney beach in 1880) like any British resort. There might be no pier, there might be sharks; but at least umbrellas were needed against the sun instead of the rain

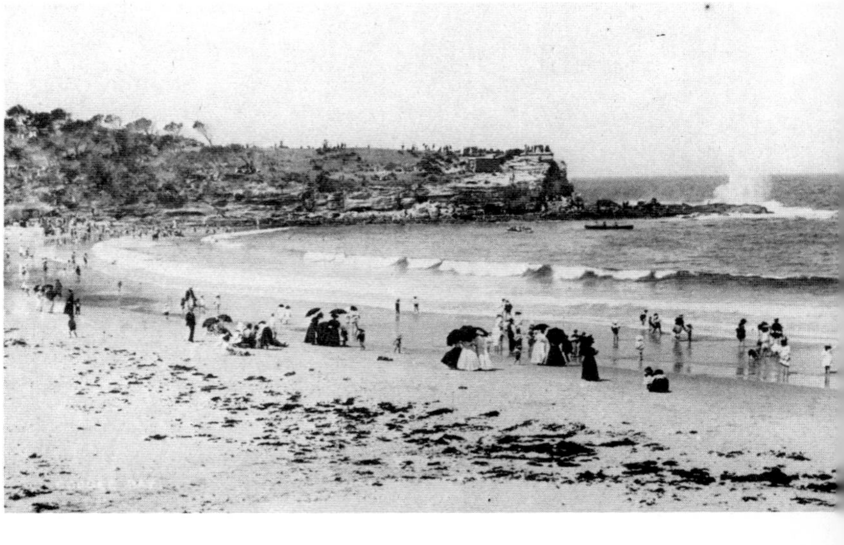

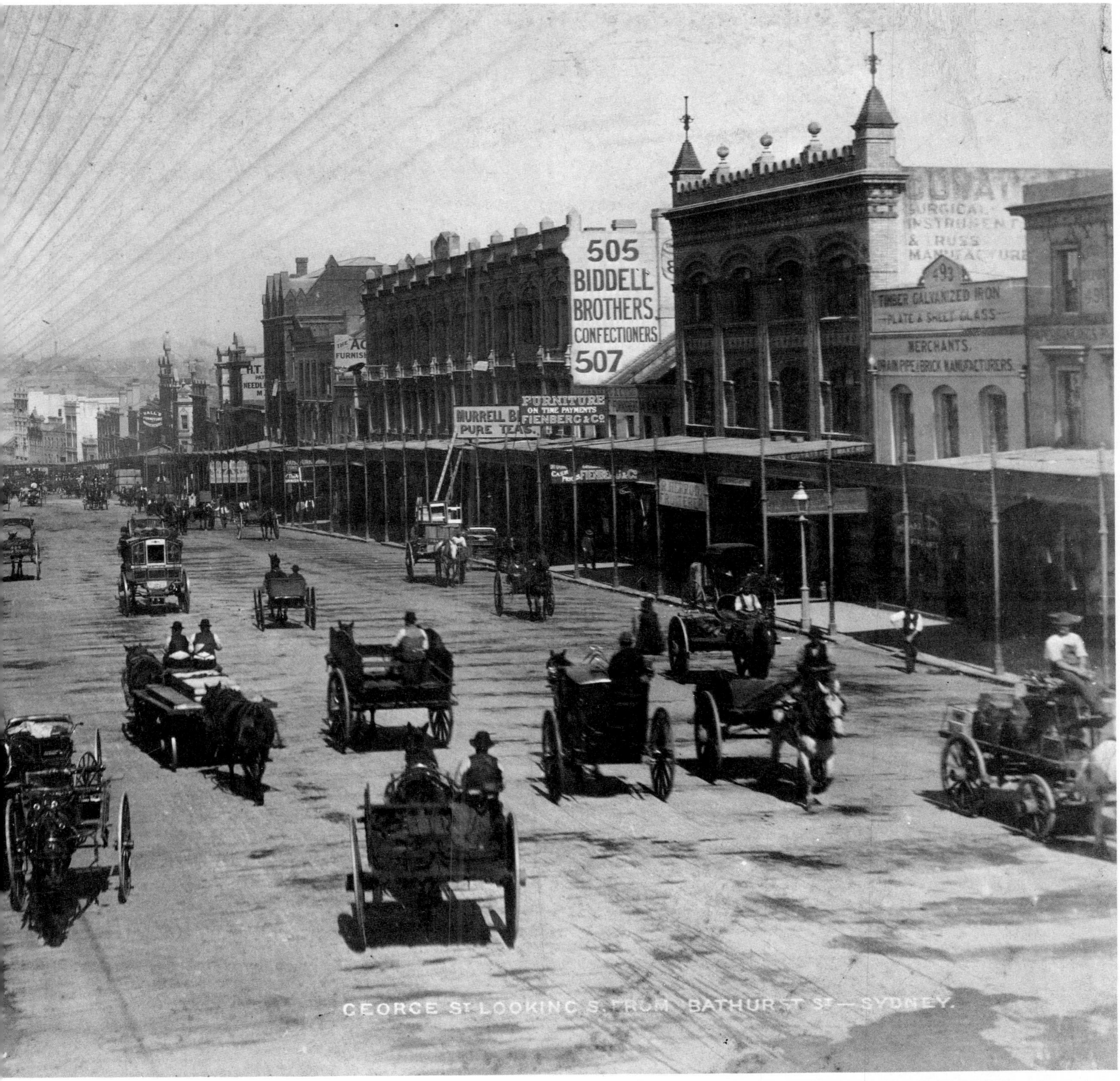
505
BIDDELL
BROTHERS
CONFECTIONERS
507
FURNITURE
ON TIME PAYMENTS
FIENBERG & Co
PURE TEAS
TIMBER GALVANIZED IRON
PLATE & SHEET GLASS
MERCHANTS
DRAIN PIPE & BRICK MANUFACTURERS
GEORGE ST LOOKING S. FROM BATHURST ST— SYDNEY

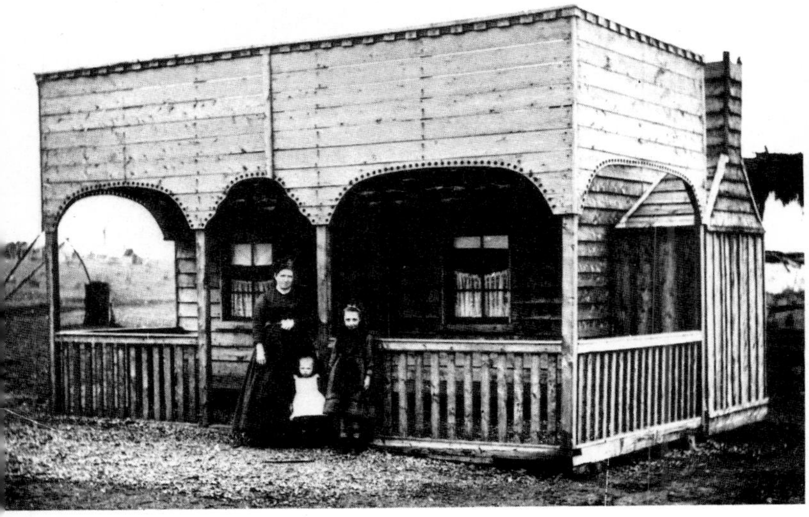

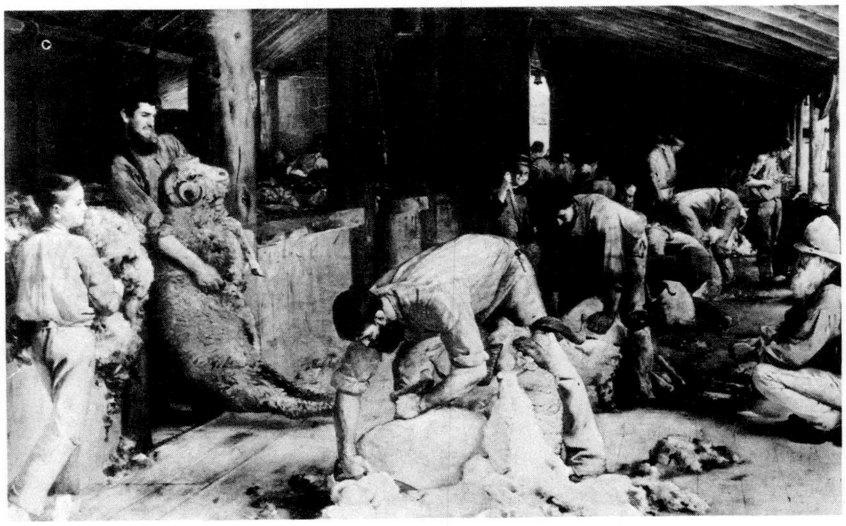

EXPANDING THE EMPIRE

Under Victoria, in the name of burgeoning trade, military expedience

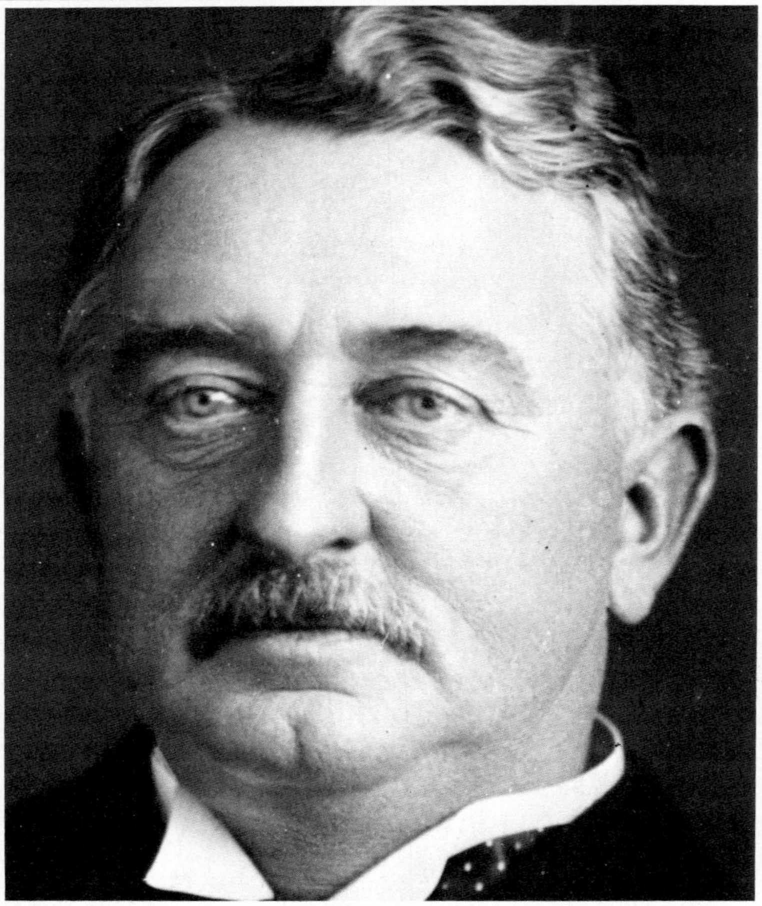

Cecil Rhodes, diamond millionaire, politician, Empire-builder, with a zeal for British expansionism that brought under the Crown the present Malawi, Zambia, Rhodesia and Botswana

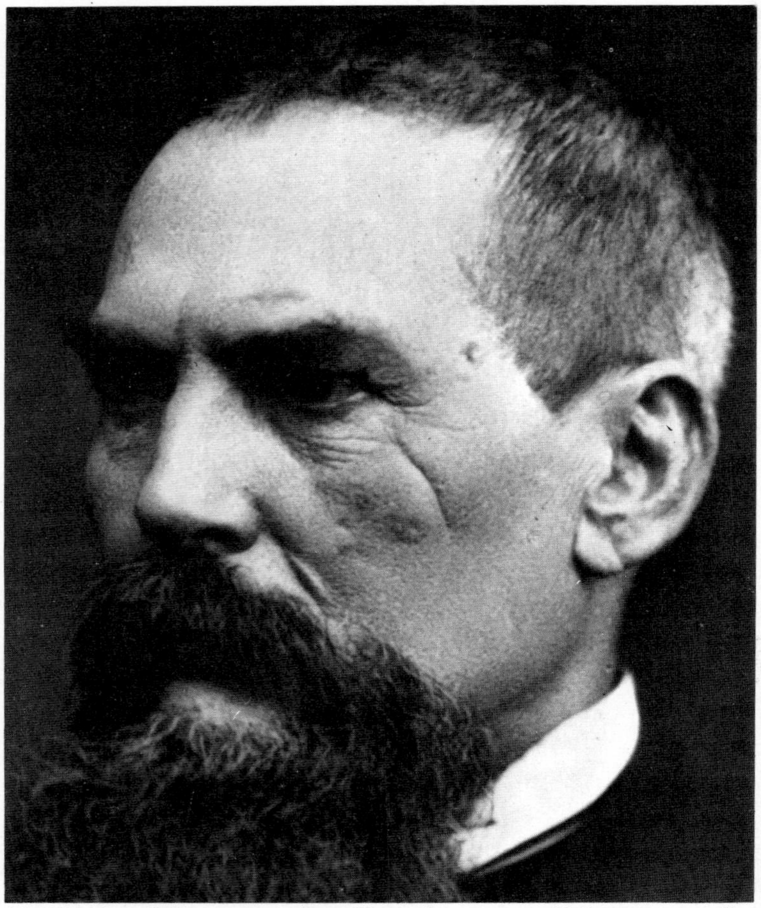

Sir Richard Burton, orientalist, adventurer, diplomat, equally celebrated for his journey to the forbidden city of Mecca, his exploration in Arabia and Africa, and his vast literary output

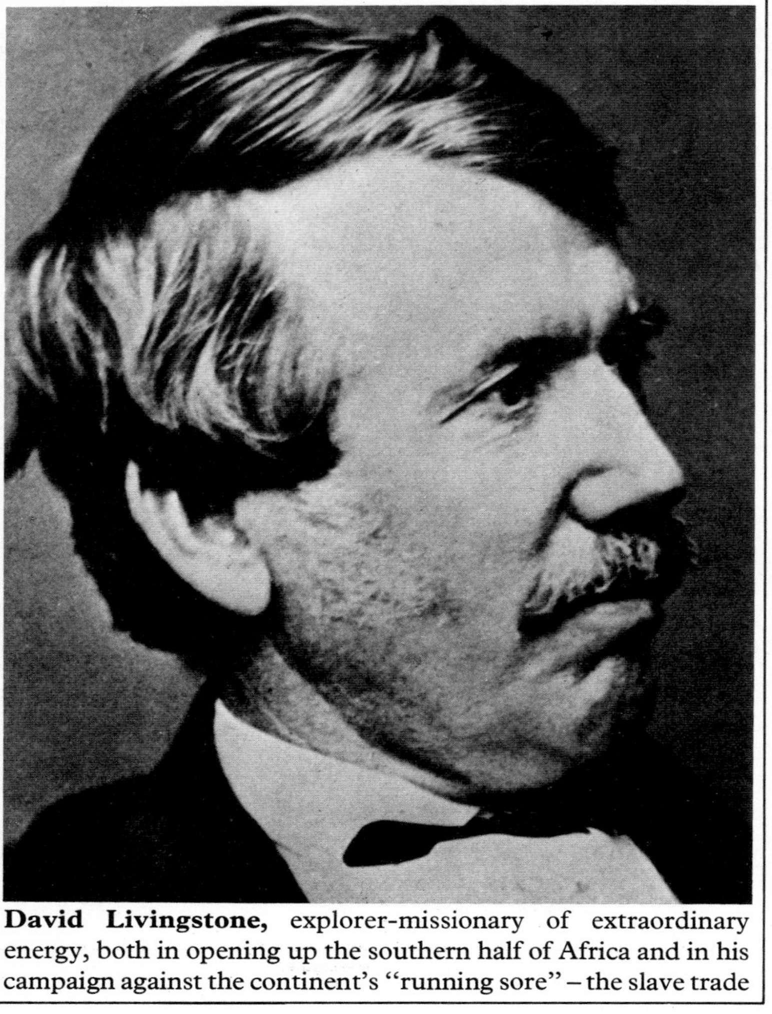

David Livingstone, explorer-missionary of extraordinary energy, both in opening up the southern half of Africa and in his campaign against the continent's "running sore" – the slave trade

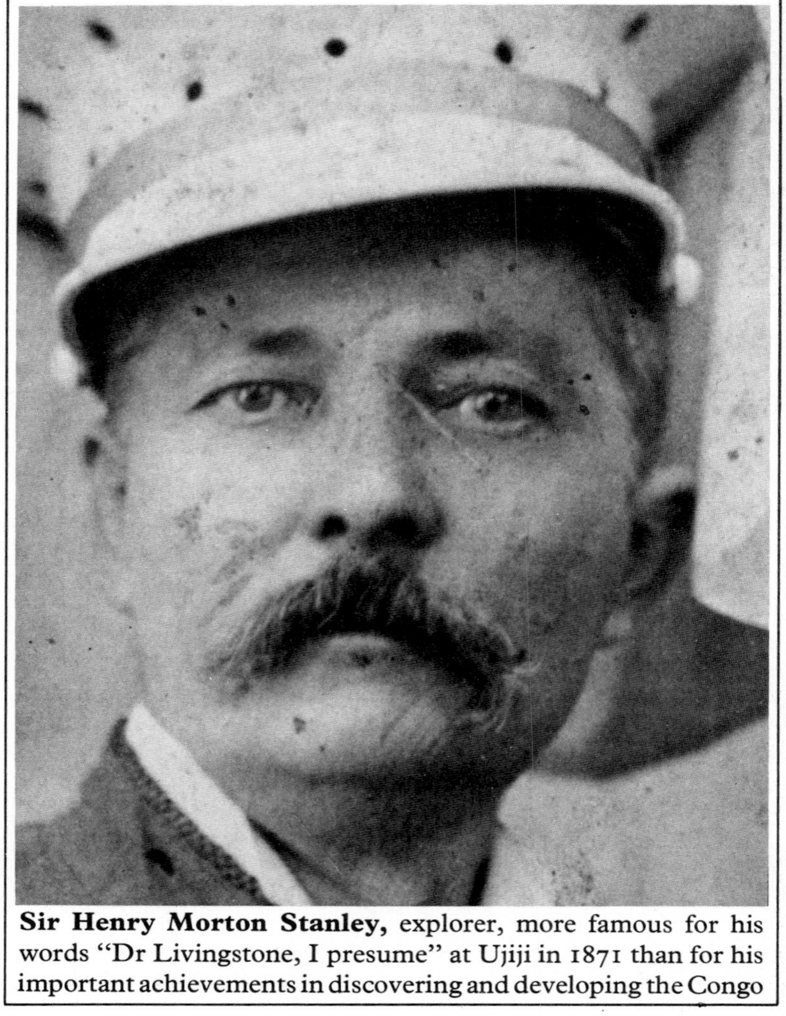

Sir Henry Morton Stanley, explorer, more famous for his words "Dr Livingstone, I presume" at Ujiji in 1871 than for his important achievements in discovering and developing the Congo

he prestigious Royal Geographical Society, the Flag was planted in increasingly unlikely corners of the uncivilised world

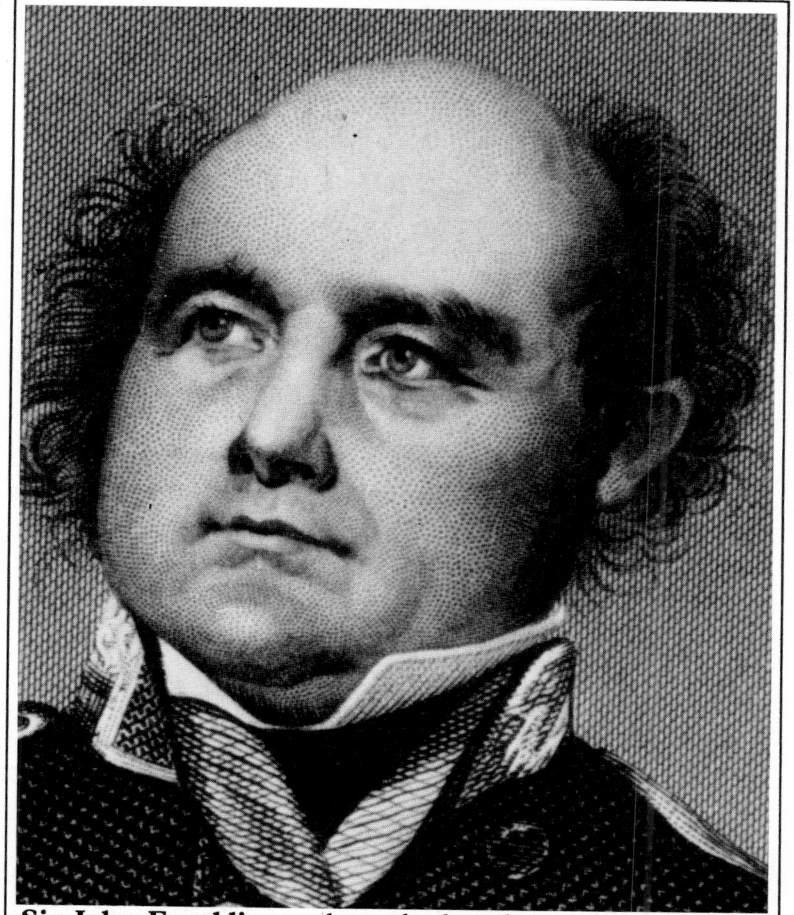

Sir John Franklin, explorer, leader of two pioneering land expeditions to the Canadian Arctic before the 1845–48 voyage, in which he and 128 men died discovering the North-West Passage

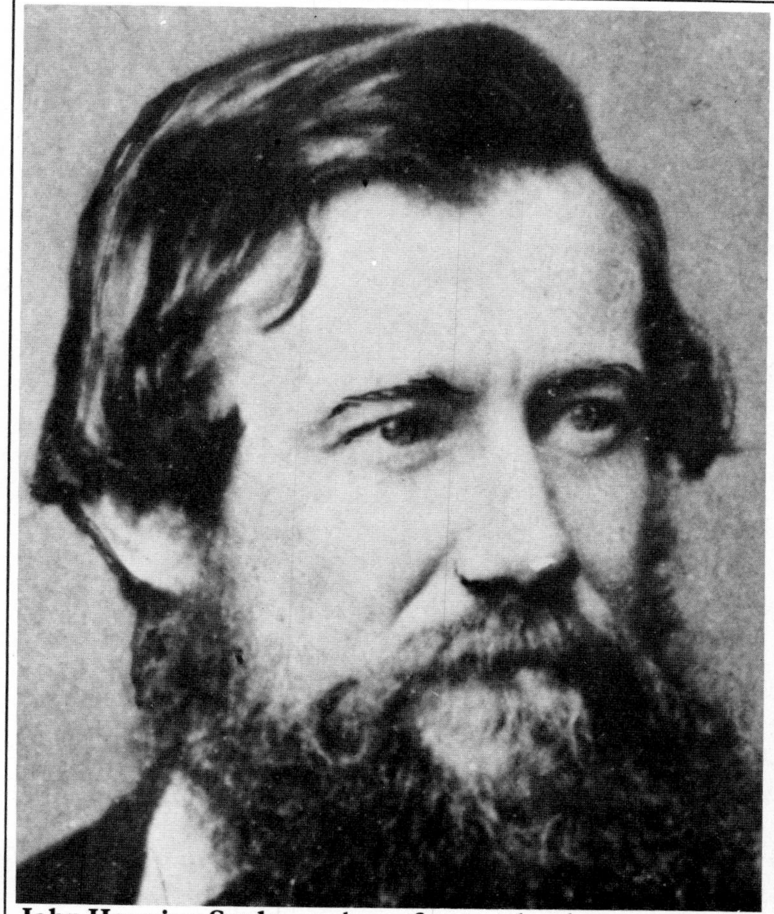

John Hanning Speke, explorer, first to solve the mystery of the Nile sources on two expeditions, one with Richard Burton, one with James Grant, from Zanzibar to the shores of Lake Victoria

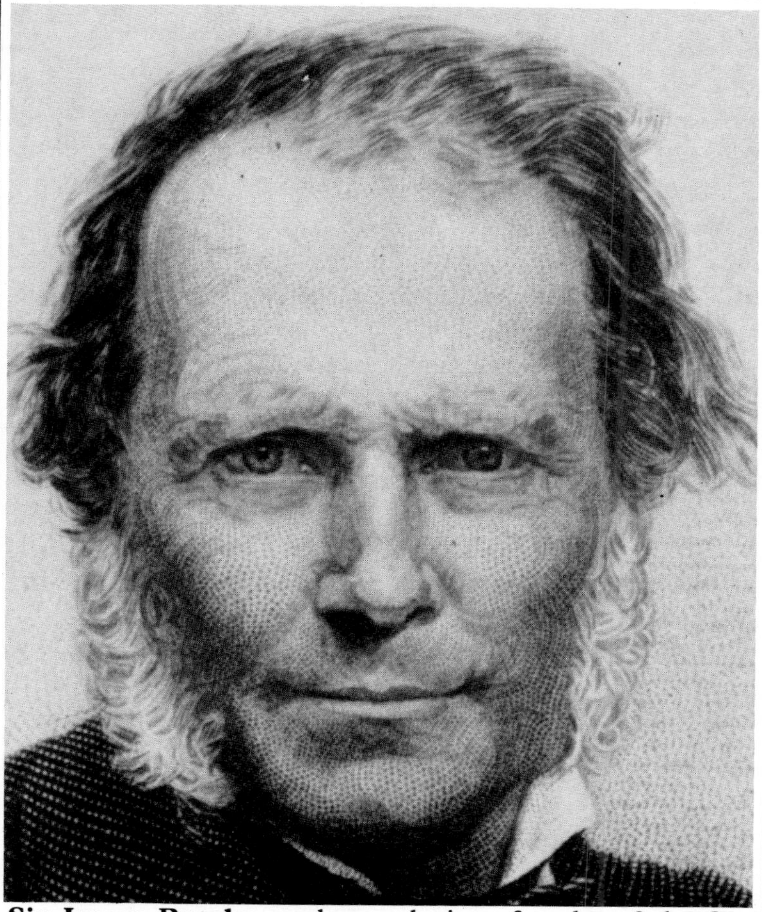

Sir James Brooke, explorer-coloniser, founder of the first British settlements in Borneo and the first in a distinguished line of benevolent dictators to rule Sarawak – the White Rajahs

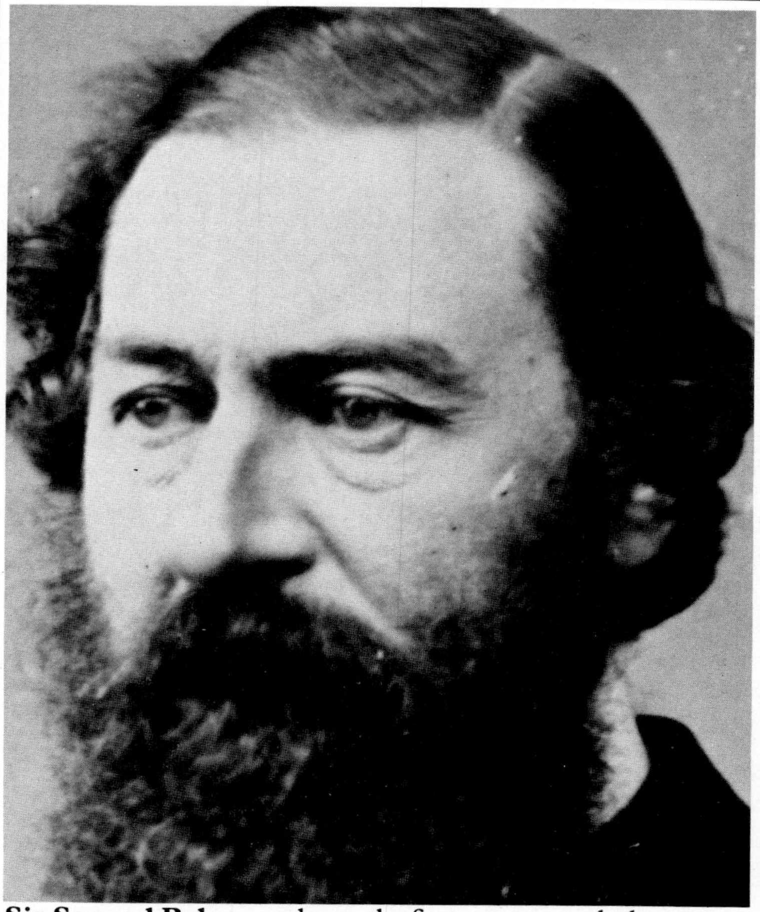

Sir Samuel Baker, explorer, the first man to reach the sources of the Nile from the north – in 1862, accompanied by his wife Florence, he sailed up the White Nile to the waters of Lake Albert

A VISION OF ROME

By Mario Amaya

Sir Laurence Alma-Tadema expressed an affinity between the British
Empire and that of ancient Rome by painting scenes
so superbly composed and imaginatively dramatised that they were
the natural precursors of the Hollywood epic

Sentiment, poetic feeling, nostalgic worlds of the past re-created through the imagination – these things have little place in an age of cybernetics and post-Freudian dissection. Yet, in the last few years we have begun to look back at such subject matter in 19th-century art. Meanwhile, those giants of the Salon and the Royal Academy who excelled in these attitudes, who were in fact praised for them, now seem more approachable and real.

Sir Laurence Alma-Tadema ranks high among them. He has suffered most from the vagaries of fast-changing taste and art revolutions, more than the Pre-Raphaelites and the *genre* painters, since his works cannot be linked entirely to direct pictographs of his times. Moreover, the paradoxes he presented to his own era have long confused the casual critic who neither knows nor cares about the rich literary and archaeological references in these 'restorations' of antiquity. The usual reaction is disdain, even ridicule, for the subject matter. If Alma-Tadema wanted to paint the excavated Roman world, then why on earth did he choose *genre* rather than heroic themes? Moreover, if he really wanted to depict mid-Victorian England, why did he choose to wrap his *nouveaux-riches* mercantile classes in togas and set them down in marble-ised halls?

Notwithstanding the superb quality in the painting, the exquisite colour, the extraordinary compositions and daring spatial concepts, it is this very paradox that makes one look again. For it becomes clear that these pictures reveal Victorian England in a rare moment off guard, as it romanticised about itself in the mirror of an antique past which it wished to emulate.

Thus, accepted themes in Victorian domestic 'high-life' could be woven into the fabric of Imperial Rome and made to re-create not only the day-to-day pastimes of ancient civilisation, but provide a parallel for modern times. Consequently, the artist managed to capture a side view of Victorian life that few painters of his generation expressed. The setting for his idle upper middle-class ladies might be St Johns Wood *or* the slopes of Vesuvius; both inhabitants led leisurely lives and were equally "exalted" as Ruskin acidly put it, "by the wealth of the capital". Therefore, it was not Gibbon's view of antiquity, with its perversions and cruelty, its decline and fall, that interested Alma-Tadema, but the sun-drenched afternoons in luxurious suburban villas outside Pompeii and Herculaneum; there the new-rich lounged in boredom, sated with materialistic comforts, but morally as decent as anyone under Victoria's reign.

These paintings exist on several levels at once: as illustrations of antique social history, as documents of newly uncovered finds, and as thinly disguised examples of what Victorian life among aspiring classes was all about. This combination was bound to force comparisons, either overt or implied, between the two greatest empires the world had known: the British and the Roman.

For Alma-Tadema, heroic feats and moral lessons were set aside. He was more interested in factual descriptions and his first truly Roman work was *Catullus at Lesbia's*, depicting the spurned Latin poet, reciting his verses to the bored and mocking *salonière*. The painting was hailed by a contemporary as the first of its type: "No one had attempted up till then," wrote one critic "to bring this intimate and personal sentiment into our dreams of the past."

In 1868, perhaps more to cause a sensation than to reconstruct the past, Alma-Tadema painted *Phideas inspecting the Frieze of the Parthenon*. It shows the sculptor standing patiently, scroll in hand, before Pericles who intently studies the work, while his teacher and later Mistress, Aspasia, nods assent. Alcibiades, arms akimbo, stands near by inspecting the warriors on the wall. Apart from the fact that the scene is set on top of a precarious scaffold under the columned portico, it might be varnishing day at the Royal Academy, with Ruskin making carping comments. It is amusing to find that seven years after Gibson exhibited his *Tinted Venus*, Victorians were still surprised and shocked to realise that Greek sculpture had been brightly coloured.

With only an occasional glimpse at Egyptian archaeology (his *Pastimes in Egypt 3,000 Years Ago* won wide acclaim) a steady procession of Roman and Pompeian subjects followed with titles any Victorian could comprehend: *Presents*; *Gallo-Roman Women*; *A Chat*; *Books*; *Home from Shopping*; *Entrance to a Roman Theatre*; *A Roman Family*, etc. In 1867 he paid tribute to one source of inspiration, Bulwer-Lytton: *Nydia* the blind girl in the novel is shown weaving wreathes of flowers while the admiring Glaucus reclines on a couch decorated with motifs that might have come from William Morris & Co. Through the door in a sunlit peristyle is a marble table-base discovered at Pompeii.

The same year he did *A Collector of Pictures* with a semi-recumbent Roman matron scrutinising a monochrome by Apelles on an easel. On the walls around the

A Coign of Vantage 1895 – Roman ladies watching the return of lovers from war in a dramatic perspective

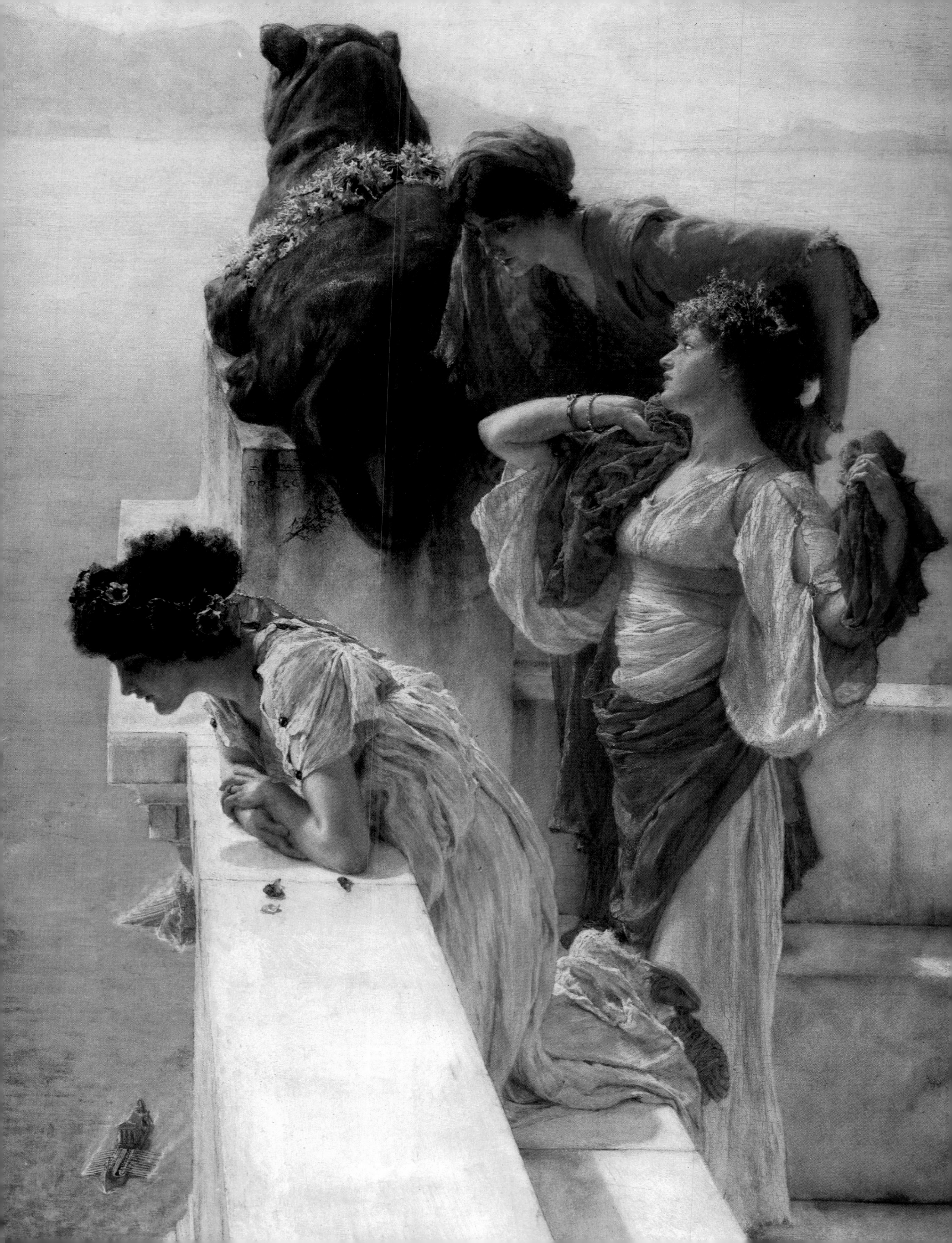

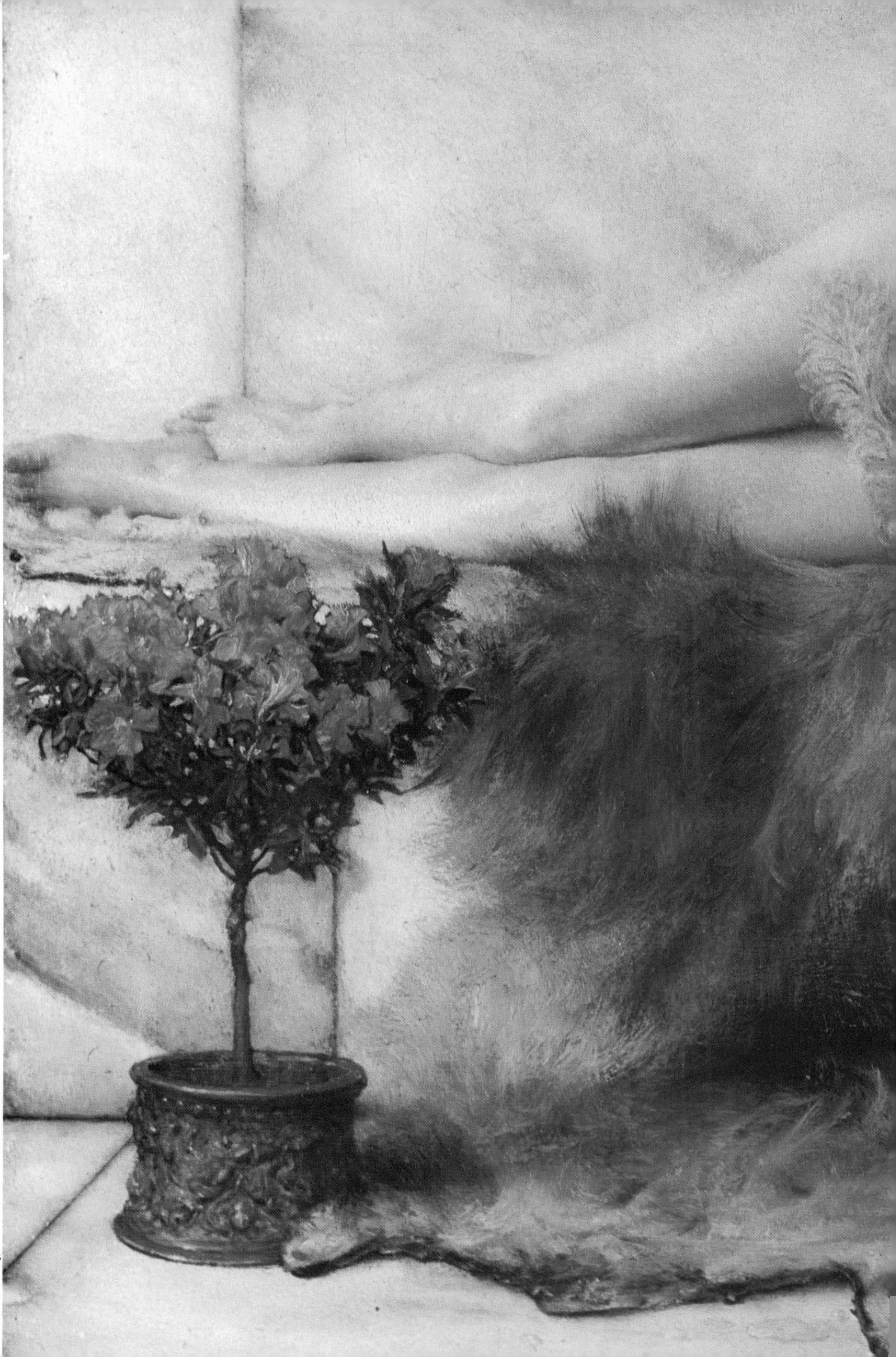

In the Tepidarium 1881 – a frankly sexual nude disguised with the trappings of antiquity – a strigil and a peacock fan

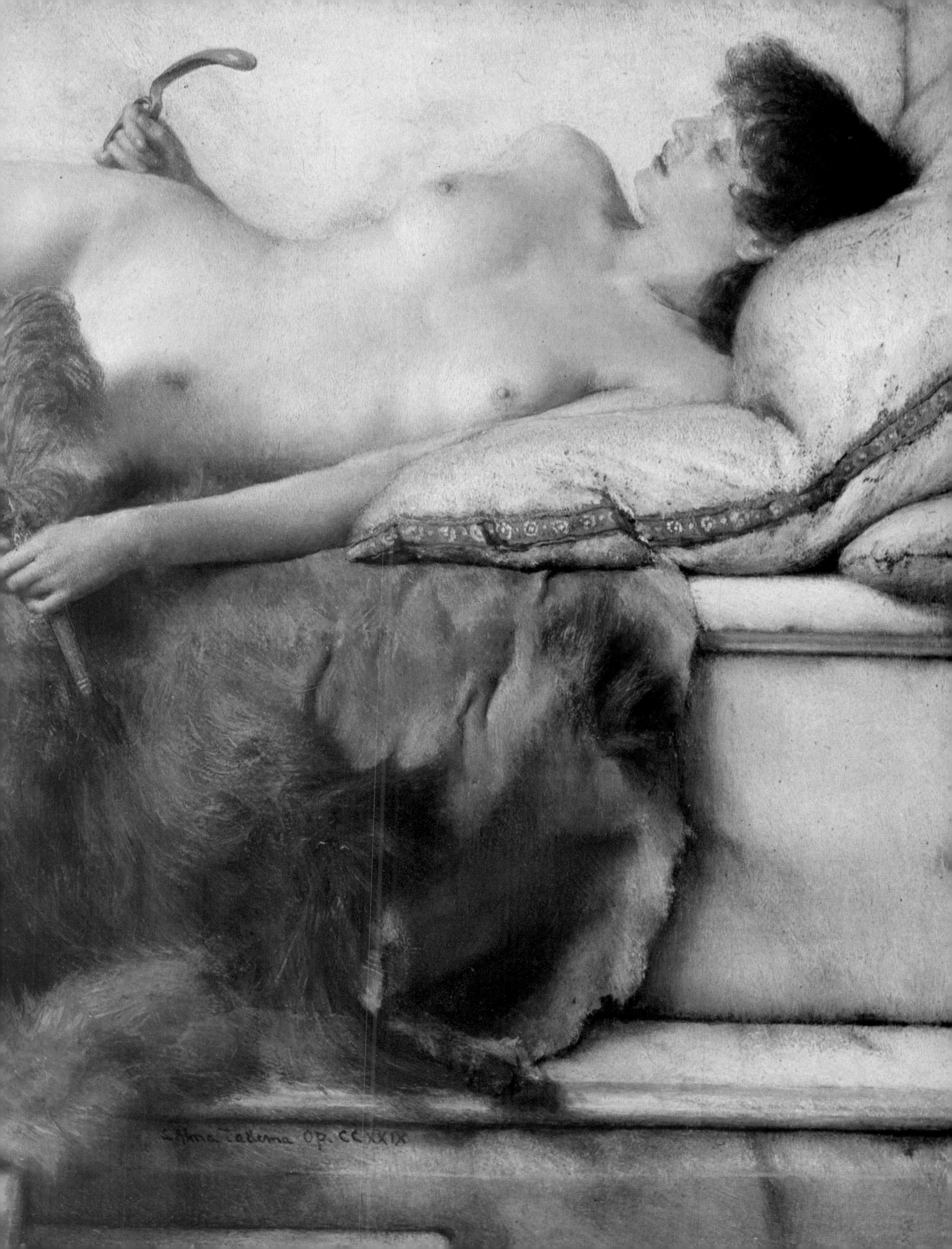
L. Alma Tadema Op. CCXXIX

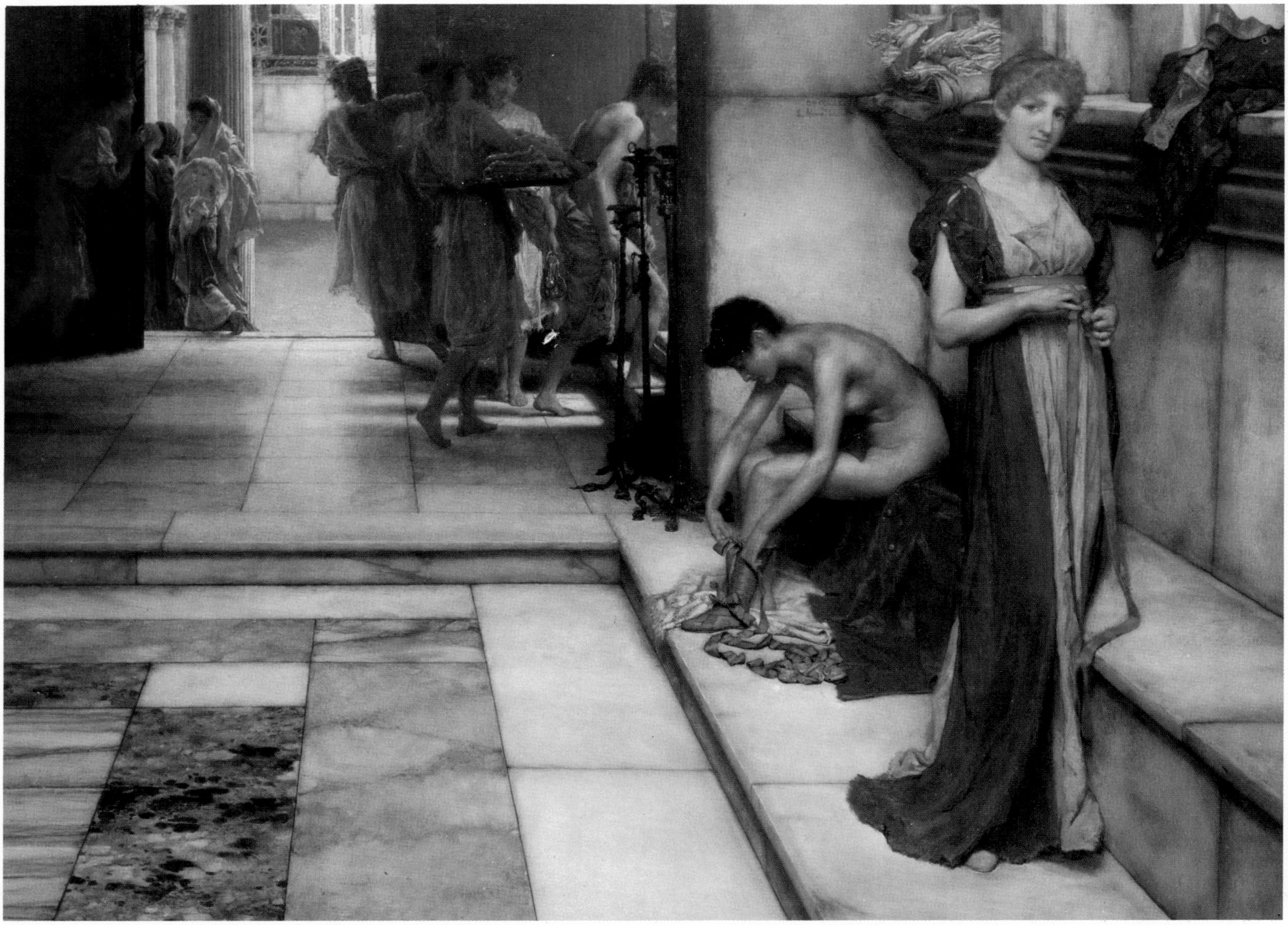

Above: *An Apodyterium* 1886 – the drawing room of a *thermae*. Below: *The Roses of Heliogabalus* 1888 – a Panavision fantasy

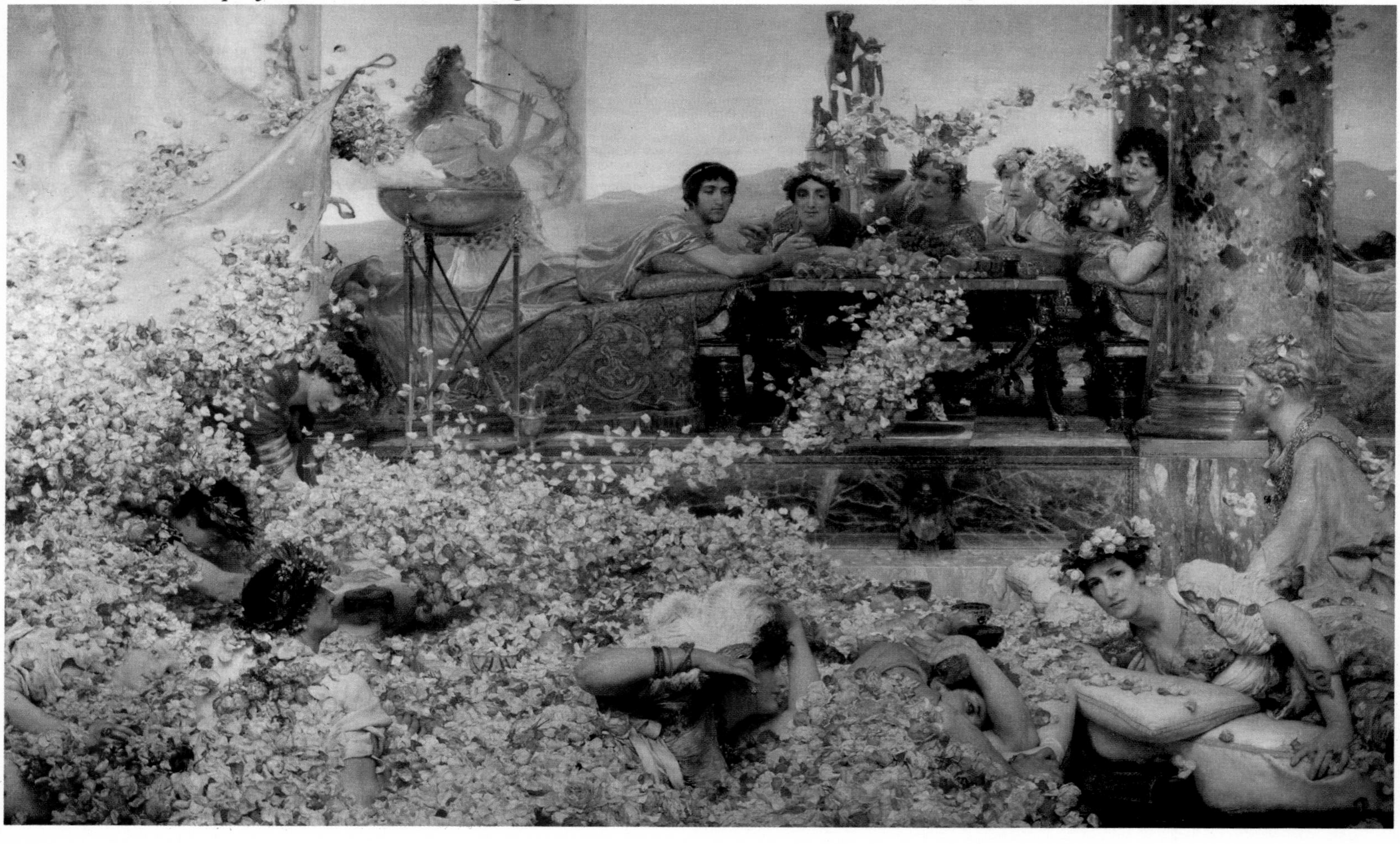

room hang a number of pictures referred to by Pliny the Elder: *Medea* by Timomachus of Byzantium which Julius Caesar had paid 80 Talents for (about £16,800); a lion by Pausias, who was the inventor of foreshortening; and the famous *Sacrifice of Iphegenia* by Timanthes of Athens, which had actually come to light in an inferior fresco copy at Pompeii. There was enough provided here for any Midlands merchant to tell his guests about after dinner, if he wanted to show off a knowledge of classical art.

Alma-Tadema did not come to settle permanently in London until 1870. Born in Dronryp, Holland, and a student of Baron Leys in Belgium, he had signed a good contract on a rising price scale with the dealer Gambart, whose clients were mainly English and American. His first wife having died in 1869, he married Laura Epps, the daughter of a physician, the following year. They set up house in a Graeco-Roman-designed interior on the Regent's Canal. A few years later they were to move to St Johns Wood, converting James Jacques Tissot's red-brick mansion into a veritable Pompeian palace, with verandahs, porches, galleries, an atrium, and even an apsed rotunda, which amazed all London. Carriages lined Grove End Road every Monday afternoon, and as guests crossed the large gardens filled with hollyhock, roses, portulaca and oleander, past the large Russian marble basin filled with goldfish, they were greeted by a SALVE over the entrance door which itself was an accurate copy of the doorway of the Building of Eumachia in the Forum of Pompeii. What more did they need to carry them back to the world of the past? No matter if their antique trance might be shattered by Paderewski or George Henschel giving a concert inside, this was antiquity itself, reconstructed and made whole again by an artist they considered a genius. A Royal Academician whom foreign heads had honoured and whom the rich and powerful patronised.

'As the Sun Colours Flowers, So Art Colours Life' was the motto inscribed in glided letters over the door of Alma-Tadema's studio. And from the Eighties until his death in 1912, he sought to colour the dreary wet London days with bright evocations of a sunny clime that could not be transplanted to England as easily as Mediterranean memories, and dreamy thoughts of the past. But the ideals of Empire themselves began to slip away through expediency and rampant commercialism, and as an imminent decadence hovered over the British horizon, so the Victorians sought to reassure themselves all the more that, as one of his painting's title proclaimed: 'The Year's At the Spring . . . All's Right with the World.' Off they poured from the easel as daily visitors to the studio watched in amazement. With a strengthening of technique, a lightening of tone and atmosphere, a new, experimental sense of composition, each picture reassured anyone who doubted that Victoria had provided for her subjects the best of all possible worlds: *Not at Home* was countered by *A Hearty Welcome*; *A Parting Kiss* preceded *A Foregone Conclusion*; and, if there was *A Difference of Opinion*, one could always make it up with *Roses, Love's Delight*.

The architectural references became more generalised, the Pompeian props became fewer, rich surfaces of marble and wide expanses of blue Mediterranean seen from the heights of Capri or Ischia began to replace the deep red and black interiors and columns of porphyry, lapis, and antique verde. The garden and loggias of his own house in Grove End Road became his favourite settings, his red-haired wife and daughters his favourite models. But often Alma-Tadema would rise to a magnificent piece of reconstruction: in 1886 he painted one of his most famous pictures, *An Apodyterium*, which was voted the picture of the year. It was a perfect piecing together of the Thermae of the Forum in Pompeii with minor interior adjustments and a great expanse of marble flooring in the foreground.

He tackled historical subjects on occasion, his *Caracalla and Geta* sited inside the Coliseum being one of his most ambitious with over 2000 figures in it. His *Antony and Cleopatra* was reproduced in every popular edition of Shakespeare. Emperors such as Claudius, Agrippa, Caligula and Heliogabalus were favourites. The latter is incorporated in a remarkable piece of virtuoso painting of a cascade of rose petals; the blossoms on which it was modelled were sent daily from the Riviera for four winter months, while Sir Laurence completed the picture. It depicts the 18-year-old emperor who declared himself a woman and took a centurion for a husband, watching his favourite sport – an orgy in which the unsuspecting participants are smothered to death by a cascade of tons of rose petals. But despite the sinister theme, there is an innocence, a playfulness in the picture.

There is no doubt that Alma-Tadema's Dutch ancestry and familiarity with 17th-century *genre* painting encouraged him in the exactness and finish of his work. He approached everything with a thoroughness of purpose and a fidelity to reality. He was as interested in light-reflecting surfaces and atmospheric effects as Vermeer. If the Impressionists could produce their 'scientific' renditions of atmospheric changes of light with flickering and broken brush-strokes, Alma-Tadema painted similar descriptions of evanescent sunlight and shadow with careful, meticulous, rendering. The difference was that he attempted not only to describe scientifically perceived reality, but to infuse a poetic mood into the subject as well.

It is unfortunate that Alma-Tadema was victimised by his own fame, for those insensitive and hard-lined etchings and reproductions of his works which have appeared in countless art journals and schoolbooks are what posterity remembers of his art, rather than the sensitive areas of rich tones, the ingenious colour relationships, the fine passages of pure paint.

Often criticised for not painting his own time, he once remarked: "You have the great question of modernity in Art, which has been so much talked of, since Courbet began to paint any low subject he came across, and Alfred Stevens, his advertisements for the Parisian dressmaker . . . These two pre-eminent apostles of the hollow notion that you must paint your own time, have, in reality, never tried to give us any *feeling* of our own time." This Alma-Tadema proved he could do, with his transfiguration of Victorian into Roman and vice versa, and with his ability to express the 19th-century taste for material things. Even the *Art Journal* in 1886, while remarking that "We think of his men and women as mere accessories," admired the beauty of his "marbles, silks, his stuffs, his textures, his silver and gold and bronze, and, occasionally his flowers . . ." In the same journal, the artist himself confessed: "Of course the subject is an interesting point in a picture, but the subject is merely a pretext under which the picture is made . . . one of the greatest difficulties is to find a subject that is really pictorial, plastic."

His admirers were legion and the most popular critics of his day outdid each other in pouring praise upon him: Cosmo Monkhouse, Professor Ebers, Percy Cross Standing (who wrote a monograph on him), and those fashionable lady critics, Mrs Edmund Gosse, Mrs Alice Meynell and Miss Helen Zimmern, were all enchanted by the learned canvases which nevertheless captured the homely sentiments of their age.

Even Whistler had recourse to refer to Alma-Tadema's "Symphonies" and "Harmonies" and Ruskin, notwithstanding his allegiance to medieval, rather than antique, daydreams, had to admit Alma-Tadema's brilliant archaeology and superb draughtsmanship. He begrudgingly wrote: "M. Alma-Tadema differs from all the artists I have ever known, except John Lewis, in the gradual increase of technical accuracy, which attends and enhances together the expanding range of his dramatic invention; while every year he displays more varied and complex powers of minute draughtsmanship, more especially in architectural detail, wherein, somewhat priding myself as a specialty, I nevertheless receive continual lessons from him."

Ruskin's position as a champion of those artists who had declared themselves enemies of the Academy made it difficult for him openly to admire Alma-Tadema, a predicament no doubt compounded when the artist was given a large exhibition at the greenery-yallery Grosvenor Gallery in 1882. He had successfully straddled the critical fence by proving he was not only a painter for the Establishment, but one for the aesthetes and the Pre-Raphaelite avant-garde as well.

Alma-Tadema's art was not only confined to easel painting. He was a photographer of some merit, as the 164 volumes of his photographs at Birmingham University prove, and he could pose a nude Neapolitan boy as artfully in a Pompeian ruin as Baron von Gloëden and Baron Corvo. He had a book of poetry published. He was an accomplished musician and the close friend of George Henschel (who founded the Boston Symphony Orchestra) as well as Paderewski. Furthermore, he was closely associated with the theatre, designing productions for Henry Irving, Beerbohm Tree and F. R. Benson.

Before the century turned, Victoria displayed her approval of his Romanised British subjects with a knighthood. He was the third painter from the Lowlands ever to be awarded an English title, his two predecessors being Rubens and Van Dyck, and he was given a splendid banquet at the Whitehall Rooms.

Alma-Tadema proved himself worthy of his knighthood. Not only was his love of hearth and home generally acknowledged by all, but he was famous for his hospitality and his friendships with rival artists. He was a loving father and devoted husband. He was said to be not against "taking a little merriment among friends" which meant he could hold his own when the port was passed around. He was a member of the Garrick and the Athenaeum, he led a rich and fulsome life in the suburbs of St Johns Wood among his antiquities and his books, and he summered on the Bay of Naples.

It is impossible to say how much his works, which were avidly collected by the new museums of America, influenced that country at the height of its building boom. Some might even go so far as to speculate whether Washington and Chicago might not have developed differently if it were not for the accurate examples of Roman architecture in his pictures. More certain is his influence over American movie spectacles, and some of his paintings look as if they could be transcribed directly onto film from canvas. His own interest in photography led him to set up compositions with a panoramic breadth of view that foreshadows the wide-angle lens and CinemaScope, and the crowd scenes which became a must in every Hollywood epic from *Ben Hur* on, in retrospect seem to have first found expression in his works.

To modern eyes, Alma-Tadema's subjects with their coyly posed women exchanging significant glances, and their repressed expressions of sentiments, might seem fraught with neurotic obsessions and hidden psychological repressions. Moreover, his fondness for painting young ladies together in a langorous state of suppressed emotions, coupled with his repeated theme of Sappho might give rise to rather obvious interpretations. However, one must see the subjects in the framework of their own time, when women dallying among themselves was considered the height of propriety and virtuousness. He supposedly painted for Edward VII a series of pornographic murals that hung at Windsor. The King gave him an O.B.E. but no trace of these panels can be found. In any event, his opulent late-Victorian nudes gave way after the turn of the century to a sort of risqué Edwardian Smoking-room humour not out of keeping with the times. One such picture is *A Favourite Custom* at the Tate Gallery. Painted in 1909 it depicts a Roman Thermae with two nude ladies in the foreground splashing each other playfully in a pool. It is a perfect example of the sort of acceptable titillation that could be infused into a reconstruction of Ladies' Night at a Roman Bath.

But for Alma-Tadema, the question of subject matter was one of triggering off the mind into a thousand avenues of thought. As he put it: "Art is imagination, and those who love Art love it because in looking at a picture it awakens their imagination and sets them thinking; and that is also why Art heightens the mind."

Neapolitan youths in Pompeii – a reference photograph taken by Alma-Tadema

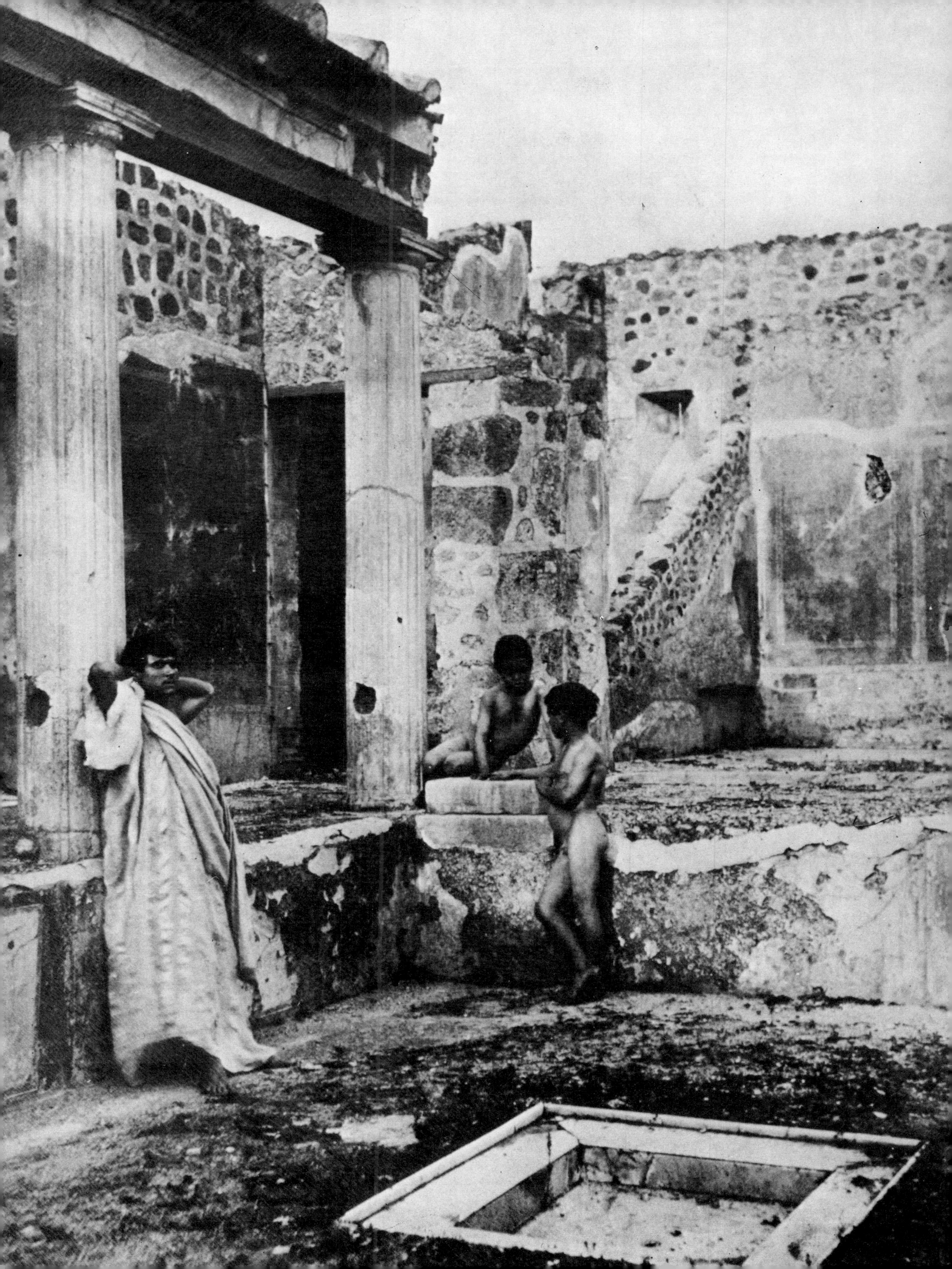

MIRRORS OF CHANGE

by Graham Reynolds. In the Victorian age painting reached a new peak of popularity. Patronage was not found only amongst the nobility and gentry; merchants and industrialists were anxious to become collectors. While these new patrons did not want religious paintings or solemn classical scenes, they did wish to acquire views of picturesque places they had seen abroad, and of peaceful British landscapes. Keenly conscious of the changes in daily life, they sought after paintings of the new steam trains and the seaside holidays which railways had made possible.

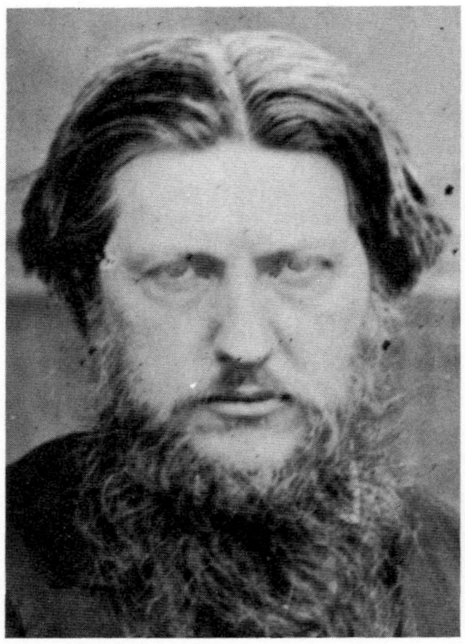

Ford Madox Brown: encouraged by the Pre-Raphaelites to paint naturalistic outdoor scenes

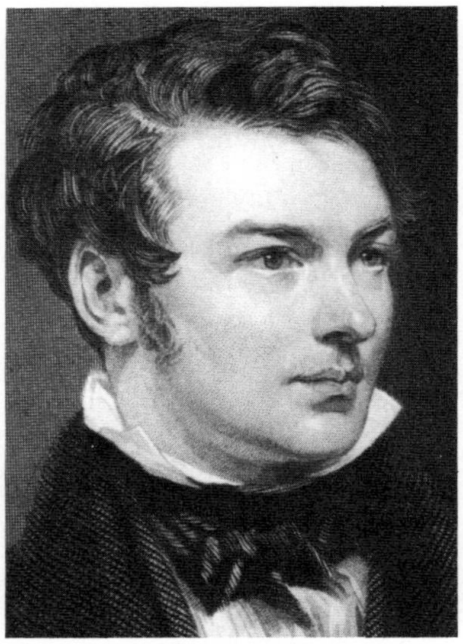

Charles Robert Leslie: literary tastes led him to subjects from Shakespeare and Molière

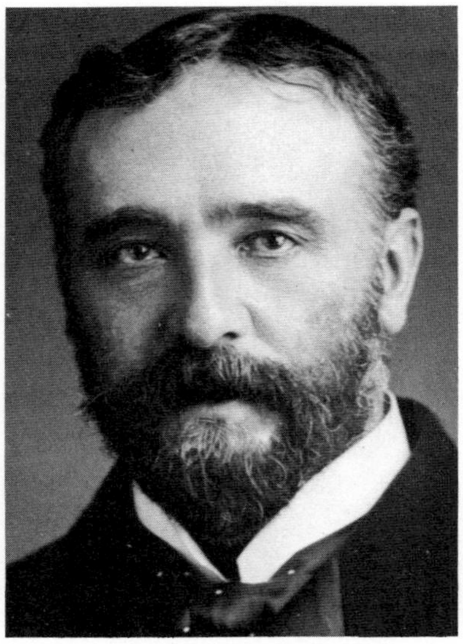

Sir Luke Fildes: illustrator of Dickens's *Edwin Drood* and fashionable portrait painter

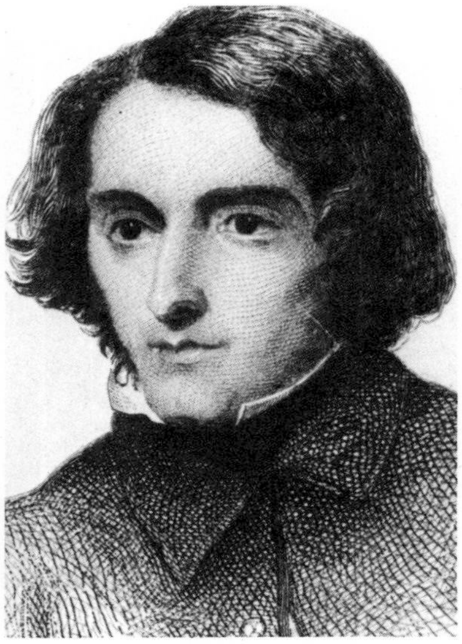

Augustus Egg: converted by Pre-Raphaelites from literary to modern themes

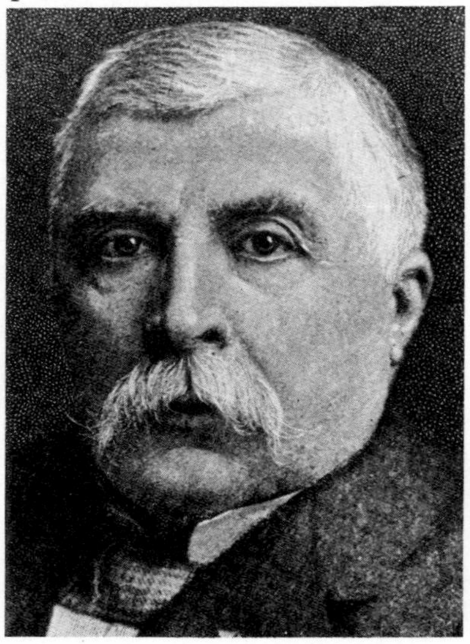

James Jacques Joseph Tissot: French exile; chronicler of London high society of the 1870s

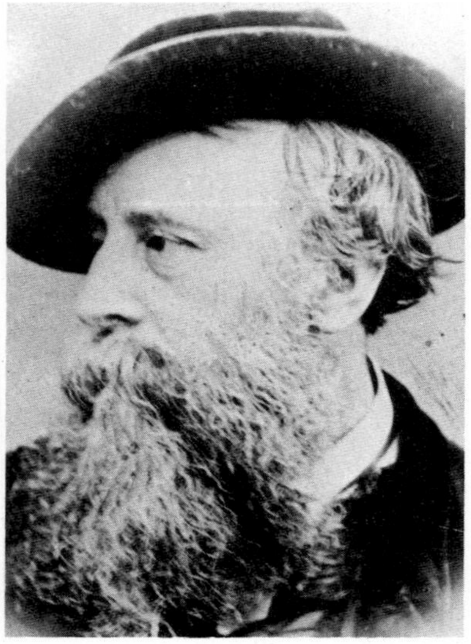

George Frederick Watts: prophet of Victorian art, famed for his allegorical painting of *Hope*

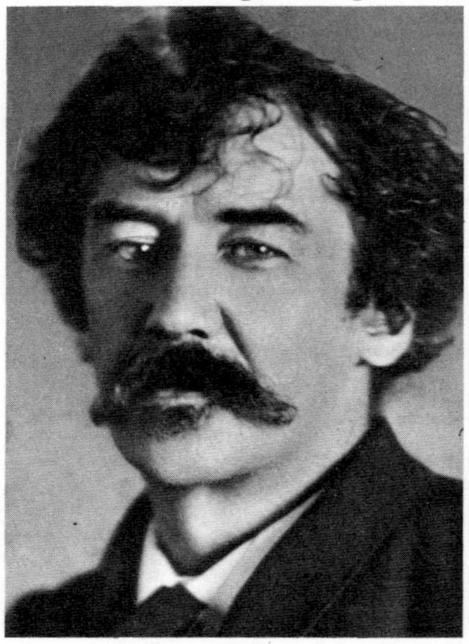

James McNeill Whistler: American innovator "flinging a pot of paint in the public's face"

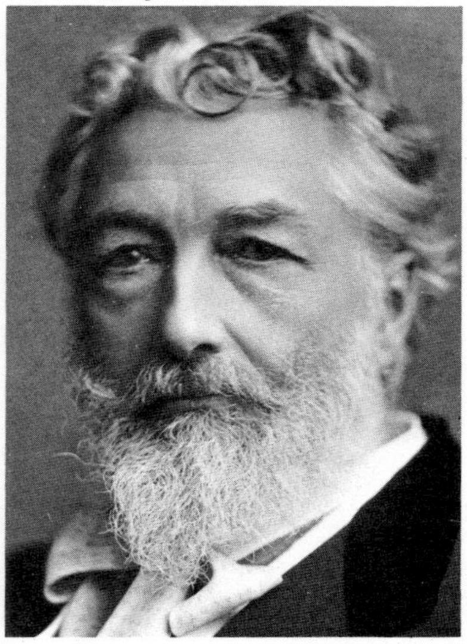

Lord Leighton: dominant figure; painted classical themes with deliberation and finish

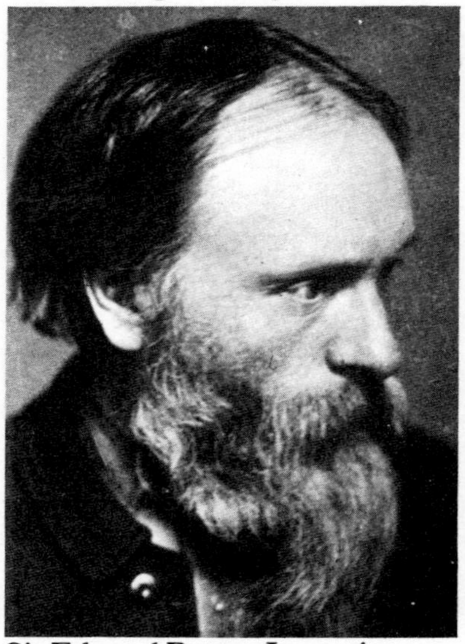

Sir Edward Burne-Jones: intense regard for Middle Ages; saw art as virtually a religion

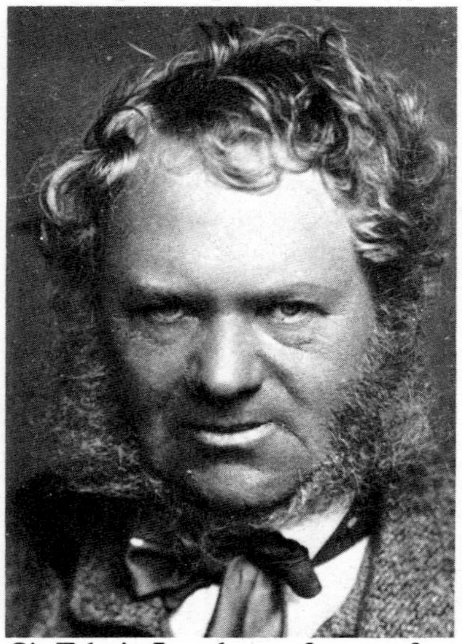

Sir Edwin Landseer: famous for *The Stag at Bay* and lions round Nelson's Column

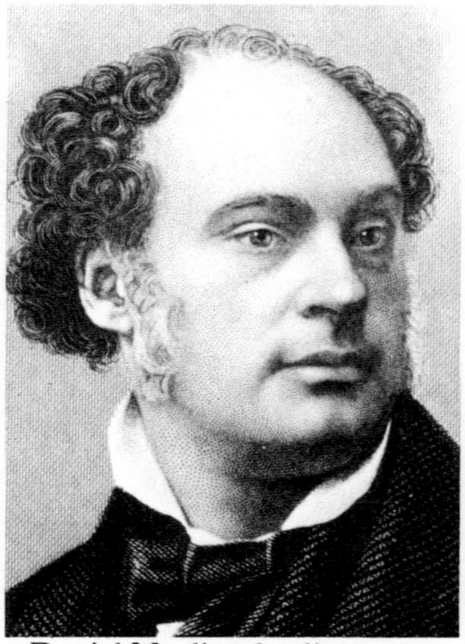

Daniel Maclise: leading artist of 1830s and 1840s; renowned for his huge frescoes

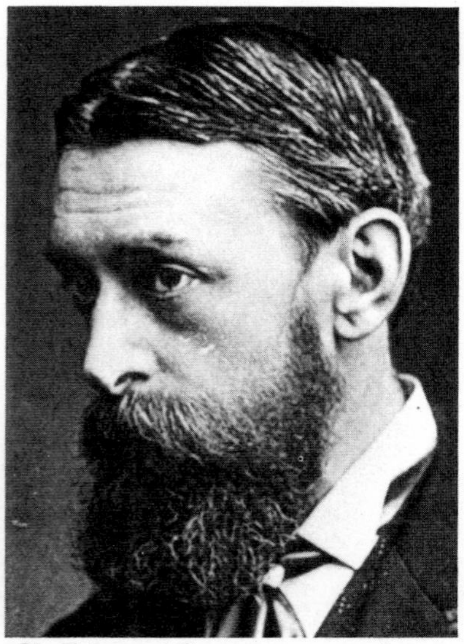

Sir Edward Poynter: prominent administrator; painter of Greek and Roman themes

There was one major revolution in painting style, when a group of ardent young men led by Rossetti, Millais and Holman Hunt founded the Pre-Raphaelite Brotherhood with a programme of 'Truth to Nature'. In practice this meant that they had recourse from painting the object out of doors to vivid, naturalistic colour and intense devotion to detail. But the misery which advanced industrialism brought in its train caused some artists to turn their backs on contemporary life and to withdraw into an ideal world. For some, such as Burne-Jones, it was the Middle Ages which held the mystery of remoteness; for others, such as Leighton, it was the antiquity of Greece and Rome. It was in this somewhat less down-to-earth mood that the Victorians confronted the exhausted emotions of the fin-de-siècle

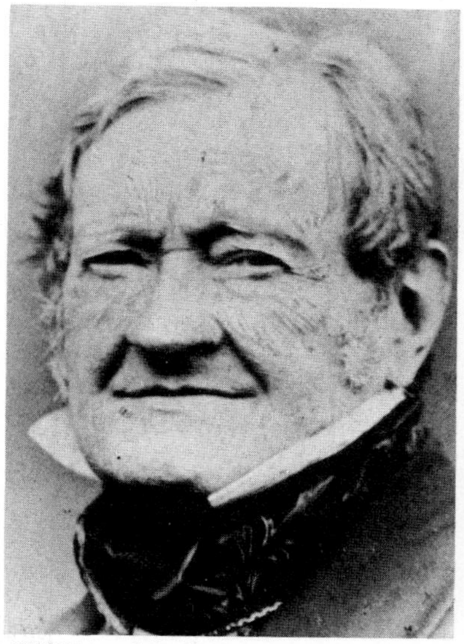

William Mulready: an Irishman working in London; a talented draughtsman of the nude

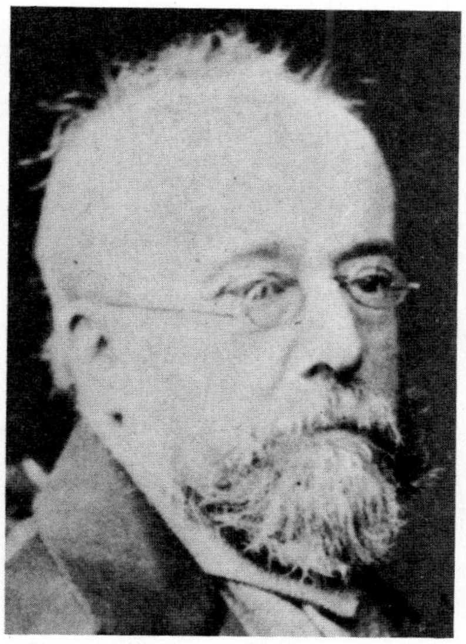

Samuel Palmer: influenced by Blake; poetic exponent of watercolour and etching

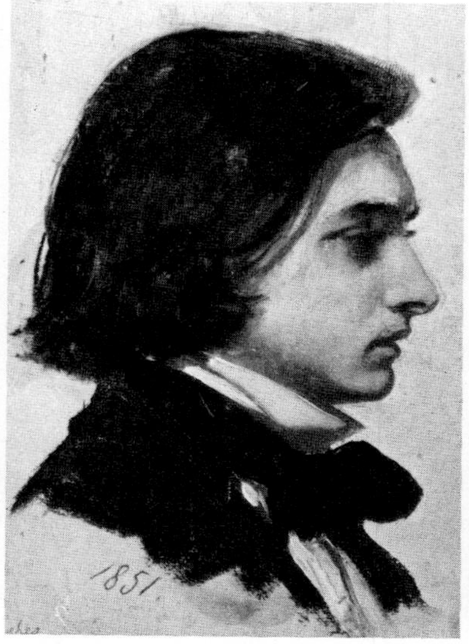
1851

Arthur Hughes: children's book illustrator; pathos, fine detail and brilliant colour

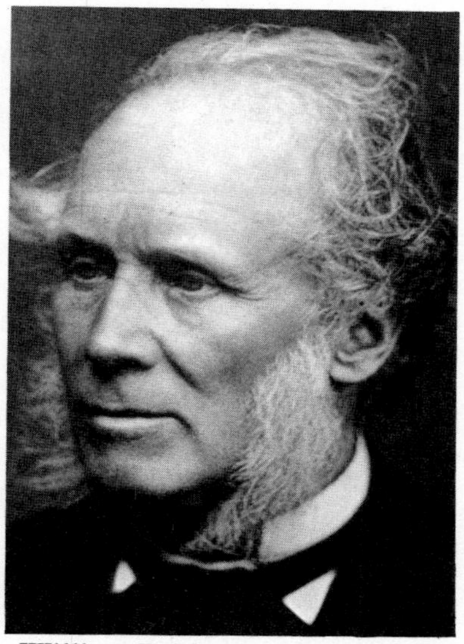

William Frith: popular painter of contemporary scenes, like *Derby Day* and *Ramsgate Sands*

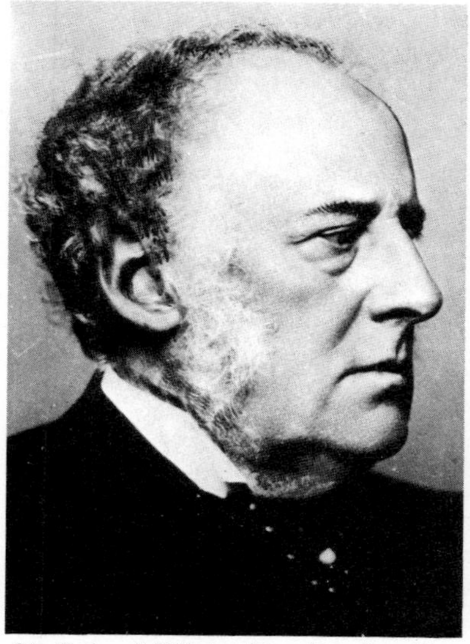

Sir John Millais: Pre-Raphaelite founder; later made £30,000 a year by fashionable portraiture

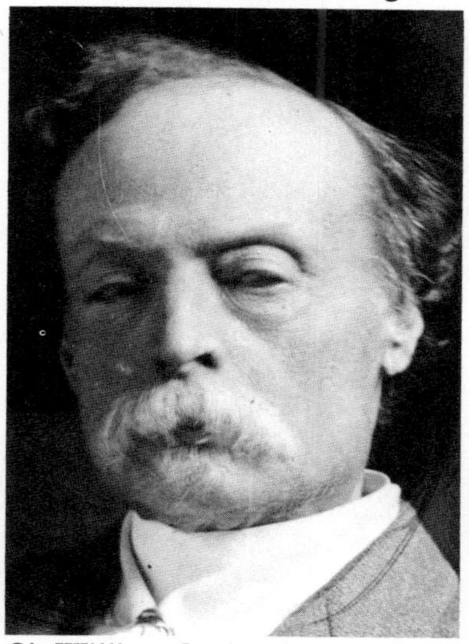

Sir William Orchardson: painter of anecdotal themes from Regency life and high society

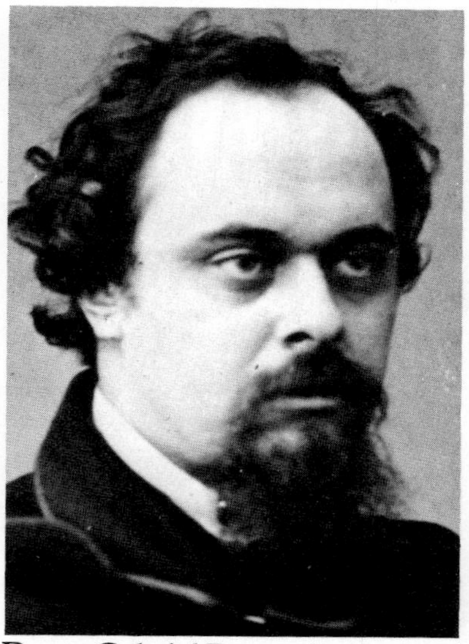

Dante Gabriel Rossetti: poet, and most imaginative of painters; co-founder of Pre-Raphaelites

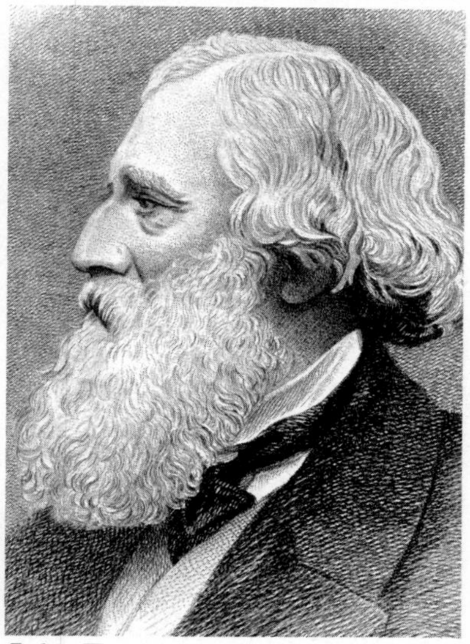

John Frederick Lewis: extensive traveller; painted harem life and brilliantly sunlit scenes

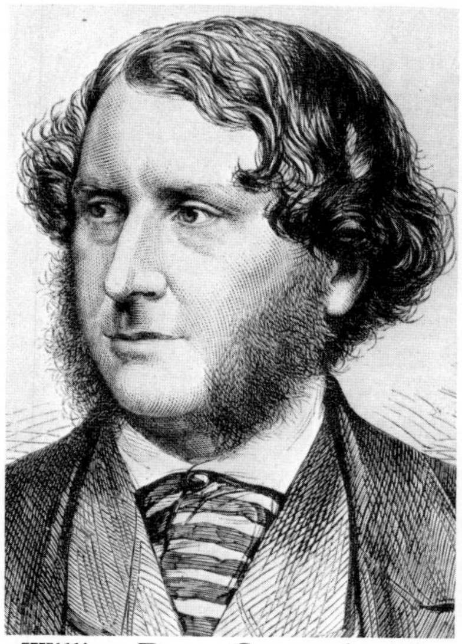

William Dyce: Germanic style admired by Prince Albert; a major force in teaching of art

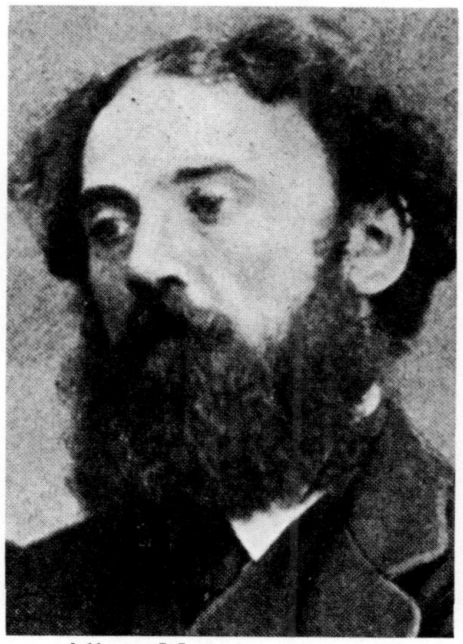

Albert Moore: painter of aesthetic experiments in Japanese form and delicate colour

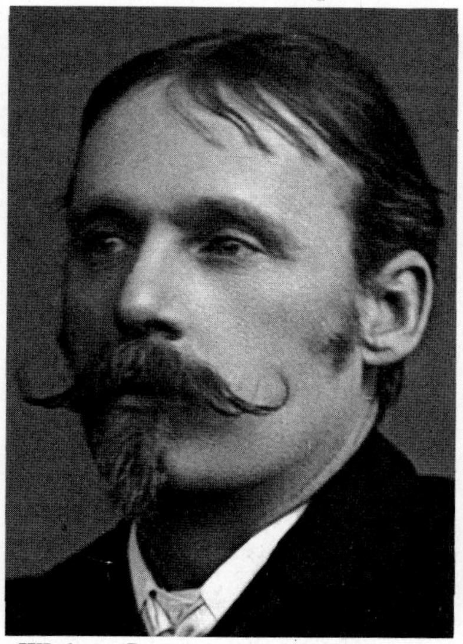

Walter Crane: children's book illustrator, designer of wallpapers and textiles

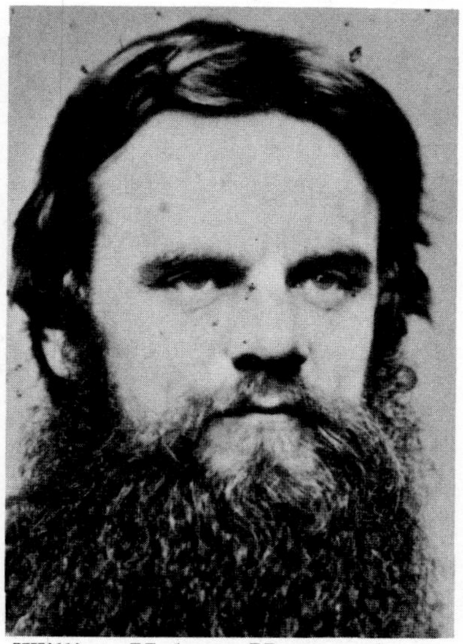

William Holman Hunt: painter of deep, moralistic themes; co-founder of Pre-Raphaelites

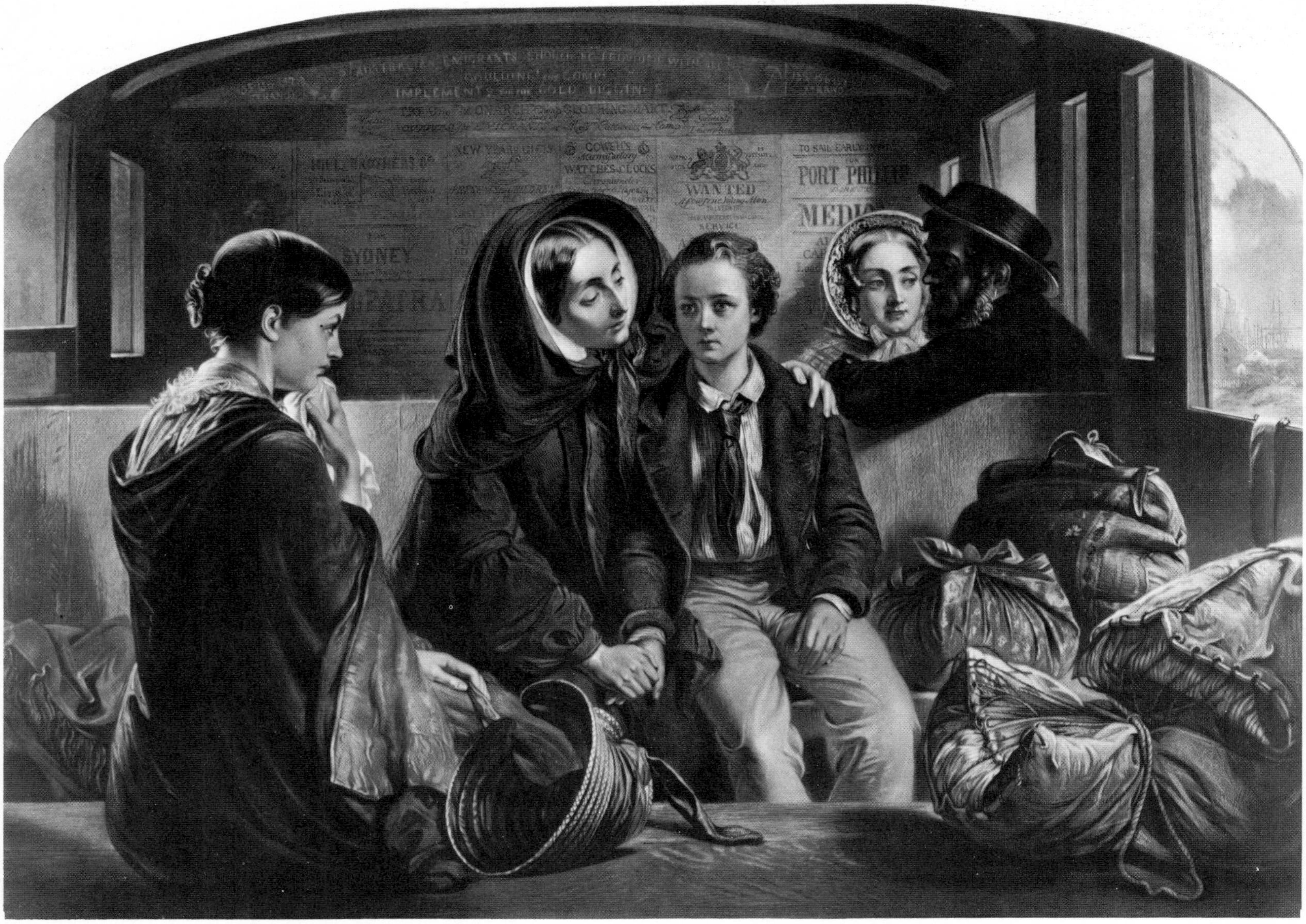
SYDNEY
WANTED

Second Class – the Parting by Abraham Solomon (1854)

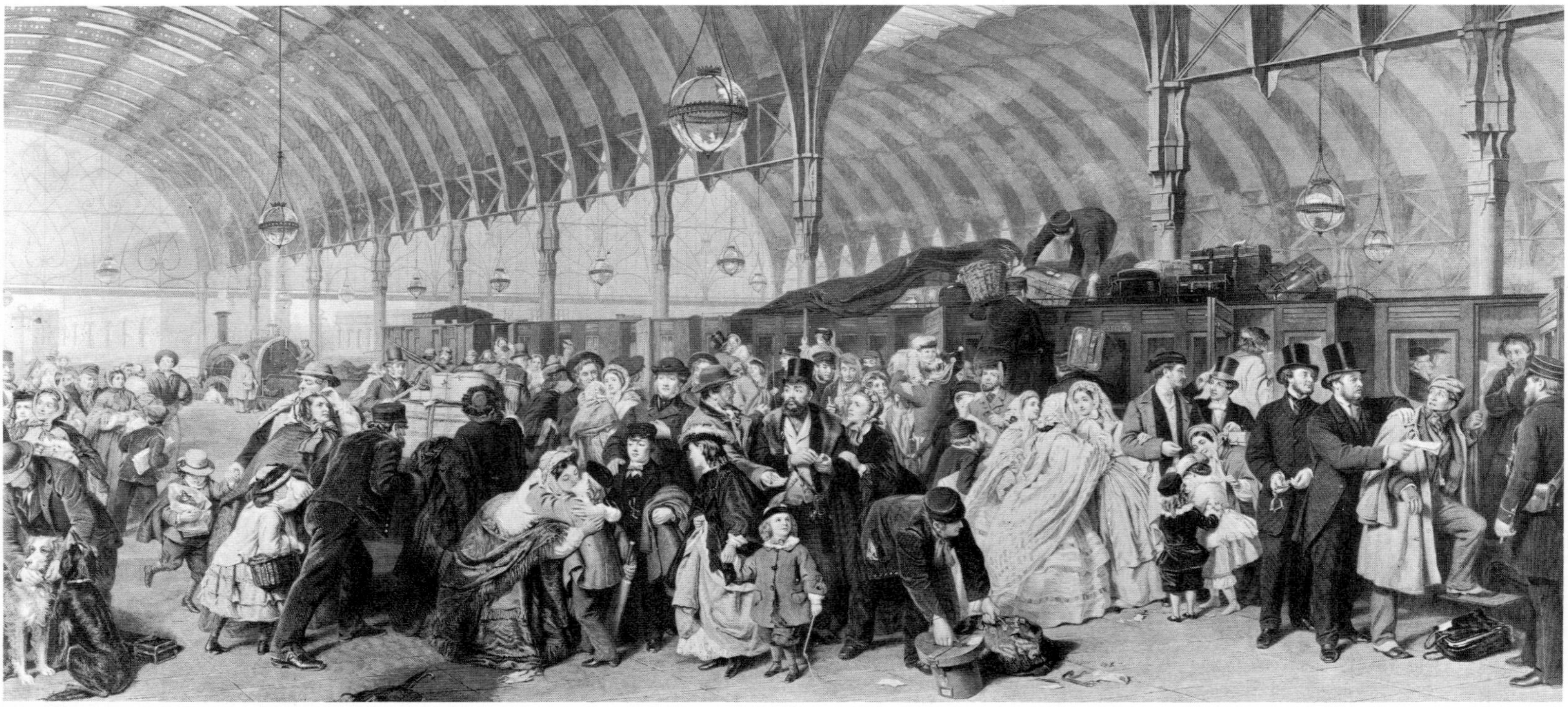

The Railway Station by W. P. Frith (1862)

As well as providing an ever-increasing market for paintings, the Victorians were pioneers in the mass circulation of reproductions. Every famous picture, and many less well known, would be the subject of an engraving of remarkable technical accomplishment, printed and sold in large quantities – it was no uncommon thing for 20,000 or 30,000 copies of these engravings to be produced. The black-and-white plates here are reproduced from a selection of these prints

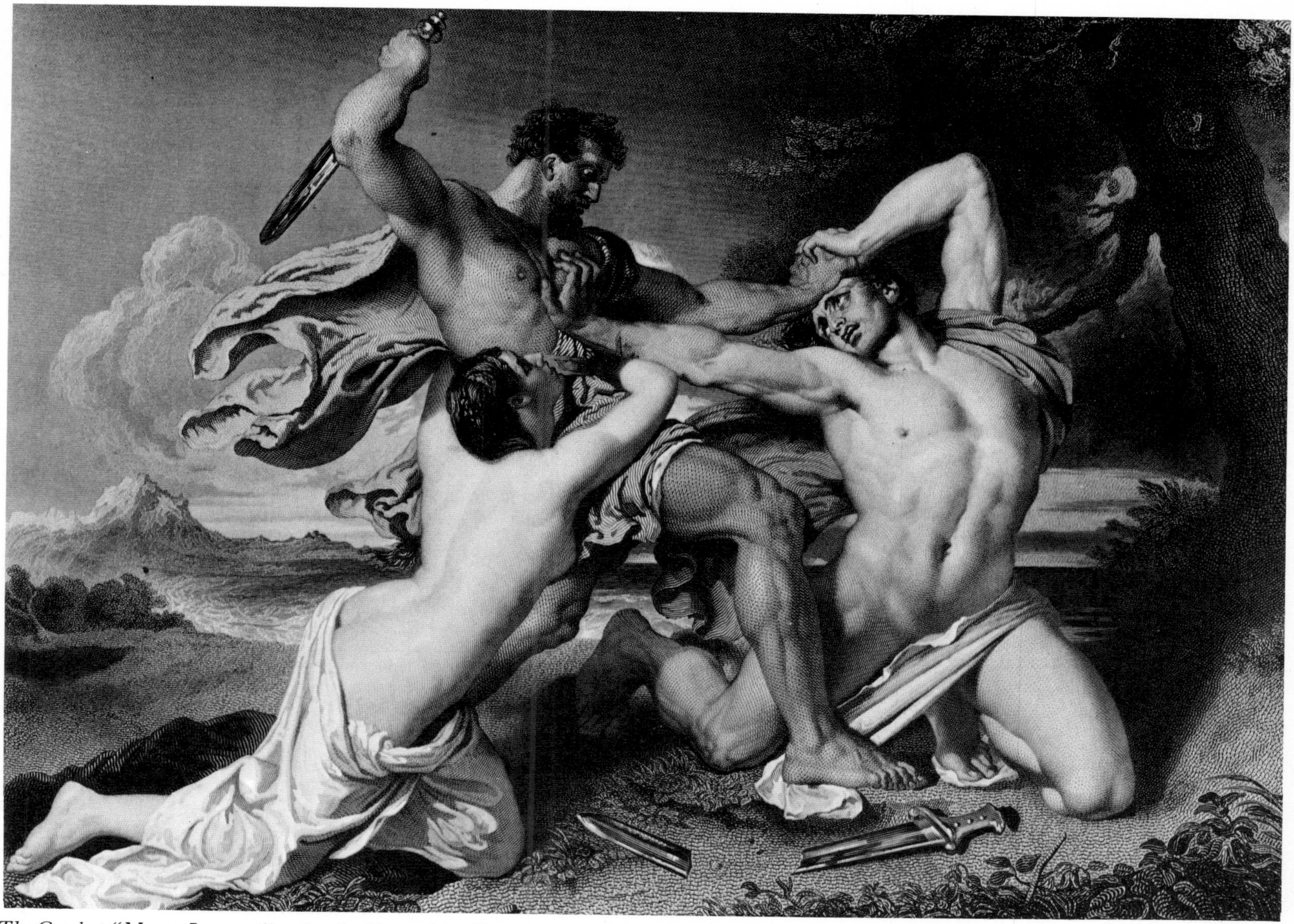

The Combat ('Mercy Interceding for the Vanquished') by William Etty (1848)

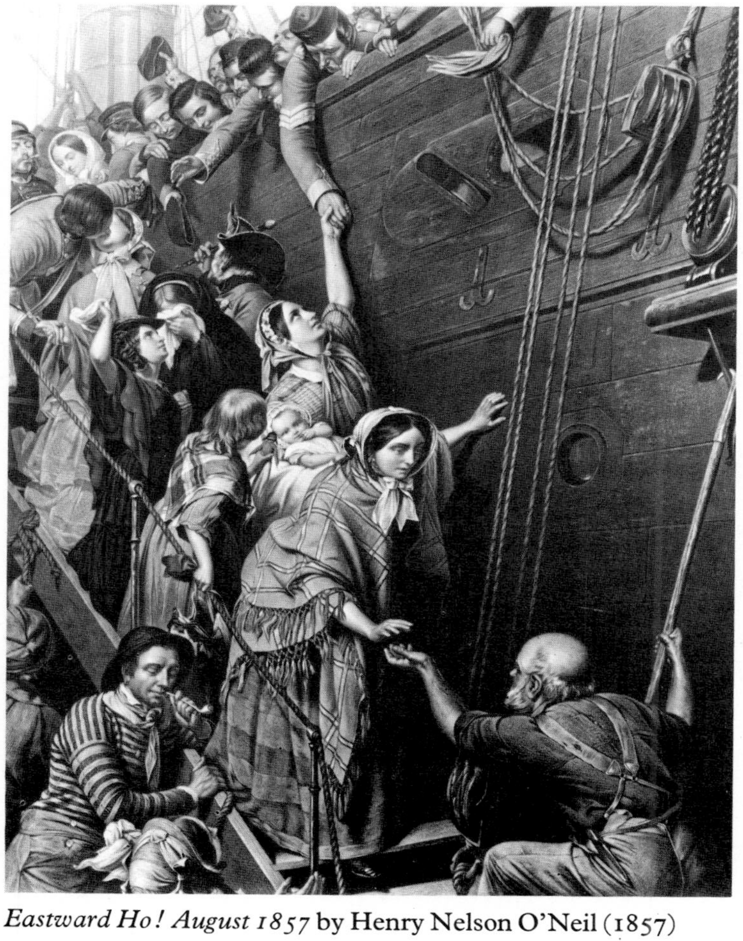

Eastward Ho! August 1857 by Henry Nelson O'Neil (1857)

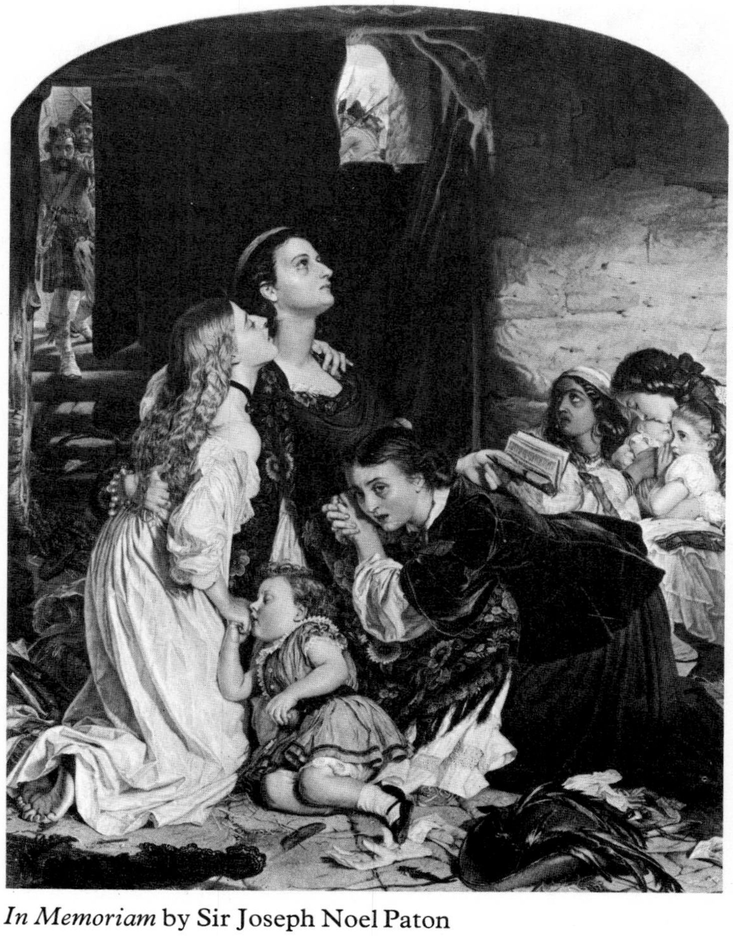

In Memoriam by Sir Joseph Noel Paton

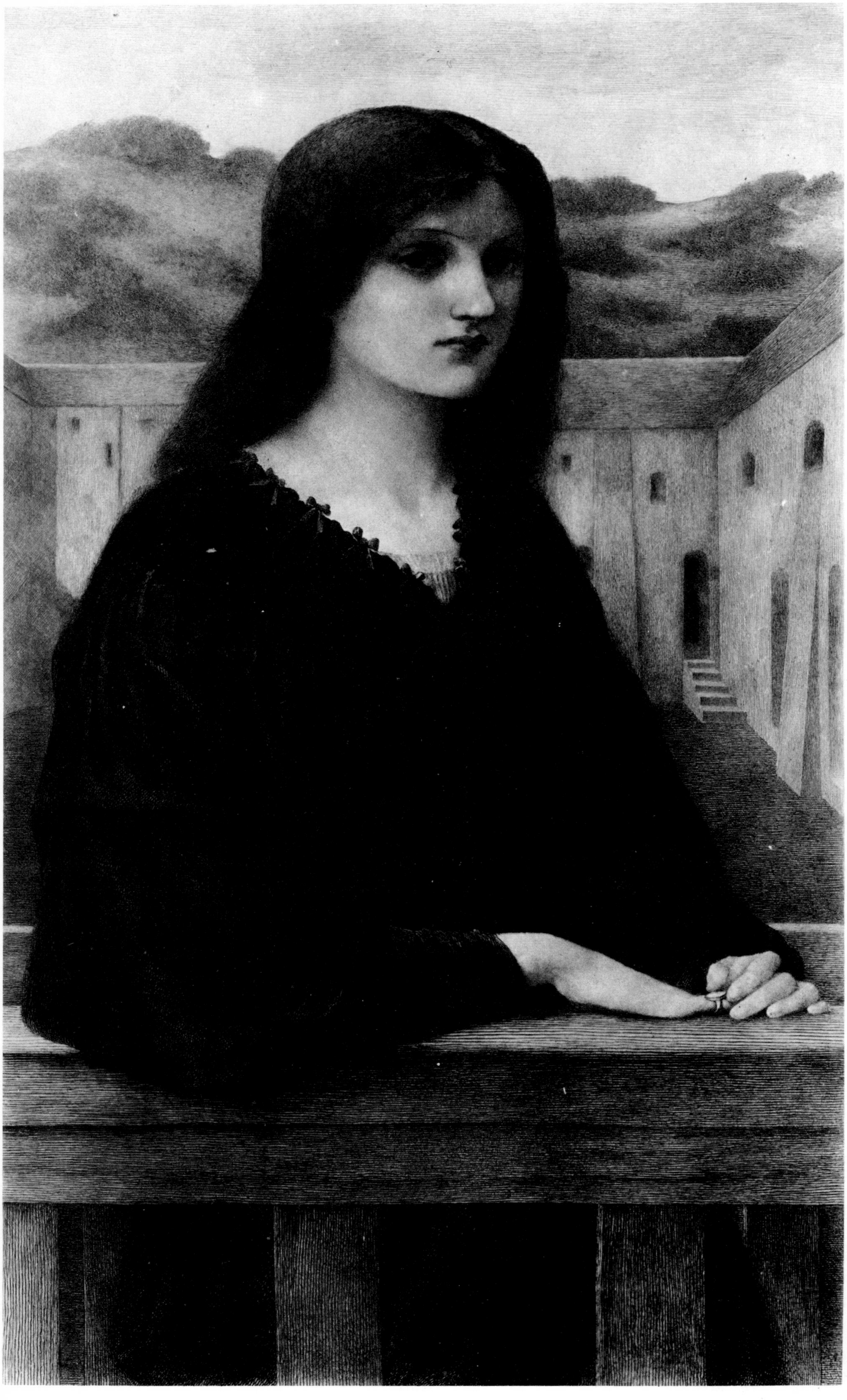

Vespertina Quies by
Sir Edward Burne-Jones
(1893)

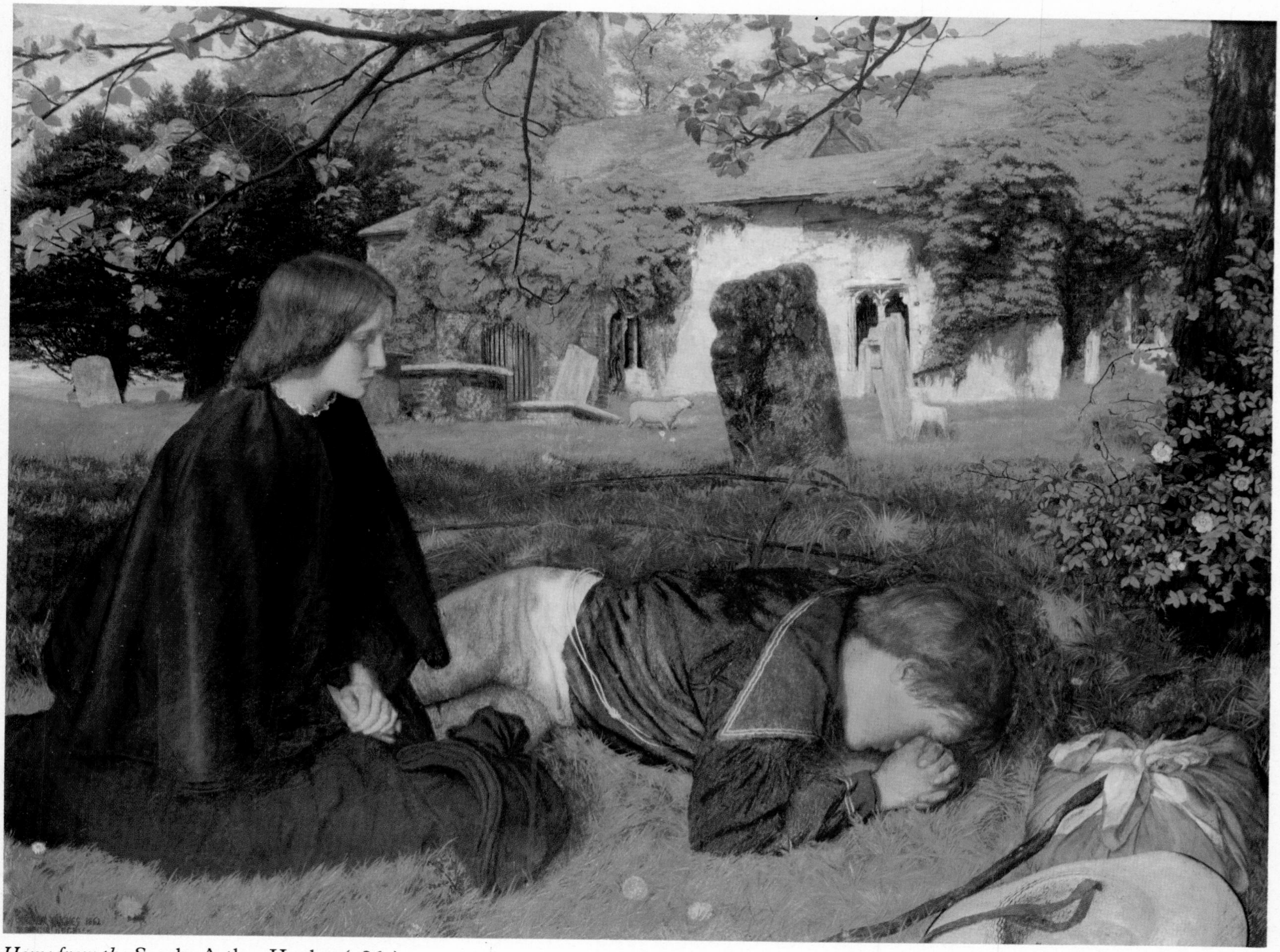

Home from the Seas by Arthur Hughes (1863)

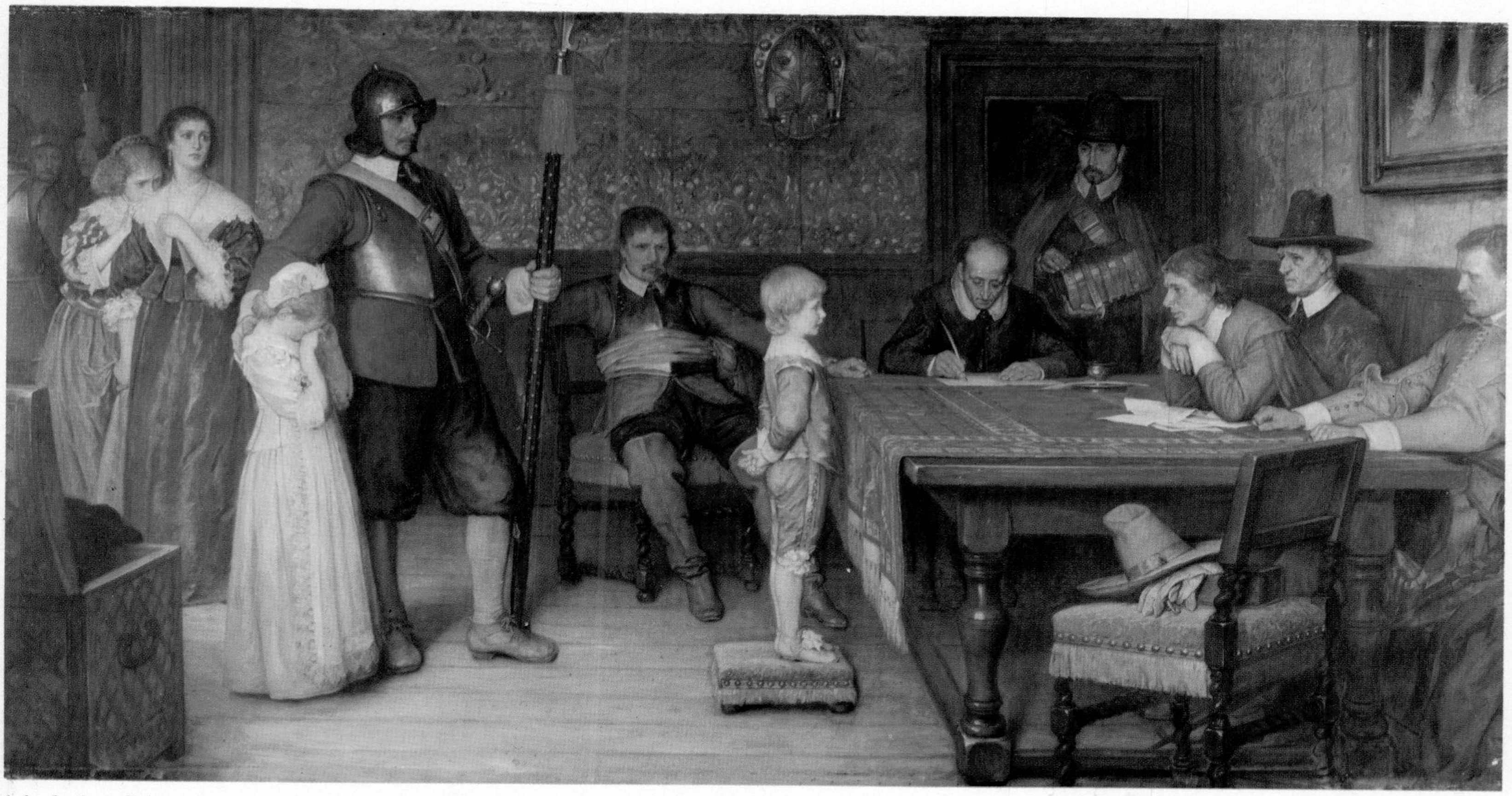

'*And when did you last see your father?*' by William Frederick Yeames (1878)

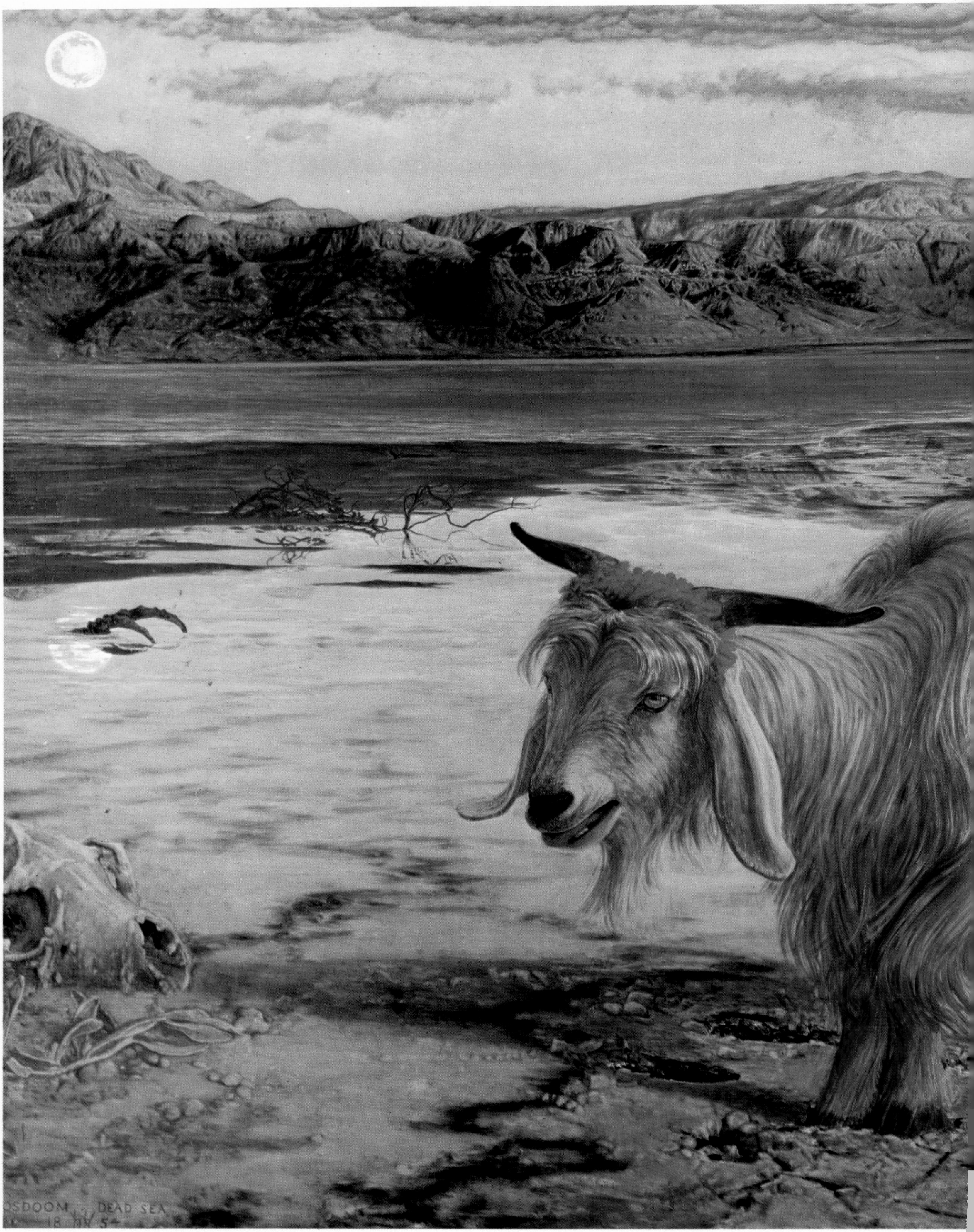
OSDOOM
DEAD SEA

The Scapegoat by William Holman Hunt (1856)

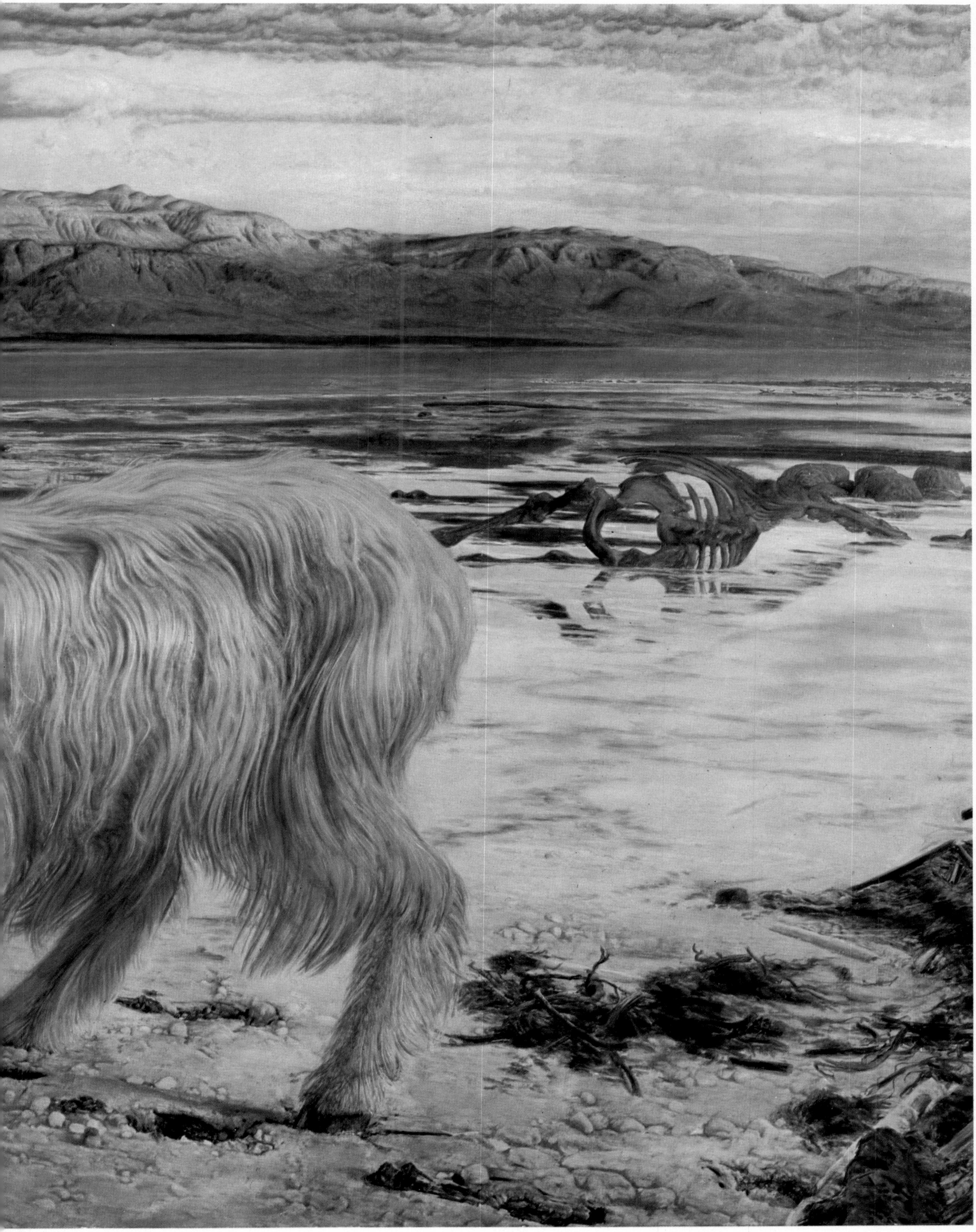

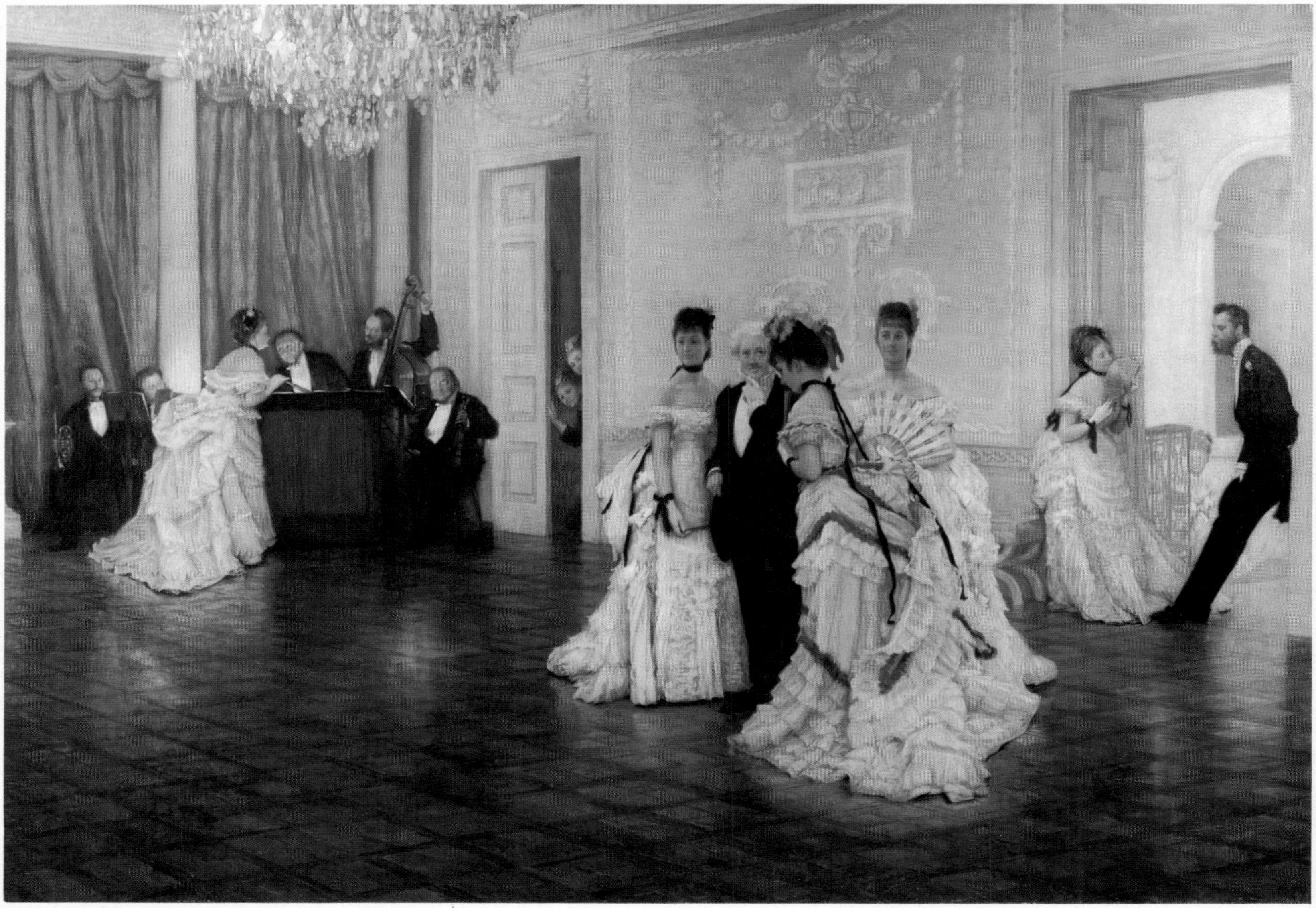

Too Early by James Tissot (1873)

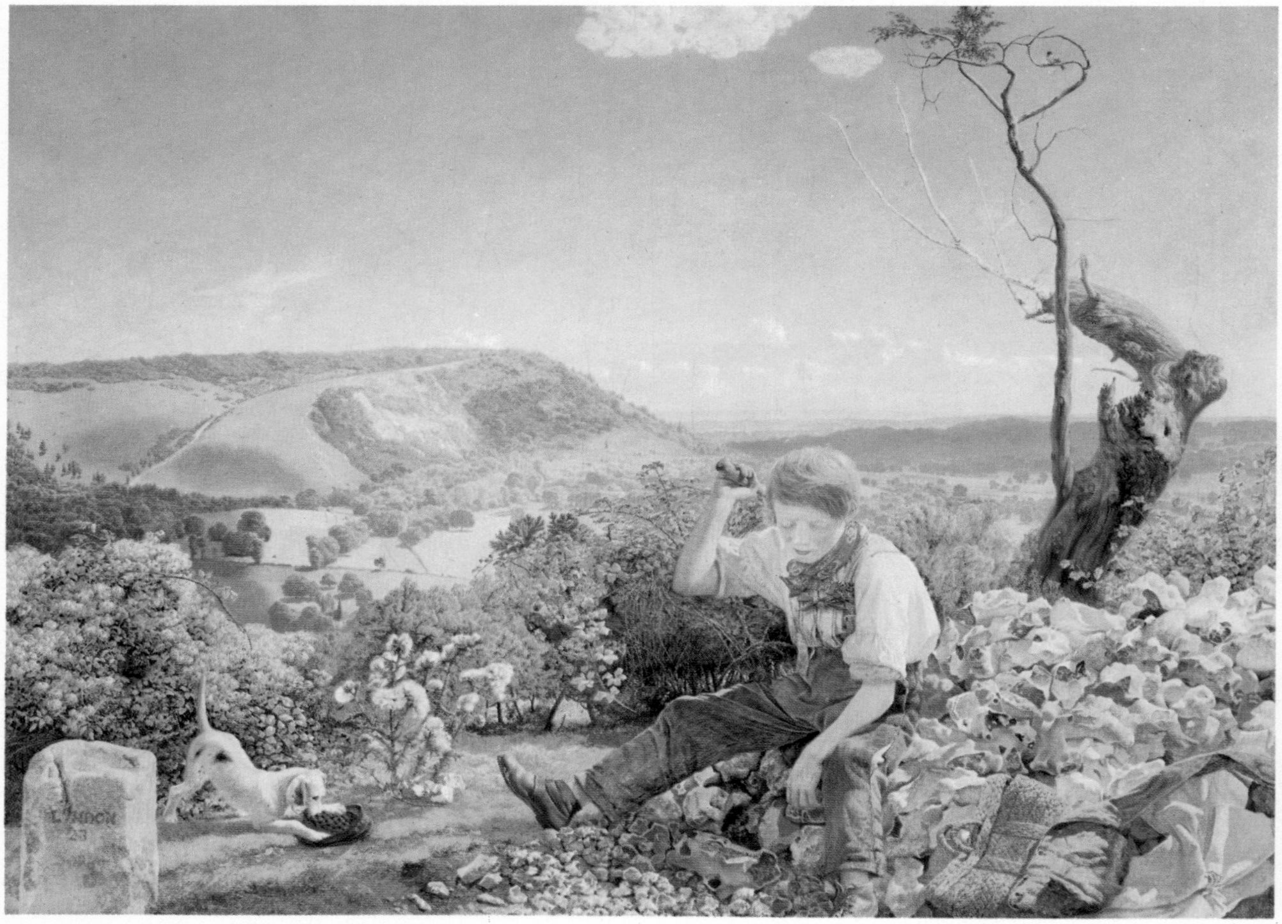

The Stonebreaker by John Brett (1858)

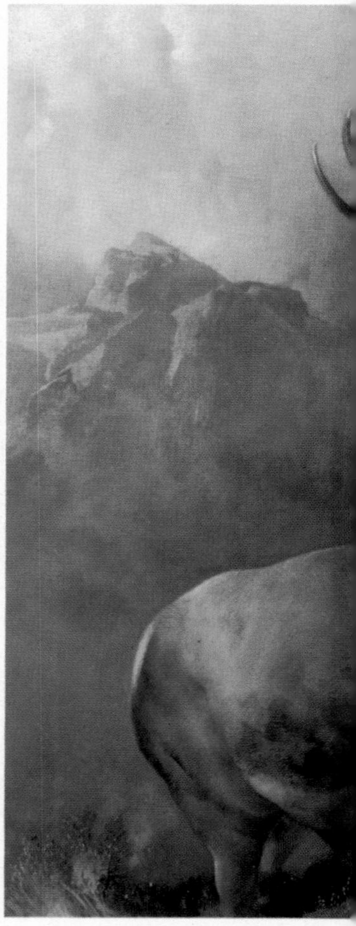

The Monarch of the Glen by Si

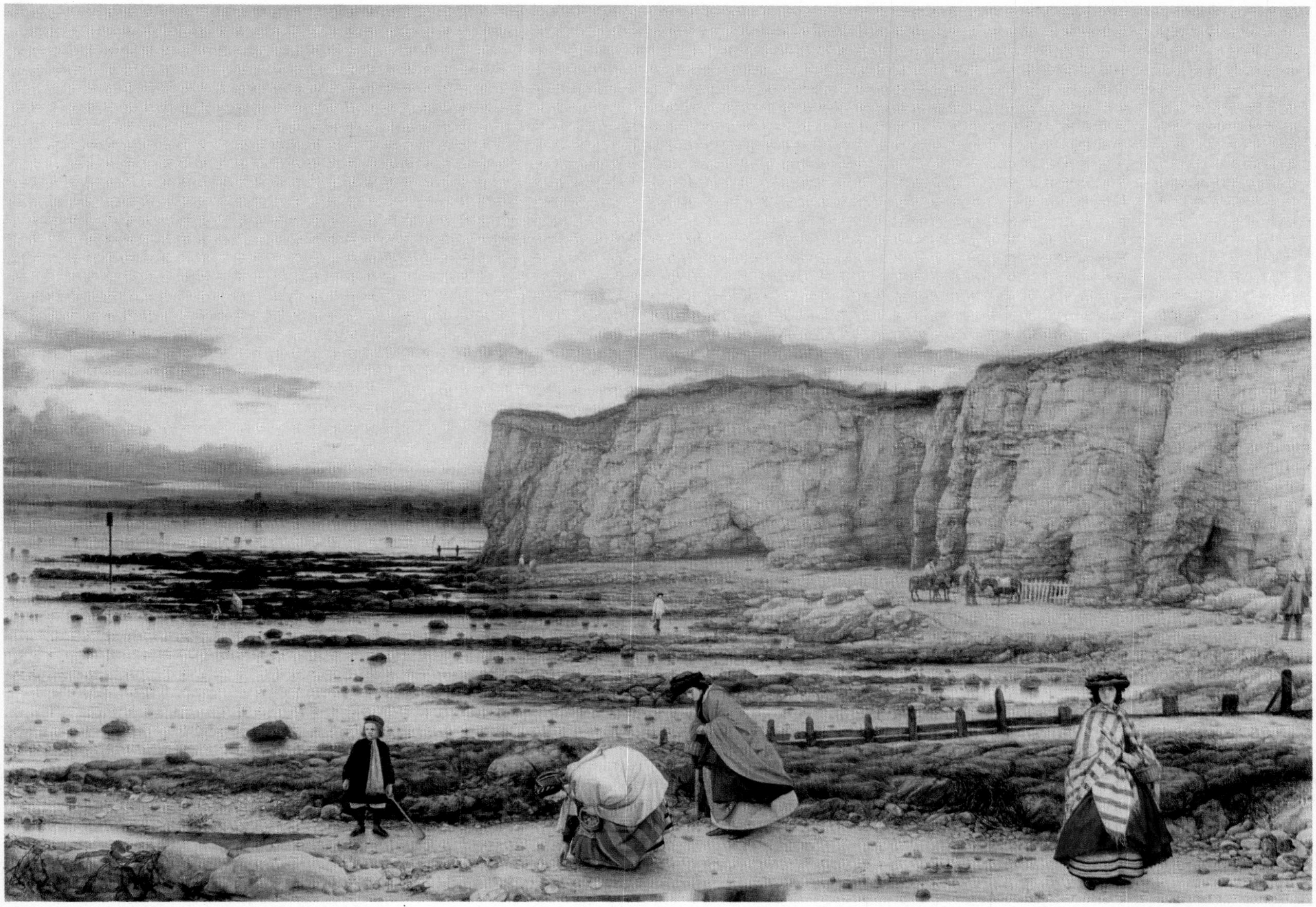

Pegwell Bay by William Dyce (1860)

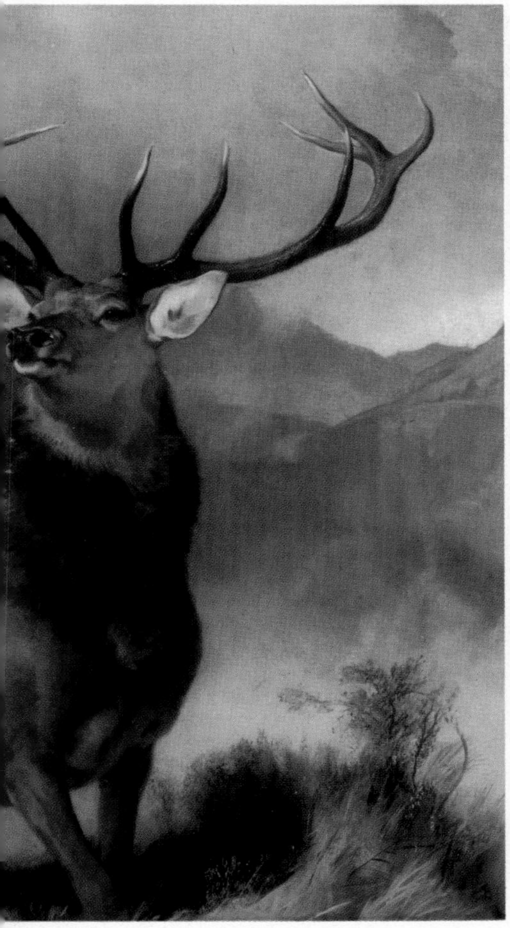

Landseer (1851)

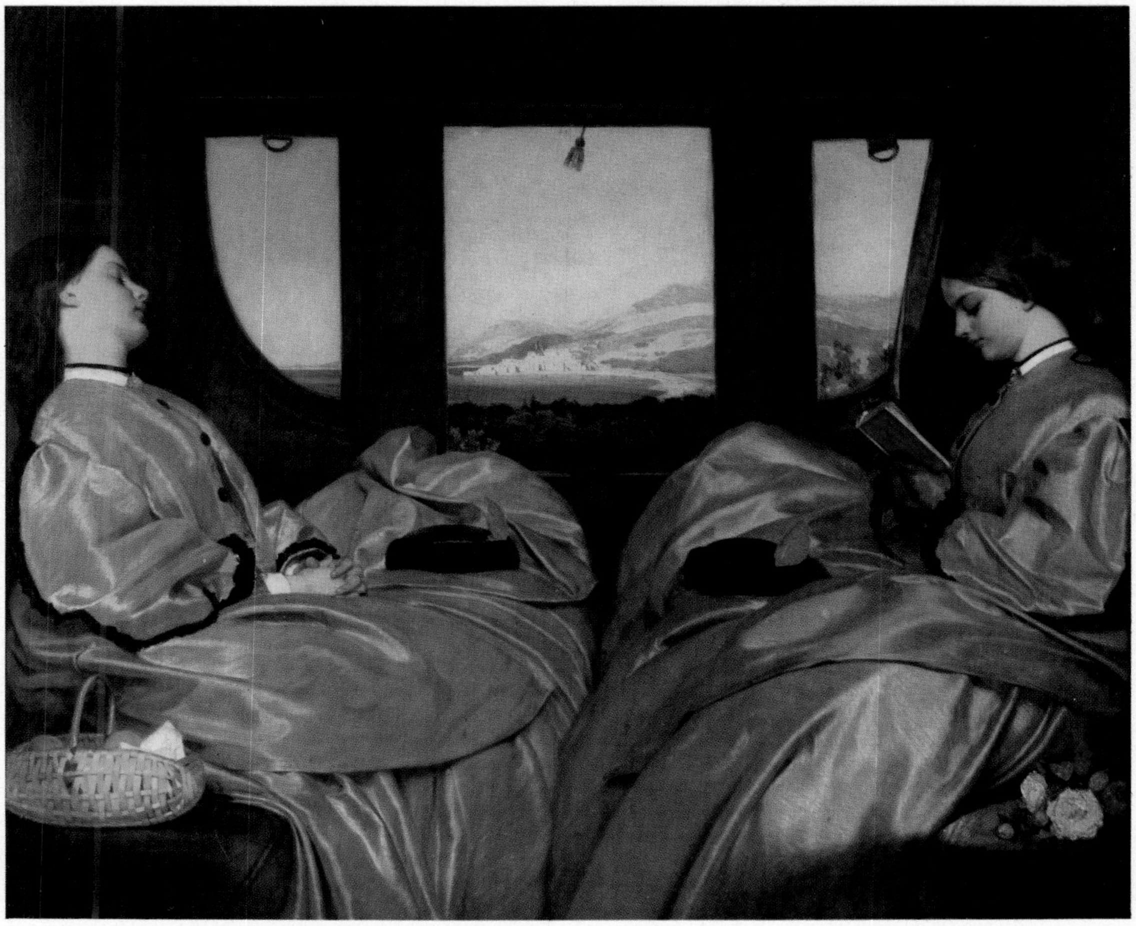

Travelling Companions by Augustus Egg (1862)

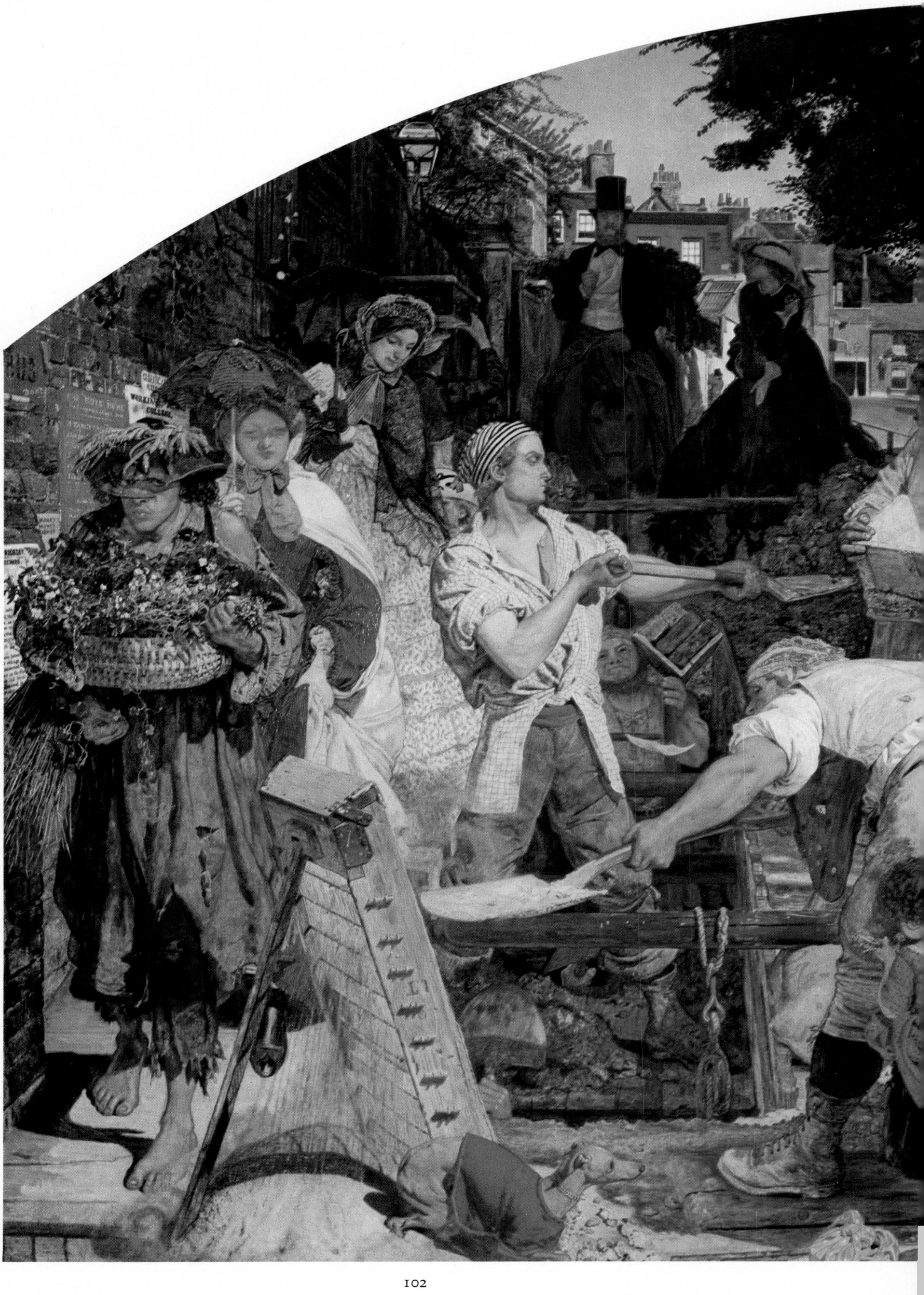

Work by Ford Madox Brown (1852–65)

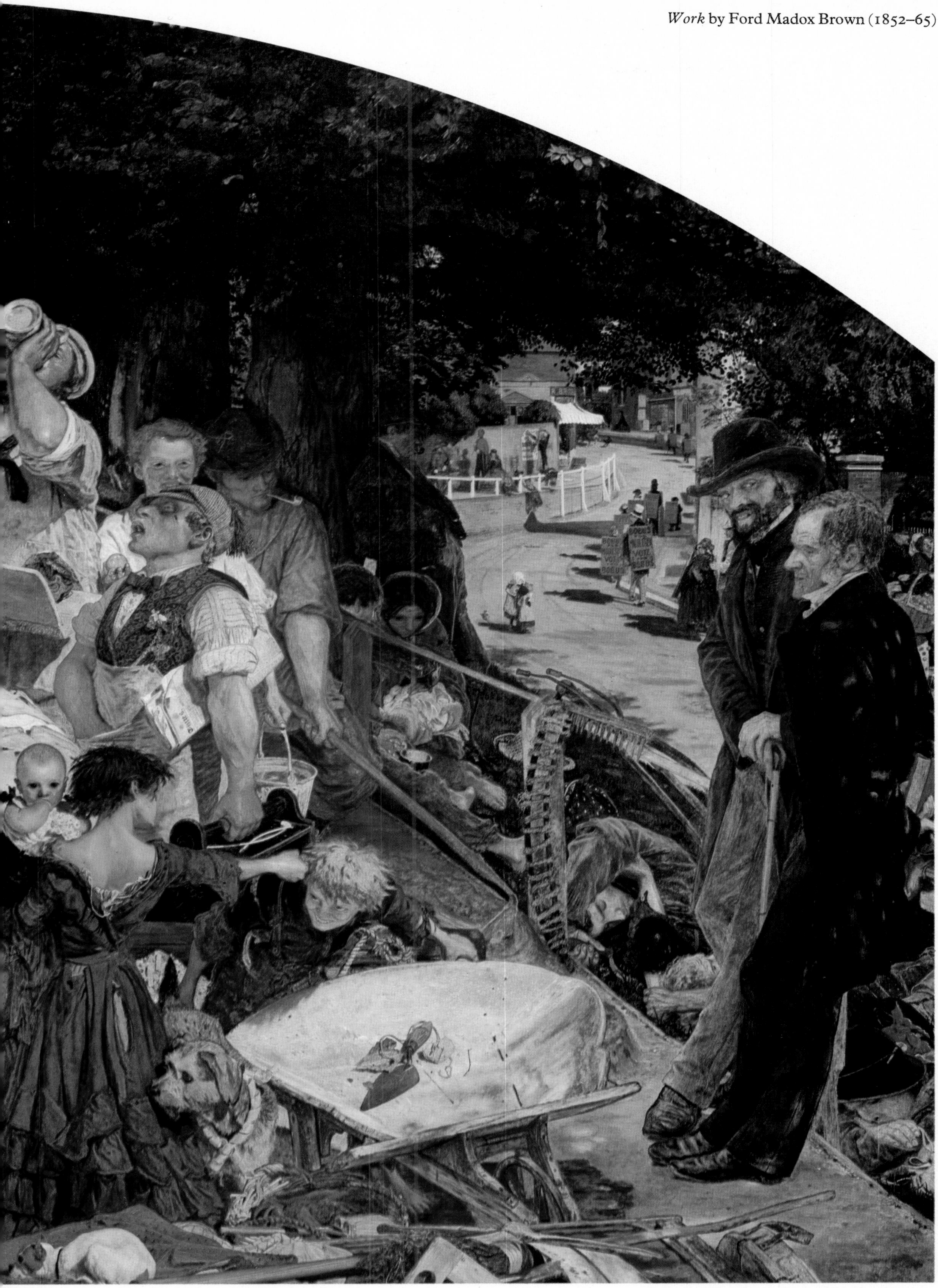

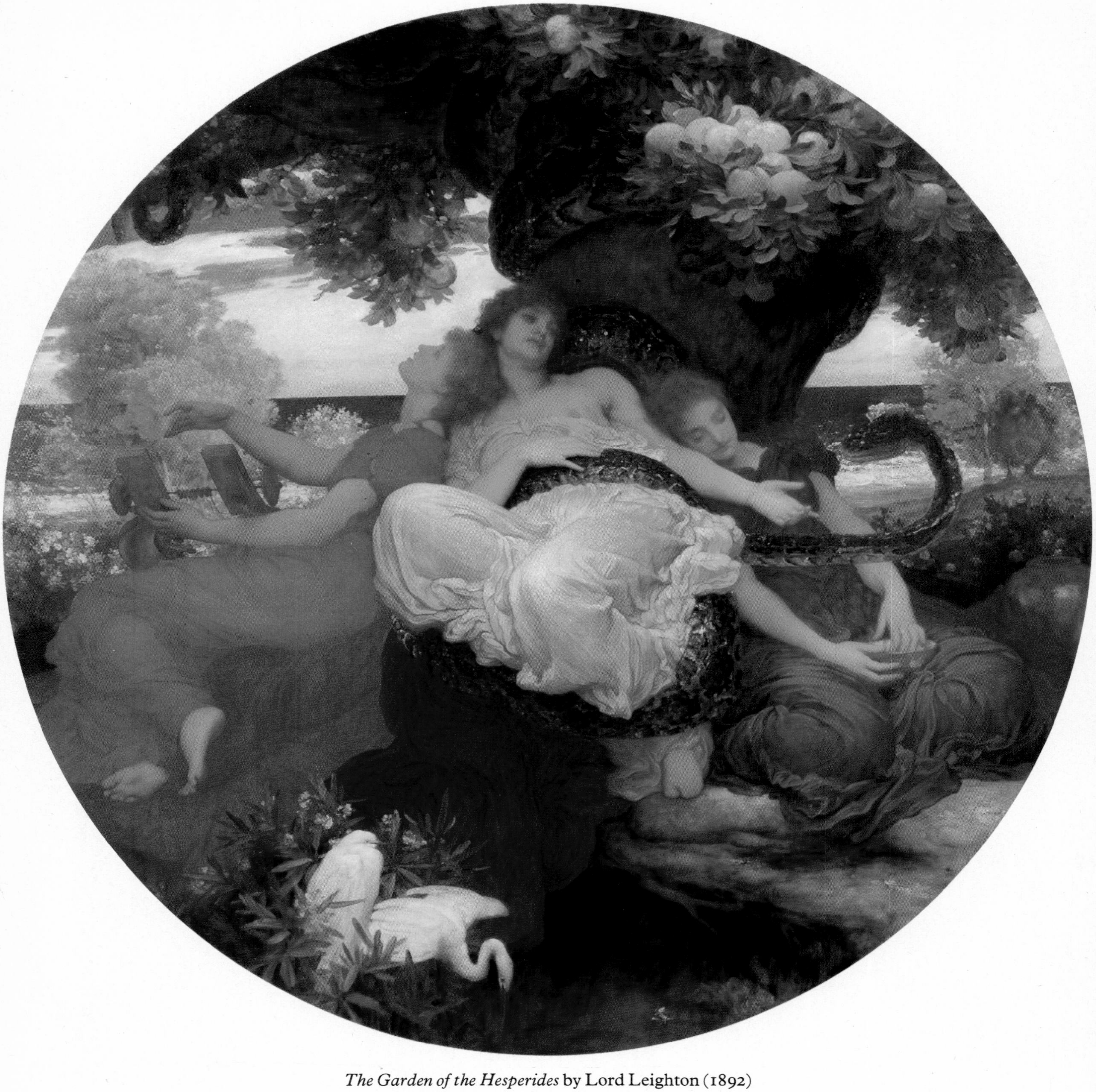

The Garden of the Hesperides by Lord Leighton (1892)

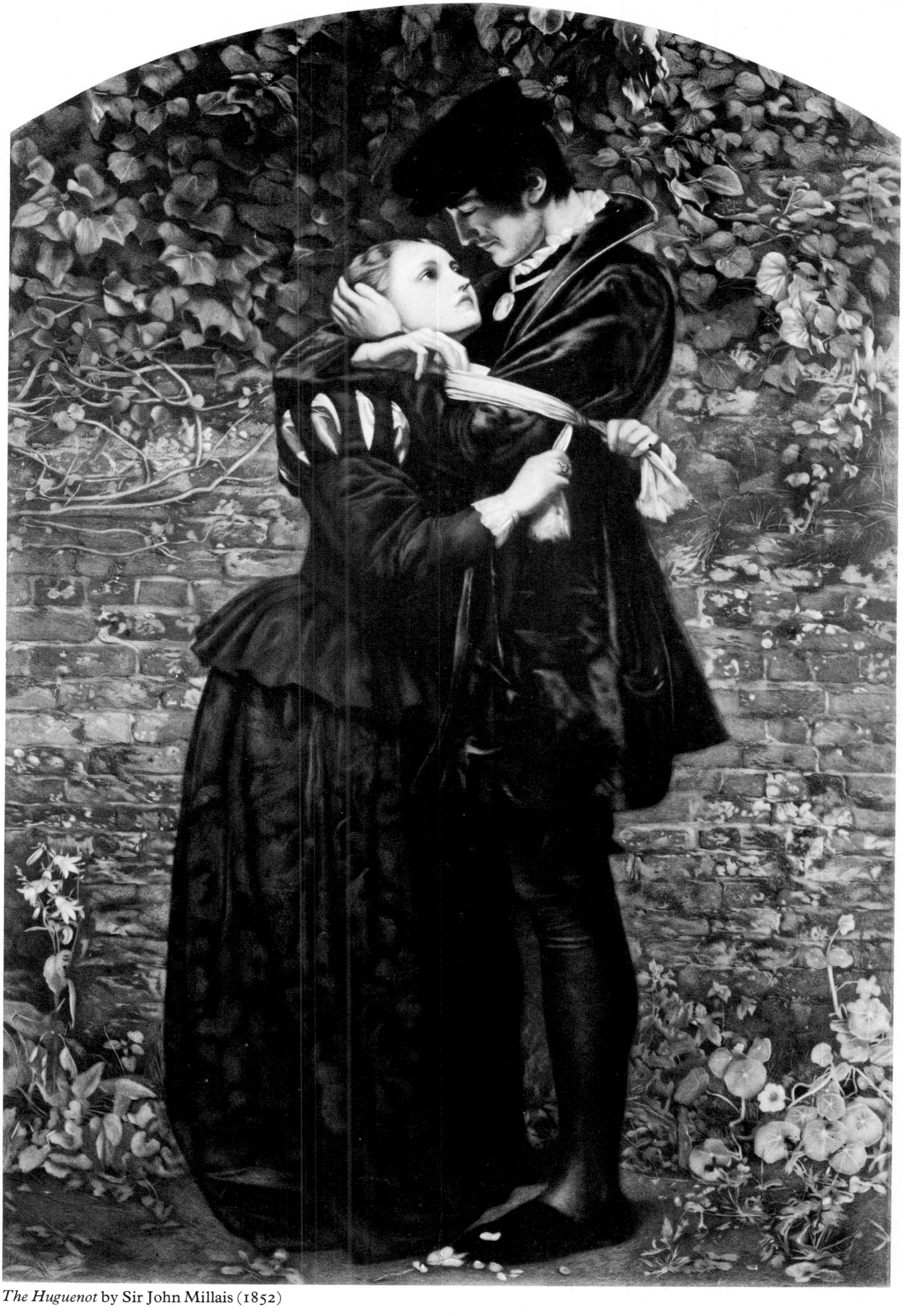

The Huguenot by Sir John Millais (1852)

THE COMING OF LEISURE

By Nicholas Mason

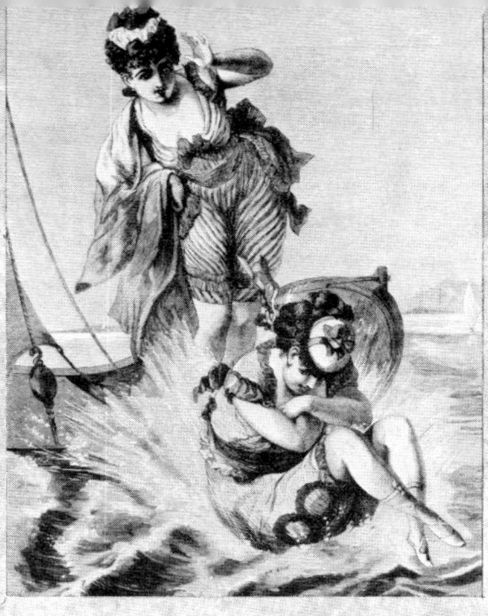

Few things do the Victorian age more credit than the way it managed to extricate itself bloodlessly from the Industrial Revolution. The Factory Acts, for the first time, ensured that a working man and his family were left with time on their hands and, with the gradual improvement in wages, a little money to save. The railways opened the seaside and the country to townspeople. From the public schools, the universities, and into ordinary life came organised sport to occupy the new-found leisure time; and hard on its heels came the multitudes not to play but to watch – first cricket matches, then, in increasing numbers, the local football team. Women responded too, graduating from croquet to the new lawn tennis and the new bicycle. The Victorians, rich and poor, had learnt to enjoy themselves

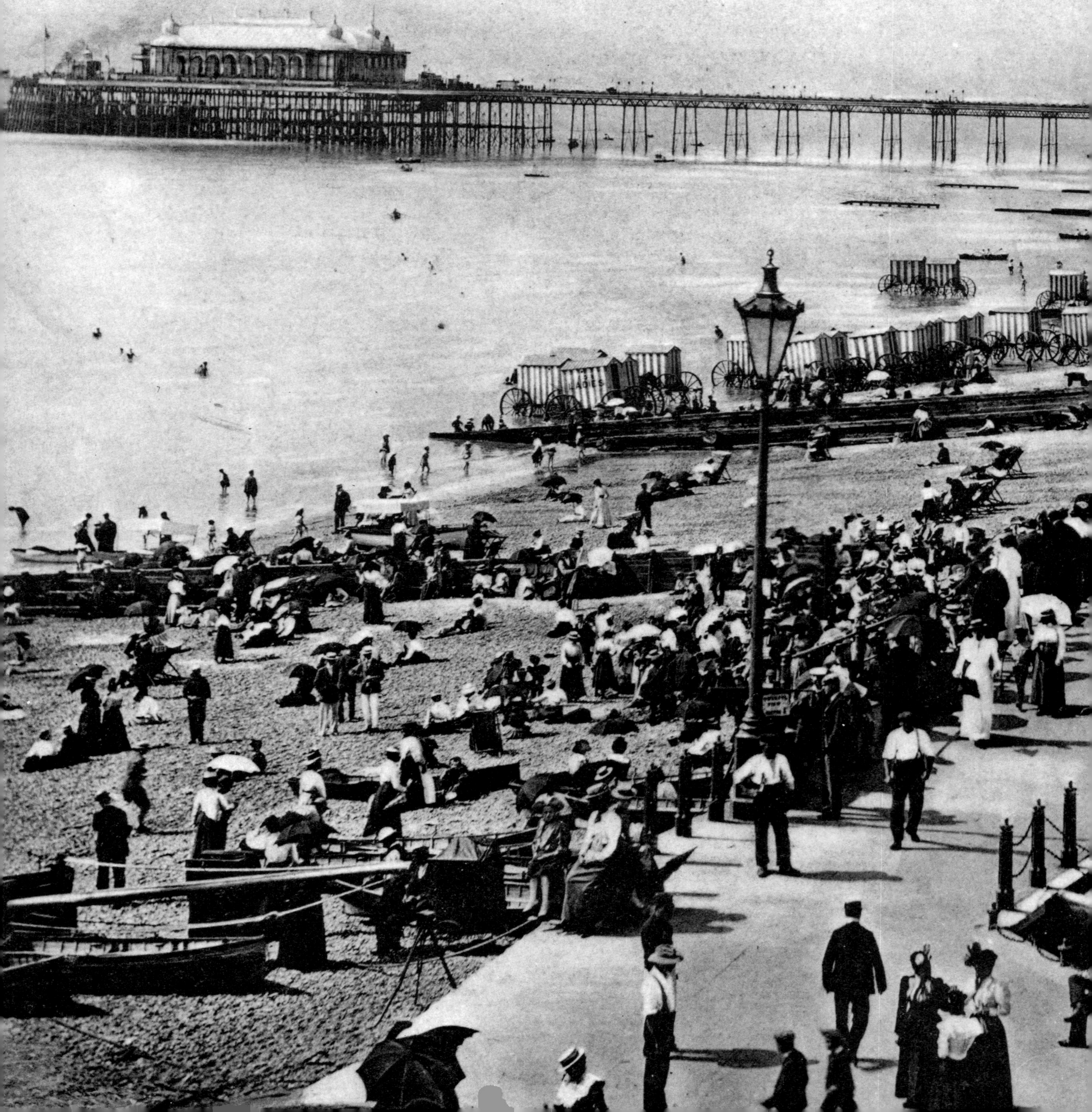

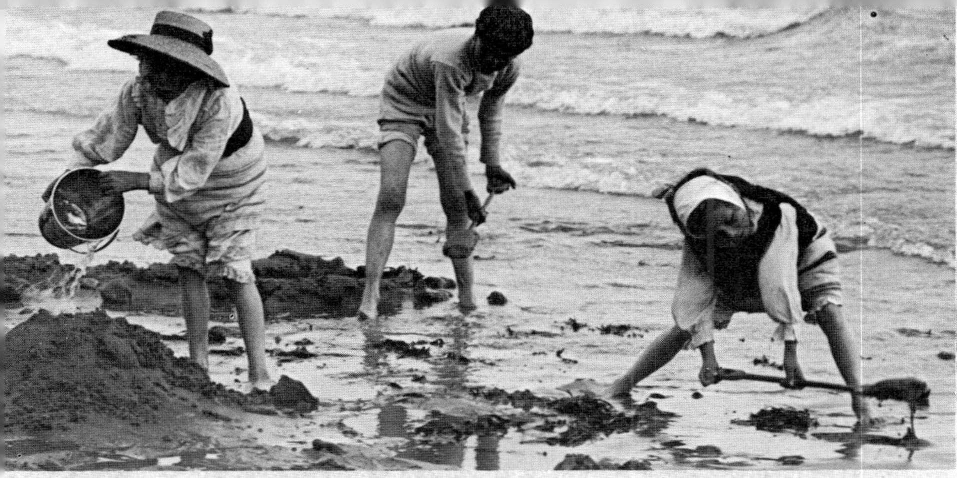

Since George IV's salty weekends in Brighton, the sea had been the universal panacea. It drew thousands of Londoners to the South Coast, and led to the explosion of sleepy fishing villages like Hastings (below) into prosperous middle-class holiday resorts

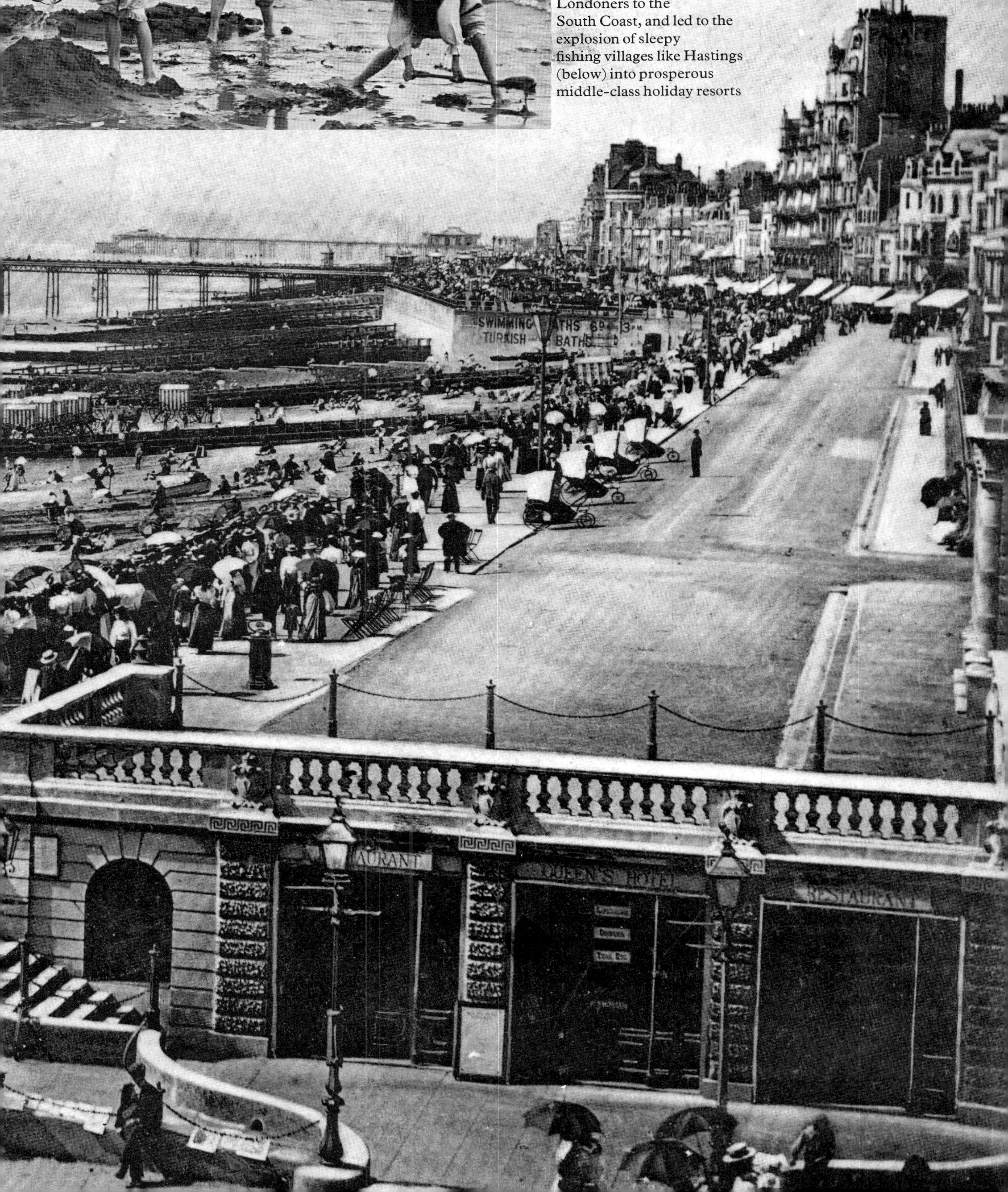
SWIMMING
TURKISH
QUEEN'S HOTEL
RESTAURANT

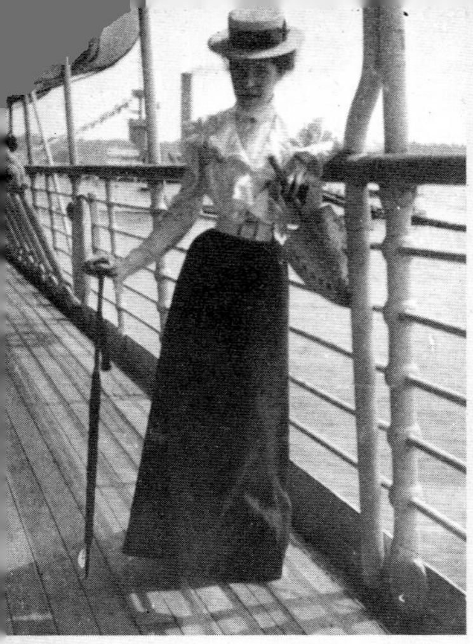
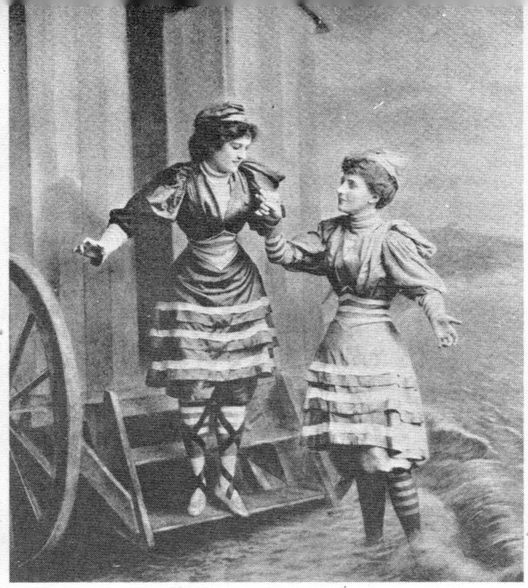
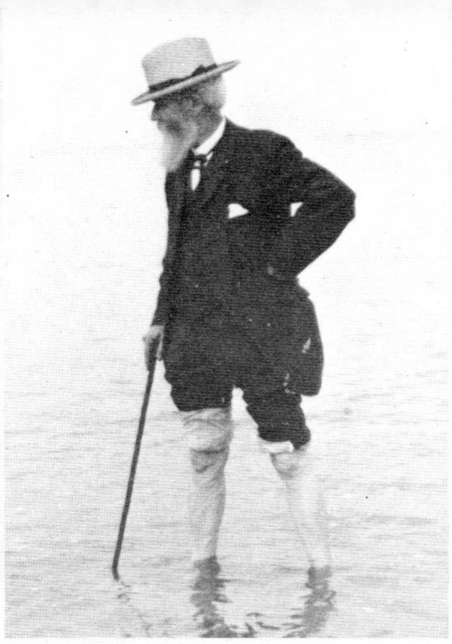

The breezes and the sunshine and the boat-trips may have been invigorating, but it was the salt in the water that did you good. Hence the clumsy, horse-drawn bathing machine (left, centre) to carry ladies into waist-deep waves where, in heavy layers of bathing garb, their unmentionable legs hidden from view by the water, they could enjoy their health-giving wade. Upright, of course – a lady did not swim

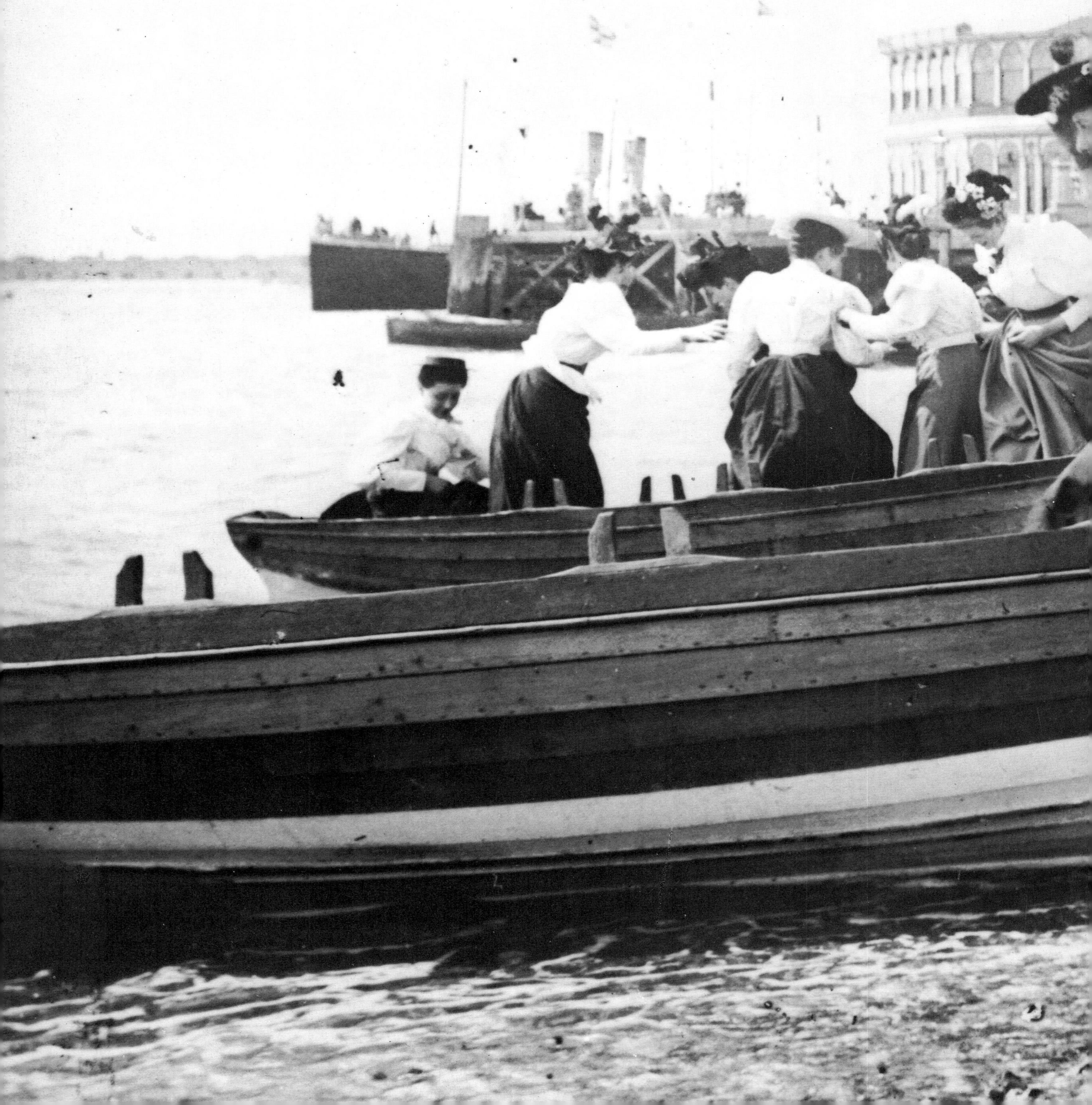

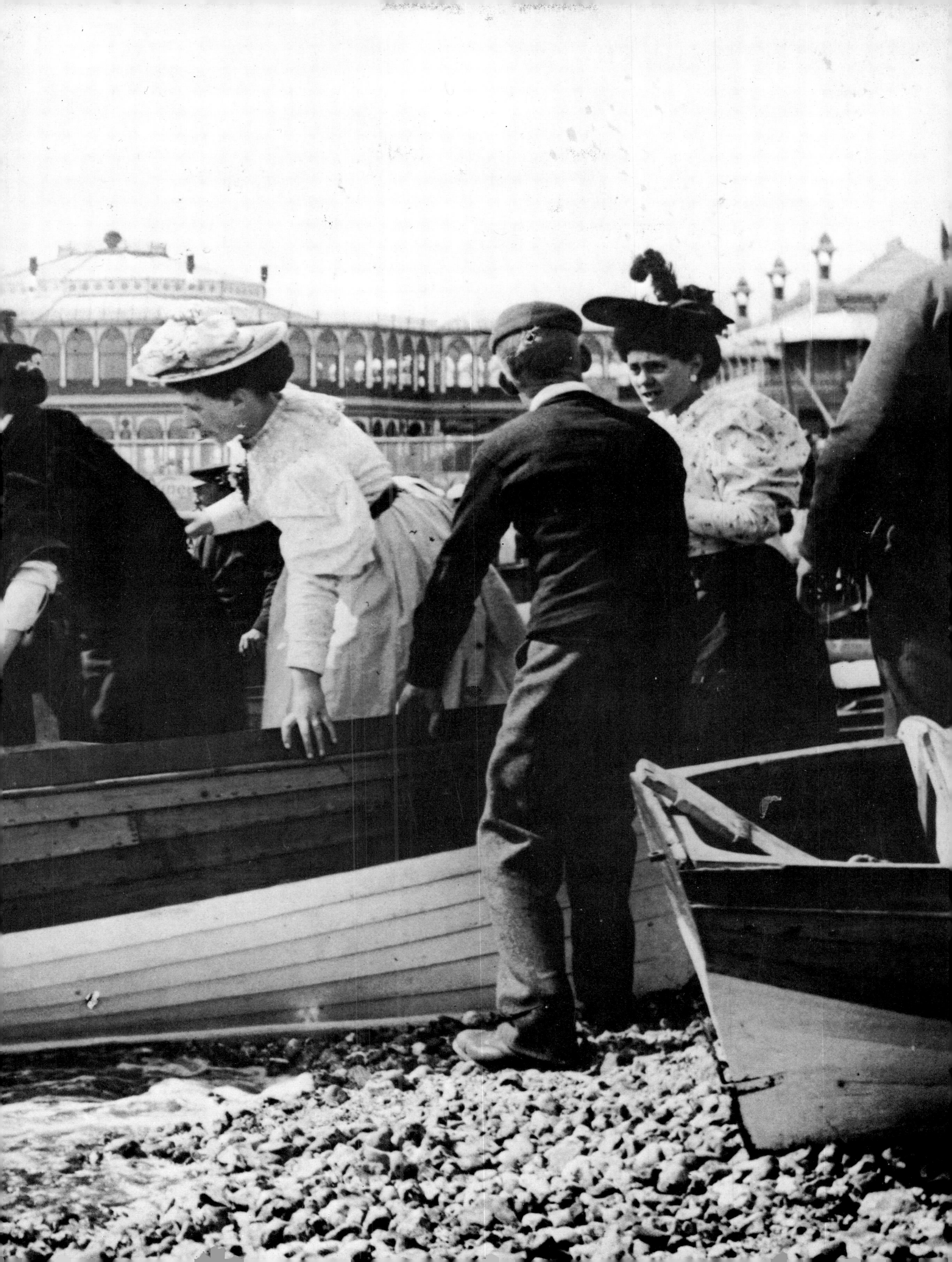

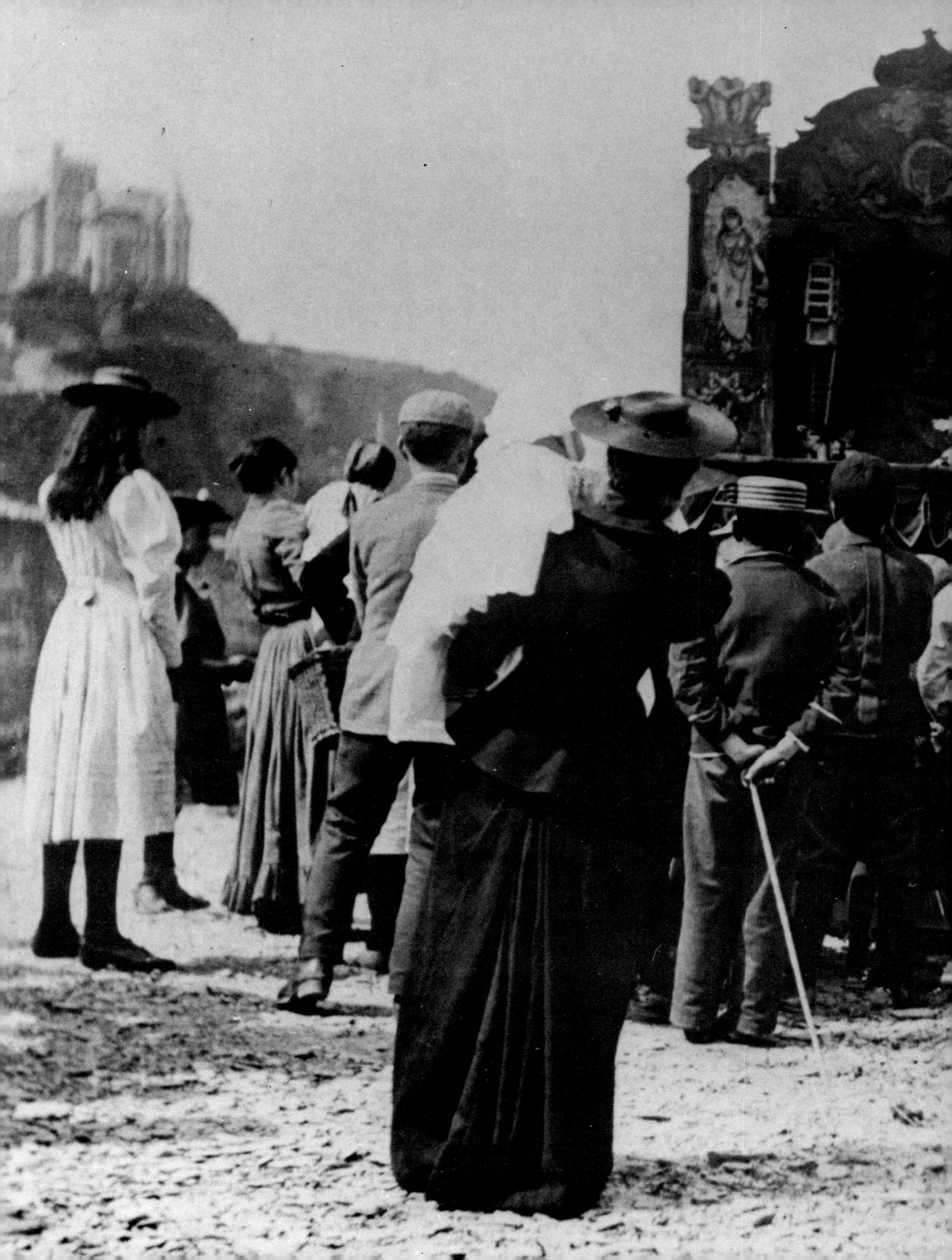

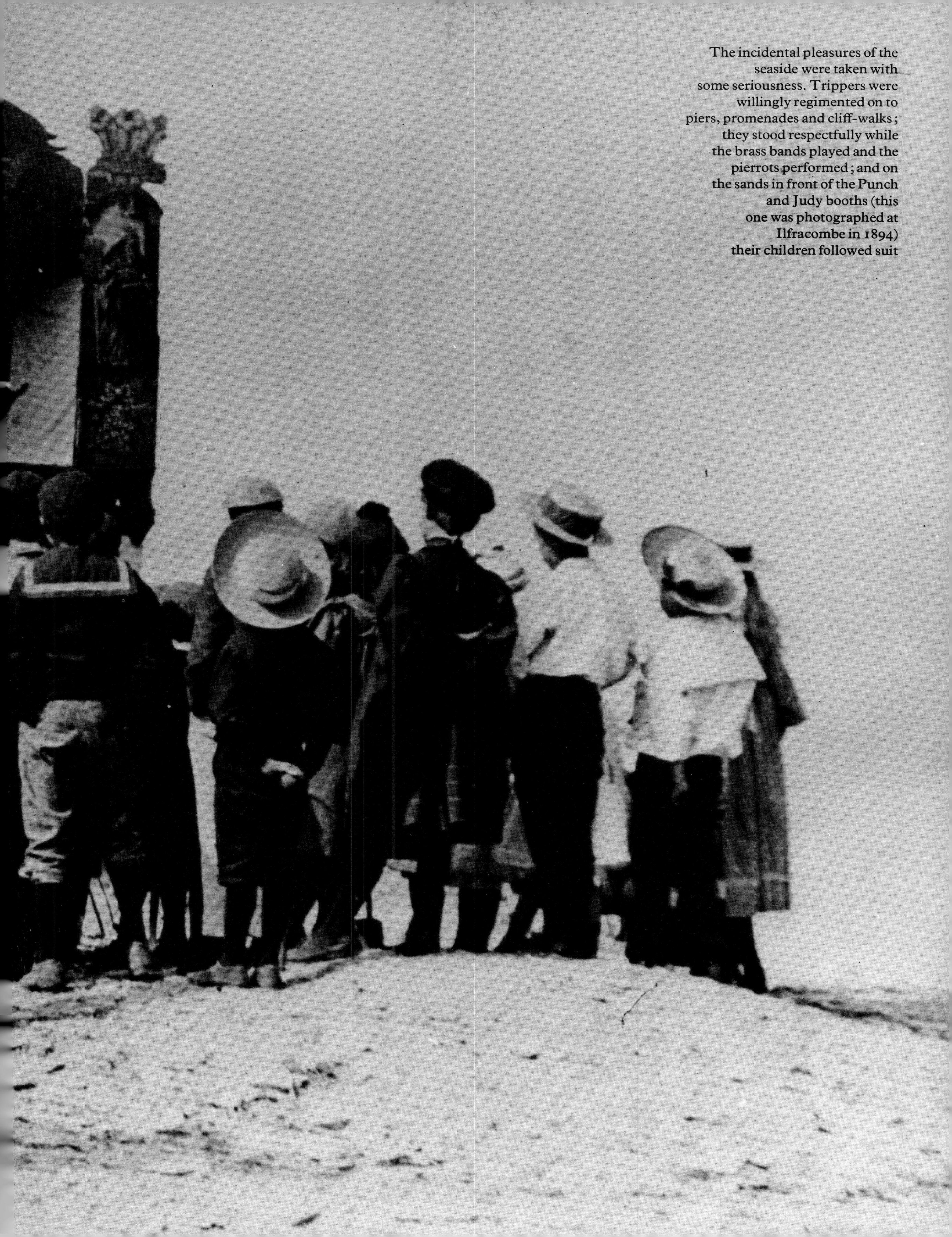

The incidental pleasures of the seaside were taken with some seriousness. Trippers were willingly regimented on to piers, promenades and cliff-walks; they stood respectfully while the brass bands played and the pierrots performed; and on the sands in front of the Punch and Judy booths (this one was photographed at Ilfracombe in 1894) their children followed suit

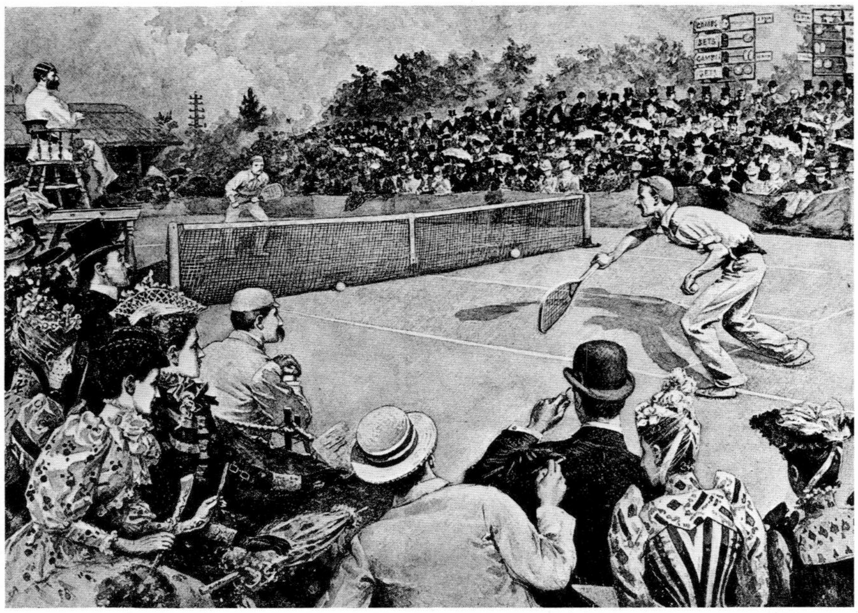

Even in leisure, invention flourished. Lawn Tennis barely existed in 1875; by 1880 it was the rage, and Wimbledon an annual event. Above: the 1891 final; William Baddeley, aged 19 and the youngest ever champion, beating J. Pym

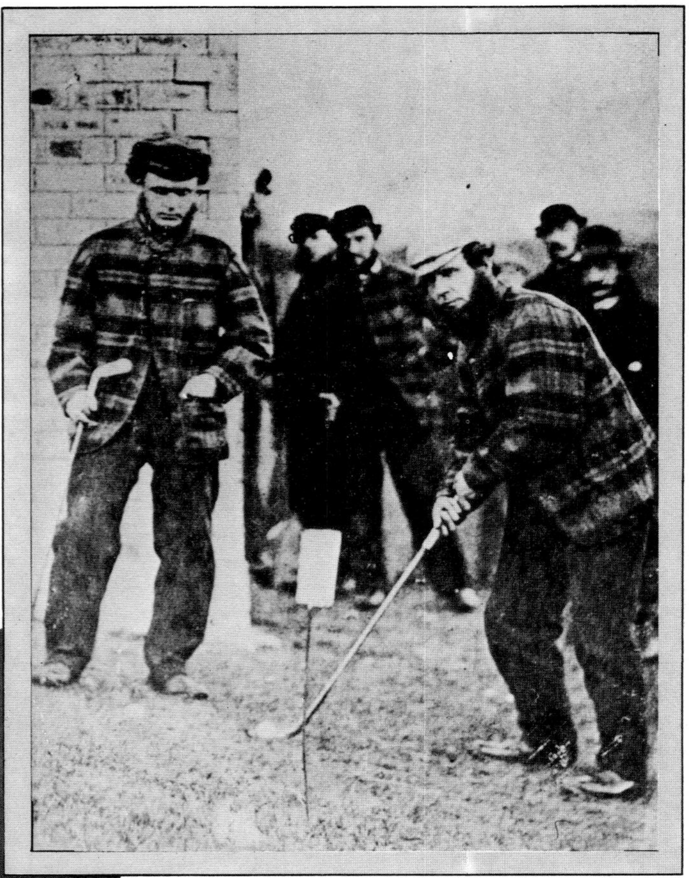

Above: the first British Open, 1860. In the mid-19th century golf, a hitherto obscure Scottish ritual, grew fast. Much of the early missionary work was done by the Prestwick Club, who staged the first Open. The legendary 'Old Tom' Morris (addressing the ball) lost that first title, but won four of the next seven

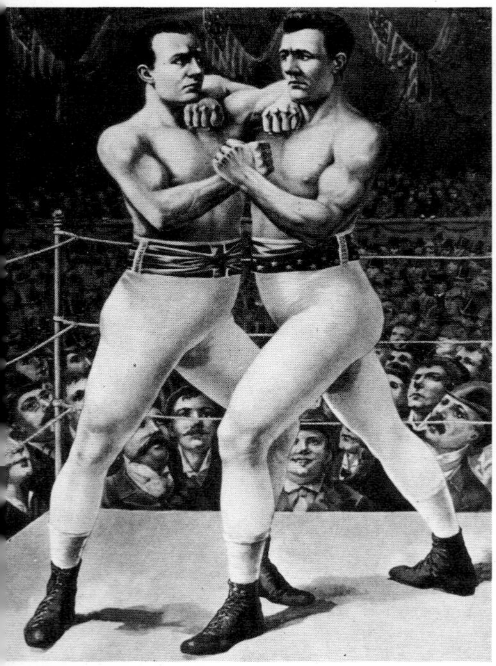

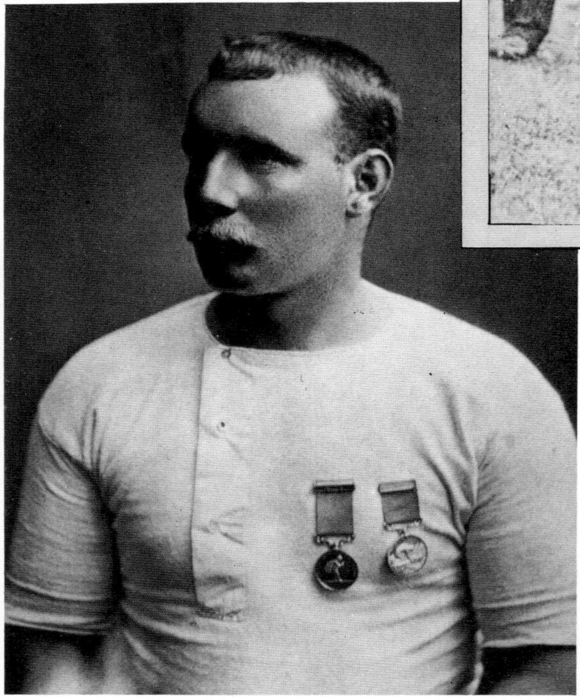

Above: Matthew Webb was first to swim the Channel (1875). Left: the Marquess of Queensberry's Rules (1865) did much to civilise boxing. Charley Mitchell (far left), first of many British fighters to visit the U.S.A. in search of a world title, was knocked out by the stylish Jim Corbett

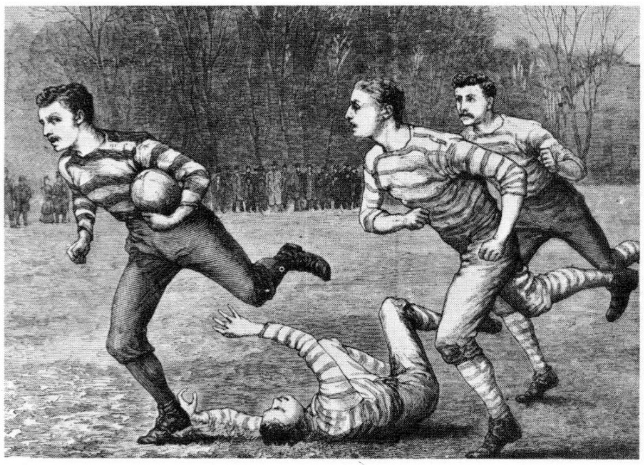

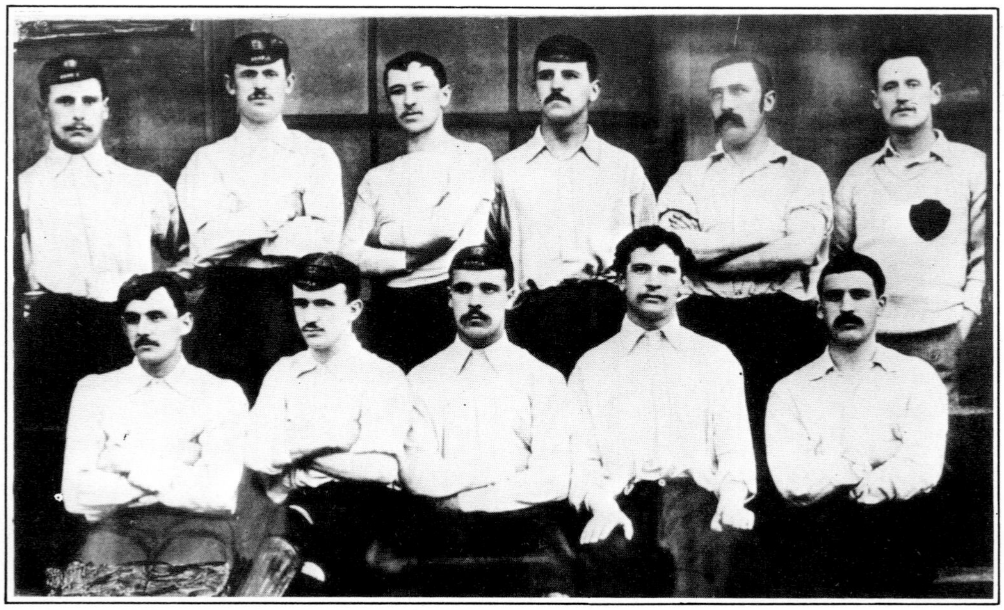

In Victoria's reign football evolved from inter-village mauls and public school kickabouts into two highly sophisticated team games. From the legendary improvisations of William Webb Ellis (who "picked up the ball and ran") at Rugby School, via the universities, came the handling game (above). From the schools, too, but eagerly adopted in the towns, came the Football Association and its kicking game. The F.A. instituted its annual Challenge Cup competition in 1871, and though the great amateur sides – Wanderers, Royal Engineers, Old Etonians, Queen's Park of Glasgow – dominated Soccer's early years, professionalism developed fast. In 1889 came the Football League, giving the powerful Preston North End team of the Eighties (left) their opportunity of the very first League and Cup double. The payment of players was less readily accepted in the South, and not until 1891 did Arsenal, captained by William Julian (right), become the first London club to turn professional

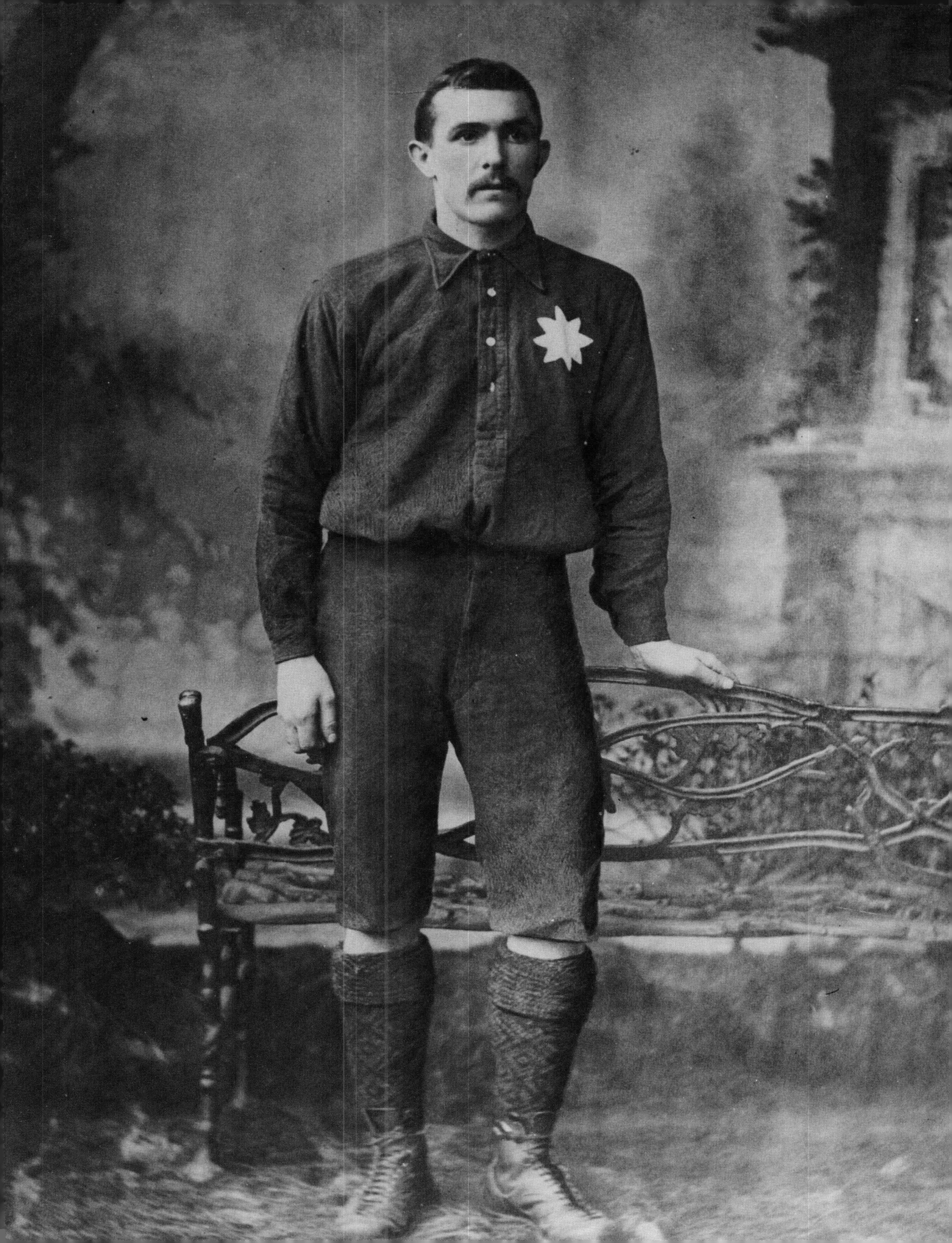

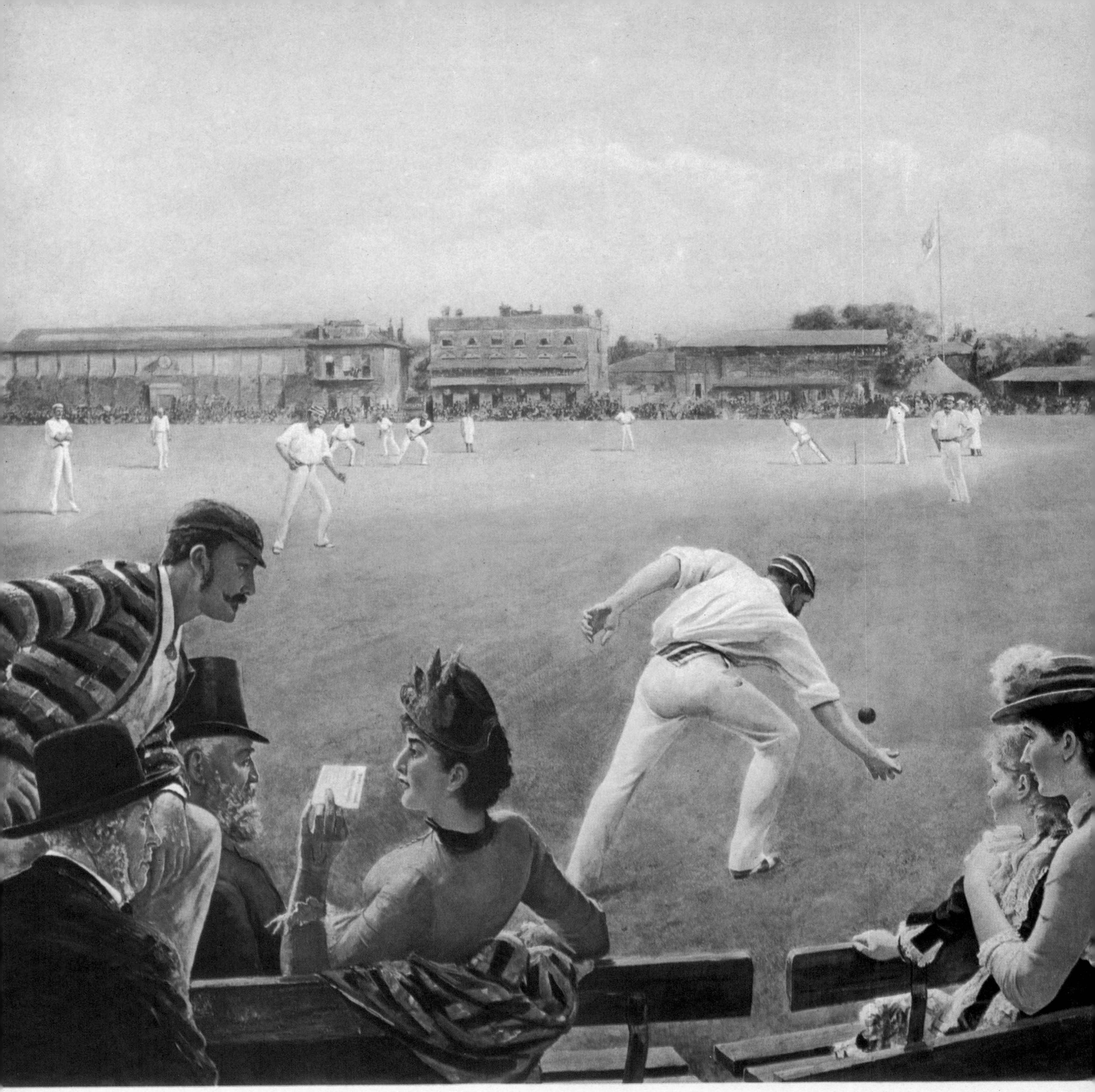

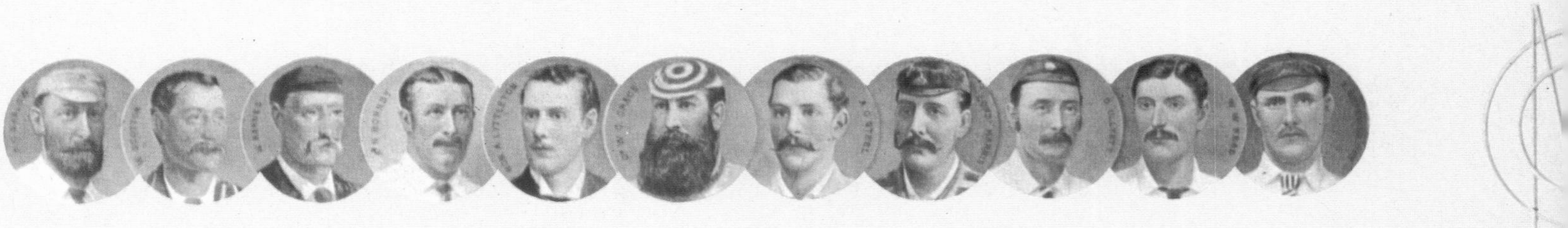

For the last half of Victoria's reign cricket enjoyed both a large popular following and an impeccable, blue-blooded patronage. This composite painting shows W. G. Grace batting at Lord's against a team of prominent Australian cricketers of the 1880s. Curiously, the match pictured here could not have taken place – these particular Australian fielders were never all on tour in England at the same time. The bowler at the

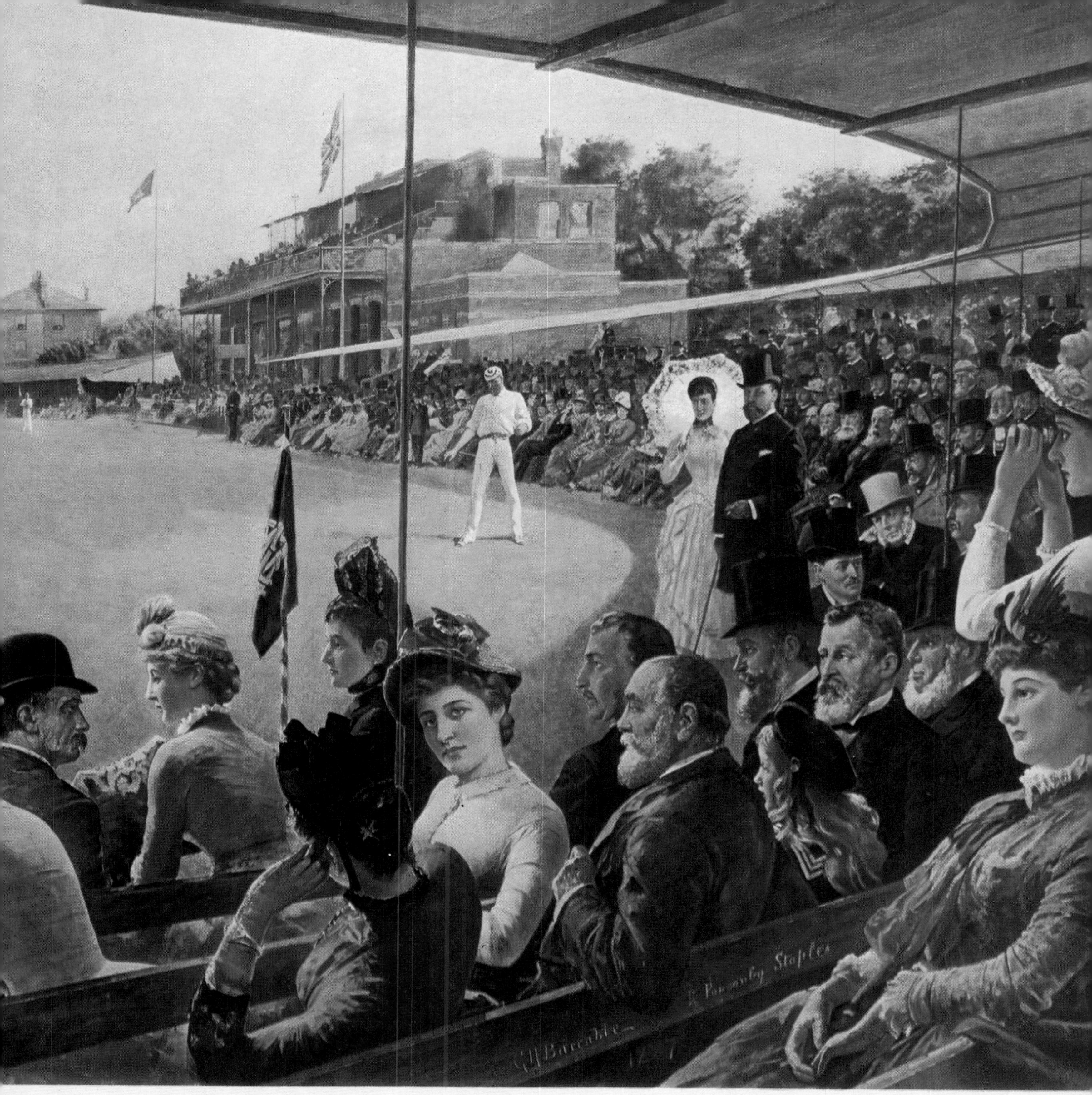

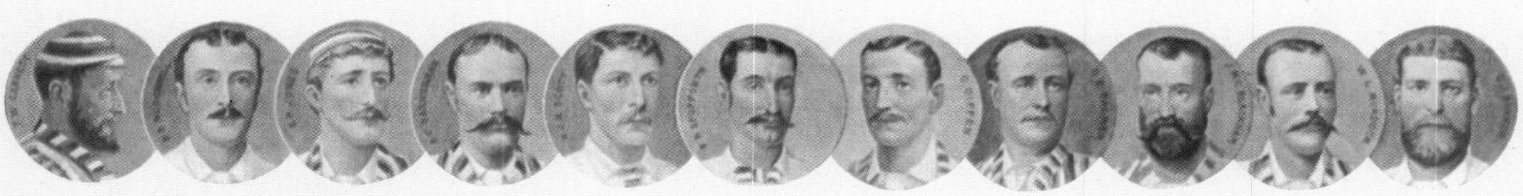

pavilion end is F. R. Spofforth, 'The Demon', the first great fast bowler of test cricket; standing among the spectators (left foreground) is Lord Harris, autocratic captain of Kent and England. The artist has, somewhat irreverently, left us in doubt as to whether the Prince of Wales (in the top hat, with Princess Alexandra at deep extra cover) has his eye on the ball or on the lady in yellow facing us – Lillie Langtry

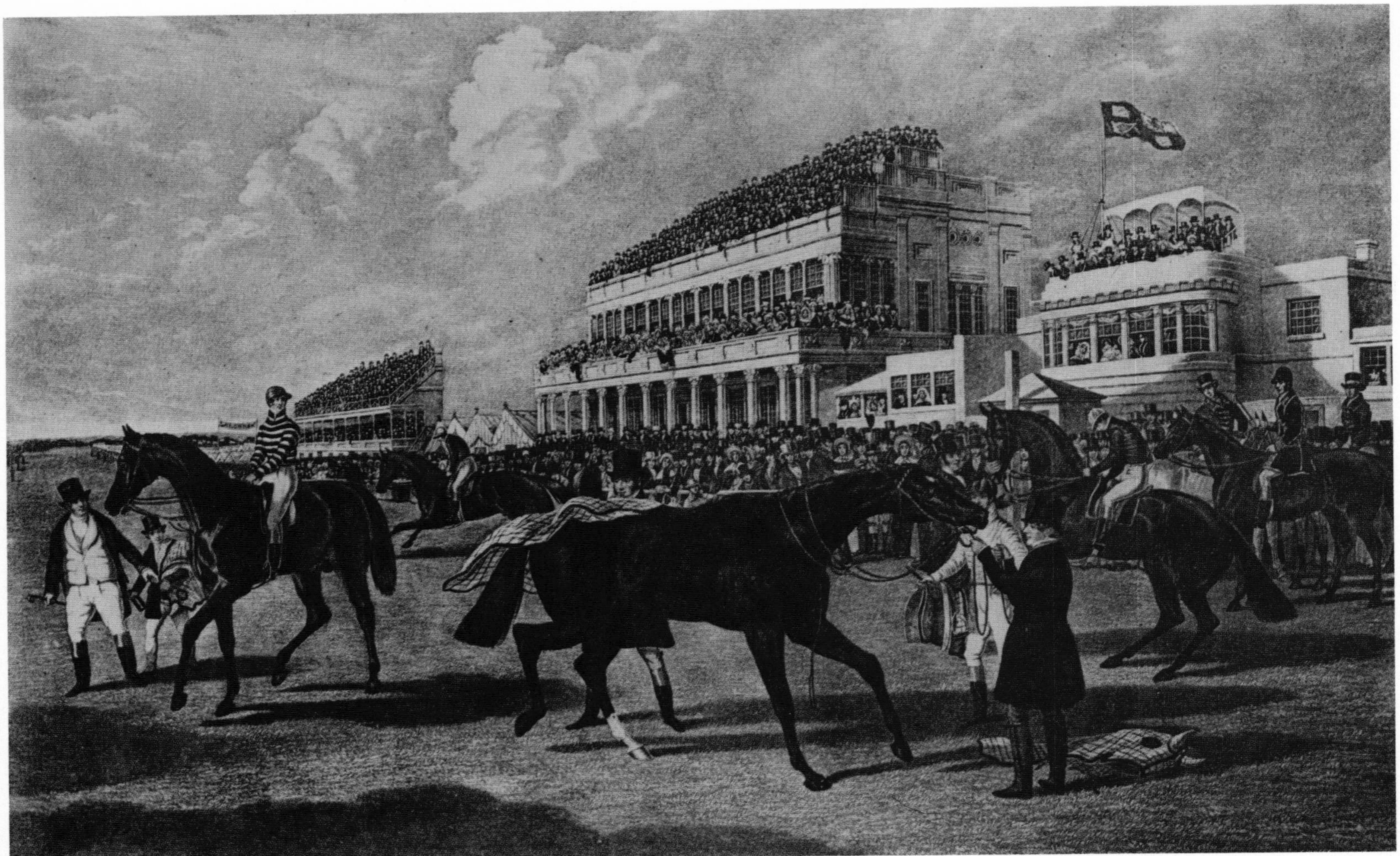

Above: Gold Cup day, 1839. Royal Ascot had been established by Queen Anne and embellished with the annual royal procession in 1828 by George IV. Victoria went regularly until Albert died. Below and opposite: Victorian cricket, with the Grace brothers prominent

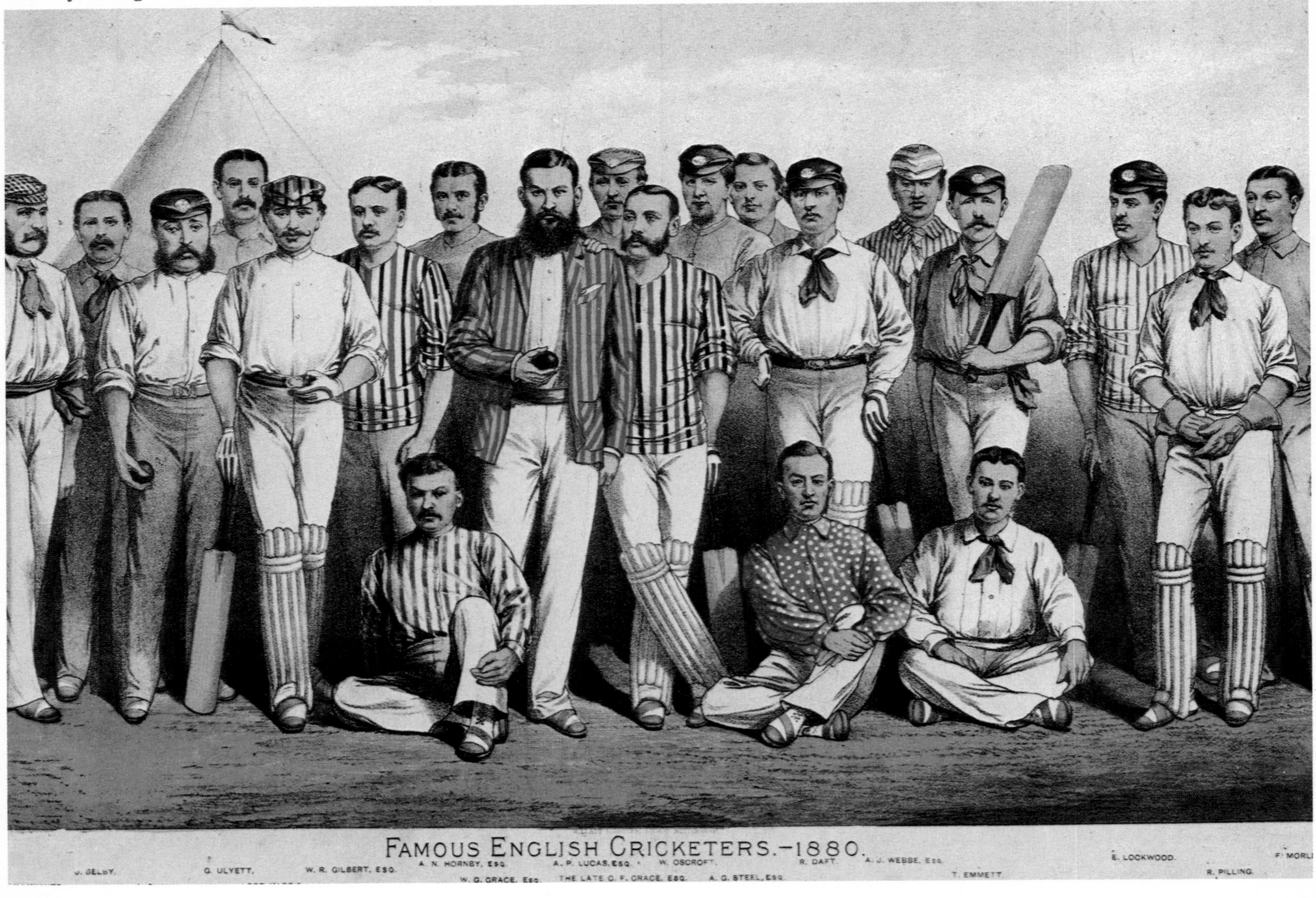
FAMOUS ENGLISH CRICKETERS.—1880.
J. SELBY.
G. ULYETT.
W. R. GILBERT, ESQ.
A. N. HORNBY, ESQ.
W. G. GRACE, ESQ.
A. P. LUCAS, ESQ.
THE LATE G. F. GRACE, ESQ.
W. OSCROFT.
A. G. STEEL, ESQ.
R. DAFT.
A. J. WEBBE, ESQ.
T. EMMETT.
E. LOCKWOOD.
R. PILLING.

MITAGE, Yorkshire.   L. GREENWOOD, Yorkshire.   H. STUBBERFIELD, Sussex.   W. A. HUMPHREYS, Sussex.   G. PINDER, Yorkshire.   G. ULYETT, Yorkshire.   H. PHILLIPS, Sussex.   J. PHILLIPS, Sussex.   J. THEWLIS, Yorkshire.   J. SOUTHERTON, Surrey.

TTERILL, Esq., Sussex.   H. B. STEEL, Esq., Lancashire.   F. WILD, Notts.   R. ABEL, Surrey.   R. PILLING, Lancashire.   J. BRIGGS, Lancashire.   W. ROBINSON, Lancashire.   F. MORLEY, Notts.   S. M. CROSFIELD, Esq., Lancashire.   R. HUMPHREY, Surrey.

MHETT, Yorkshire.   W. EVERSHED, Esq., Derbyshire.   E. LAMB, Esq., Yorkshire.   E. PEATE, Yorkshire.   H. JUPP, Surrey.   M. W. READ, Esq., Surrey.   R. PEEL, Yorkshire.   W. H. PATTERSON, Esq., Kent.   W. CROPPER, Derbyshire.   GEO. PARR, Notts.

KWOOD, Yorkshire.   L. G. DOCKER, Esq., Derbyshire.   I. GRIMSHAW, Yorkshire.   W. E. ROLLER, Esq., Surrey.   M. READ, Surrey.   R. HENDERSON, Surrey.   J. SHUTER, Esq., Surrey.   W. LILLYWHITE, Sussex.   W. CHATTERTON, Derbyshire.   A. SHREWSBURY, Notts.

ARRISON, Yorkshire.   A. APPLEBY, Esq., Lancashire.   R. BARLOW, Lancashire.   R. P. SMITH, Esq., Derbyshire.   Dr. W. G. GRACE, Gloucestershire.   Dr. E. M. GRACE, Gloucestershire.   E. ROPER, Esq., Lancashire.   A. N. HORNBY, Esq., Lancashire.   A. WATSON, Lancashire.   W. A. WOOF, Gloucestershire.

ENWOOD, Yorkshire.   C. MARRIOTT, Esq., Lancashire.   J. JUNIPER, Sussex.   Hon. M. B. HAWKE, Yorkshire.   A. P. LUCAS, Esq., Middlesex.   A. J. WEBBE, Esq., Middlesex.   C. T. STUDD, Esq., Middlesex.   W. OSCROFT, Notts.   R. DAFT, Notts.   J. SELBY, Notts.

HILL, Yorkshire.   W. MYCROFT, Derbyshire.   G. F. GRACE, Esq., Gloucestershire.   T. WARREN, Leicestershire.   J. A. BUSH, Esq., Gloucestershire.   W. R. GILBERT, Gloucestershire.   W. BARNES, Notts.   Lord HARRIS, Kent.   E. F. S. TYLECOTE, Esq., Kent.   F. SILCOCK, Essex.

TYRE, Lancashire.   J. HUNTER, Yorkshire.   J. WHEELER, Leicestershire.   LOUIS HALL, Yorkshire.   W. O. MOBERLY, Esq., Gloucestershire.   F. TOWNSEND, Esq., Gloucestershire.   E. O'SHAUGHNESSY, Kent.   G. G. HEARNE, Kent.   W. BATES, Yorkshire.   J. HIDE, Sussex.

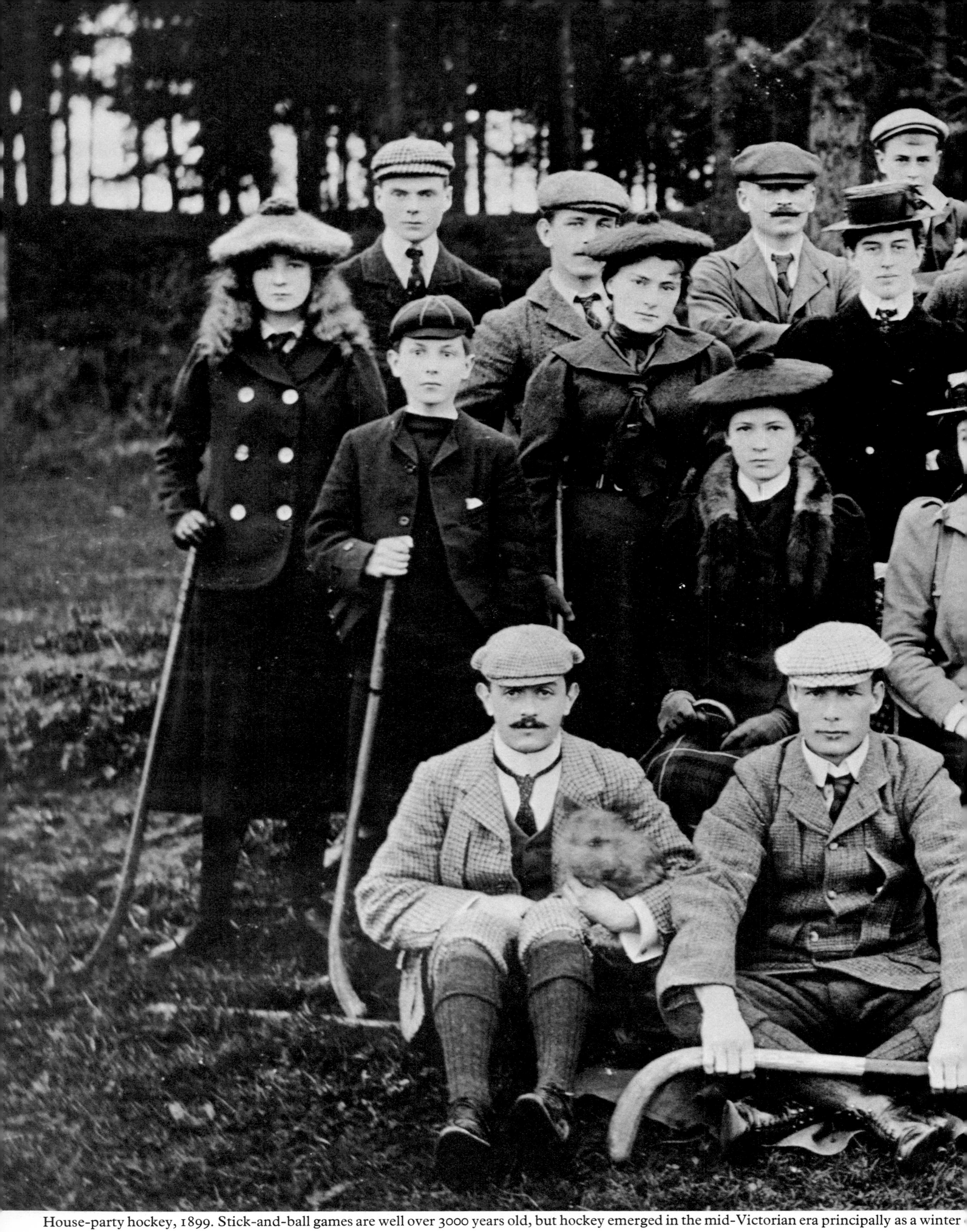

House-party hockey, 1899. Stick-and-ball games are well over 3000 years old, but hockey emerged in the mid-Victorian era principally as a winter

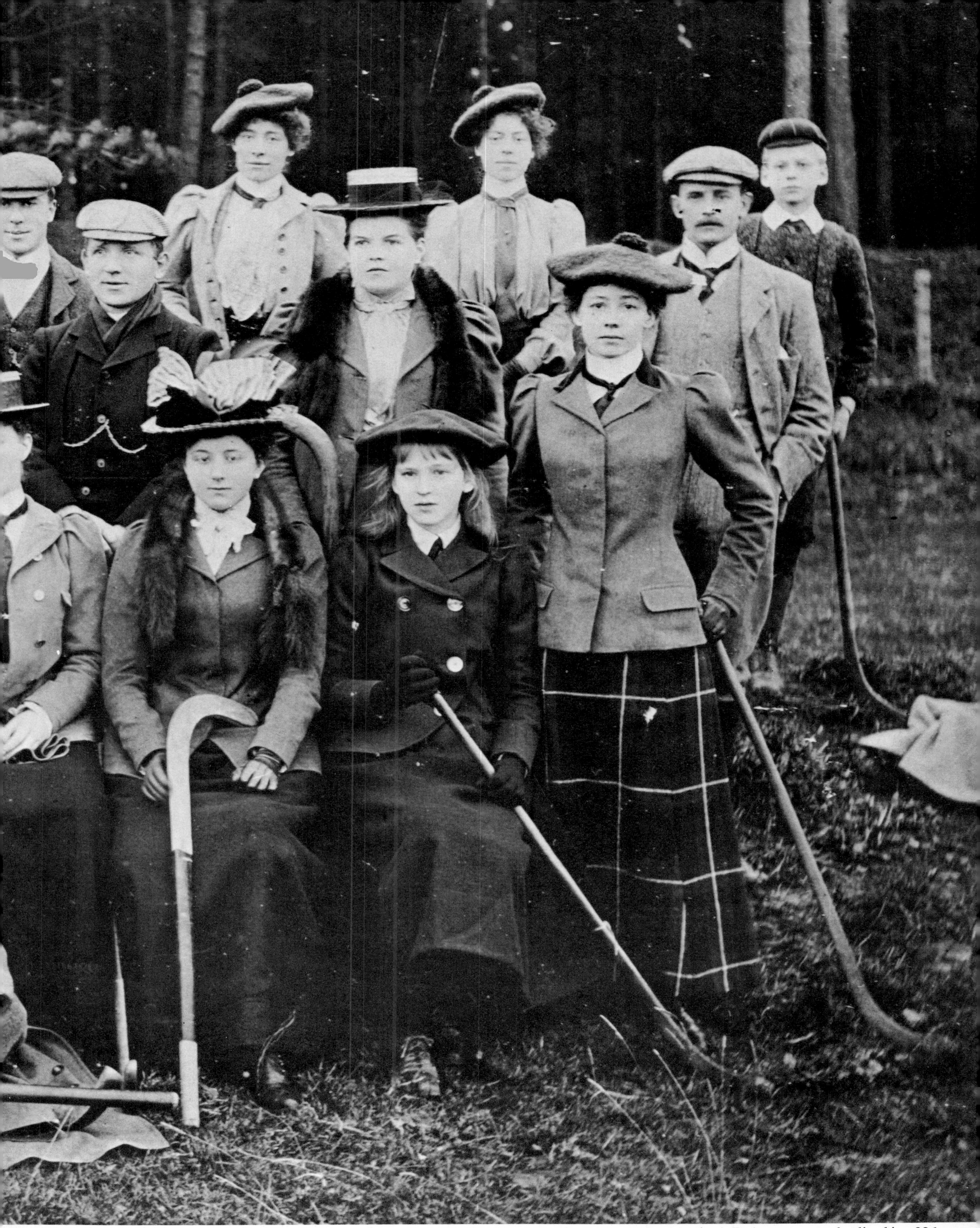

cise for cricketers (this affinity presumably lent it the necessary respectability for men and women to play together). Rules were standardised in 1886

Tennis's Age of Innocence outlived the century: the players remained amateurs and sportsmen, international competition was as yet unknown, an

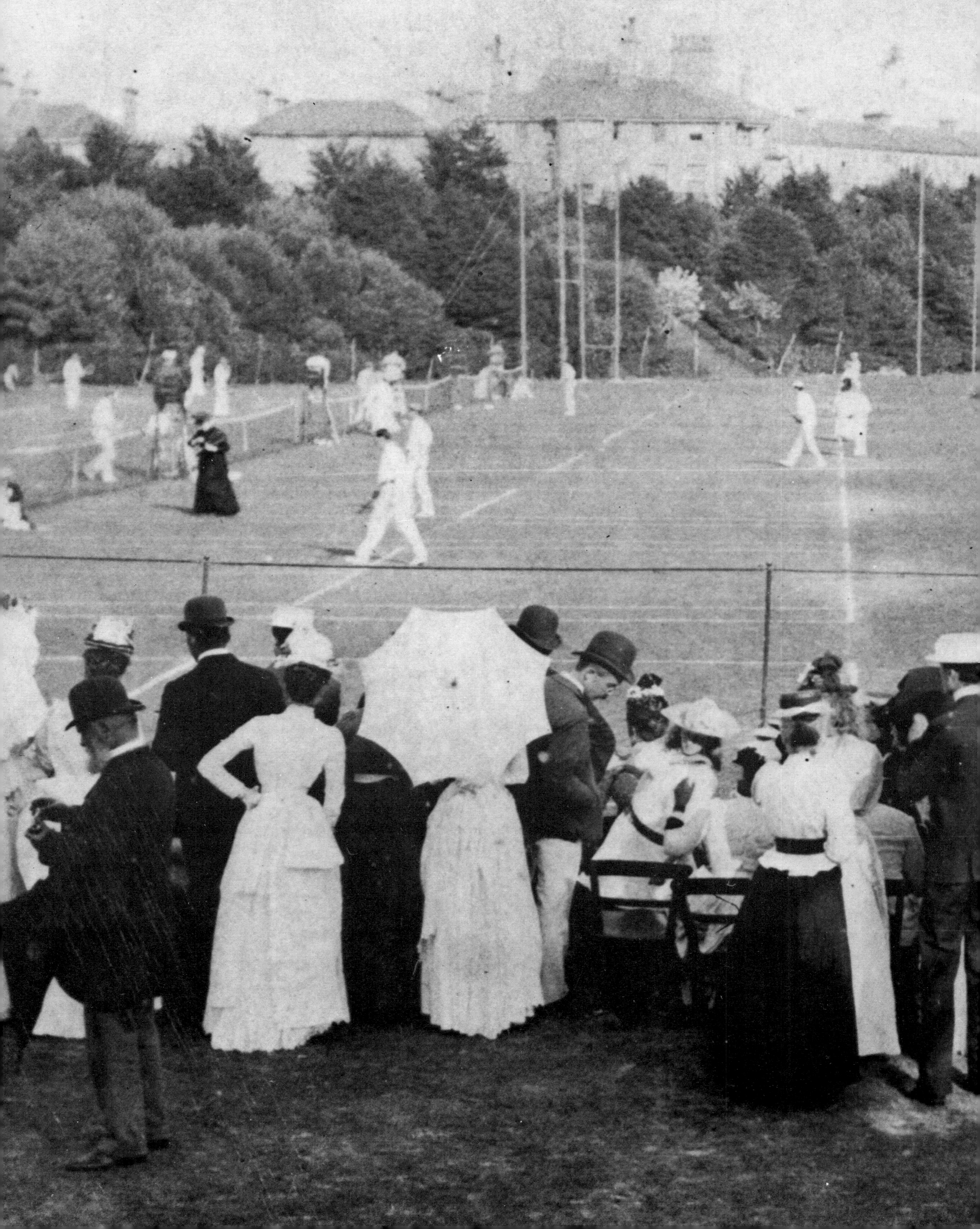

rnaments, like this one at Eastbourne in 1889, retained a relaxed, almost country-house, gentility

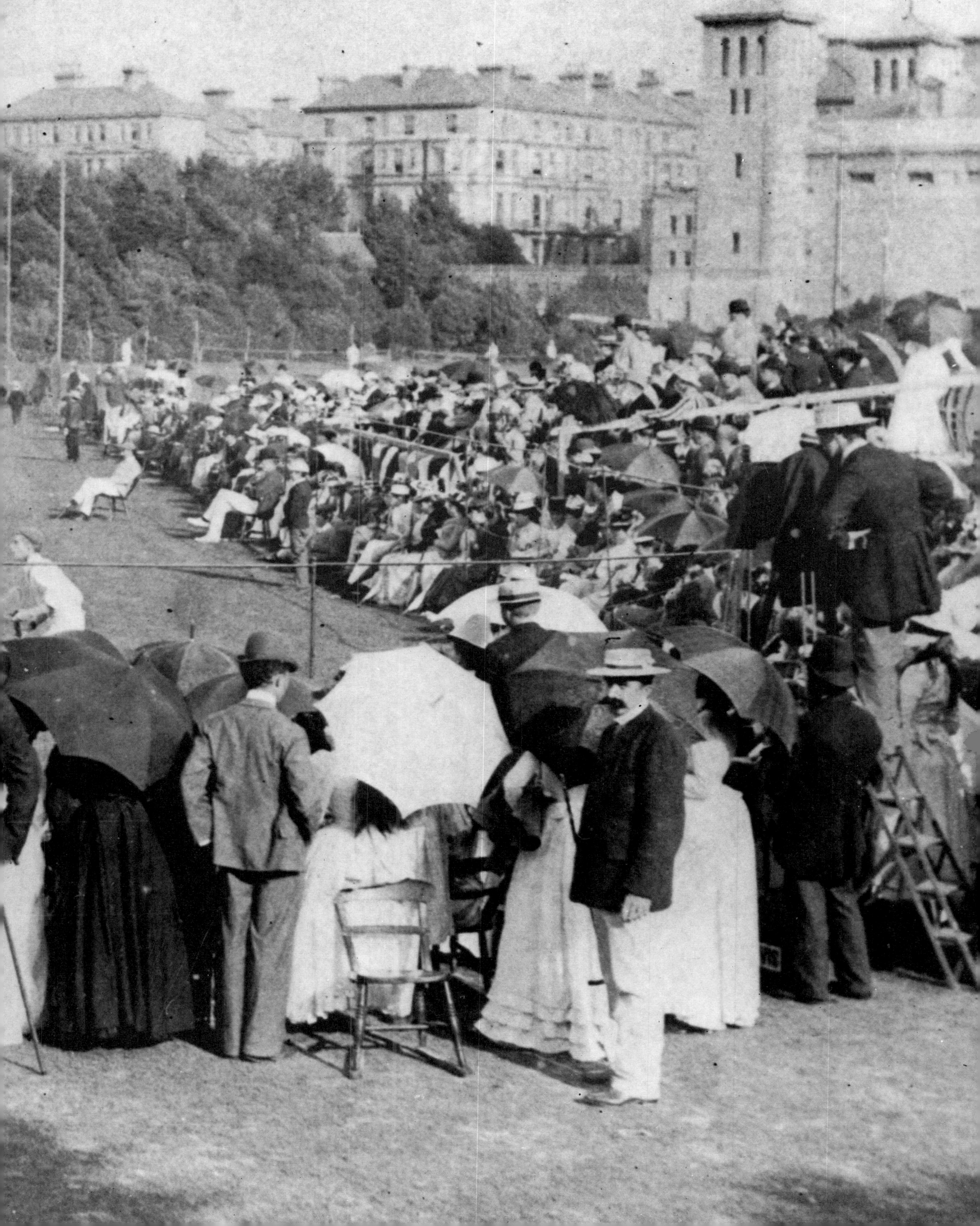

THE VOICE OF THE THUNDERER

By A. P. Ryan

Under the inspired and untiring editorship of John Thadeus Delane, *The Times*
of London achieved a matchless reputation for high-speed
newsgathering, fearless campaigning and objective reliability

"By Jove, John, what do you think has happened? I am Editor of *The Times*!" The year was 1841, the speaker John Thadeus Delane, and the place, the lodging he shared with John Blackwood in St James's Square.

The age of the new Editor was 23. He held the chair for 36 years, giving it up only when his health had broken.

The circulation of the paper in his day more than doubled. By 1855 it was 58,000; more than twice the sales of all its rivals put together.

Competition was fierce. Scoops were fought hard for, and money was spent freely on news-gathering. *The Times* hired special trains and steamships, and, on one occasion, organised at short notice a camel service for bringing messages across the desert.

Master of his editorial house in Printing House Square, Delane also lived a strenuous social life. Every night he was in his room at the office by half past 10 or 11, and he stayed there till five in the morning. Sir William Russell, the famous Crimean War correspondent, said that no man had seen the dawn rise over London so often as Delane.

Delane married the widow of a previous Assistant

Early automation – an 'eight-feeder' installed in 1862

Editor, the daughter of Horace Twiss. But after only a few years of wedlock she was separated from her husband (whom she outlived) and placed under medical care.

An invitation to dine at his home in Sarjeant's Inn was coveted. Delane kept an excellent French cook and cellar. He himself drank only sparingly and did not smoke. He was a familiar figure paying his morning calls, with a groom following behind to hold his horse. He rode to hounds, shot, fished and stalked. He seldom missed the Derby, never in his later years Ascot, and he often went to Goodwood, and he got Admiral Rous, the dictator of the Turf in those days, and a friend, to write on racing

matters, making *The Times* almost a sporting paper.

To follow Delane day by day through his diary is to be amazed at his physical toughness. He had been a boxer at Oxford, and was remembered for having stood up to the Chicken of Wheatley, a redoubtable, retired prize fighter. He needed stamina to keep up with the double life between his modest, gaslit office in Printing House Square and his attendance at long Parliamentary debates, enlivened by looking in at society balls.

How cool a customer he was comes out most vividly in a letter he wrote to Russell, with whom he kept up a long and friendly correspondence. It begins by apologising for not having answered one from Russell more promptly, adding: "I have had a tolerably sufficient excuse." It was that:

"I have lost an eye and for a long time was prohibited from writing a line that I could avoid. Of course, I did not give up work, *but I had to dictate, which I cannot at all manage, and to be read to, which I detest. Now, at last, the fear of sympathetic inflammation is over, and I can do my best with my remaining eye; but it is one instead of two, and I am urgently pressed to be what I could never be – careful."*

That was dated 1861. Delane had another 16 years of those long nights poring over the small print of mid-Victorian proofs.

He never made the mistake of trying to use his editorial strength as a lever for careering in politics. He stuck to his last as a journalist. When Lord Derby warned the Press that, if it aspired to exercise the influence of statesmen, it should accept the responsibilities of statesmen, *The Times* replied in forthright terms:

"The purposes and duties of the two Powers are constantly separate, generally independent, sometimes diametrically opposite. The dignity and freedom of the Press are trammeled from the moment it accepts an ancillary position. To perform its duties with entire independence and consequently with the utmost public advantage, the Press can enter into no close or binding alliance with the statesmen of the day, nor can it surrender its permanent interests to the convenience or the ephemeral power of any Government. The first duty of the Press is to obtain the earliest and most correct intelligence of the events of the time, and instantly, by disclosing them, to make them the common property of the nations. The Press lives by disclosures."

That declaration of a journalist's faith – as valid today as it was when it appeared in *The Times* of 1852 – was not first expressed by Delane. It had been asserted by his predecessor, Thomas Barnes, in the face of threats at Cabinet level and other powerful pressures from the

WALTER PRINTING PRESS
(PRINTING "THE MAIL")
A TRI-WEEKLY REPRINT OF THE "TIMES"
JOHN WALTER ESQ. M.P.
PRINTING HOUSE SQUARE BLACKFRIARS.

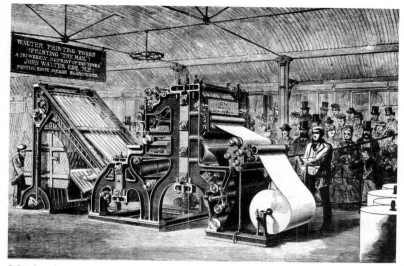

Mechanical progress – *The Times* pioneered rotary presses

early 19th-century Establishment. Politicians before Barnes had been accustomed to bribe and bully newspapers – including, in its early years, *The Times*. By Delane's day, they wooed it.

As soon as he succeeded Barnes, Delane was approached by Greville, the diarist and holder of many State secrets, with an offer of continued off-the-record help for the paper. Cabinet Ministers gave the Editor confidential information with a freedom that seems astonishing now that a monstrous regiment of public relations officers has been recruited to provide political smoke-screens.

Aberdeen, Palmerston and Disraeli, among others, helped *The Times* keep its readers in the picture. Some politicians resented the hold of the paper on the Westminster Square Mile. "I am aware," Lord Russell once wrote with characteristic petulance, "that Mr Delane was angry that I did not ask to kiss his hand instead of the Queen's when I was appointed to succeed Palmerston; but I would rather not be in office than hold it on such humiliating conditions."

Queen Victoria herself, stung by comment in *The Times* on her "protracted seclusion" as a widow, wrote an indignant complaint in her own hand. It was published under the discreet heading "The Court".

A colleague of Delane's referred to his "flashes of sure intuition". It was plainly apparent that he had a nose for news and the courage to be led by it.

Meeting a doctor at the Athenaeum he was told that Lord Northbrook had been asking how a hot climate would be likely to suit his daughter. Quickly following this trail, *The Times* astonished the official world by announcing next day that Northbrook was going to India as Governor-General. "But it is altogether premature to congratulate me," the new Viceroy exclaimed. "It was only settled this morning, and how *The Times* got hold of it I cannot imagine, for no one but myself and Gladstone have even discussed it."

Delane had chanced his arm on that talk with the doctor and risked a prophecy that came true. The most famous of Delane's coups – breaking the news that the Corn Laws were about to be repealed – was based on information from Lord Aberdeen.

Some of Delane's campaigns shook the nation. *The Times* in peacetime took the lid off the railway scandal – a 19th-century South Sea Bubble. In wartime it exposed the bloodcurdling inefficiency of the Crimean campaign.

Keeping in touch with events and shaping the work of his staff left Delane little time for writing, except letters. As a correspondent he was terse, racy, colloquial and always to the point. Leader writers were never left in doubt as to what he expected from them. When Russell proposed to stand for Parliament in Chelsea, Delane wrote to him asking: "Do you really mean to go to the poll? Or are you making a diversion for some Tory swell? That you should be serious in defence of the Irish Church seems quite unintelligible to yours as ever, J.T.D."

Keen, especially in his early years, on the stage, and keeping an eye on all sides of the paper, he put main news and leading articles first and: ". . . would never allow publication to be delayed even five minutes for a musical or theatrical critique."

When the news of his impending retirement became known, Disraeli speculated on: "Who will undertake the social part of the business? Who will go about in the world, and do all that which Mr Delane did so well?" He certainly had a genius for making and keeping friends, in the City as well as at Westminster. A chance encounter in a barber's shop with Lionel Rothschild led to a long and close intimacy with the great financial family. But the social was only one – valuable – side of Delane.

He remained to the end what Kinglake had called him, after they had visited the Crimea together during the war: "A man of great ardour, great eagerness, and one passionately imbued with the spirit of journalism."

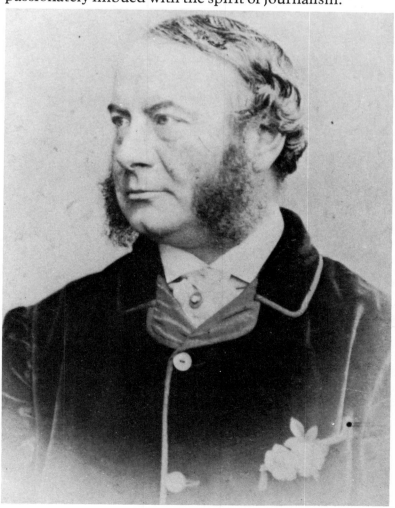

John Thadeus Delane – the homes of the great opened to him

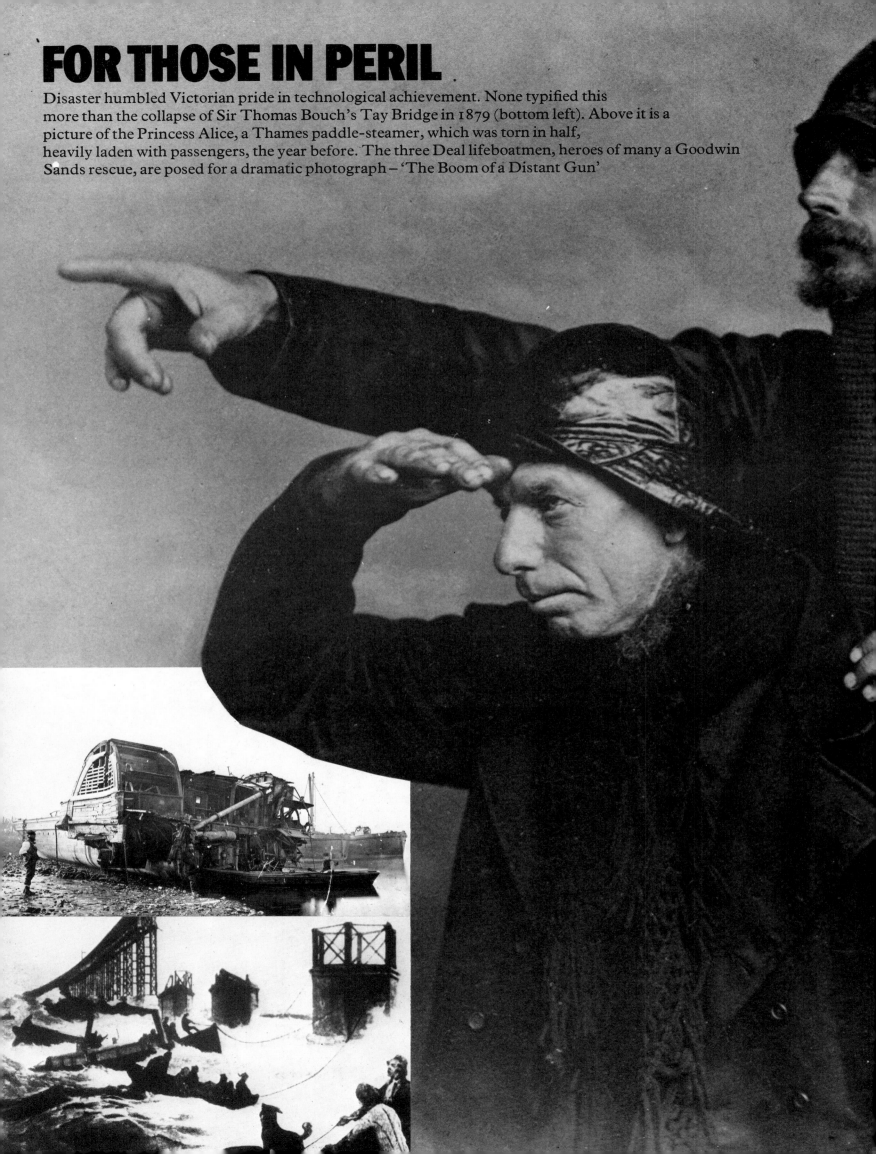

FOR THOSE IN PERIL

Disaster humbled Victorian pride in technological achievement. None typified this more than the collapse of Sir Thomas Bouch's Tay Bridge in 1879 (bottom left). Above it is a picture of the Princess Alice, a Thames paddle-steamer, which was torn in half, heavily laden with passengers, the year before. The three Deal lifeboatmen, heroes of many a Goodwin Sands rescue, are posed for a dramatic photograph – 'The Boom of a Distant Gun'

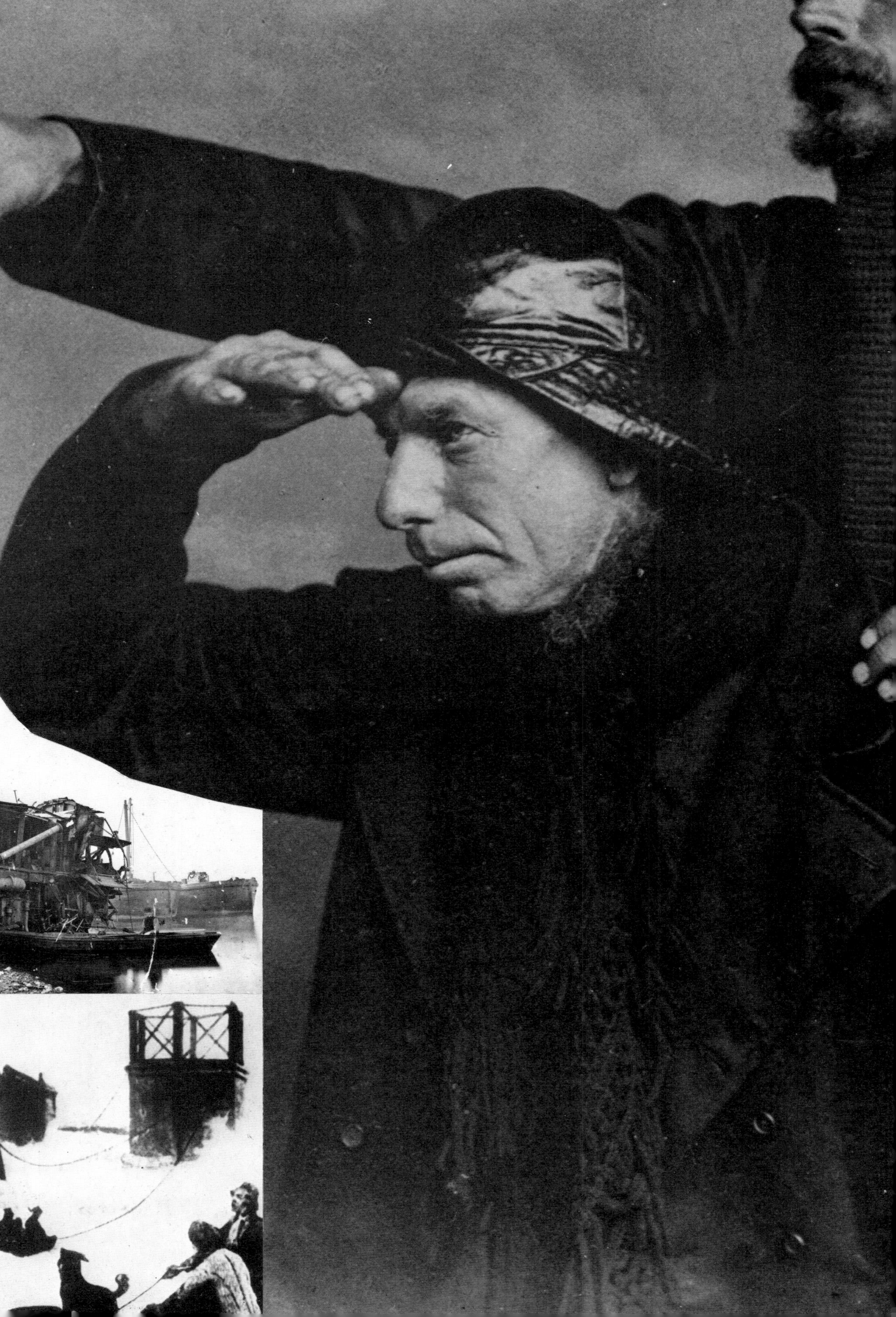

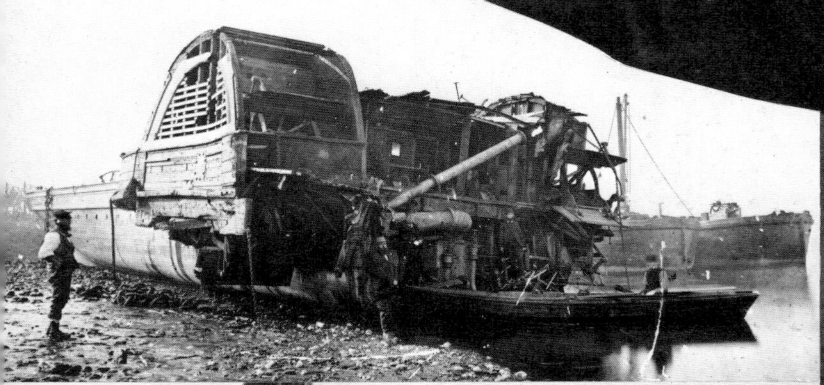

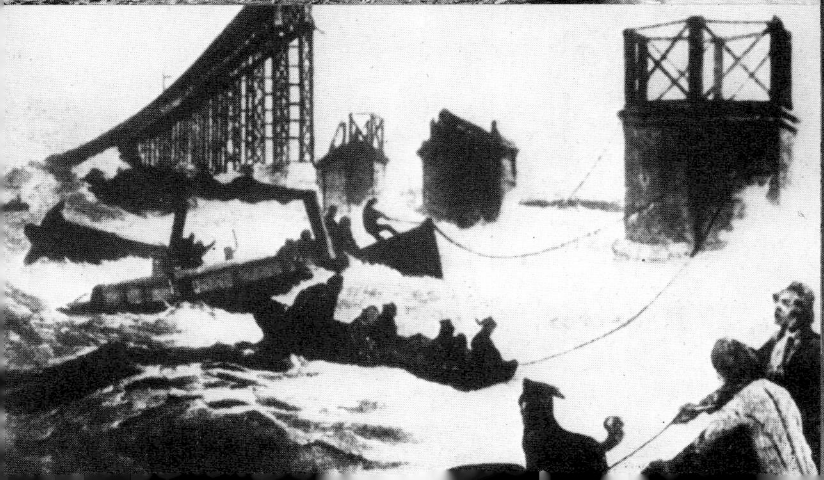

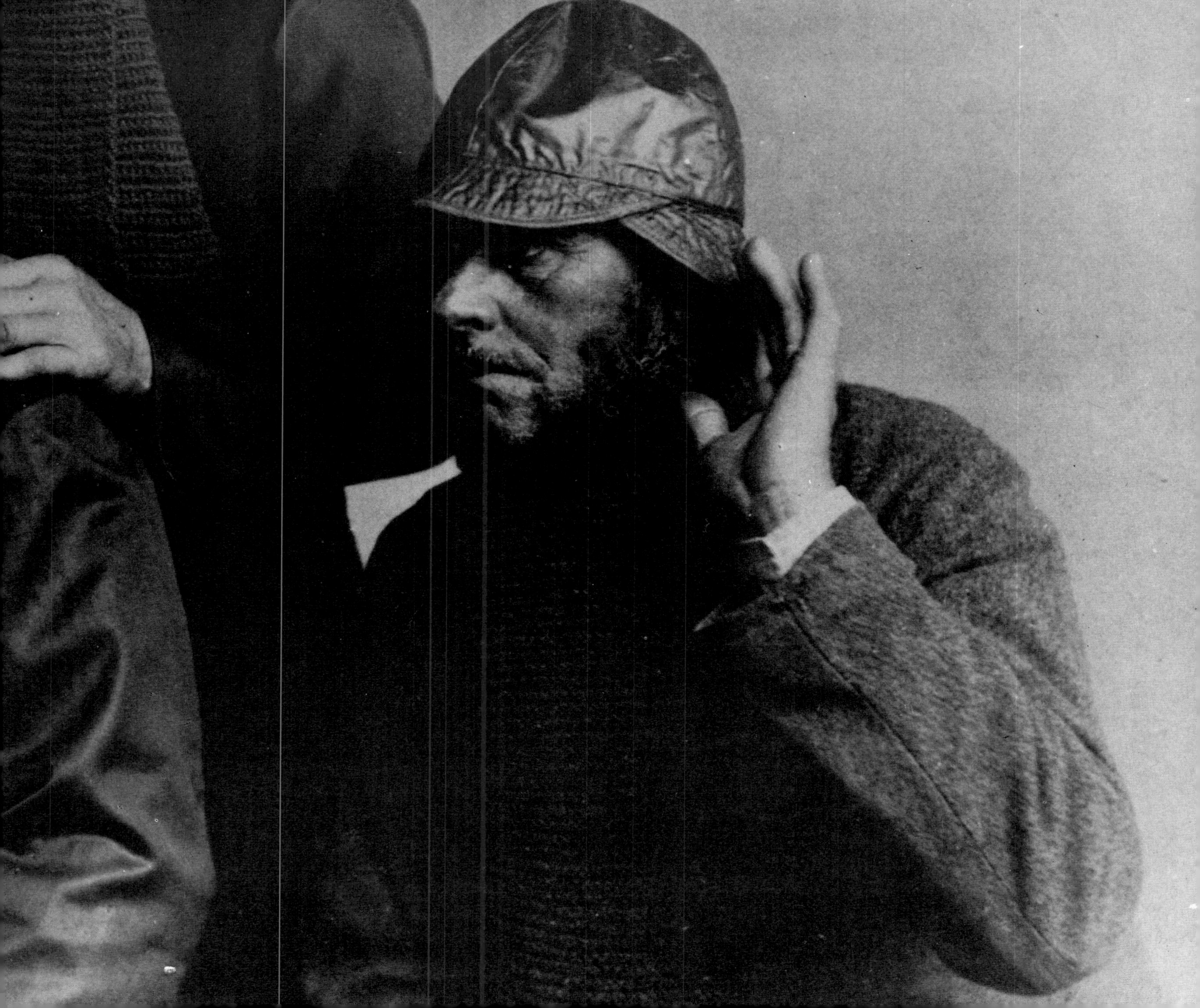

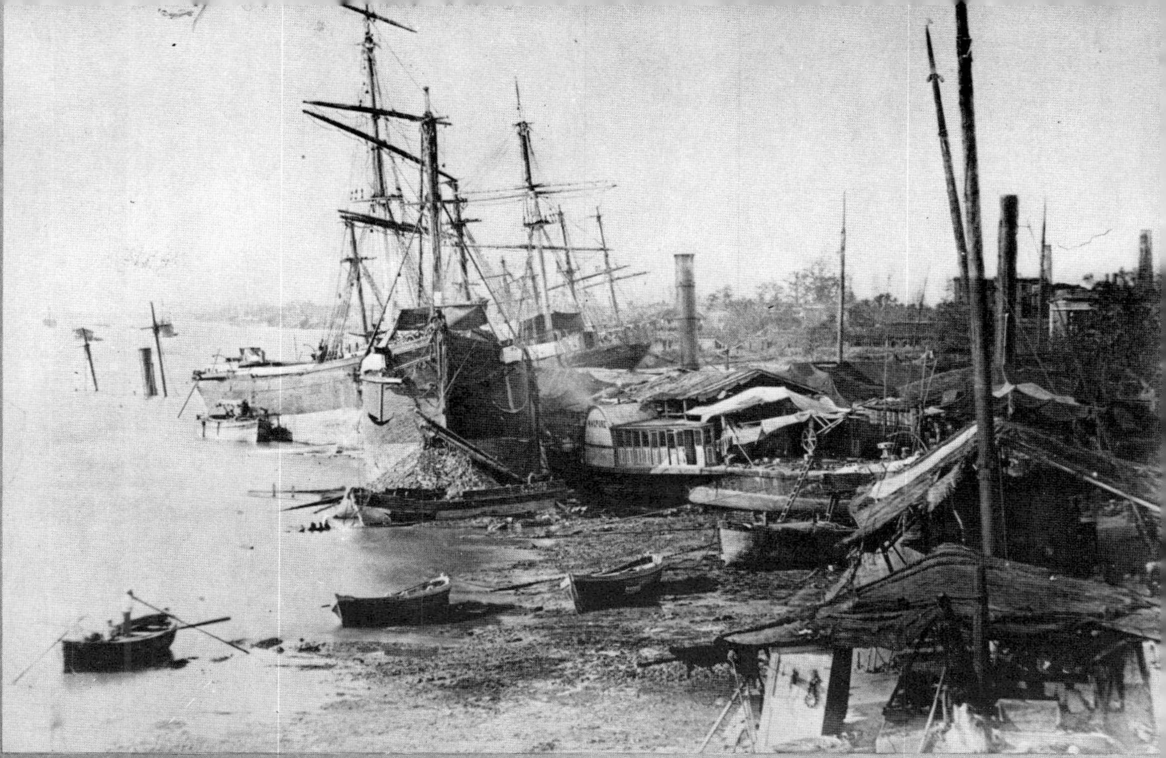

The debris of disaster after a bitter storm in the Bay of Bengal: the devastated harbour of Bombay photographed in 1856. Several steamers can be seen among the distressed vessels

The rugged coastline of Cornwall, traditional lair of the wreckers, maintained its fair share of wrecks. The Gibson family m

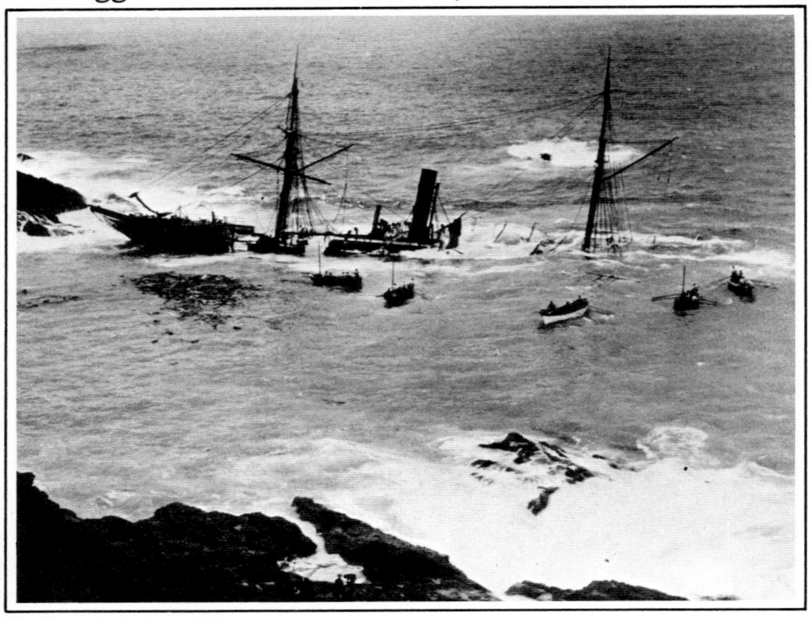

In October 1889 the S.S. Malta drove ashore in dense fog just south of Botallack Head, near St Just on the west coast of Cornwall. All on board were able to escape, but the ship was completely wrecked

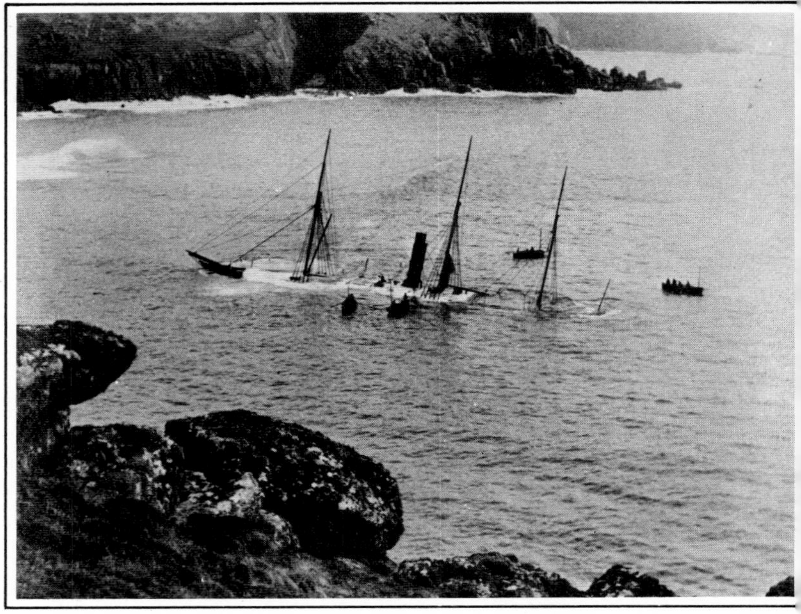

In 1884 the Cunard steamer Baalbec, bound for Le Havre from Liverpool, was holed when she struck a rock near the Longships, off Lands End. The captain ran her aground in Millbay Cove to save crew lives

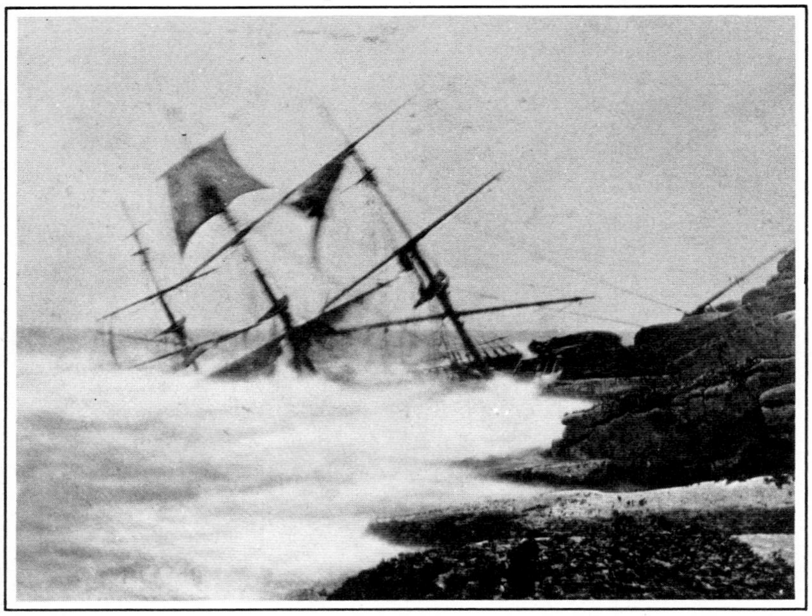

Ten men, including the captain, were drowned in 1871 when the four-masted barque Minnehaha was wrecked in thick fog on Peninnis Head in the Scillies. She was on her way from Falmouth to Dublin

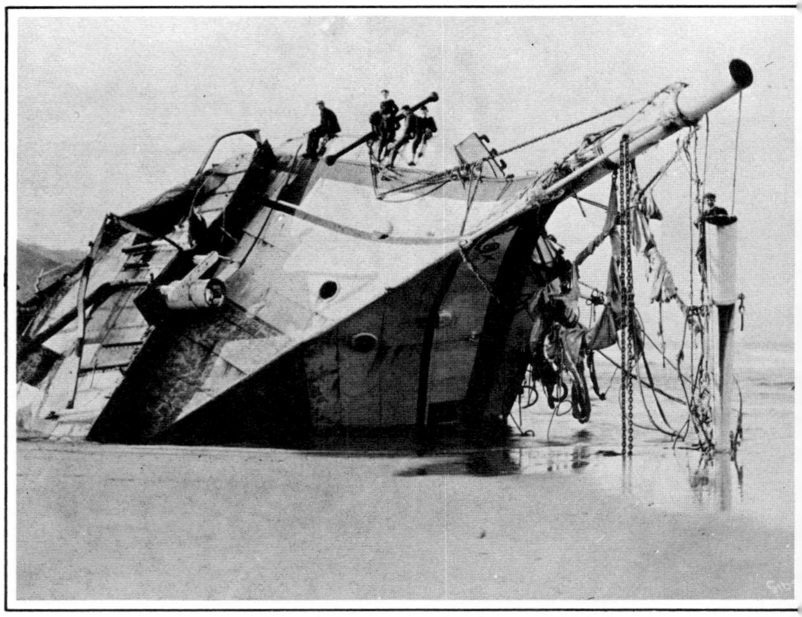

The wreckage of the French barque, the Seine, which came to grief at Perranporth in 1900. The vessel had been heading for Falmouth, carrying a cargo of saltpetre. The deck was torn away by the heavy seas

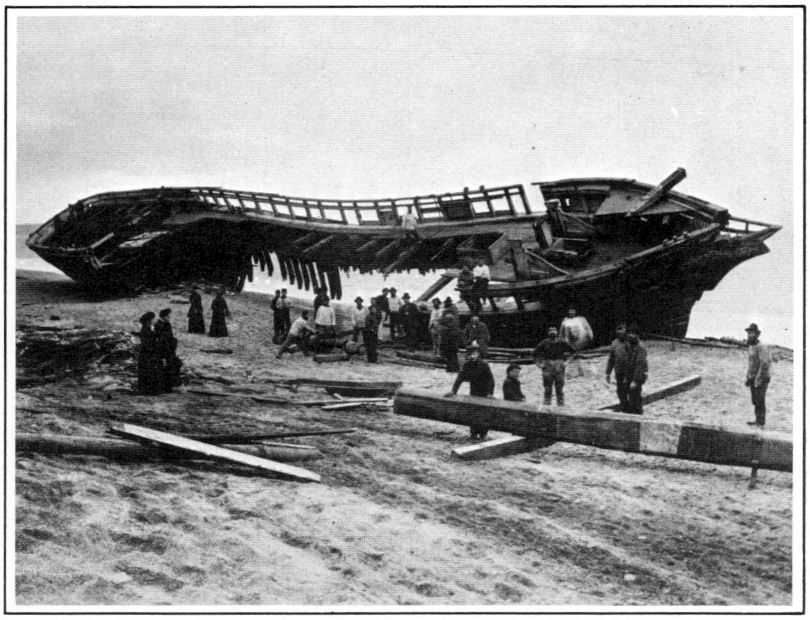

Wreckage of the Civet after a storm at Porthleven in 1884. Porthleven, a tiny seaport and fishing harbour midway between Penzance and the Lizard, was famed for the distinguished record of its lifeboatmen

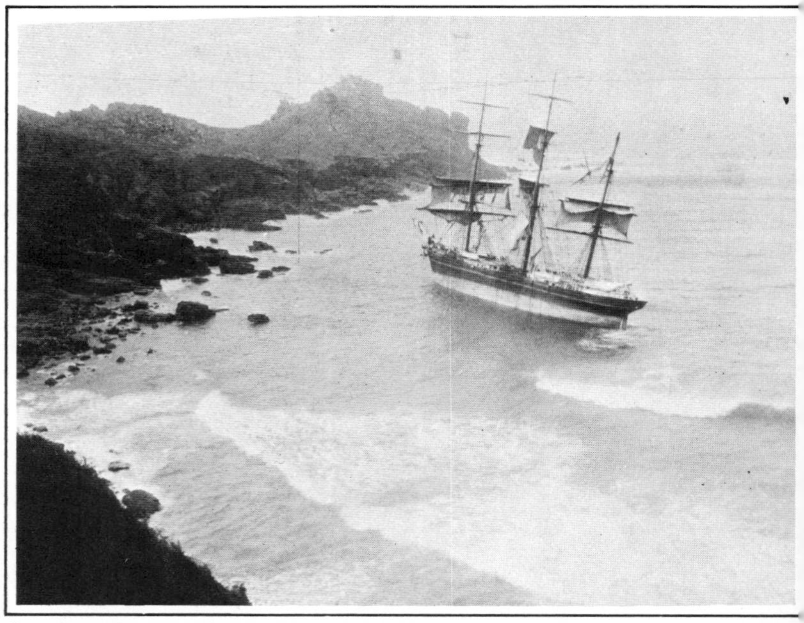

In 1896 Gurnard's Head was the scene of the wreck of the Alexander Yeats, bound from Georgia to Devonport with a cargo of pitch-pine. Fog and a north-west gale combined to drive the vessel aground

a practice of photographing every shipping disaster on the county's shores; all these pictures come from their early archives

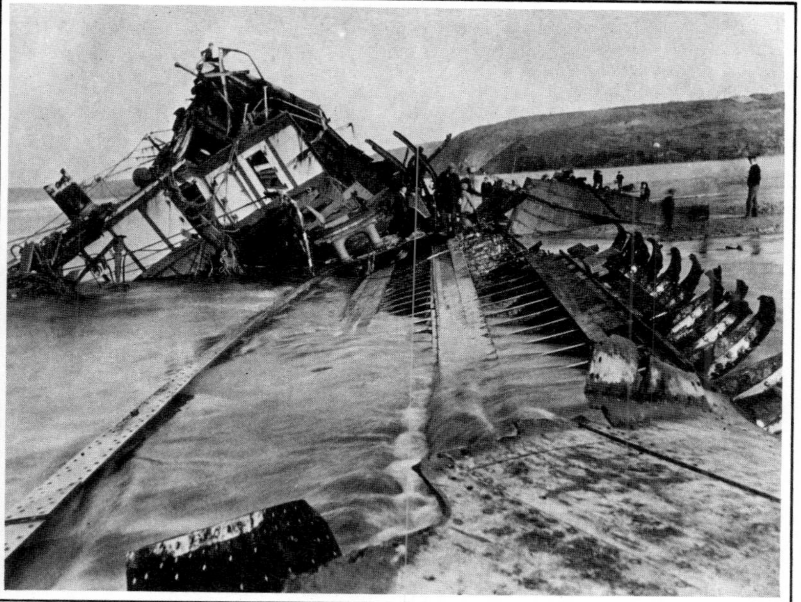

In November 1895 The Granite State, bound for Swansea from La Plata, was deliberately run aground near Porthcurno, after striking the Runnelstone Rocks. The seas broke up the ship the following day

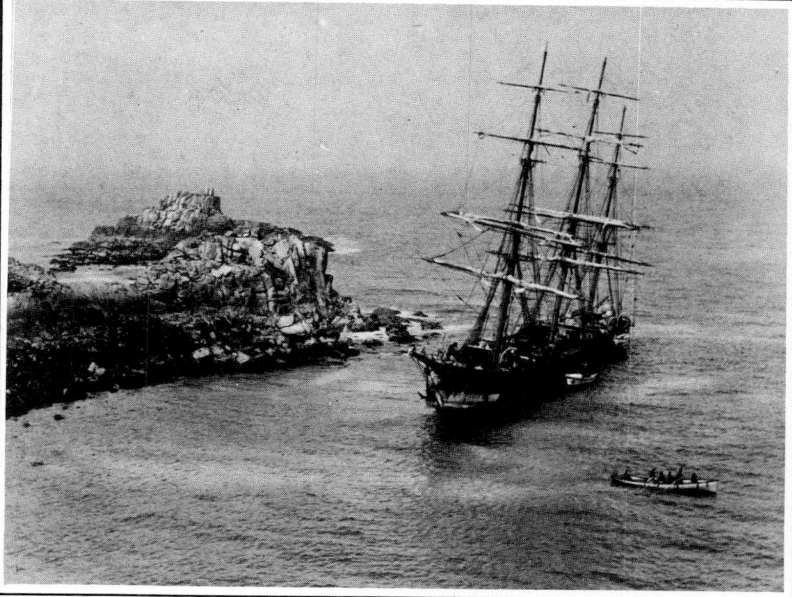

Aground off St Martin's, Isles of Scilly, in April 1893, is Horia, a full-rigged ship laden with grain. Attempts to refloat her were unsuccessful, and she foundered in deep water. All the crew were saved

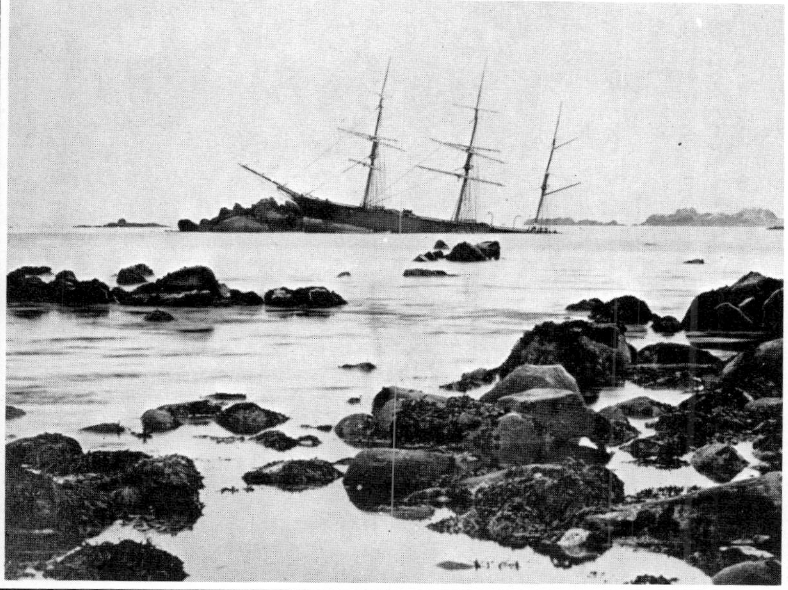

A dense summer fog claimed the Liverpool barque River Lune in July 1879. She foundered on rocks off the Scillies. All hands were saved, together with the ship's figurehead – now on the island of Tresco

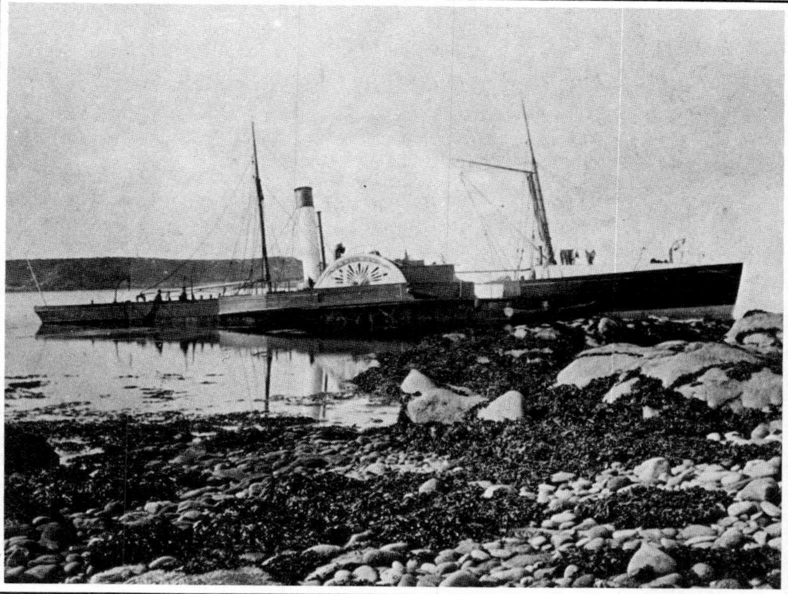

The Earl of Arran, a railway paddle-steamer, was wrecked after being washed on to the rocks of Normour in the Isles of Scilly in 1872. The rugged shoreline of the Scillies is the graveyard of many ships

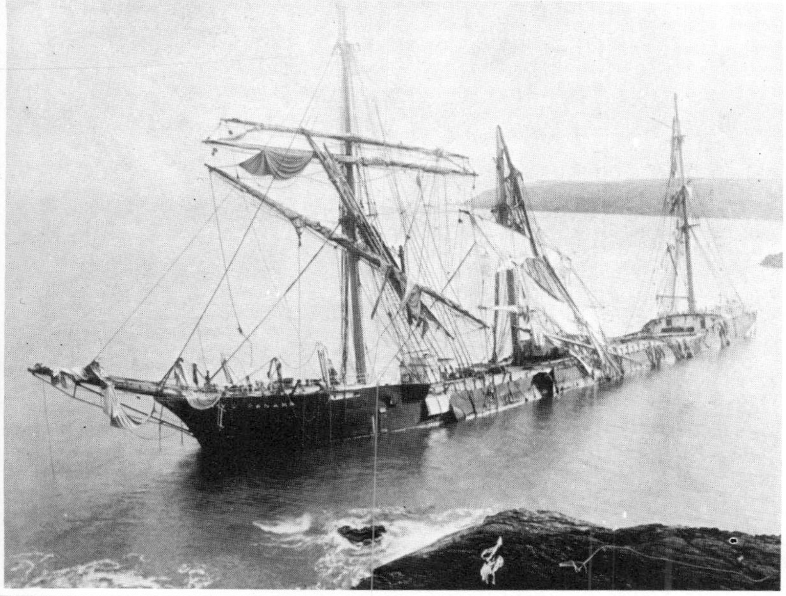

The Bay of Panama was wrecked on the Lizard in the great blizzard of March 1891. The bodies of most of the crew of this ship, bound for Glasgow with a cargo of jute, were found frozen to the rigging

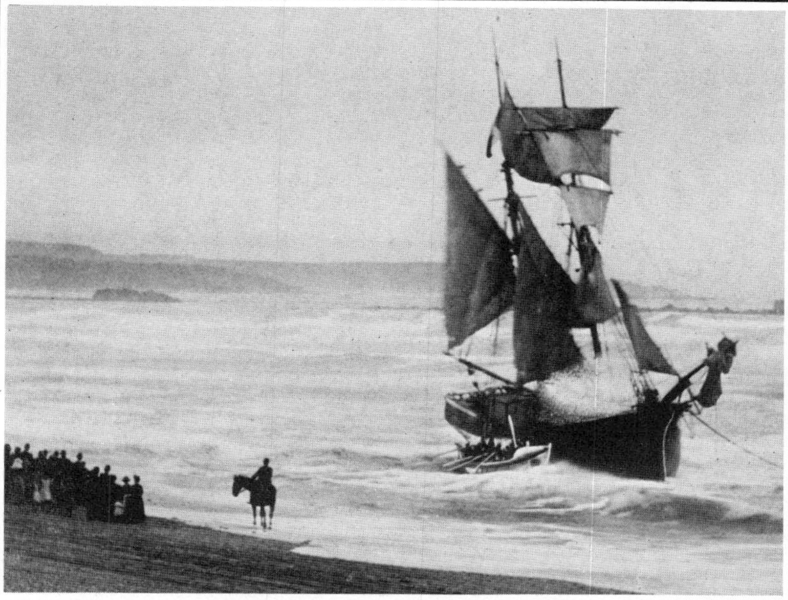

The Jeune Hortense, a French brig, went aground in a coastal gale at Penzance in 1886 and beached in the lee of St Michael's Mount. The local lifeboat, Dora, was brought up for the rescue by horse team

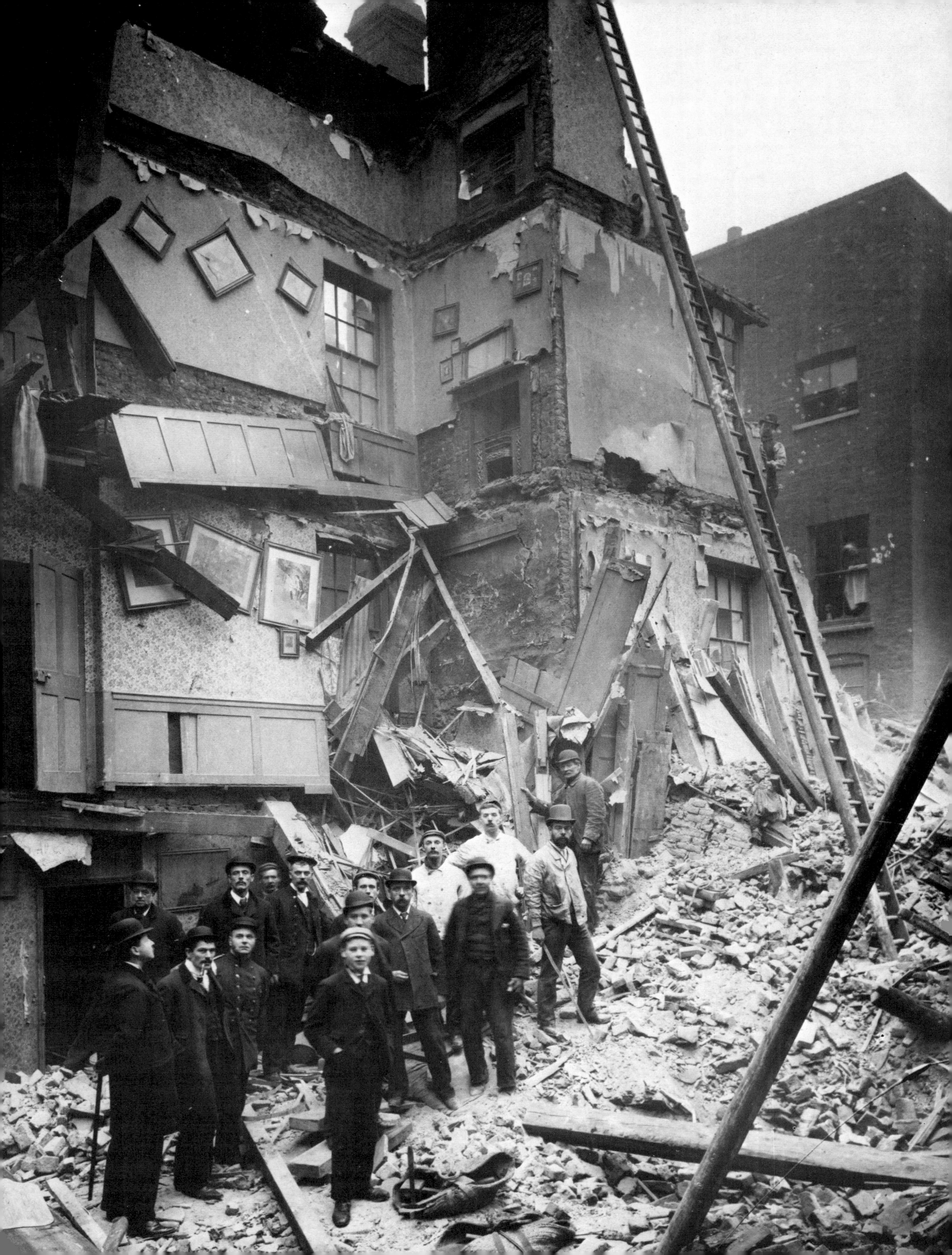

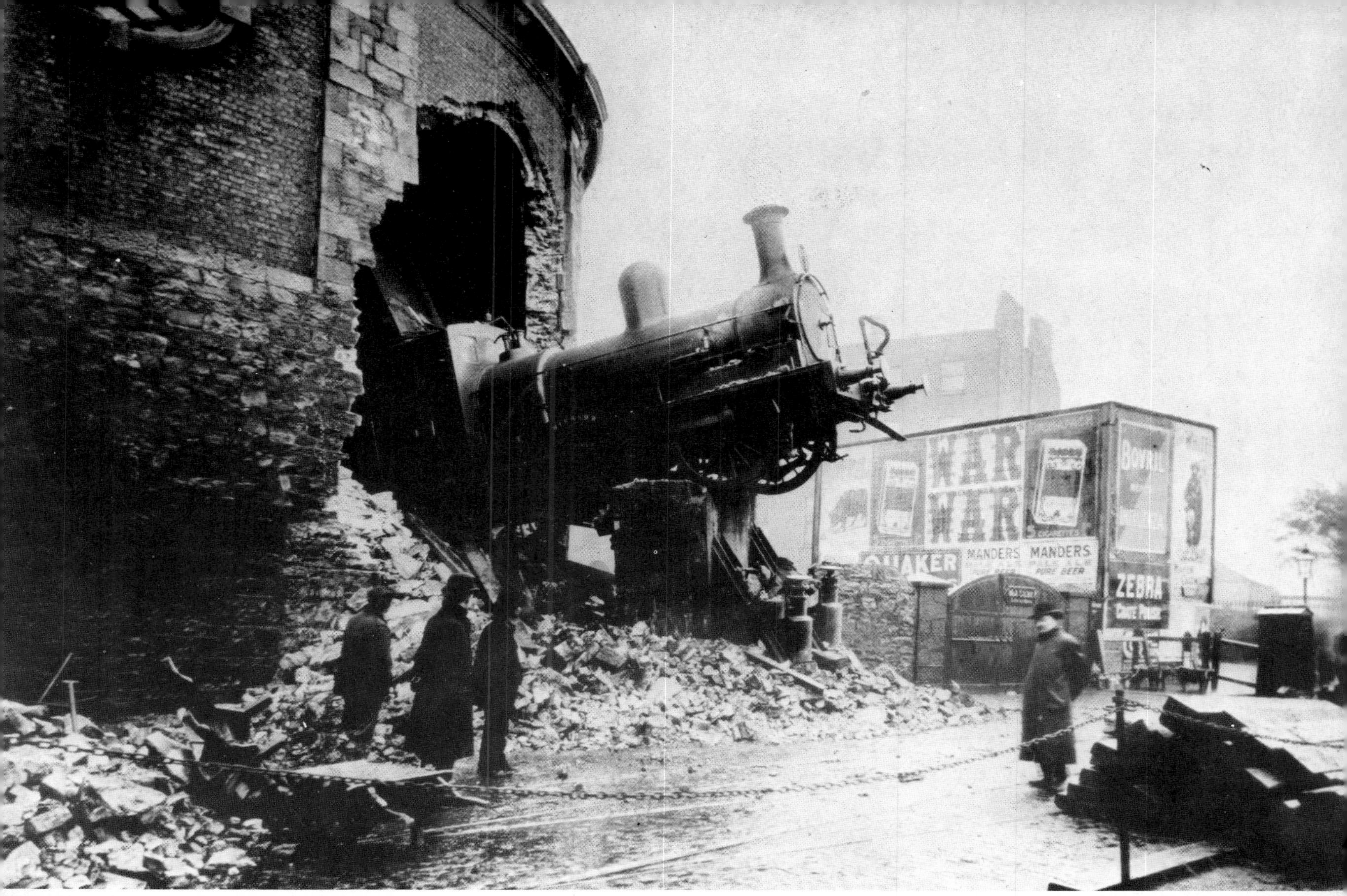
WAR
WAR
BOVRIL
MANDERS
MANDERS
ZEBRA

It was not only at sea that the Victorians faced disaster; pictures of other mishaps provide an uncanny preview of the Blitz – a devastating gas explosion in the Strand (left), a spectacular fire in the City of London (below) and a misdirected engine in Dublin (above). All-too-frequent pit accidents were bread and butter to lurid illustrators (right), but in 1899, when Mr Sewell and Major Nitrobe became the first motor fatalities (bottom), car accidents were a distinct novelty

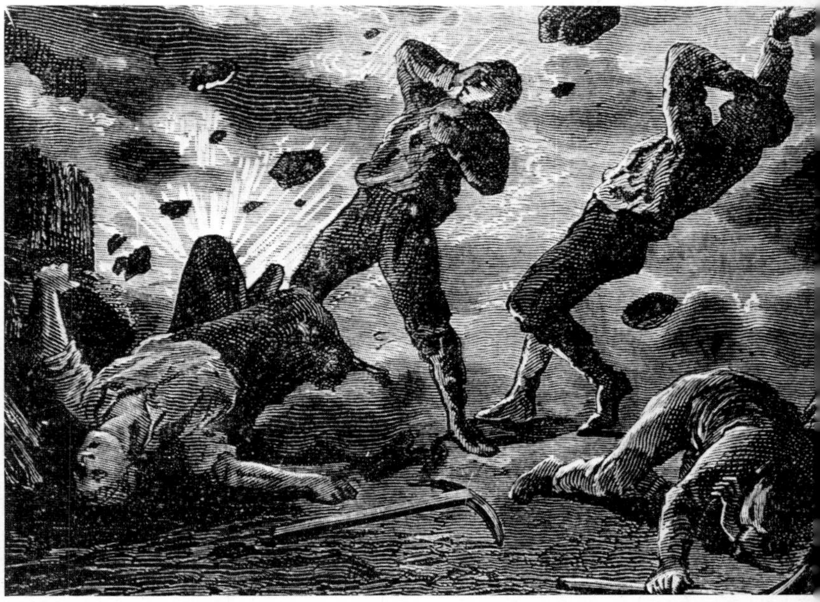

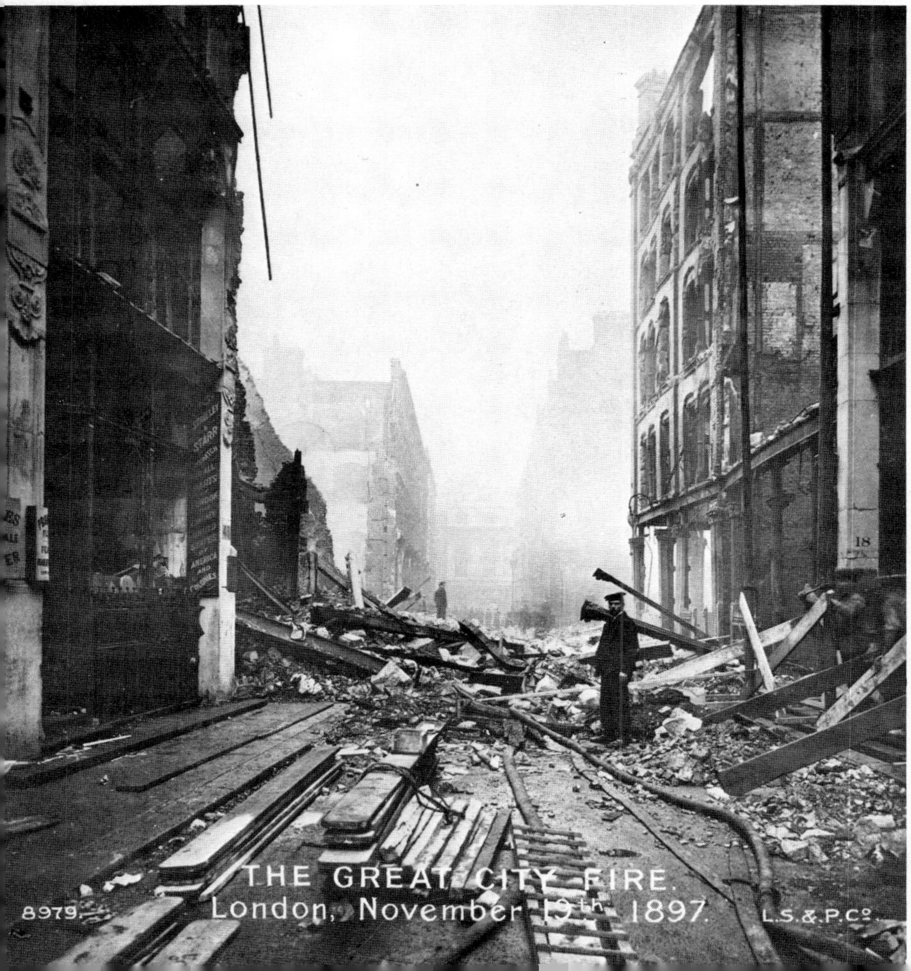
THE GREAT CITY FIRE.
London, November 19th 1897.
8979
L.S.&P.Co

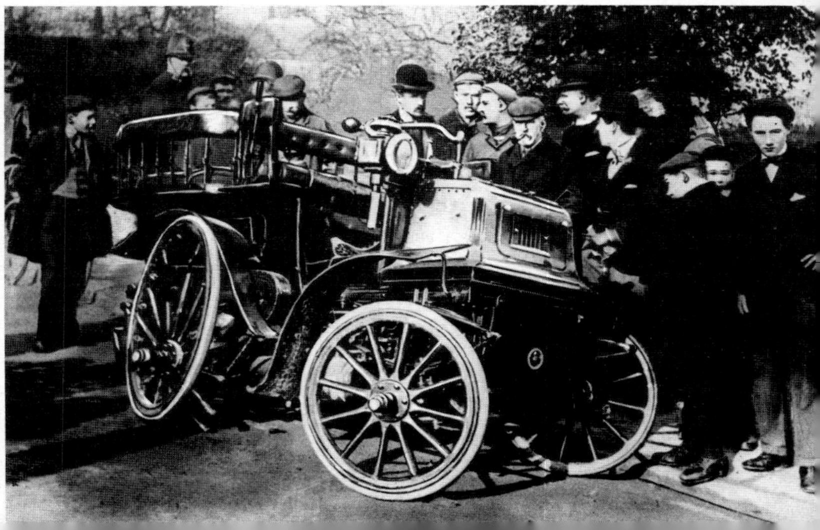

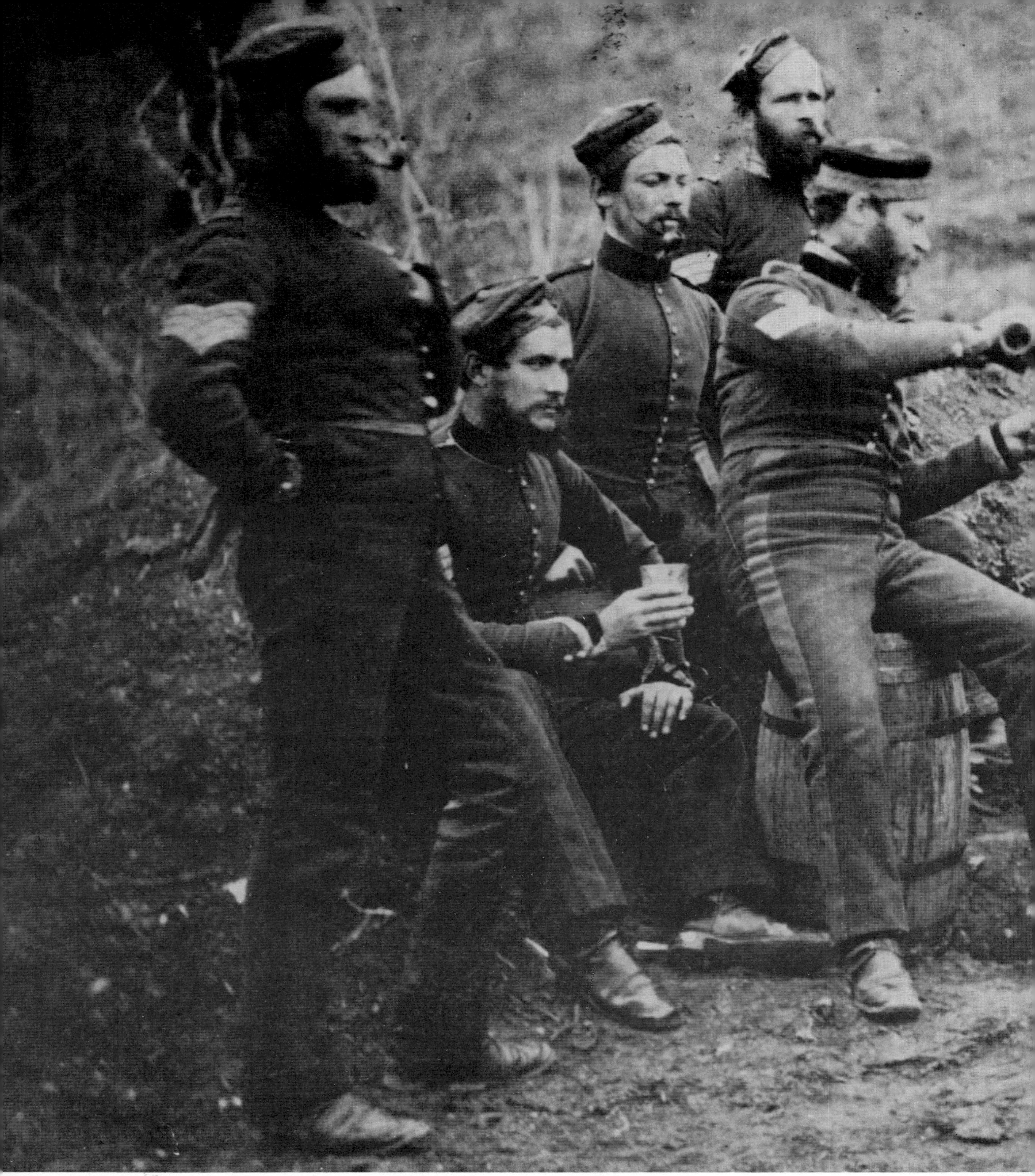

SOLDIERS OF THE QUEEN

By Graham Norton

The army changed in Victorian times from a rabble led by wealthy aristocrats into something approaching a professional fighting force. Before the Cardwell reforms commissions were generally purchased and private regiments equipped and maintained by members of the nobility, striving to outdo each other in the splendour of their uniforms. The British soldiers above, at the Crimea, are entertaining a French colleague and sampling the new-fangled cigarettes

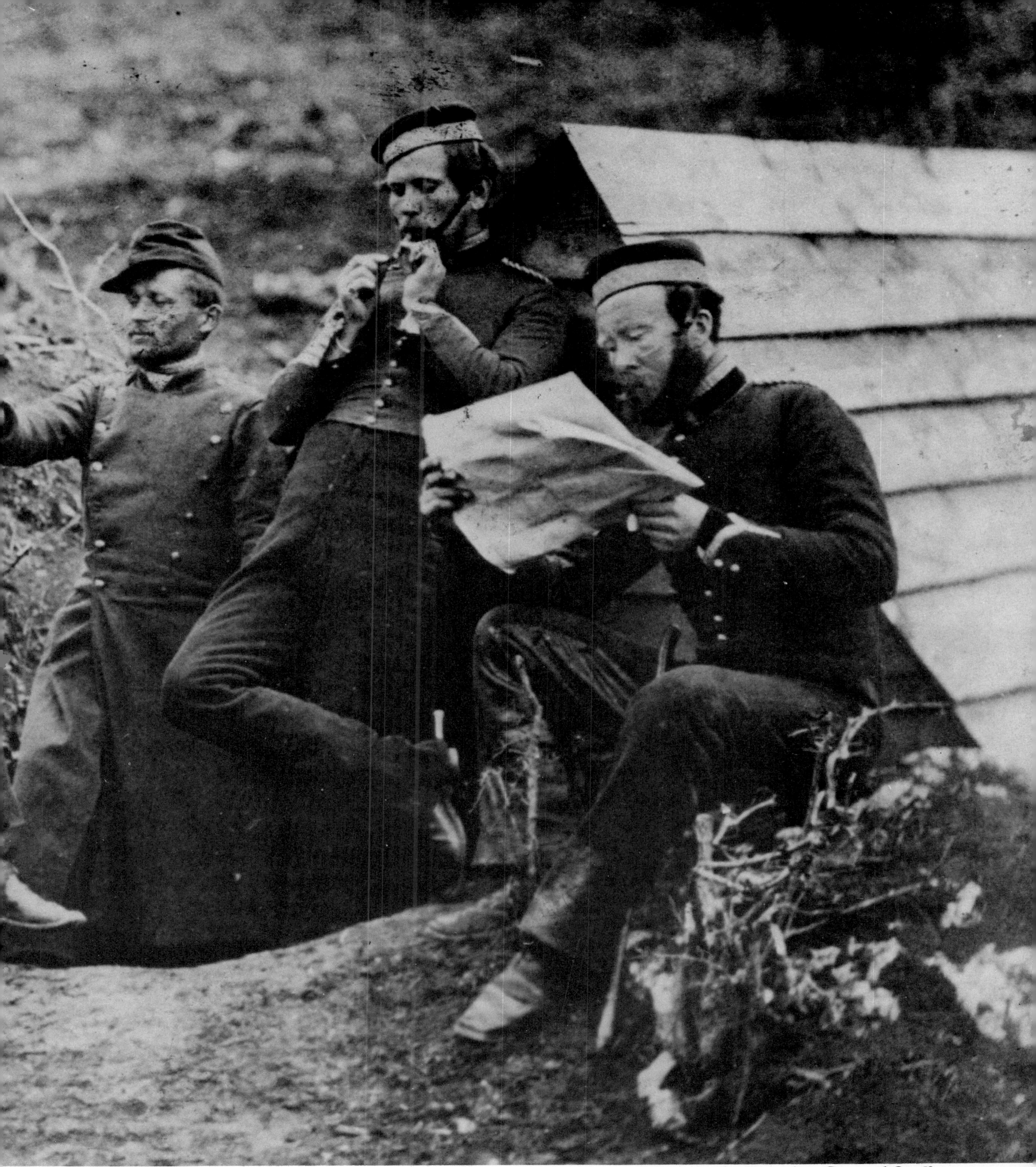

In 1864, when war was imminent between the German states and Denmark, Palmerston threatened to land the British army on the Prussian coast to block the invasion.

What, somebody asked Bismarck in Berlin, would he do if the British army landed? The reply was tart: "Send a policeman and have it arrested."

Queen Victoria's army held no terrors for the highly professional soldiers on the Prussian General Staff, or to the French who had been our allies and witnessed our logistic debacle in the Crimea. Military attachés, war correspondents and parliamentary committees had spelt out our humiliating incompetence to anyone who cared to read about it.

When the war broke out in 1854 the tough, flexible

Roger Fenton's famous study of Lord Raglan (seated) with his staff in the Crimea

weapon which had been Wellington's supreme creation had stood still for forty years. But, with its appropriations continually cut by cheese-paring Parliaments, something had to go. Wellington himself sacrificed his splendid commissariat, the supply and support of the whole army, so that at least the fighting regiments were able to survive.

It was a peacetime army. And it was an army of dandies. The trend was established after Waterloo – it was perhaps natural for the victors to preen themselves. But the royal head of this victorious force was the Prince Regent. He, who had never heard a shot fired in anger, infinitely preferred decorativeness to military efficiency. Uniforms became so tight that officers and privates alike could hardly get into them: "A wrinkle is unpardonable," said George.

Dandyism was not easily eradicated. The Earl of Lucan and the Earl of Cardigan commanded the cavalry at Balaclava. Beside their rank, they had other things in common. They were brothers-in-law; they had an undisguised hatred for each other; they were devoted to military show and had a martinet obsession with the details of drill. Cardigan led the Charge of the Light Brigade in the brilliant uniform of the 11th Hussars, a design that he had superintended in 1840. Then *The Times* had written: "The brevity of their jackets, the irrationality of their headgear, the incredible tightness of

their cherry-coloured pants altogether defy description." The *ensemble* was completed by little Hungarian jackets of royal blue, with thick gold embroidery on the front, and on the fur-trimmed pelisse slung over the left shoulder. It was a magnificent suit of clothes to meet death in, and for it Lord Cardigan paid hugely. On the uniforms for the troopers, and on horses for them better than the War Office could afford, he spent £10,000 a year.

Basically, the British political class preferred the army inefficient. It must never constitute a challenge to their own supremacy. The precautions they took were curious. Troops had to march out of any town where an election was taking place – a Secretary-at-War who failed to issue this order could be impeached. There was a prejudice against barracks; the army could be built up inside them without people knowing. So half the nation's soldiers were kept permanently under canvas, being moved into empty barns and similar places in very cold weather.

The doctrine of the old constitution – that only those who had property of their own could be trusted with any sort of power, "a stake in the country" it was usually called – applied to officers. It would be highly dangerous, Lord Palmerston said "if the connection between the army and the higher class of society were dissolved". The way would be opened to military adventurers.

He was defending the practice of the purchase of commissions. Officers usually paid cash, often at a public

The debris of the Crimea War. A shattered redoubt after bombardment

auction, for each step up in rank. Lord Cardigan paid a reputed £40,000 to become a colonel. Officers' pay was so low that it was quite inadequate for such purchases. Indeed, it might not be enough to pay the bills of the military tailor.

With few exceptions, a commission was confined to gentlemen of means. They often regarded the army as their private property, a lounge-annexe for their class. It faithfully reflected the values of the country gentry. The qualities of the fox-hunting man were those most admired in the mess. Such attitudes persisted until the end of the century, with the general exception of the Indian Army, the unfashionable garrison gunners ("They are all mad, married or Methodists" ran the jibe) and the highly professional corps of Royal Engineers.

Even after the shock of the Crimea the army went out of its way to appear unprofessional, to be the province of gallant but amateur gentlemen. Officers wore their uniform in public as rarely as possible, and the Household Brigade, so gorgeous on parade, changed into ordinary black evening clothes for the mess. An ethos more different from continental armies, particularly the Prussian, could not be imagined.

But it was also very different from the approach to life which we identify as 'Victorian' – a belief in progress, in science, a religious seriousness, professionalism.

After 1851 the middle class became convinced that the whole need for an army would shortly be outdated. The Great Exhibition was the herald of an era of universal peace. We would never again fight a civilised power. In any case, we had the navy to protect us. All Victorian books on the army make it plain that the army came a poor second to the Royal Navy in its importance to national defence.

But sometimes an army was needed. And as the reports streamed back from the Crimea, the first war in history to be fully reported – the circulation of *The Times* and the *Illustrated London News* rocketed – the middle class and Members of Parliament asked: But need the army be like *this*?

The great scandal, an army decimated not by enemy action, but by bungling and inefficiency, by lack of food, of proper clothing, of medical supplies, demanded action. In the middle of war, reforms were made. For the first time in her history, Britain now had a minister solely responsible for the army – the Secretary of State for War. Before, the army had been divided between seven departments.

Only the Commander-in-Chief, Queen Victoria's cousin George, Duke of Cambridge, remained outside the system. His royalness was often to be regretted, for he later became an arch-conservative and remained at his his post until 1895. He was usually strongly supported by the Queen, who felt that she had a very special relation-

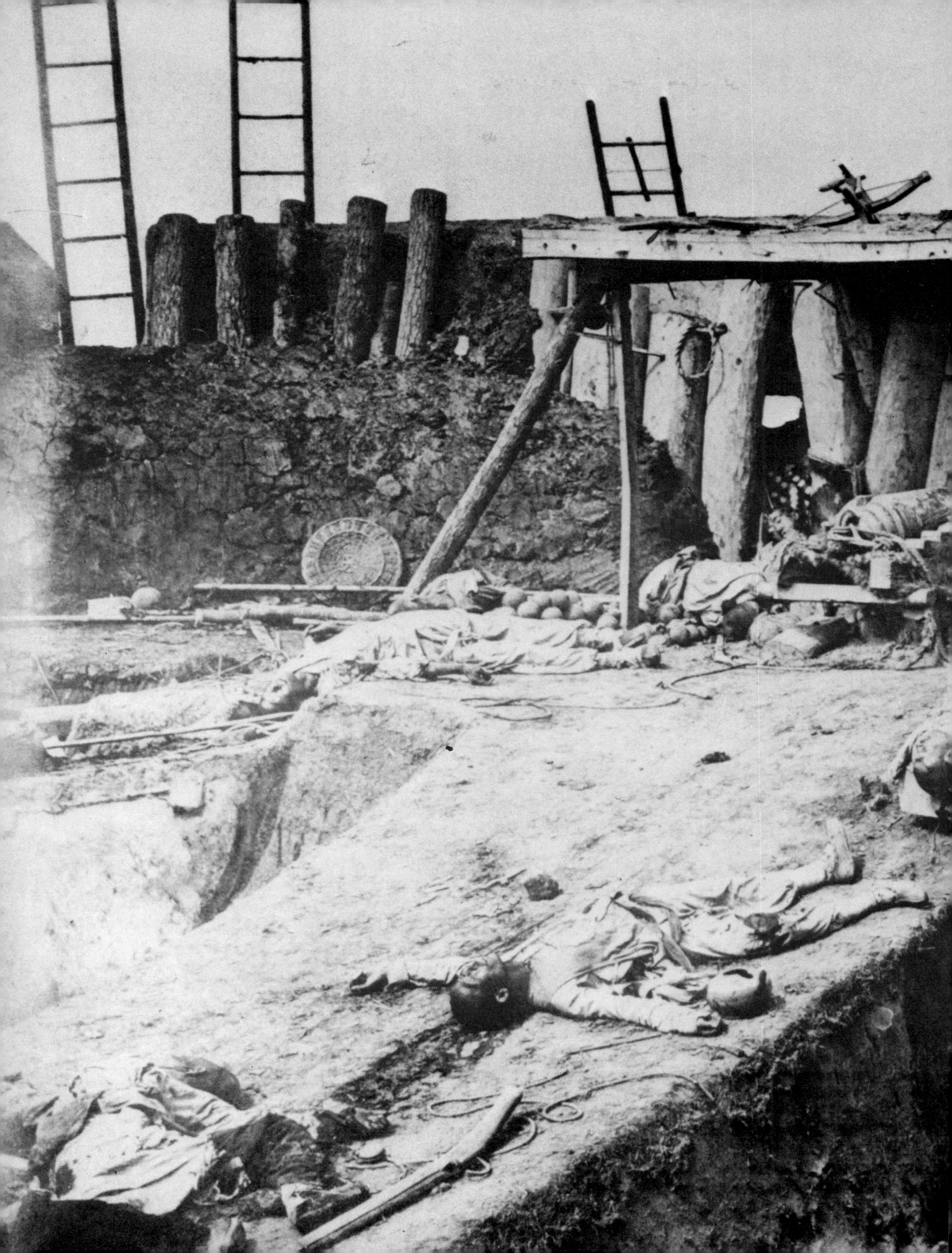

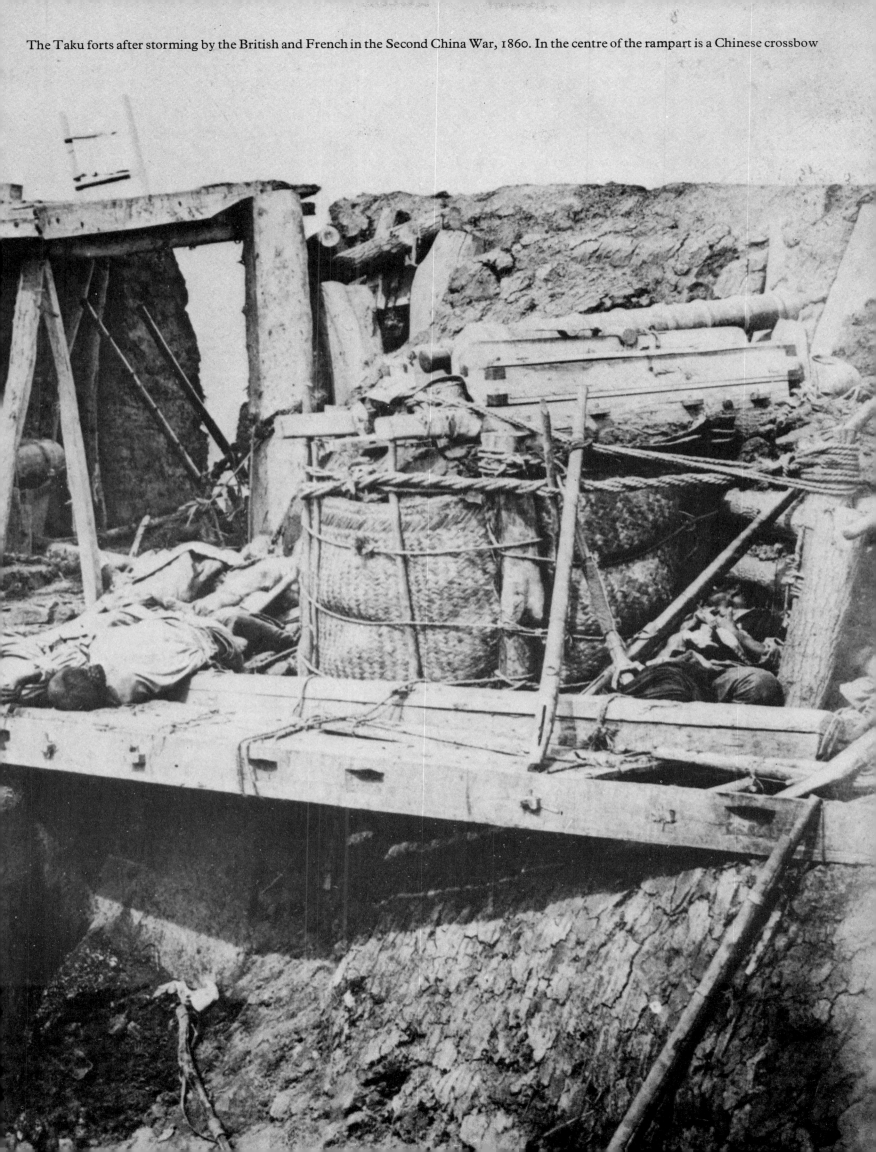

The Taku forts after storming by the British and French in the Second China War, 1860. In the centre of the rampart is a Chinese crossbow

Army life could still be hazardous. This is the last picture of Major Sir Louis Cavaguari, murdered at Kabul in 1879

ship with *her* army, and having a member of the family as C.-in-C. drove the point home.

But the younger Cambridge set up the Camberley Staff College in 1857. A great period of military building began. Barracks rose in the garrison towns. The Woolwich Royal Arsenal was doubled in size, and Aldershot was laid out. The avenues and buildings within that huge military encampment were to be named after the great army towns in India.

Before the Indian Mutiny, India was administered by the Honourable East India Company, one of those chartered companies which had advanced the frontiers of empire since the 17th century. It had an army of 10,000 European troops and 230,000 natives, divided between three Presidencies. Fortunately, only the sepoys of Bengal mutinied, but it took from 1857 to 1859 to subdue them.

There was also a separate, regular British army establishment in India, of 30,000 men. On these 'Queen's troops' rested the brunt of the early stages of the Mutiny, the defence of Lucknow and Delhi, the treacherous massacre of Cawnpore.

The mutiny was a dreadful reminder of the dangers that the handful of British faced in the great subcontinent. Never again could they relax. Native troops were not to outnumber Europeans in Bengal again by more than two to one.

The aftermath was bloody. Sepoys were drawn up on countless parades to witness who was master. There

were executions. The rebel gunners suffered the regulation British army penalty: strapped down alive over the muzzles of their own guns, they were blown to pieces. They were the last Indian gunners. Never again were natives permitted to be artillerymen.

India would now be the army's strategic base for operations in the East. Though the mid-Victorian consensus held that Free Trade had made the empire an encumbrance and it would soon wither away this just did not happen. The army was to be kept busy, suppressing uprisings – even in Canada, with the Red River expedition in 1870 – and bringing to account those who dared to twist the lion's tail. When imperialism came back into fashion in the 1880s, it expanded the frontiers of empire by its conquests. And it mounted punitive expeditions, like those to Abyssinia and China.

British merchants had long wished for access to the Chinese market. So had the French. Opium was a significant item of the trade, grown in India by the Honourable East India Company, taxed on export to provide a significant contribution to the Government of India's revenues. The Third China War of 1860 – the last of the so-called Opium Wars – was a result of the refusal of the Chinese to ratify the trading concessions they had granted as a result of previous encounters with European arms. An attempt by a British admiral to convey diplomatic representatives up the Peiho with the treaty for the Emperor's signature was repulsed by the Taku forts at the river's mouth.

British and Sikh officers at the time of the Indian Mutiny. Only the Bengalis rebelled

This could not be allowed. Troops were sent from India and the Cape of Good Hope. Great attention was paid this time to medical matters, with a fleet of well-equipped hospital ships standing offshore. The Taku forts were a formidable example of Chinese military architecture. Their walls were high and thick, and were protected by two broad ditches. The ground before them was studded with sharp bamboo spikes. Allied tactics were to land north of the forts and bombard them from landward. For the first time, the British army used breech-loading field guns – Armstrong 12-pounders, with rifled barrels. Some of these blew up, and the British army, alone in Europe, reverted to muzzle-loaders.

The artillery punched holes in the walls of the forts, the infantry swam the ditches, swarmed up the scaling ladders and raised their colours triumphantly on the ramparts. Many of the Chinese gunners lay dead at their posts. They had touched off their cannon with port-fires of smouldering rope, which they attached to their wrists; the story circulated that they were tied to their guns to stop them running away. A howl went up for the army. Regiments in many of the self-governing colonies were brought back. Fortifications were built around the coasts. Volunteers drilled.

The Franco-Prussian war provided the final frightening lesson. In 1871, Cardwell's Army Act began a great and cumulative era of army reform. The purchase of commissions was abolished. (Thrown out by the Lords, the bill was accomplished by the use of the Royal Prerogative.) The curious rule which gave ranks in the Guards a higher equivalent in the line – a Guards captain held the army rank of Lt-Colonel, out-ranking all other regiments' majors – was dispensed with.

The essence of Cardwell's measures lay in recruitment and in the reserve. The old line regiments lost their numbers, and were re-christened with the names of counties. They were then linked with county militia in a common organisation based on a local depot. There were now to be four battalions to a regiment, two regular and two militia, and it was envisaged that one regular battalion would always be away, usually in India, though colonial wars and troubles in Ireland meant that both were often absent. Enlistment was to be for twelve years, six with the colours and six with the reserve.

The last punitive expedition that the old army of numbered regiments undertook was the Abyssinian War. It was a splendid success, and did a great deal to restore army morale. It also earned it the respect of opinion at home and abroad. A great deal of the credit was due to Sir Robert Napier, the C.-in-C., a sapper who had been commanding in Bombay.

The Emperor Theodore of Abyssinia had imprisoned the British Consul and a number of missionaries and other Europeans in his remote fortress of Magdala, located among a range of almost inaccessible mountains 300 miles inland from the Red Sea. Napier's first task was to get to the Europeans and rescue them before Theodore could himself get to Magdala and put them to

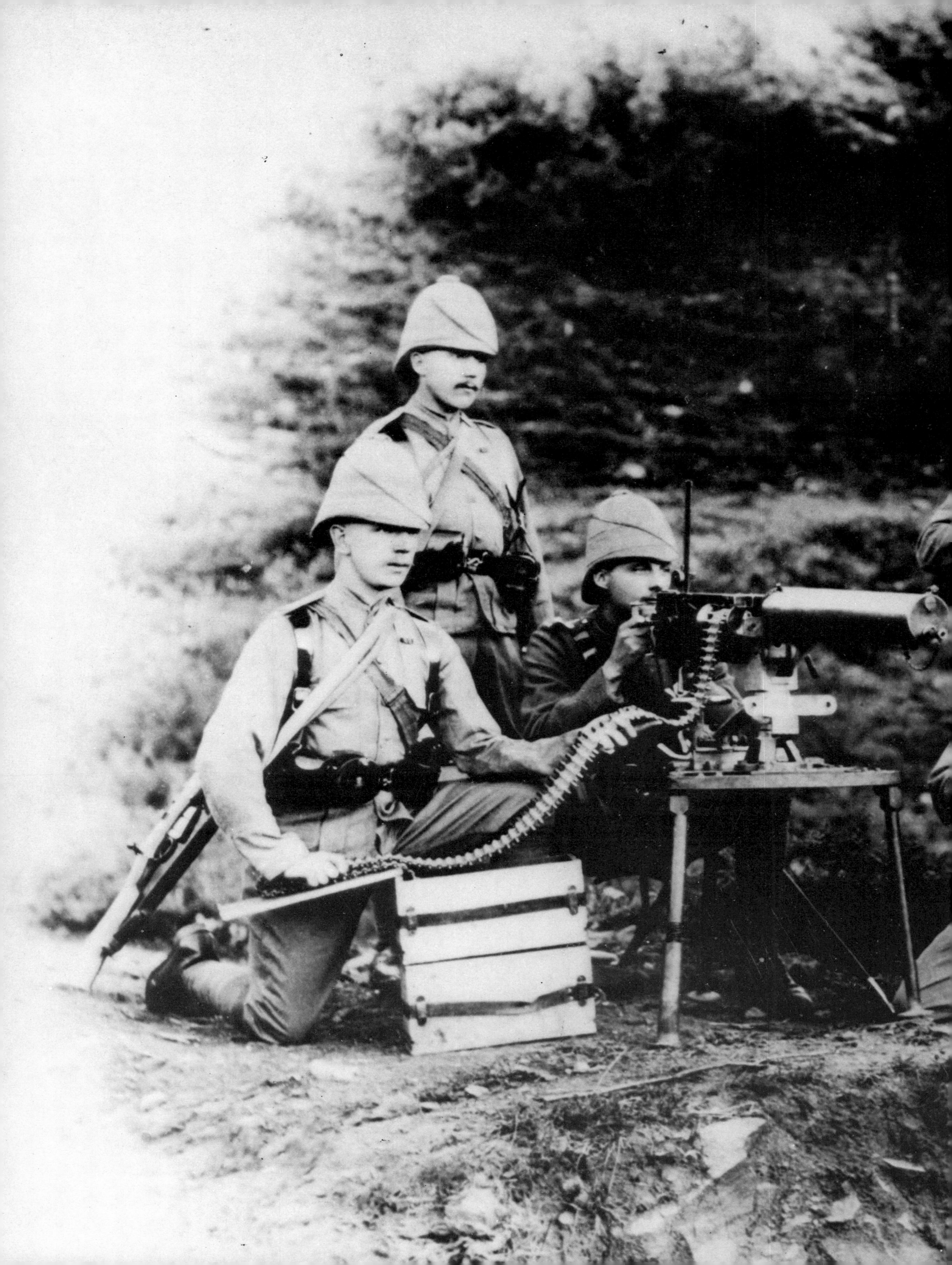

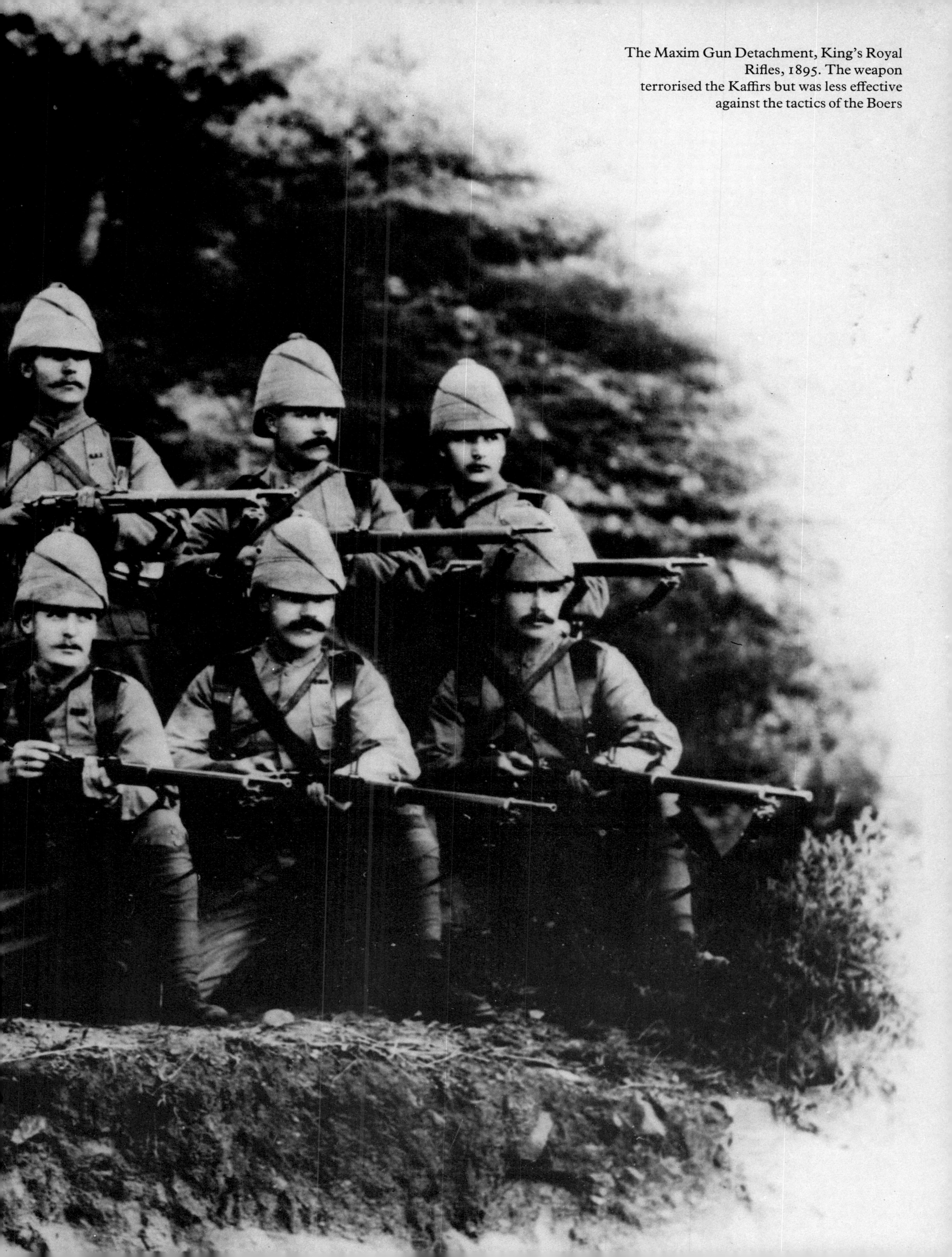

The Maxim Gun Detachment, King's Royal Rifles, 1895. The weapon terrorised the Kaffirs but was less effective against the tactics of the Boers

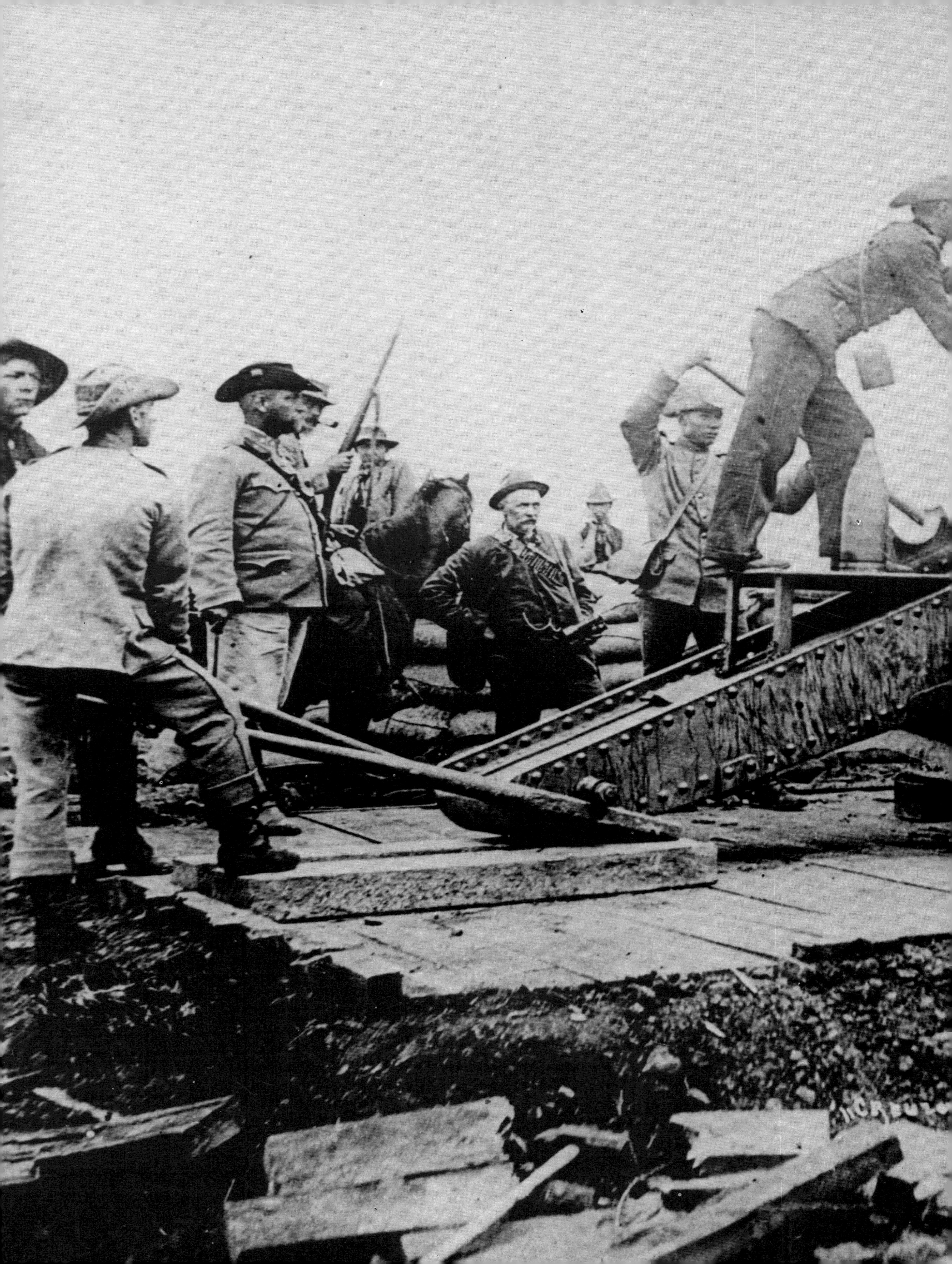

The Boers bombarded Mafeking almost daily with Long Tom. Baden-Powell returned their fire with an improvised cannon

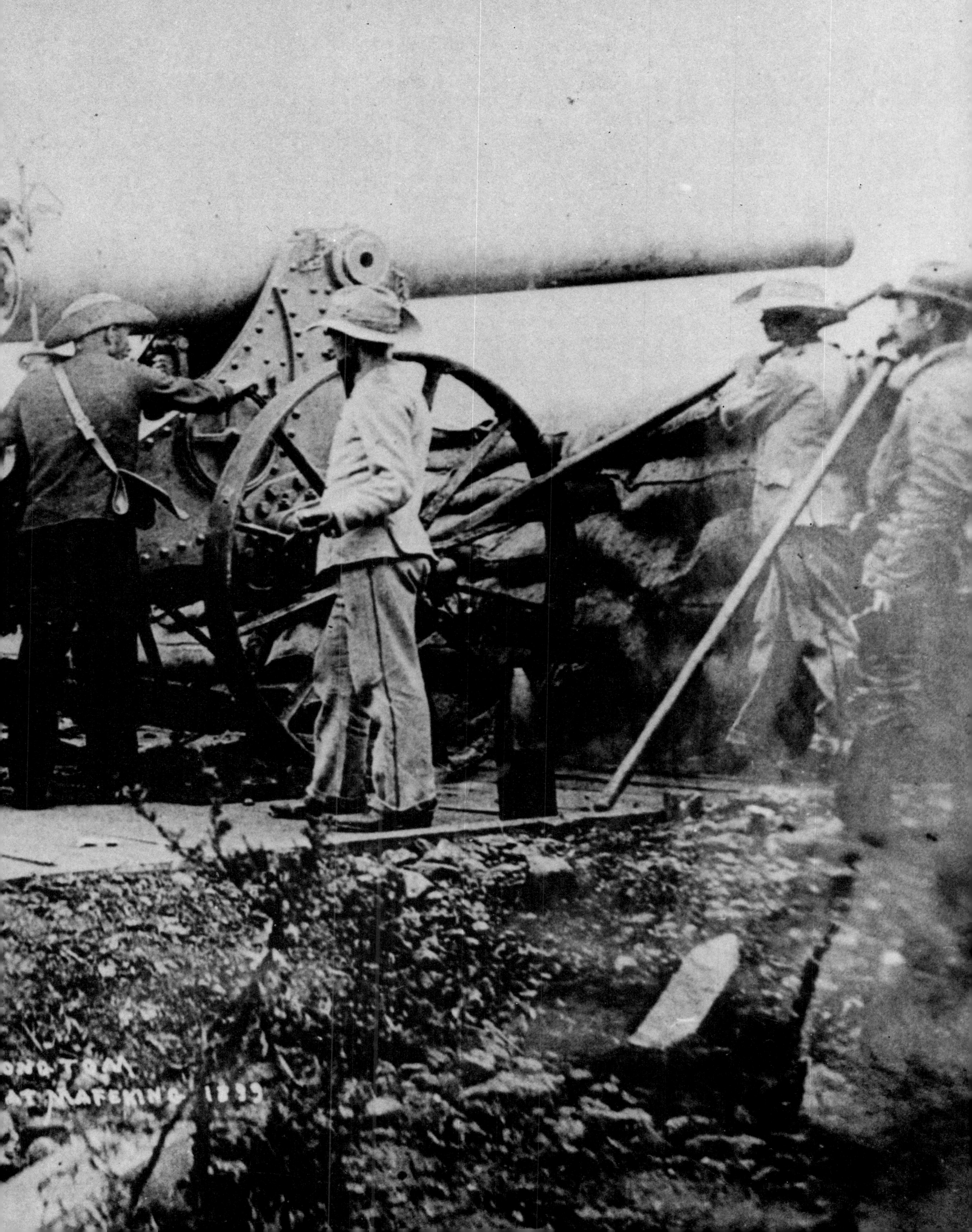
ONG TOM
AT MAFEKING 1899

Colonel Pilcher with his officers, after action at Sunnyside in the Boer War

death. It was the first time that an Engineer had been appointed G.-in-C. in the field, and Napier mounted his expedition scientifically. Though the terrain was difficult, he laid a field telegraph, built a short railway and carried advanced equipment to bore wells. Water on the arid coast was provided by steam condensers. There was even a sort of 'Mulberry Harbour' made of iron.

Though the Emperor won the race to the fortress, when confronted by Napier's force he gave up his prisoners in an attempt to placate the British. But Napier demanded his surrender, and on it being refused Magdala was stormed. Theodore shot himself through the mouth with an elaborately mounted pistol – a present from Queen Victoria.

The experience gained in China and Abyssinia was drawn upon by the brightest rising star in the whole army, Garnet Wolseley, a General at 40. He had himself been at Taku. In his *Soldier's Pocket-Book*, which he first published in 1869, he set out to provide a practical and portable book which dealt in minute detail with the likely duties required of an officer in the field from the moment war was declared. No better picture of the Victorian army can be found.

Wolseley, an infantryman from an impoverished Anglo-Irish family, had earned his promotions largely on active service (where purchase did not apply). As an Ensign in his teens he first went to war in the 1852 Burma campaign, fighting in the steamy heat of the jungle wearing white buckskin gloves and a thick scarlet jacket buttoned close under the chin. In the *Pocket-Book* he campaigns for a more sensible uniform, suggesting an adaption of the Norfolk jacket. The modern army uniform clearly descends from this aristocratic shooting garment. Wolseley was satirised as a "know-all" – he was W. S. Gilbert's "Modern Major-General" – but he was determined to make the army efficient and humane.

In his book he impresses officers to treat their men well, and to share their discomforts and burdens. "We have been too much educated to believe the British soldier is simply a machine, incapable of noble impulses." Such impressions must be eradicated. There was an art in getting the best out of the men, so that they, like the good officer, will covet honour and perform daring deeds.

It was not only the men who had to be looked after. Transport in the British army meant pack-animals, and at the commencement of every campaign the mule-raising districts of the world, particularly the Levant, were scoured for the animals and their drivers, both of which were an invariable source of continuing trouble. Wolseley's preference would have been for light horse-drawn vehicles. Traction engines had been tried; usually the inclines were too much for them, but he had hopes for a make called the "Steam Sapper". The ways of bullocks, elephants and camels are discussed, and of course "in many of our small wars transport coolies have played a notable part".

An officer should know how to make army tack as palatable as possible. In the field, each soldier was

Lord Kitchener enters Johannesburg in triumph after defeating the Boers

allowed 1½lb of salt meat, 1lb of bread, 2oz of compressed vegetables, and before an action, as a treat, 4oz of sausage and a dram of rum. This seemed as plentiful as it was in the navy – not a thing Wolseley liked.

In the Ashanti War of 1873, the first major expedition he commanded, Wolseley picked his staff for their energy, quickness of mind and courage. The war was a model of its kind, not only a triumph over savage arms, but economical as well – he managed it on £800,000, less than a tenth of the cost of the Abyssinian adventure.

With honours heaped upon him, Wolseley rose in the high command. From now on the army was to be continuously occupied abroad. In the ten years after the Ashanti campaign there was the Duffla expedition in the Naga Hills, Perak, Barbados (to quell riots), the Jowakhi campaign, the Ninth Kaffir War, the Zulu War. the Second Afghan War, the First South African War, the Egyptian War, the Suakin Expedition, and the Sudanese War in which Wolseley, who had seen his old friend Gordon off at the station, was unable to reach him before the fall of Khartoum. Gladstone's delay in mounting the relief expedition was blamed.

Wolseley became C.-in-C. in 1895, H.R.H. the Duke of Cambridge being at last removed. He and the select band who had accompanied him to Ashanti and who were known, particularly by their opponents, as the 'Ring' now set about bringing their ideas on the modern army into practice. Africa, now that reborn imperialism was partitioning the continent, was a principal concern.

In Southern Africa, gold and diamonds, an immense wealth of minerals had been found. The Matabele and Bechuana were cowed. Cape to Cairo – it could be done. Kitchener, an R.E. officer with a ruthlessness no other general possessed, reconquered the Sudan.

Wolseley put the army into khaki, but by the time the Second Boer War broke out in 1899 his ideas had made little impact on the two-edged regimental system. It was strong – so strong that men would die for their regiment. But this devotion also meant resistance to any change in cherished tradition. The early stages of the Boer War bore a resemblance to Wolseley's criticism of a Kaffir War in the conduct of the generals, who commanded "in a slow barrack-yard field-day fashion, although strictly according to regulation". It led to disaster at the hands of the Boer farmers.

Lord Roberts and Kitchener went in. Better tactics were improvised. As Queen Victoria lay dying in January 1901 she knew that her confidence in her army was justified . . . the possibility of defeat no longer existed.

What she would have said as the war dragged on, and Kitchener pushed the Boer women and children into internment camps, no one knows. She would have disliked intensely the massive public inquest that followed, a Royal Commission on the war. It was a general indictment of the army. It was fortunate, coming when it did, the Boer War. There were just ten years to rectify the system, ten years to prepare for Armageddon.

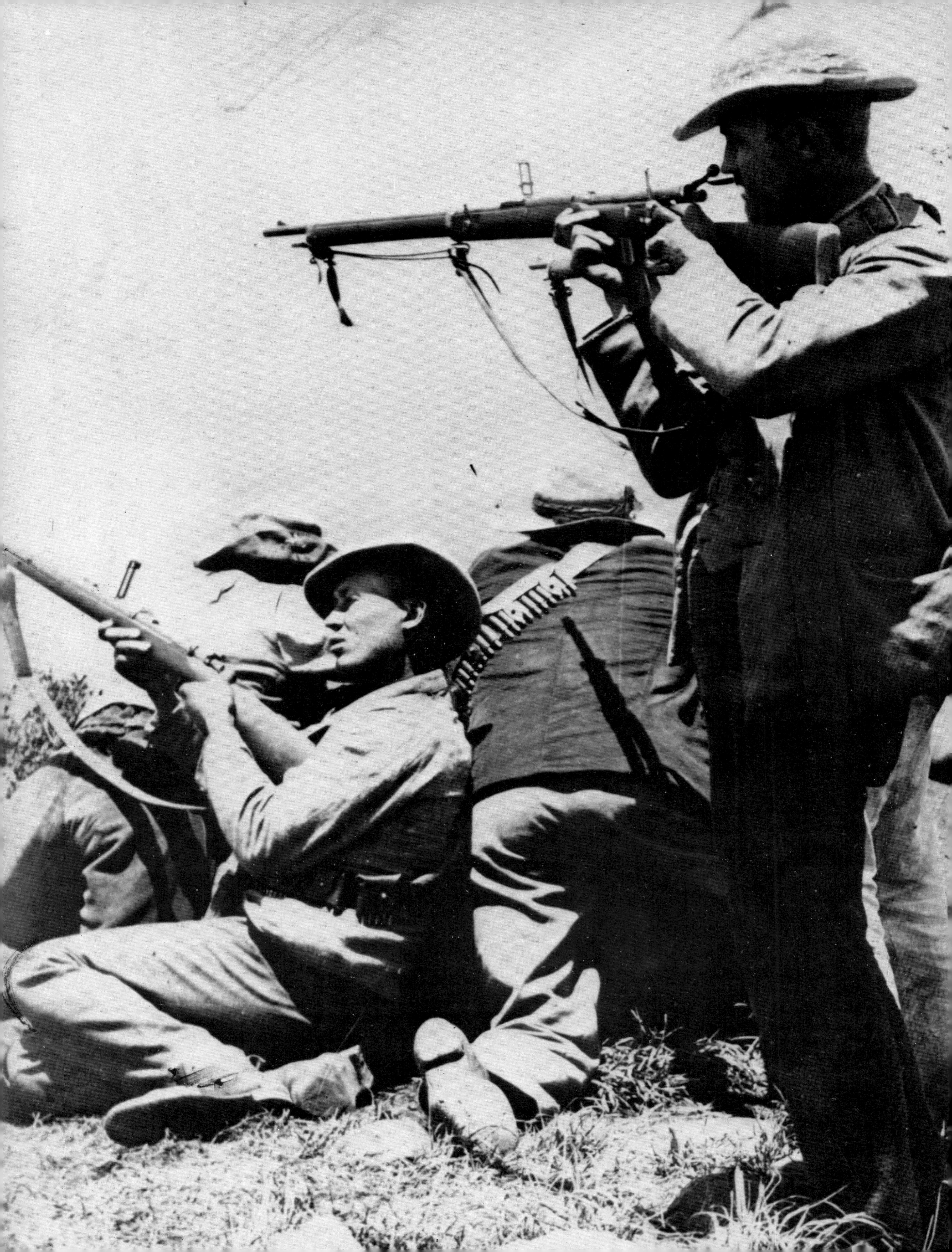

The Boers in action against British troops near Ladysmith. The Boers were the first white opponents of the British army for over 40 years

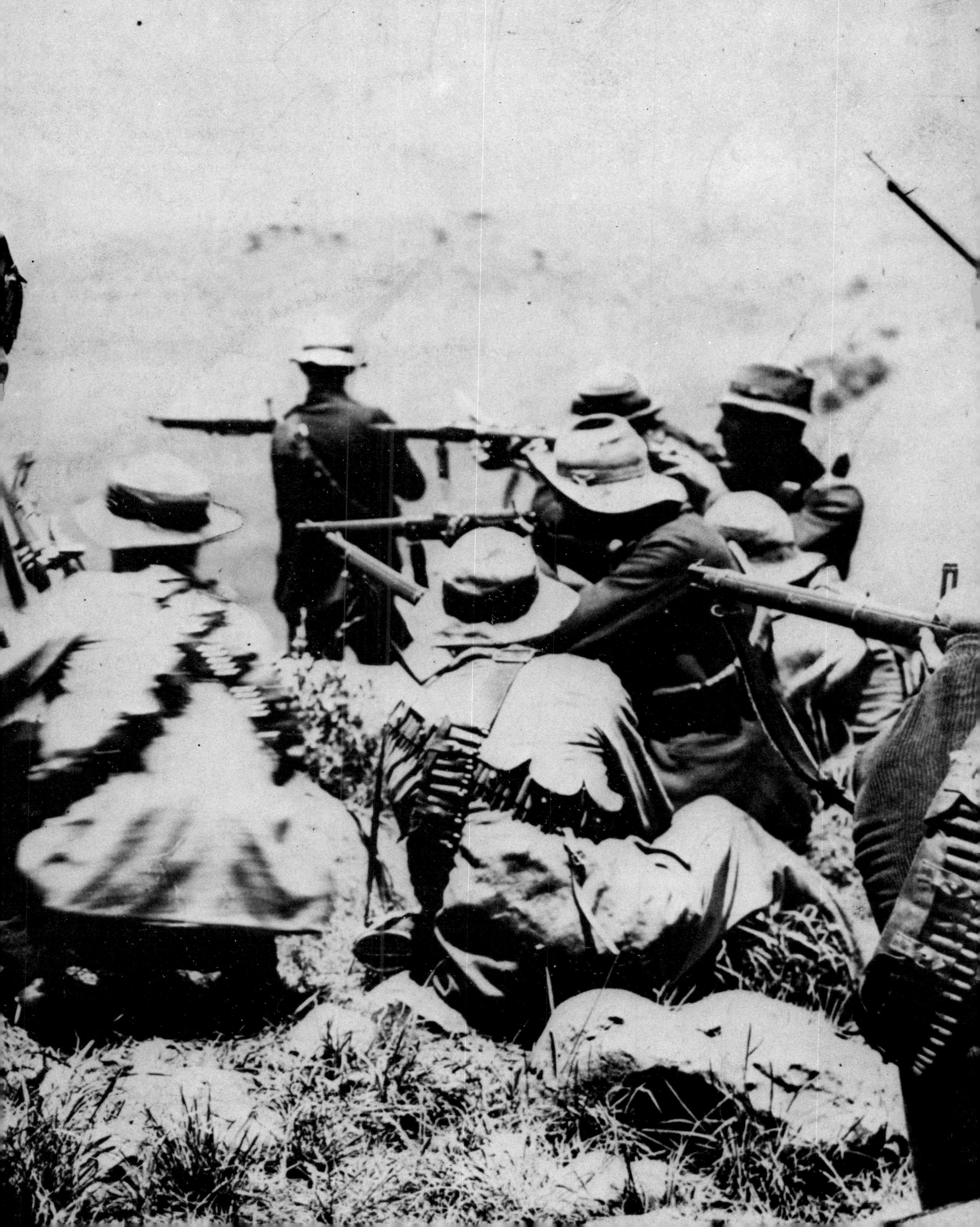

RULING THE WAVES

By James Morris

Britain's sea power in the 19th century was unassailable. The Royal Navy epitomised Victorian assurance and self-confidence, and the merchant fleet held profitable sway over the whole world's shipping

During one of the Armenian massacres in Turkey – those perennial Congos of an earlier day – an officer of the Royal Navy, Captain William Packenham, went ashore from his ship to restore order in a particularly violent village near the southern coast. He was accompanied only by a midshipman and a Turkish interpreter, both very frightened, and he was dressed in every refinement of British naval elegance, his buttons blinding, his beard impeccable, his high white collar stiffly starched. The village toughs suspended their atrocities to gather round this incongruous visitor from the sea, fingering their weapons and cursing, and presently Packenham called for silence. "Let us begin," he said to his interpreter. "Tell these ugly bastards that I am not going to tolerate any more of their bestial habits."

There spoke the voice of late Victorian England, a sea-kingdom of immense authority and assurance. Packenham had grown up in the noonday of British naval power, and he behaved with the careless and humorous arrogance of supremacy. He had no doubts. He was an officer of the Royal Navy, and bestial habits on the Anatolian shores could not be tolerated. Victorian England's sense of privileged immunity arose partly from illusions of divine favour, and partly from technical achievement, but fundamentally from command of the sea. "Splendid Isolation", that wistful euphemism for the condition of having no allies, had its roots in this command, which set England apart from all other nations, and convinced its public that niggers began at Calais. "I do not say the French cannot come," Lord St Vincent had declared not so long before the opening of the era, "I only say they cannot come by sea." They never had, and for nearly a century after Trafalgar the British were able to enjoy the ultimate comfort of national security, a blessing denied most super-Powers.

If they were ill-adjusted in many ways, High

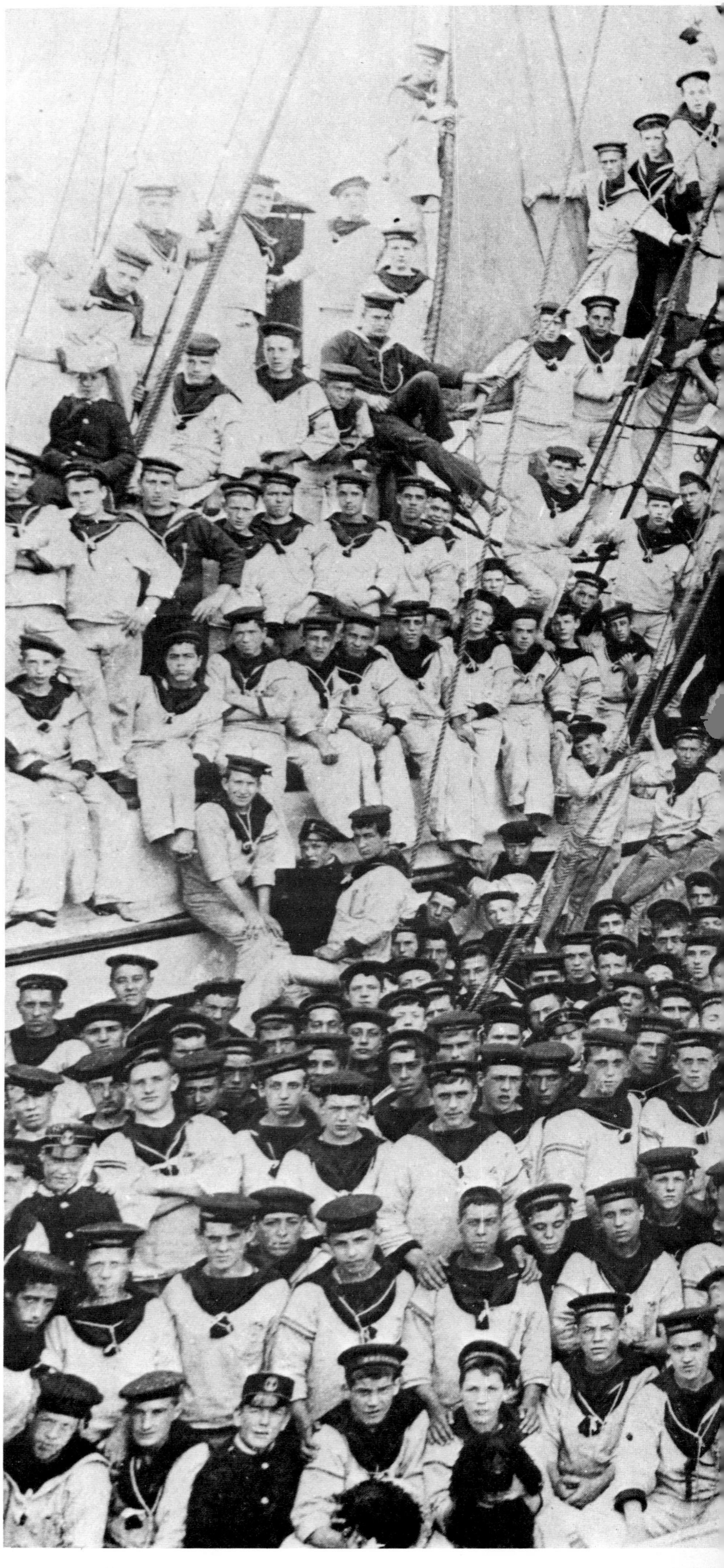

Ship's company, HMS The Hope of Scotland, 1896. Overleaf: section of HMS Duke of Wellington; although the ship was steam-powered and screw-driven it follows the layered gun-deck style of Nelson's day

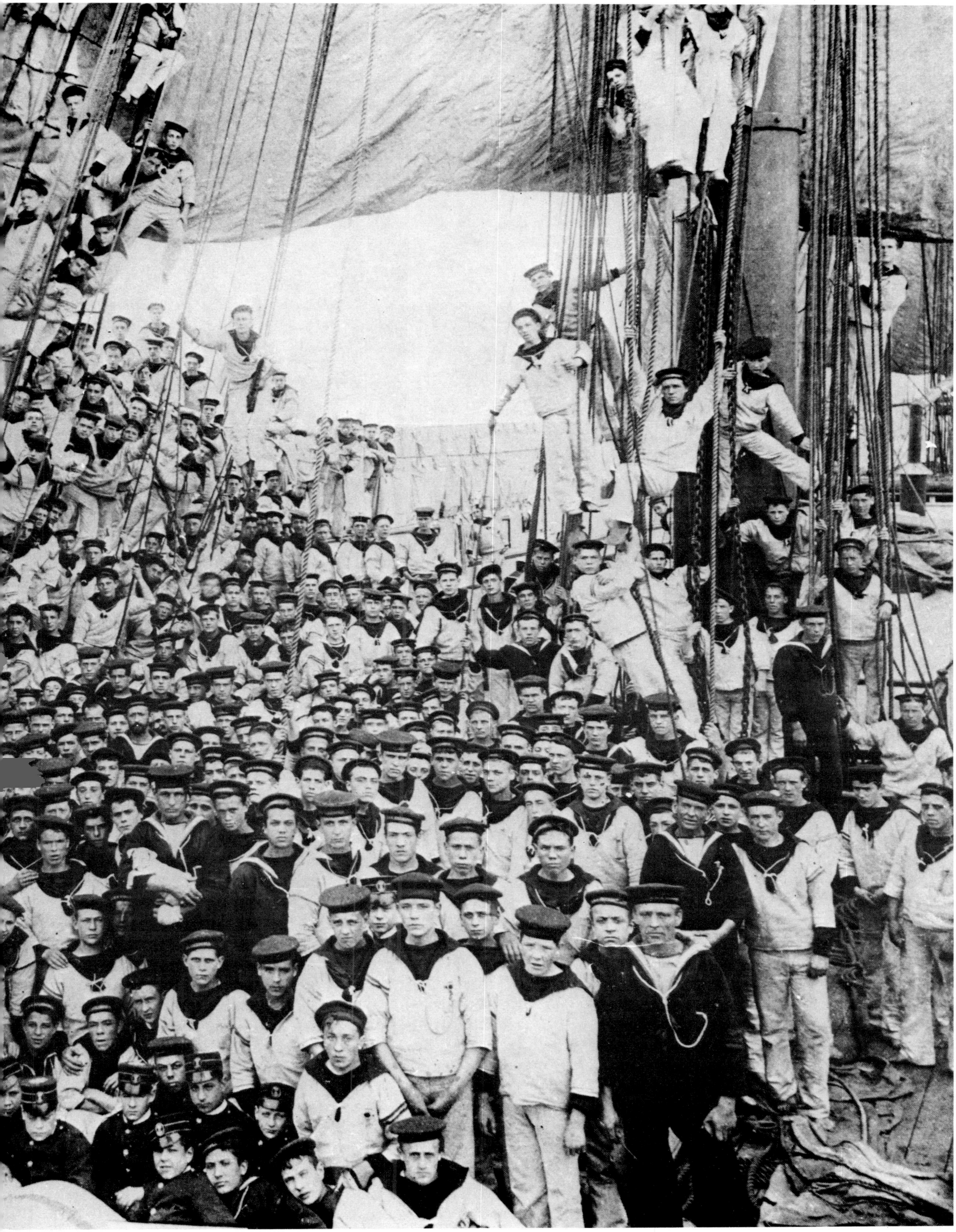

WAR SH

SCREW STEAM SHIP D

LAUN

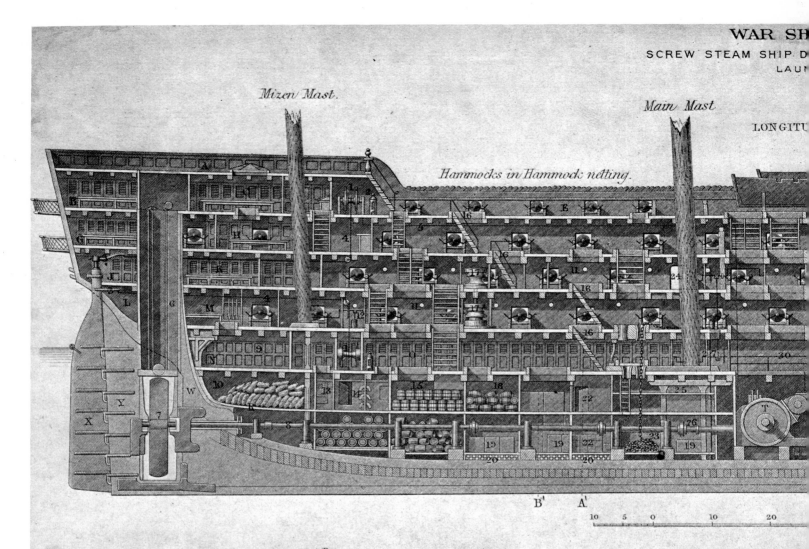

Mizen Mast.
Main Mast
LONGITU
Hammocks in Hammock netting.
B'
A'
10 5 0 10 20

A. Poop.
B.B. Upper Deck.
C. Captain's Cabin.
D. Waist.
E. Quarter Deck.
F. Forecastle.
G.G. Main Deck.
H. Admiral's Apartment.
I. Sick Berth.
J.J. Middle Deck.
K. Ward Room.
L.L. Gun Deck.
M.M. Gun Room.

Cross Section at

A'
B'
N

Cross Section

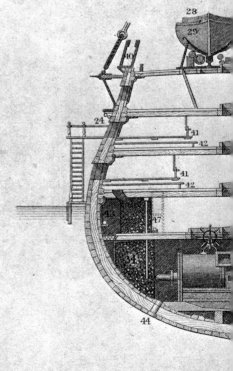

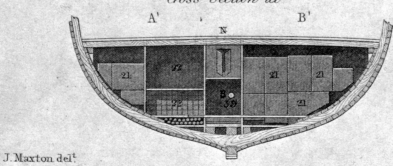

J. Maxton delt.

1.1. Steering Wheels.
2.2. Binnacles.
3.3. Tiller.
4.4. Tiller Ropes.
5. Telegraph Wire from Steersman to Engine.
6. Apparatus for raising and lowering Screw.
7. Screw.
8. Screw Shaft.
9.9. Pursers Issue Room.
10. Bread Room.
11.11. Scuttles for Light and Air.
12. Wash Deck Pumps.
13. Light Room.
14. After Magazine.
15. Provision Room.
16.16. Hatchways.
17.17. Capstans
18. Spirit Room.
19. Paint, Oil, Yarn, &c.
20.20. Shot Lockers
21.21. Water Tanks.
22. Shell Room.
23. Chain Cable Locker.
24. Entrance Port.

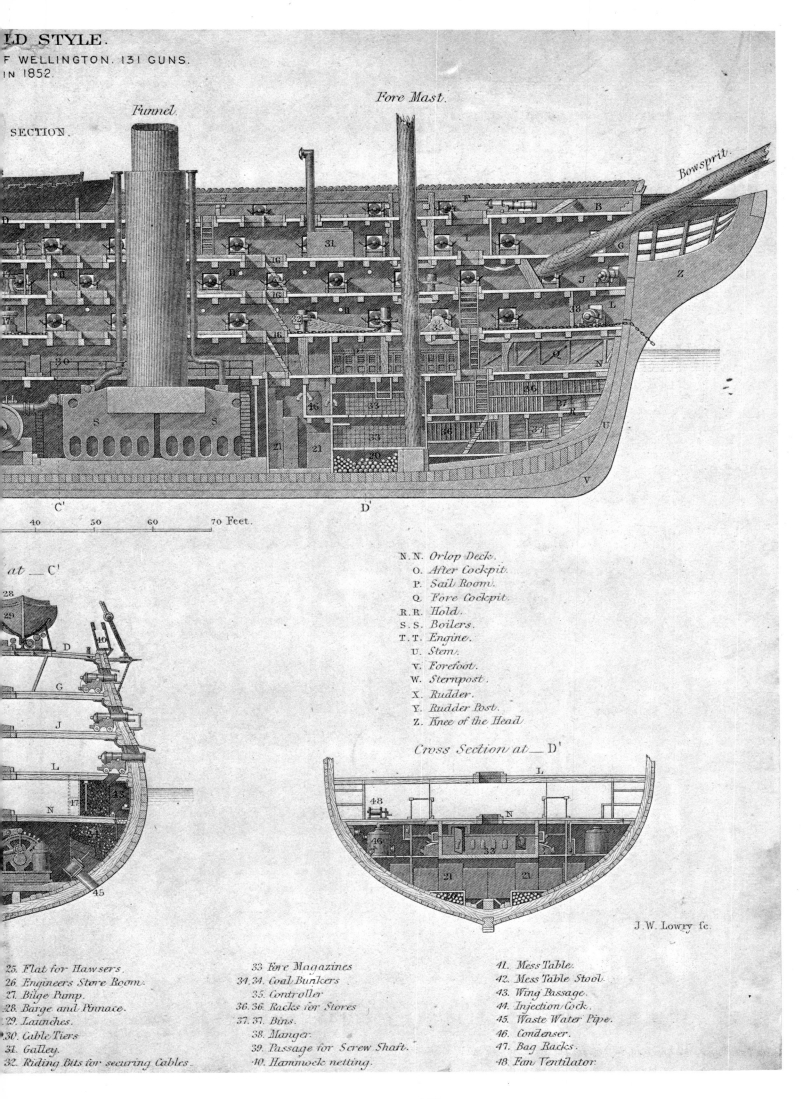

LD STYLE.
F WELLINGTON. 131 GUNS.
IN 1852.

SECTION.

Funnel.   Fore Mast.   Bowsprit.

40   50   60   70 Feet.

at __ C'

N.N. Orlop Deck.
O. After Cockpit.
P. Sail Room.
Q. Fore Cockpit.
R.R. Hold.
S.S. Boilers.
T.T. Engine.
U. Stem.
V. Forefoot.
W. Sternpost.
X. Rudder.
Y. Rudder Post.
Z. Knee of the Head

Cross Section at __ D'

J.W. Lowry fc.

25. Flat for Hawsers.
26. Engineers Store Room.
27. Bilge Pump.
28. Barge and Pinnace.
29. Launches.
30. Cable Tiers
31. Galley.
32. Riding Bits for securing Cables.

33. Fore Magazines
34.34. Coal Bunkers.
35. Controller
36.36. Racks for Stores
37.37. Bins.
38. Manger.
39. Passage for Screw Shaft.
40. Hammock netting.

41. Mess Table.
42. Mess Table Stool.
43. Wing Passage.
44. Injection Cock.
45. Waste Water Pipe.
46. Condenser.
47. Bag Racks.
48. Fan Ventilator.

149

Victorians looked out to sea with few inhibitions. They were sure their Navy was unbeatable – that its storm-tossed battleships, as the American Admiral Mahan romantically phrased it, could still deny any upstart conqueror the dominion of the world. They knew that their merchant fleets, their systems of communications, their forts and harbours and coaling stations, dominated the sea-routes. The Victorians often laughed or even sneered at themselves and their institutions, as any old volume of *Punch* demonstrates, but they seldom made fun of their association with the sea. It was too close to the nerve. A soldier in the family might be a disgrace: a sailor was always a cause for pride.

It was against this background of specialised certainty that the complex drama of Victorianism was enacted. Whatever else might happen to the British, the sea was safe. This maritime confidence sometimes fluctuated, but the tremendous excitement of the age was fuelled throughout by the knowledge of sea-power. Victoria's Britons were islanders always, and proud of it.

To the British sea-power was more than brute force and money. It was an inherited vocation. They believed themselves to be naturally better sailors than anyone else. Nelson's legendary dash and romance was not merely a tradition, but a kind of technique, and was the basis of the British naval system. The Royal Navy was built upon panache, discipline and fine seamanship – sailing-ship qualities – and its manner was essentially aristocratic. Its deck officers, in Nelson's day mostly the sons of poor gentlemen, became grander as the reign wore on, and in the High Victorian decades were likely to have names like Bateman-Champain, De Montmorency or Umfreville: by 1897 the Navy List included two princes, two dukes, a viscount, a count, an earl, four lords by courtesy, eight baronets and 35 honourables. The engineer officers were generally not gentlemen at all – their mamas, as one radical officer observed, were not asked to take tea with other mamas – and were probably called Samuel Rock or Elijah Tricker. The ratings, whose living quarters at sea were horribly primitive, and who ate with their fingers because cutlery might be prejudicial to naval discipline, were splendidly cocky nonetheless, and seen beside the mustachio'ed, music-hall matelots of continental navies, looked proper seamen through and through.

Among them all, duke to deckboy, there was a grand comradeship. Every witness testifies to it. A photograph of the ship's company of the cruiser Flora, taken in the 1890s, well illustrates its style. The men are crowded all over the foredeck, all over the bridge, up the rigging, leaning against the rails or squatting cross-legged on the deck. They are not at all smart or self-conscious. Their caps are on any-old-how, their jerseys look grubby, they are smoking pipes and cigarettes. Some have beards, and some might be thought by matinée audiences to be in need of haircuts. Yet for all the informality of the scene, there is to the foredeck of HMS Flora a suggestion of formidable punch. The men look happy, pleased with themselves, proud of their ship and even fond of each other. They look as though they would jump to it with a will – like a family, long since accustomed to each other's

ways, and bound by that sense of brotherhood which was the happiest of all Nelson's legacies. Often in fact such a small warship was a unit all on its own, far from a higher command, and left to potter through the Tropics very much to its own devices. "Well boys," the captain would say to his wardroom in the morning, "where shall we go today?"

It was a showy service. It loved eccentricity and display – the Admiralty was patron to the church living of Alston with Garrigill and Humshaugh – and it was superb at showing the flag. Its ships were gaily painted: white all over in tropical waters, black with orange funnels and white upperworks elsewhere – and nothing could be swankier than a warship of Queen Victoria's navy entering a foreign port. At its stern fluttered a truly gigantic White Ensign, on its bridge its officers stood about urbanely, swords at their sides, sometimes laughing at a joke, or strolling with measured step towards the flying bridge to keep an eye on the bumboats. A band would probably be playing somewhere, *Hearts of Oak* or *The Girl I Left Behind Me,* and from stem to stern the ship would gleam with spit, polish and embellishment (officers often paid for extra brasswork out of their own pockets, as they chipped in to augment the pay of a particularly urbane wardroom steward). Everywhere the barefoot ratings were vigorously on the move, chivvied by petty officers. And if the ship were in Mediterranean waters, presently, when she had dropped her anchor, out would swing from her deck a colourful Maltese gondola, with a colourful Maltese boatman, to take the officers merrily ashore for the evening's pleasures and remind the local populace that this was an imperial navy.

All this was the show of supremacy. The substance was less absolute. The Royal Navy was easily the largest in the world throughout the Victorian era. In the 1880s the Two-Power Standard, guaranteeing a fleet equal in size to any two European navies, became the basis of official policy: by 1897 the Navy, with a volunteer recruitment of 96,000 men, had 332 major ships to France's 95, Russia's 86, Germany's 68, America's 56 and Italy's 53. In warlike technique and modern *matériel*, though, the Royal Navy of the High Victorian era was distinctly rusty. A century of peaceful pride had diluted the old skills. There were no such things as war plans, most naval officers regarding the Navy less as an instrument of war than as a police force of a national pageantry. The officers themselves, cloistered within the service since boyhood, were often fearfully ignorant of the wider world, and generally as conventional in professional matters as they were bold in private habit. The Navy's gunnery was a disgrace – as late as the 1890s an Admiral's annual report on his squadron made no report at all on its gunnery – and this was almost the last navy in the world to retain muzzle-loading guns. Half those 332 ships were obsolete – too weak to fight, too slow to run away – and most of their captains had only the haziest notion what to do if a war broke out. Smartness of appearance was the principal object of naval activity: guns were fired as seldom as possible, because the blast might blister the paintwork, and almost until the end of the

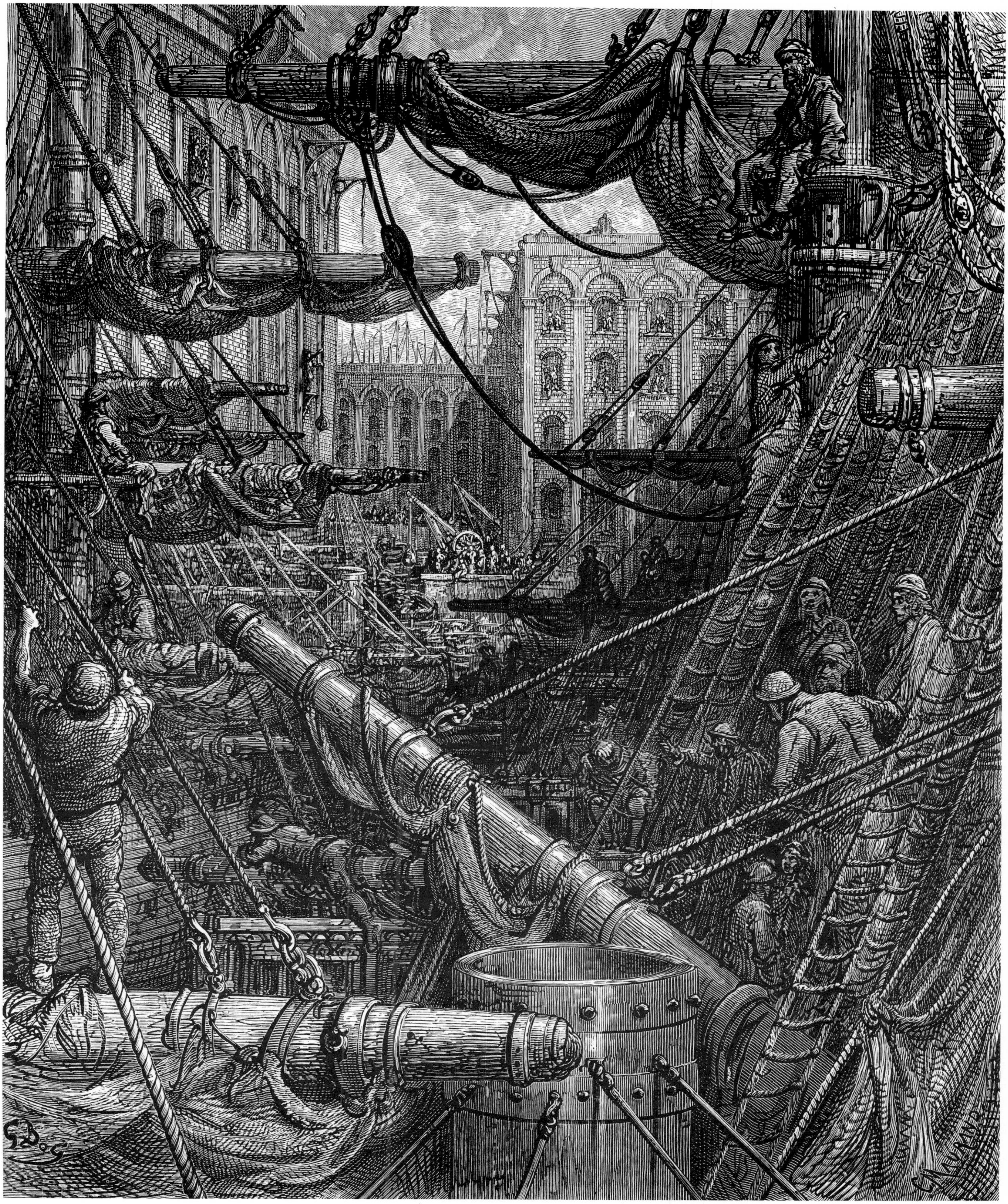

Merchant shipping in the London Docks, drawn by Gustave Doré

century it was not uncommon for commanders to have ammunition thrown overboard rather than shoot it off.

A few furious reformers, like John Fisher and the gunnery specialist Percy Scott, already concerned themselves with these deficiencies; from time to time there were Navy scares, and the newspapers were full of awful warnings about German building programmes, terrible new French torpedoes, or the prospect of becoming a Second-Class Power – always a preoccupation among the late Victorians. The Queen's ministers were often all too aware how narrow the margin of power really was, and

Tennyson himself fell upon those in high places who seemed to be letting the Navy rot:

You – you – if you have failed to understand –
The Fleet of England is her all in all –
On you will come the curse of all the land
If that Old England fall,
Which Nelson left so great . . .

But the alarms seldom lasted long, and were never directed at the sailors themselves, only at their political masters, or at the Admiralty. The country at large had a passionate confidence in its Navy. Had it not always won in the past? Did it not possess 332 ships? Was it not the very same fleet that Nelson led? Had any nation been impertinent enough to challenge it, since those famous victories long ago? Well, then.

High Victorian England loved those diagrammatic maps which purport to show the movement of trade: thick red arrows circumnavigating the continents, or blobs to represent the ships of the merchant marine plodding along the trade routes. Every schoolboy's primer emphasised Britain's dependence upon overseas commerce, and when towards the end of the century the Victorians shifted into their highest imperial gear (in both modern senses of the word, for they loved both speed and epaulettes) it was the far-flungness of their possessions that most excited them. Such a small island of the misty north, linked by so many Tall Ships (or

Comradeship on the high seas: marines in a ship's galley, about 1890

Ocean Greyhounds, or Argosies) with such remote dominions and exotic markets of the East!

The British set the pace of international communication, playing the same role in the control of shipping routes and cable links as the Americans now play in the development of telecommunications. In 1885 a third of all sea-going ships were British, and four-fifths of all steamships. By 1896 it was claimed that at any one moment 200,000 British seamen were at sea, and 200,000 passengers were travelling on British ships, while British exports were running at more than £250 million a year. Even on the North Atlantic routes British companies had overwhelmed their American competitors, and Cunard was one of the great New York institutions.

On the imperial routes – which meant in particular all sea-routes between east and west – the advantage was

even more apparent, for most of the coaling stations were British, and most of the cable stations too. A captain sailing his ship from western Europe to the Far East need never be deprived of British services: at Gibraltar or Malta, Alexandria, Port Said or Suez, Aden, Bombay, Colombo, Calcutta or Singapore – everywhere British coal awaited him, British telegraph offices, British insurance brokers, victuallers, ship surveyors, marine engineers – until at last, sailing into the celestial harbour of Hong Kong beneath the Union Jack on the Peak flagstaff, he dropped anchor in the shadow of China. Even in foreign waters the British often imposed an unofficial hegemony. In the Persian Gulf and the Red Sea, for instance, despairing of persuading the Turks to erect proper navigation aids, they simply put up lighthouses for themselves, some of them manned by British lighthouse keepers: the most miserable overseas post open to an Englishman must have been the supervision of the lighthouse erected by the P and O Company on the blistering and uninhabited Daedalus Reef, near the head of the Red Sea off nowhere in particular.

There was an element of noblesse oblige to all this. Just as the Royal Navy considered itself, as one officer put it, "guide, philosopher and friend to the merchant ships of all nations", so the British were, in their lordly way, happy to share their facilities with the lesser maritime powers. When in 1889 they declared their intention of opening to navigation the Karun River, in Persia, they declared it to be "for the advantage of all nations" (and so it was, growled the Russian Foreign Secretary, Nicholas de Giers, "in a manner of speaking"). The Navigation Acts, which had limited trade within the British Empire to British ships, had been repealed in 1849, and vessels of all nationalities were now free to carry coals to Newcastle or mangoes home from Penang. No charge was made for the benefits of the Daedalus Reef lighthouse, and captains of every merchant fleet really were grateful for the philosophic guidance of the Royal Navy, just as mariners from Alaska to the South Seas now happily accept the succour of the Stars and Stripes.

But it was, as the Russian said, all a manner of speaking. It was upon Free Trade that the British Empire had based its prosperity, and this opening of the waters to the world did the British no harm. Fifty years after the repeal of the Navigation Acts, only one half of one per cent of British coastal cargoes were carried by foreign ships, and by the end of the century Britain had a bigger proportion of the ocean traffic than ever before in her history. A thousand new British ships were launched in 1896 and 1897: of every thousand tons of shipping passing through the Suez Canal in the 1890s, 700 tons were British (95 were German: *two* were American).

Nowhere indeed could the power of Victorian Britain be better grasped than from a vantage point upon the banks of Suez, as the daily convoy sailed through: there, one after the other through the wasteland, passed the British merchantmen from the East, their ensigns fluttering: fine big steamships painted in reds and blacks, their captains to be discerned portly in white ducks upon their bridges, their passengers in the scarlets and white muslins of Empire clustered at the rail.

Even then people often saw something rather comic to the way the British ran their passenger ships. Kipling wrote that British India provided "freedom and cockroaches", while P and O acted as though "'twere a favour to allow you to embark".

The style of passenger accommodation in the High Victorian steamship set the tone of sea travel for half a century to come, and was above all genteel. To a British liner there was none of the rococo flamboyance that characterised, for example, a Mississippi river-boat. The Orient Line's *Guide* of 1888, describing the interiors of its newest ships, gives a fairly drear impression of dark-stained woods and potted palms, heavy buttoned sofas in alcoves of the Music Saloon, velvet-curtained portholes, elaborately carved dining-room chairs and pictures like *The Old Squire* and *On The Coast of Banffshire*. The Austrian traveller Baron von Hübner, travelling on one such British ship to Australia in the Nineties, was aghast at the gloomy decorum of a British seaboard Sunday. Whist and bezique were forbidden, and even smoking was frowned upon. "Young M. caught with a novel in his hand: a lady looks at him fixedly, utters the word 'Sunday', takes away the novel and slips into his hand a hymnbook instead."

But these were the big ships. In every corner of the world, too, tramps, coasters and river-boats carried the Red Ensign into the remotest trading areas and spheres of interest. Look hard at almost any picture postcard of a late 19th-century seaport, anywhere on earth, and you are likely to find a British merchantman somewhere about – an essential feature of the seascape. The Welsh captain and the Scottish engineer were familiar to every waterside bar, Hamburg to San Francisco, and all through the islands of the Tropics sailed the sweaty sea-going opportunists of Conrad's world, with their tatty schooners or thumping run-down steamers. The British presence at sea was inescapable: to the world at large the British Empire was pre-eminently an empire of the sea, and the Briton was first of all a sailor.

At home there were hundreds of thousands of Britons who had never set eyes on the sea. It was true that nobody in the islands lived farther than 70 miles from tidal waters, and that the railways had brought the seaside resorts within reach of a vast new clientele: but the great concentration of industry in the Midlands had created new populations altogether cut off from maritime contact. Yet this was still a nautical nation to a degree we have almost forgotten. During the Victorian era some eight million people, for a start, had boarded ship to emigrate: ocean travel was an experience that vast numbers of British households shared, if only vicariously in the persons of Uncle Jack or Cousin Mary's youngest.

There were towns still whose populations were almost exclusively concerned with the sea – Liverpool, for instance, was entirely a port, and Portsmouth almost entirely a naval base. Even London seemed far more a seaport in those days, and its waterfronts were rich in the characters of W. W. Jacobs's stories, the barge-hands, the pilots, the ferrymen and the schooner captains. Few

Collision of the Camperdown and the Victoria in 1893; 300 lives lost

Victorian artists failed to paint their seascapes, and few of the great English poets ignored the imagery of the sea, from Arnold listening to the melancholy roar of the tide on Dover Beach to Browning pressing a patriotic hand to his heart off Trafalgar. Britain was consciously an island, but except in a geographical sense she was anything but insular. The sea had given her people an unequalled breadth of experience, making the powers of the Continent parochial by comparison.

And when, in the last decades of the century, the imperial idea reached its apogee, and Victorian responsibility acquired a new dimension, this old familiarity with the sea easily accustomed the British to the role of global authority. The seamanlike Americans, their Yankee heritage obscured by the influx of Central European immigrants – landlubbers to a man – were turning their backs upon the Atlantic, and concerning themselves more and more with their landlocked hinterland. The British, as their island became more crowded, tamed and threatened, looked ever more fervently to sea. Business people, faced with powerful new foreign competition, looked for new markets, financiers for new fields of investment, prospectors for new goldmines, Jingos for new battlefields, emigrants for new homesteads. The steamship had made possible a new kind of empire, tighter-knit, and the expansionist Britons of the New Imperialism, that infatuation of the Nineties, depended even more than their predecessors upon maritime skills and instruments. The sea that had given Britain insular security now offered her imperial control – even perhaps a measure of universal sovereignty, the immemorial dream of conquerors. The resurgent powers of the Continent threatened to overwhelm Britain in military strength and industrial capacity: Britain's reaction in the Victorian era was not to join them, but to turn once more to that other world, of water and movement and distance, which her people best understood.

Within a couple of decades the greatest British armies in history would be engaged on the battlefields of continental Europe. Within the lifetimes of men already born, the British would be trying desperately to merge their destinies with those same European land-States, and would deny any number of times, before a French cock could crow, that they were really islanders at all.

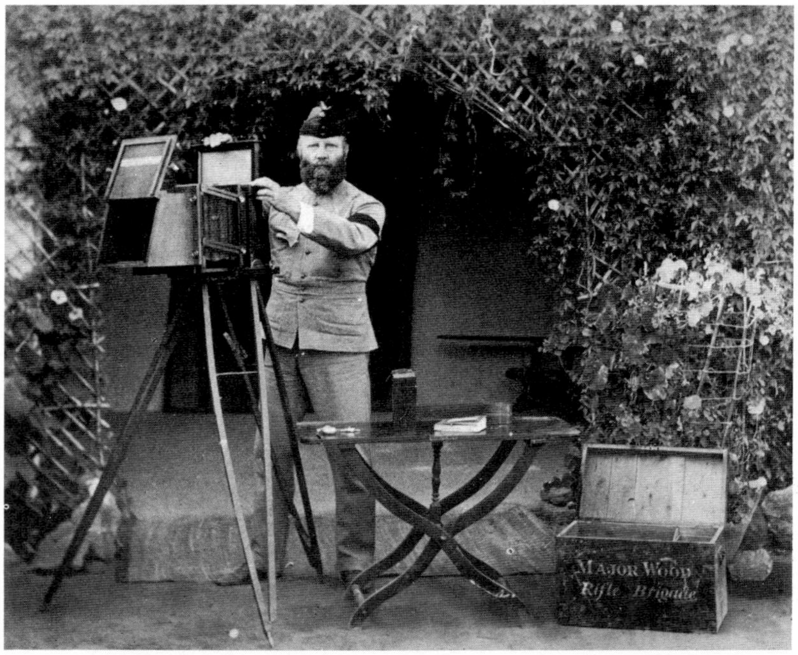
MAJOR WOOD
Rifle Brigade

FAMILY LIFE OF A SOLDIER

In 1848 Henry Wood left St Peter's College, Radley, and joined the army. Six years later he was in the Crimea, and wrote to his father from Sebastopol: "I am very glad I came out here and shall stay as long as I can." In 1859 he transferred to the Rifle Brigade and went to India. There in 1866 he married but his wife died only three years later, at the age of 22, leaving a son and a daughter. He married again in 1871 and had four daughters by his second wife. A riding accident left him permanently lame and he finished his army career as commander of the 9th Regimental District Norfolk. Colonel Wood was a typical Victorian professional soldier. He had a passion for photography and the selection of hitherto unpublished pictures from his great collection convey an impression of life in the vast colonial dependency of India. Above: Colonel Wood in his early days in India, in mourning for his first wife. Opposite: in camp on a survey expedition in the Northern India hills. Charlotte, Colonel Wood's second wife, was permitted to accompany the party. Here they sip tea on chintz-covered chairs in the evening sun

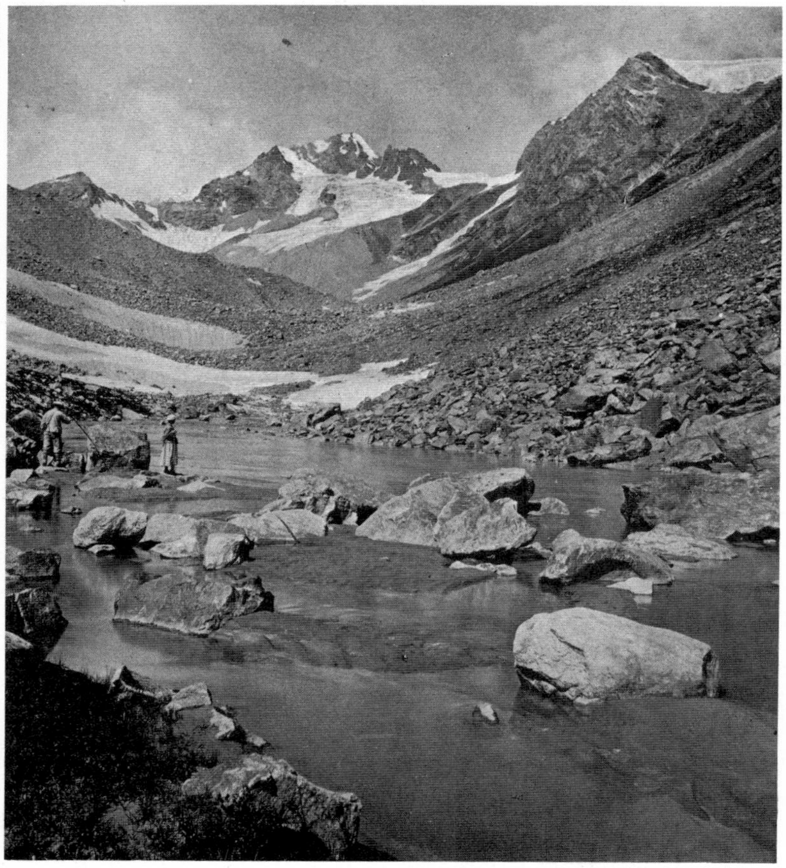

The second Mrs Wood stands by a river at the base of a glacier in Kaghan, Northern India

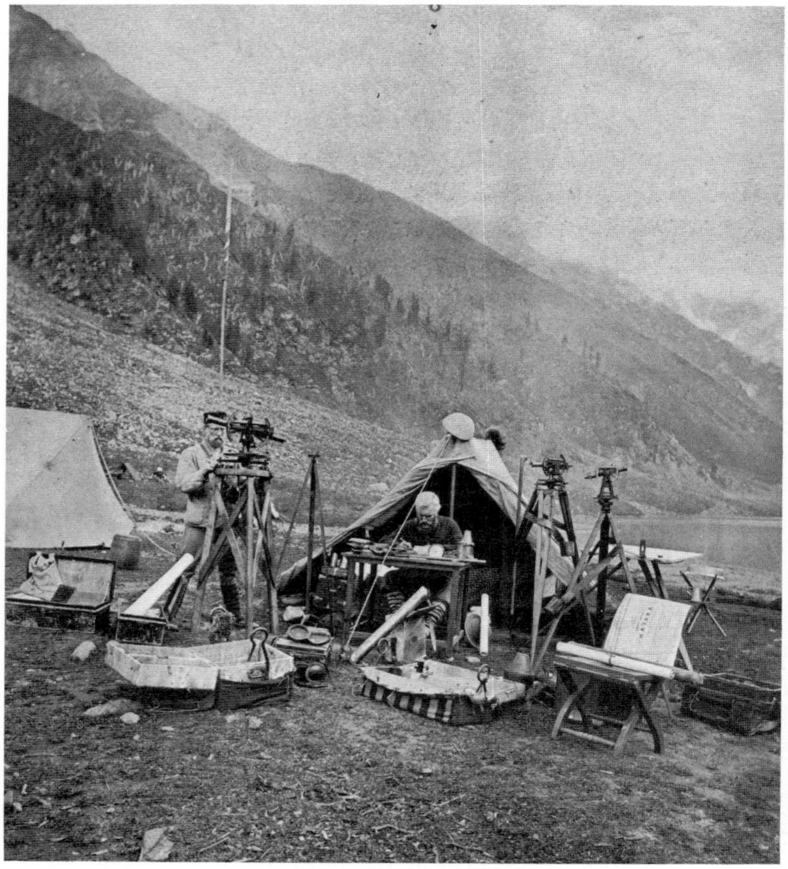

Two officers in the survey team take measurements with a massive array of instruments

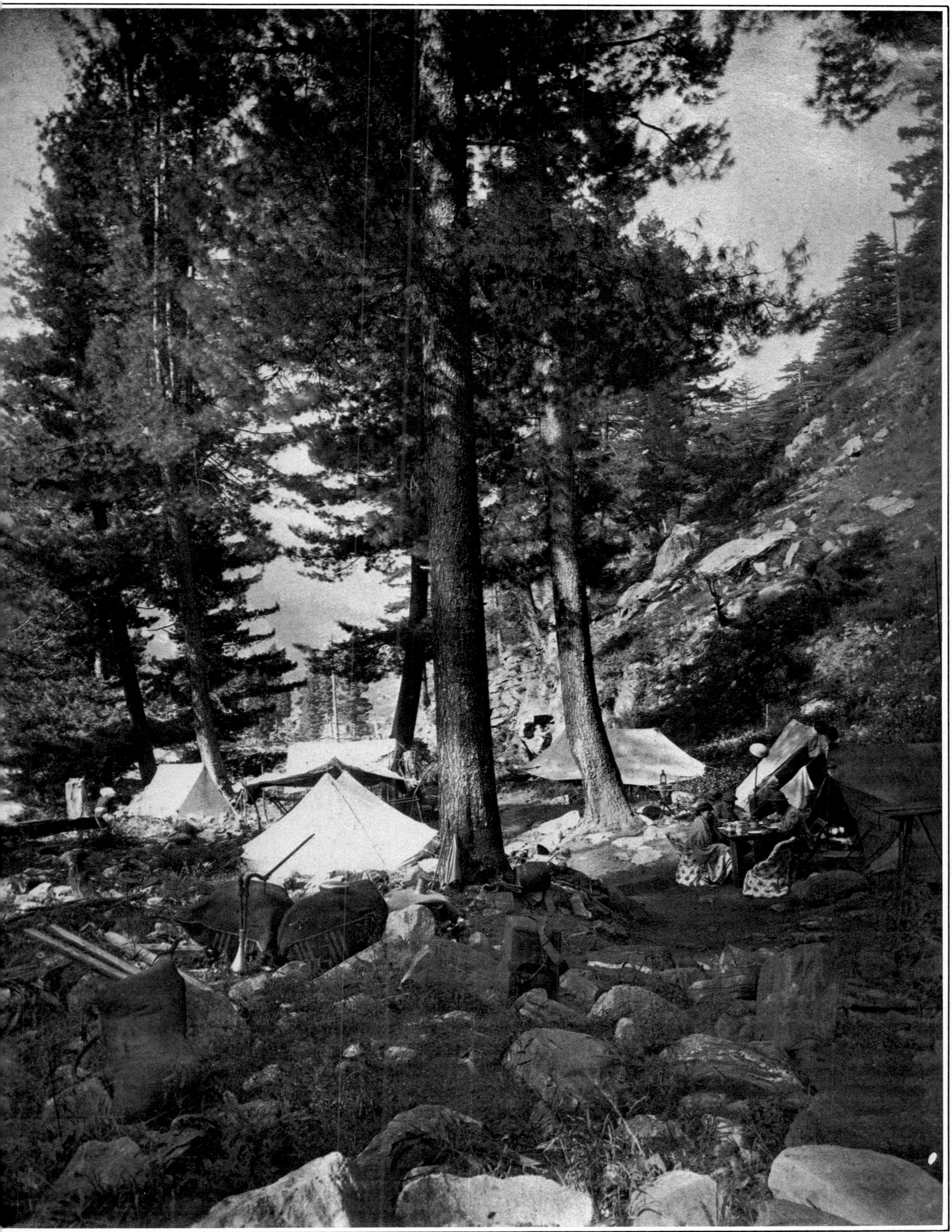

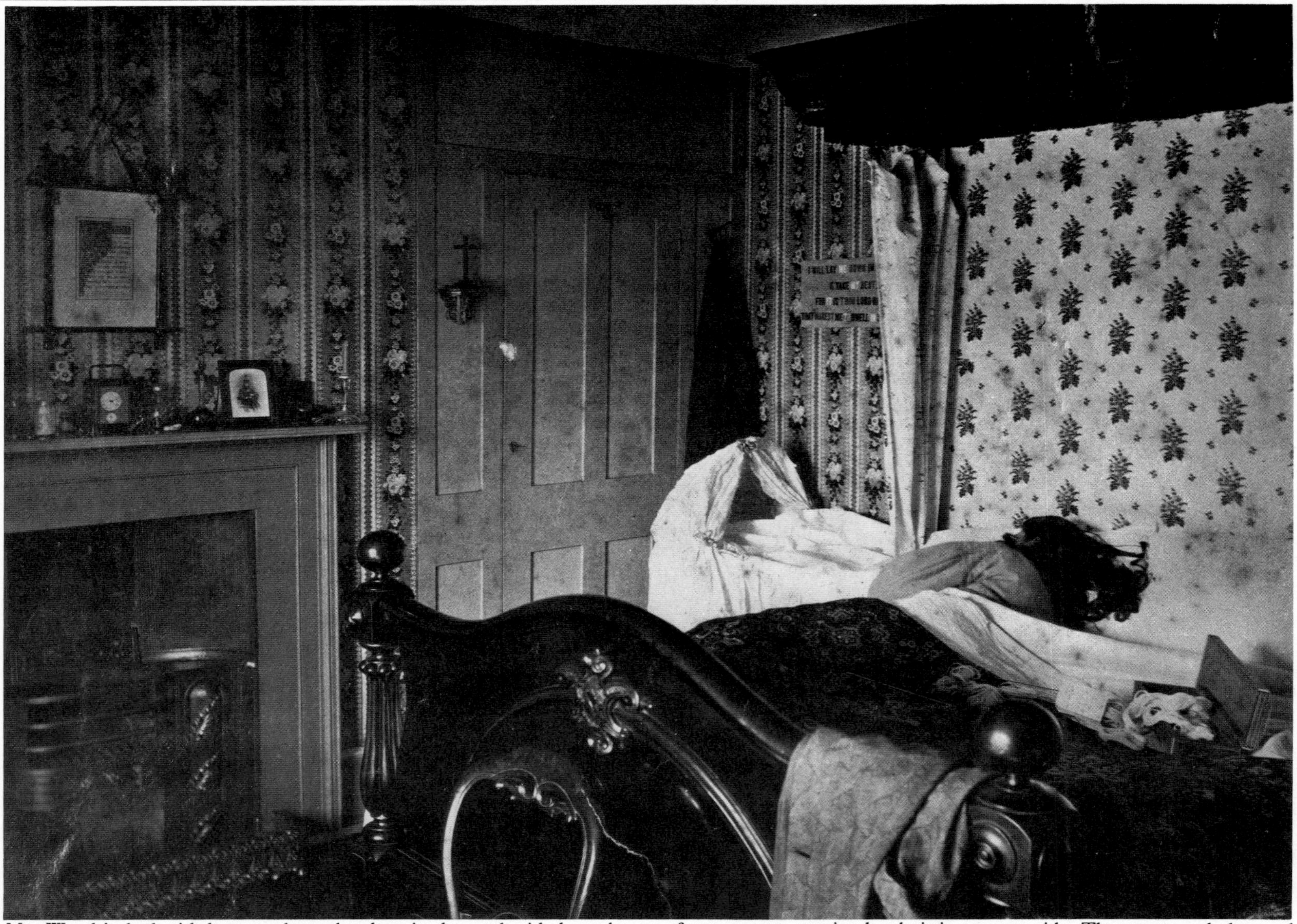

Mrs Wood in bed with her new-born daughter in the cot beside her takes an afternoon rest, putting her knitting on one side. The ornate and cluttered atmosphere of a Victorian bedroom comes across strongly in this photograph. The second Mrs Wood bore four daughters, Hazel, Myrtle, Olive and Holly

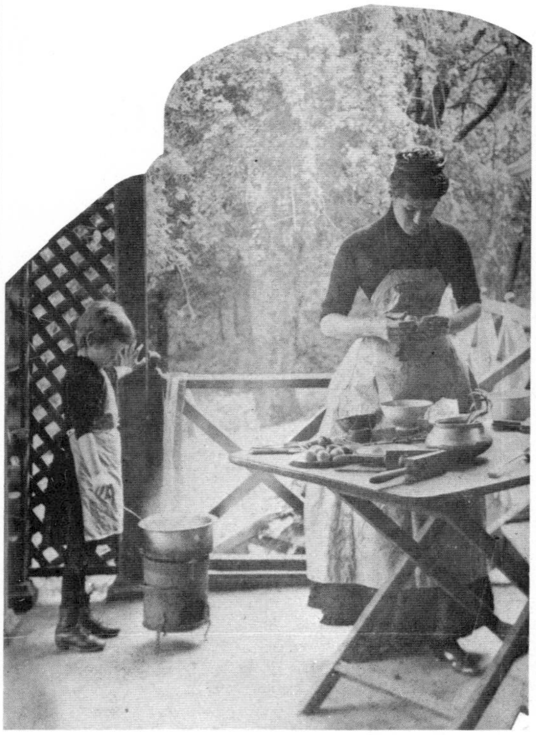

Olive helps her mother to prepare a meal on the verandah of their house

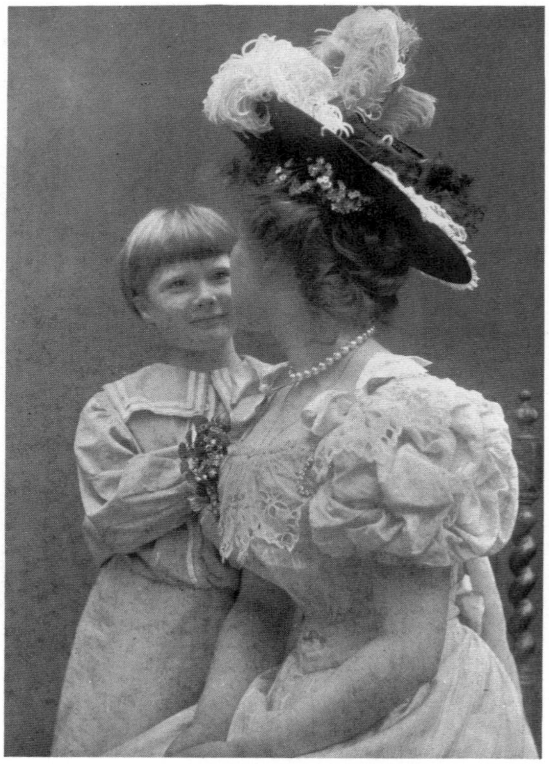

A more mature Olive, dressed for theatricals, is admired by Myrtle

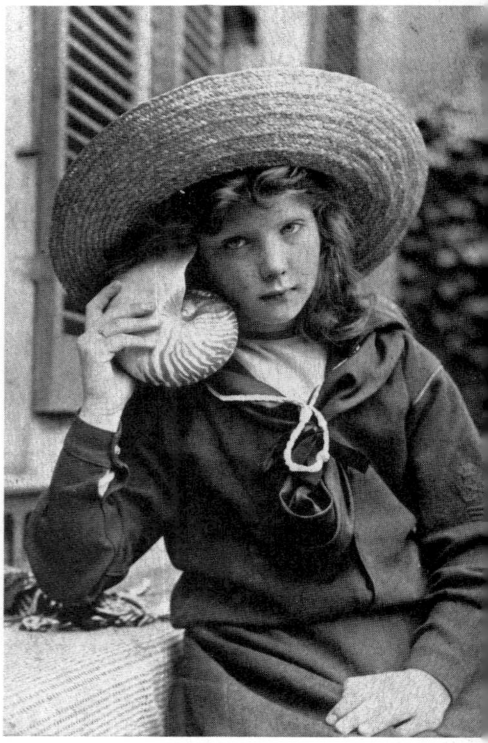

Olive with a shell, one of the Colonel's favourite photographs. He experimented with various ways of printing it

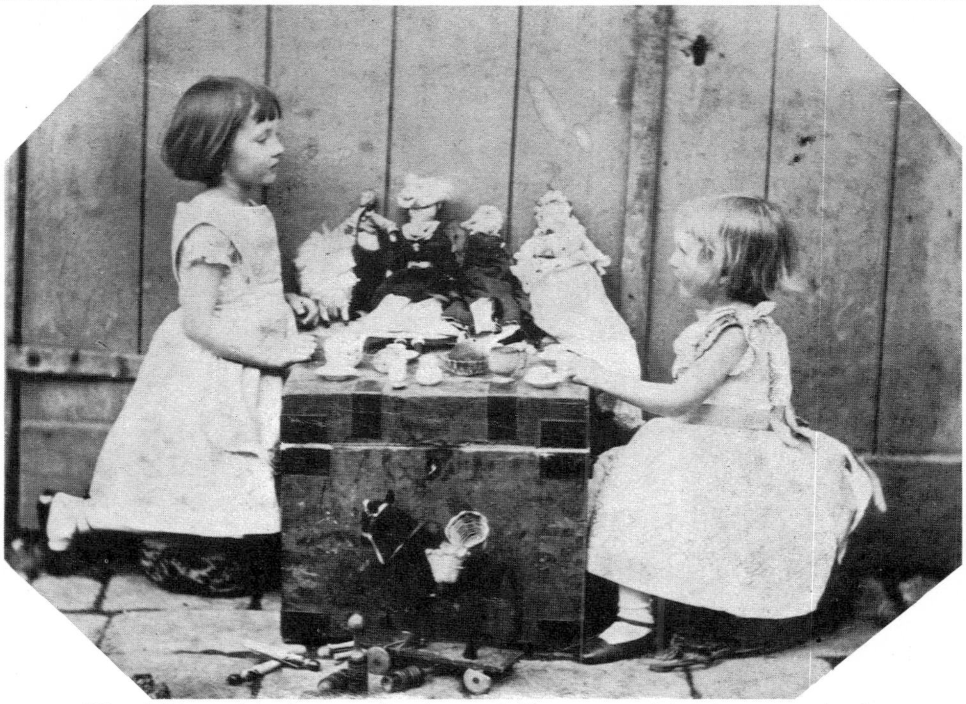

The children of the first marriage have a doll's tea party. Little boys wore frocks and were indistinguishable from their sisters. Cecil is on the left

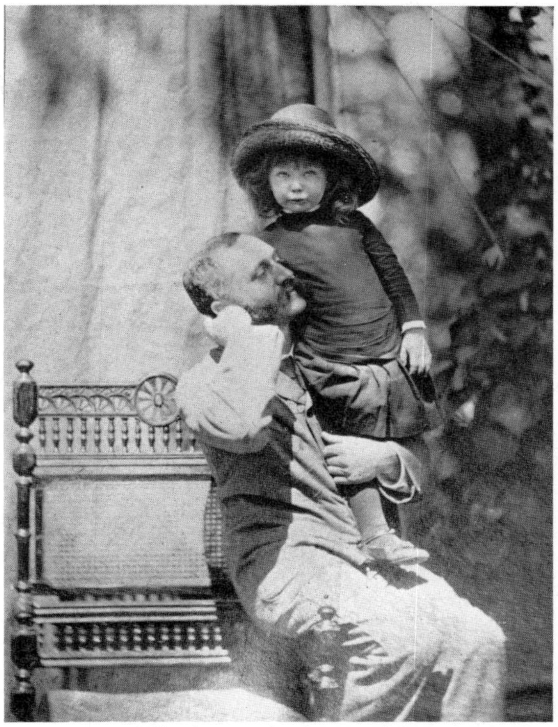

Olive in a sunhat poses with a friend of her father

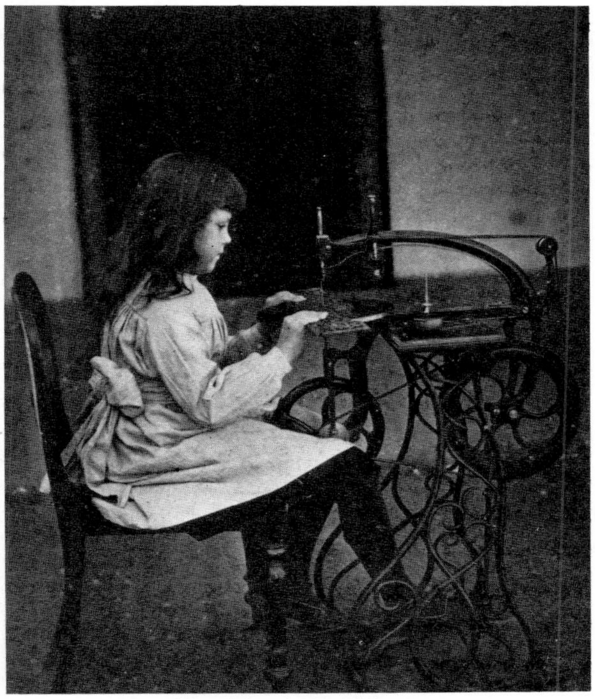

Hazel, in a holland dress, uses the family sewing machine

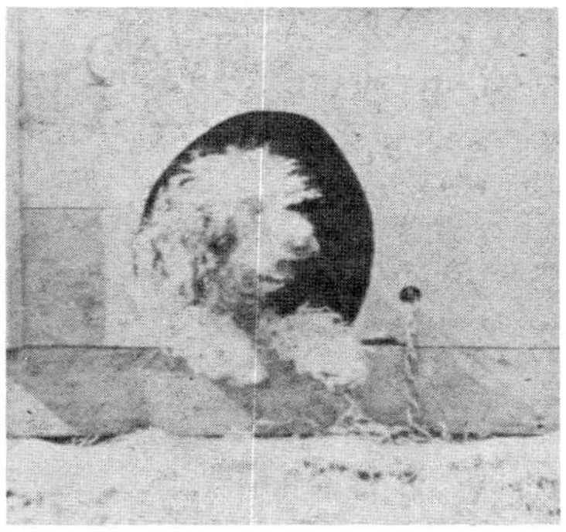

Rose, the family dog, looks out of its kennel

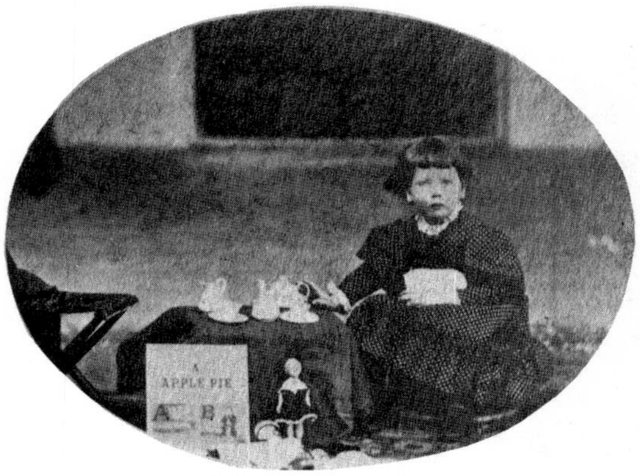
A
APPLE PIE

Olive at three with a doll, alphabet book and tea set

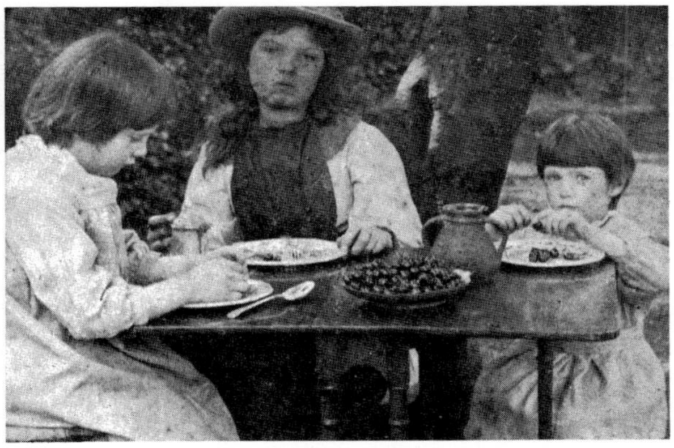

Olive, Hazel and Myrtle under a tree in the garden of the Woods' home at Murree

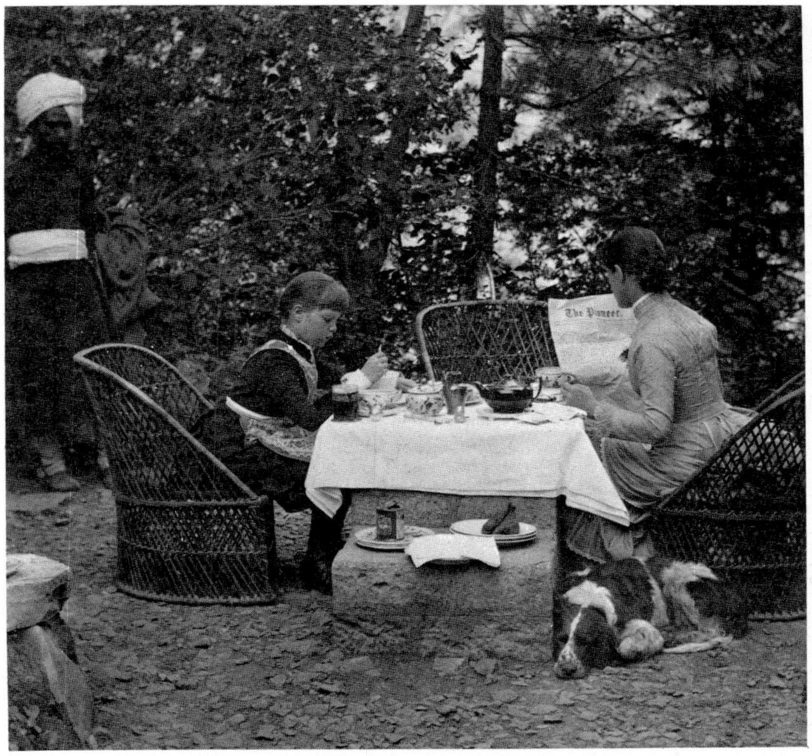

Olive and her mother breakfast in the garden with Teak the dog. In the background Mustafa the *klutmatgar* (butler) attends

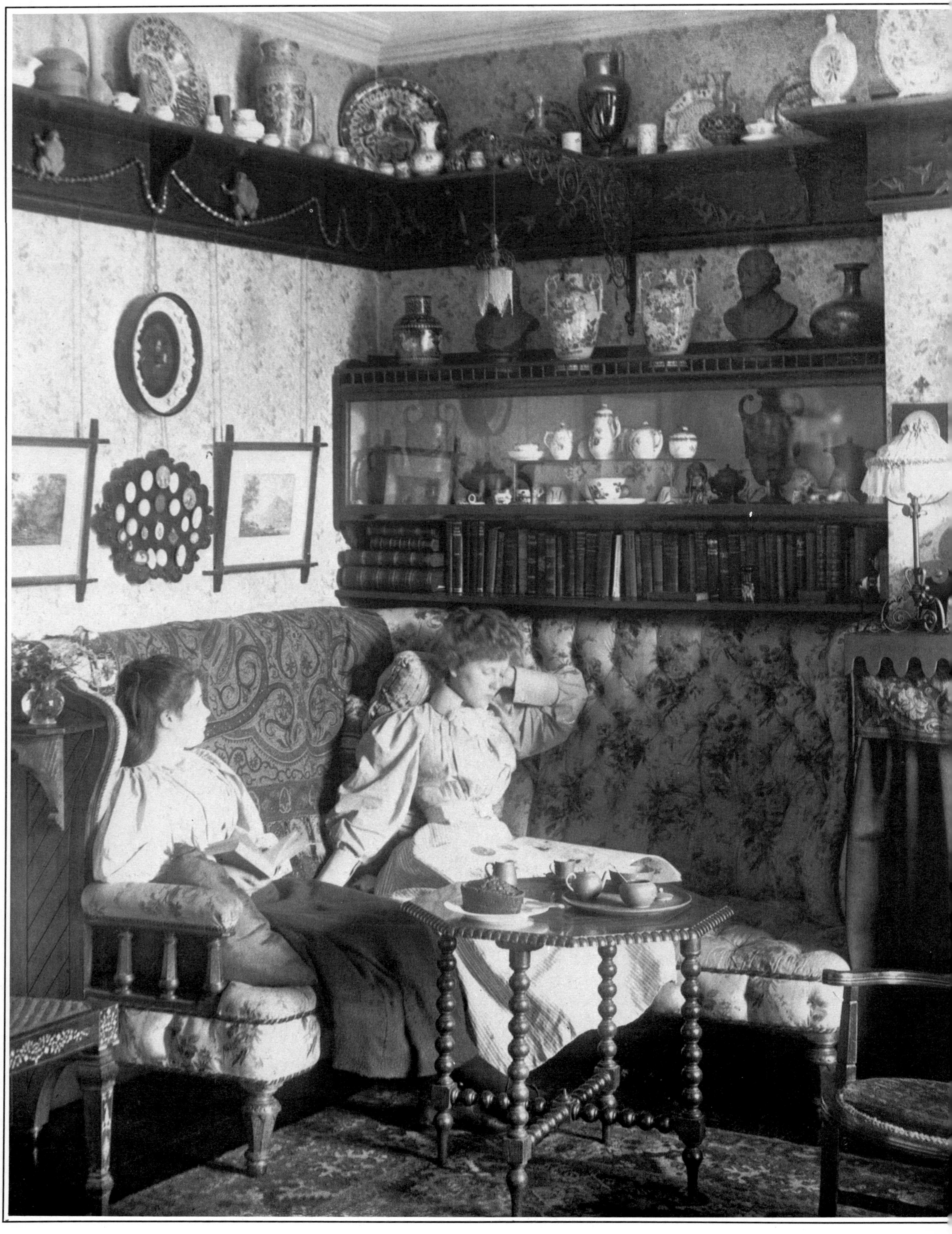

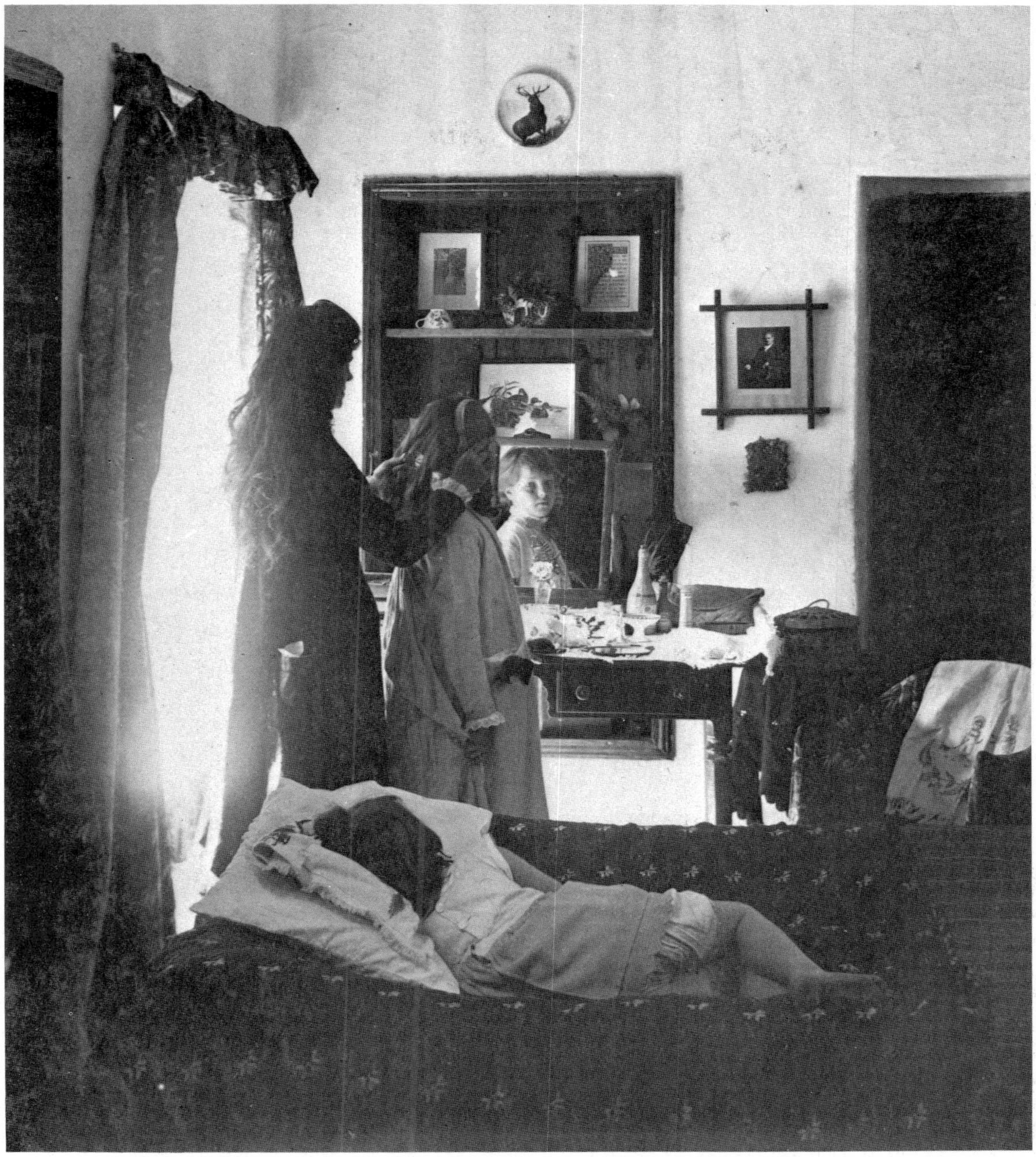

The family rises from afternoon rest. Few Victorian photographs achieve the informality of this picture. Opposite: years later the family lived in Norwich. Olive is grown-up and Myrtle is in her teens

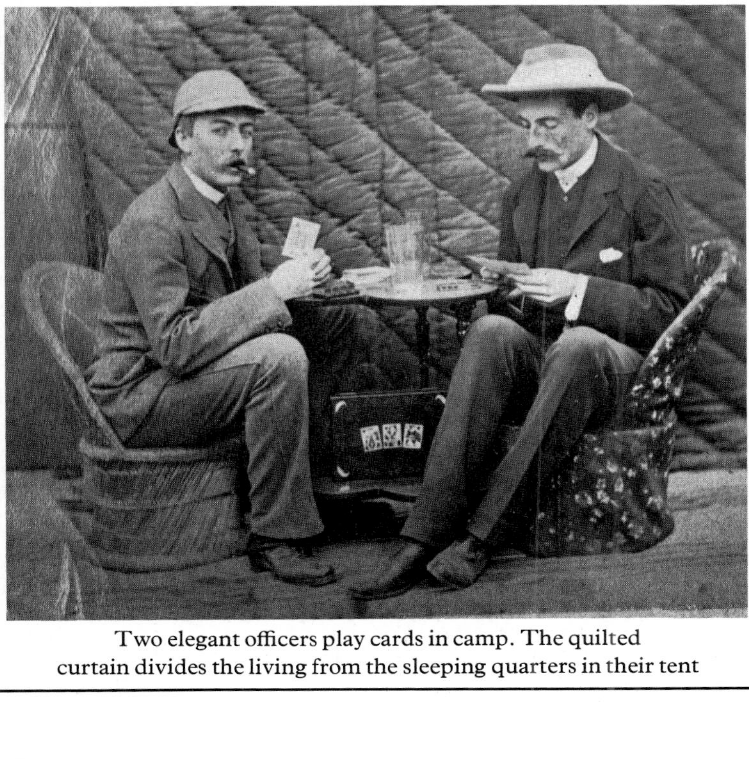

Two elegant officers play cards in camp. The quilted curtain divides the living from the sleeping quarters in their tent

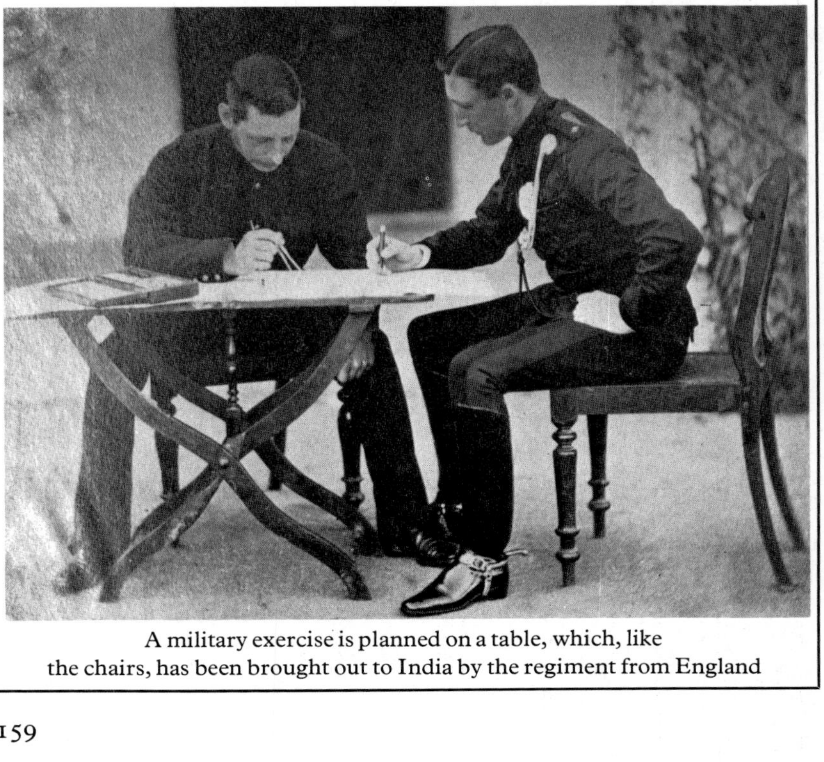

A military exercise is planned on a table, which, like the chairs, has been brought out to India by the regiment from England

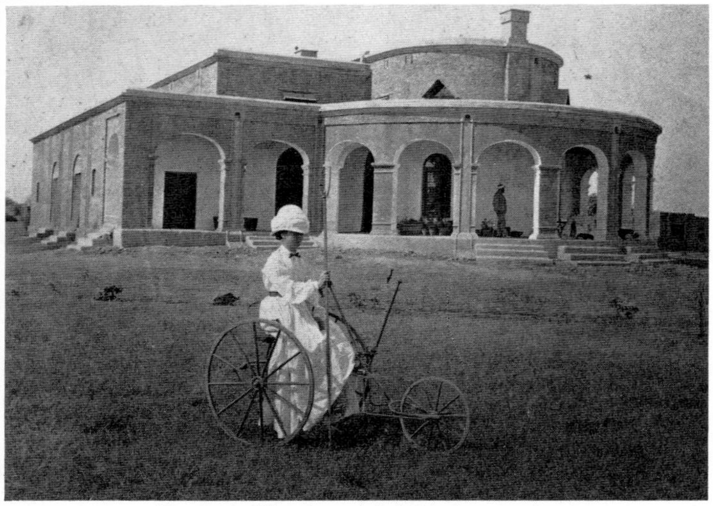

Charlotte Wood, married for six months,
poses as Britannia on the lawn of Marlborough Lodge, Rawalpindi.
Her father, General Smith, is on the verandah

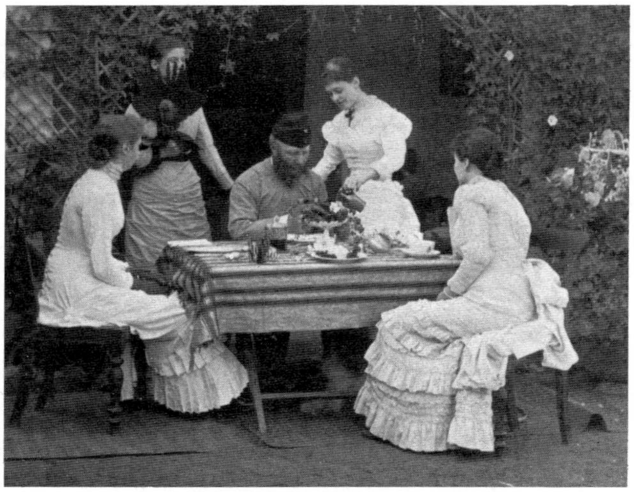

Colonel Wood breakfasts in style on his
verandah with his wife and some of their friends.
The bustle has now arrived

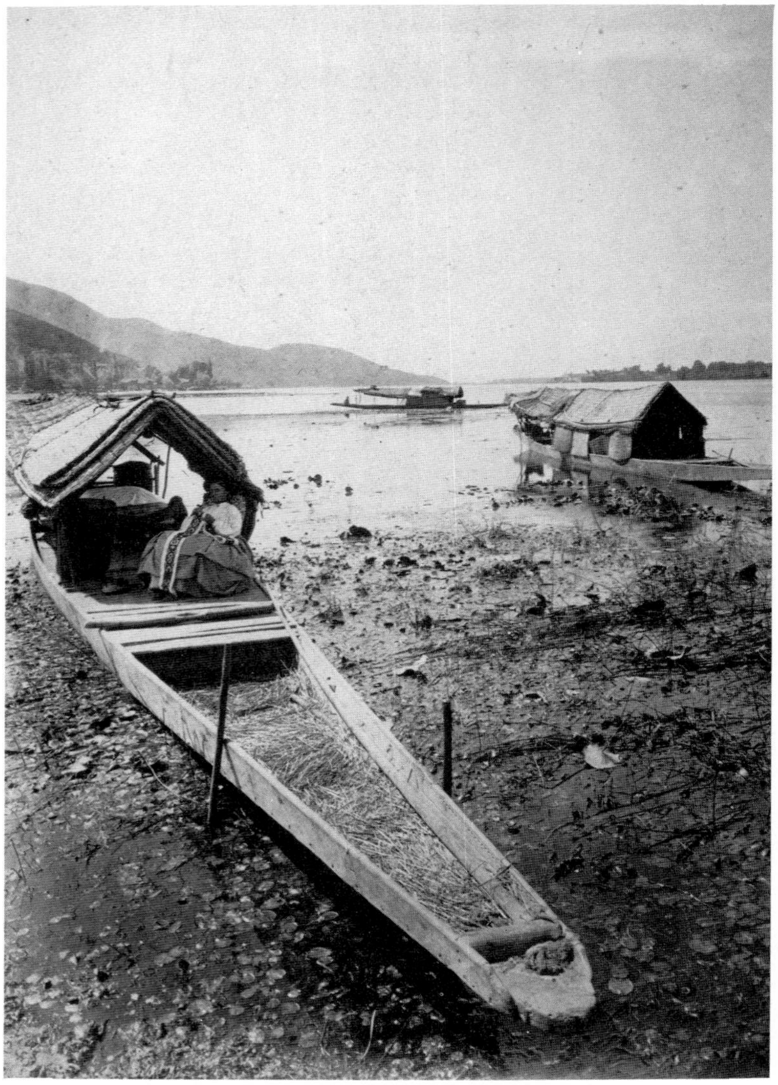

On holiday in Kashmir.
Charlotte Wood sits under the matting shade,
embroidering a bell rope in Berlin wool

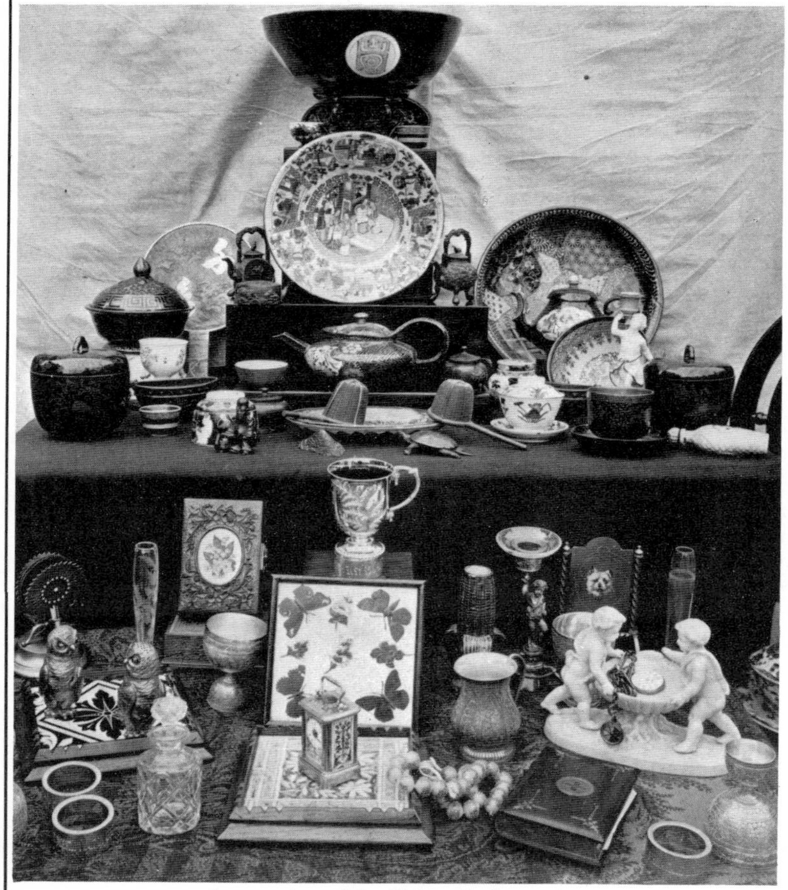

A grouping of the Colonel's favourite
ornaments, to make a still life for his camera

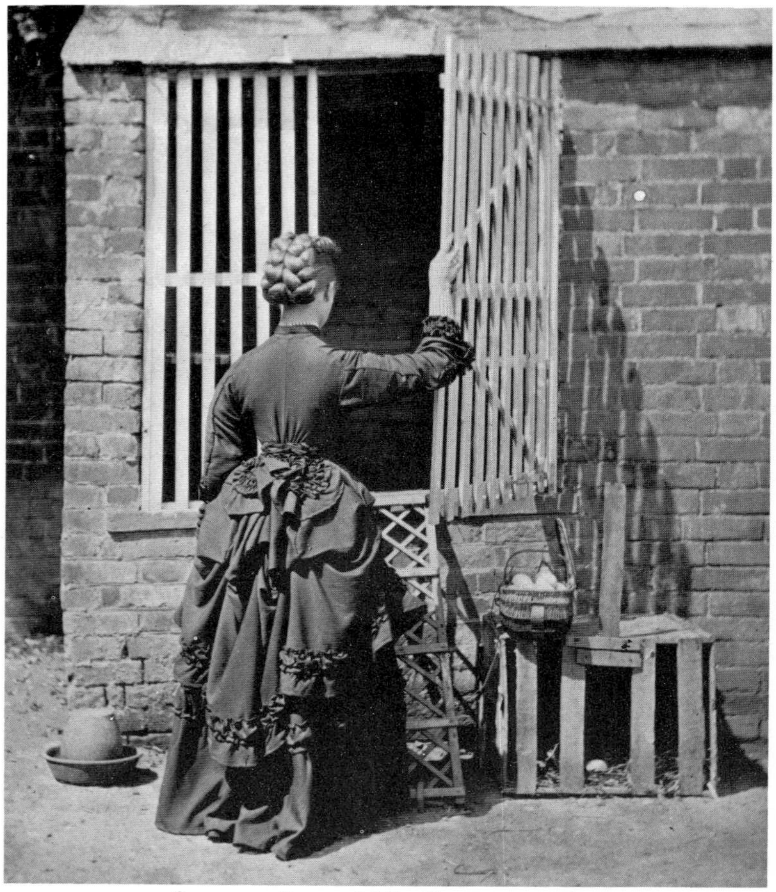

Summer 1872, and Alice Brown, a cousin
of the Woods, collects the eggs from the henhouse

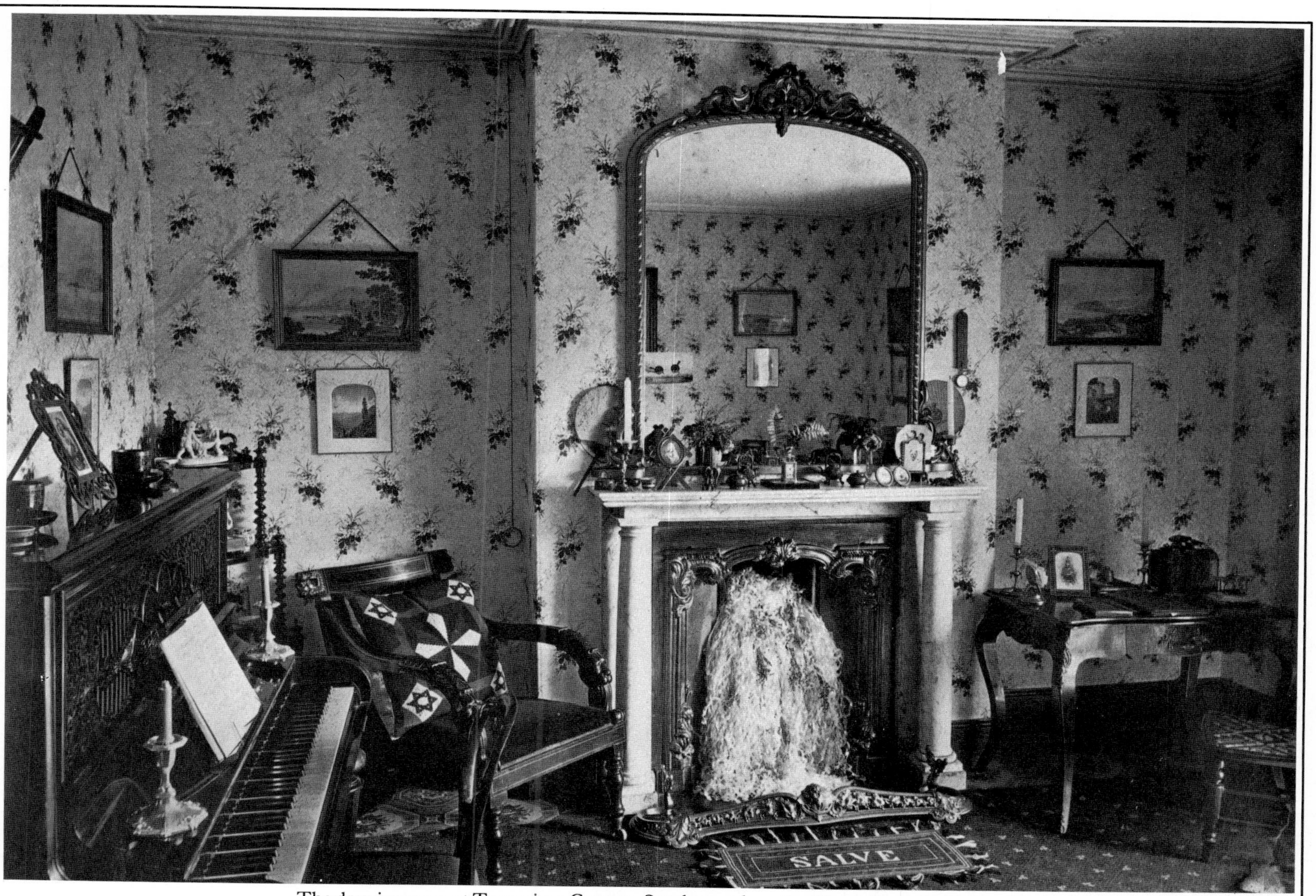
SALVE

The drawing room at Trapezium Cottage, Southsea, where the Woods lived during one of their sojourns in England. A typical Victorian interior, the clue that it is summer is provided by the 'paperfall' in the grate

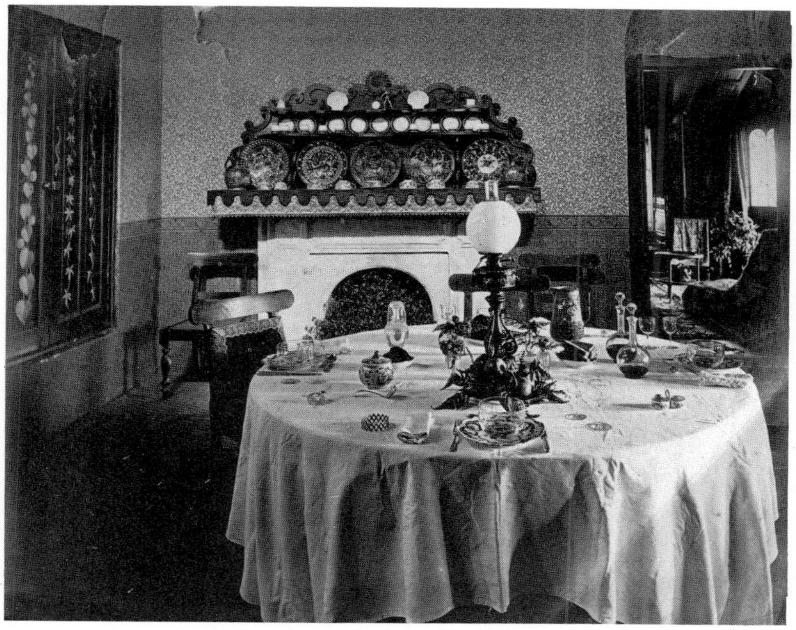

Dining room at Murree, India. The drawing room can be glimpsed through the open doorway

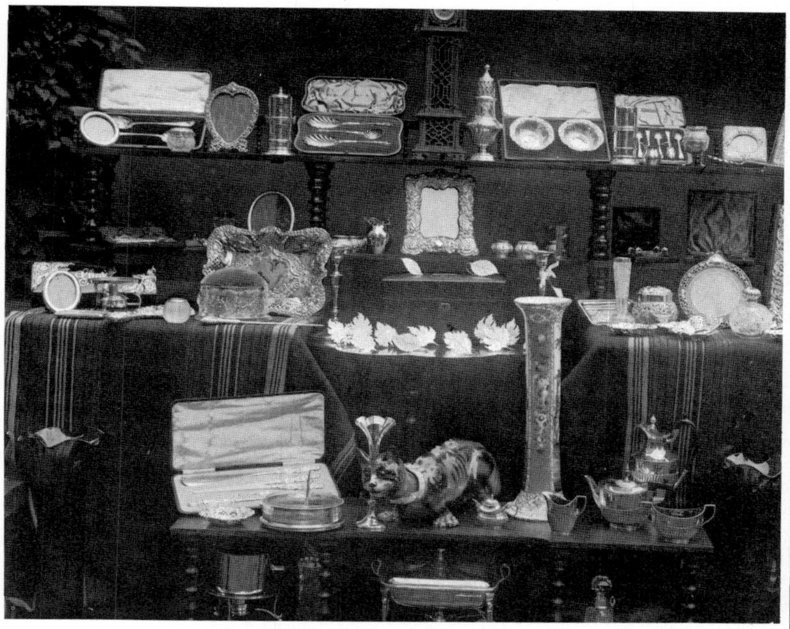

A still life of the family silver, with a china nodding cat in the foreground for light relief

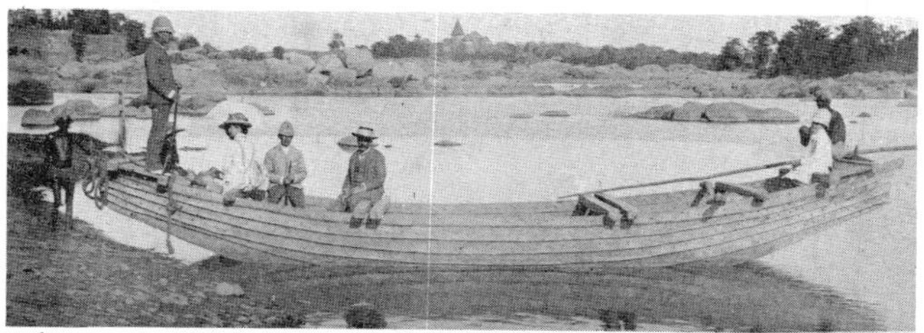

An elegant family picnic on the river, with two boatmen in attendance

BUILDING TO LAST

By Nicholas Taylor. There had never before been such an era of building in Britain as the Victorian age. This was scarcely surprising: the population increased almost threefold and houses were needed for the people to live in. But it was a mobile population too, and a people with money in its communal pocket; it needed great public buildings, from the railway stations – and all the associated edifices from bridges to engine houses which went with a railway system – to the places of public resort, like the Albert Hall and the exhibition buildings. Iron and steel came to the aid of architects, particularly in helping to solve the problem of how to roof over vast concourses. York railway station, below, is one of the most satisfying results, with the great train shed

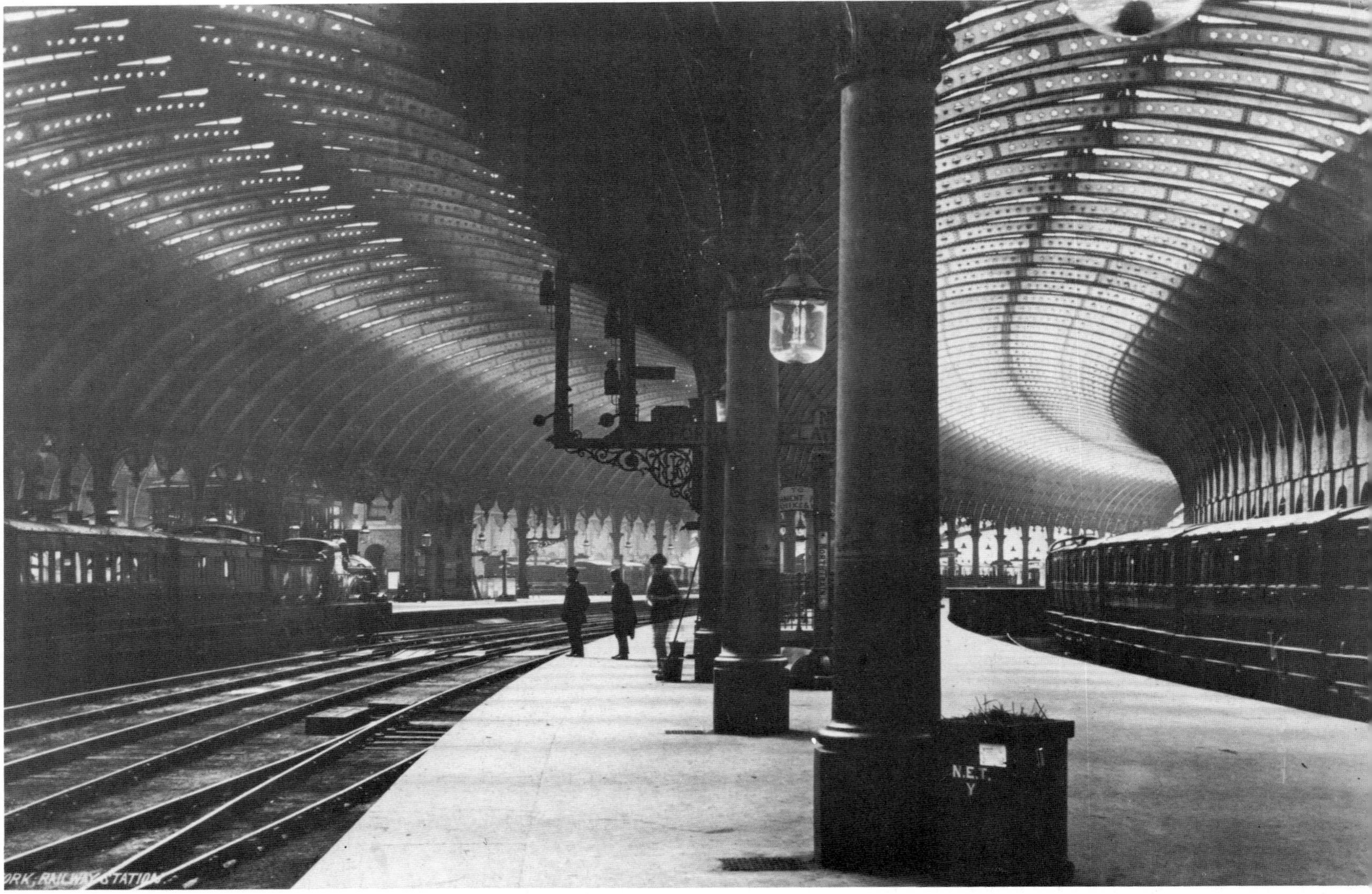
N.E.T.
Y

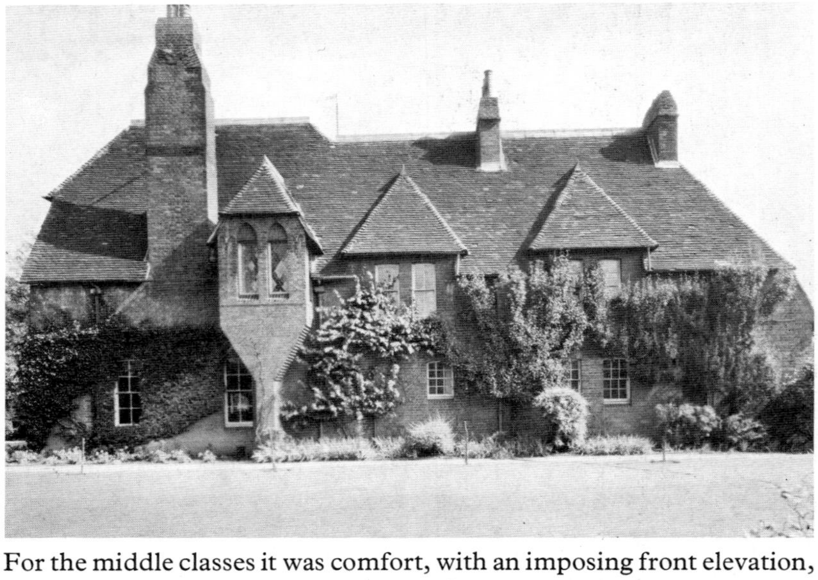

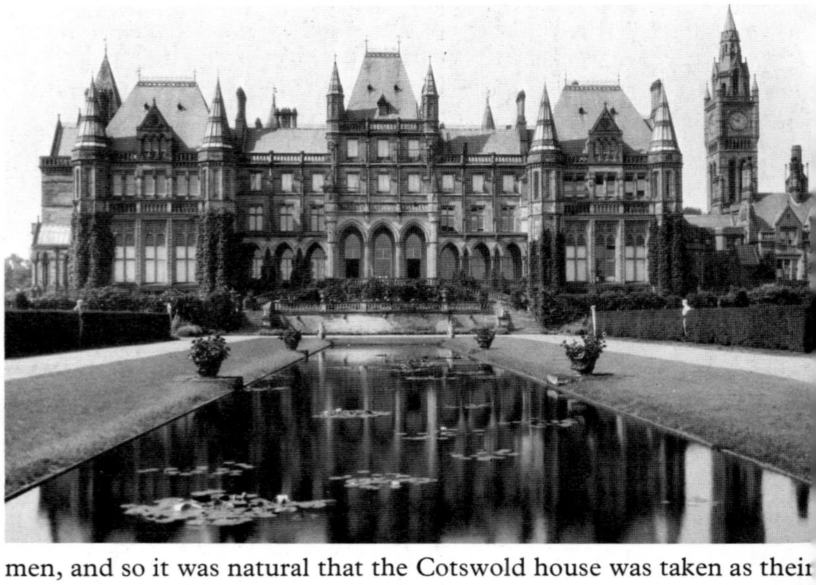

For the middle classes it was comfort, with an imposing front elevation, that a man looked for. As the classical Regency villas degenerated into pretentious Italianate and mass-produced Gothic ornamentation, the intellectuals began to be disturbed. Repelled by the vulgarity they saw springing up around them, they adopted a purist line. William Morris went for functional medievalism, and turned to English vernacular architecture. Morris and so many of those around him were Oxford men, and so it was natural that the Cotswold house was taken as their model. Philip Webb built the Red House (above left) at Upton for Morris in 1859. He stressed sound construction, well laid bricks, basic form rather than ornament, everything, in fact, which is insisted upon today. The aristocracy, however, wanted a more literary and fantastic Gothic. Eaton Hall (above right), which Alfred Waterhouse remodelled for the Duke of Westminster was one of the most notorious examples.

following the pleasing curve of the existing line. All is in iron, from the fretting which closes off the top of the shed at either end – York is not a terminus – to the great ranks of corinthian columns which march along the platforms. It is still there. A planned relationship between factory and dwelling was unusual, but not unknown – the idea went back to Robert Owen and the previous century. Saltaire, the creation of Sir Titus Salt, a model town just outside Bradford also stands today as a mid-century example. The great factory was opened in 1853 with a gigantic temperance banquet for two and a half thousand workers and over a thousand other guests. Opposite the factory Salt built a Congregational church. The model town to house the workers is built on a grid system, with schools, baths, wash-houses and other amenities all in a good workmanlike Venetian Gothic. The engraving below shows it in a pleasantly sylvan setting romanticising industry.

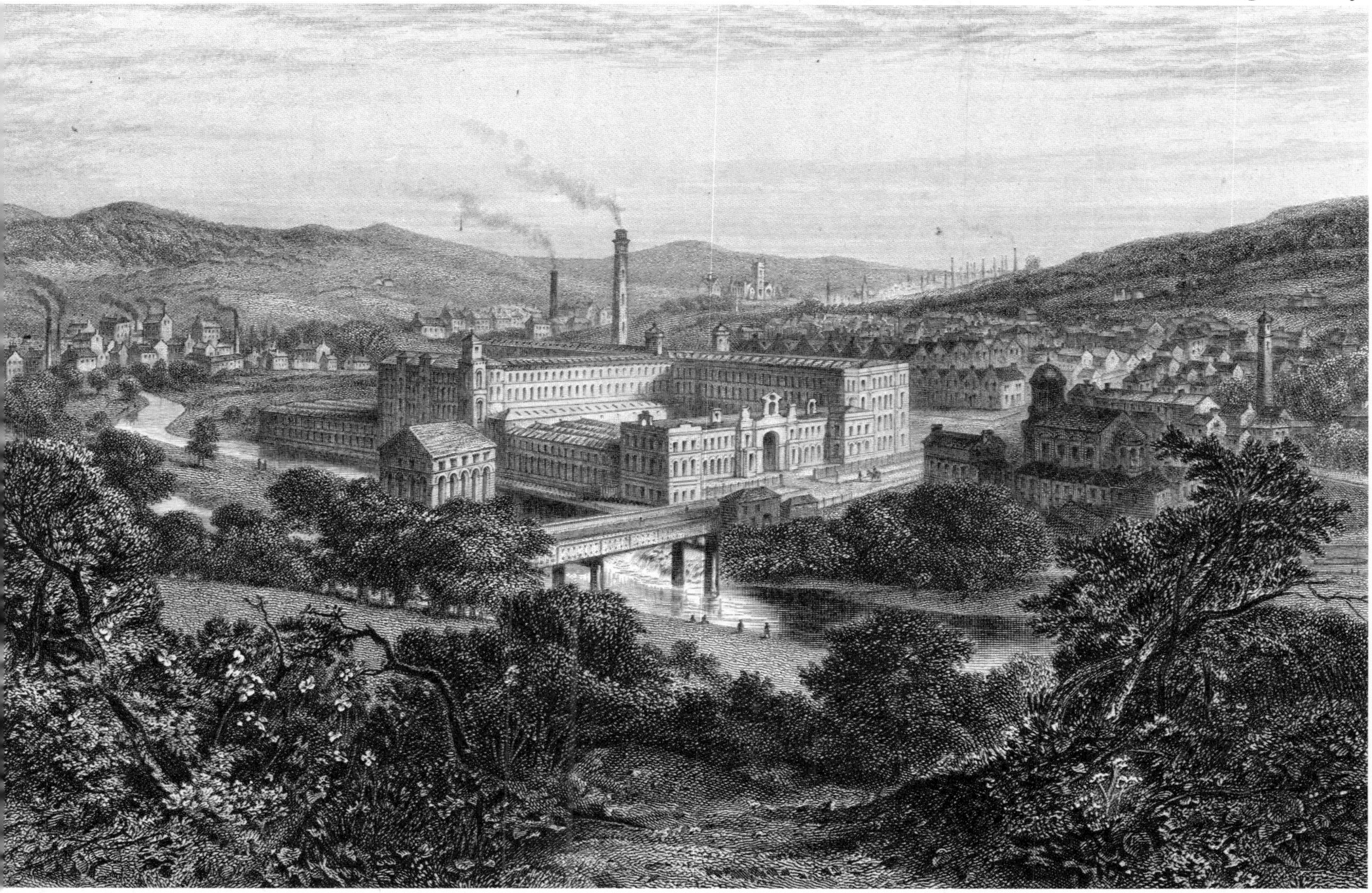

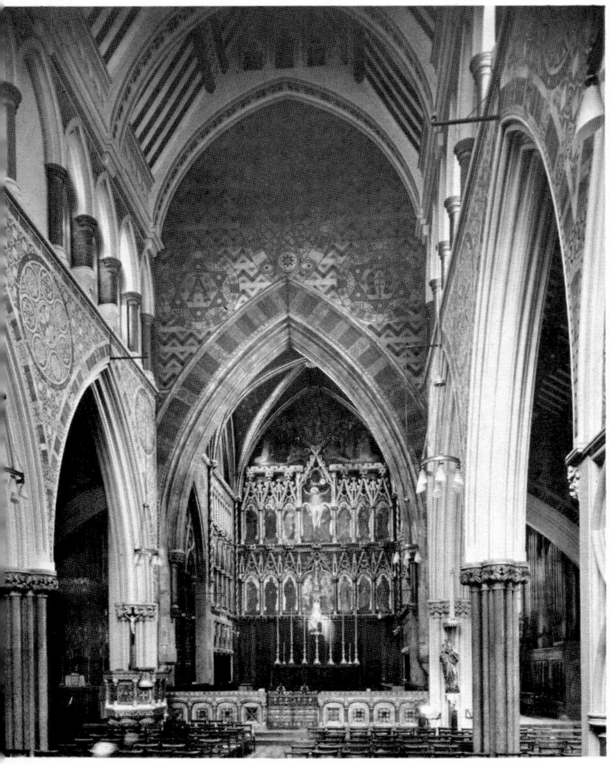

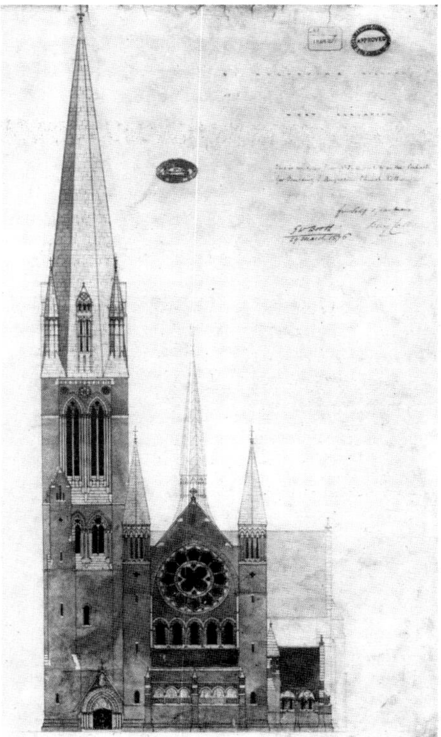

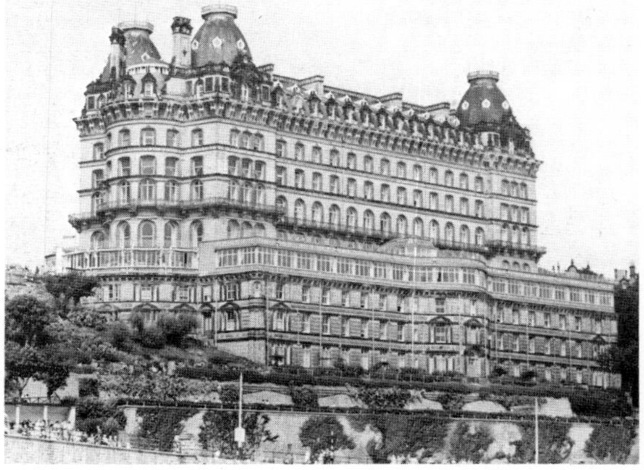

Comfort, too, was what hotels were for. Few buildings could be uglier than Cuthbert Broderick's Grand Hotel, Scarborough (above), but its curious style does at least convey solidity. Churches could rarely be anything other than Gothic. All Saints, Margaret Street (far left), in London, is curiously, an example of Gothic as a modern style. Butterfield, who built it, insisted that only the materials of the age were to be used. The more delicate, scholarly St Augustine's, Kilburn (left), is by the fastidious J. L. Pearson

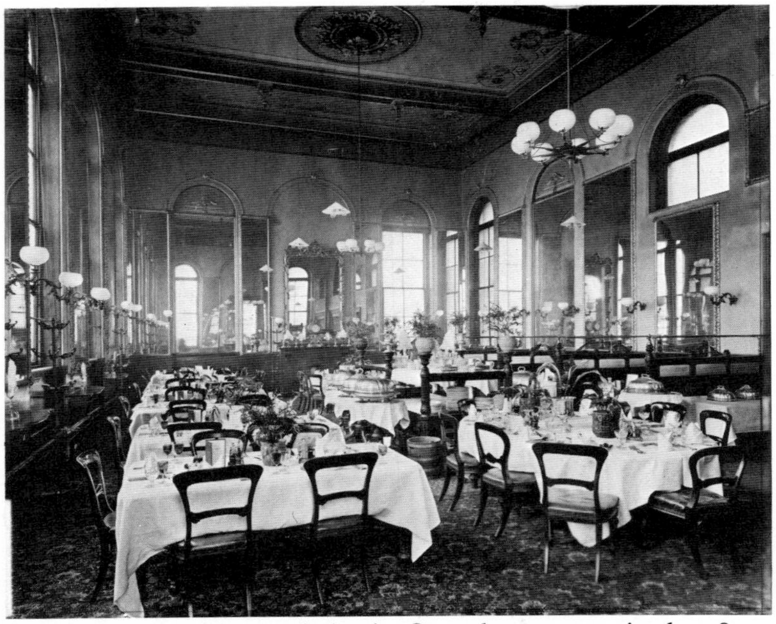

Public interior: Simpson's in the Strand restaurant in the 1890s

By the end of the century, the proud towers of the Gothic revival punctuated the sky-line of England: innumerable churches, even an Anglican cathedral, brand new, at Truro. And Gothic became the official imperial form for public secular building, too: town halls and government offices, which had in the early years of Victoria's reign followed a classical pattern – Rome and Athens, the great ancient republics, were clearly the best architectural inspiration for good government. Palmerston had vetoed a Gothic Foreign Office, and even the Renaissance Italian substitute was seen as a compromise. But now the Goths carried all before them

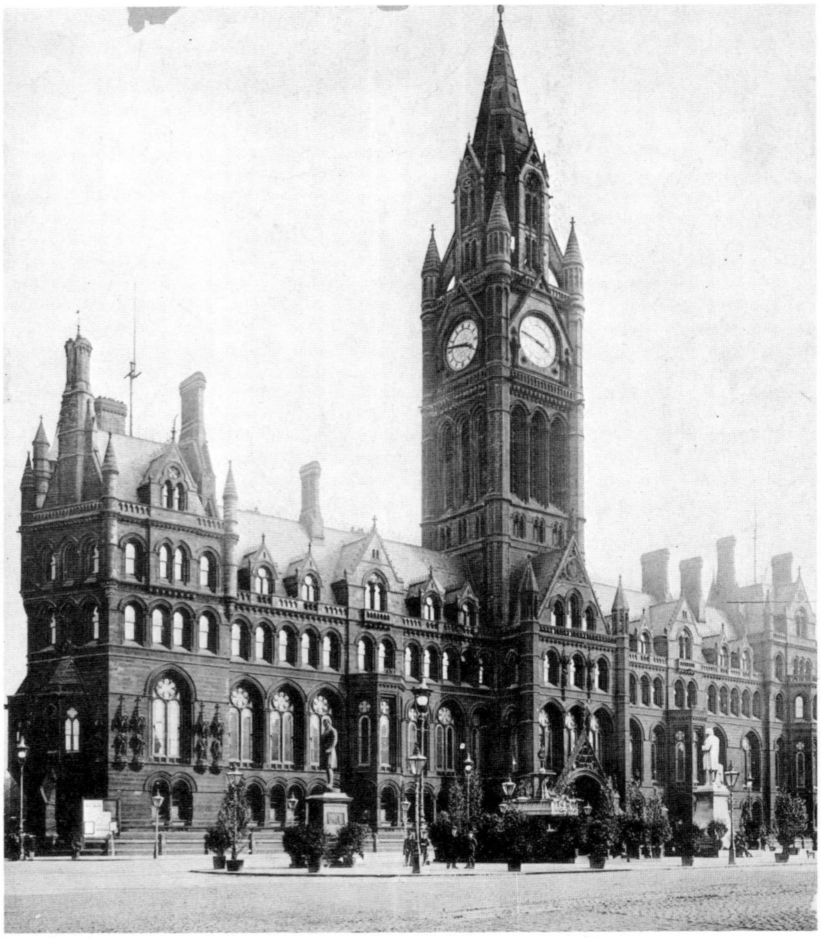

Public exterior: Manchester Town Hall, by Alfred Waterhouse, c. 1868

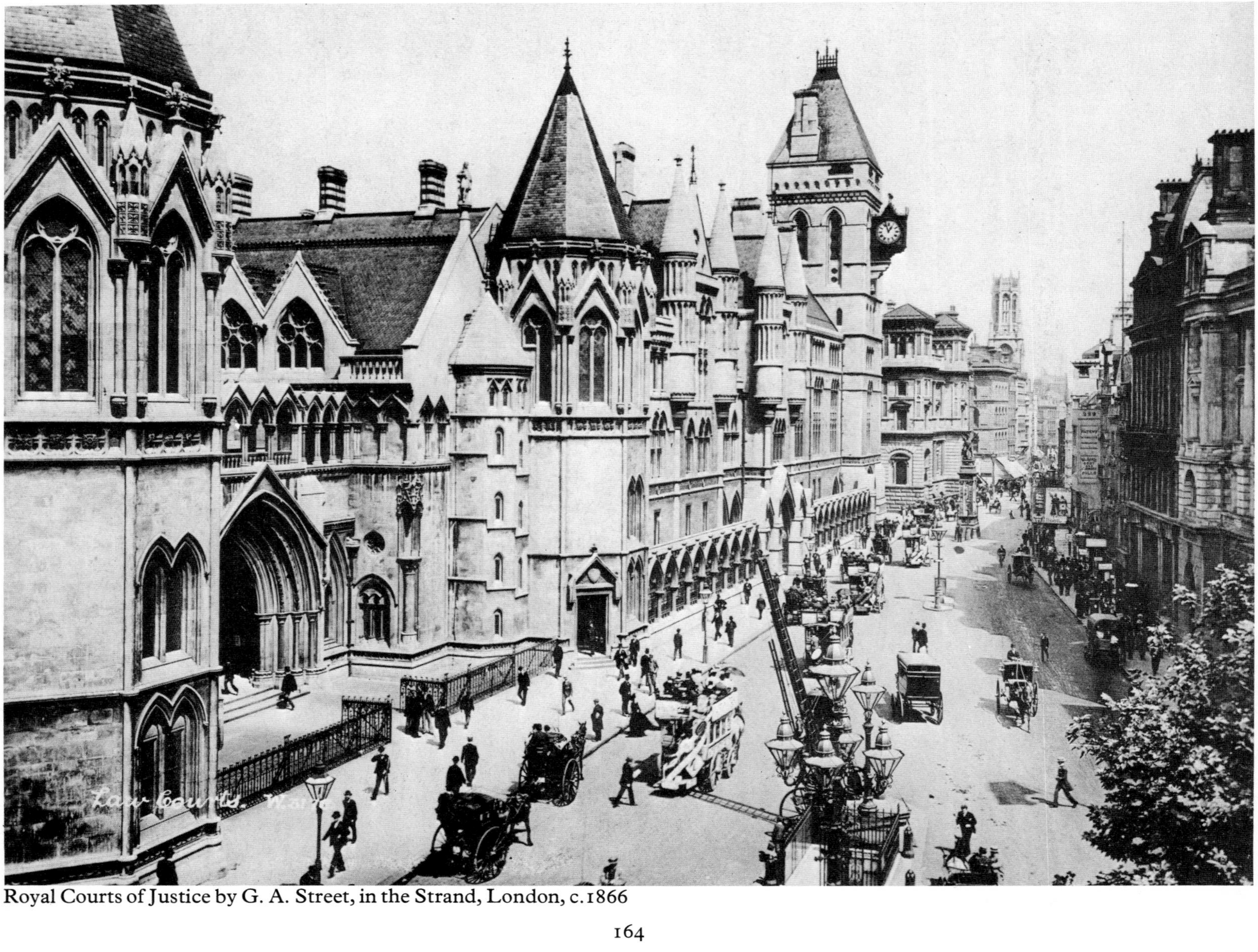
Law Courts.

Royal Courts of Justice by G. A. Street, in the Strand, London, c.1866

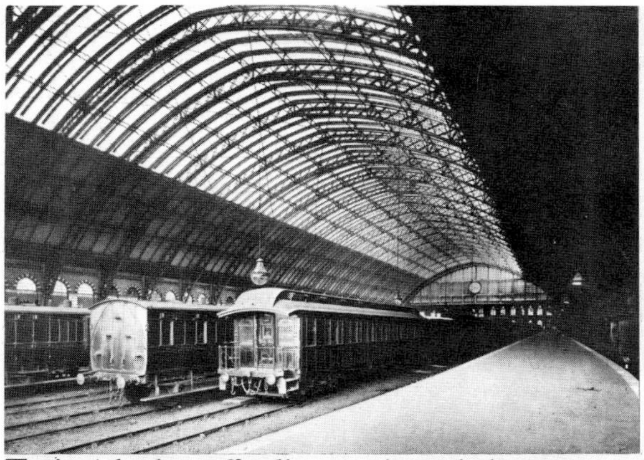

Train sheds, affording unimpeded cover to trains, platforms and passengers, provided one of the great challenges to architects. St Pancras has the finest of all, designed by W. H. Barlow

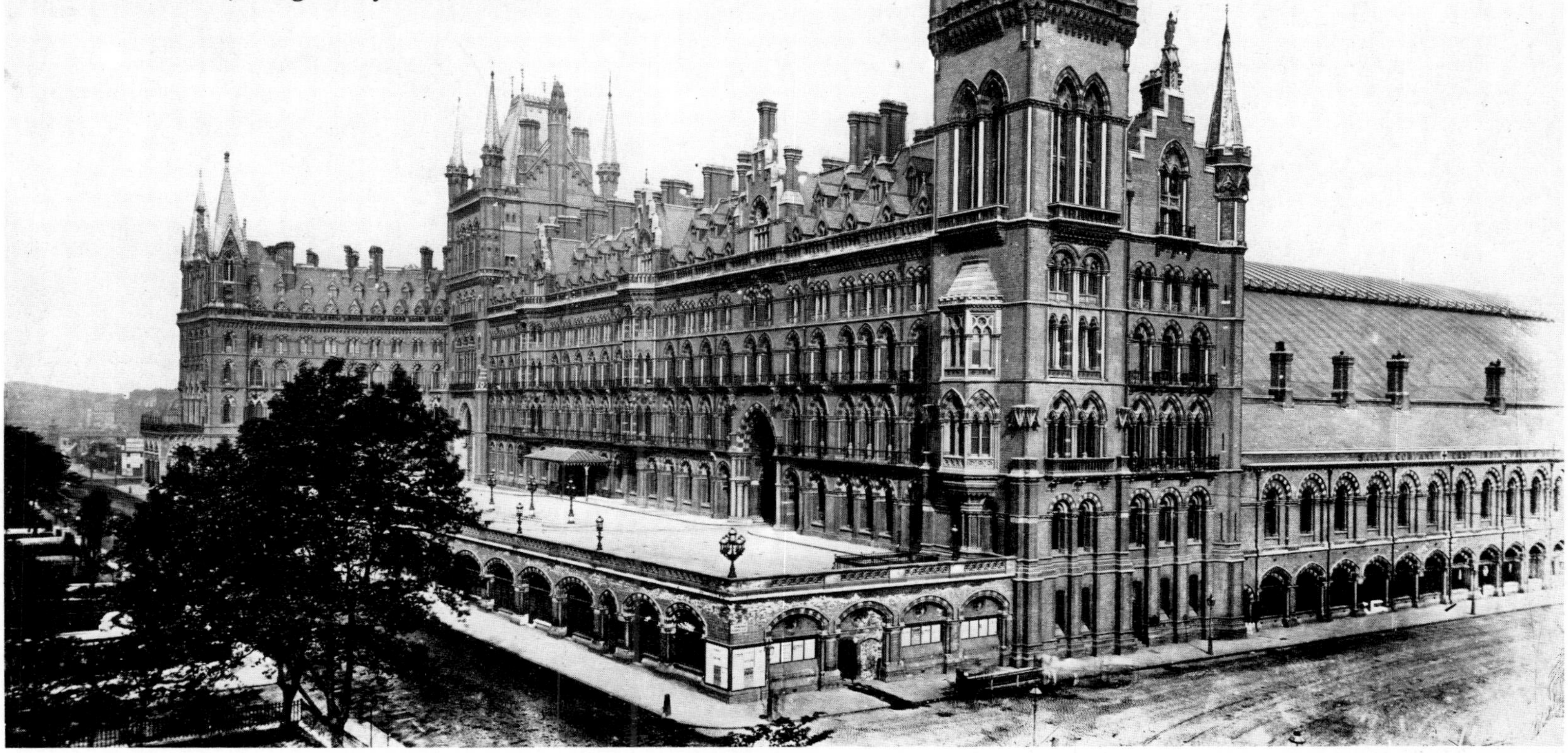

The hotel at St Pancras station (above, 1874), a Gothic façade for Barlow's superb iron arched shed, was the work of Sir Gilbert Scott, designer of the Albert Memorial. No expense was spared to make it the pride of the London and Midland Railway, as the fine encaustic tiling of the stairway shows (below left). In Glasgow Charles Rennie Mackintosh anticipated much of the architecture of the 1930s. The main façade of his Glasgow School of Art (below right), with the big metal windows of the studio and the art nouveau detail, dates from 1896–9

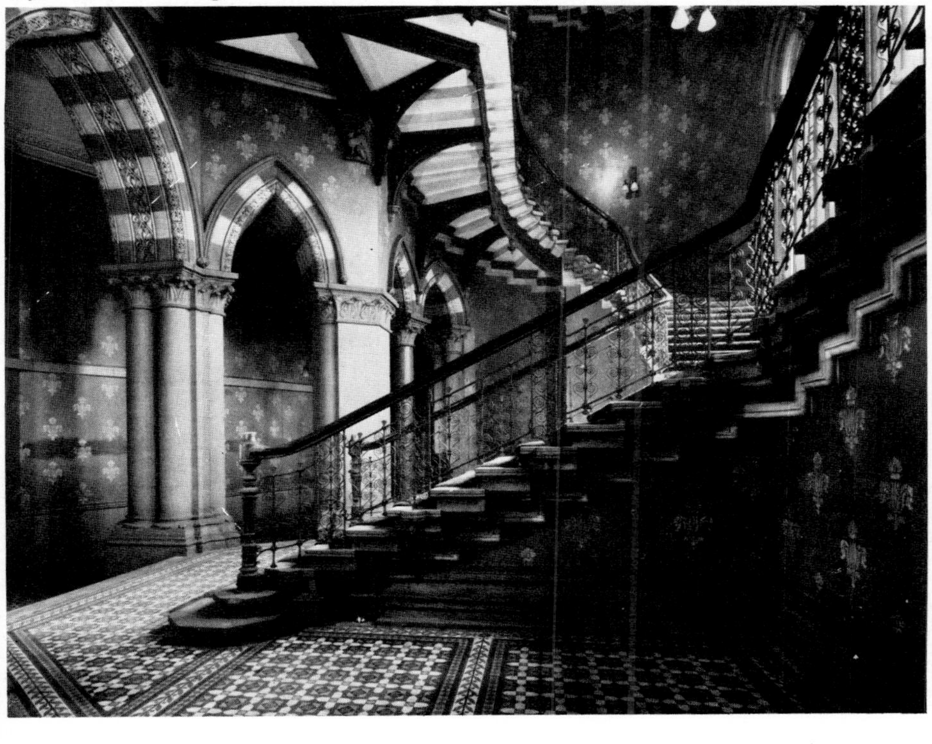

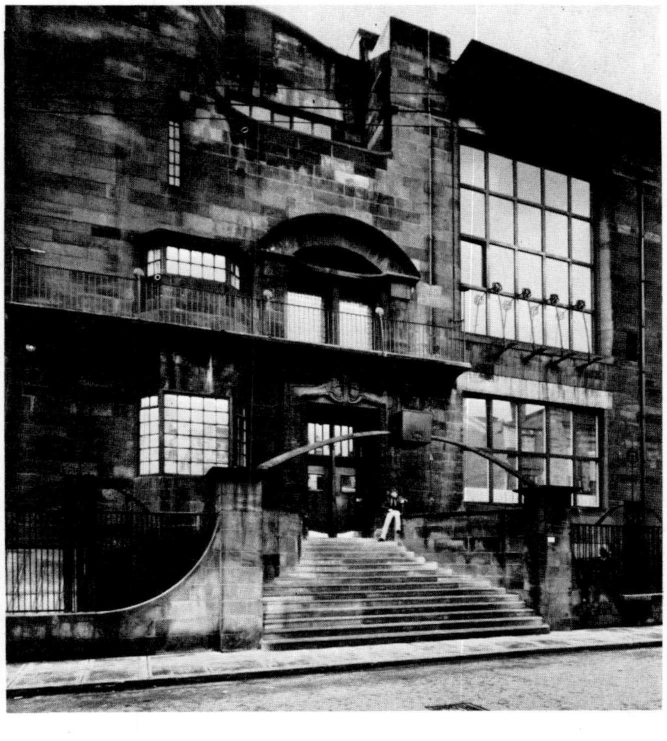

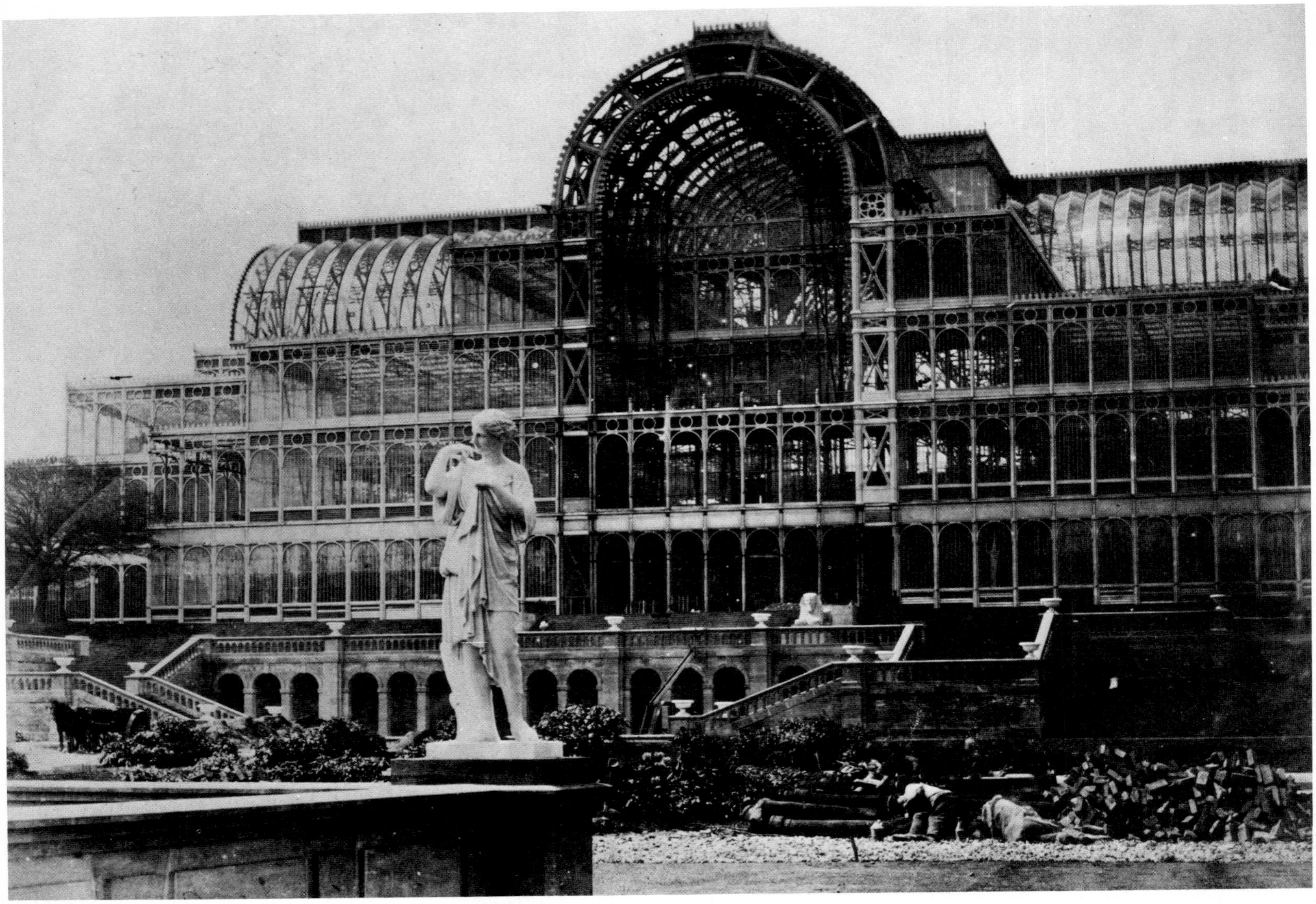

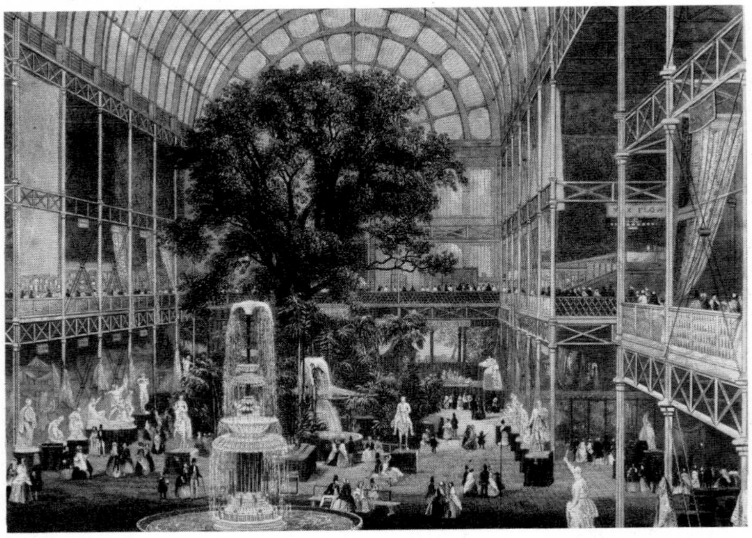

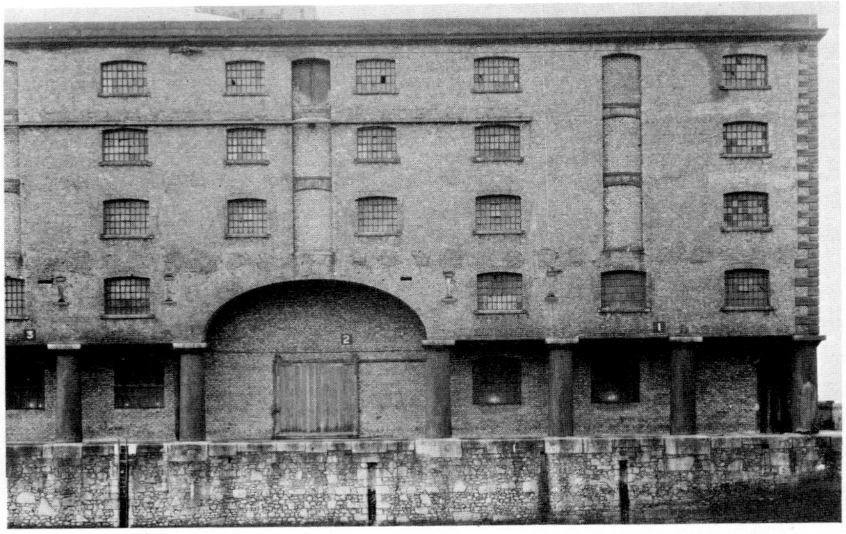

Trains and steamships combined to make London – the country's leading port in Victorian times – a magnet for the rest of England in the way it had never been before. Larger than many continental countries in population, it was itself visited every year by tens of thousands of foreigners, many from the United States or the British colonies. Architecture called on the skills of the engineer and the two professions now began to meet. Nothing dramatised more London's pre-eminent position as a world centre than the Great Exhibition of 1851. Conceived by Prince Albert as an occasion to demonstrate the high state of manufacturing and an opportunity for all the world to display its products, the Exhibition was planned on a vast scale. The nature of the building to house all the exhibits and the great crowds confidently expected presented a considerable problem. Heavy, lumpish and conventional designs were being considered when Joseph Paxton, who had begun life as a gardener's boy, quickly sketched his gigantic greenhouse on the famous piece of blotting paper at a committee meeting – the Crystal Palace. It caught the public imagination, and itself became the symbol of the exhibition and the first factor in its enormous success. It can serve as an object lesson in Victorian technology. Prefabricated in standard iron and glass sections, it could be put up quickly, and just as easily taken down again. The tubular iron pillars in the pavilion (bottom left) were hollow, and carried rainwater away from the roof. And the great elm trees of Hyde Park flourished happily as never before inside the great greenhouse. So popular was the Palace that a cry of outrage went up when it was proposed to scrap it when the Exhibition was closed. A company was hastily formed, and the Crystal Palace was re-erected (top picture), and indeed extended, to survive on the heights of Sydenham in South London until it was destroyed by fire in 1936. Some of the best Victorian buildings which survive today are by practical men, like

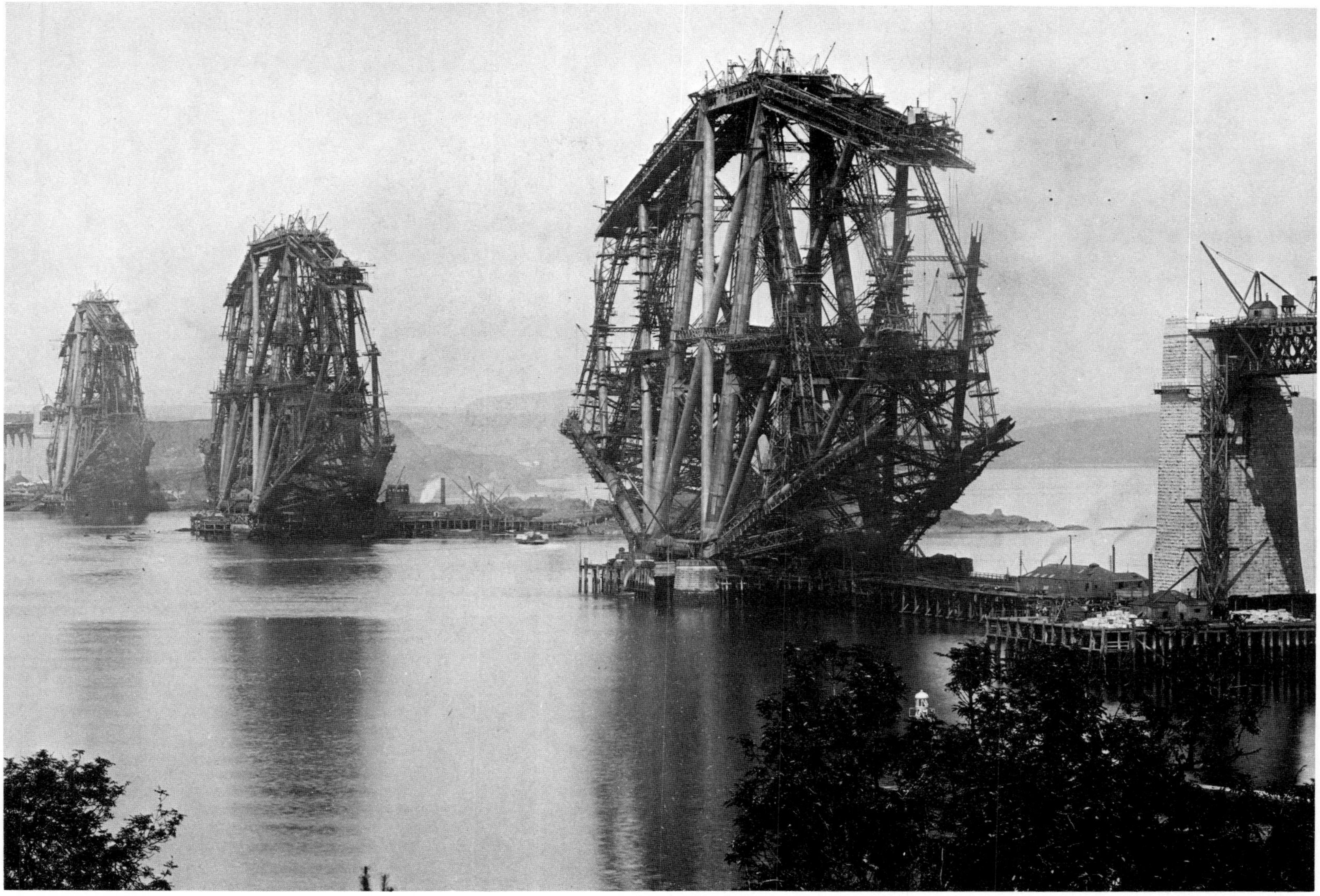

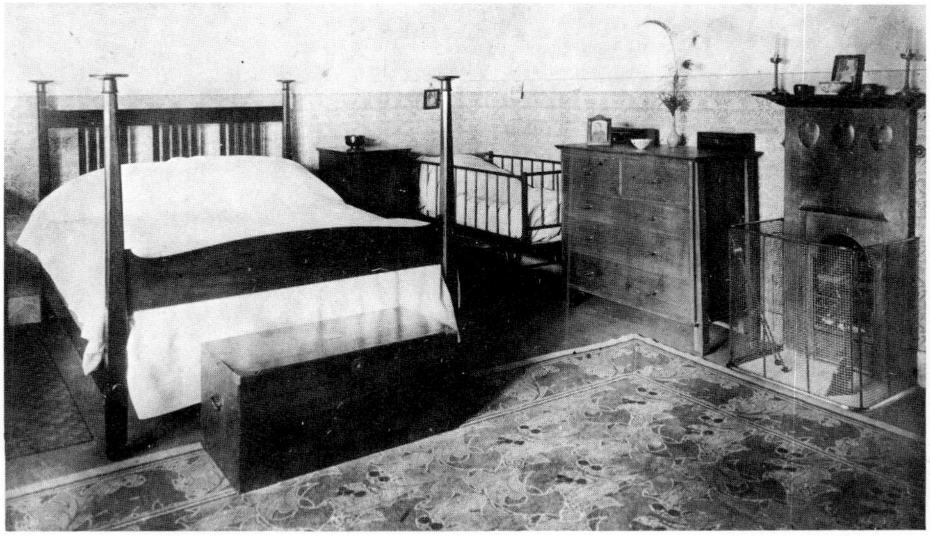

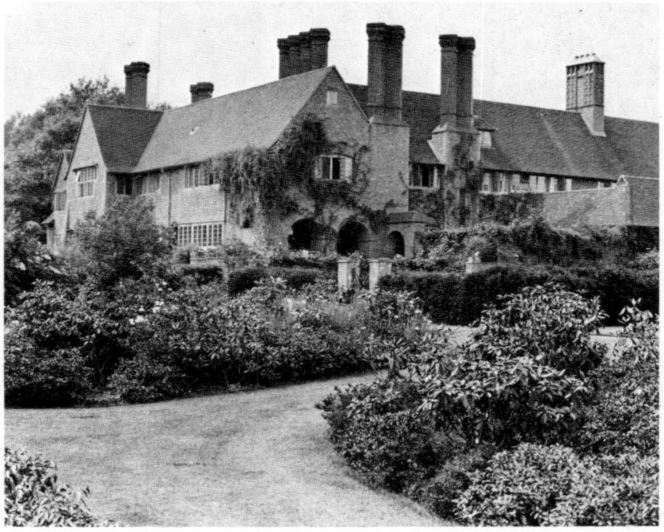

Paxton, with no polite university education. Engineers often had a superb sense of style. Brunel's aquaducts and tunnel entrances are handsome, to be admired in their own right. The prince of the dock builders was Jesse Hartley, who was Dock Engineer at Liverpool between 1824 and 1860. He inherited dock buildings of sandstone, he left a great system of durable granite. Hartley delighted in the strength of his material, and he reflected this in the buildings he designed around his great harbour system. Here is strength – for his walls he used the biggest blocks possible – and the complex has a feeling of the classical about it. His greatest triumph was the Albert Dock (opposite page, bottom right), with its doric-columned warehouses. Even an undecorated and purely engineered structure often had an infectious rhythm about it – perhaps more so than the pretentious academic building. The Forth railway bridge (top) was the largest built in Britain during the century, and was the most celebrated triumph of the 1880s. The huge tubes were fabricated on site, and a number of machines and techniques were specially invented. In domestic architecture, too, Britain had gained admiration – not for the run-of-the-mill terraced house or semi, but for the movement which had begun with Morris's Red House. The fine interiors of C. F. A. Voysey (above left), with their white painted woodwork, fine textiles and wall-papers and furniture of oak unpainted and unpolished, designed for the lovely proportions of the room, were raved about on the Continent. Perhaps Sir Edwin Lutyens is thought of more today for his pompous offices in London and his work at New Delhi. But he began with romantic, vernacular country houses. Orchards (above right) represents a crowning achievement of this phase of his wide-ranging career. It is at Goldalming, in Surrey, in warm red brick with ample red roofs, tall chimney stacks, deep entrance ways – an idealised, eminently habitable house in the country.

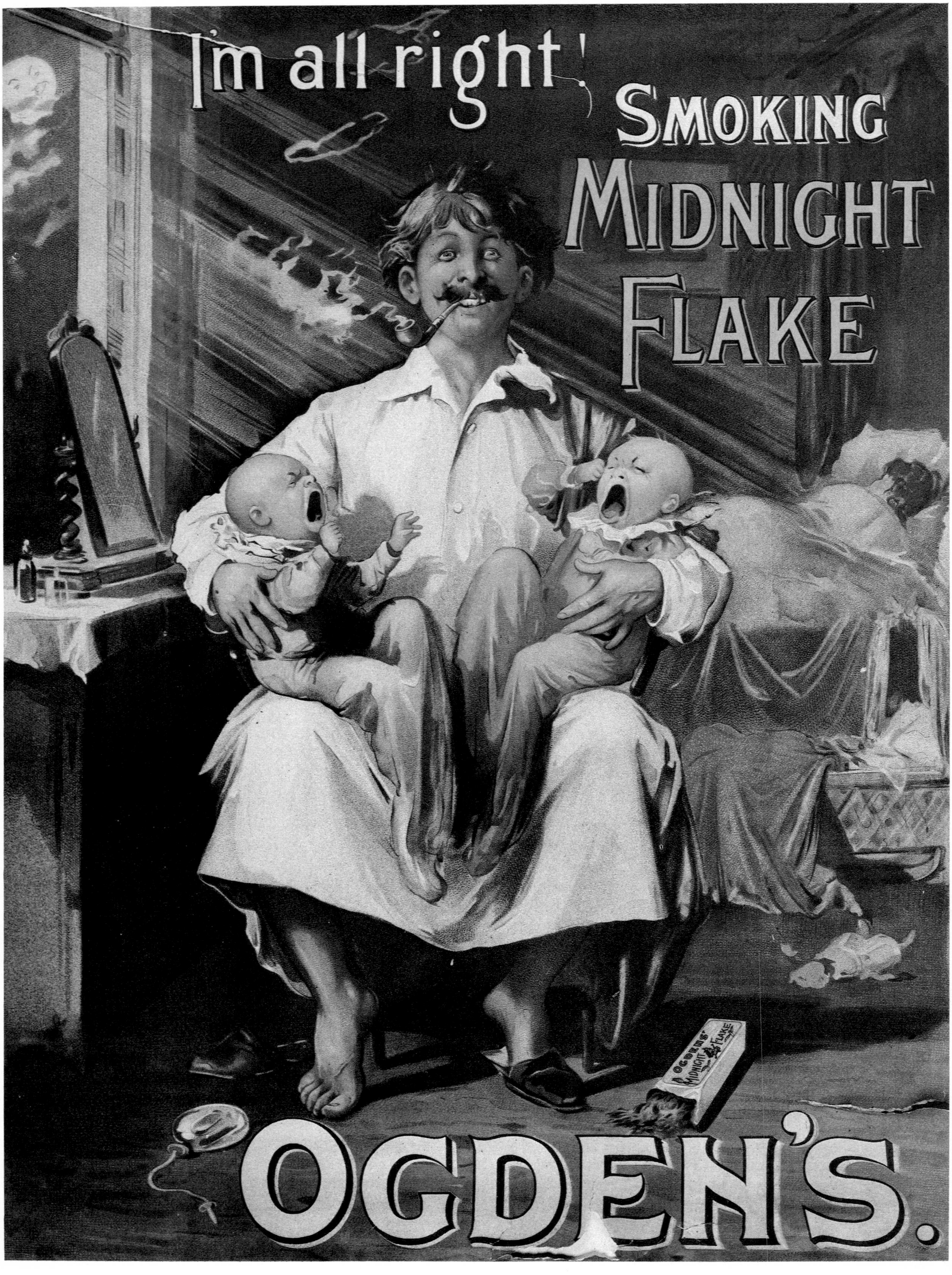
I'm all right!
SMOKING
MIDNIGHT
FLAKE
OGDEN'S
MIDNIGHT FLAKE
OGDEN'S.

A NATION OF SALESMEN

By Graham Norton

Advertising became, in Victorian times, an organised business which threatened to get out of hand. Even the Queen herself appeared on the poster sites drinking branded tea

"Good Morning! Have you used Pears' Soap?" Lillie Langtry had, and her signature – *and* Patti's, plus endorsements from Professor Sir Erasmus Wilson, FRS ("the greatest English authority on the skin") and the eminent American preacher Henry Ward Beecher – confronted the Victorians everywhere they went, from hoardings, display cards, hand bills and magazine advertisements. Empire builders could not escape, for the advertisers had quite often gone before them, painting slogans on the savage rocks of the Sudan or the demure city streets of Durban. In America, before blocking tariffs, British soap went west with the waggons, and in the Civil War Holloway's Pills printed special posters in the United States showing wounded Union soldiers stretching out their grateful hands for this British specific – which would do little for their wounds, but would, however, effectively and quickly purge their bowels.

All that pent-up 19th-century energy which pushed back the frontiers of technology, left no corner of the world unexplored and no child nominally unschooled and unchurched spilled over into advertising. The beginnings of mass production needed promotion to provide purchasing impetus, whipping up demand to cope with the ever-increasing supply: the profits which could come from massive large-scale production had been discovered.

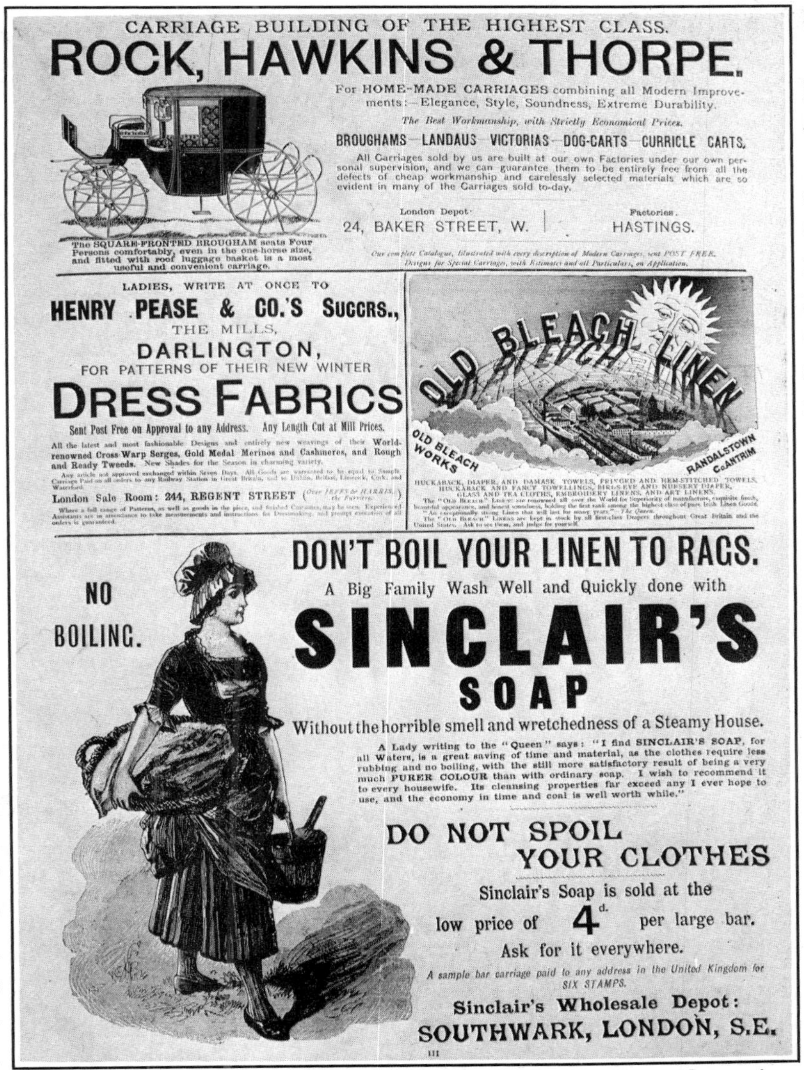

CARRIAGE BUILDING OF THE HIGHEST CLASS.
ROCK, HAWKINS & THORPE.
For HOME-MADE CARRIAGES combining all Modern Improvements:—Elegance, Style, Soundness, Extreme Durability.
The Best Workmanship, with Strictly Economical Prices.
BROUGHAMS—LANDAUS—VICTORIAS—DOG-CARTS—CURRICLE CARTS.
All Carriages sold by us are built at our own Factories under our own personal supervision, and we can guarantee them to be entirely free from all the defects of cheap workmanship and carelessly selected materials which are so evident in many of the Carriages sold to-day.
London Depot: 24, BAKER STREET, W.
Factories. HASTINGS.
The SQUARE-FRONTED BROUGHAM seats Four Persons comfortably, even in the one-horse size, and fitted with roof luggage basket in a most useful and convenient carriage.
LADIES, WRITE AT ONCE TO
HENRY PEASE & CO.'S SUCCRS.,
THE MILLS,
DARLINGTON,
FOR PATTERNS OF THEIR NEW WINTER
DRESS FABRICS
Sent Post Free on Approval to any Address. Any Length Cut at Mill Prices.
All the latest and most fashionable Designs and entirely new weavings of their World-renowned Cross Warp Serges, Gold Medal Merinos and Cashmeres, and Rough and Ready Tweeds. New Shades for the Season in charming variety.
London Sale Room: 244, REGENT STREET
OLD BLEACH LINEN
OLD BLEACH WORKS
RANDALSTOWN Co. ANTRIM
HUCKABACK, DIAPER, AND DAMASK TOWELS, FRINGED AND HEM-STITCHED TOWELS, HUCKABACK AND FANCY TOWELLINGS, BIRDS-EYE AND NURSERY DIAPER, GLASS AND TEA CLOTHS, EMBROIDERY LINENS, AND ART LINENS.
DON'T BOIL YOUR LINEN TO RAGS.
NO BOILING.
A Big Family Wash Well and Quickly done with
SINCLAIR'S SOAP
Without the horrible smell and wretchedness of a Steamy House.
A Lady writing to the "Queen" says: "I find SINCLAIR'S SOAP, for all Waters, is a great saving of time and material, as the clothes require less rubbing and no boiling, with the still more satisfactory result of being a very much PURER COLOUR than with ordinary soap. I wish to recommend it to every housewife. Its cleansing properties far exceed any I ever hope to use, and the economy in time and coal is well worth while."
DO NOT SPOIL YOUR CLOTHES
Sinclair's Soap is sold at the low price of 4d. per large bar.
Ask for it everywhere.
A sample bar carriage paid to any address in the United Kingdom for SIX STAMPS.
Sinclair's Wholesale Depot:
SOUTHWARK, LONDON, S.E.
III

Above: a page from Pears Christmas Annual 1891. Opposite: humour was one of the basic and most effective advertising methods

The first to realise this were the pill-pushers – Victorians relied enormously on patent medicines; they were cheap, and in those pre-antibiotic days there was very little that orthodox medicine could do. Backed by extensive advertising as an aid to faith, the psychological effect of an over-the-counter powder or pill might be a good deal more effective than a prescription. And just as the pill-maker's advice to the sick was the simple message to take more if the first dose didn't cure, so his own business salvation lay in the same direction – take more advertising if the public was slow to buy.

The printing industry had not been left behind in the great wave of improvements: years before Queen Victoria *The Times* and other newspapers had been printed by steam. For the poster, besides crude wood-cuts, lithography had been available since the early 19th century.

There were, however, man-made obstacles in the way, as irritating as the man with the red flag who stood in the way of the motor car. The first of these was the tax on newspapers in general. Until 1855 all daily and weekly papers had to be stamped. Anyone who looks up *The Times* or the *Illustrated London News* in a library can still see the red imprint, with its tiny bit of fugitive lead foil, impressed somewhere on the design. There was also a tax on newsprint, and a further tax on advertisements, which was fixed in 1833 at a flat rate of 1s. 6d. even for one line in the personal column.

The Inland Revenue interpreted this tax in the strictest way. A favourable reference to any saleable commodity in a newspaper's editorial pages was construed as an advertisement – the civil service plainly believed that the journalist could be easily bought – and claimed accordingly. Book reviews were forced to leave out the name of the publisher, and even then a rave review might still be the cause of a claim for 1s. 6d. An item reporting the arrival of the new season's vegetables might be subject to a similar swoop. However, in 1853 the tax was abolished – its principle was revived in the 1960s by the television advertisement levy – and the paper duties went in 1861. Coupled with recent advances in the art of printing the press lay ready for the taking. At the same time, the hoardings which littered the centres of Britain's great cities, from London to Leeds – all being rebuilt to accommodate the railways and the business they were bringing – were not to be left naked.

Up to the 1860s, war was the natural state between the bill-stickers. Out would go bands of "the boiled flour

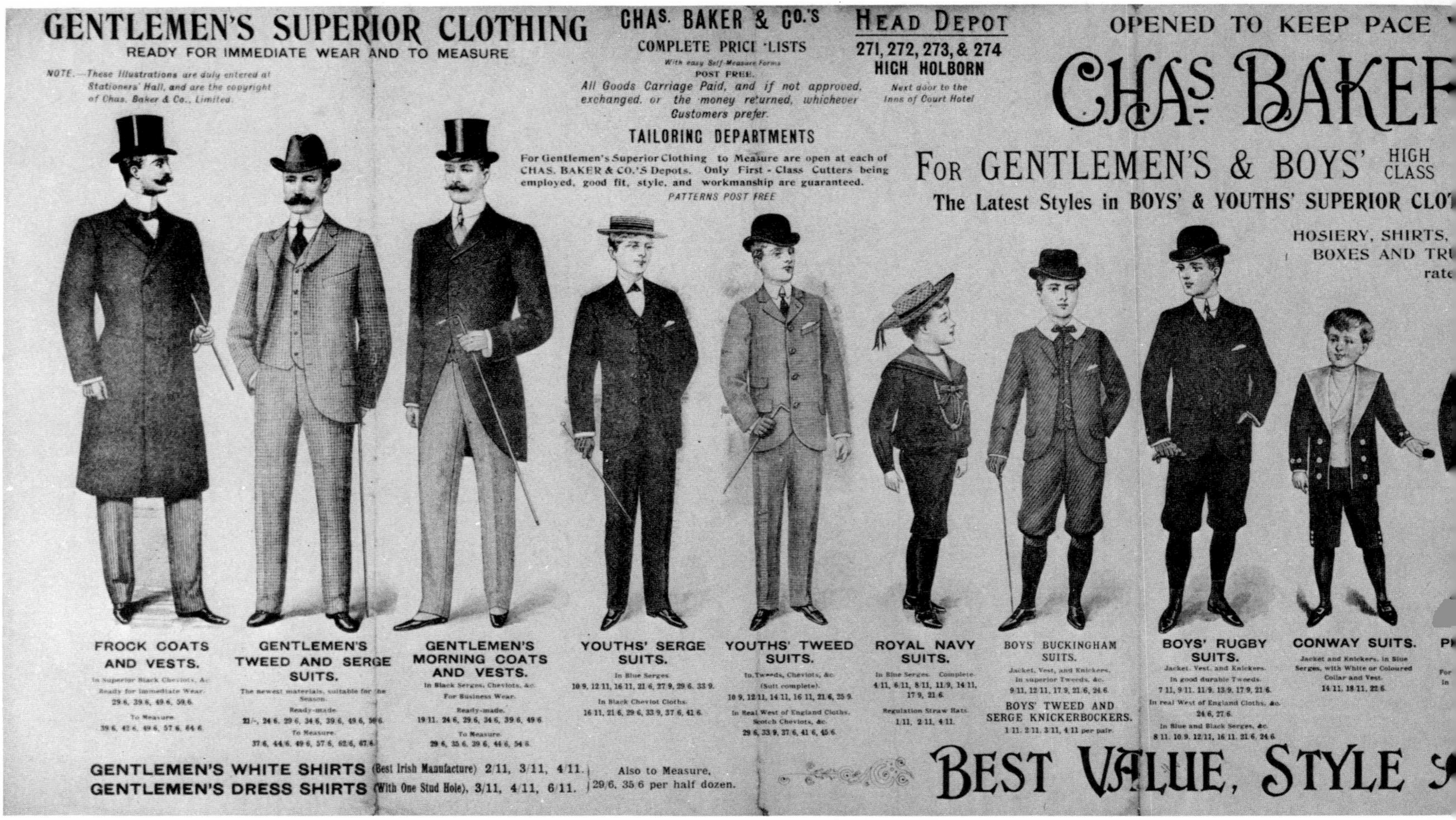
GENTLEMEN'S SUPERIOR CLOTHING
READY FOR IMMEDIATE WEAR AND TO MEASURE
NOTE.—These Illustrations are duly entered at Stationers' Hall, and are the copyright of Chas. Baker & Co., Limited.
CHAS. BAKER & CO.'S
COMPLETE PRICE LISTS
POST FREE.
All Goods Carriage Paid, and if not approved, exchanged, or the money returned, whichever Customers prefer.
TAILORING DEPARTMENTS
For Gentlemen's Superior Clothing to Measure are open at each of CHAS. BAKER & CO.'S Depots. Only First-Class Cutters being employed, good fit, style, and workmanship are guaranteed.
PATTERNS POST FREE
HEAD DEPOT
271, 272, 273, & 274
HIGH HOLBORN
Next door to the Inns of Court Hotel
OPENED TO KEEP PACE
CHAS BAKER
FOR GENTLEMEN'S & BOYS' HIGH CLASS
The Latest Styles in BOYS' & YOUTHS' SUPERIOR
FROCK COATS AND VESTS.
GENTLEMEN'S TWEED AND SERGE SUITS.
GENTLEMEN'S MORNING COATS AND VESTS.
YOUTHS' SERGE SUITS.
YOUTHS' TWEED SUITS.
ROYAL NAVY SUITS.
BOYS' BUCKINGHAM SUITS.
BOYS' TWEED AND SERGE KNICKERBOCKERS.
BOYS' RUGBY SUITS.
CONWAY SUITS.
GENTLEMEN'S WHITE SHIRTS (Best Irish Manufacture) 2/11, 3/11, 4/11.
GENTLEMEN'S DRESS SHIRTS (With One Stud Hole), 3/11, 4/11, 6/11.
Also to Measure, 29/6, 35/6 per half dozen.
BEST VALUE, STYLE

frescoists" as the more flowery writers called them, to paste up their fly-posters over any "dead wall", hoarding, house, shopfront or door – it was not uncommon for people to be pasted in and unable to get out in the morning.

It all happened at night. In spite of unauthorised bill-sticking being illegal, the police were powerless to stop the gangs of bill-stickers not only slapping up their own posters but also tearing down those of their rivals. Gangs had pitched battles to gain control over favoured sites, and would go out armed not only with paper and paste, but also with blacking to smear over posters put up by the enemy.

Also out were the vehicles in the shape of monster top-hats or cabbages or Egyptian obelisks which jammed the streets of Dickens' London (he conducted an interview once going through the city on one of these carts). These were banned in 1853, though advertisers occasionally got away with eccentric designs if they could show that they were first and foremost used to carry goods around. But better opportunities were opening up for the advertiser. Colour posters came in. First used in England, to publicise "blood and thunder" melodramas like *Maria and the Red Barn*, they were printed by lithography, using different stones for each colour. Crude but effective, the process was vastly improved by Jules Chéret, who learnt the technique in England, and then went back to Paris and perfected it. French standards of graphic design were better than the British before this: now they excelled.

Chéret began working at the close of the Second Empire, and his work reflected the adoration of healthy young girls which was such a pleasing feature of the period. Chéret not only pioneered the full-colour poster –sometimes using as many as fourteen 'stones' in the process. He also put pretty girls on posters. They have been kept there ever since.

If Chéret's softly seductive girls made the mouths of English visitors water, sending them panting to crowd the Moulin Rouge, it was only to be expected. For at home there was nothing like this. The newspapers and magazines in particular kept to a sober note. It was the age of the loud-spoken journalist – every editor thought of himself as a thunderer – and there was general agreement that the word must be mighty, would be mightier yet, and must on no account be distracted from by allowing any kind of illustration in advertisements.

Advertisers were also trammelled by editorial insistence that rules ran down the edges of columns, and would remain there. It was an advertising doctrine of the time anyway that promotion meant the repetition of the name of the product, so down the columns went such notices as HARLENE FOR THE HAIR in endless sequence. Sometimes a pendant sentence was added, like:

SCRUBB's Cloudy AMMONIA
Household
Try it in your bath

Pictorial journalism had come in in the 1840s, with *Punch* and the *Illustrated London News*. The latter rose to have the highest circulation of any weekly or daily paper in the country, selling nearly 200,000 copies, and being able to charge seven times more than *The Times* for advertising space. Illustrated advertisements were not however at first allowed, but the advertisers were not entirely dismayed; cutting picture blocks in the 1840s

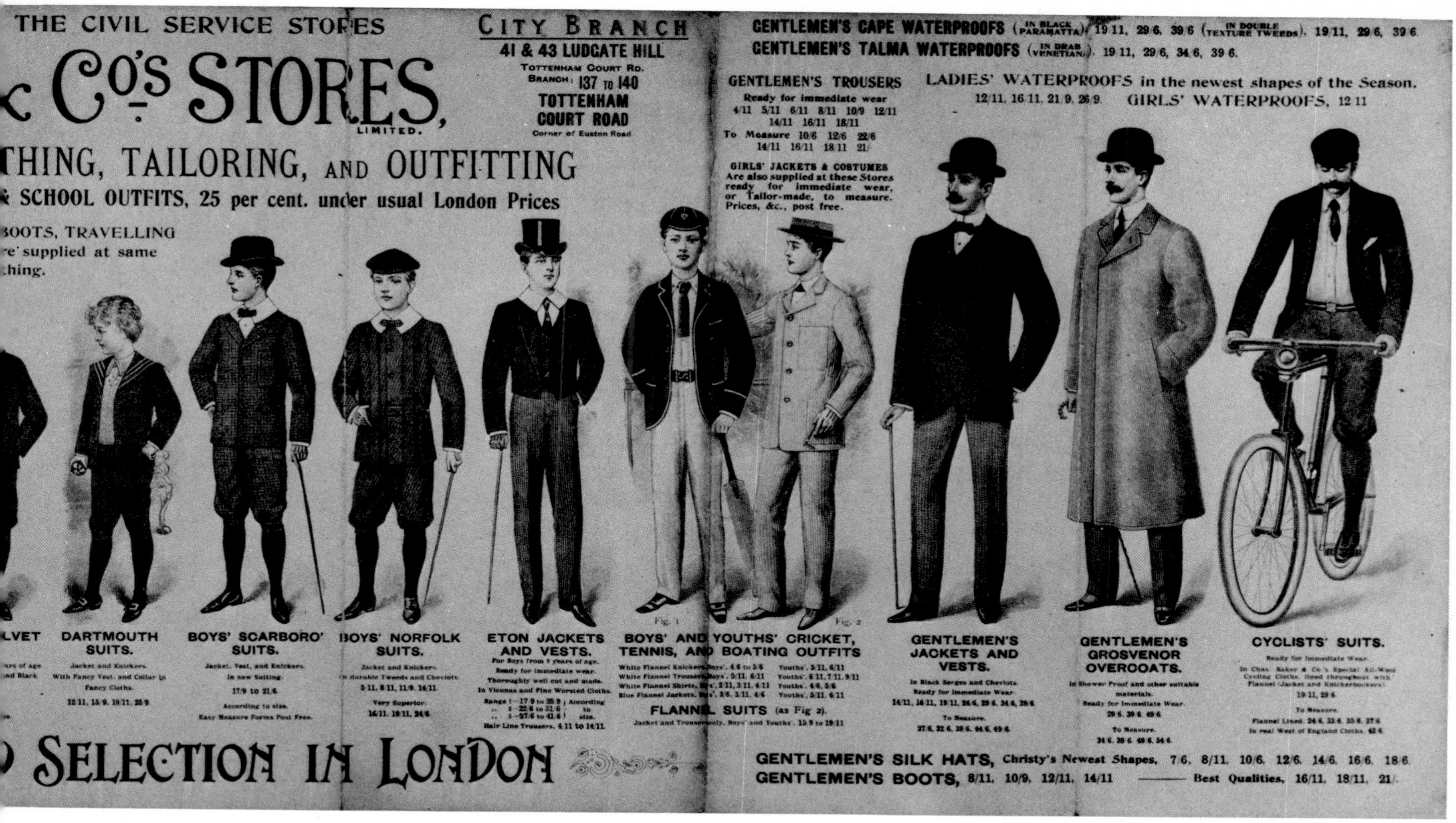
THE CIVIL SERVICE STORES
CITY BRANCH
41 & 43 LUDGATE HILL
TOTTENHAM COURT RD. BRANCH: 137 TO 140 TOTTENHAM COURT ROAD
Corner of Euston Road
Co's STORES,
LIMITED.
THING, TAILORING, AND OUTFITTING
SCHOOL OUTFITS, 25 per cent. under usual London Prices
BOOTS, TRAVELLING
re supplied at same
thing.
GENTLEMEN'S CAPE WATERPROOFS (IN BLACK PARAMATTA) 19/11, 29/6, 39/6 (IN DOUBLE TEXTURE TWEEDS). 19/11, 29/6, 39/6.
GENTLEMEN'S TALMA WATERPROOFS (IN DRAB VENETIAN). 19/11, 29/6, 34/6, 39/6.
GENTLEMEN'S TROUSERS
Ready for immediate wear
4/11 5/11 6/11 8/11 10/9 12/11 14/11 16/11 18/11
To Measure 10/6 12/6 22/6 14/11 16/11 18/11 21/
GIRLS' JACKETS & COSTUMES
Are also supplied at these Stores ready for immediate wear, or Tailor-made, to measure. Prices, &c., post free.
LADIES' WATERPROOFS in the newest shapes of the Season.
12/11, 16/11, 21/9, 26/9.
GIRLS' WATERPROOFS, 12/11
LVET
DARTMOUTH SUITS.
Jacket and Knickers.
With Fancy Vest, and Collar in Fancy Cloths.
12/11, 15/9, 19/11, 25/9.
BOYS' SCARBORO' SUITS.
Jacket, Vest, and Knickers.
In new Suiting.
17/9 to 21/6.
According to size.
Easy Measure Forms Post Free.
BOYS' NORFOLK SUITS.
Jacket and Knickers.
In durable Tweeds and Cheviots.
5/11, 8/11, 11/9, 14/11.
Very Superior.
16/11, 19/11, 24/6.
ETON JACKETS AND VESTS.
For Boys from 9 years of age.
Ready for immediate wear.
Thoroughly well cut and made.
In Vicunas and Fine Worsted Cloths.
Hair Line Trousers, 4/11 to 14/11.
Fig. 1
BOYS' AND YOUTHS' CRICKET, TENNIS, AND BOATING OUTFITS
FLANNEL SUITS (as Fig 2).
Fig. 2
GENTLEMEN'S JACKETS AND VESTS.
In Black Serges and Cheviots.
Ready for Immediate Wear.
14/11, 16/11, 19/11, 24/6, 29/6, 34/6, 39/6
To Measure.
27/6, 32/6, 39/6, 44/6, 49/6.
GENTLEMEN'S GROSVENOR OVERCOATS.
In Shower Proof and other suitable materials.
Ready for Immediate Wear.
29/6, 39/6, 49/6.
To Measure.
34/6, 39/6, 49/6, 54/6.
CYCLISTS' SUITS.
Ready for Immediate Wear.
19/11, 29/6.
To Measure.
SELECTION IN LONDON
GENTLEMEN'S SILK HATS, Christy's Newest Shapes, 7/6, 8/11, 10/6, 12/6, 14/6, 16/6, 18/6.
GENTLEMEN'S BOOTS, 8/11, 10/9, 12/11, 14/11 —— Best Qualities, 16/11, 18/11, 21/.

The Victorians firmly believed in showing the product to the customer; this catalogue display employs detailed line engravings

was a highly skilled art – they were carved on small squares of box-wood, which were jigsawed together for the larger pictures, at a cost which went up pro rata according to size.

Ten years later small illustrations were accompanying advertisements, much in the style of those two-inch 'bargain' squares for greenhouses or specialist bras that papers from *The Times* to the *News of the World* carry today.

Then came *The Field* (1853) with half-page drawings of the things country gentlemen would be needing – carriages, tools, farm machinery. *The Queen* in 1861 saw the first advertisements for underwear, ladies in what looks like a large bolster secured by ribbons. Full pages began to be taken, though often by eccentrics like the owner of Eno's Fruit Salts, who preached and packed their space with high-sounding sermons and quotations.

It was outer rather than inner cleanliness which woke advertising up: soap showed what could be done. A small traditional manufacturer, A. & F. Pears, was in a bad way, and a young man of 24, Thomas J. Barratt was taken into partnership. "Any fool can make soap", he said; "it takes a clever man to sell it." Barratt was the man. Pears, when he joined them, spent £80 a year pushing the product. Ten years later, when the young brash cuckoo pushed the family directors out of control and took charge, Barratt spent over £100,000.

Pears had to become the word for soap. The public had to be hypnotised so that it became an unconscious reaction. The name Pears was everywhere, and then other tricks began – red puzzle posters, optical illusions – were plastered all over Britain.

The Victorian age was one of deference. A common advertisement ploy was the aristocratic endorsement. Minor German and Balkan royalty were bought up to endorse the most unlikely products – at one point, if the advertisements are to be believed, the whole of the Almanach de Gotha was anticipating democratic Scandinavian royalty by going everywhere by bicycle.

If royalty was not to be bought, then it was used anyway. A chance remark in favour of a product by the Princess of Wales or another royal lady (The Duchess of York says: "She thinks the Flower Shield a most ingenious invention and wishes it success" – this for a corsage protector for "Balls, Receptions and Assemblies of the *élite*") and it would be proclaimed for years.

More entertaining, the Royal Family were regarded as common property by advertisers, and were imaginatively and patriotically drawn into helping sales along. A simple colour portrait of the Queen might preside over:

"The Subject's Best Friend"
HUDSON'S DRY SOAP
Home and Clothes as Sweet as a Rose

but she was also pictured more actively, in the act of sipping Mazawattee tea.

In spite of her fondness for whisky, which did much to popularise it as a society drink, she was not as far as is known depicted with this Highland tipple (which to be fair, she used with great moderation: her continental nickname of Whiscatoria was undeserved).

The Prince of Wales, however, featured in a whole series of ads for Bushmills whisky in 1889. He was shown urging the drink upon the Shah of Persia, at that time visiting London and Paris. At the Paris Exhibition the Prince is saying: "*This, your Majesty, is the celebrated Bushmills Whisky which you tasted in England, and liked so much.* I feel sure it will win the Gold Medal."

Then we are told: "The Prince was right. BUSHMILLS has obtained the ONLY GOLD MEDAL". The international consequences of this alleged action of the Prince's might have been severe, and if faithful Persians had read the *Illustrated London News* in which this interesting observation had been recorded the Shah, as a Muslim sovereign who was sworn never to touch liquor, might well have lost his throne. Fortunately, it would seem that Persia never got to hear of it.

One famous endorser did lose by it all. Lillie Langtry had signed one of her many statements for Pears, and her signature was reproduced in facsimile. An enterprising forger copied it, and persuaded her bank to let him take out her jewels, worth £40,000, which she had deposited for safe-keeping. Well, it was all extra publicity for Pears.

Deference was also rendered to art, particularly art shown at the Royal Academy and painted by Academicians. Barratt saw the possibility, and bought *Bubbles*, by Sir John Millais, a somewhat sentimental picture of a golden-haired boy making soap bubbles with a clay pipe. It was first reproduced in lavish and expensive colour, including a gilt frame, and posted up in this simple form all over the country. The hoardings, said Barratt, were to be the poor man's art gallery. Later versions however bore the name of Pears on the soap tablet which lay on the ground at the boy's side.

Barratt's action caused an aesthetic outcry, and the artist was criticised. Millais was not however in anyway involved – his picture had been bought first by Sir William Ingram of the *Illustrated London News* (whose fortune rested originally on patent pills). The great art vogue grew: W. P. Frith, whose great canvases were a talking point at the Academy, had his painting of a little girl holding up a whiter than white dress, *The New Frock,* bought by Lever to spread the virtues of Sunlight Soap.

New pictures by great names were conned for some association with the product; a Landseer did very well for dog biscuits, and those cardinals who caroused their way through the last Victorian decades provided excellent business for wines and brandy.

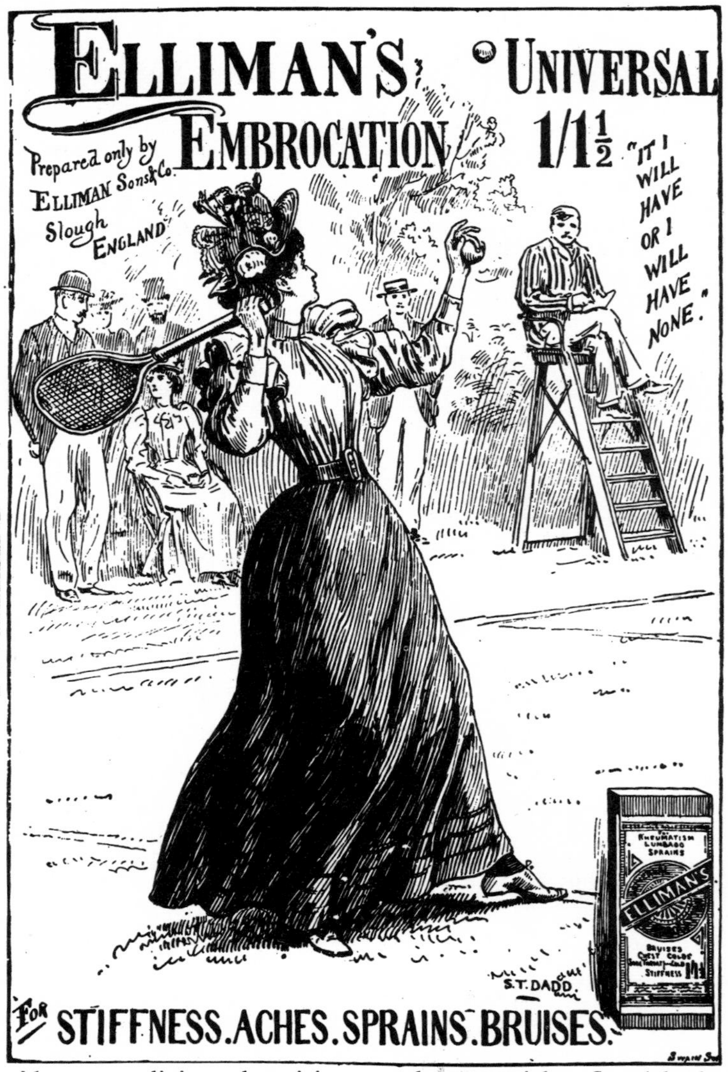
ELLIMAN'S UNIVERSAL
EMBROCATION 1/1½
Prepared only by ELLIMAN Sons & Co. Slough ENGLAND
"IT I WILL HAVE OR I WILL HAVE NONE."
S.T. DADD.
FOR STIFFNESS. ACHES. SPRAINS. BRUISES.

Above: medicine advertising – and pretty girls – flourished. Opposite: it is a strange fireman who pauses to drink cocoa

The Pope himself wrote that he appreciated the effects of Mariani Tonic Wine, though His Holiness was not confined to beverages which could at a pinch play their part in a pontifical mass: "Two Infallible Powers. The Pope and Bovril" depicted a smiling pontiff with a giant beaker of steaming brown fluid.

Frys and Cadburys advertised extensively. Frys used a poster of the Ten Little Nigger Boys, which was reduced and sold commercially as a successful postcard. Untroubled by post-imperial guilt or anti-racialist lobbies, the Victorians often used the little nigger boy theme in their advertising material. Blacks pranced in the lime juice cordial advertisements (not only Roses then – there was also Stower's and Montserrat Lime-Fruit juice) and naturally enough in the soap ads of Hudson's and Pears', like that on page 177. These advertisements were issued before the imperialism of the last years of Victoria's reign really got under way, and when, in the afterglow of emancipation and the triumph of the North over the South in the American Civil War, the majority of Victorians were sympathetic to the Negro cause. It would be interesting, if it could be ever found out, to see what effect these advertisements had on the subconscious mind of the next generation, which began to use "nigger" as a term of contempt, and began to think of the coloured races as an inferior breed altogether.

To 1880s people, however, there was no doubt about one thing – if it was British, the product was, it went without saying the best obtainable. (Exceptions were made for champagne and luxury articles from France.) Advertisements for overseas sales campaigns showed local brands being thrown contemptuously away upon the arrival of the superior British product. Out went the salesmen full of a self-confidence which would send today's Board of Trade and the British National Export Council into raptures.

The 1890s brought a reaction against excess promotion, and in the year 1894 came a law forbidding the use of Army or Navy uniforms for advertising purposes – before this it was a common sight to see processions of down-and-outs clad in the Queen's scarlet (even to the rank of staff officer) handing out leaflets in the streets. A spate of restrictive regulations and by-laws were soon to follow: law had come to the frontier, and the wildest days of advertising were over.

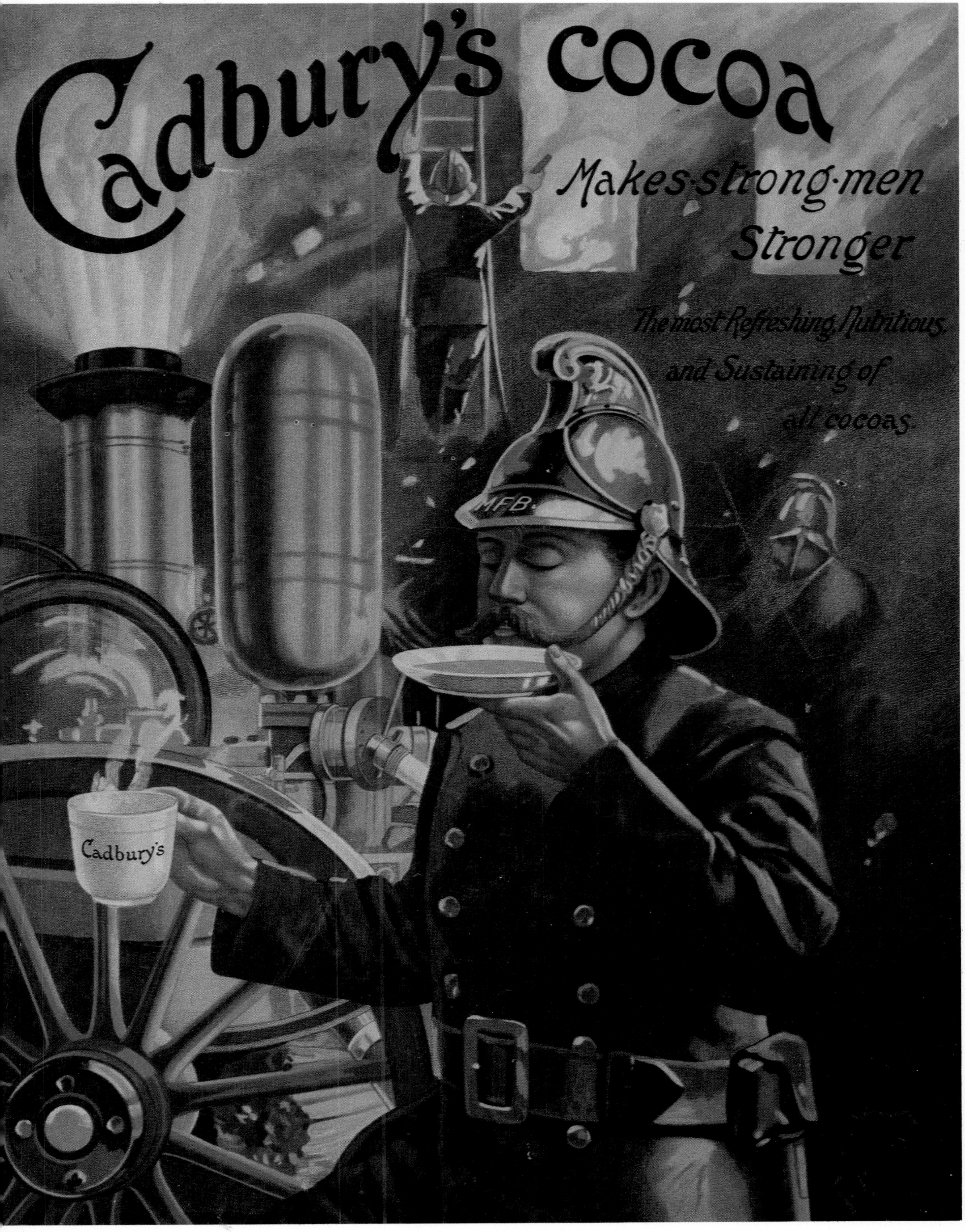
Cadbury's Cocoa
Makes·strong·men
Stronger
The most Refreshing, Nutritious,
and Sustaining of
all cocoas.
MFB
Cadbury's

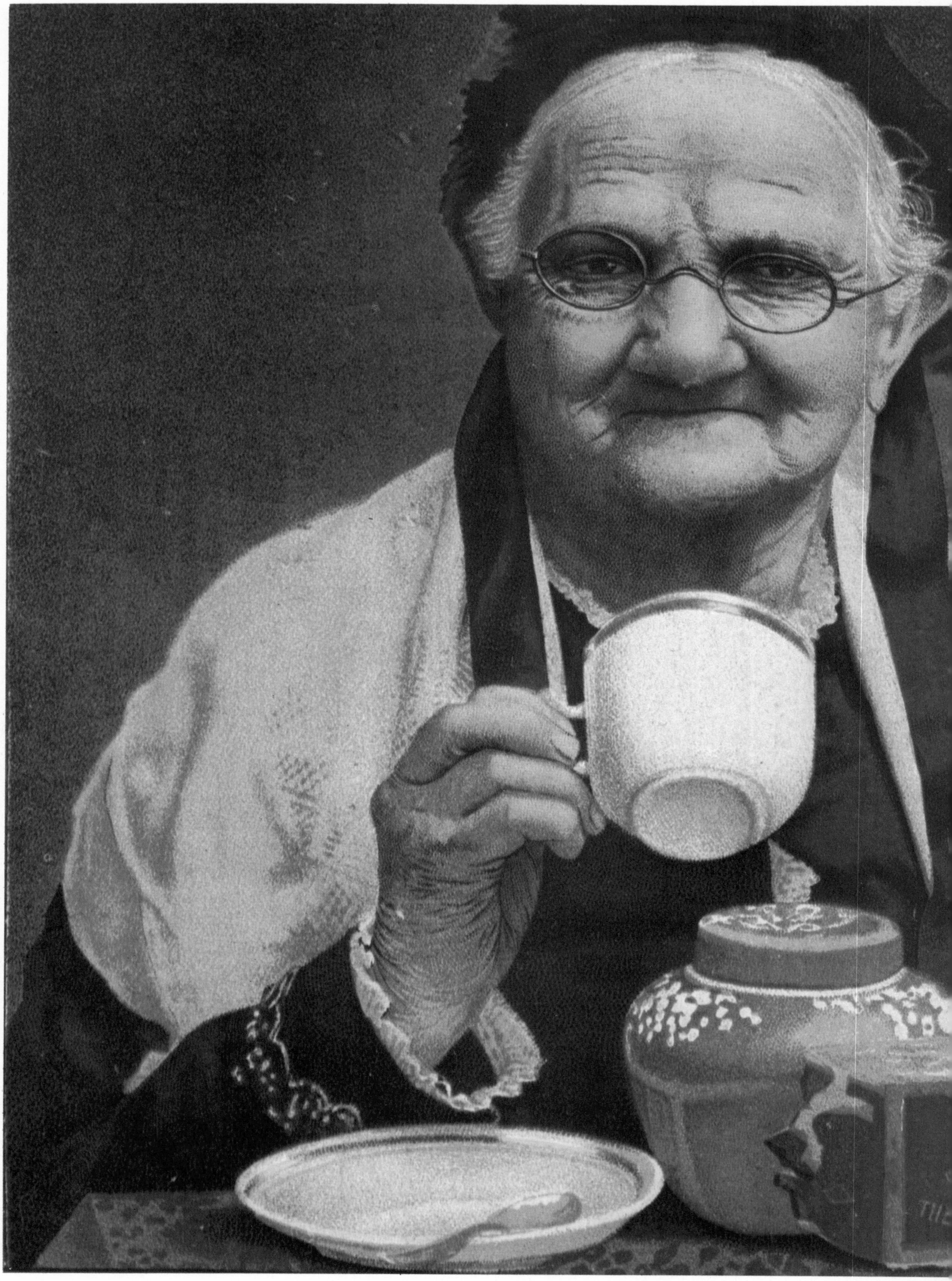

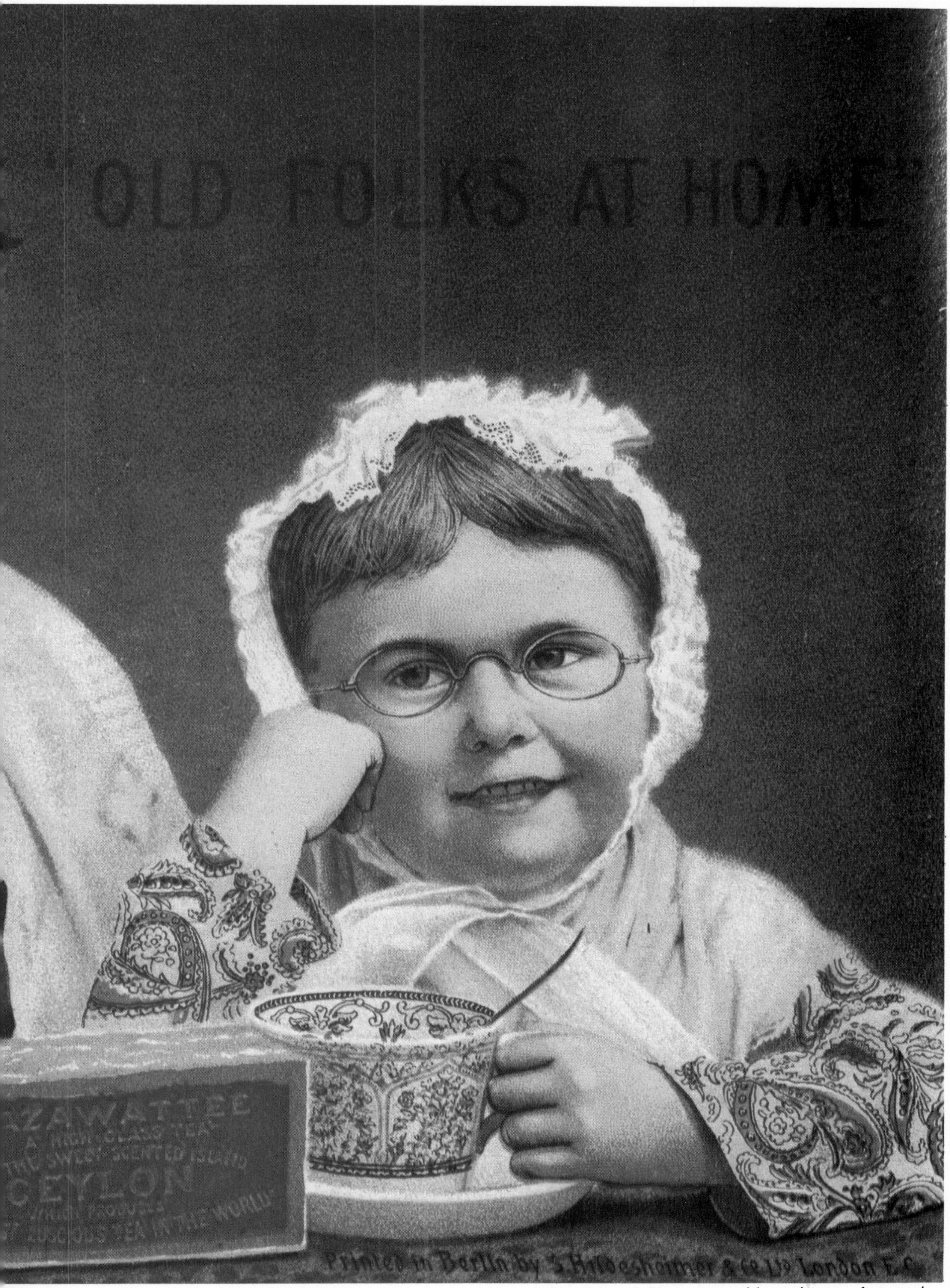
'OLD FOLKS AT HOME'
ZAWATTEE
A HIGH-CLASS TEA
THE SWEET-SCENTED ISLAND
CEYLON
WHICH PRODUCES
LUSCIOUS TEA IN THE WORLD
Printed in Berlin by S. Hildesheimer & Co. Ltd. London E.C.

Fine artwork, with an impeccably rendered pack somewhere in the picture, could make a subtle statement without vigorous sloganeering

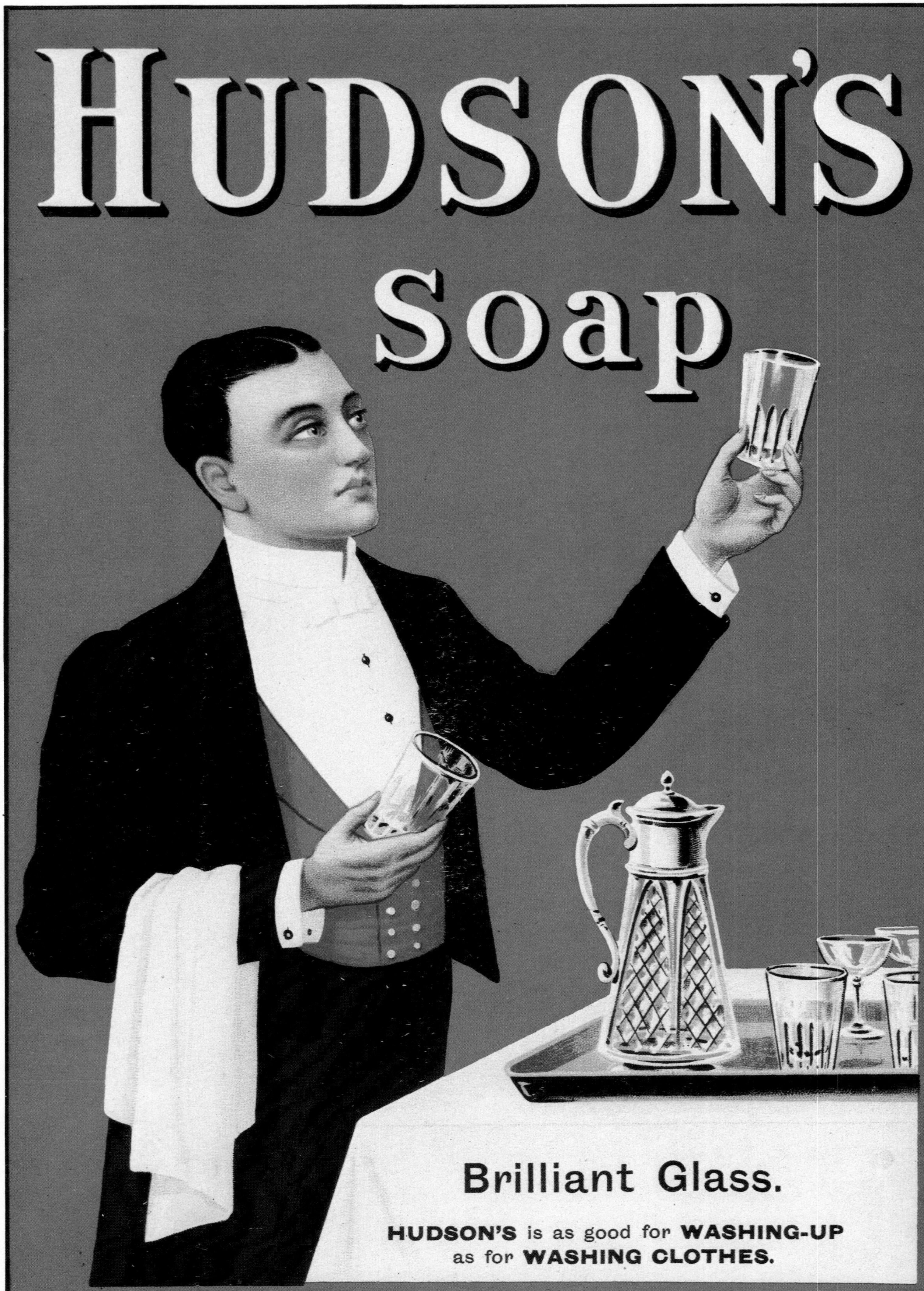
HUDSON'S
Soap
Brilliant Glass.
HUDSON'S is as good for WASHING-UP
as for WASHING CLOTHES.

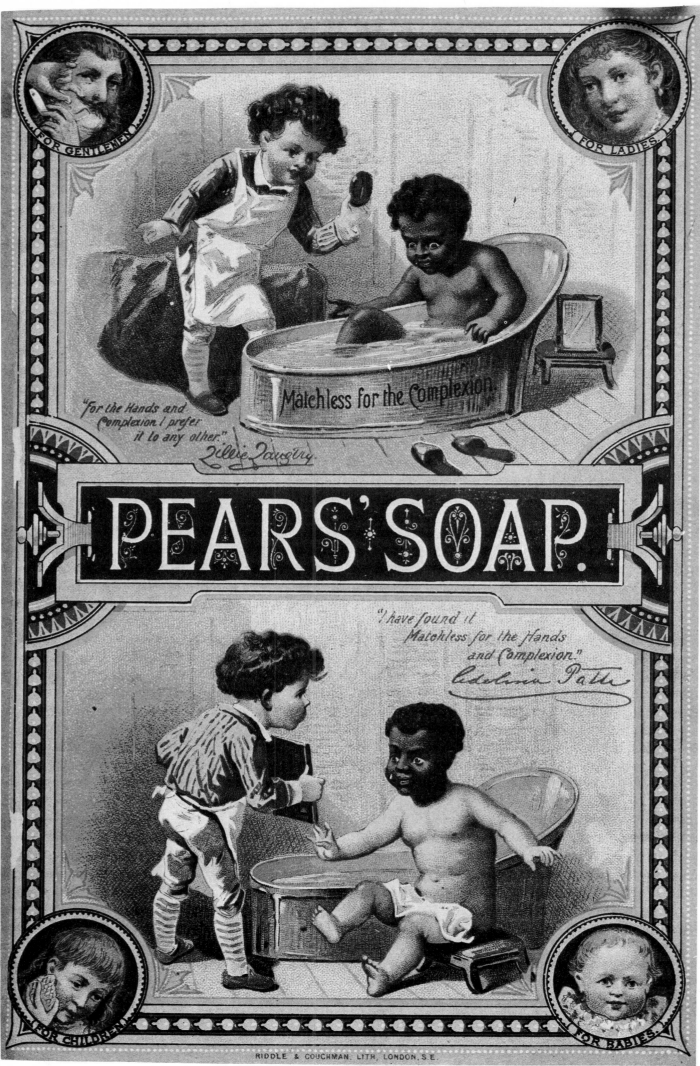

"For the Hands and Complexion I prefer it to any other." Lillie Langtry.

Matchless for the Complexion.

"I have found it Matchless for the Hands and Complexion" Adelina Patti

PEARS' SOAP.

FOR GENTLEMEN.

FOR LADIES.

FOR CHILDREN.

FOR BABIES.

RIDDLE & COUCHMAN. LITH. LONDON. S.E.

Jokes about coloured people were acceptable in Victorian advertising, when today a complaint to the Race Relations Board would inevitably lead to prosecution. Endorsements from Langtry and Patti are allowed to clutter the layout. Opposite: the immaculate footman is a reminder of how a large below-stairs class was taken for granted

THE DOUBLE STANDARD

By O. R. McGregor

Victorians were of two minds where sex was concerned. On the one hand London had 80,000
prostitutes, on the other uncovered piano legs were alleged to
bring blushes to womanly countenances. In fact, Victorian sexual attitudes were remarkably robust.
The nymphet opposite is putting across an unambiguous message

The Victorians inherited a strict moral code. They got it from evangelical religious teachers who imposed it on the new middle class, the executive agents of their expanding industrial economy, and planted it, as far as they could, on their lower orders. Their bookshelves carried the weight of such typical products of the evangelical outlook as Thomas Bowdler's *The Family Shakespeare. In which nothing is added to the Text; but those Words and Expressions are omitted which cannot with Propriety be read aloud in a Family.* These ten volumes reached a sixth edition in 1831, six years before the 18-year-old Victoria came under the influence of her first prime minister, a cultivated Whig who had been heard to respond to an evangelical sermon with the observation that "things are coming to a pretty pass when religion is allowed to interfere with private life". 'That d...d morality' which disturbed Lord Melbourne did not only result from religious enthusiasm. Differing provisions for the inheritance of property were also important. The sexual waywardness of aristocrats in the later 18th century did not endanger the integrity or succession of family properties regulated by primogeniture and entail. Countless children of the mist played happily in Whig and Tory nurseries where they were no threat to the security of family property or to the interests of the heirs.

But middle-class families handled their accumulating industrial wealth within a system of partible inheritance which demanded a severer morality imposing higher standards upon women than upon men. As the Lord Chancellor explained during the parliamentary debates on the proposal to set up a divorce court in 1857, a wife would not be damaged by her husband's adultery and could forgive him "without any loss of caste" but "no one would venture to suggest" that he could in any way consider condoning her adultery because it "might be the means of palming spurious children upon him". In these circles, such a wife would have been guilty of undermining the very foundations of her family by

"That girl seems to know you, George"

admitting a fraud to the succession of its property.

Women in well-off families could be easily made to accept a double standard of morality which applied within and without marriage. Marriage was the only respectable and fulfilling vocation open to them and, within it, their sphere of usefulness was restricted to mirroring their husband's social status, to bearing children and to supervising servants. Ladies had to endure what Florence Nightingale called "the petty grinding tyranny of a good English family. What I complain of the Evangelical party for is the degree to which they have raised the claims upon women of 'Family'. It is a kind of Fetichism." But the status of marriage was hard to acquire in a society carrying far more women than men in the marriageable age groups. Women, especially upper-class women, had to compete for a limited supply of husbands and a breach of the rule which imposed chastity on them would have ruined their chances of marriage. The rule was rarely broken because girls, constantly supervised by relatives, never enjoyed dangerous opportunities.

It was different for men. Of course, they were formally required to observe the rule of no sex outside marriage. They mostly had to marry very late because convention insisted that a bride was entitled to expect in her husband's home the same standards of comfort that she had enjoyed in her father's. Given the late age of marriage of middle-class men, the expectation that they would have some wild oats to sow and the rule of chastity for their sisters, it is easy to understand why Lecky, in common with other Victorian moralists, described prostitutes as eternal priestesses of humanity, blasted for the sins of the people, preserving the purity of upper-class womanhood.

There was nothing new in early-Victorian ignorance of the physiology and psychology of sex. What was new was the urban setting in which it operated. By severing their country connections these town dwellers could try to maintain a conspiracy of silence about sex for there

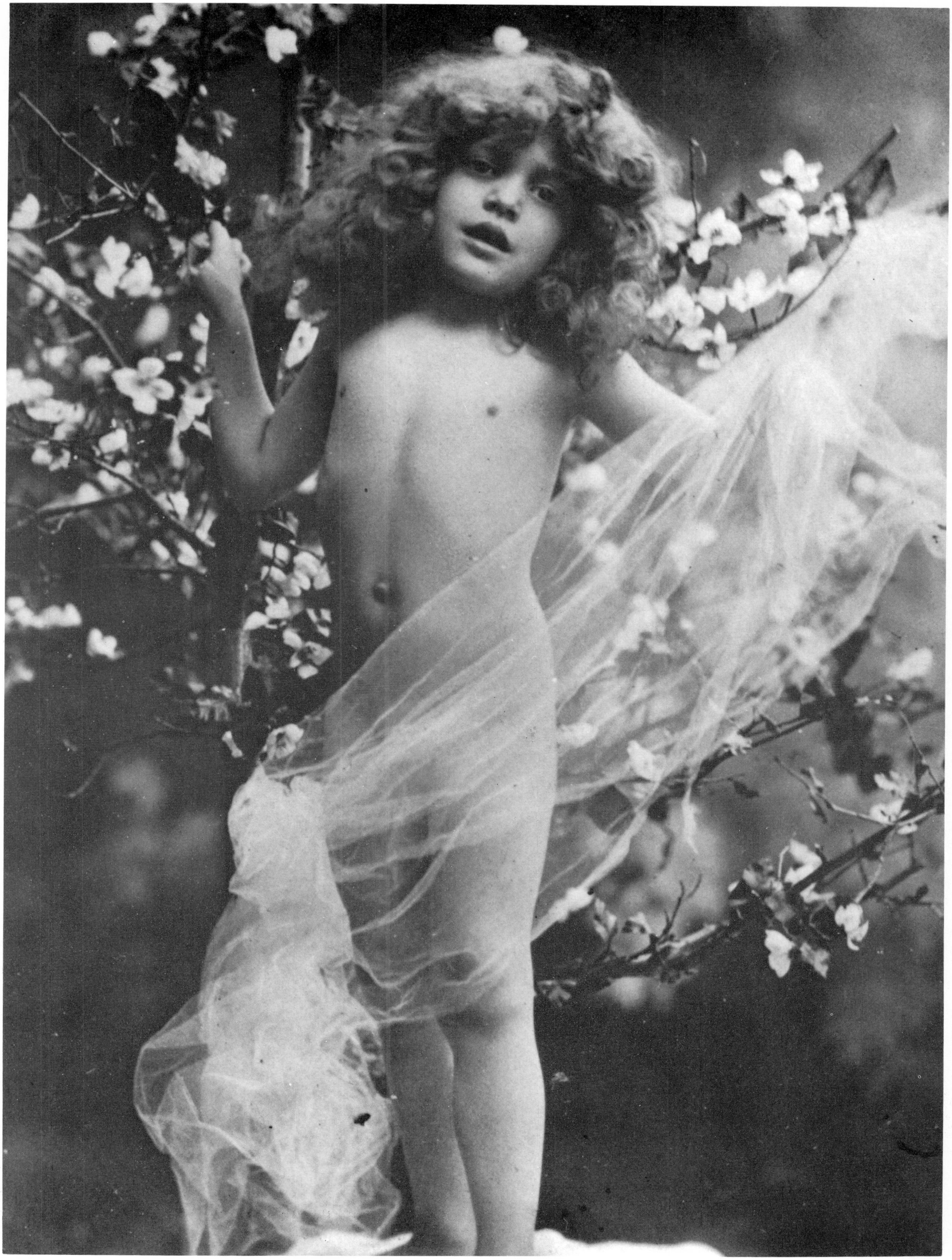

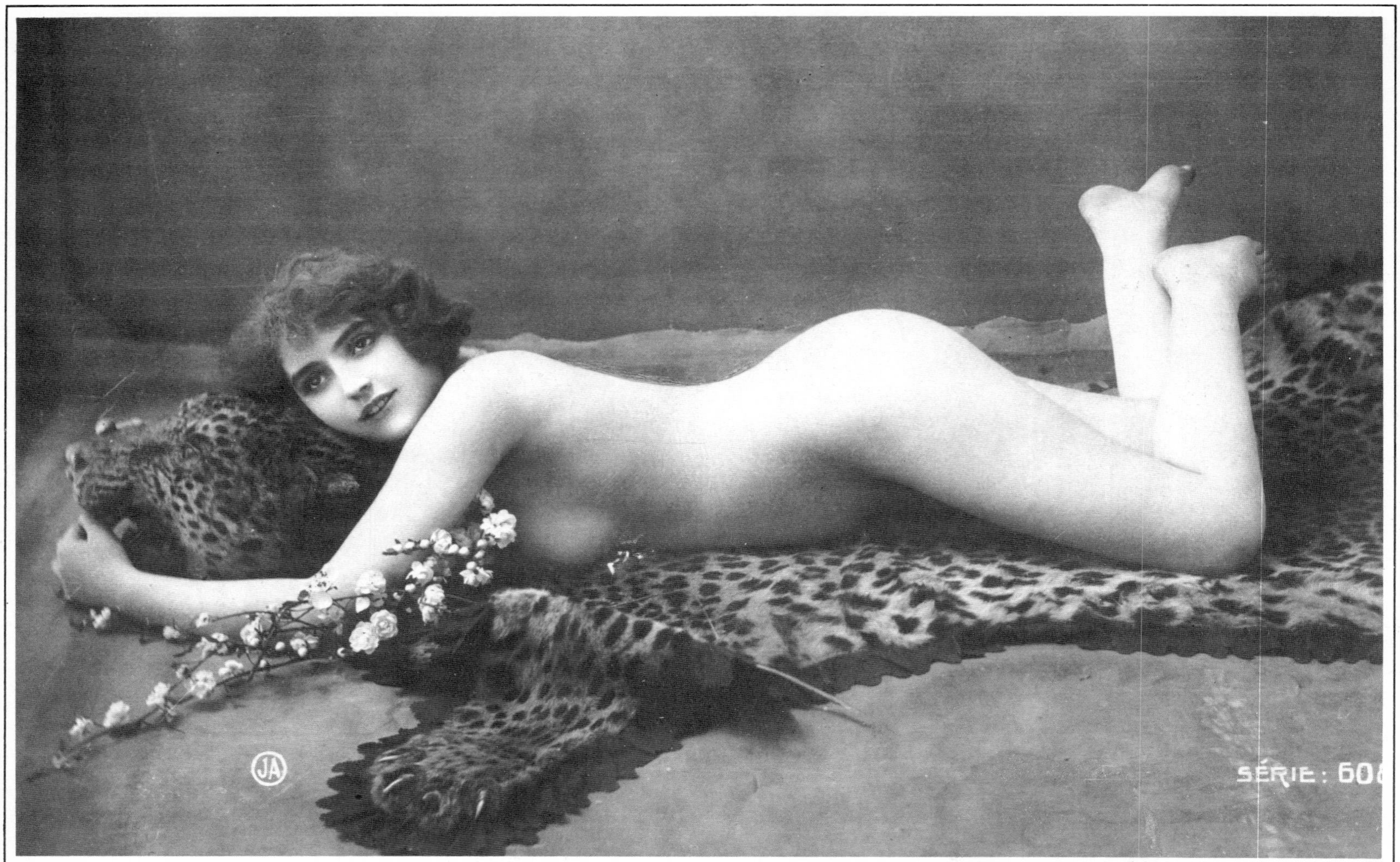
JA
SÉRIE: 60
Classic pin-up pose 1 – baby on animal skin rug

are no sexual secrets in farmyards, and city doctors soon discovered that moral women derived no pleasure from sex or the sexual act itself.

A reputable London surgeon, William Acton, set out in his *The Functions and Disorders of the Reproductive Organs* of 1857 what was probably the representative medical view of the day. "As a general rule, a modest woman seldom desires any sexual gratification for herself. She submits to her husband but only to please him; and, but for the desire of maternity, would far rather be relieved of his attentions. No nervous or feeble young man need, therefore, be deterred from marriage by any exaggerated notion of the duties required from him." Female sexual satisfactions came only from child-bearing and issued in pain and suffering. Only men and immoral women knew and sought sexual pleasures. Accordingly, conventional early- and mid-Victorians thought of sexual relations in marriage as situations in which men wreaked their lust upon their joylessly submissive wives.

The Victorian conspiracy of silence about sex was an aspiration not an achievement. It is partly the invention of those who have looked at life in the period through the double meanings of some novels. It is true that Mr Bowdler would have been able to read to his family with equanimity almost every sentence in those scenes describing the relations of Becky Sharp and the Marquis of Steyne.

Nevertheless, others were not so mealy-mouthed. Only two years and a parson's stock separated the gentle allusiveness of *Mary Barton* in 1848 from the rough directness of *Alton Locke* which showed why the daughters of the makers of cheap clothes and nasty had to "eke out their miserable earnings by prostitution". Charles Kingsley's theme was external pressures forcing a choice between sin and starvation. A generation later, in 1880, George Gissing described in his first novel his own experience of marriage to a prostitute who went back to the streets to earn the drink that he could not afford. Even in literature the conspiracy of silence had but a patchy hold; in life all sorts of events helped to break it up.

Prostitution itself became a political issue at the end of the 1860s and held its place until the 1880s. By the 1860s the military authorities were disconcerted by the crippling consequences of venereal diseases which took such a toll of sailors that ships could not be got to sea after periods of shore leave. They persuaded Parliament to pass in 1864 without debate the first of a series of Contagious Diseases Acts which, by the end of the decade, put in force an elaborate system for regulating prostitution. It applied to 18 garrison towns and ports in England and Ireland; it required the registration and compulsory periodical medical examination and treatment of prostitutes; and it was enforced by plainclothes sanitary police specially recruited from the Metropolitan force.

Very soon this branch of laissez faire principles came under violent political attack from a women's movement enraged by a scheme which discriminated

Classic pin-up pose 2 – dishevelled, black-stockinged maid

against women by applying severe sanctions to prostitutes but not to their consorts. Led by Mrs Josephine Butler, the repealers forced the issue into violently fought by-elections. It finally erupted in 1885 with the publication by W. T. Stead, then editor of the *Pall Mall Gazette*, of four special issues under the title *The Maiden Tribute of Modern Babylon* reporting under such headings as 'Liberty for Vice', 'The Violation of Virgins', 'The Confessions of a Brothel Keeper', 'How Girls are Bought and Ruined' how he and other repealers went out and purchased a young virgin. After the furore the purchased girl was sent to Paris in the charge of the Salvation Army to sell copies of the *War Cry*, the acts were repealed and Stead went to gaol for three months charged with abduction because he had neglected to obtain the consent of the child's father. It is an ironic comment on the moral delicacy of the 1880s that when Stead wished his counsel, Sir Charles Russell, to ask for the mother's marriage lines, he was refused because, Russell said, "I will never be a party to such licence of cross-examination." But the abducted child was later discovered to be illegitimate and Stead need never have served his sentence.

In 1877, another notorious case had contributed to public discussion of sexual matters and to the break up of the conspiracy of silence. Charles Bradlaugh, atheist and republican, and Annie Besant, an Anglican parson's wife recently converted to Free Thought and separated from her husband, deliberately invited prosecution by re-issuing an American pamphlet which first circulated

in England in the early 1830s and had been on sale ever since. Written by a doctor, Charles Knowlton, *The Fruits of Philosophy; or, the Private Companion of Young Married Couples* recommended douching as the best method of contraception. They were tried before Lord Chief Justice Cockburn for unlawfully intending "to vitiate and corrupt the morals as well of youth as of divers other subjects of the Queen and to incite . . . to indecent, obscene, unnatural, and immoral practices . . ." by publishing an "indecent, lewd, filthy, bawdy, and obscene book".

The immediate result of the trial was widespread though mainly hostile publicity in the press and a jump in the sales of the pamphlet from some 700 a year to 125,000 in four months. In a model summing-up Lord Cockburn thus presented to the special jury, containing among its members Dr Augustus Voelcker, consulting chemist to the Royal Agricultural Society, and Arthur Walter of *The Times*, "that part of the case on which your verdict must hinge . . . Over-population, says Knowlton, is productive of abundant misery. How can we prevent this over-procreation of the species? If you check marriage, prostitution takes it place; and, therefore, the only possible way in which you can grapple with it is to allow legitimate intercourse between men and women after marriage, but to prevent procreation by applying artificial checks after conjugal and connubial intercourse." The question was whether such behaviour ran "contrary to the law of God and man, and contrary to the sound morals which ought to prevail". The jury's

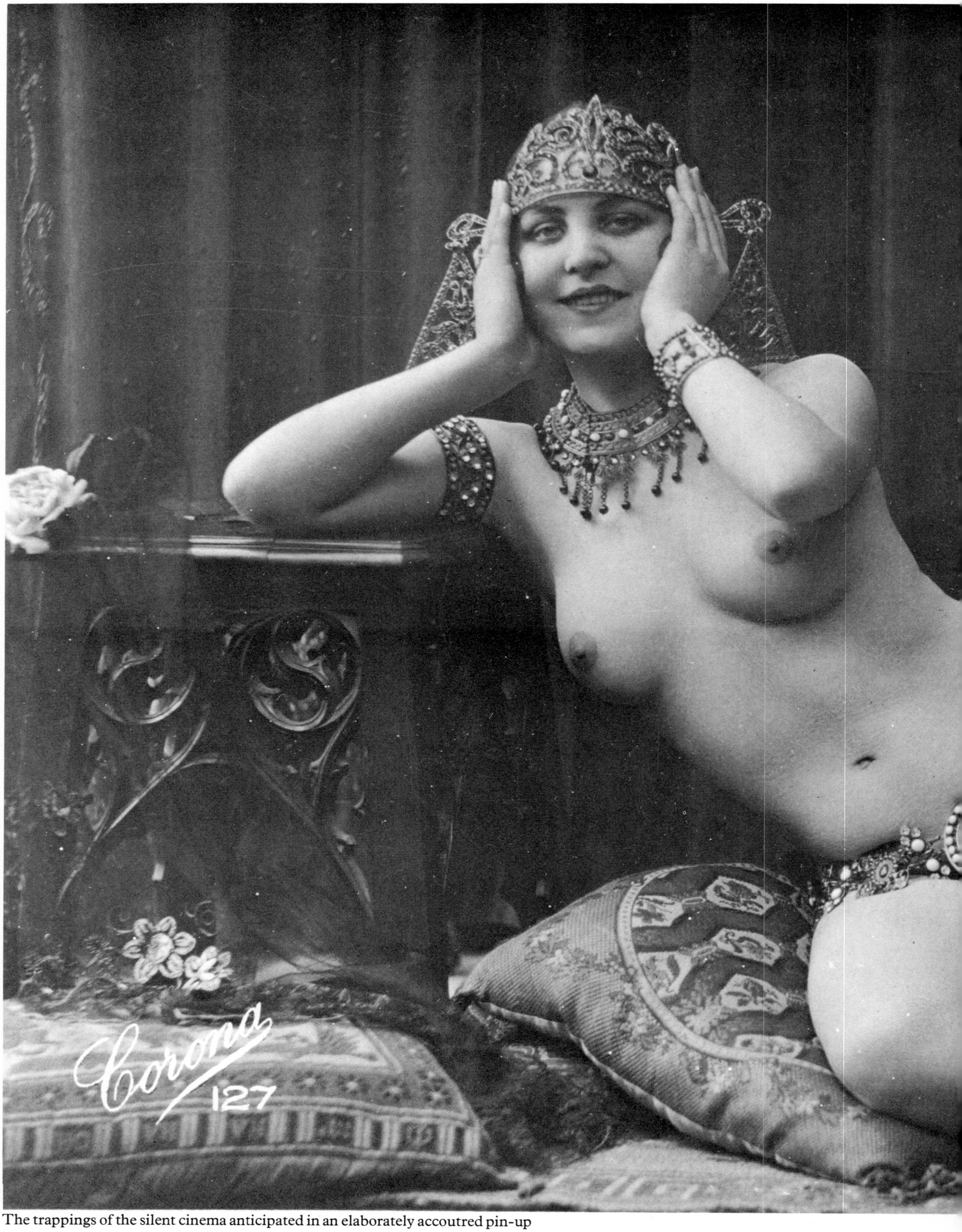
Corona
127
The trappings of the silent cinema anticipated in an elaborately accoutred pin-up

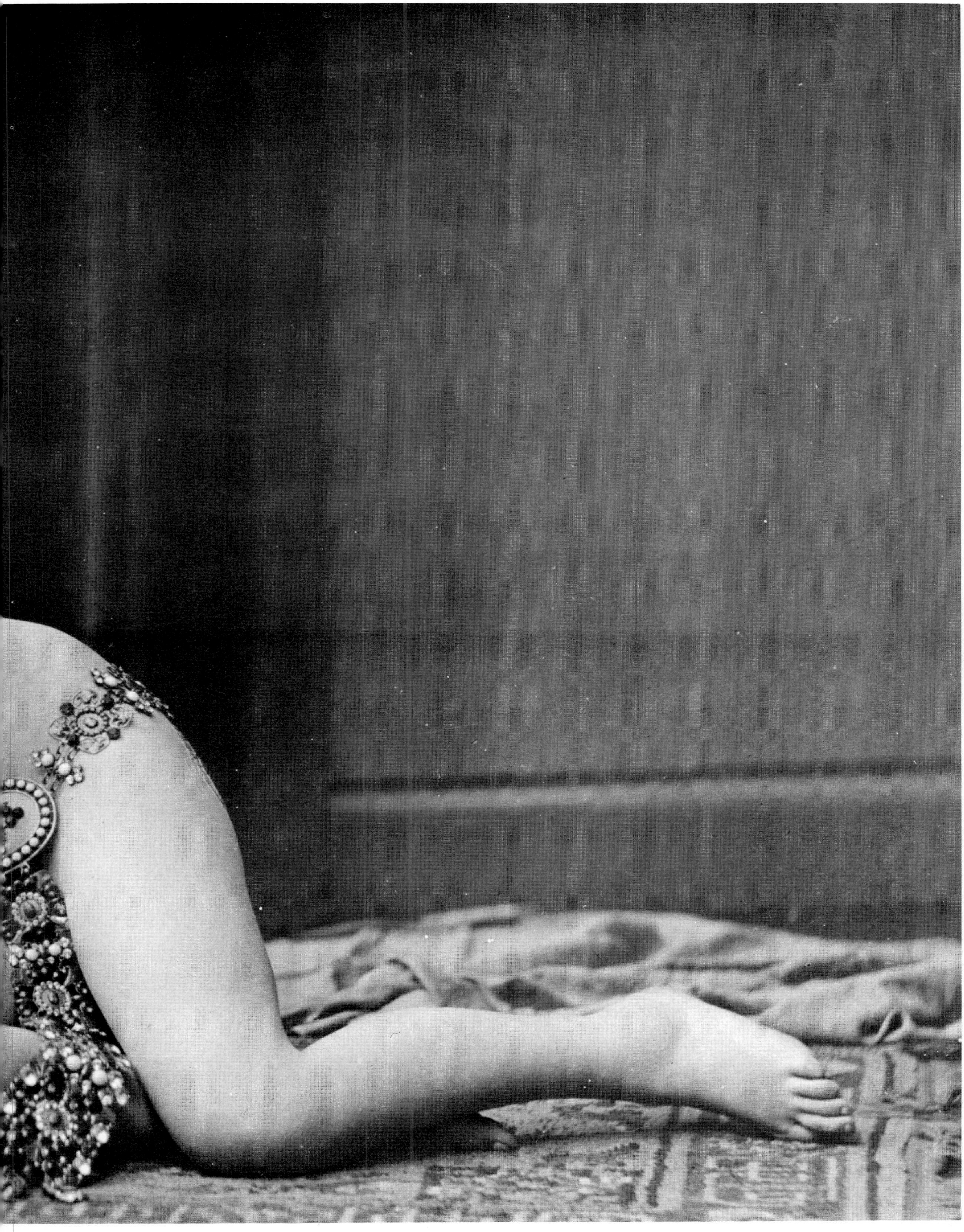

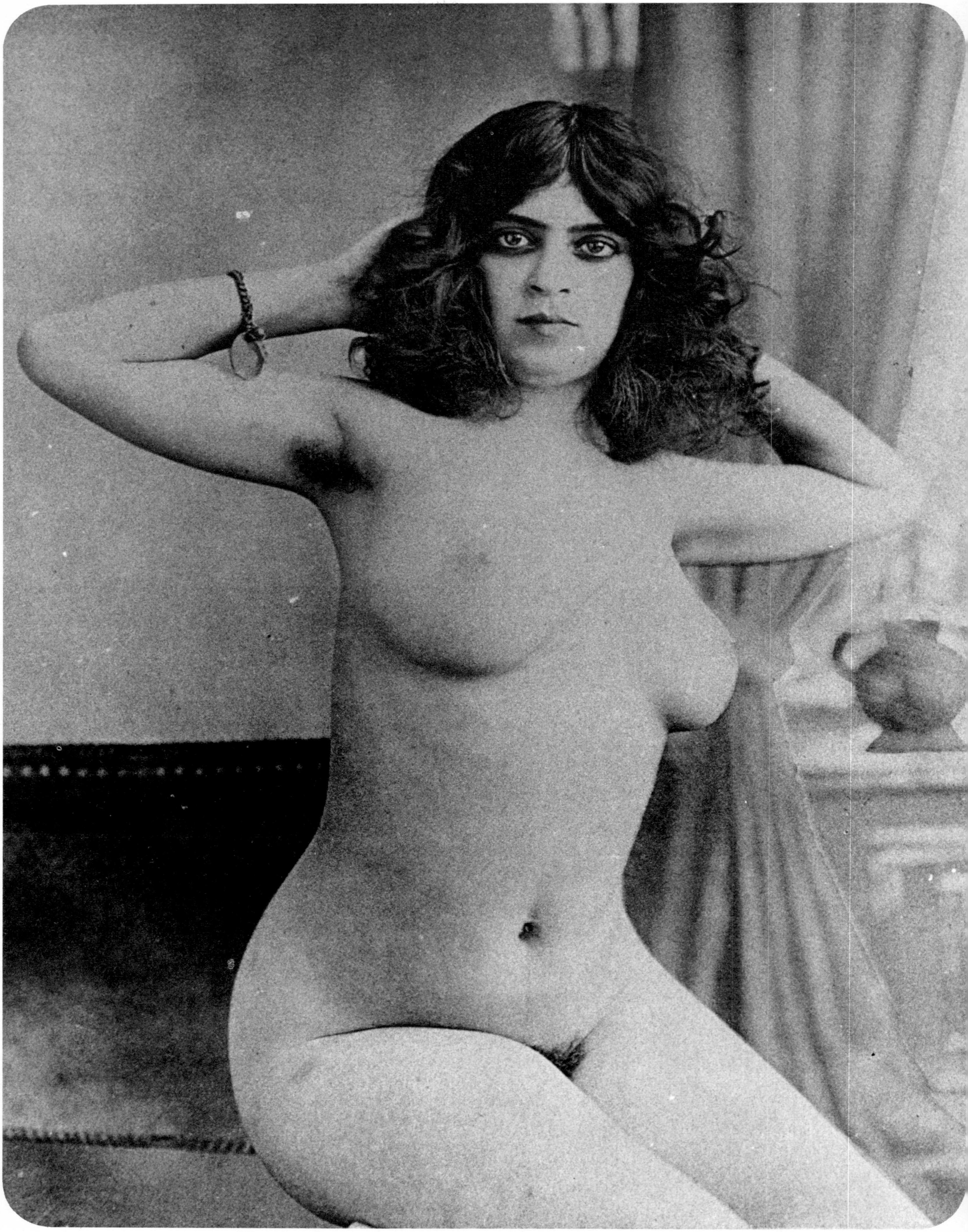

Victorian pin-up with the unabashed frankness of today's girlie magazines

verdict was equivocal, ducking away from a positive stand on one side or the other. They found the book obscene and calculated to deprave public morals, but they entirely exonerated Bradlaugh and Mrs Besant from any corrupt motives in publishing it.

Lord Cockburn's question must have been put to each other by many husbands and wives in upper-class bedrooms in the 1870s. No doubt it was easier to face up to in private for having been debated in public. This was the decade in which the wealthy began to limit the size of their families. Before then there had been little conflict between the religious injunction to be fruitful and multiply and the social obligation upon parents to do their best for their children. In practice this meant equipping them with the means to achieve in adult life a social status no lower than that of the parents and higher if possible. But the costs of processing children were then becoming so much heavier that parents could only do their duty by a restricted number. The habit of mild reproduction among the well-to-do spread later to poorer folk whose family expenditures ate further into inelastic wages as compulsory schooling to a certain age and other measures kept their children from work and earning.

Conscious control of family size among the upper classes coincided both with the crumbling of their loyalties to religion and with the growth of scientific knowledge. First medicine, then psychology, helped to liberate bodies and minds from old restrictions. The forlorn petition of 65 London doctors to the Privy Council in 1853 that physiology be taught to working-class children had become by the 1880s a flow of cheap books for the literate denouncing tight-lacing and corsets with stiff blades in pregnancy and advocating fresh air, plain diet and exercise for nursing mothers. The movement towards rational dress which Amelia Bloomer had tried to pioneer in the 1850s was promoted by the sports which middle-class women took up from the mid-1870s, roller-skating and lawn tennis especially. But, above all, it was the bicycle which finally put women into breeches and liberated them from their chaperones. Psychologists, too, were digging around the foundations of Victorian sexual morality. Havelock Ellis published the first volume of his *Studies in the Psychology of Sex* before Victoria's death, and he helped many to a realisation of women as independent human beings with their own legitimate sexual needs and satisfactions. By the turn of the century, there was a ferment of adjustment to new knowledge, to new ideas and to new conceptions of the relationship of men and women in what was now a fast-changing society.

This was evident in the preoccupations of all those who had to be sensitive to the connections between belief and behaviour. The Rev. the Hon. Edward Lyttleton, headmaster first of Haileybury and then of Eton, gave some conventional touches to his *Training of the Young in Laws of Sex*, published in 1900 to counsel parents how to cope with "the normal growth of animal desires, far stronger in the male than in the female, at least in England".

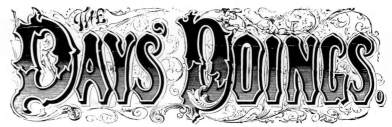

The Days' Doings.
An Illustrated Journal of Romantic Events, Reports, Sporting & Theatrical News, at Home & Abroad.
Vol. II.—No. 38. All Rights Reserved.
PUBLISHED AT No. 300, STRAND, LONDON, W.C.—SATURDAY, APRIL 15, 1871.
PRICE THREEPENCE. Registered at the G.P.O. as a Newspaper
EASTER MONDAY.—HIGH HOLIDAY IN GREENWICH PARK.

Bank holiday frolics – a racy magazine cover

But the substance of his book was a powerful and savage denunciation of the double standard of Victorian sexual morality. "There are scores of 'men of the world', fathers of boys at school, who show a real anxiety about their boy's school career being free from scandal, and . . . from vice. But only a small percentage of these are anxious to anything like the same extent that the same boys should be saved from the sin of fornication . . . The important thing to notice is that the question is settled wholly irrespective of the claim of women . . . to a fair measure of humane consideration." In this headmaster's view, the attitudes of upper-class men were "nothing but barbarous".

So it is easy to understand why Grant Allen's *The Women Who Did* of 1895 should hold marriage to be morally repugnant to a free woman. "I know what marriage is – from what vile slavery it has sprung; on what unseen horrors for my sister women it is reared and buttressed; by what unholy sacrifices it is sustained and made possible. I know it has a history. I know its past: I know its present: and I can't embrace it . . . (but) I am yours, take me and do as you choose with me. That much I can yield, as every good woman should yield it, to the man she loves, to the man who loves her." Sensitive forward-looking radical that he was, Grant Allen was still sufficient of a Victorian to make his emancipated heroine 'yield'.

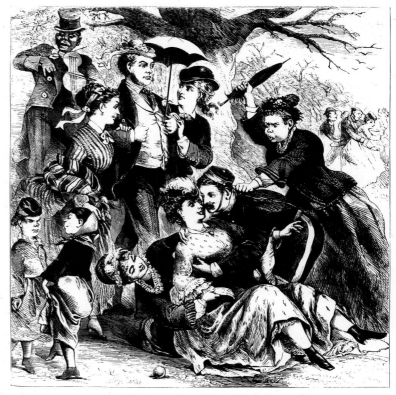

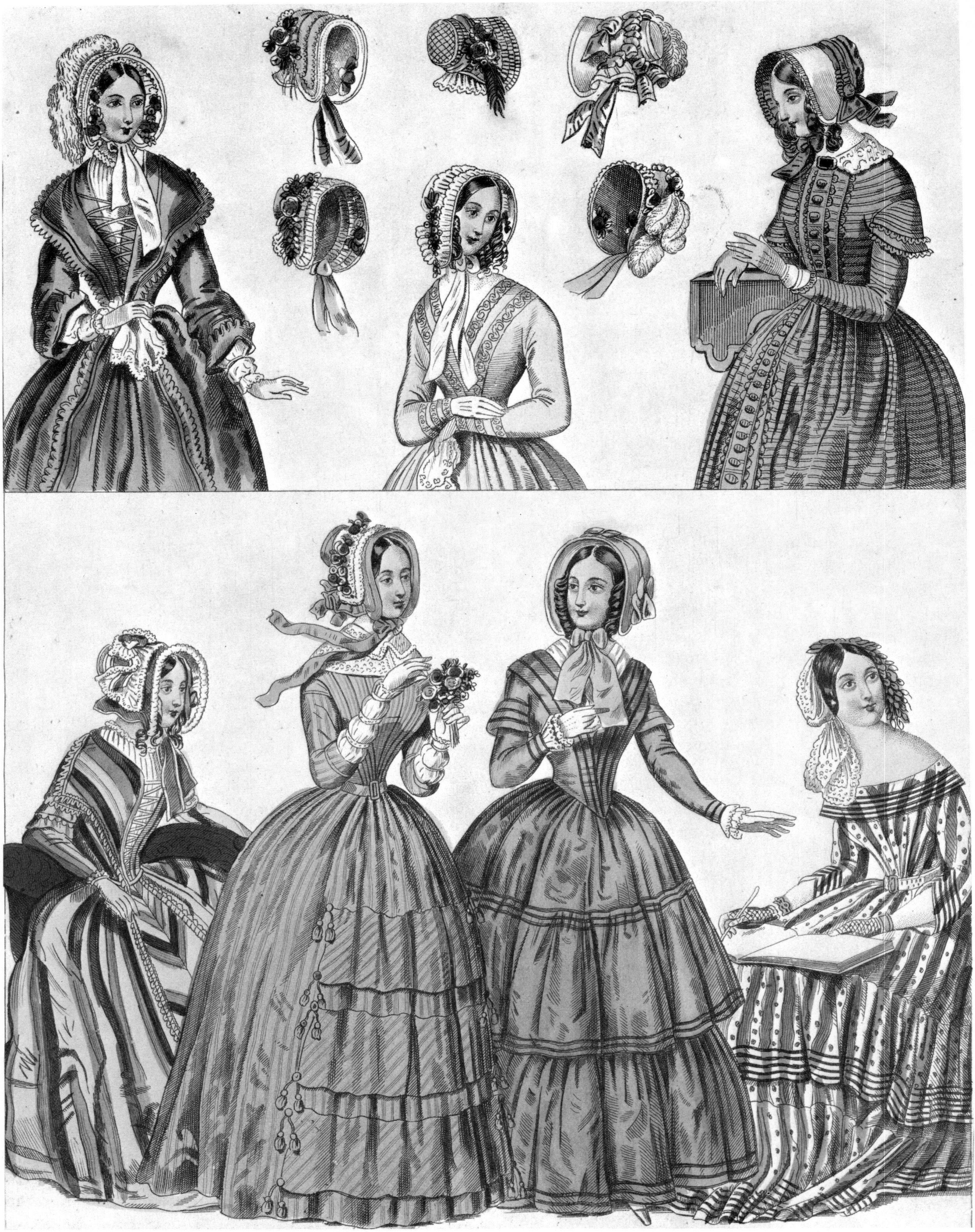

THE FASHION PICTURE Elaborate hair and dress, tight bodices and the armour of corsetry set the pattern for women's fashion. Fluttering ribbons, lace trimmings, flowers, ringlets, and jewellery were essential. So were a lace cap to wear at home and a hat for paying calls or shopping

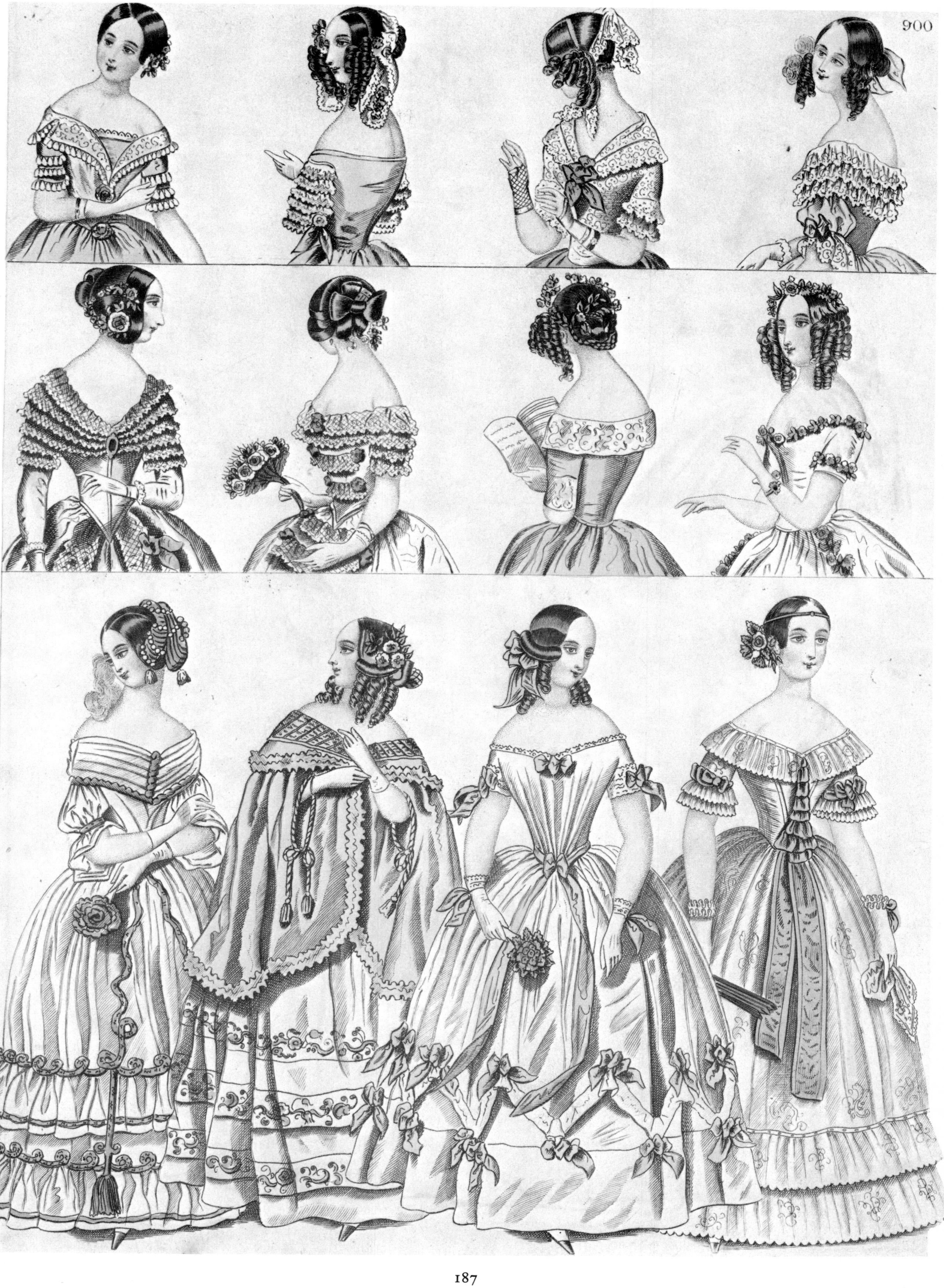
900

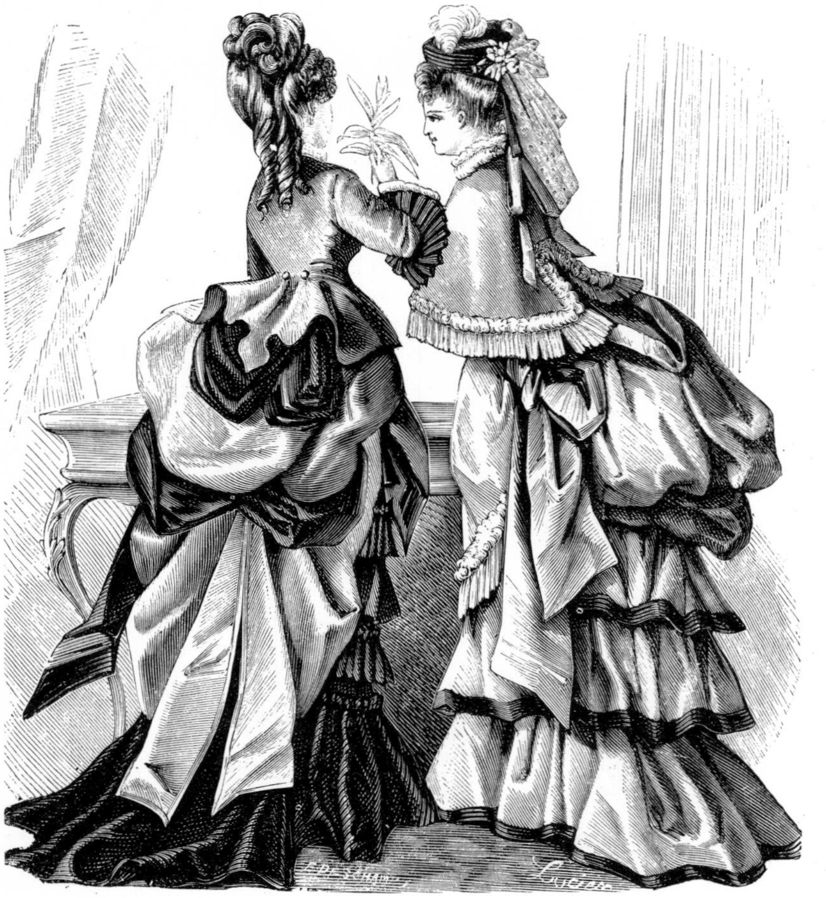

Close-fitting shoes, clothes and corsets reflect the restraints fashion placed upon young women entering society (above), and their well-dressed brothers (below)

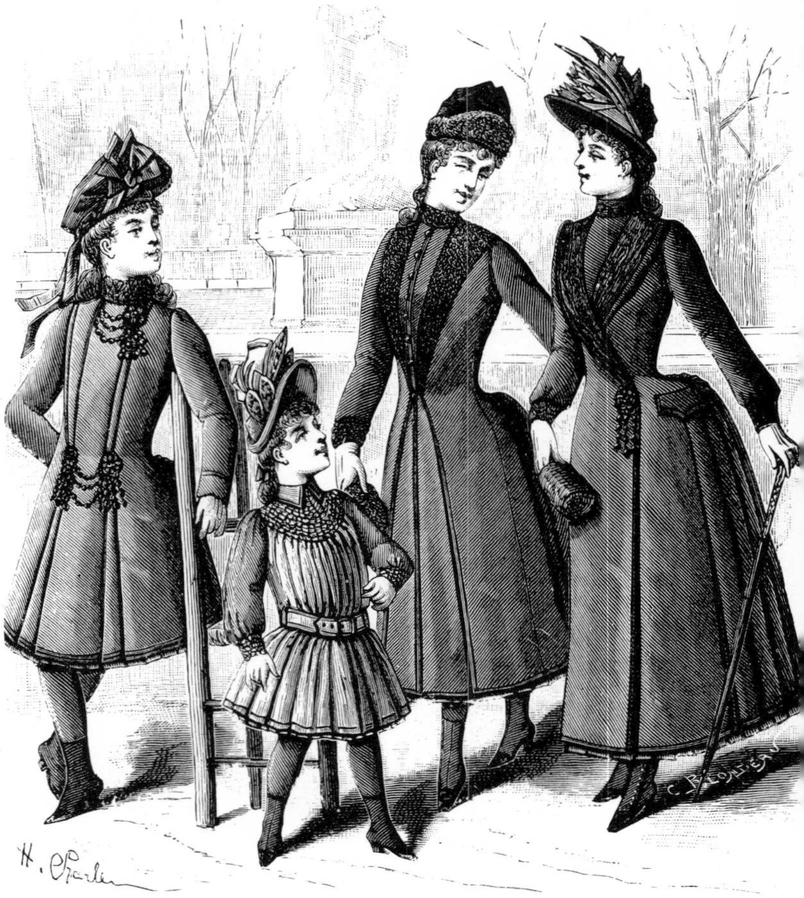

Clothes were a conspicuous display of a family's wealth and social pulling-power, proving they were rich enough not to work. Even young girls were corseted from an early age

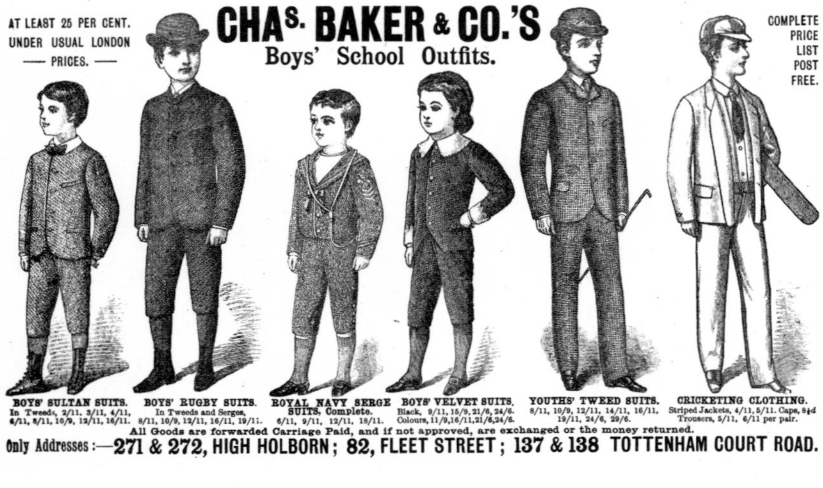

AT LEAST 25 PER CENT. UNDER USUAL LONDON PRICES.
CHAS. BAKER & CO.'S
Boys' School Outfits.
COMPLETE PRICE LIST POST FREE.
BOYS' SULTAN SUITS. In Tweeds, 2/11, 3/11, 4/11, 6/11, 8/11, 10/9, 12/11, 16/11.
BOYS' RUGBY SUITS. In Tweeds and Serges, 8/11, 10/9, 12/11, 16/11, 19/11.
ROYAL NAVY SERGE SUITS, Complete. 6/11, 9/11, 12/11, 18/11.
BOYS' VELVET SUITS. Black, 9/11, 15/9, 21/6, 24/6. Colours, 11/9, 16/11, 21/6, 24/6.
YOUTHS' TWEED SUITS. 8/11, 10/9, 12/11, 14/11, 16/11, 19/11, 24/6, 29/6.
CRICKETING CLOTHING. Striped Jackets, 4/11, 5/11. Caps, 8½d Trousers, 5/11, 6/11 per pair.
All Goods are forwarded Carriage Paid, and if not approved, are exchanged or the money returned.
Only Addresses:—271 & 272, HIGH HOLBORN; 82, FLEET STREET; 137 & 138 TOTTENHAM COURT ROAD.

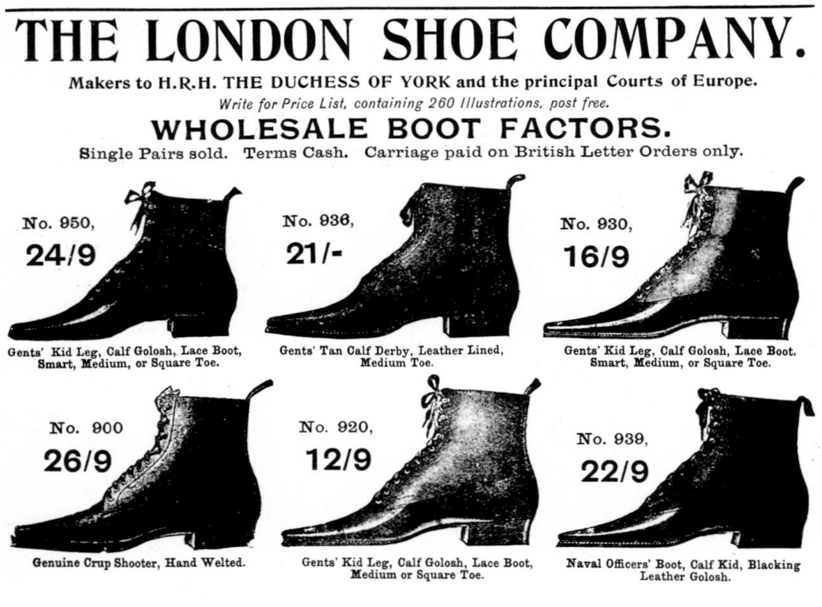

THE LONDON SHOE COMPANY.
Makers to H.R.H. THE DUCHESS OF YORK and the principal Courts of Europe.
Write for Price List, containing 260 Illustrations, post free.
WHOLESALE BOOT FACTORS.
Single Pairs sold. Terms Cash. Carriage paid on British Letter Orders only.
No. 950, 24/9
Gents' Kid Leg, Calf Golosh, Lace Boot, Smart, Medium, or Square Toe.
No. 936, 21/-
Gents' Tan Calf Derby, Leather Lined, Medium Toe.
No. 930, 16/9
Gents' Kid Leg, Calf Golosh, Lace Boot. Smart, Medium, or Square Toe.
No. 900 26/9
Genuine Crup Shooter, Hand Welted.
No. 920, 12/9
Gents' Kid Leg, Calf Golosh, Lace Boot, Medium or Square Toe.
No. 939, 22/9
Naval Officers' Boot, Calf Kid, Blacking Leather Golosh.

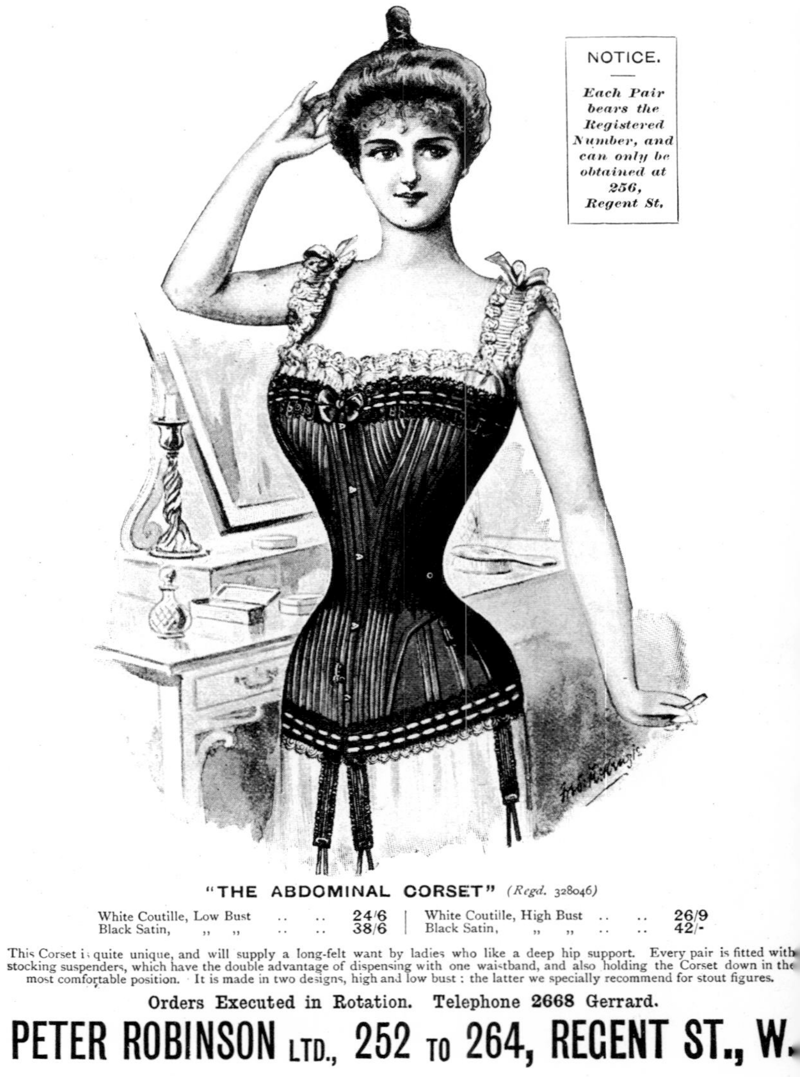

NOTICE.
Each Pair bears the Registered Number, and can only be obtained at 256, Regent St.
"THE ABDOMINAL CORSET" (Regd. 328046)
White Coutille, Low Bust 24/6
Black Satin, ,, ,, ... 38/6
White Coutille, High Bust 26/9
Black Satin, ,, ,, ... 42/-
This Corset is quite unique, and will supply a long-felt want by ladies who like a deep hip support. Every pair is fitted with stocking suspenders, which have the double advantage of dispensing with one waistband, and also holding the Corset down in the most comfortable position. It is made in two designs, high and low bust: the latter we specially recommend for stout figures.
Orders Executed in Rotation. Telephone 2668 Gerrard.
PETER ROBINSON LTD., 252 TO 264, REGENT ST., W.

THE "SPÉCIALITÉ CORSET"

REGD. DESIGN No. 2517

IS A DREAM OF COMFORT.

Above: a corset, stiffened with whalebone and steel, described as comfortable enough to sleep in.
Tight lacing was the cause of many internal injuries

Below (left and right): still corseted, covered with lace and frills, to a mid-Victorian woman of fashion this was informal wear for the family circle

LE MONITEUR DE LA MODE

Modèles de Lingeries de la Maison Colas 17, rue Vivienne

LE MONITEUR DE LA MODE

Modèles de Lingeries de la Maison Colas 10, rue Vivienne

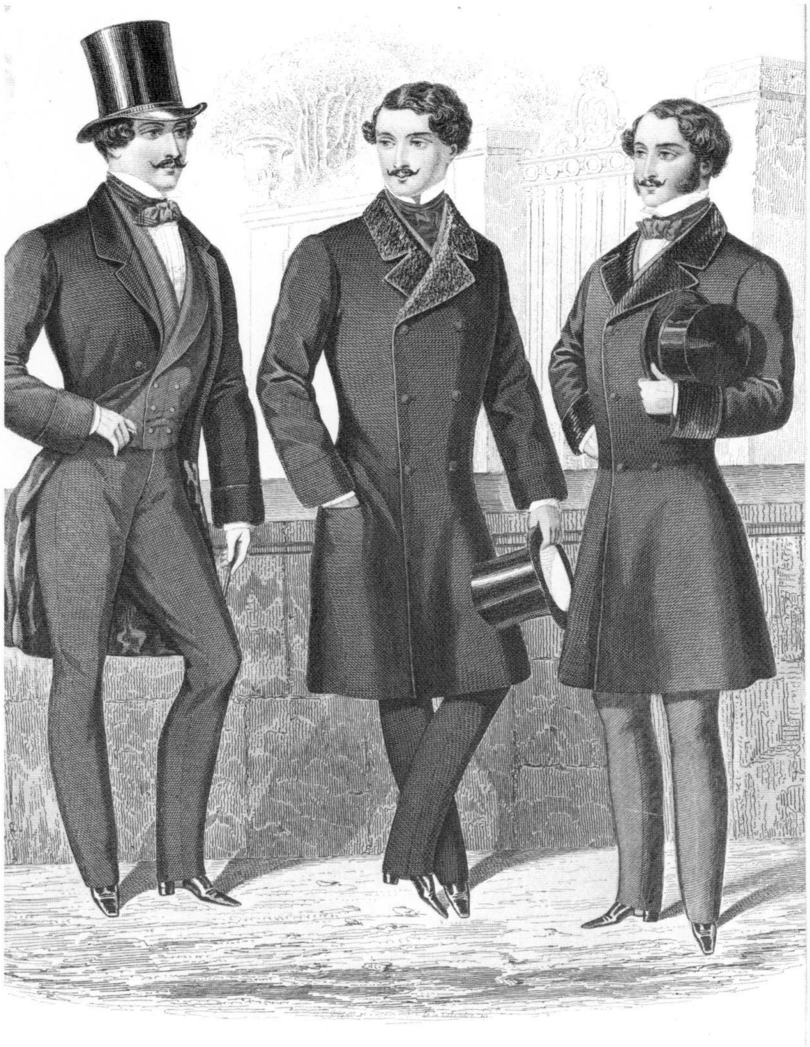

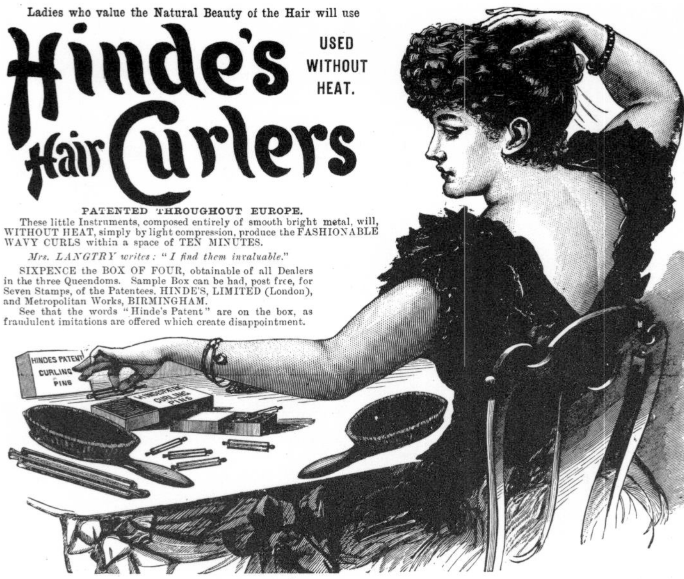
Ladies who value the Natural Beauty of the Hair will use
Hinde's Hair Curlers
USED WITHOUT HEAT.
PATENTED THROUGHOUT EUROPE.
These little Instruments, composed entirely of smooth bright metal, will, WITHOUT HEAT, simply by light compression, produce the FASHIONABLE WAVY CURLS within a space of TEN MINUTES.
Mrs. LANGTRY writes: "I find them invaluable."
SIXPENCE the BOX OF FOUR, obtainable of all Dealers in the three Queendoms. Sample Box can be had, post free, for Seven Stamps, of the Patentees, HINDE'S, LIMITED (London), and Metropolitan Works, BIRMINGHAM.
See that the words "Hinde's Patent" are on the box, as fraudulent imitations are offered which create disappointment.
HINDES PATENT CURLING PINS

A lady's hair was fancifully curled

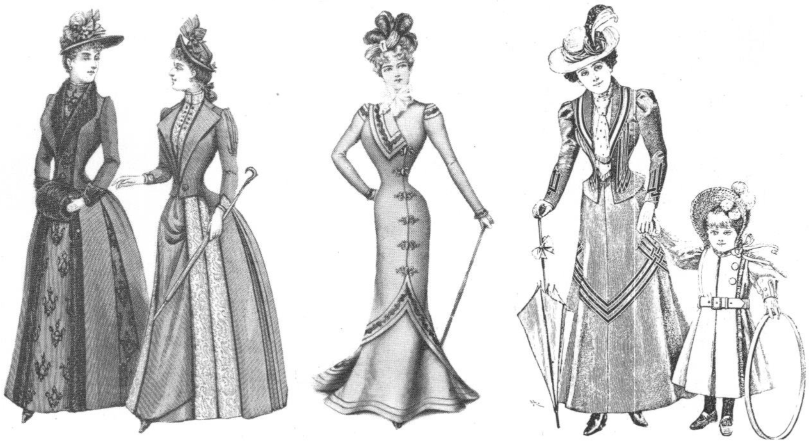

Above: men's street dress of the 1850s. To be recognised as a gentleman was all-important: clothes, along with stance and manner, were the outward signs

Late in the century women's fashion was still expensive, formal and ornate, even for children. Great attention was paid to the overall appearance

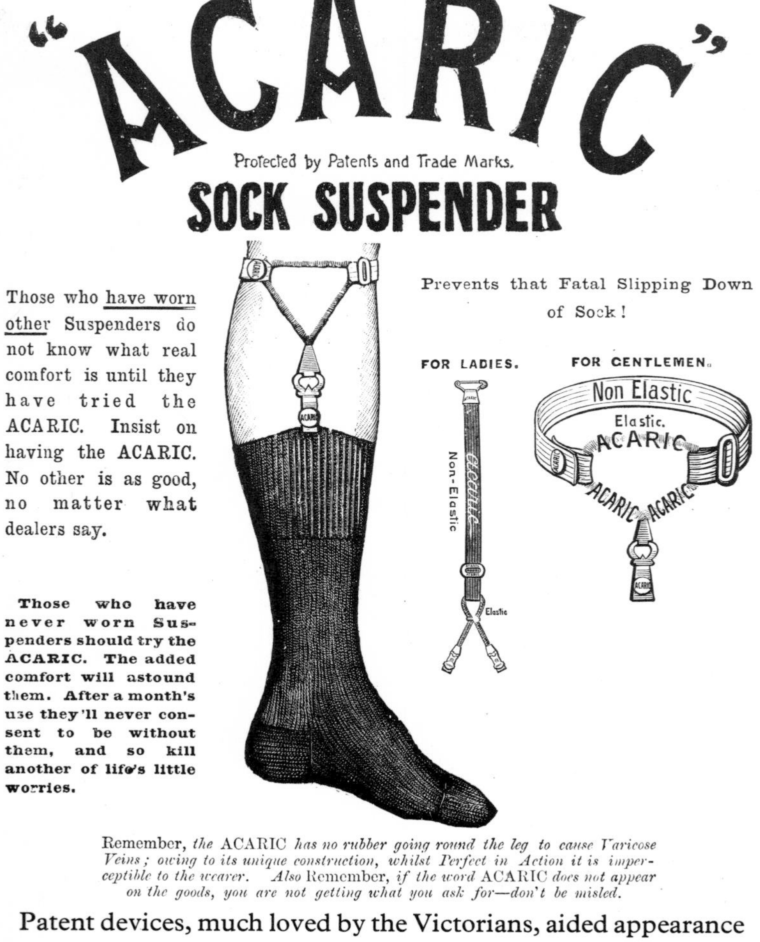
"ACARIC"
Protected by Patents and Trade Marks.
SOCK SUSPENDER
Prevents that Fatal Slipping Down of Sock!
Those who have worn other Suspenders do not know what real comfort is until they have tried the ACARIC. Insist on having the ACARIC. No other is as good, no matter what dealers say.
FOR LADIES.
FOR GENTLEMEN.
Non Elastic
Elastic.
ACARIC
Non-Elastic
Elastic
Those who have never worn Suspenders should try the ACARIC. The added comfort will astound them. After a month's use they'll never consent to be without them, and so kill another of life's little worries.
Remember, the ACARIC has no rubber going round the leg to cause Varicose Veins; owing to its unique construction, whilst Perfect in Action it is imperceptible to the wearer. Also Remember, if the word ACARIC does not appear on the goods, you are not getting what you ask for—don't be misled.

Patent devices, much loved by the Victorians, aided appearance

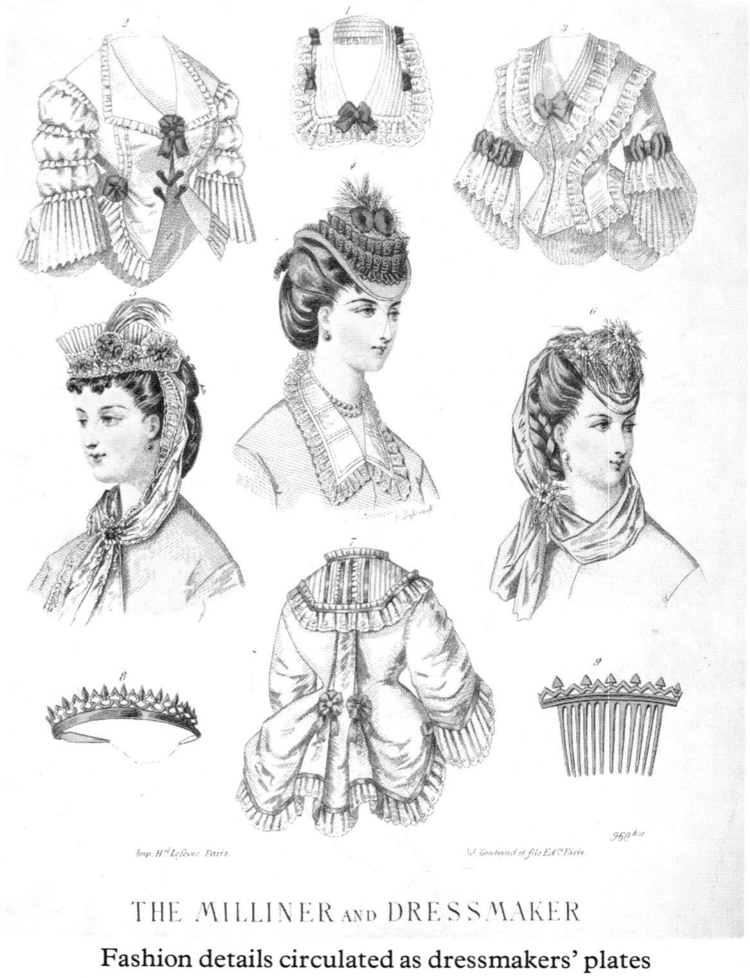
THE MILLINER AND DRESSMAKER

Fashion details circulated as dressmakers' plates

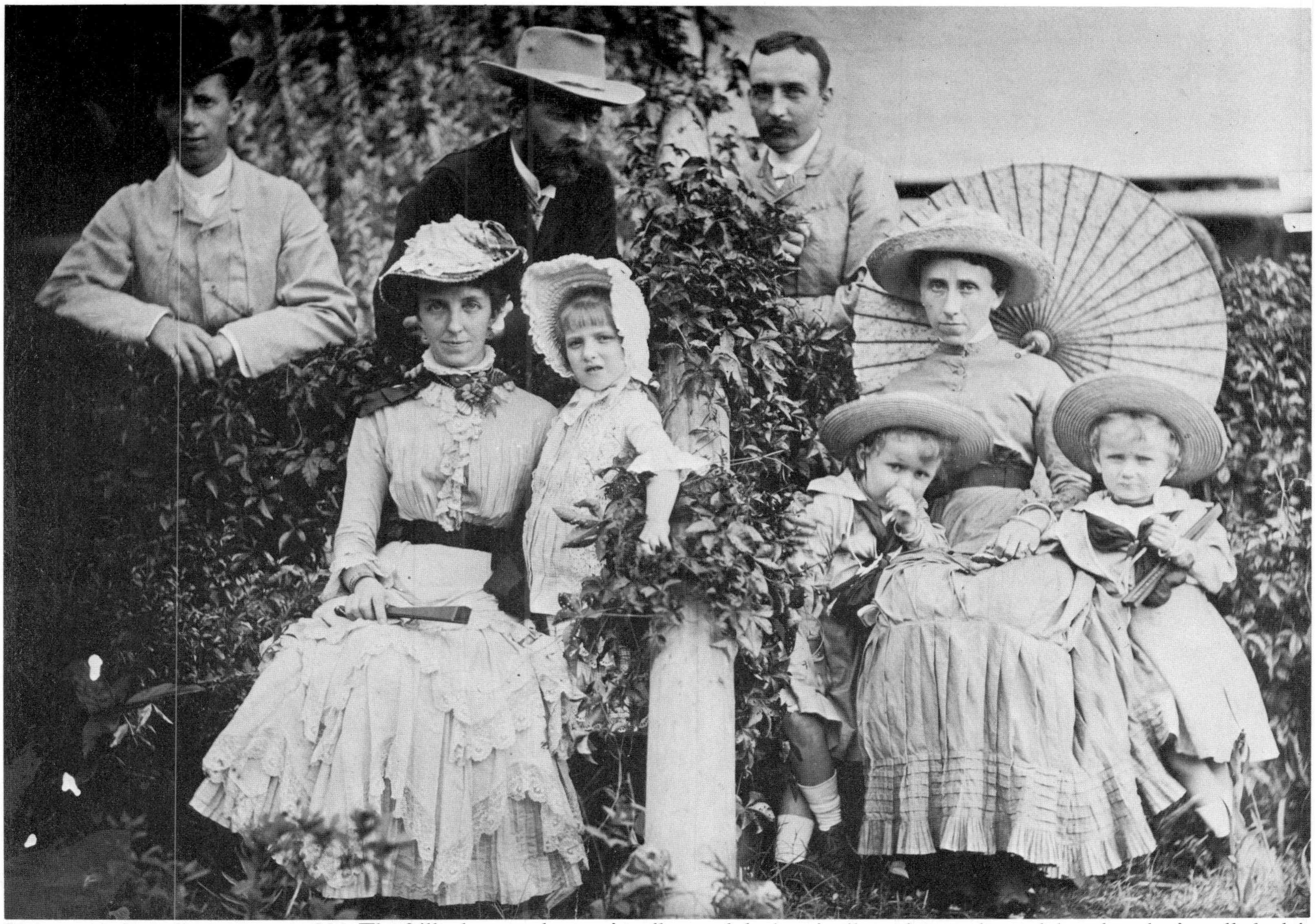

Elaborate informality, summer 1886. The frilly dresses, the men's collars and the boys' sailor suits may be cool, but they don't really look it

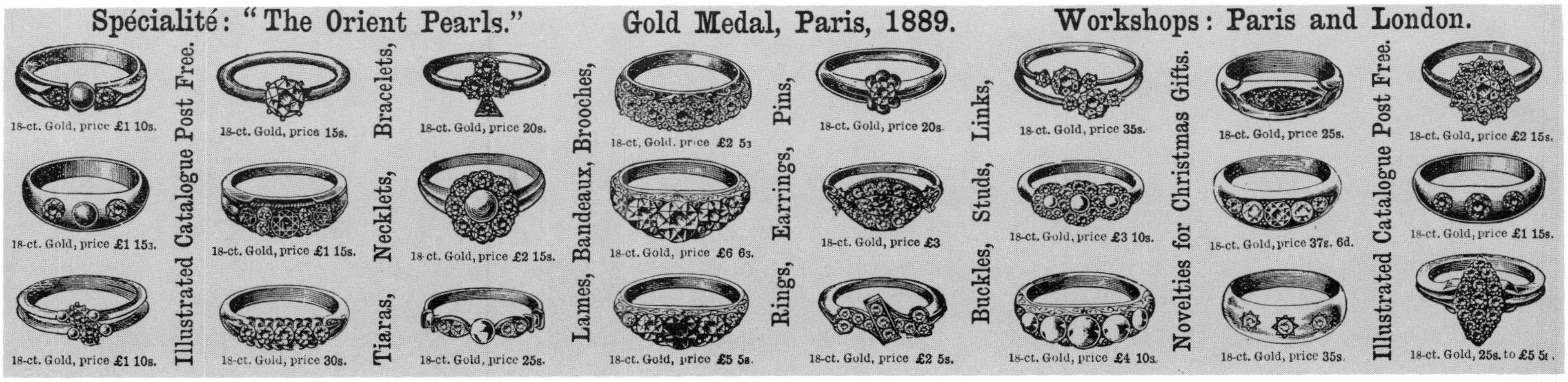

Spécialité: "The Orient Pearls." Gold Medal, Paris, 1889. Workshops: Paris and London.
18-ct. Gold, price £1 10s.
18-ct. Gold, price £1 15s.
18-ct. Gold, price £1 10s.
Illustrated Catalogue Post Free.
18-ct. Gold, price 15s.
18-ct. Gold, price £1 15s.
18-ct. Gold, price 30s.
Tiaras, Necklets, Bracelets,
18-ct. Gold, price 20s.
18-ct. Gold, price £2 15s.
18-ct. Gold, price 25s.
Lames, Bandeaux, Brooches,
18-ct. Gold, price £2 5s.
18-ct. Gold, price £6 6s.
18-ct. Gold, price £5 5s.
Rings, Earrings, Pins,
18-ct. Gold, price 20s.
18-ct. Gold, price £3
18-ct. Gold, price £2 5s.
Buckles, Studs, Links,
18-ct. Gold, price 35s.
18-ct. Gold, price £3 10s.
18-ct. Gold, price £4 10s.
Novelties for Christmas Gifts.
18-ct. Gold, price 25s.
18-ct. Gold, price 37s. 6d.
18-ct. Gold, price 35s.
Illustrated Catalogue Post Free.
18-ct. Gold, price £2 15s.
18-ct. Gold, price £1 15s.
18-ct. Gold, 25s. to £5 5s.

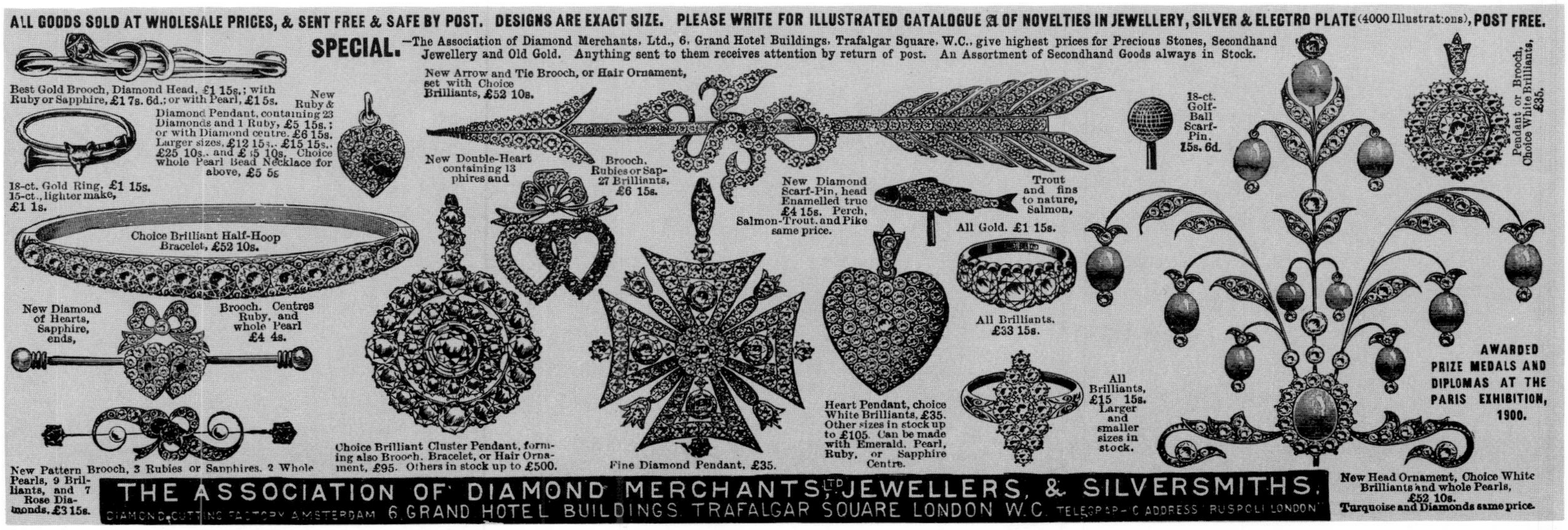

ALL GOODS SOLD AT WHOLESALE PRICES, & SENT FREE & SAFE BY POST. DESIGNS ARE EXACT SIZE. PLEASE WRITE FOR ILLUSTRATED CATALOGUE OF NOVELTIES IN JEWELLERY, SILVER & ELECTRO PLATE (4000 Illustrations), POST FREE.
SPECIAL.—The Association of Diamond Merchants, Ltd., 6, Grand Hotel Buildings, Trafalgar Square, W.C., give highest prices for Precious Stones, Secondhand Jewellery and Old Gold. Anything sent to them receives attention by return of post. An Assortment of Secondhand Goods always in Stock.
Best Gold Brooch, Diamond Head, £1 15s.; with Ruby or Sapphire, £1 7s. 6d.; or with Pearl, £1 5s.
New Ruby & Diamond Pendant, containing 23 Diamonds and 1 Ruby, £5 15s.; or with Diamond centre, £6 15s. Larger sizes, £12 15s., £15 15s., £25 10s., and £35 10s. Choice whole Pearl Bead Necklace for above, £5 5s.
18-ct. Gold Ring, £1 15s. 15-ct., lighter make, £1 1s.
New Arrow and Tie Brooch, or Hair Ornament, set with Choice Brilliants, £52 10s.
New Double-Heart Brooch, Rubies or Sapphires and 27 Brilliants, containing 13 £6 15s.
18-ct. Golf-Ball Scarf-Pin, 15s. 6d.
Pendant or Brooch, Choice White Brilliants, £35.
Choice Brilliant Half-Hoop Bracelet, £52 10s.
New Diamond Scarf-Pin, head Enamelled true to nature, £4 15s. Perch, Salmon-Trout, and Pike same price.
Trout and fins to nature, Salmon,
All Gold. £1 15s.
All Brilliants, £33 15s.
New Diamond of Hearts, Sapphire, ends,
Brooch. Centres Ruby, and whole Pearl £4 4s.
Heart Pendant, choice White Brilliants, £35. Other sizes in stock up to £105. Can be made with Emerald, Pearl, Ruby, or Sapphire Centre.
All Brilliants, £15 15s. Larger and smaller sizes in stock.
AWARDED PRIZE MEDALS AND DIPLOMAS AT THE PARIS EXHIBITION, 1900.
New Pattern Brooch, 3 Rubies or Sapphires, 2 Whole Pearls, 9 Brilliants, and 7 Rose Diamonds, £3 15s.
Choice Brilliant Cluster Pendant, forming also Brooch, Bracelet, or Hair Ornament, £95. Others in stock up to £500.
Fine Diamond Pendant, £35.
THE ASSOCIATION OF DIAMOND MERCHANTS LTD. JEWELLERS, & SILVERSMITHS.
DIAMOND CUTTING FACTORY AMSTERDAM 6 GRAND HOTEL BUILDINGS TRAFALGAR SQUARE LONDON W.C. TELEGRAPHIC ADDRESS "RUSPOLI LONDON"
New Head Ornament, Choice White Brilliants and whole Pearls, £52 10s. Turquoise and Diamonds same price.

Engagement rings became popular; like the jewellery with which he adorned his women, they were indicators of a man's prosperity and status

PLAYS AND PLAYERS

By Philip Oakes

In 1800 there were only ten theatres in London. By 1840 – three years after Queen Victoria's accession – there were twenty-two, reflecting a surge in popular taste. Before Victoria, the theatre had relied on support from the Court and the monied upper classes, but as the century entered its fourth decade, a genial revolution swept the boards. The stalls were packed with the new bourgeoisie; workers thronged the galleries.

When Victoria came to the throne only two theatre managers – those of Drury Lane and Covent Garden – had the right to present spoken drama. The other so-called minor theatres in London were obliged to present 'illegitimate' drama, or burlettas in which spoken dialogue had to be accompanied by music. Writers, artists and businessmen banded together and in 1843 the Theatre Regulations Act ended the monopoly.

New acting styles and reputations burgeoned. Dion Boucicault wrote *London Assurance*, a comedy which leaned towards a more realistic contemporary drama. The great tragedian Henry Irving (who invented the stage black-out in which scenery was changed) introduced naturalism to the classics. Actor-managers such as Frank Benson, Forbes-Robertson, Cyril Maude and

John Martin-Harvey created repertory companies in which egos were rampant but talent was fostered. Acting itself became almost respectable; even Charterhouse, the public school, thought it fitting to book the Haymarket Theatre for a special matinée in 1899 (above).

Only the music-hall held out against rising propriety. Its tunes were patriotic (right), but its manners lacked polish. The reasons are plain. In the 1850s the halls drew their talent from the old Song and Supper Rooms, where the entertainment, designed for men only, was of an 'erotic and Bacchanalian order'.

The halls had as much to live down as they had to live up to. But mixed audiences reduced the spice in variety to a palatable level. By 1868, London had over 270 variety theatres, and the rest of the country had 300 more. Architecture was ample, gaslight gleamed on glass and brass, seats were upholstered, scenery was solidly built, and dioramas – which were landscapes painted on a continuous backcloth – rattled through rollers.

Halls, large and small, were conceived as people's palaces. And the sovereignty of the stars depended not only on their versatility, but also on the proof that they had that vital spark – the common touch.

SIEGE OF LADYSMITH

GRAND DIVERTIMENTO

COMPOSED BY

THEO. BONHEUR.

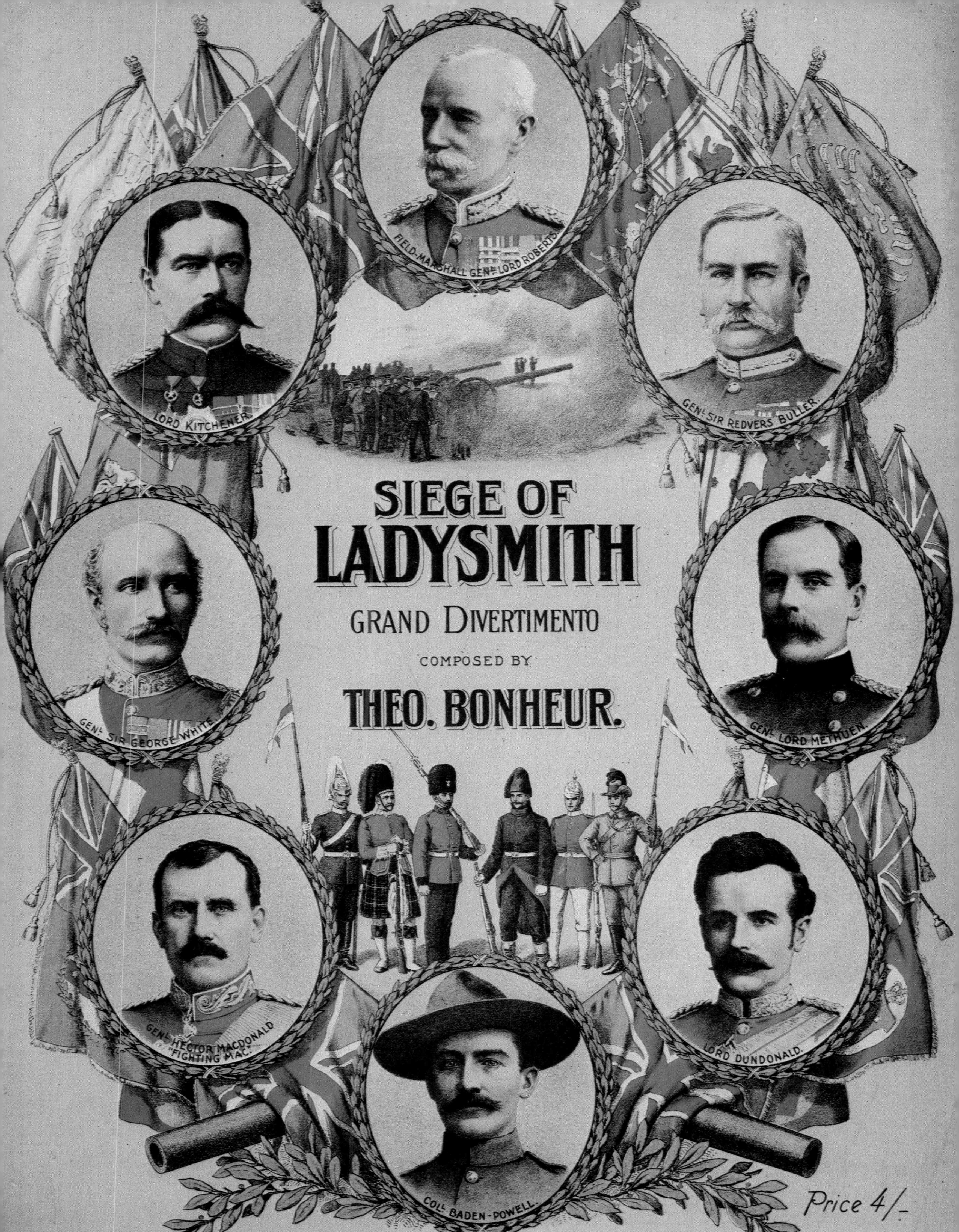
FIELD-MARSHALL GENL. LORD ROBERTS.
LORD KITCHENER.
GENL. SIR REDVERS BULLER.
GENL. SIR GEORGE WHITE.
GENL. LORD METHUEN.
GENL. HECTOR MACDONALD "FIGHTING MAC."
LORD DUNDONALD.
COLL. BADEN-POWELL.

Price 4/-

MOORE SMITH & Co. 43A ROLAND ST LONDON W.

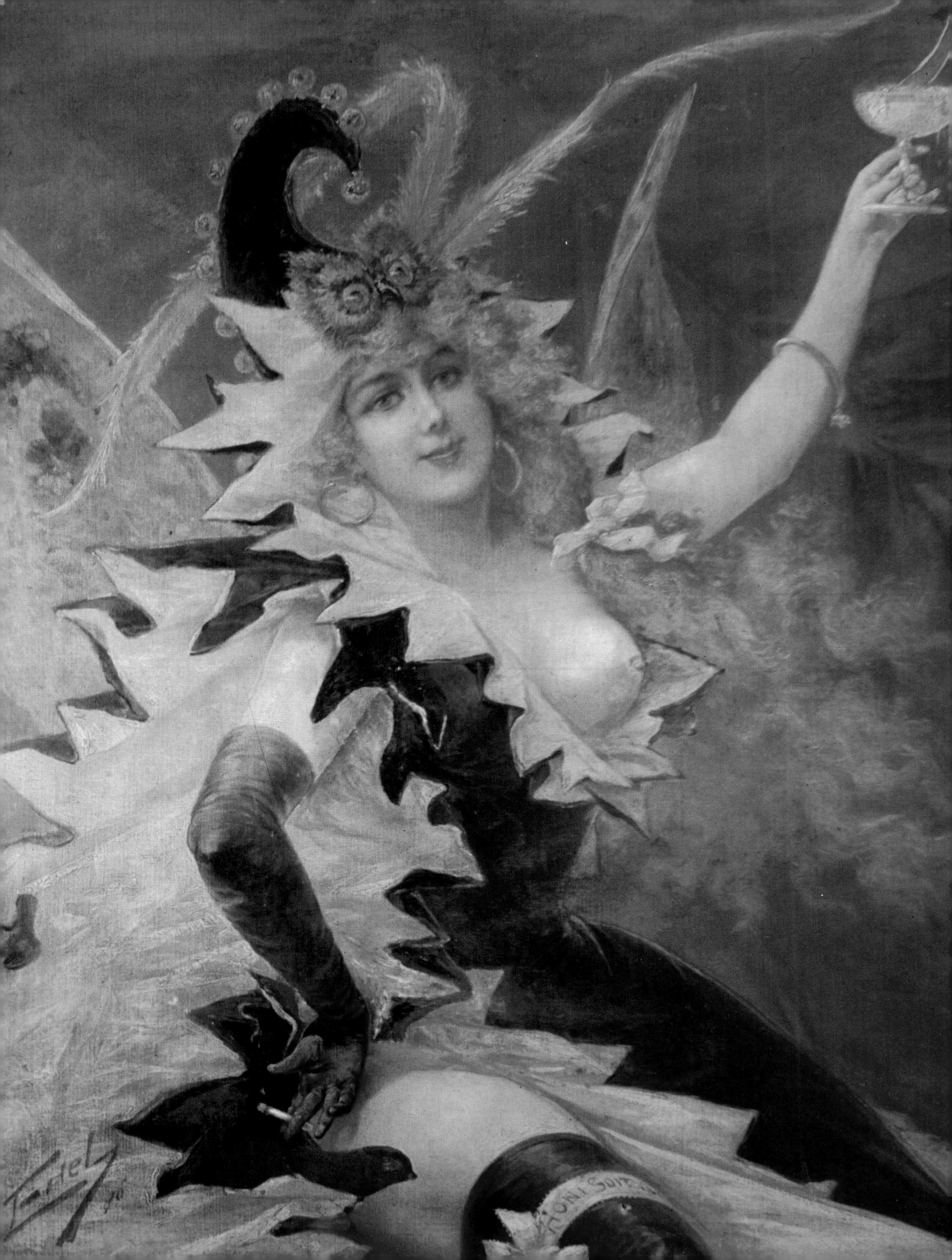

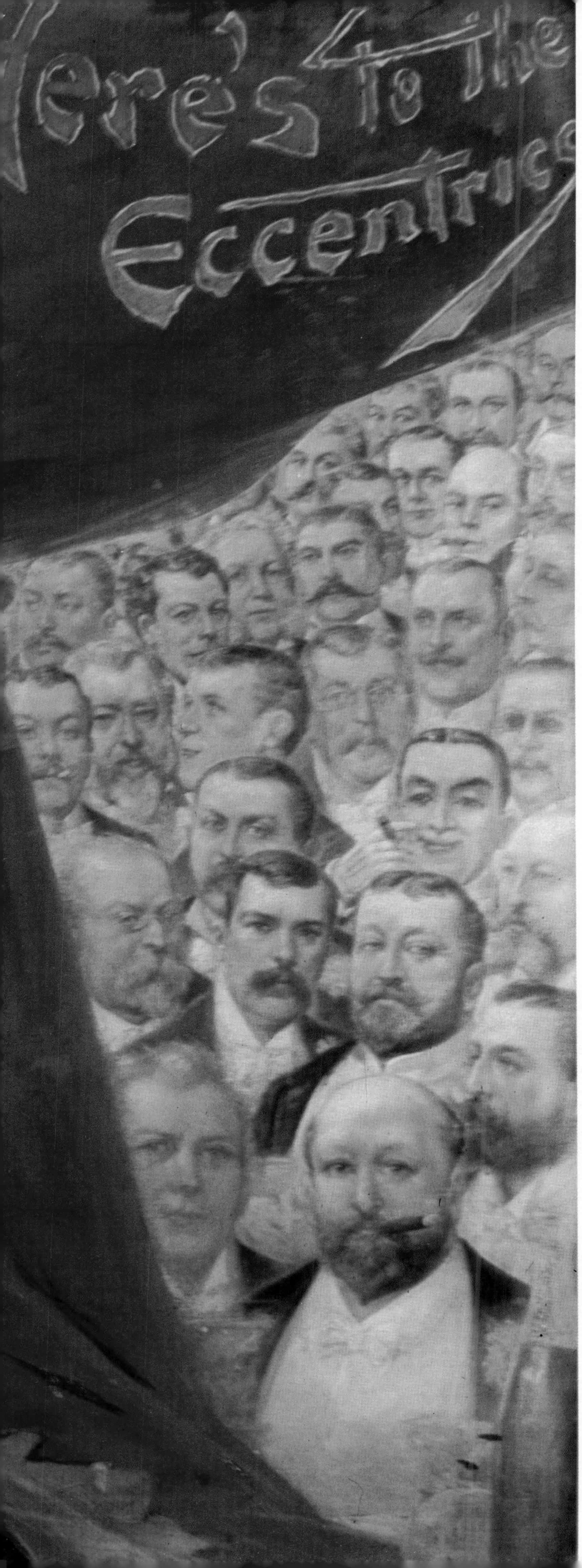
ere's to the
Eccentric

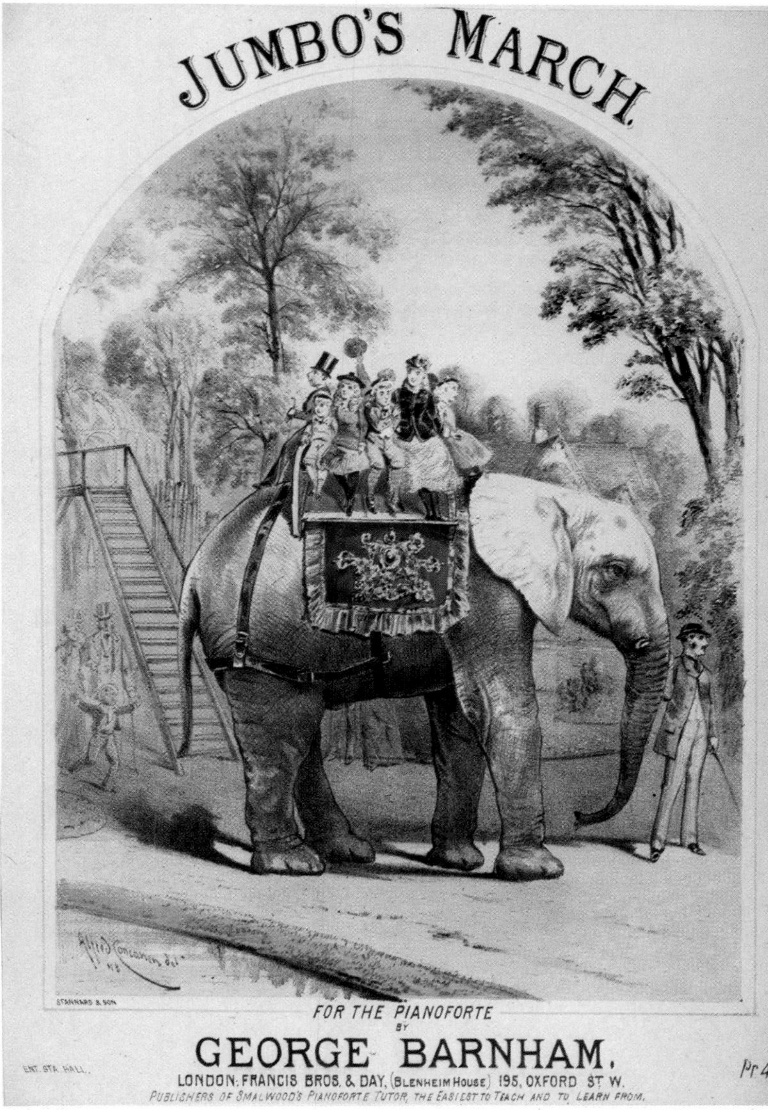
JUMBO'S MARCH.
STANNARD & SON
FOR THE PIANOFORTE
BY
GEORGE BARNHAM.
ENT. STA. HALL.
LONDON: FRANCIS BROS. & DAY, (BLENHEIM HOUSE) 195, OXFORD ST W.
PUBLISHERS OF SMALWOOD'S PIANOFORTE TUTOR, THE EASIEST TO TEACH AND TO LEARN FROM.
Pr 4/-

Stage-door Johnnies (left) courted music-hall queens. The garter worn by the buxom beauty seen toasting members of the Eccentrics Club bears the royal motto. And the cigar-smoking customer close by is a notable Eccentric, the Prince of Wales himself. His mother Queen Victoria was not amused. She was more tolerant of popular songs (above) which celebrated London Zoo's most famous elephant, subsequently bought for his show by Phineas Barnum. But variety theatres, like the Palace (below), prospered regardless

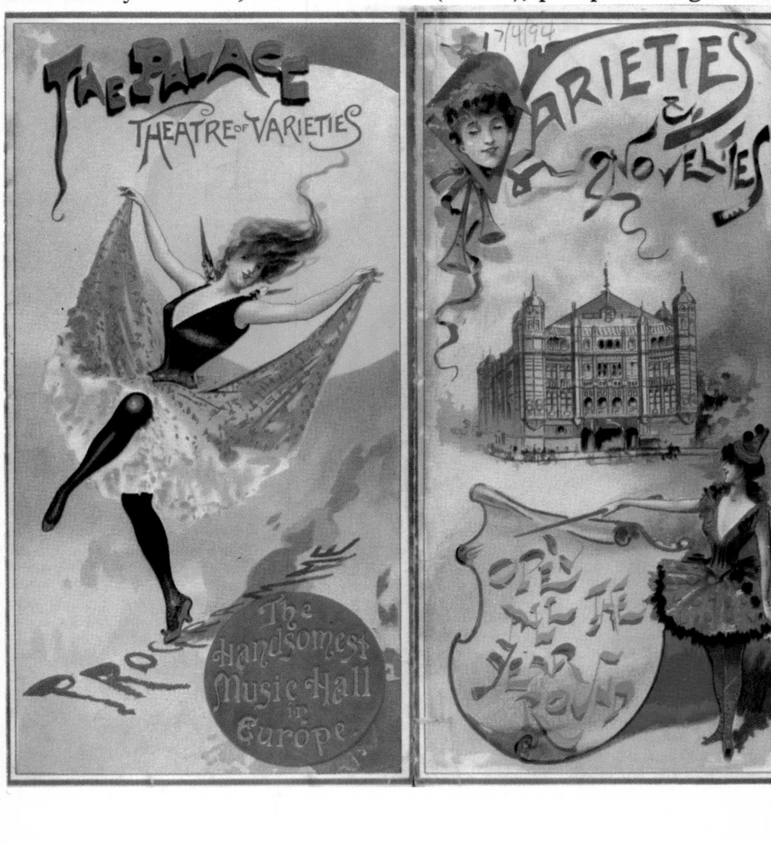
THE PALACE
THEATRE OF VARIETIES
PROGRAMME
The Handsomest Music Hall in Europe
VARIETIES & NOVELTIES
OPEN ALL THE YEAR ROUND

THE·HIT·OF·THE·SEASON.

THE NINETEENTH·CENTURY·BOYS.

POPULAR MARCH SONG AND CHORUS.

Written by
ARTHUR J. LAMB,

FATHER TIME UP-TO-DATE

Composed by
W.M. FRED.K PETERS

SUNG WITH THE GREATEST SUCCESS BY

THE·SISTERS·LEVEY.

Copyright for all Countries. LONDON: CHARLES SHEARD & Co. Music Publishers & Printers, 192, HIGH HOLBORN, W.C. Price 2/=net.
SANDUSKY. O. U.S.A. THE PETERS Music Publishing Co
Copyright 1895 by The Peters Music Pub Co

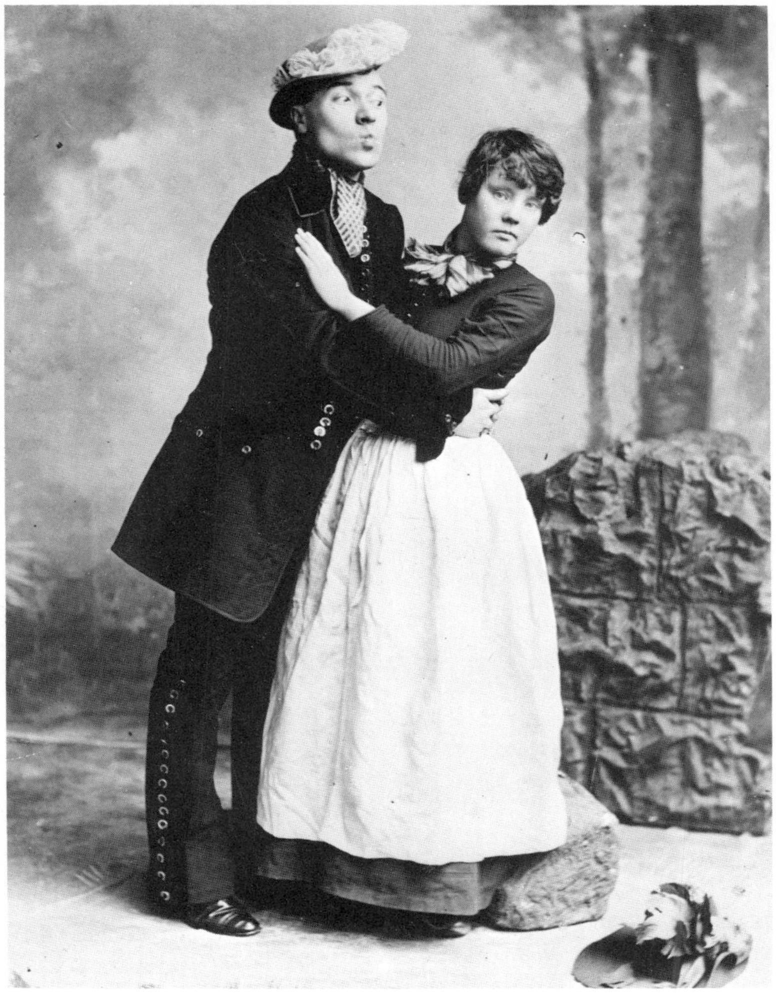

Music-hall stars. Albert Chevalier wore traditional 'pearly' garb, sang Cockney songs, and claimed title of 'the Coster Laureate'

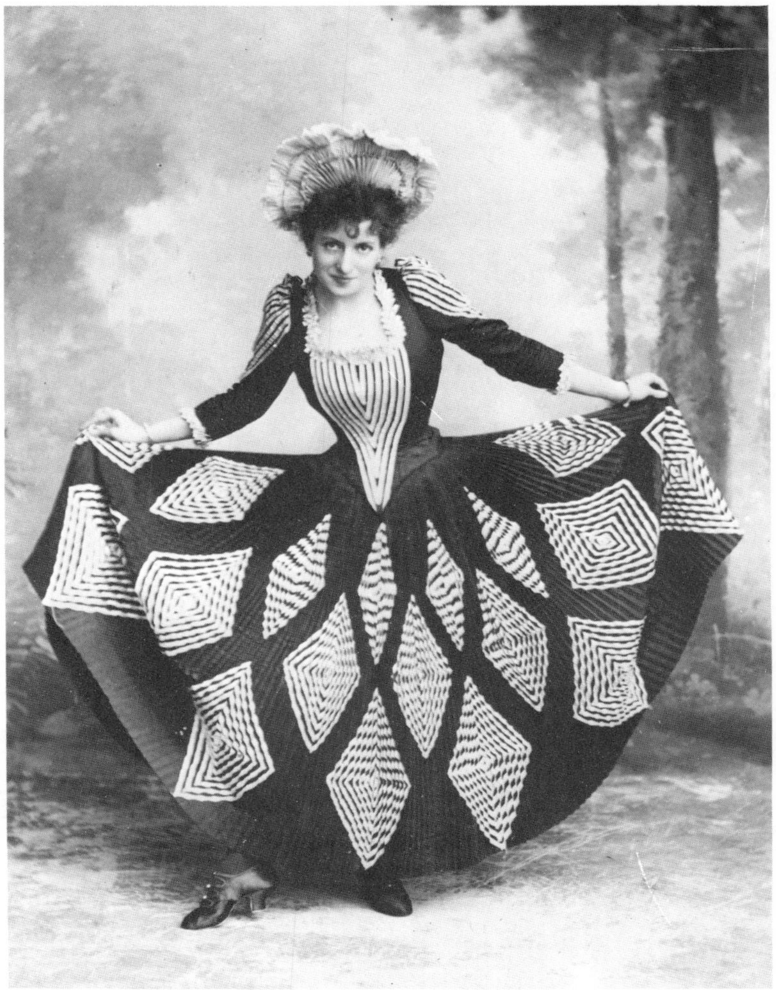

Lottie Collins, first known for her 'abandon dance', which the audience 'encored until she was exhausted'. Fame brought decorum

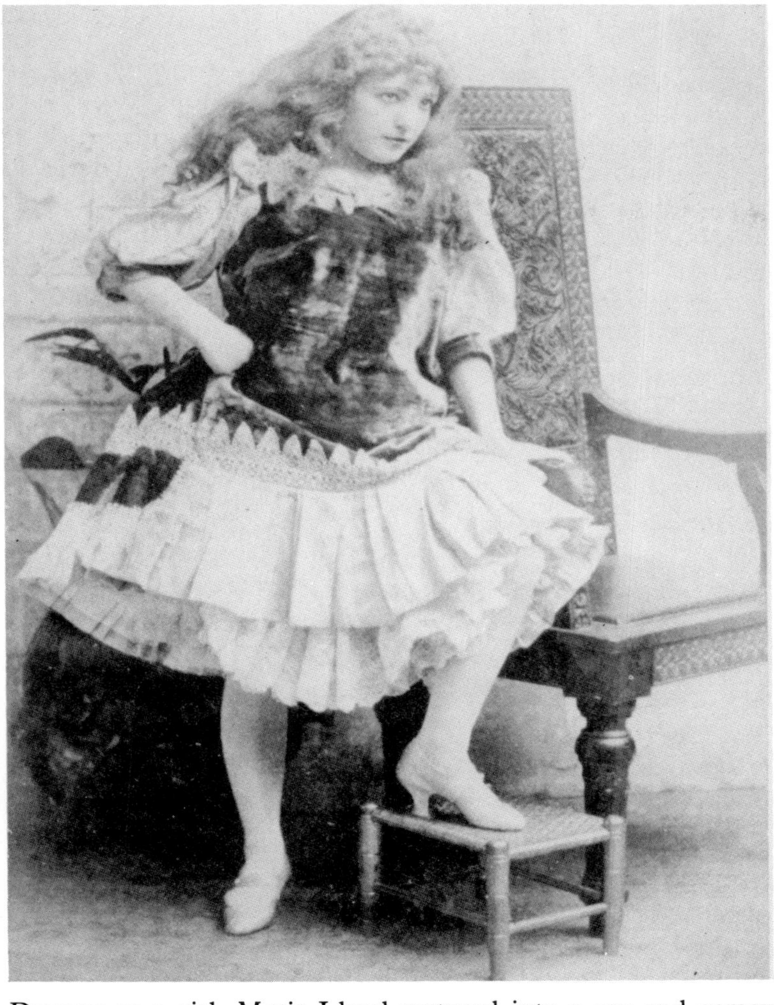

Demure as a girl, Marie Lloyd matured into a gay and gamey comedienne, whose songs seemed wholly innocent until sung by her

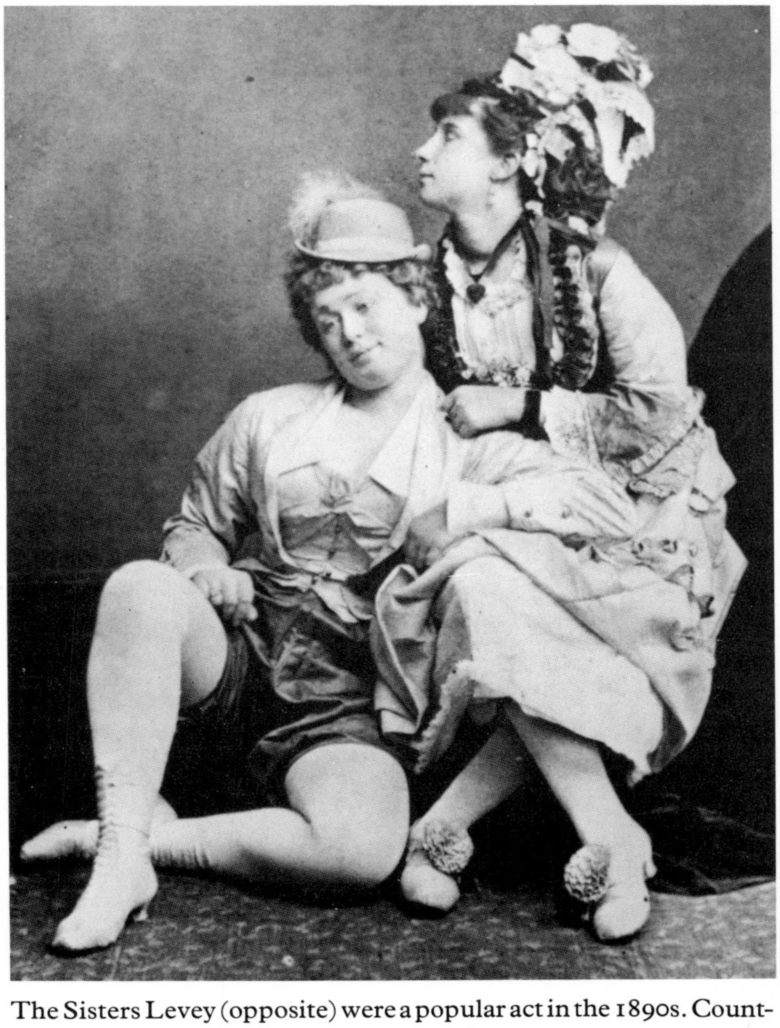

The Sisters Levey (opposite) were a popular act in the 1890s. Countless other artists, not featured on song sheets, are now anonymous

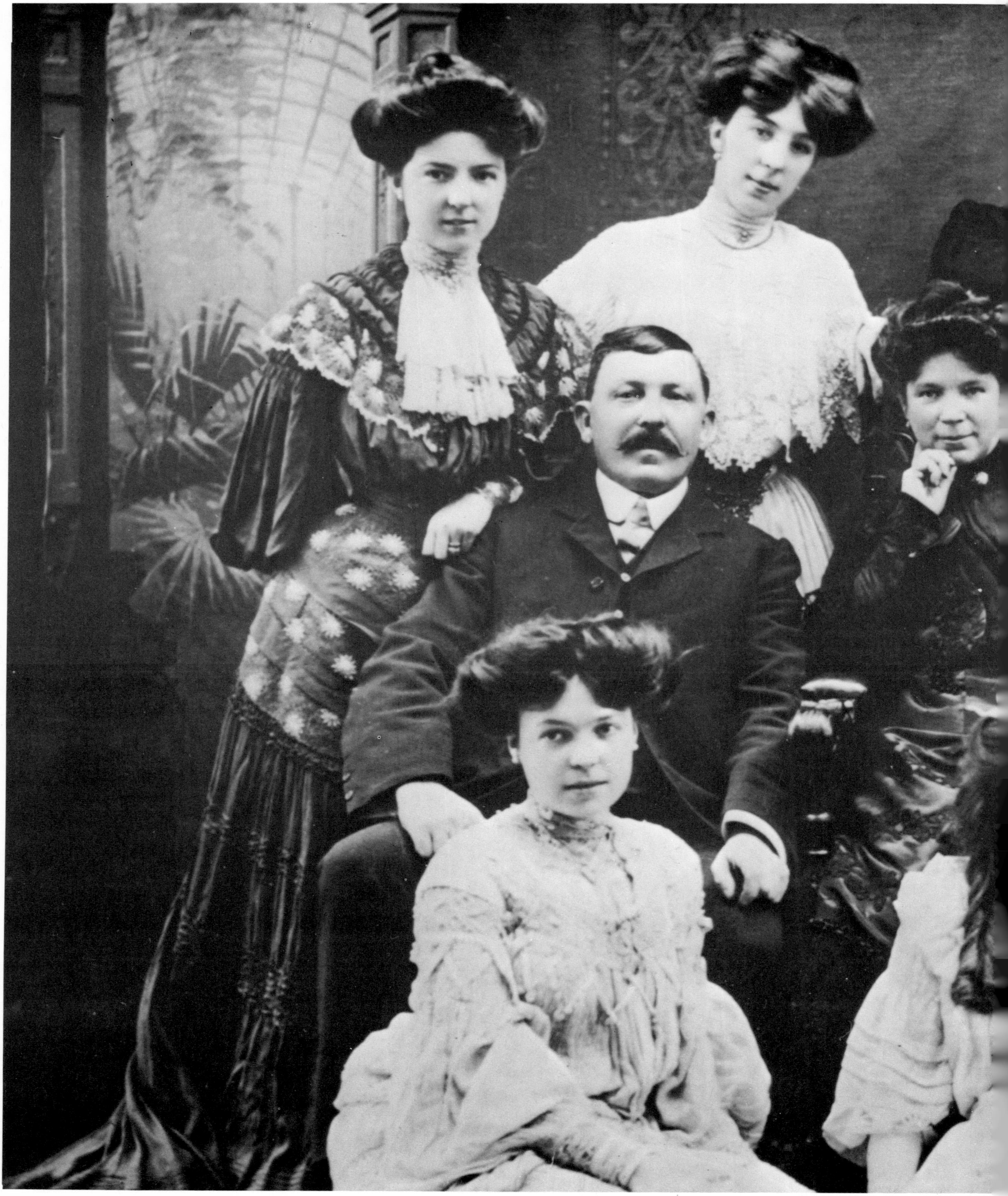

The Lloyds of East London. Marie Lloyd (right, centre row) was the stage name of Matilda Alice Victoria Wood. Her father (beside her mother, centre row) made artificial flowers in Hoxton. Her sisters Daisy, Rosie, Grace, and Alice (back row with brother John) followed her into the profession; not so sisters Annie and Maud (with brother Sydney, front row). At 15 she appeared at a hall attached to the Eagle

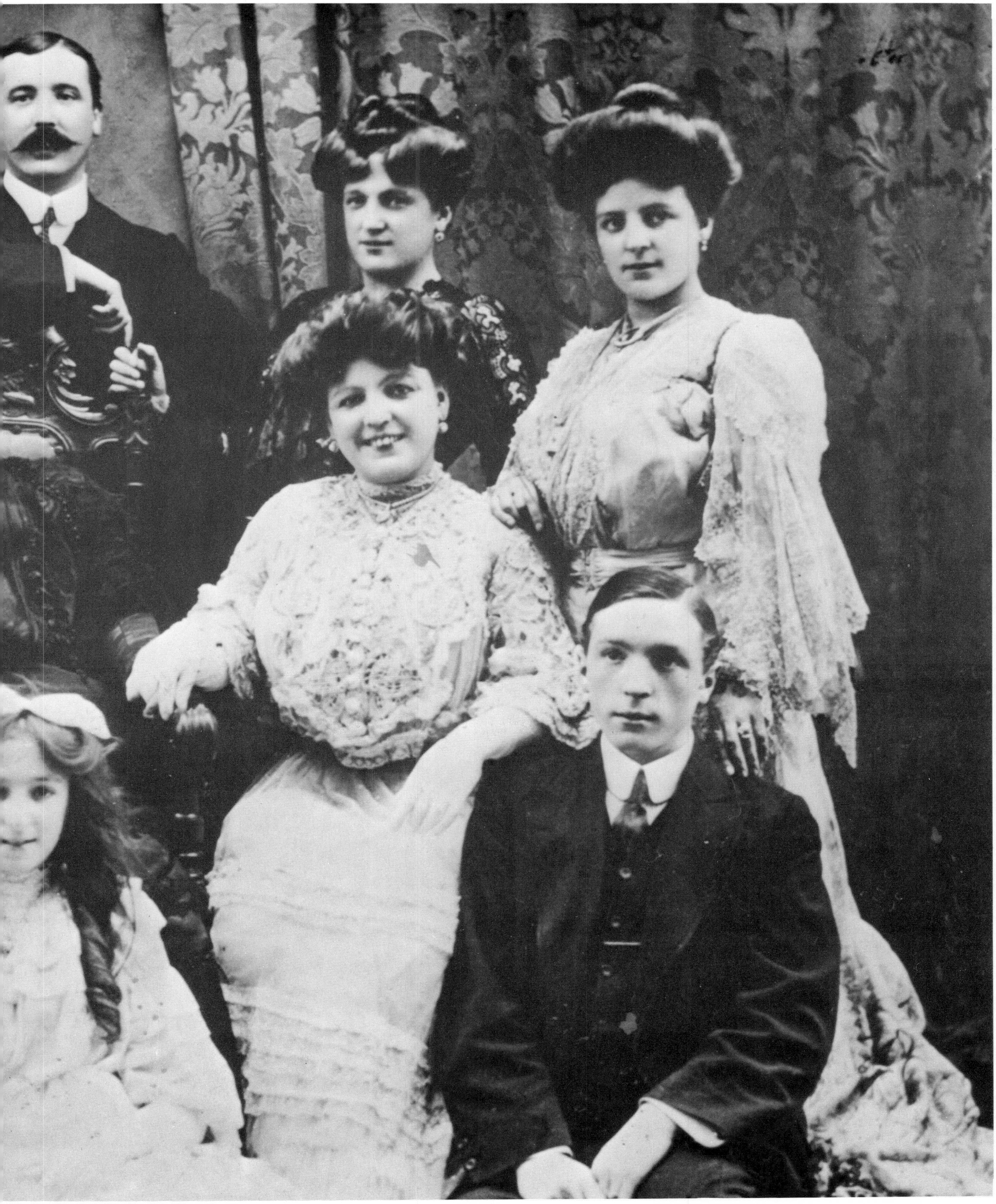

Tavern in City Road, London, under the name of Bella Delmare. On the advice of a manager she took the name of a Sunday newspaper of the day and became Marie Lloyd. Within two years her salary rose from 15 shillings to £100 a week – most of which she insisted on giving away. Audiences loved her for her golden vulgarity. She married three times, and died at the age of 52. Her funeral was attended by 50,000 mourners

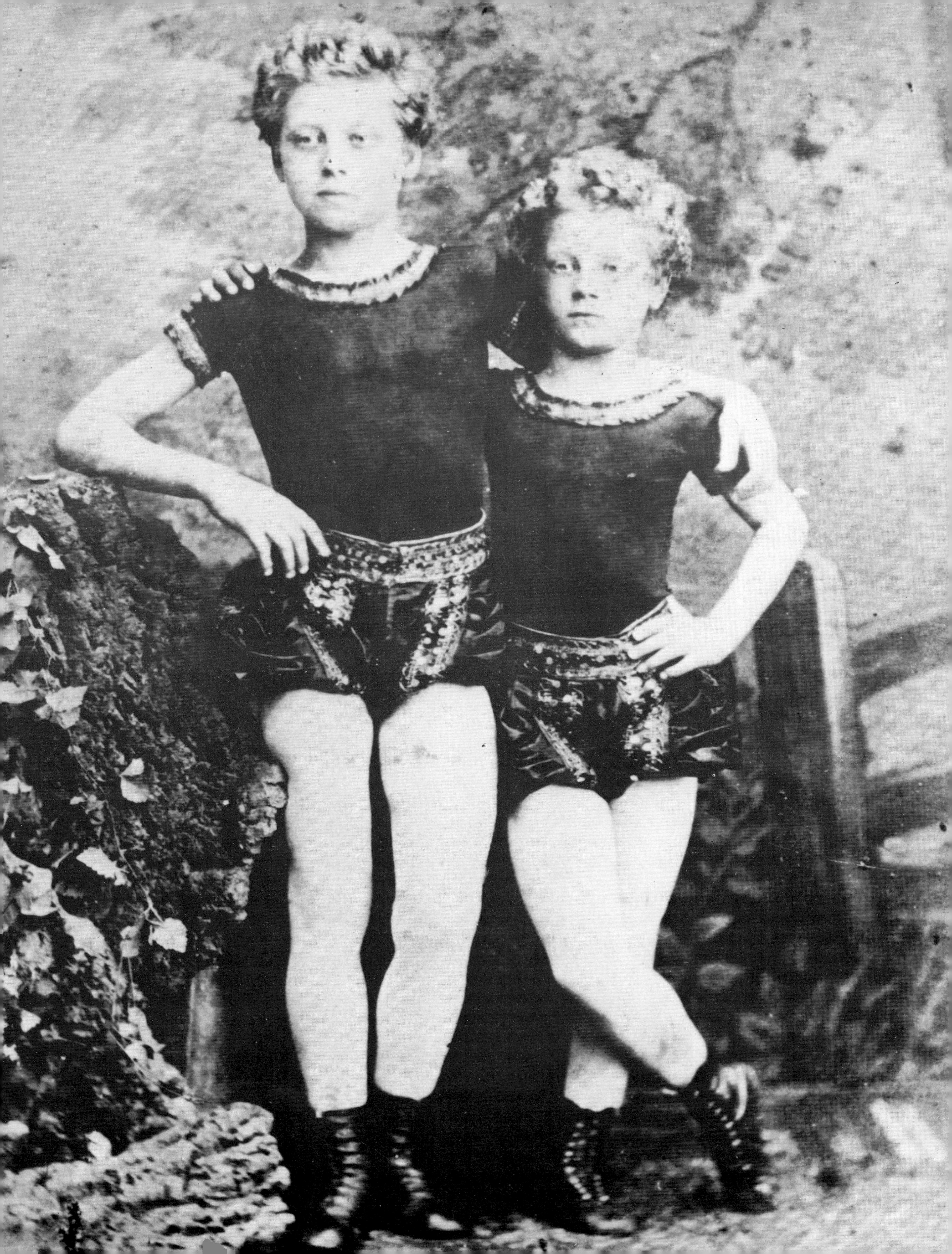

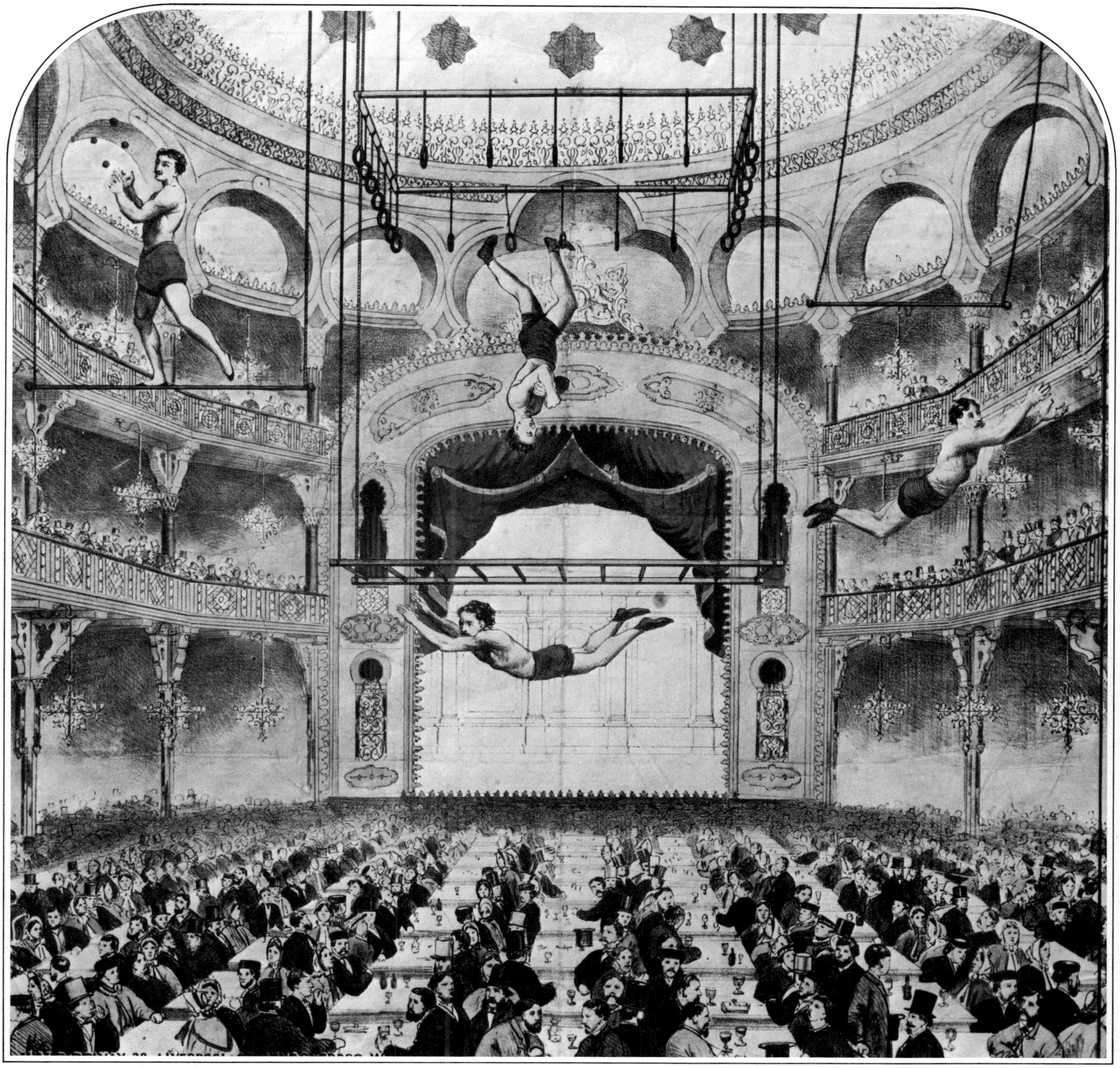

Music halls began as tavern entertainment. Singers and acrobats (opposite and above) vied with dinner

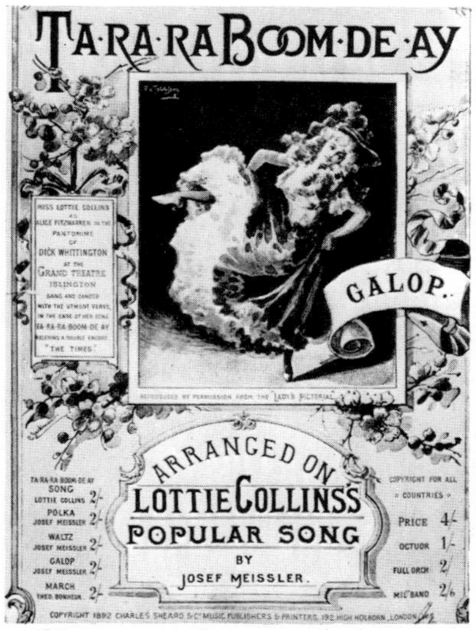
TA·RA·RA BOOM·DE·AY
MISS LOTTIE COLLINS AS ALICE FITZWARREN IN THE PANTOMIME OF DICK WHITTINGTON AT THE GRAND THEATRE ISLINGTON
"THE TIMES."
GALOP.
ARRANGED ON
LOTTIE COLLINS'S
POPULAR SONG
BY
JOSEF MEISSLER.
SONG LOTTIE COLLINS 2/-
POLKA JOSEF MEISSLER 2/-
WALTZ JOSEF MEISSLER 2/-
GALOP JOSEF MEISSLER 2/-
MARCH THEO BONHEUR 2/-
COPYRIGHT FOR ALL COUNTRIES
PRICE 4/-
OCTUOR 1/-
FULL ORCH 2/
MIL BAND 2/6
COPYRIGHT 1892 CHARLES SHEARD & Co MUSIC PUBLISHERS & PRINTERS, 192 HIGH HOLBORN, LONDON

Singers made songs their own

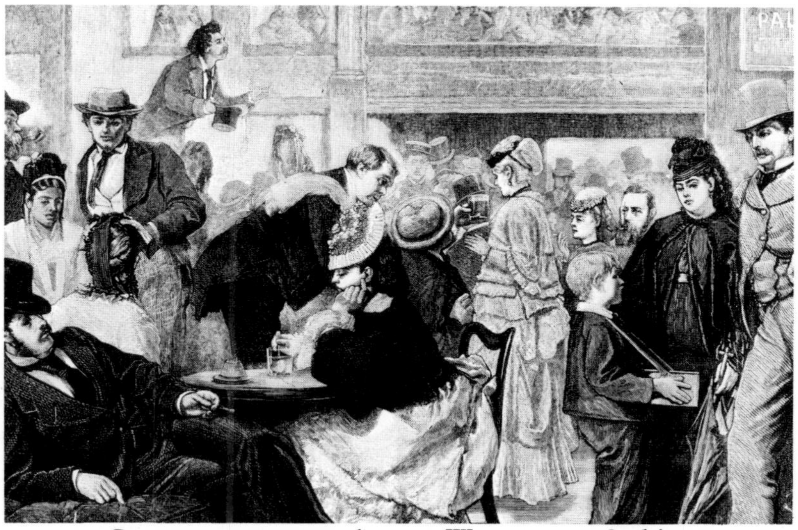

Customers were mostly men. Women were for hire

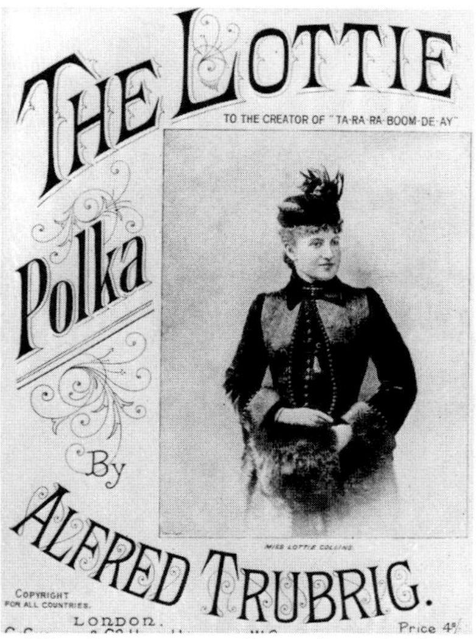
THE LOTTIE
TO THE CREATOR OF "TA-RA-RA-BOOM-DE-AY"
Polka
By
ALFRED TRUBRIG.
MISS LOTTIE COLLINS
COPYRIGHT FOR ALL COUNTRIES.
LONDON.
Price 4/

The image weathered maturity

By the end of the 19th century show business had infiltrated, then been adopted by, the Establishment. Theatrical knights featured frequently in the honours lists, and Queen Victoria commanded the D'Oyly Carte Opera Company to bring their production of *The Mikado* to Balmoral. Shakespearean actor-managers led their companies on tours of Canada and South Africa – perhaps the first-ever cultural safaris. Ibsen's *Ghosts* reached London in 1891. Sir Henry Irving coaxed artists such as Burne-Jones, Ford Madox Brown, Gustave Doré and Alma-Tadema to design for the theatre, and stage equipment underwent a technical revolution. But doubts were stirring. Sarah Bernhardt (opposite) was dubbed 'The Divine Sarah' by fashionable London. But her success did little to lull her fears for the future. In 1910 she made a three-reel movie version of *Camille*, and announced: "I rely on these films to make me immortal."

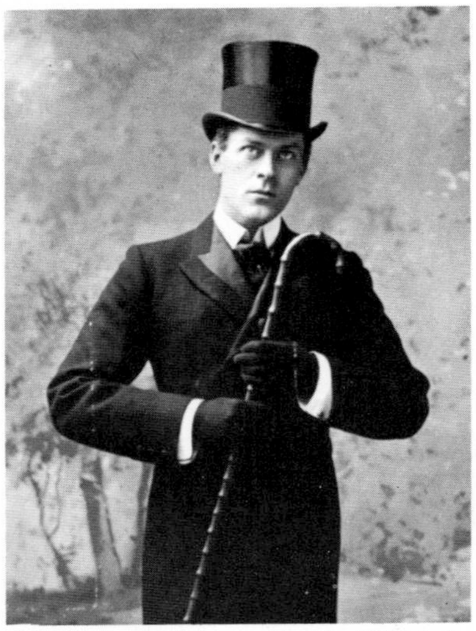

Sir George Alexander in Wilde's *The Importance of Being Earnest*

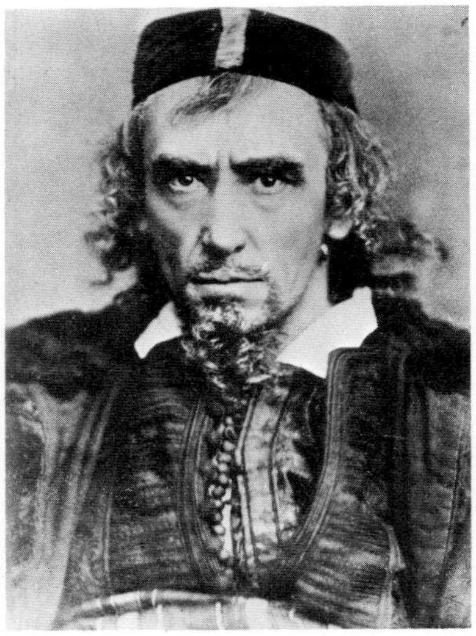

Sir Henry Irving as Shylock. The accent was on production

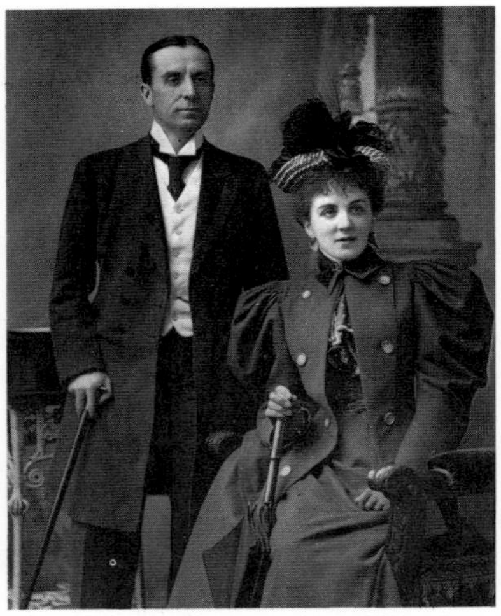

Gentleman-entertainer Weedon Grossmith, with his wife

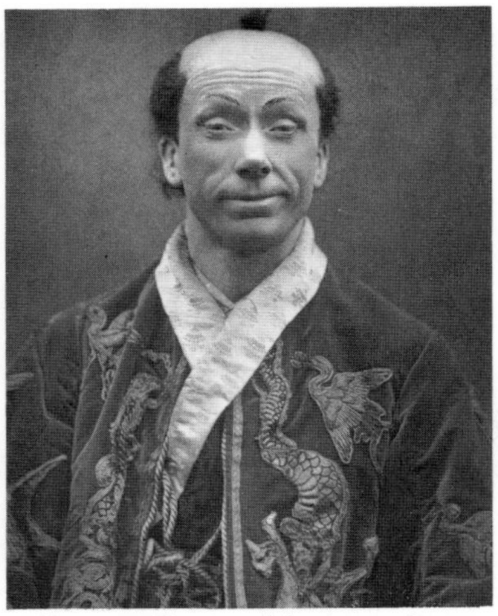

George Grossmith, star of ten Gilbert and Sullivan operas

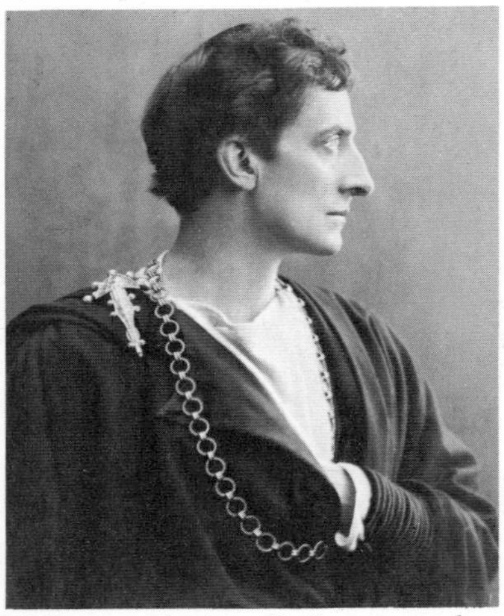

Johnson Forbes-Robertson, the most romantic of Hamlets

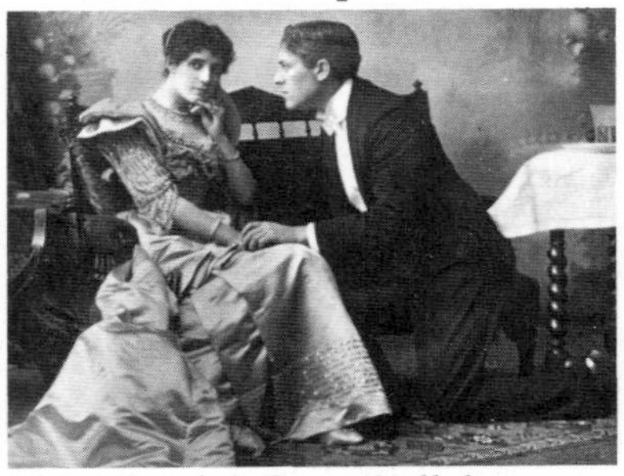

Mrs Patrick Campbell, later to shock London in *Pygmalion*

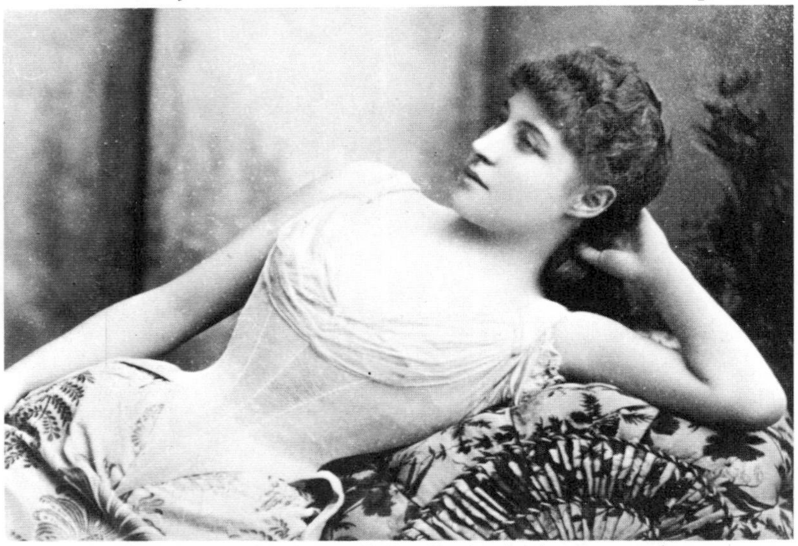

Lillie Langtry – the Jersey Lily; limited talent, great beauty

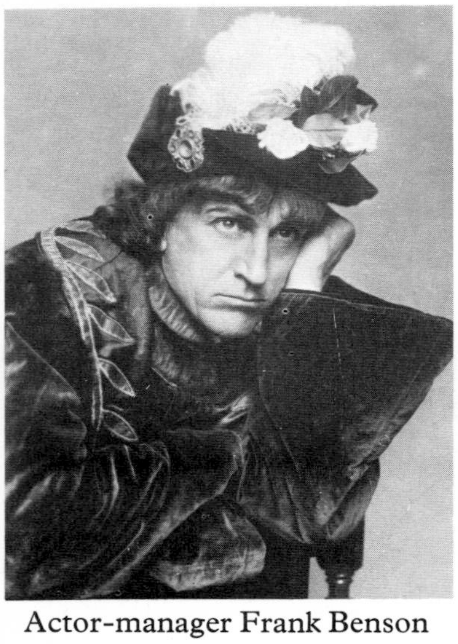

Actor-manager Frank Benson chose casts for their cricket

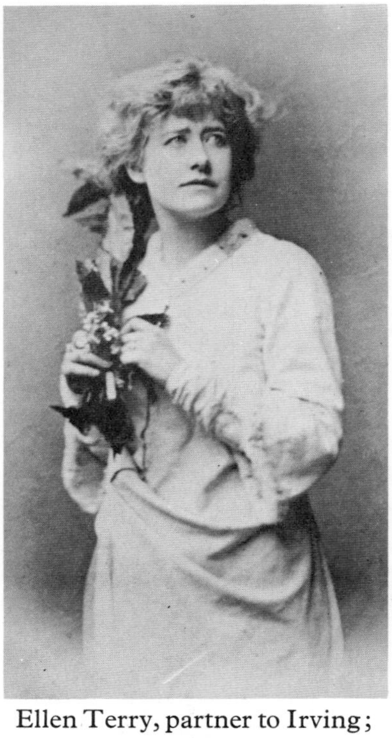

Ellen Terry, partner to Irving; 30 years as leading actress

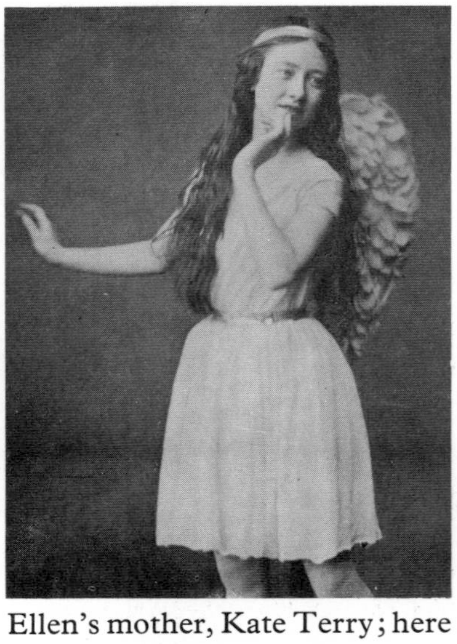

Ellen's mother, Kate Terry; here seen as Ariel in *The Tempest*

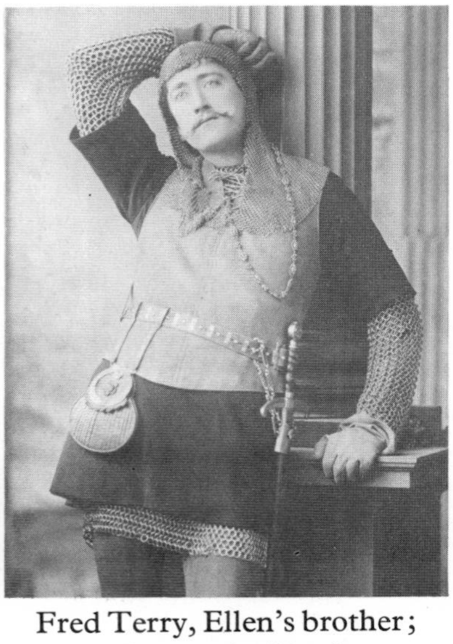

Fred Terry, Ellen's brother; as Laertes in *Hamlet*

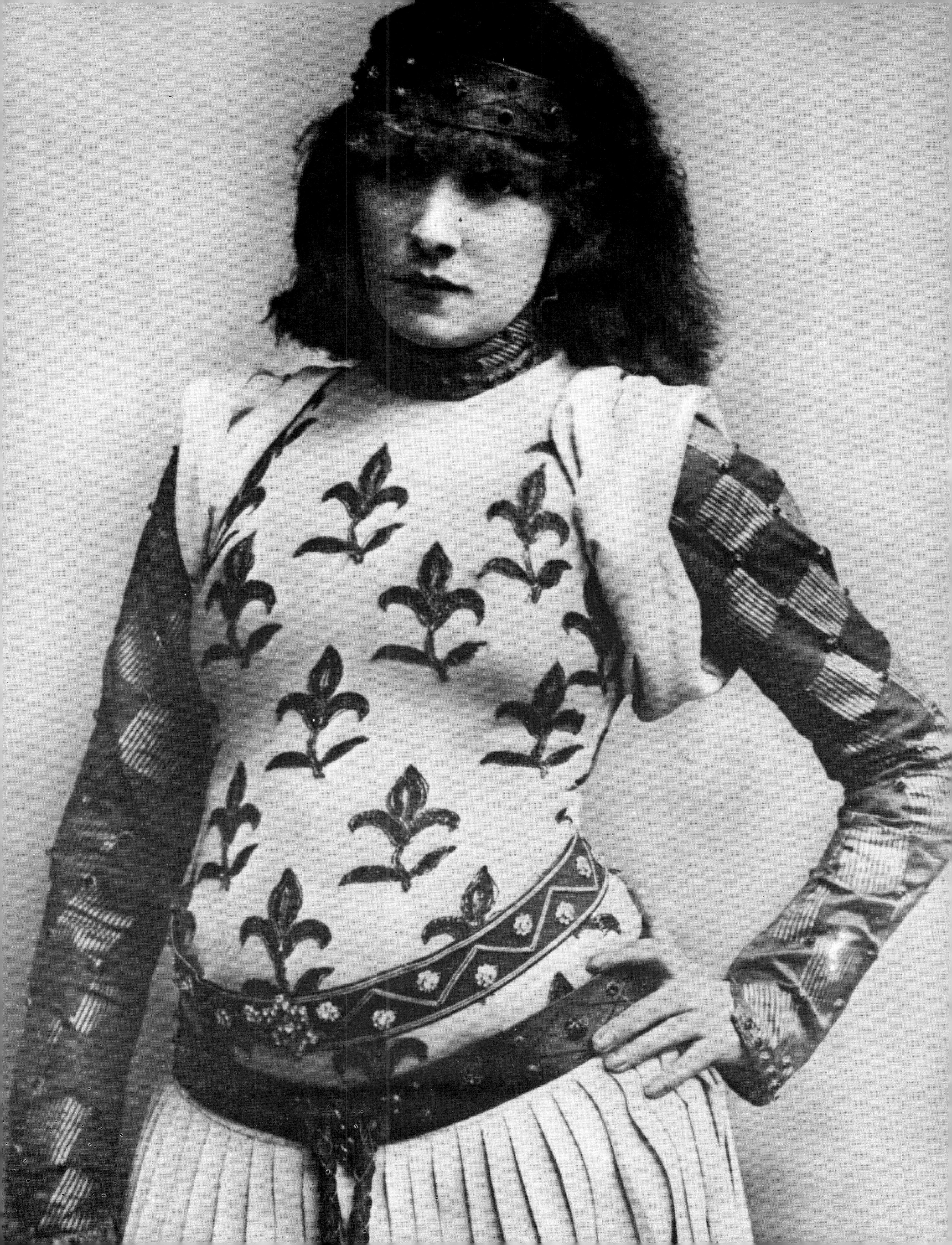

THE UBIQUITOUS PILL

By Graham Norton

Many fortunes were founded on the manufacture of beneficent nostrums. It was
an age that all but submerged under a swirling
tide of patent medicines, neatly packaged in every kind of pill box, and consumed
by the million to a fanfare of uninhibited advertising

"IT IS SAID THAT BEECHAM'S PILLS FIND GREAT FAVOUR WITH THE CZAR,

Insomuch that he frequently carries a box in his pocket, and may be seen swallowing a couple before he sits down to meat."—

EXTRACT FROM FOREIGN CORRESPONDENCE.

"Worth 5 guineas a box" – the most celebrated pill

Making money was to the Victorians a virtue which took precedence only to cleanliness and godliness. It was an essential part of the popular spirit of the age. A weekly popular magazine, *The Inventor*, proclaimed on its masthead that it was for inventors, engineers and capitalists. The greatest praise of all was given to those who started with nothing, and yet made the desert of their personal fortune blossom like the Royal Horticultural Show. Like Thomas Holloway.

Holloway was completely the self-made capitalist. That vast fortune had grown from a beginning literally the size of a dried pea – Holloway's Pills, which he and his wife rolled themselves from 4 am to 10 pm until the Pills began to prosper.

It was in the year of the Queen's Coronation, 1837, that Holloway, a man as old as the century, launched Pills and Ointment onto the world. How far the formula was his, and how much it owed to an Italian product he had previously promoted, is uncertain. If the origins of Holloway's Pill are obscure, as to its effect, *The Times* said in 1883: "Of the intrinsic merits of these much vaunted drugs we cannot pretend to be informed. If they possessed one-tenth of the wonderful virtues that have

been assigned to them, their discovery may surely be set down as marking an era of no small importance in the progress of curative art. Certain it is that they have been before the public for many years, that they have commanded the confidence of millions, and that no bad consequences have been proved to follow from their use."

Holloway claimed much more. "A Key to Health!!! The Hollowayian System of Medicine . . ." To him, the key to wealth came through advertising. He ploughed back every penny he could into taking space in the papers, and where at first he didn't have the money, he ran up enormous bills. In 1839 *The Times* foreclosed on him for a comparatively small debt, and he spent a small period in a debtor's prison. Holloway never read *The Times* again.

But in 1842 he was spending £5000 in advertising, in 1845 £10,000, in 1864 £40,000, and in the year he died £50,000. He had had "Take Holloway's Pills" written up on the Great Pyramid, and plastered all over London, New York and other major cities of the world. During the Civil War in the United States, wounded Union soldiers could be seen on Holloway's posters stretching out imploring hands for Holloway's Ointment. Holloway advertised in China, he advertised in Peru. His profits became so great that he was supposed to have found it impossible to spend the proportion on advertising that he intended: there just wasn't the space available. He made, nevertheless, £5 million.

But it was largely the poor who took the Pill, who feared the expense that might arise from treatment other than self-medication. The pamphlet that came with the Pills prescribed them for over fifty complaints, from gout, paralysis, liver complaints, bronchitis, tumours, wounds, floodings and the whites, youthful indiscretion, impotency and indigestion to constipation, the stone, scrofula and diarrhoea. What did this miracle that brought in five million contain? The British Medical Association did an analysis some time after Holloway's death. Chemical and microscopic examination showed the presence of aloes, or a preparation of aloes, powdered ginger and soap.

For his philanthropy to the middle classes, Holloway got no knighthood. He died childless. If he had founded a dynasty of pillmasters then perhaps his name would survive on the roll of baronets, like that of Beecham. Thomas Beecham opened a chemist's shop in Lancashire

JOHN DURANT'S
CONTAINING
FLEXIBLE
O
CAPSULES
PURE BALSAM COPAIBA.
MANUFACTURED IN ENGLAND
BEDMINSTER, BRISTOL.

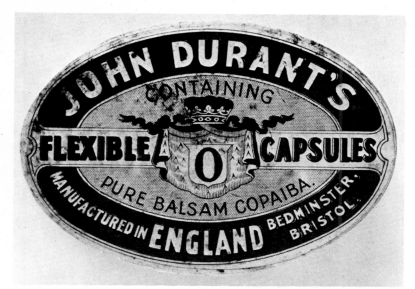

A profitable variation on the pill's traditional shape

in 1845. Like many local chemists, he put out remedies made up by himself. In 1847 he first licensed his Pills, and in 1857 he moved to St Helen's, where, from a chance remark of a lady who bought his product, he picked up the slogan which was to make the Pill famous, and himself a millionaire: "worth a guinea a box". They actually sold for 1*s* 1½*d*. The prime cost of 50 Beecham's Pills, as estimated by the BMA in the early years of this century, was about half a farthing.

Oddly, analysis of Beecham's Pills found them to be of the same ingredients as Holloway's – aloes, ginger and soap. And the same pattern for success was there. A great factory was built at St Helen's in 1885, others in New York and other places abroad. And the advertising for Beecham's similarly saturated the Press and appeared on hoardings all over the cities of this country, beside the railway lines and in beauty spots and bathing beaches. A million Beecham's Pills were swallowed every day. Thomas Beecham's son, Joseph, entered the business in 1866 and gave it a great push forward. Now the company faced American competition from Carter's Little Liver Pills in particular. Other American products followed Carters. Ten years after the death of Queen Victoria, a House of Commons Committee reported, more than 15 million packages of an annual value of £400,000 were coming in from the US. In 1899, well over £2 million was paid by the British public for patent medicines.

In the penny press, the giant pill companies rubbed shoulders with advertisements for "female complaints", for the restoration of lost manhood and for the cure of venereal disease. Against these quacks, who did real damage and who could sometimes be brought to court, the *Medical Circular* raged relentless war in the 1880s. The publishers of cheap religious and 'servant's hall' papers made fat profits in concert with the sordid vendors of useless remedies. When public opinion was alerted, and a demand was made for the exclusion of such advertisements, the proprietors of the papers increased the charges for this type of small-ad some 300–400 per cent.

Of all the entrepreneurs who entered the patent medicine field in the hope of emulating the great Holloway, or just making money fast, the most brazen were the three brothers Chrimes. In 1896 they began to sell through the post 'Lady Montrose's Miraculous Female Tabules', an obvious abortifacient to those looking for one. Thousands of orders came in. The tablets were actually innocuous, but the name of every woman who purchased was recorded, and on October 7 1898 the brothers posted off a circular letter to over 8000 women. Signed 'Charles J. Mitchell, Public Official', it began:

"Madame,

I am in possession of letters of yours by which I can positively prove that you did on or about ________ commit the fearful crime of abortion by preventing or attempting to prevent yourself giving birth to a child. Either of these constitutes a criminal act punishable by penal servitude and legal proceedings have already been commenced against you, and your immediate arrest will be effected unless you send me on or before Tuesday morning next the sum of £2 2*s*, being costs already incurred by me, and your solemn promise on oath before God that never again will you prevent or attempt to prevent yourself giving birth to a child . . ."

In two or three days over £800 came in. But a husband had intercepted a letter, informed the police, and the Chrimes brothers were imprisoned. But the exploitation of the ignorant, playing on fear and promising a cheap, quick cure, was not so easy to put down. Only the advance of education and medical science, together with legislative sanctions (and a free health service) could confine patent medicines to that vague zone of minor illness where the psychological effect of clever advertising has as much credit for cure as what has been put into the pills that it pushes so persuasively.

DROPSY PILLS
RACKHAM'S
LIVER PILLS
TWINBERROW'S
DANDELION, CHAMOMILE & RHUBARB
PILLS
PAGE WOODCOCK'S
WIND PILLS
ORIENTAL PILLS
FOR ALL LIVER AND STOMACH ILLS
THOMASSO'S
PER BOX

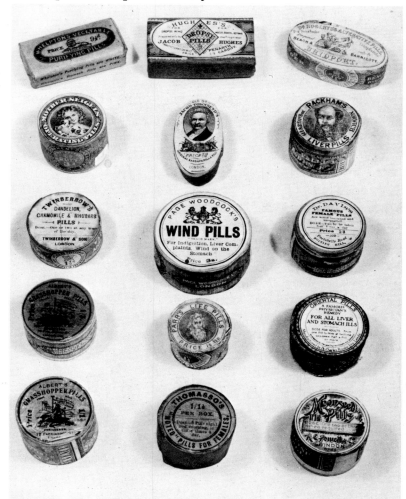

The pillmasters' wares – a formidable array

BALLIOL AND THE WORLD

By E. M. Nicholson

The Oxford of the Victorian
era, and in particular Balliol College under Benjamin
Jowett (below), placed a firmer stamp
than any other seat of the Victorian establishment on the
future of British political thought

"I thought once of giving myself up to political economy, but I happened to become a Professor of Greek," said Benjamin Jowett with a flash of insight into the fate of which he was both a victim and an agent. He also happened to become Master of Balliol and the great formative influence on Oxford in the decisive Victorian days. He thus indirectly made himself a principal moulder of modern Britain. Only now can we see how he himself was moulded, and why his personality and career took their characteristic shape, which was to leave such a mark on history. Even so the contradictions which baffled his intimates are still often inscrutable to us. It is equally easy to portray him as a high-minded, pure-hearted, clear-headed teacher and friend of the cream of young Victorian manhood, or as a comical, cynical, muddled and power-loving hypocrite, or as one of the most adroit and objective of Victorian operators in academic, and indirectly in national, politics. If we judge by results, however, two seemingly contradictory verdicts become inescapable. He was the outstanding inspirer and virtuoso of the great tutorial system of Oxford, and is probably the most successful and influential of all modern British university leaders, when viewed in broad and long perspective. Nevertheless his teaching and preaching made him the main carrier of a highly contagious, virulent and persistent intellectual and social disease, from which even today many of Britain's rulers and instructors are hardly beginning to convalesce.

This peculiar comparison perhaps best covers Jowett, who was in so many ways an admirable and likeable man, from becoming regarded as himself a monster because his life work had, quite unintentionally and unconsciously, as we can now see, such calamitous results for Britain. That this should have happened to Jowett was, however, no accident. He invited it by his own internal contradictions. "He tried to be a philosopher, moralist and preceptor all at once", not to mention a politician and an administrator, regardless of the fact that, as a close friend and disciple wrote: "his mind seemed often to be in a state of flux. Some of his opinions varied not merely

from decade to decade but from conversation to conversation."

A clergyman, brought up an evangelical, but early attracted by the Oxford Movement, he flirted with the idea of becoming a Roman Catholic. Later, as a keen Platonist and moral stoic who "thought with the rationalists but felt with the Christians", he was justly suspected of no longer qualifying even as a genuine Anglican. In politics he wavered between Liberalism and Conservatism, for which he was given every excuse by the muddled leadership of Gladstone and Disraeli. Seeing himself as a "political economist" *manqué* he sent an extraordinary letter on Christmas Day 1884 to Marshall, who was just taking over the Chair at Cambridge, in which he wrote: "We shall be able by the

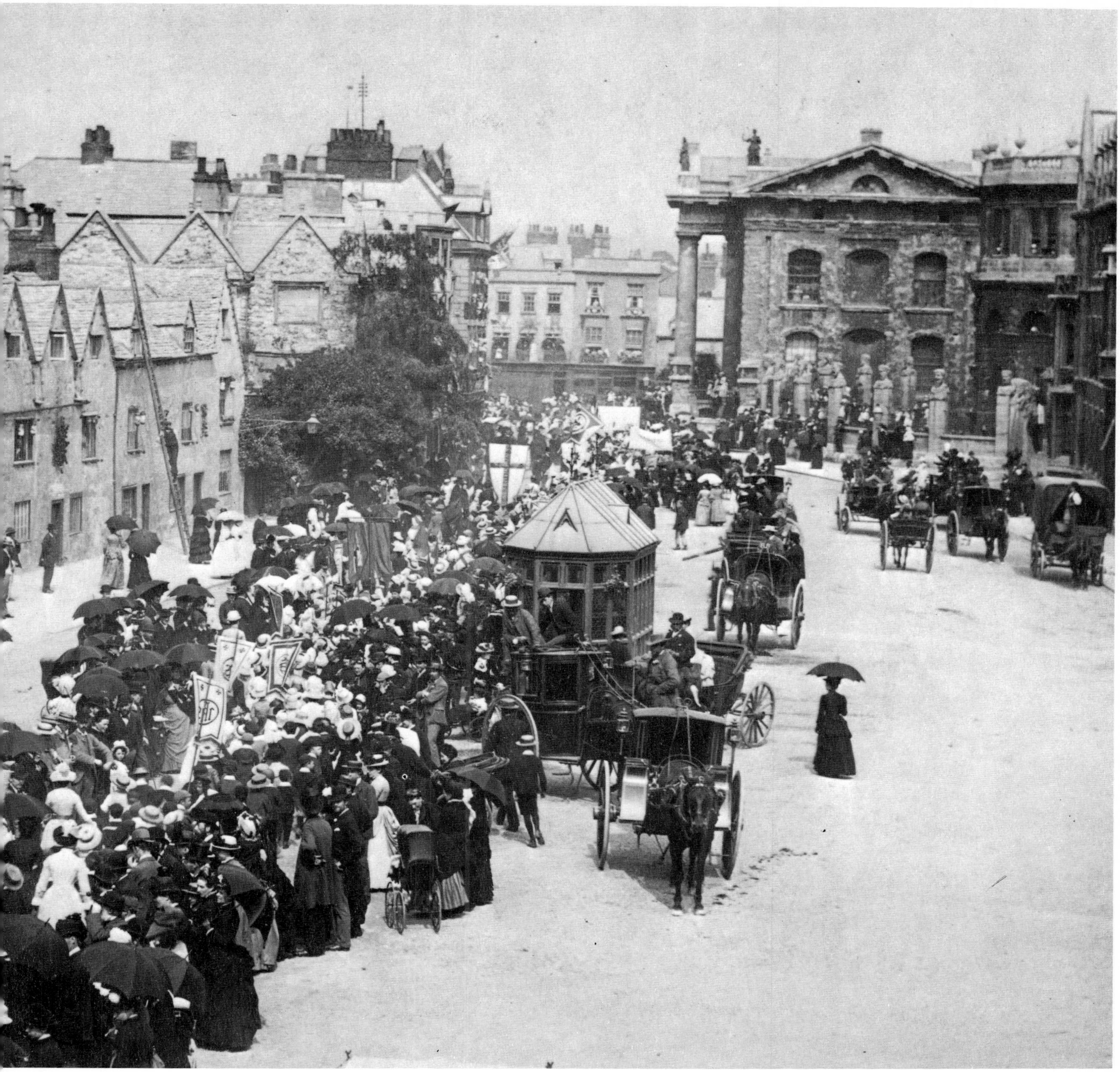

Non-political Oxford – a Jubilee procession in Broad Street, 1887

help of Political Economy to look communist movements in the face; to predict them a few days or weeks beforehand, and to make the best use of the interval." He aimed at Balliol "to bring the peer and peasant together", but in fact a strongly marked growth of sets and cliques, divided by class barriers, was permitted to nullify this aspiration. He saw more of a few pupils who united great ability with high rank than of many other pupils who had the ability without the rank. He defended such rank snobbery because "social eminence is an instrument wherewith, even at the present day, the masses may be moved". But his Sayings contain the comment: "I do not doubt that one day such distinctions will vanish. While they remain, I wonder at any one not taking advantage of them." It is characteristic of Jowett so to have hedged his bets, and to have exploited snobbery with open eyes as well as practising it.

More crudely he disseminated the notorious maxim "Never retract. Never explain. Get it done and let them howl." Another statement which he quoted with approval was: "We are all dishonest together, and therefore we are all honest."

As we read such remarks in his own words and gaze at his portraits we can almost hear him "giving utterance to generally cynical sentiments in his pleasantly falsetto voice" otherwise described as a "cherubic chirp". Except for his commanding forehead, his soft effeminate features and his "infantine smile" could hardly have been impressive. It must have been his power to charm

Balliol College as it appeared during Jowett's period as Master, 1870–93

and persuade key people in small groups, rather than his public image, which established his ascendancy. He could be shy and taciturn in company, and rarely opened up with unintellectual persons, or with those whom he disliked.

Oxford, as Jowett first got to know it, was a celibate university. Although his views on the admission and education of women were progressive for his time he found himself at home in a Platonic environment, whether in college or on the famous Balliol reading parties during vacation. The nearest he came to matrimony was an intense but highly intellectual affair with Florence Nightingale, to whom he imparted his keen feeling of responsibility "when I see men passing through the College or in the university to whose course I might have given a twist in the right way, if only I had the time or energy." Temperamentally it suited him best to be wedded to his vocation.

His vocation changed however, as time went on. During his first quarter-century, up to about 1865, he was mainly a tutor, engaged in politics and administration on the side. From then until he died in 1893 the relationship was reversed. Around the same time he developed a keen interest in international affairs, taking a long view which does him credit in retrospect. Within a week of the outbreak of the Franco-Prussian War of 1870 he wrote of Napoleon III: "I fear this will be the end of his dynasty and the ruin of France . . . we have need of both France and Prussia in Europe . . . France will fight again as soon as she recovers her strength," and he rightly dreaded the long-term prospect of "her abiding hatred of Prussia".

His ideas about the wise handling of both Ireland and India make a lot of sense in the light of later history. He was discreetly critical of the narrowness of the Indian Civil Service and the unwisdom of official parsimony which "may do a great deal of harm in an undeveloped country if it leads to the discontinuance of public works required for health or agriculture. Saving money by any means is barbarous finance."

Writing this in 1888 he must have reflected that this Service was the outcome of the new system of 1853 which he as a Commissioner had played a large part in framing. He realised that something had gone badly wrong, but although he lucidly analysed many secondary faults the fundamental deficiency escaped him. Yet the Home Civil Service, whose reconstitution had swiftly followed, was almost a carbon copy of the Indian, and its similar failings have had even more unfortunate results, since its leverage on events has been so much greater.

As a scholar at St Paul's – the best of his day – Jowett had become unshakably attached to two archaic pedagogic methods – the learning by heart of great slabs of Latin and Greek poetry and the retranslation into Greek or Latin of passages which one had previously translated from these tongues into English. Such techniques, eked out by Platonic philosophy and Socratic dialogue, became early imprinted on his mind as the highest form of education. By a fatal coincidence the overpoweringly emotional Oxford Movement, promoted by the Tractarians with such unhappy results in sterile sectarian controversy, almost exactly synchronised with the strong liberal drive for reform extending to the university and to English higher education, and with the reconstruction of the Indian and Home Civil Services. Jowett, arriving in Oxford in 1835, was first swept away on this torrent, and later deformed and exhausted in his efforts to escape from it and to stem and tame it. Thus he was in no shape to comprehend and absorb the immediately succeeding great wave of scientific thought.

This was a tragedy for Jowett, for Oxford and for British higher education. So near was he to seeing the light of science that he even attended unobtrusively meetings of the British Association, and expressed regrets at his own scientific illiteracy. Unhappily his early entanglements with theology and the educational stance he had adopted led him to declare war upon science as menacing "the higher conception of knowledge and of the mind", and as antagonistic to "morals and religion and philosophy and history and language". "It seems to me," he wrote in 1884, "that all those who, like ourselves, are entrusted with the care of ancient studies, have a hard battle to fight against the physical sciences which are everywhere encroaching, and will certainly lower the character of knowledge if they are not counteracted." "Unless we all unite, the 'repulsive' persons who will only believe what they can hold in their hands will be too much for us." Jowett was at this time Vice-Chancellor of Oxford. He thus laid down the Snow line which has been so disastrous for Britain. He considered the *Origin of Species* one of the greatest books of the century, but he dismissed *The Descent of Man* without giving any reasons beyond "I don't believe a word of it." Research was alien to his outlook, and he therefore took up an attitude of implacable opposition to the wise proposals of Mark Pattison for giving greater weight to the claims of advancement of learning and for developing Oxford beyond the role of a glorified grammar school. Jowett held that a University should be above all a place of tuition, and although in his young days he stigmatised Cambridge as being "eaten up by examinations" his own approach led inexorably to that same end for Oxford.

For Jowett the object was frankly to pick and train winners. Provided they worked and succeeded the system must be right. He hated failure. A star pupil, Curzon, who achieved only Second Class Honours, lamented: "In the public eye I am of course stamped with the brand of respectable mediocrity." To which Jowett responded, not very convincingly, that "it should be regarded as an accident". What was no accident was the highly efficient and aptly named "colonising of the rest of Oxford by Balliol men" and the much broader take-over operation performed by Balliol on the Civil Service, the Church and other key centres of power. Archbishop Tait; Stafford Northcote, the Parliamentarian; and Farrer, Permanent Secretary of the Board of Trade, established this trend as undergraduate contemporaries of Jowett, but he brought it to a crescendo with his matchless output of Cabinet Ministers, heads of government departments, bishops, viceroys, bankers

Dr Jowett, flanked by two colleagues

and leading academics. He certainly achieved his famous ambition "to inoculate the world with Balliol".

Perhaps Asquith, the brilliant Prime Minister who let his country drift into the First World War, and so nearly lost it before a less peculiarly educated successor replaced him, best personifies the strengths and weaknesses of Jowett's products. He said of Jowett: "He never at any time . . . had anything definite to teach, being always an eclectic with a horror of onesidesness . . . The secret of his power lay . . . in what he was – a person with the magnetism of an apostle and the shrewdness of a man of the world."

It was Jowett's misfortune, and ours, that his own initial education was so old-fashioned even for its time; that he was wrongly pressed into the Church and led to spend so much energy in sermonising, theologising and philosophising for which he was not truly suited; that he accordingly missed getting abreast of the two great formative movements of his time in the unfolding of science and the creation of a genuine higher education on the Continent and in the best of the American universities; that by his ambiguities and confusions he turned his pupils out with a dislike of research and of fact-finding, a reluctance to look forward and an aloofness from lesser breeds of men. Worst of all he encouraged them to be over-proud and complacent, closing their minds and hearts to new ideas. He also profoundly influenced the tone and style of British life, and by his apparent endorsement of Victorian snobbery and religiosity he did much to buttress and extend their sway. His qualities and achievements were great, but his influence in the long run can only be judged catastrophic.

INTELLECTUAL EMINENCE

The social and industrial ferment of the Victorian age was reflected in the energy and versatility of the men who shaped its opinions; political, educational, moral and scientific theorists all played their part in moulding the attitudes of future generations

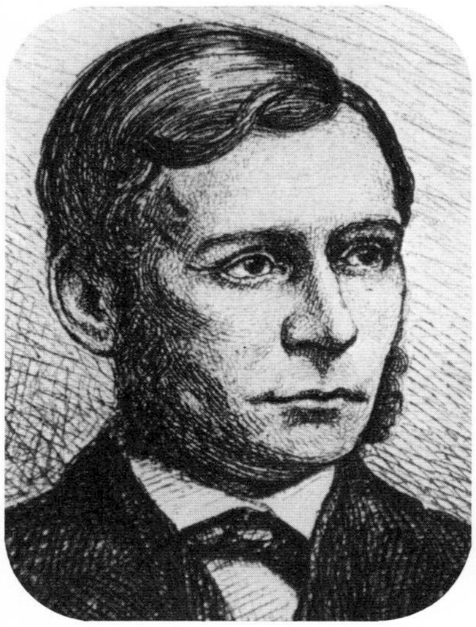

T. H. Green – philosopher viewing man's 'self consciousness'

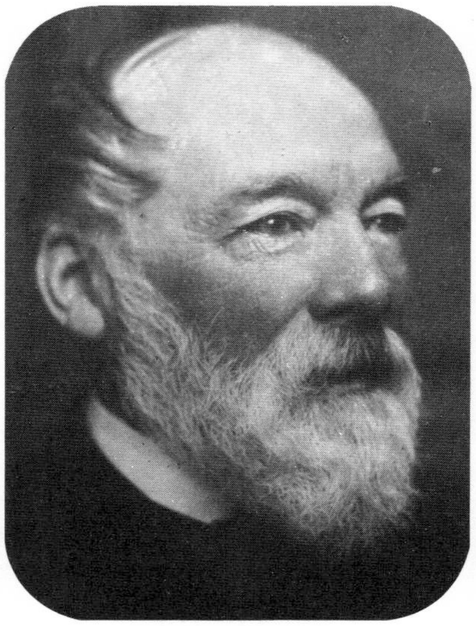

Samuel Smiles – polemicist preaching the virtues of self-help

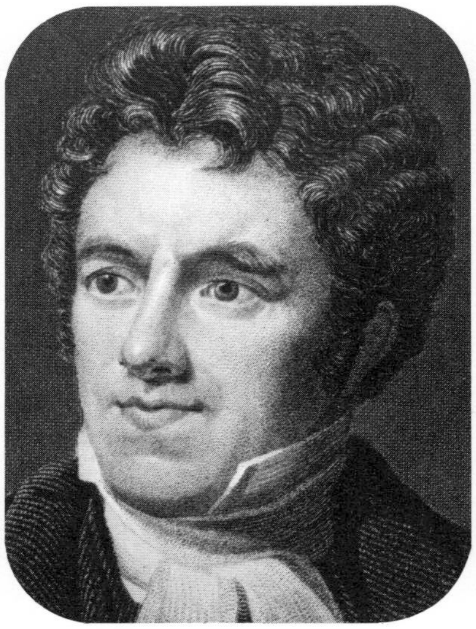

Thomas Arnold – educationist reforming the public school system

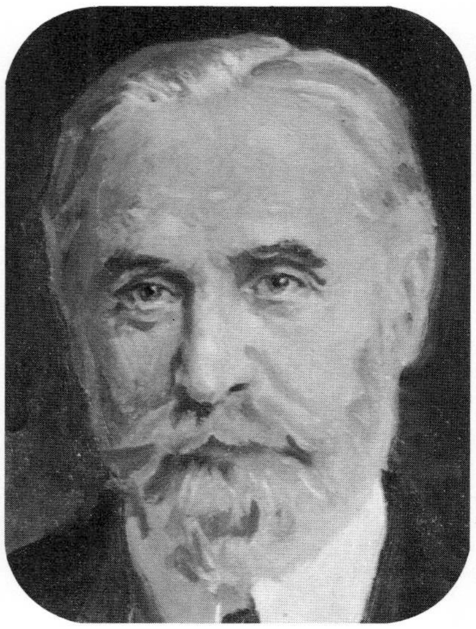

F. H. Bradley – philosopher propounding Absolute Idealism

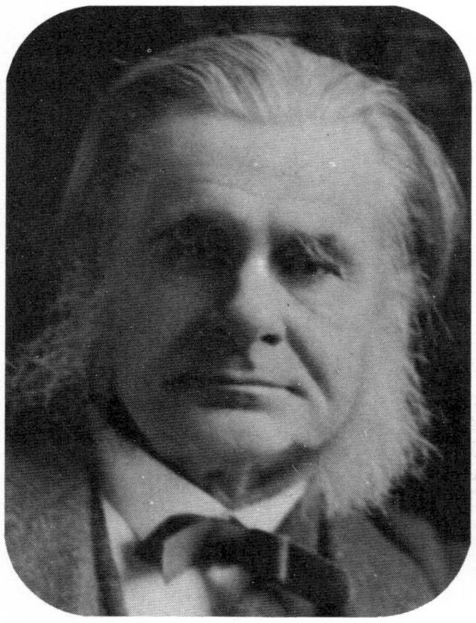

T. H. Huxley – biologist led by science towards agnosticism

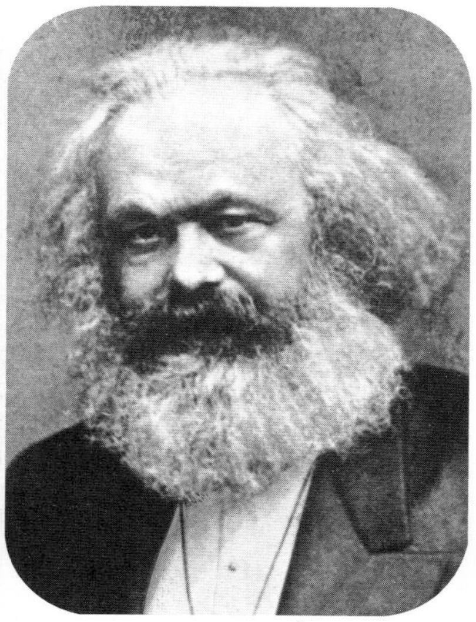

Karl Marx – political theorist attacking the capitalist system

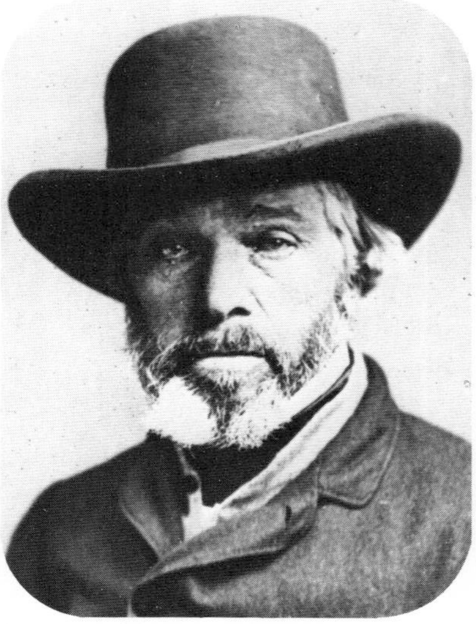

Thomas Carlyle – prophet regarding history as Divine Scripture

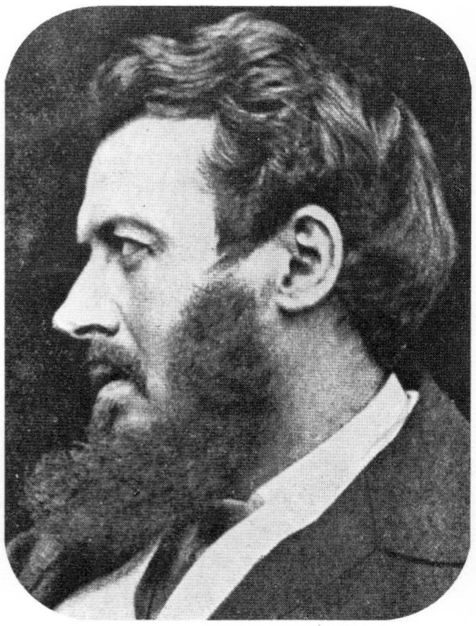

Walter Bagehot – historian championing the Constitution

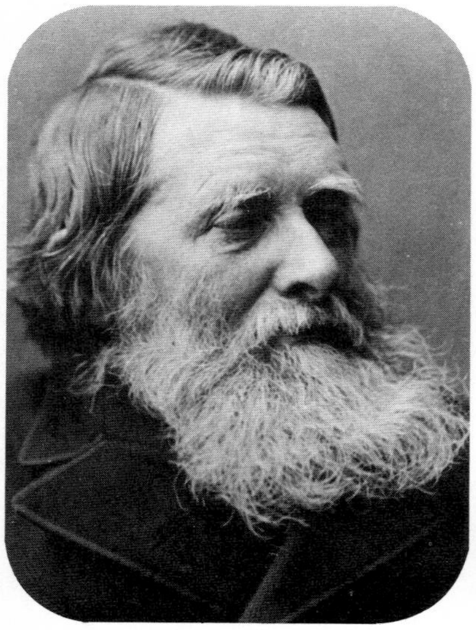

John Ruskin – critic recoiling from industrial chaos

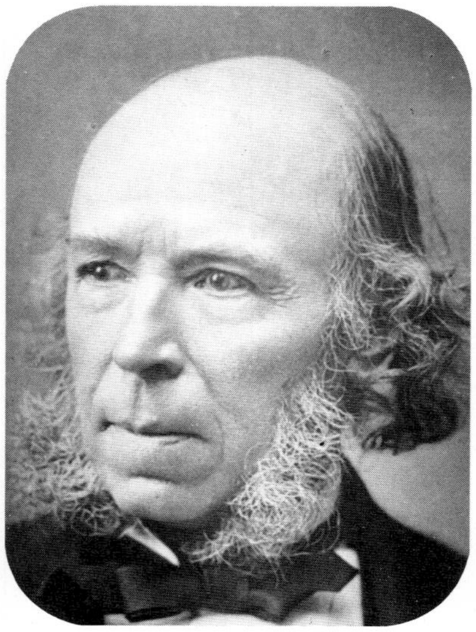

Herbert Spencer – philosopher placing individual above society

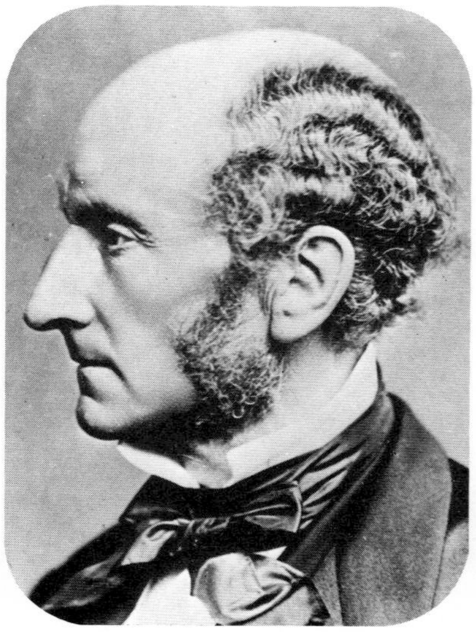

John Stuart Mill – thinker epitomising the new liberalism

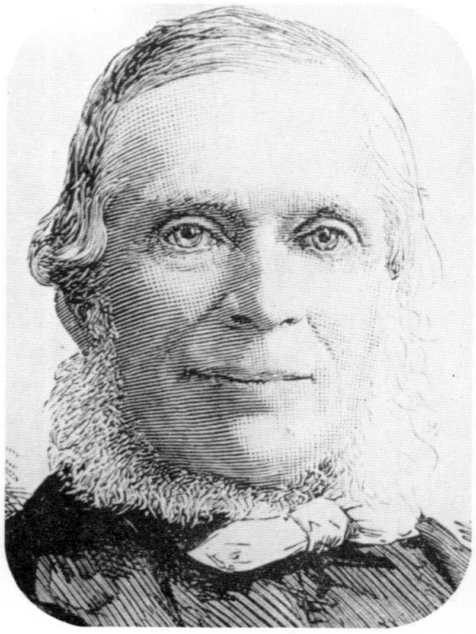

Edward Thring – educationist redefining role of the school

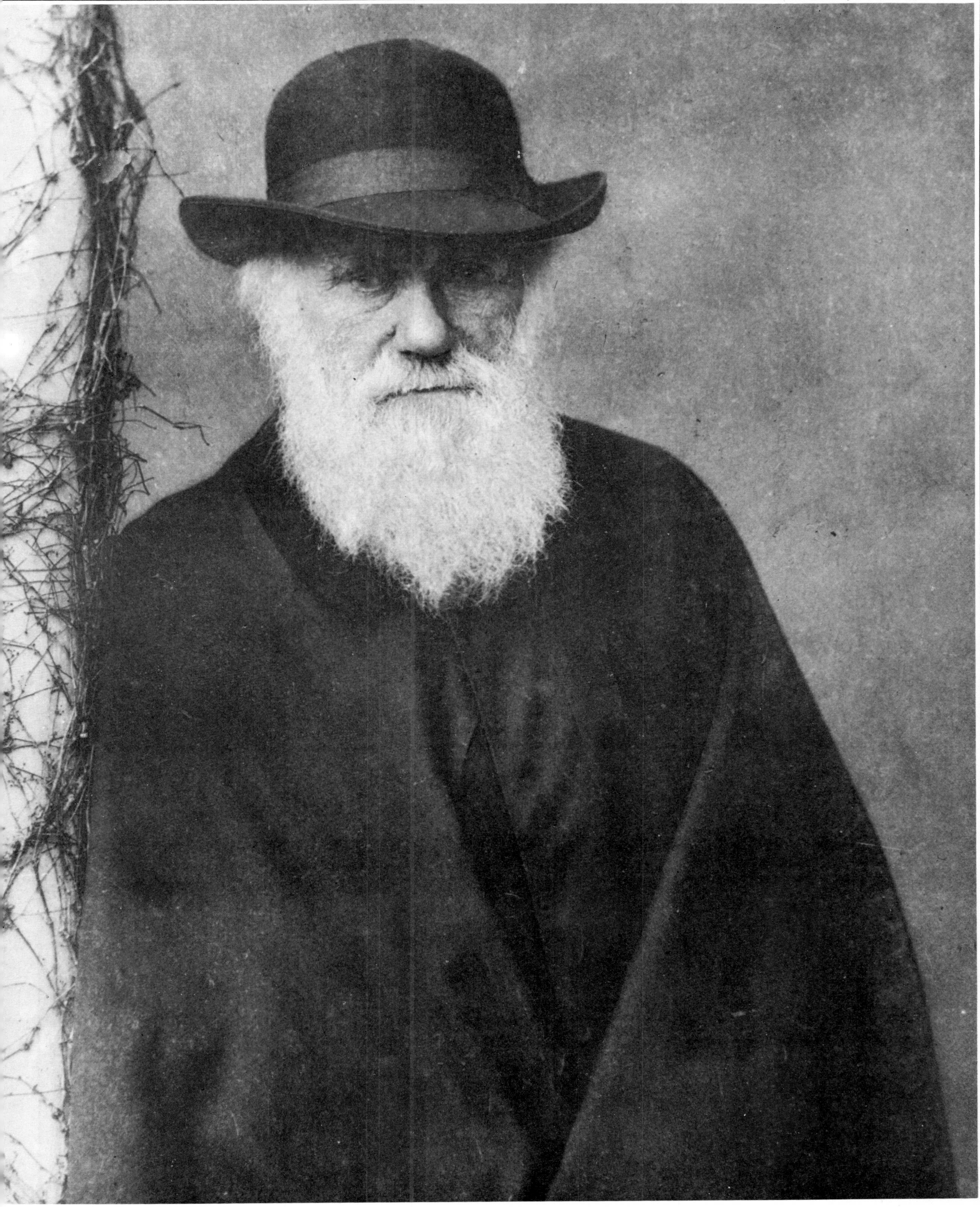

Charles Darwin – biologist and scientific giant
proving through *Origin of Species* his theory of organic evolution

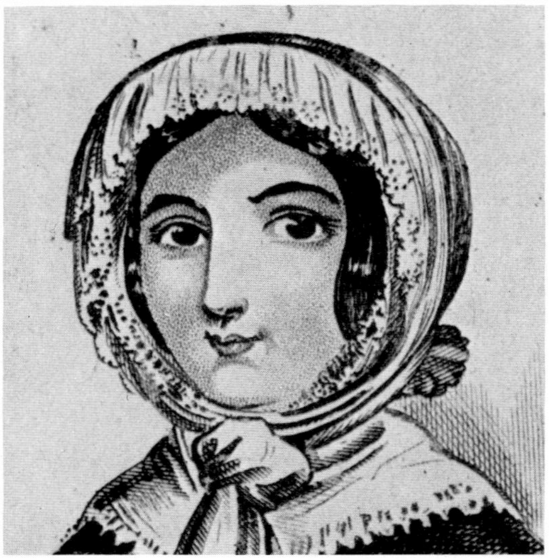

Formidable Maria Manning murdered her lover for his money with her husband's help, later left the husband. Hanged in 1849

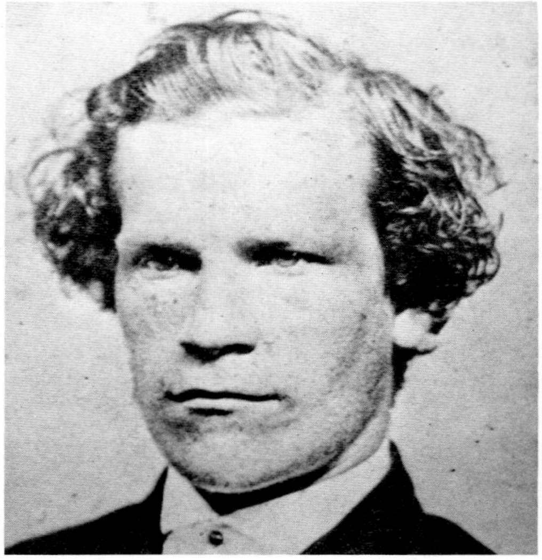

The first railway murder – near Hackney on the North London Line, 1849. German Franz Muller (above) killed Thomas Briggs

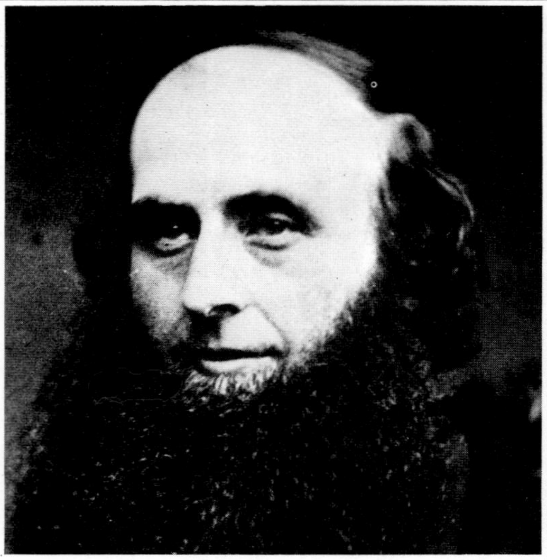

Edward William Pritchard, doctor, amorist. Poisoned wife and mother-in-law with aconite and antimony. Hanged in 1865

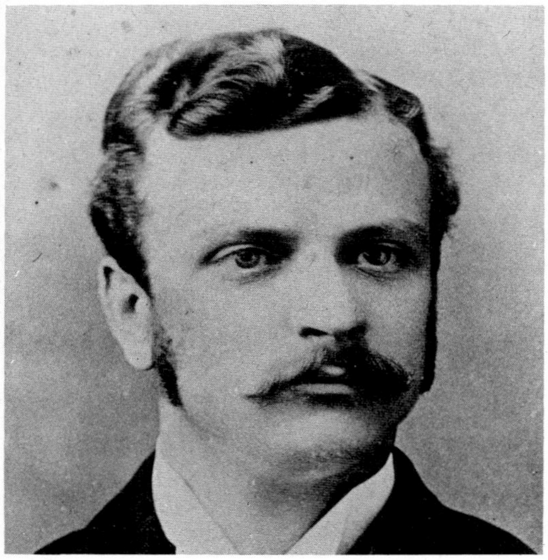

James Canham Read, bookkeeper with wife, seven children, several mistresses, one of whom he shot. Hanged in 1894

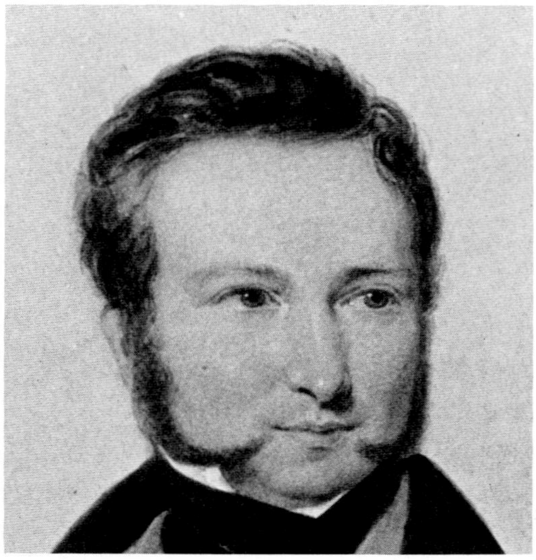

William Palmer. Doctor and gambler. Poisoned, mostly for money. Number of victims unknown. Hanged 1856

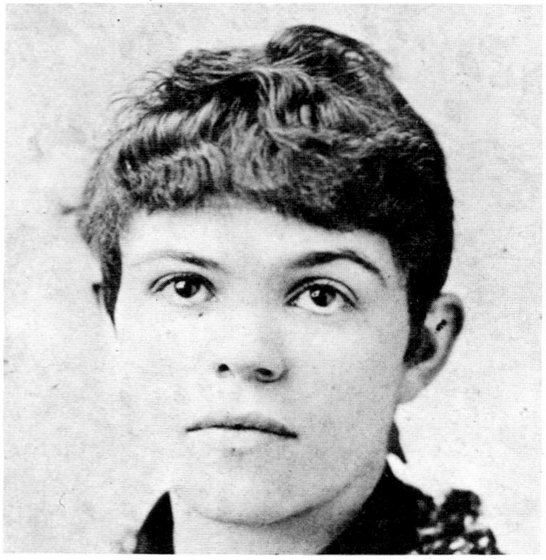

Adelaide Bartlett, acquitted in 1886 of poisoning her husband because no one could say how she administered it

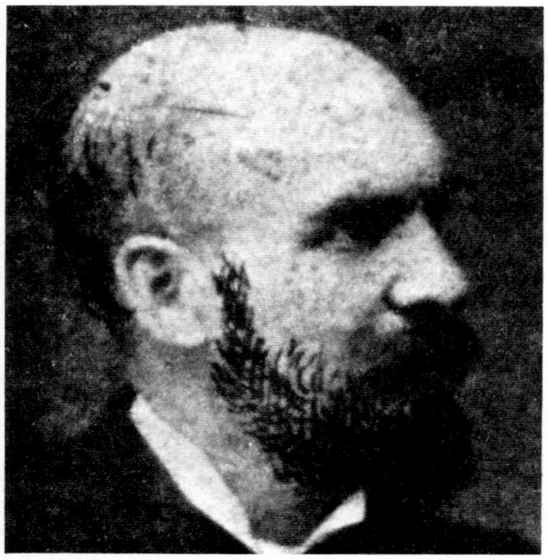

Thomas Neil Cream, doctor, petty swindler. Killed several prostitutes with strychnine. Caught and hanged in 1892

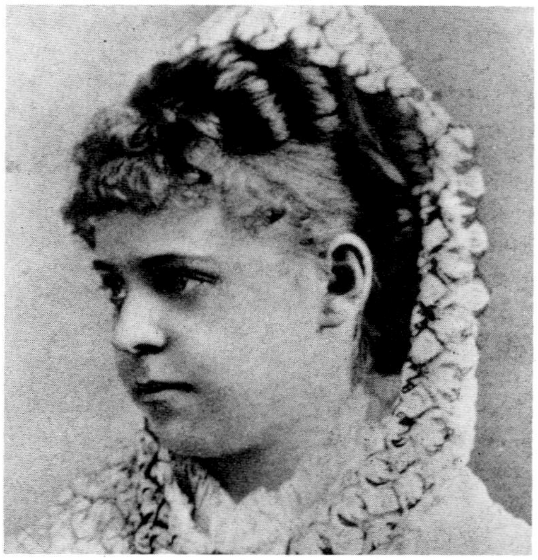

Florence Maybrick. Poisoned husband in 1889, using arsenic soaked out of fly-papers. Death sentence commuted

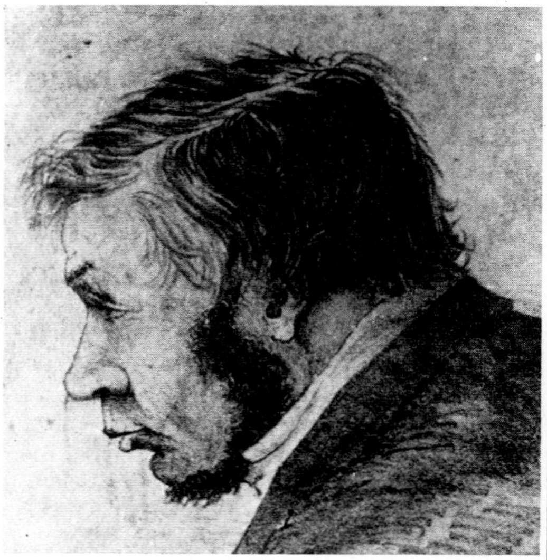

William Rush. Tenant farmer who killed his Norfolk landlord and son, 1848. Wig and whiskers disguise did not save him

THE CRIMINAL CLASSES *By Julian Symons*

In murder, as in beer and biscuits, British is best. Perhaps national hypocrisy is the reason, apparent respectability covering extreme violence. Charles Peace, opposite, is the super-hypocritical criminal. After killing a neighbour in Sheffield he settled in London where, before he was hanged, he lived in a house with his mistress, his wife occupying the basement; he attended church, gave musical soirées and went out housebreaking with his tools in his violin case

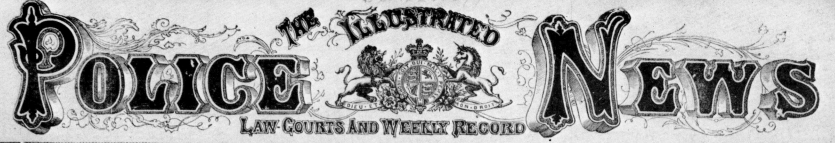

THE ILLUSTRATED POLICE NEWS
LAW-COURTS AND WEEKLY RECORD

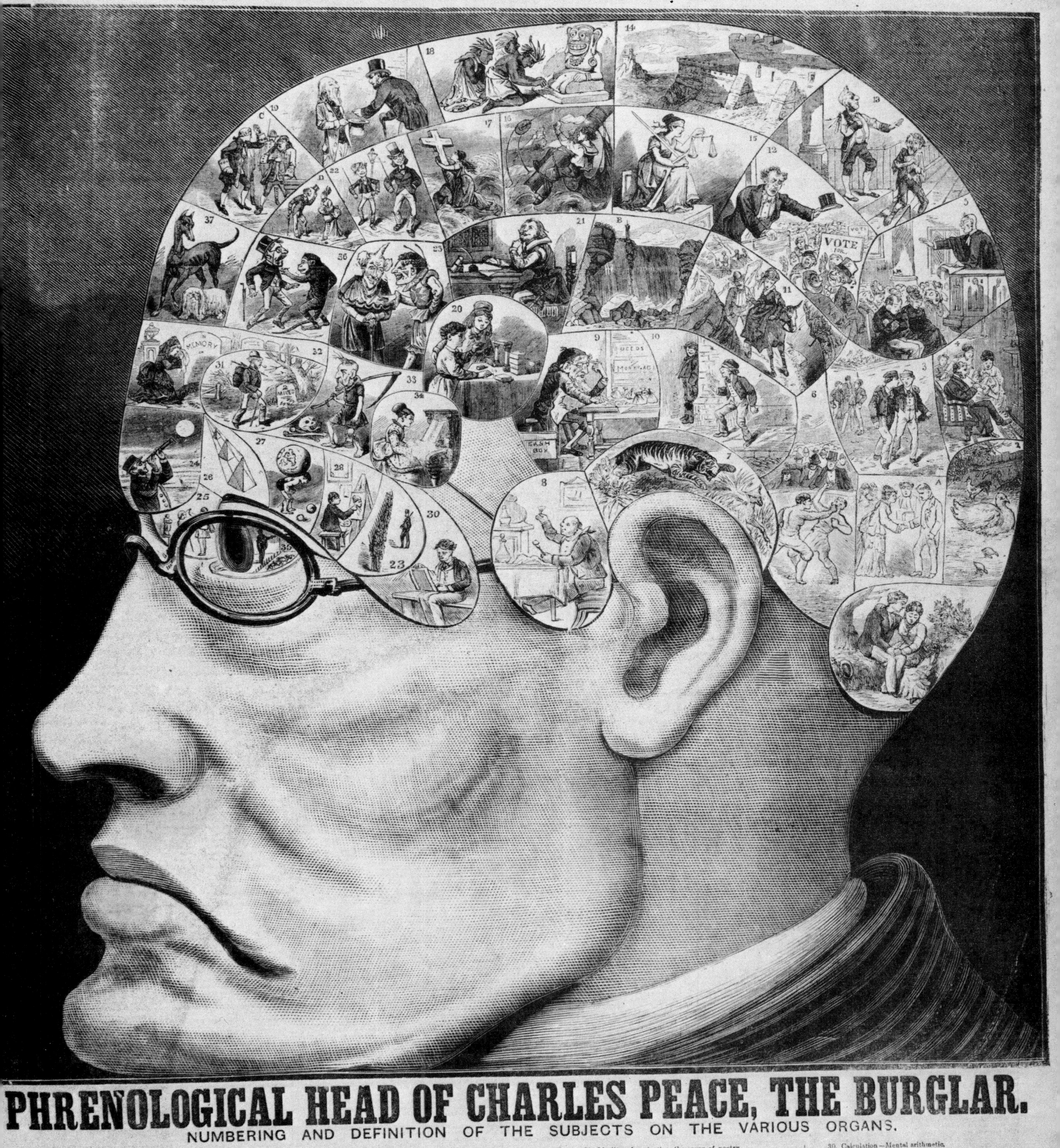
VOTE

PHRENOLOGICAL HEAD OF CHARLES PEACE, THE BURGLAR.

NUMBERING AND DEFINITION OF THE SUBJECTS ON THE VARIOUS ORGANS.

1. Amativeness—Love between the sexes.
A. Conjugality—Matrimony, love of one, &c.
2. Parental Love—Regard for offspring.
3. Adhesiveness—Friendship, attachment.
4. Inhabitiveness—Love of home.
5. Continuity—One thing at a time.
6. Combativeness—Pugnacity, resistance.
7. Destructiveness—A disposition to destroy, murder, &c.

11. Cautiousness—Prudence, care, caution.
12. Approbativeness—Love of approbation and applause.
13. Self-Esteem—Having a high opinion of oneself.
14. Firmness—Strength of will, immovable.
15. Conscientiousness—Fair dealing, sense of justice.
16. Hope—Expectation, self-reliance.
17. Spirituality—Religion, faith, credulity.
18. Veneration—A tendency to worship.
19. Benevolence—Compassion, kindness, charity.

21. Ideality—Imagination, the organ of poetry.
B. Sublimity—Love of grandeur.
22. Imitation—Fondness for mimicry.
23. Mirthfulness—Cheerfulness, jocularity, &c.
24. Individuality—Observation of external objects.
25. Form—Putting things into shape.
26. Size—Measuring things by the eye.
27. Weight—Carrying, balancing, &c.
28. Colour—Having an eye for the arrangement of colour.

30. Calculation—Mental arithmetic.
31. Locality—Recollection of places.
32. Eventuality—Memory of past events.
33. Time—One common evening.
34. Tune—Sense of harmony: an ear for music.
35. Language—Expression of ideas.
36. Causality—Apply causes to effects.
37. Comparison—Contrast, inductive reasoning.
C. Human nature—Perception of motives.
D. Agreeableness—Pleasantness, suavity.

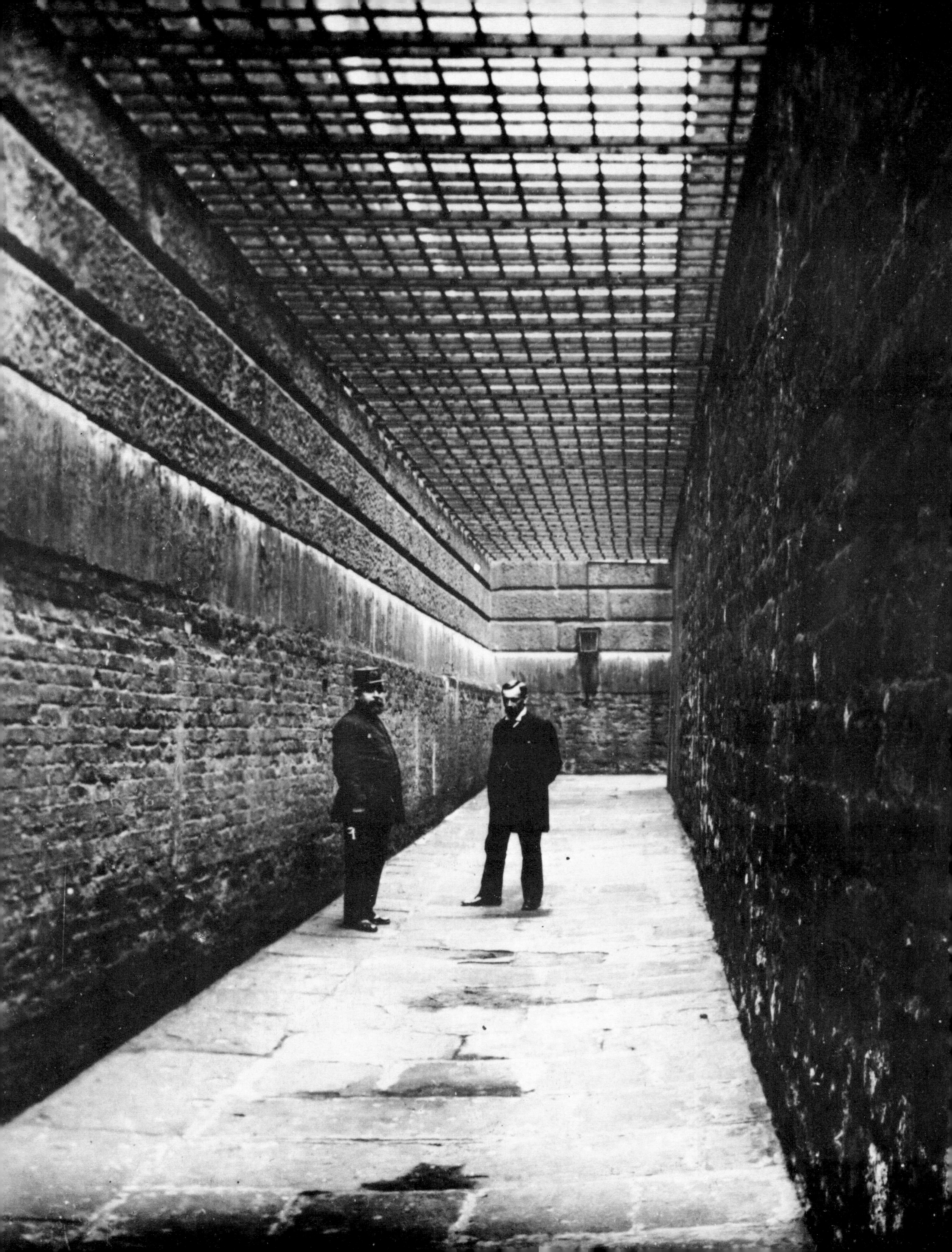

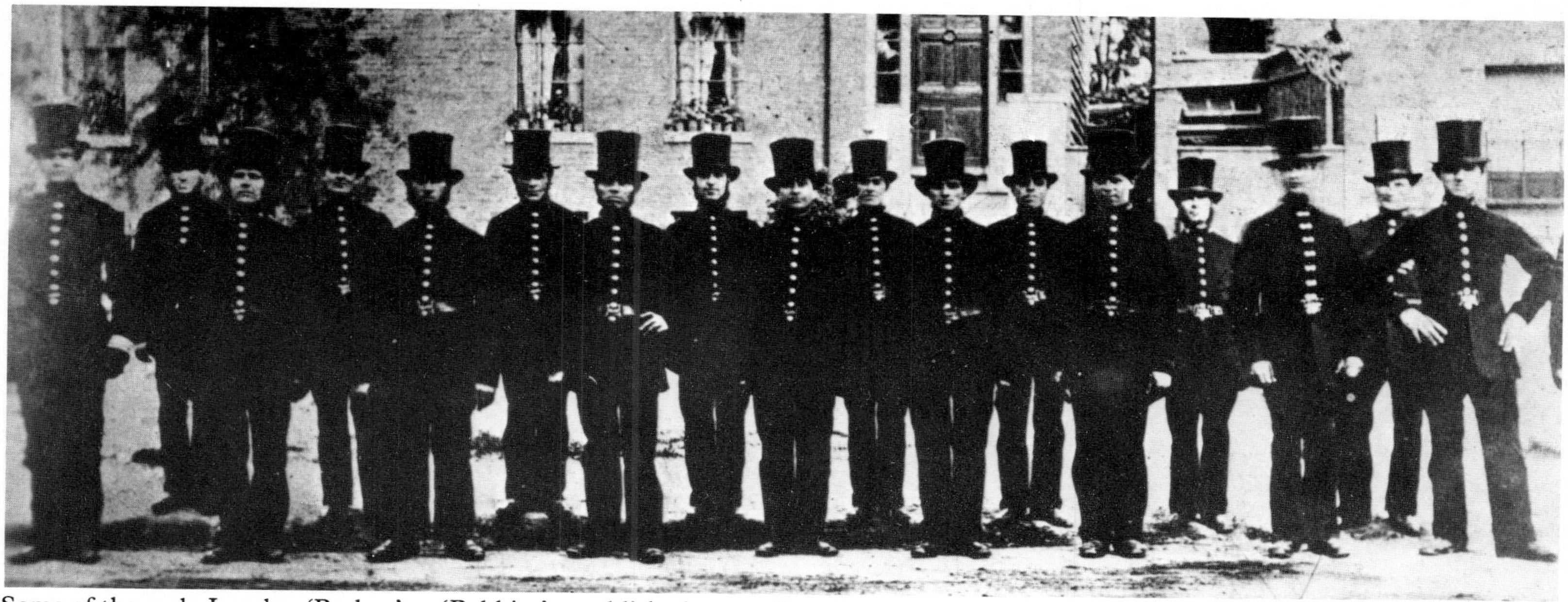

Some of the early London 'Peelers' or 'Bobbies', established as a police force in the early 1830s under Sir Robert Peel's Police Bill. They wore a chimney-pot hat, a blue cloth uniform with a high collar that made it difficult to turn the head, and carried rattles to call for help

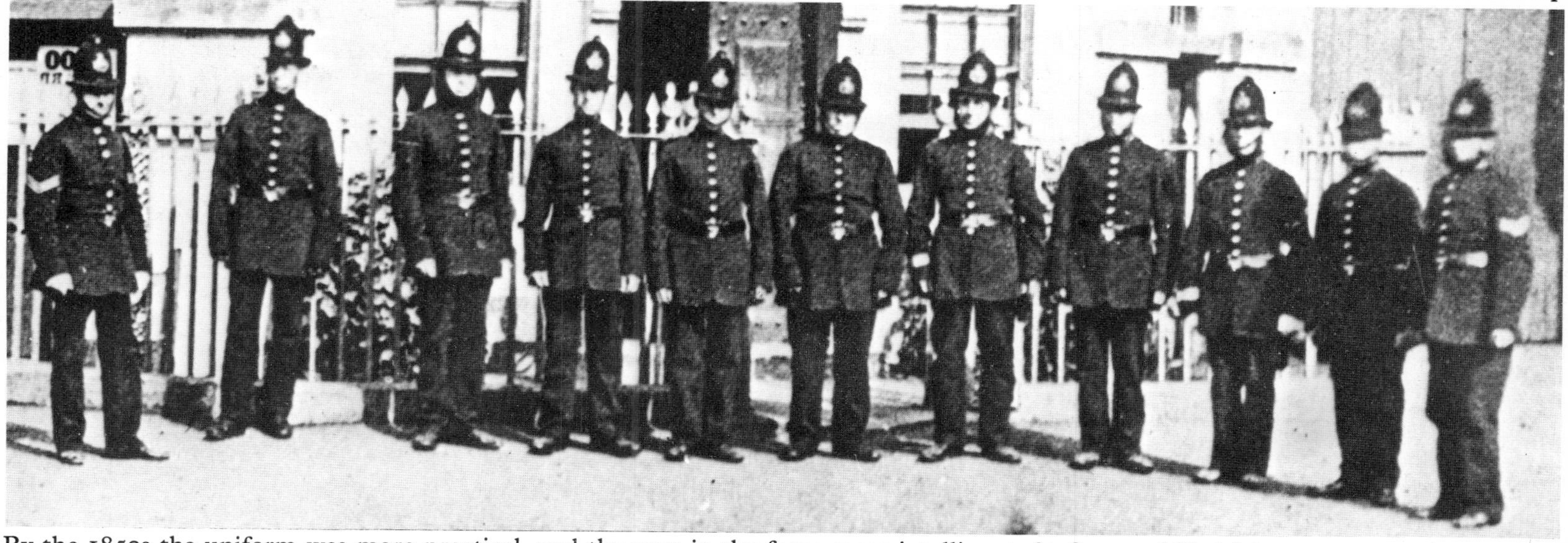

By the 1850s the uniform was more practical, and the men in the force more intelligent. At first unskilled labourers were taken on, and the turnover was rapid. Later on education was regarded as necessary, but it was generally of a rudimentary nature. Rattles were still in use

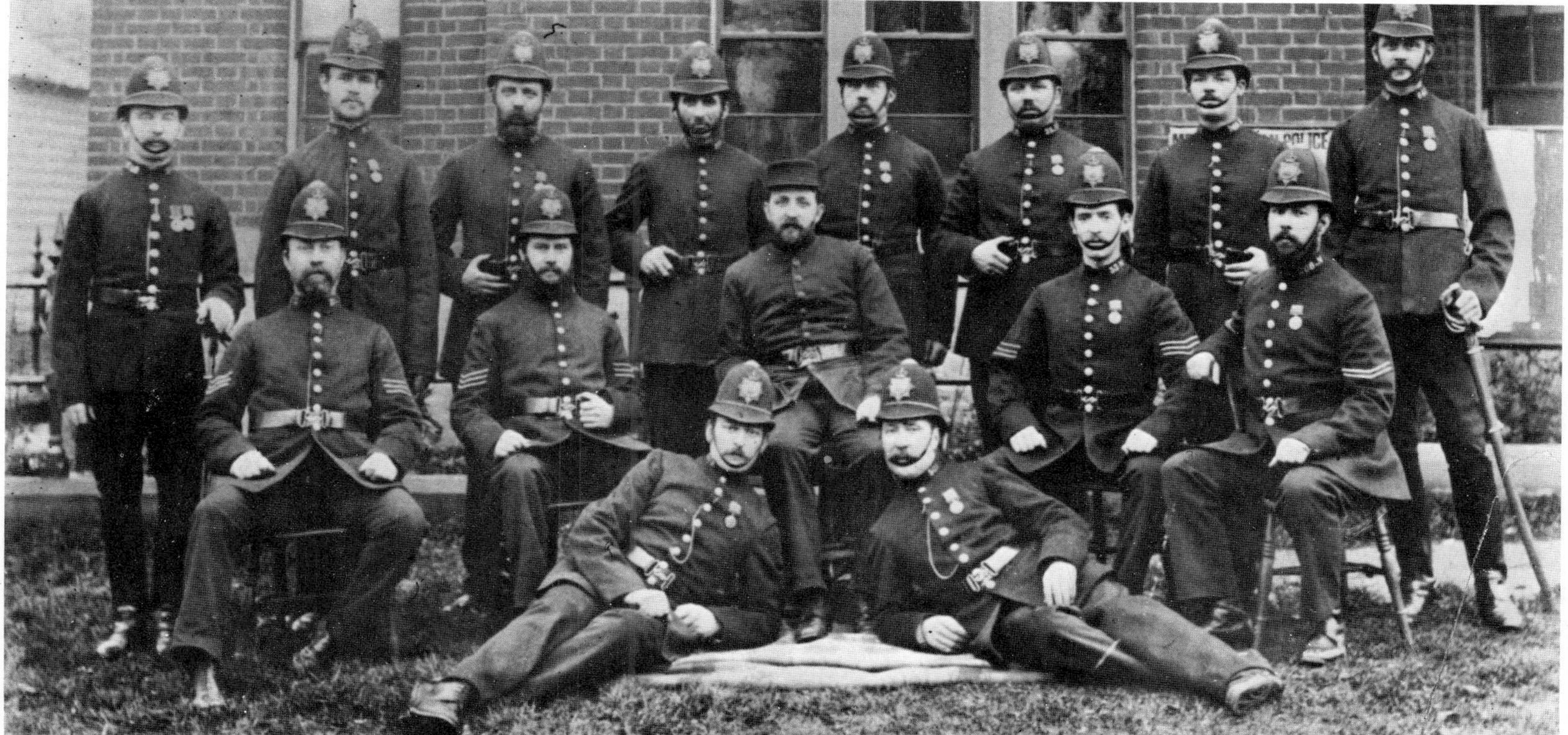

A group of policemen in the 1890s. The rattle had been replaced by the whistle in 1880 (whistles can be seen on the two men sitting in front of the group). Great strides had been made in scientific detection of crime, and these were filtering down to some men on the beat

Left: prison officers in the passage from Newgate Prison to the old Central Criminal Court, beneath which executed prisoners were buried

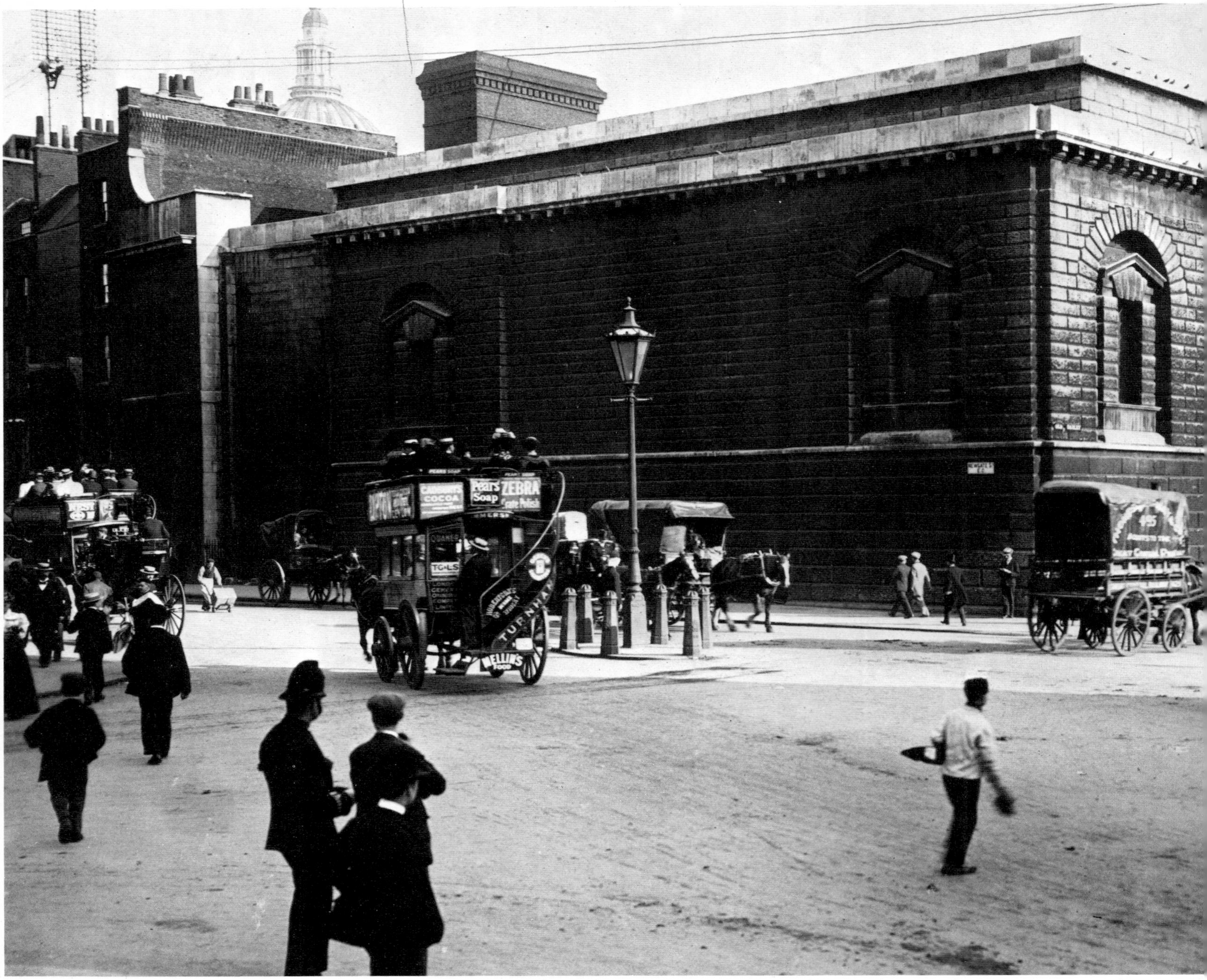
CADBURY'S COCOA
Pears' Soap
ZEBRA
TURNHAM
MELLIN'S FOOD

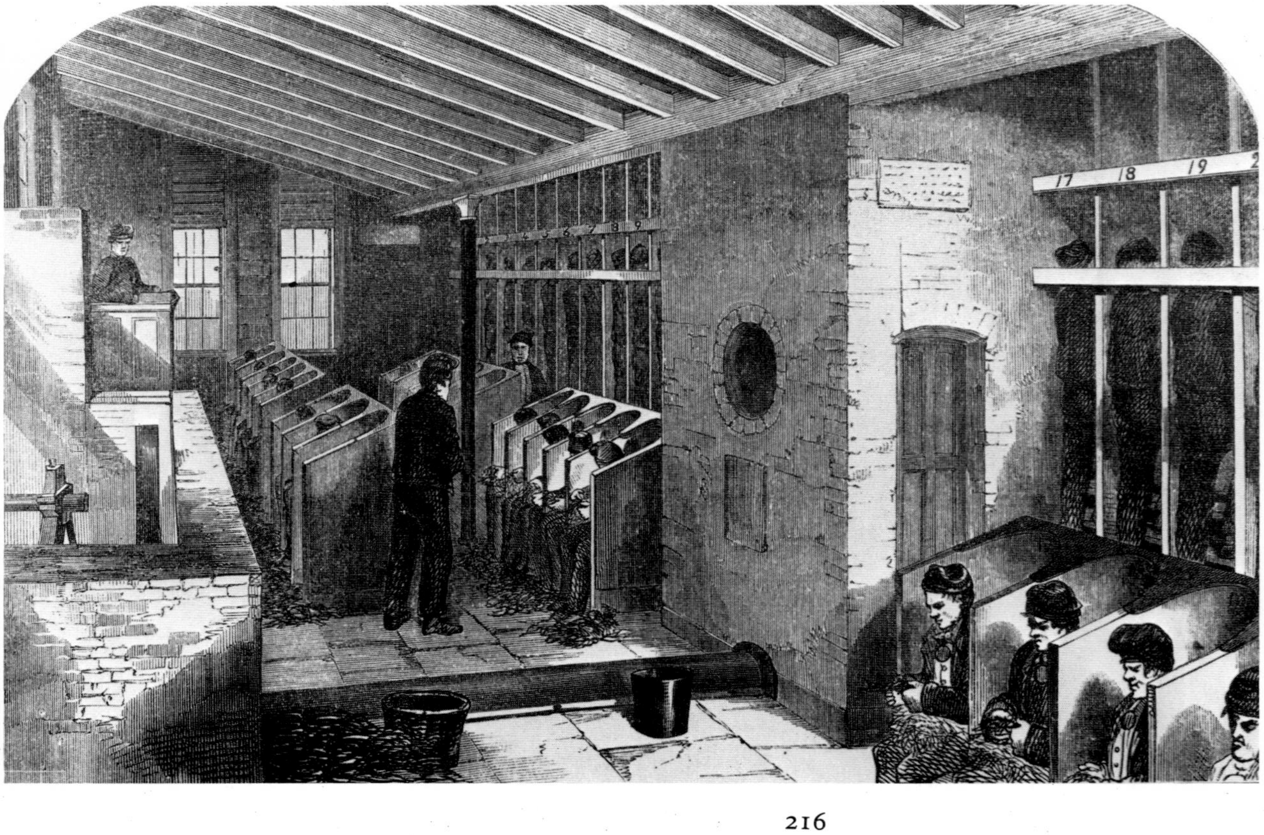
17
18
19

Above: in Newgate, as in many Victorian prisons, there was little attempt at classification. Homosexuals were shut up with young boys, first offenders with violent criminals. Bribery of warders was common. In the 1840s and 1850s reforms were effected through the Separate System (every prisoner kept apart) and the Silent System (prisoners allowed to work together, but not to speak). Left: prisoners at Holloway picking oakum and working on the treadmill. Right: a male convict at Pentonville, a woman at Millbank Prison. The man is masked, to emphasise his anonymity. The idea that suffering purified the soul was firmly applied to convicts. By the end of the century, though, the thought that they might do useful work was just beginning to seep through

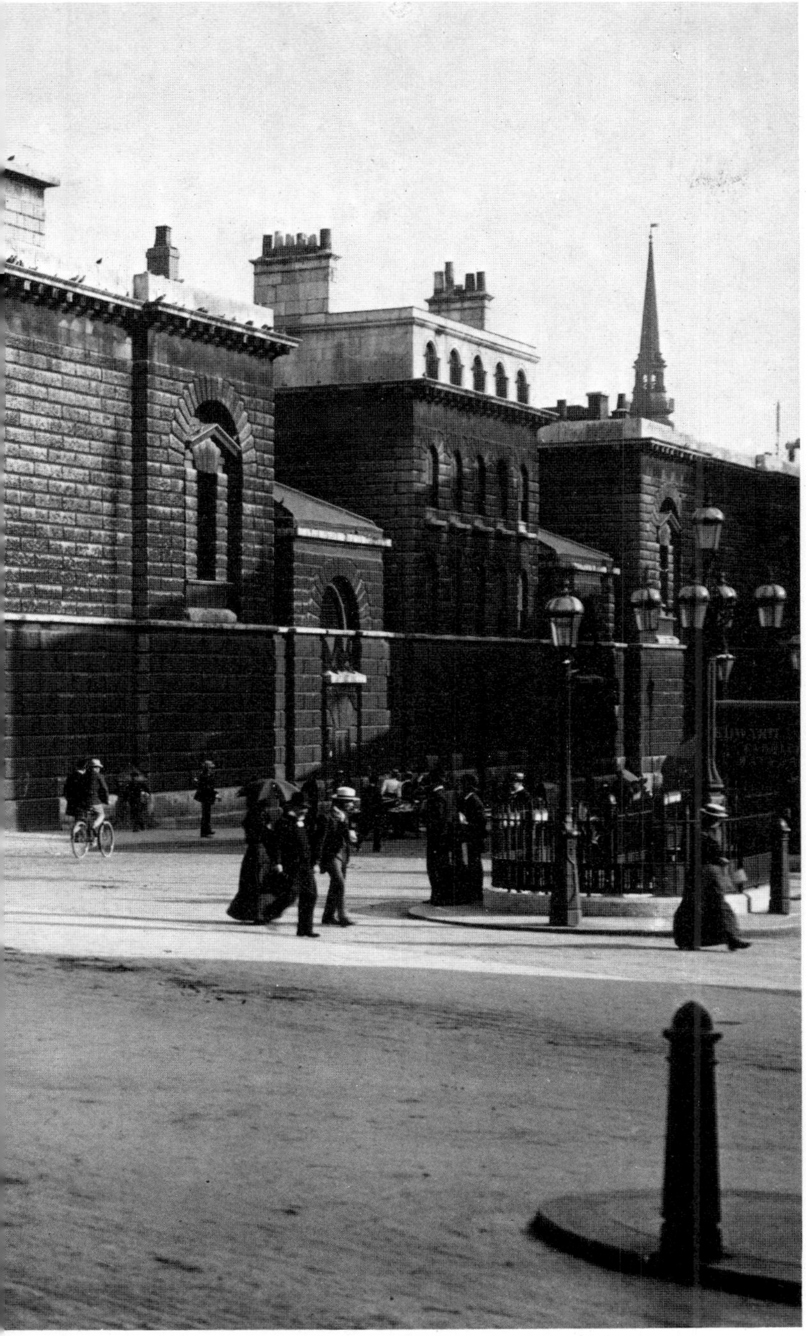

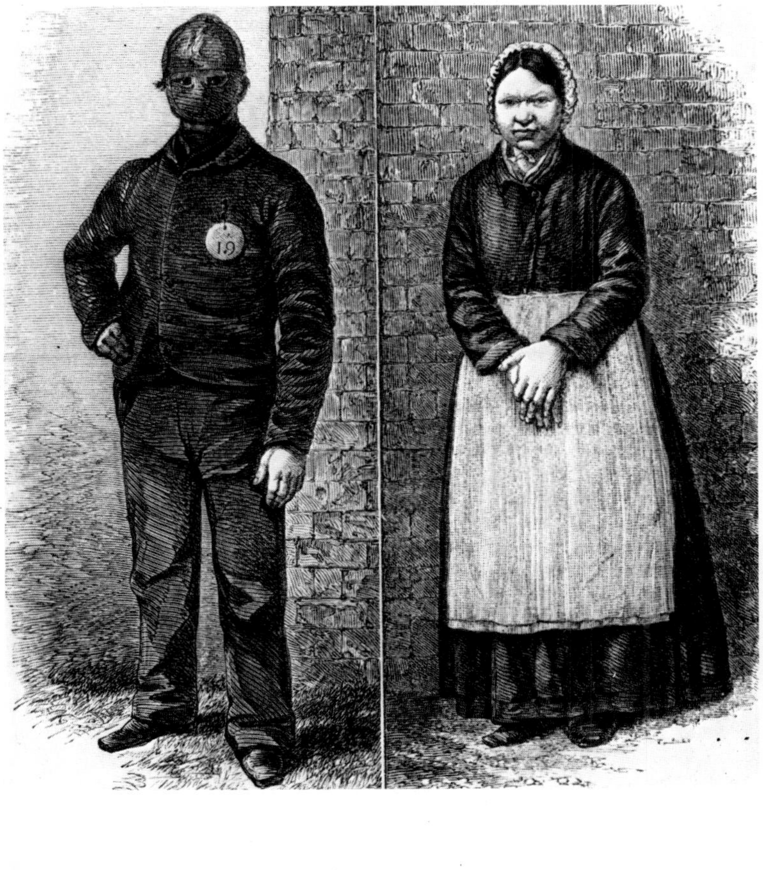
19

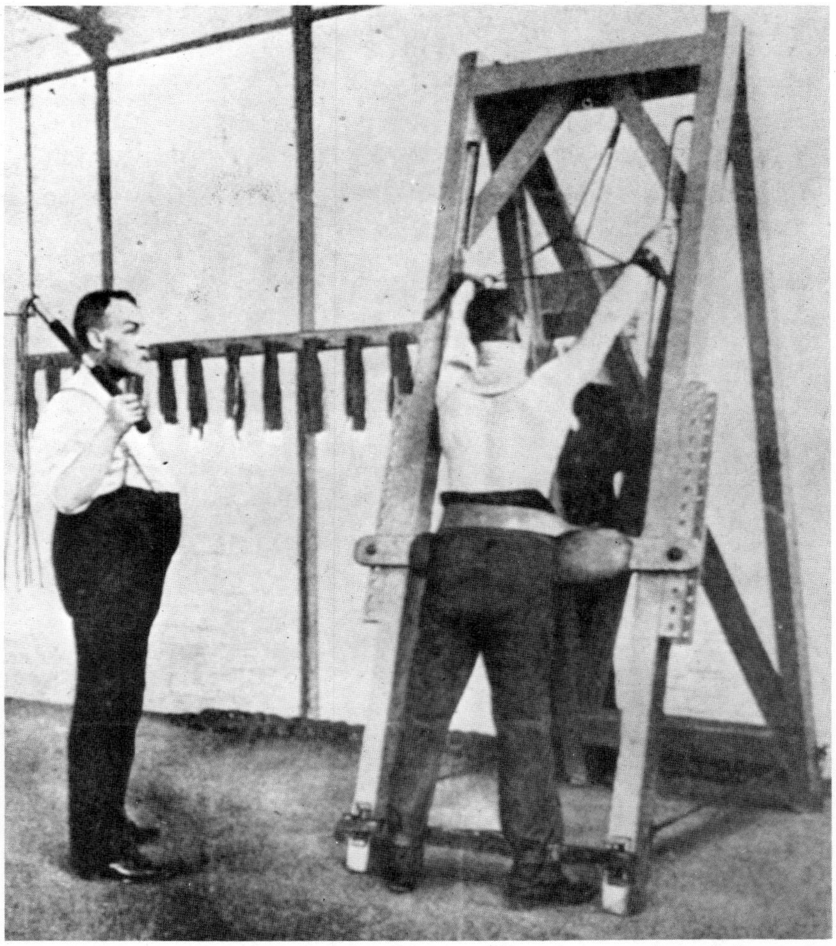

Above: prisoner fixed to flogging frame. Flogging continued throughout Victoria's reign, but in 1873 it was restricted to offences involving personal violence. The reform was regretted by many judges. Below: the execution chamber at Newgate, showing the lever controlling the 'drop'

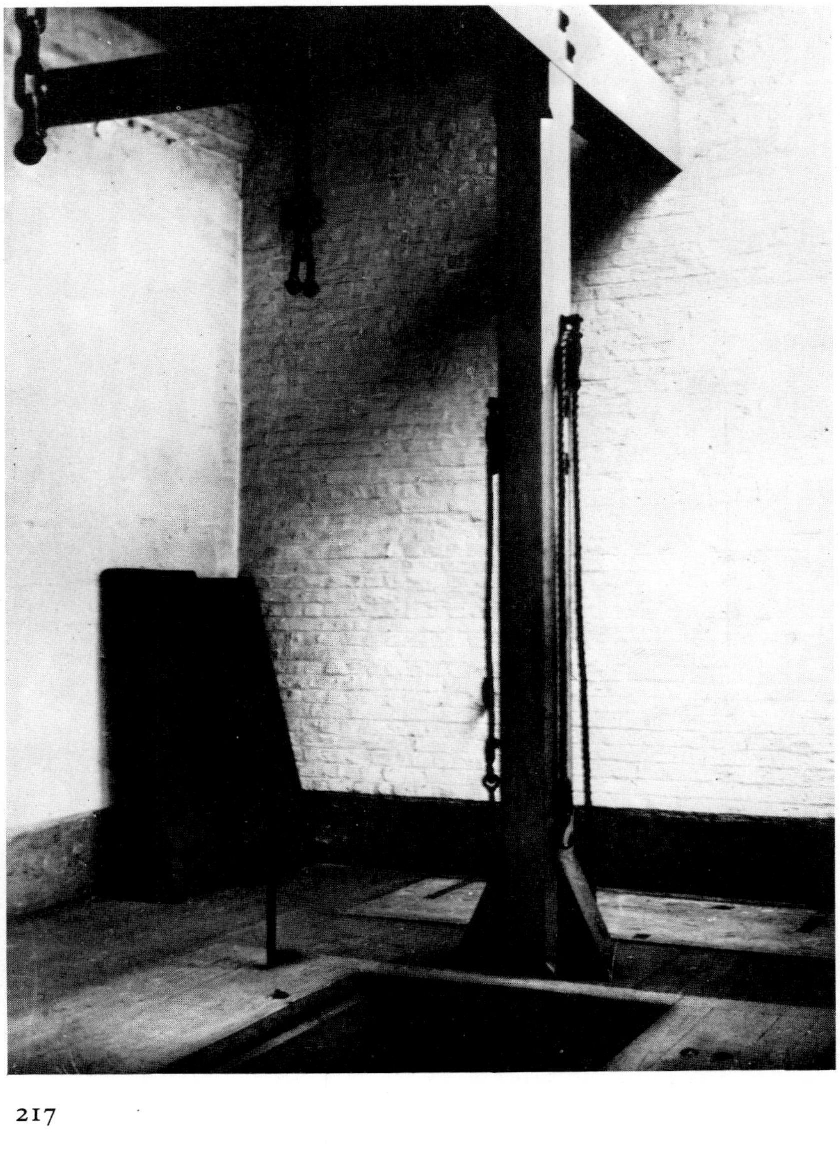

Jack the Ripper committed only half a dozen murders, or just possibly seven, a modest number as mass murderers go. His fame endures because his activities were so brief and carried out with such bravado, because of the unforgettable directness of his celebrated nickname, and because his identity remains a mystery. All his murders were carried out between August and November 1888 in London's East End. Six prostitutes were killed, all having their throats slit, after which they were savagely mutilated. In one case the intestines were pulled out and draped over the shoulder, in others they were removed. Since five of the murders took place outdoors, although after dark in badly-lit streets, the Ripper obviously had some surgical skill. After November, when the East End was in turmoil, and London's Press in a furore of lurid speculation, the crimes simply stopped. Who was Jack the Ripper? A man possibly trained as a surgeon, with a hatred of women, very likely one who had caught venereal disease from a prostitute. For a long time the principal candidate was George Chapman, really Severin Klosovski, who was hanged in 1903 for poisoning three women. Chapman was a surgeon, and looked rather like descriptions of the Ripper. The Inspector in charge believed that he was the man, but a butcher of women who was also a poisoner seems improbable. Other candidates: a seaman, a midwife, a policeman, the royal Duke of Clarence, even a Tsarist secret agent.

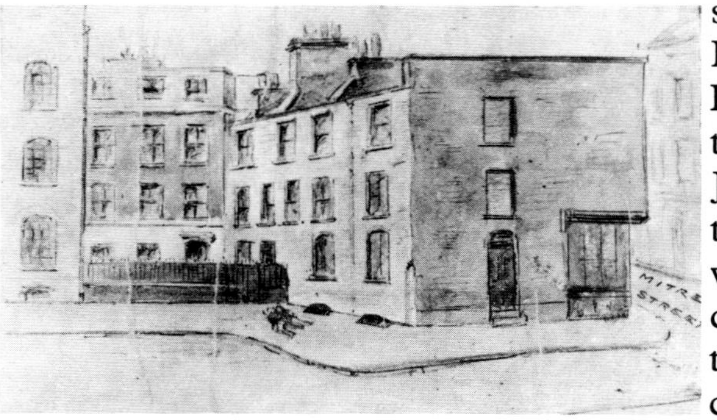
MITRE STREET

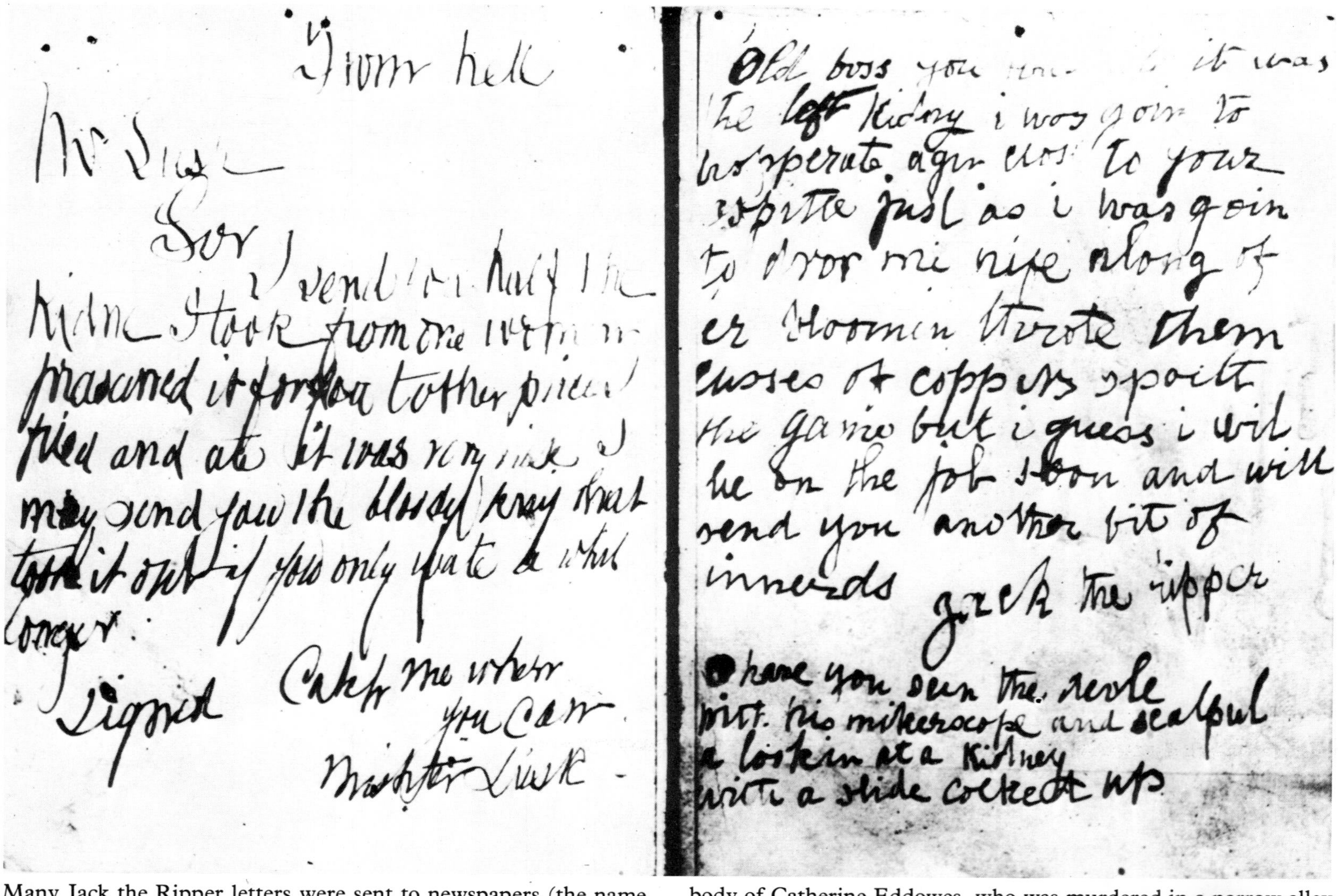

From hell

Mr Lusk

Sor

I send you half the
Kidne I took from one women
prasarved it for you tother piece I
fried and ate it was very nise I
may send you the bloody knif that
took it out if you only wate a whil
longer.

signed Catch me when
you Can
Mishter Lusk

Old boss you was rite it was
the left kidny i was goin to
hoperate agin close to your
ospitle just as i was goin
to dror mi nife along of
er bloomin throte them
cusses of coppers spoilt
the game but i guess i wil
be on the job soon and will
send you another bit of
innerds
jack the ripper

O have you seen the devle
with his mikerscope and scalpul
a lookin at a kidney
with a slide cocked up

Many Jack the Ripper letters were sent to newspapers (the name came from the first of them), and almost certainly some were genuine. The letter above refers to sending a kidney taken from the body of Catherine Eddowes, who was murdered in a narrow alley near Mitre Square (top). The promise to send "another bit of innards" is quite characteristic of the Ripper's ghastly jocularity

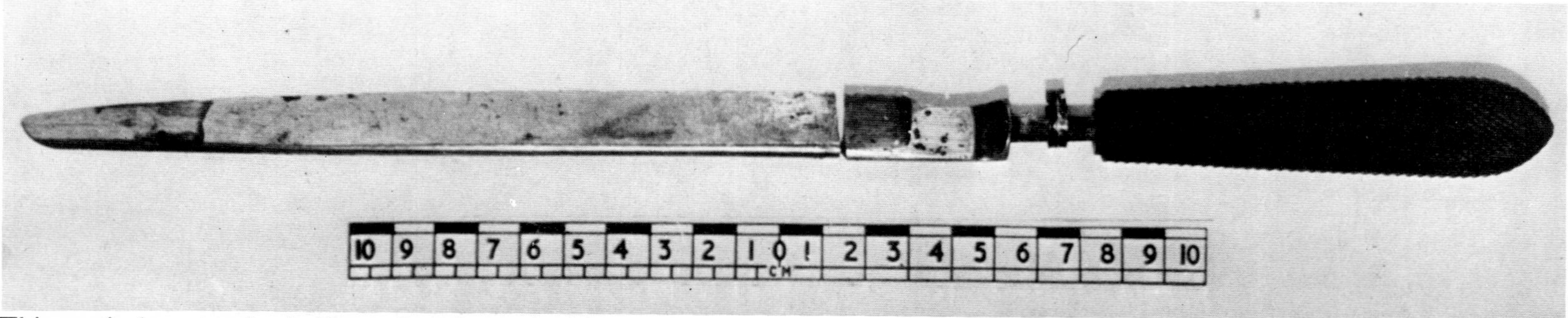
10 9 8 7 6 5 4 3 2 1 0 1 2 3 4 5 6 7 8 9 10
CM

This surgical amputation knife was found near the body of one of the murdered prostitutes, and had almost certainly been used for the crime

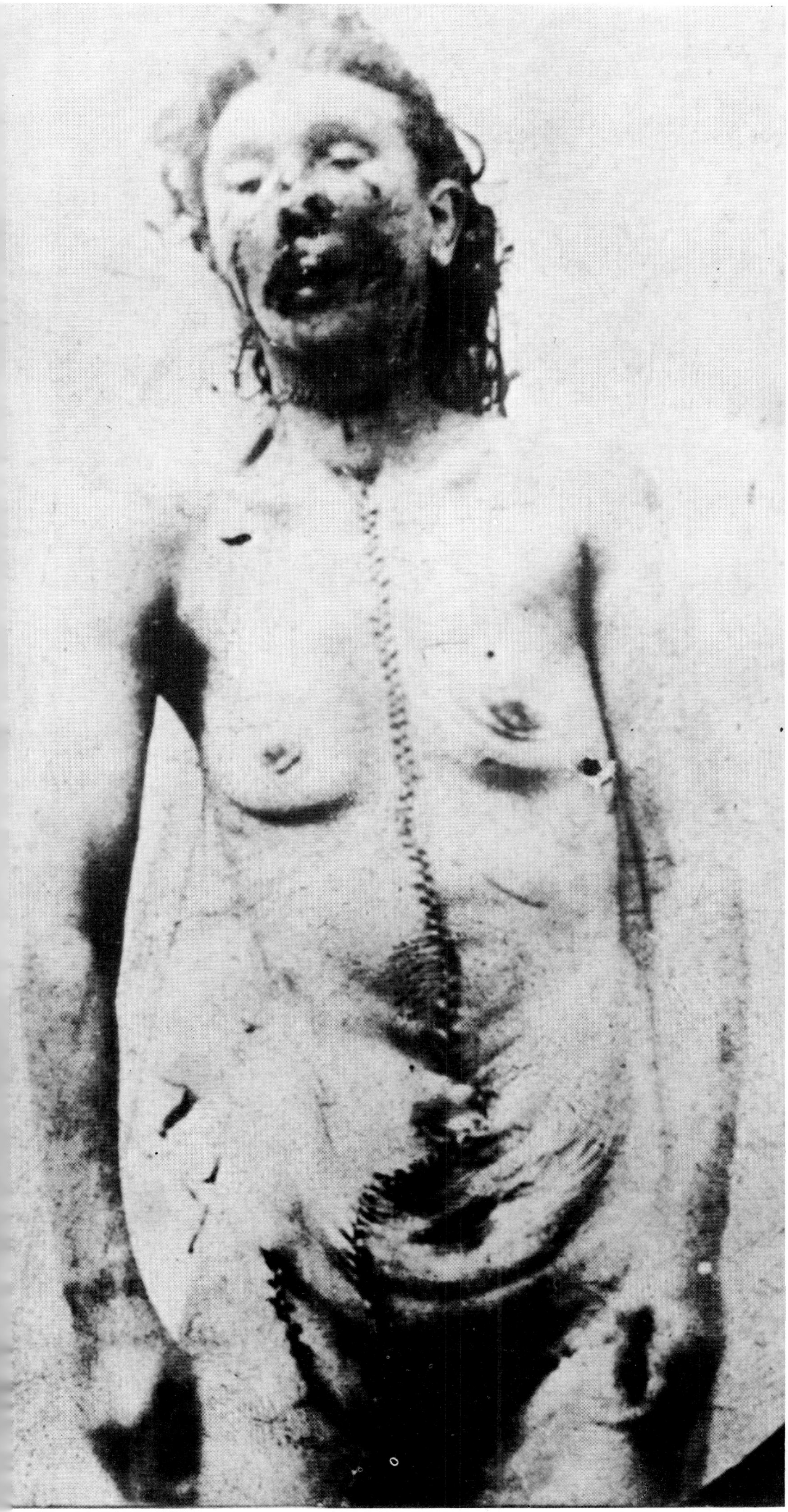

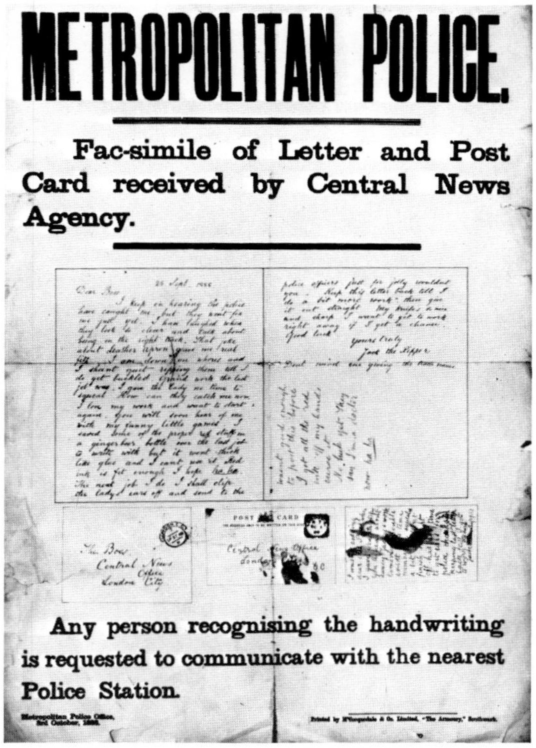

METROPOLITAN POLICE.

Fac-simile of Letter and Post Card received by Central News Agency.

Any person recognising the handwriting is requested to communicate with the nearest Police Station.

A police notice of another Ripper letter and a postcard. Suspiciously lacking in detail, both the documents had probably been faked

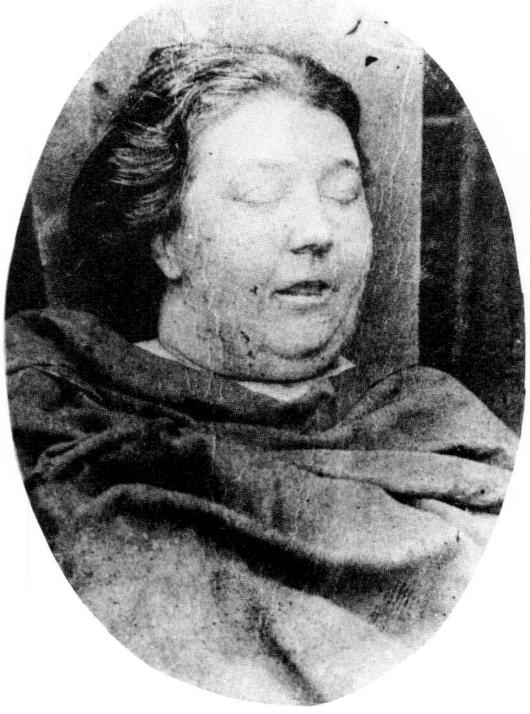

Martha Turner (above), probably the Ripper's first victim. Stabbed 39 times, no mutilations. Catherine Eddowes (left) met the Ripper near Mitre Square. Within fifteen minutes – a police constable was patrolling the area – she had been murdered and disembowelled. All the murders took place within half a mile of Whitechapel Road (below)

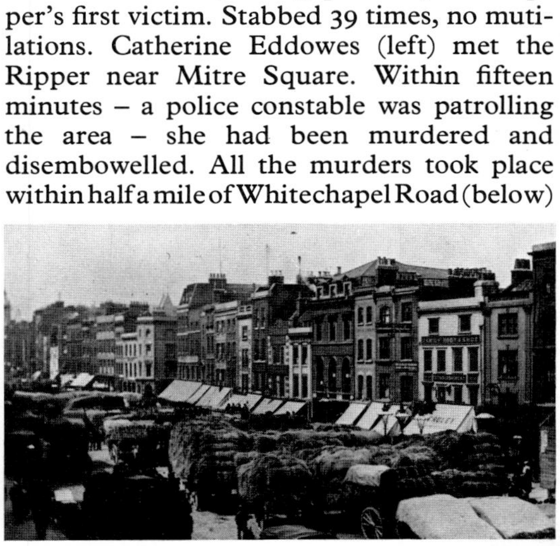

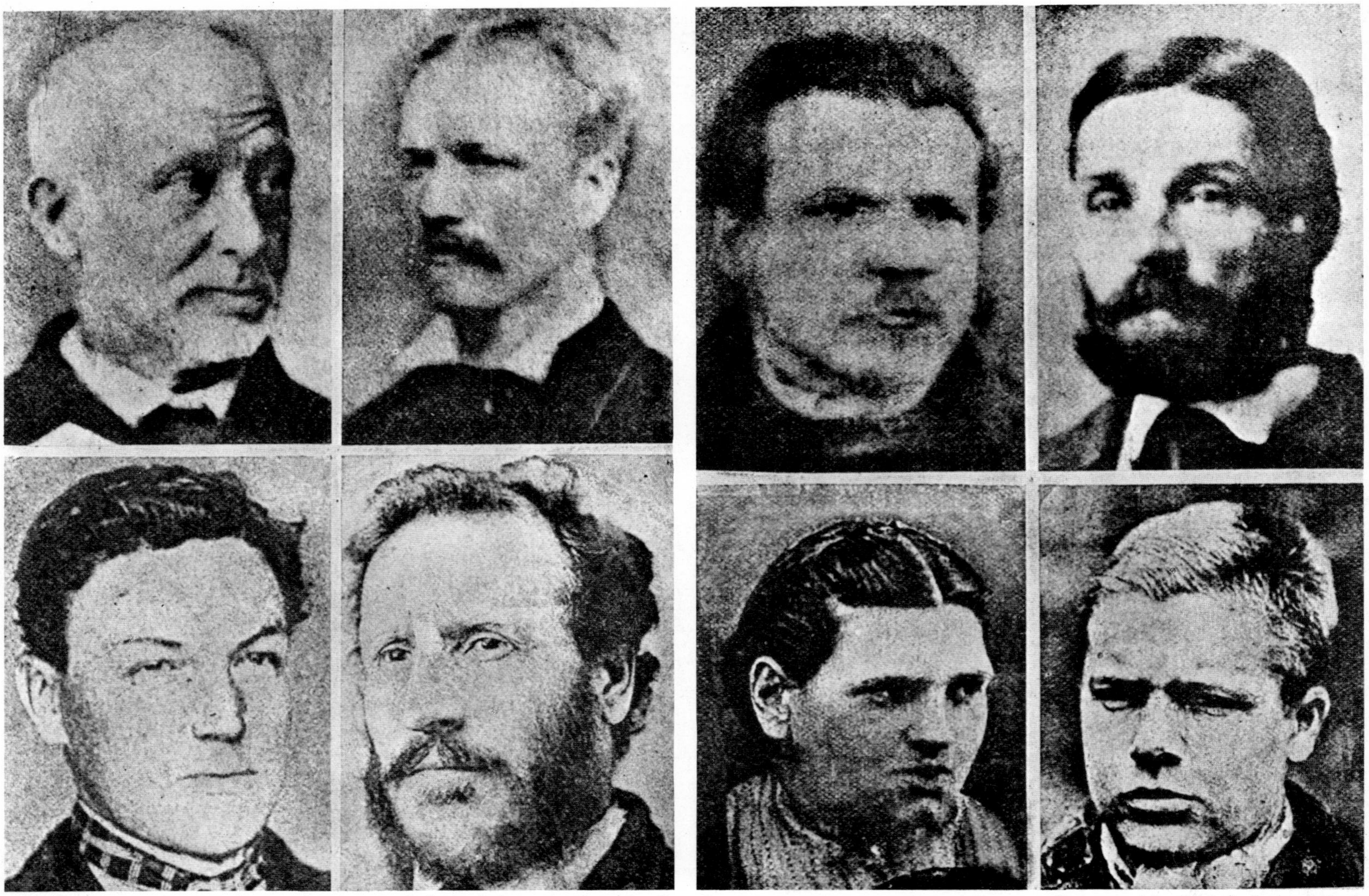

According to Havelock Ellis's book *The Criminal* these are heads of average London criminals chosen almost at random. Ellis, walking in Cesare Lombroso's footsteps, thought that they could be identified by details of nose, forehead, ears, hair. There was supposed to be a ten per cent greater chance of men with dark hair and dark eyes being criminals, while lunatics were more inclined to be fair. Bodily appearance was also thought important. A prison surgeon noted many convicts with large nipples and undescended testicles

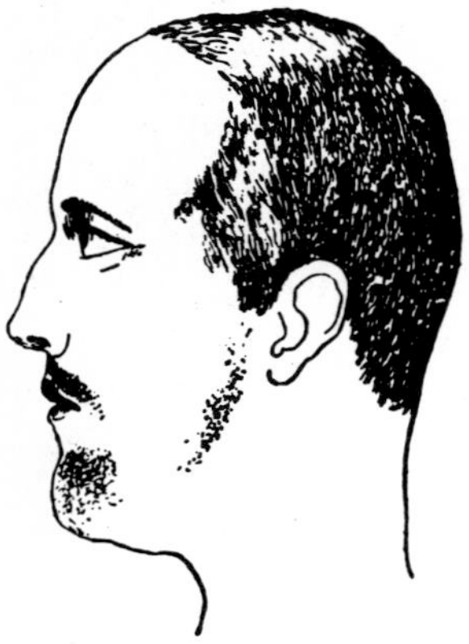

Murderer. Ellis notes "massive forehead, small compressed mouth, villainous expression"

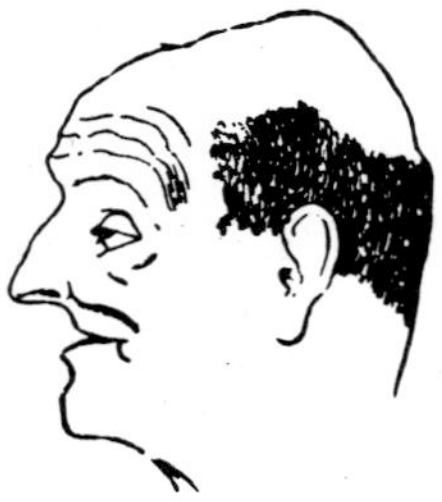

Gardener, aged 86. Typical sugar-loaf criminal head, bulging at the back

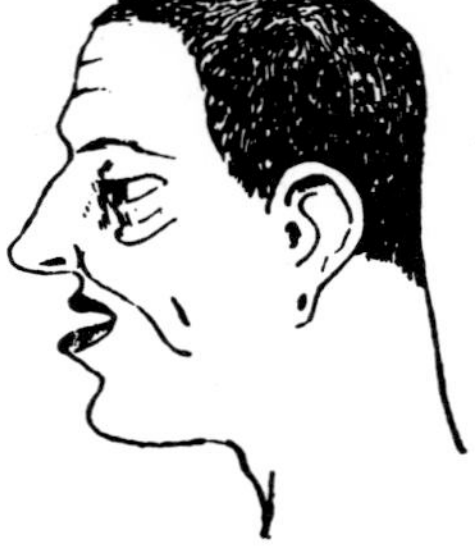

Weak-minded cattle stealer from Paisley. Criminal jug-handle ears

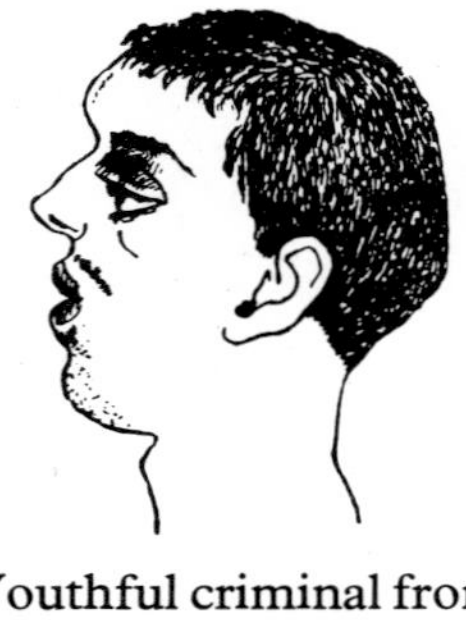

Youthful criminal from Portsea. Bulging forehead a bad sign

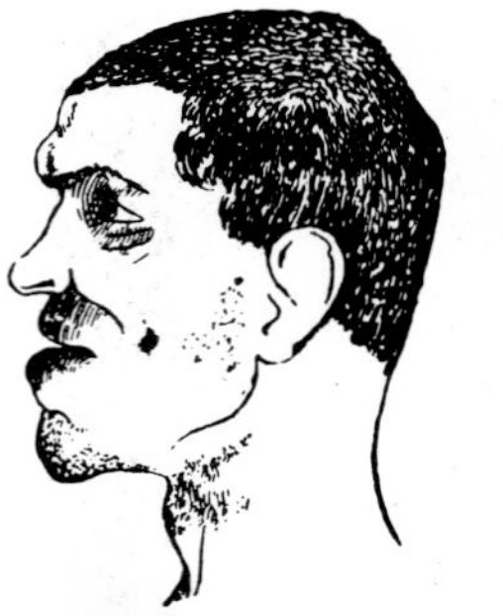

Soldier, would-be murderer, with "low or flat-roofed skull characteristic of degeneration"

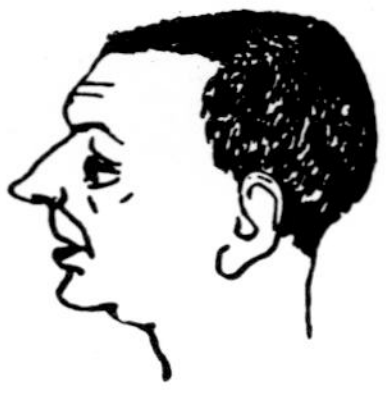

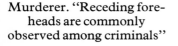

Murderer. "Receding foreheads are commonly observed among criminals"

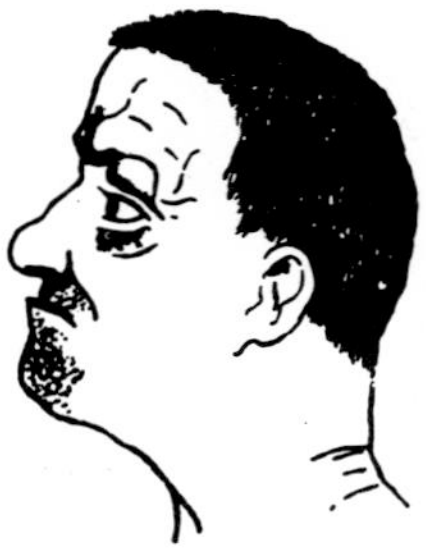

Farm labourer, petty thief, low mentality, confirmed by prognathous jaw

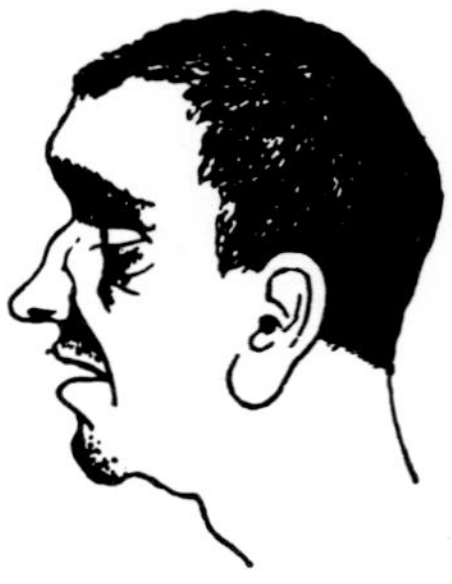

"The frontal crest is often strong among criminals and the insane"

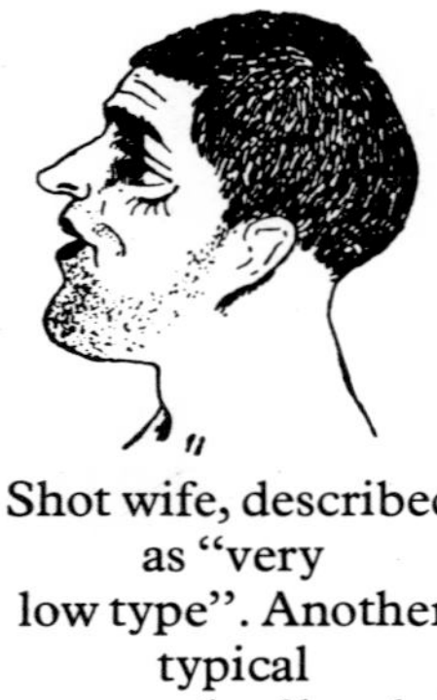

Shot wife, described as "very low type". Another typical sugar-loaf head

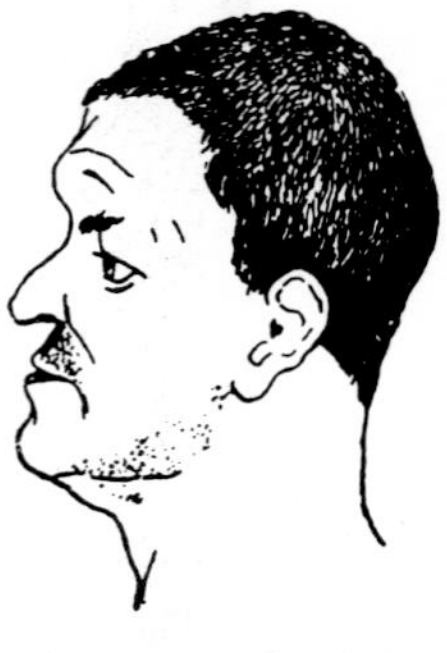

Another sugar loaf. Dock labourer, killed wife's lover. Undeveloped genitals

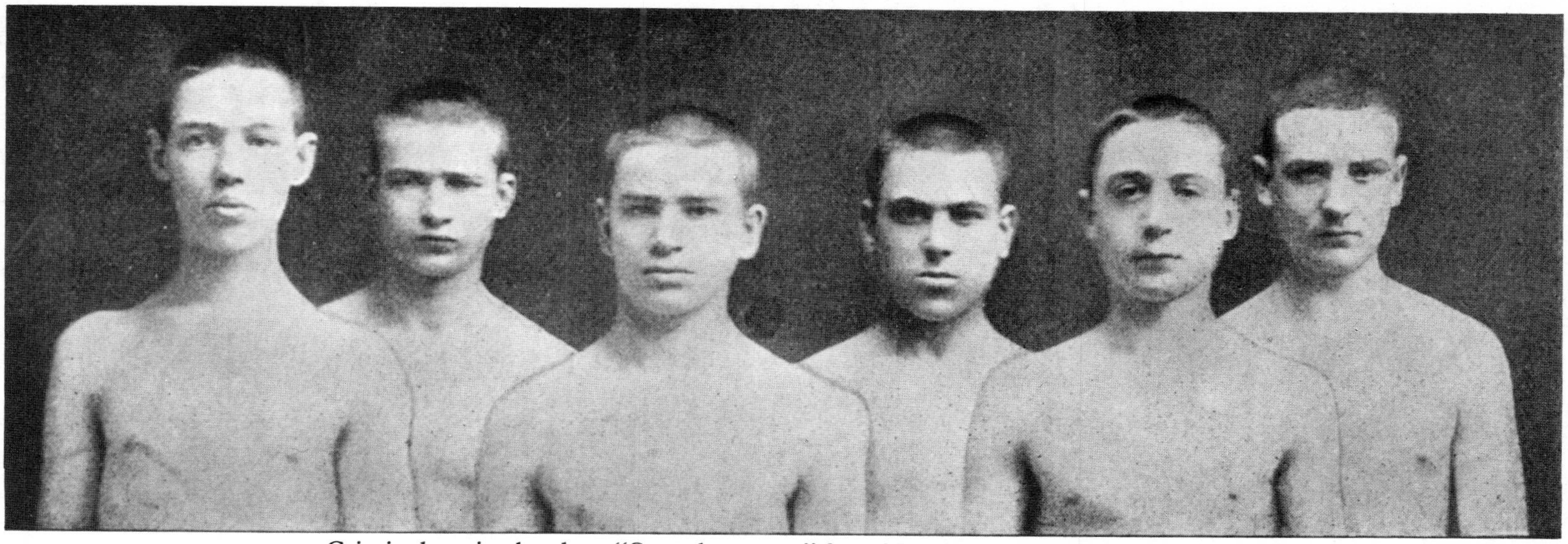

Criminal-typing by class. "Sexual perverts" from New York's Elmira reformatory

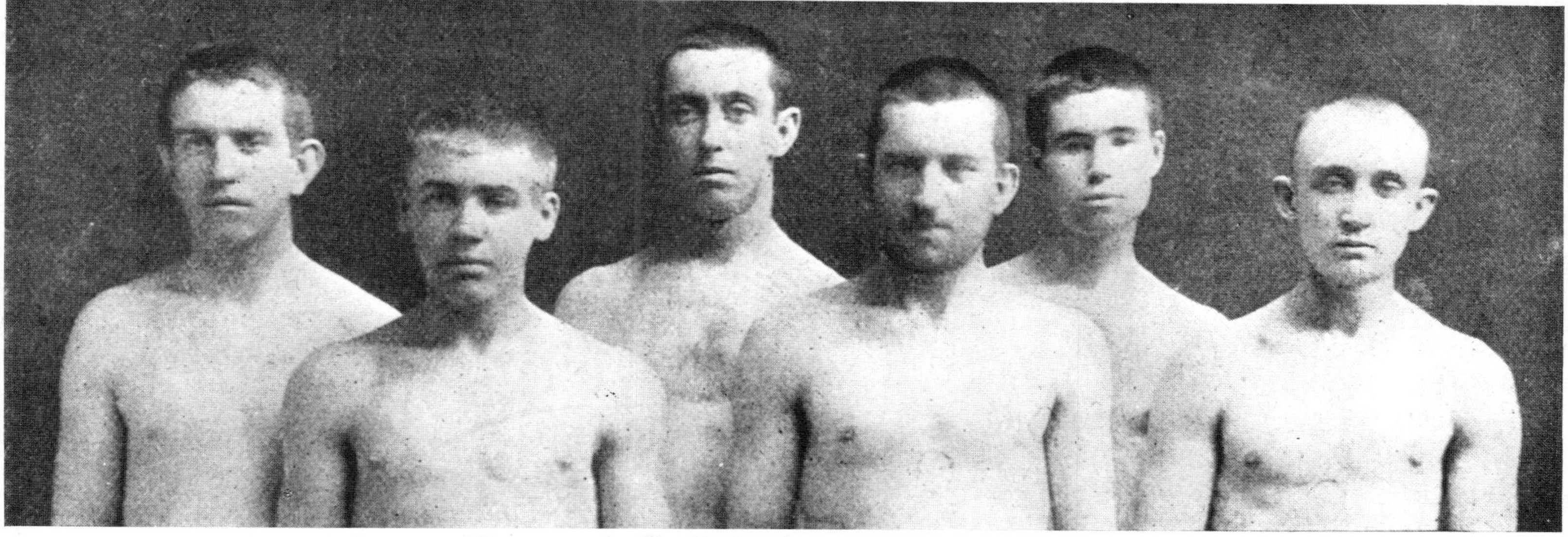

A group of "low mental calibre", also photographed at the Elmira reformatory

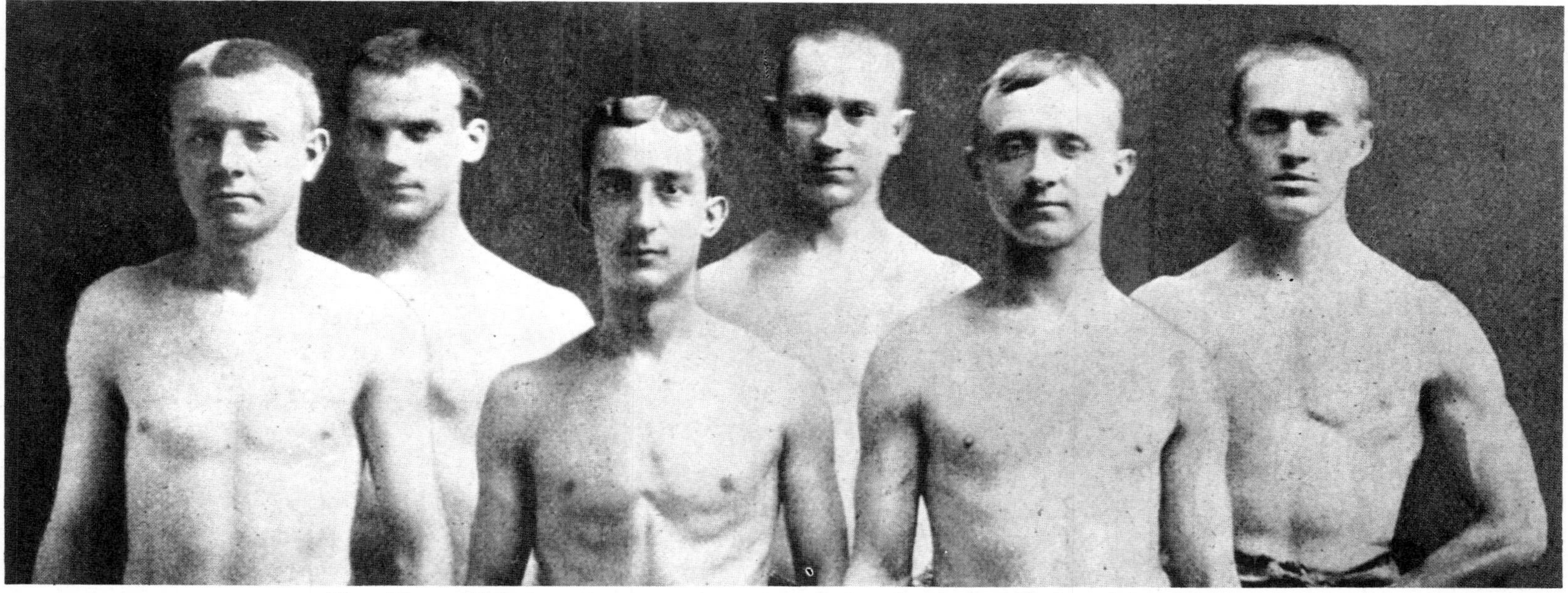

"Intelligent" Elmira prisoners, who responded to physical and industrial training

Immense strides were made in scientific investigation of crime during the century. Fingerprints came at the end of it, but they were preceded by Alphonse Bertillon's anthropometrical system, which involved exact measurements for identification, and by Cesare Lombroso's attempts to classify criminal types. Lombroso used comparatively sophisticated means of measurement to discover whether a man was born with criminal tendencies. His many followers were more naïve, and never asked whether 'ordinary people' also showed similar characteristics. The results were often almost comic, as can be seen in the plates from Havelock Ellis's book. By the end of the century it realised that environment was as important as heredity in making a criminal, and real attempts were being made in a few reformatories to change bad citizens into good ones through training and education

The rapid development of new printing methods and the spread of literacy enabled the Victorians to read as people in Britain never had before. Circulating libraries, part-works, railway bookstalls and a burgeoning periodical industry helped to satisfy the public appetite. There were many popular novelists to meet the demand, some who have survived

THE MIGHTY PEN

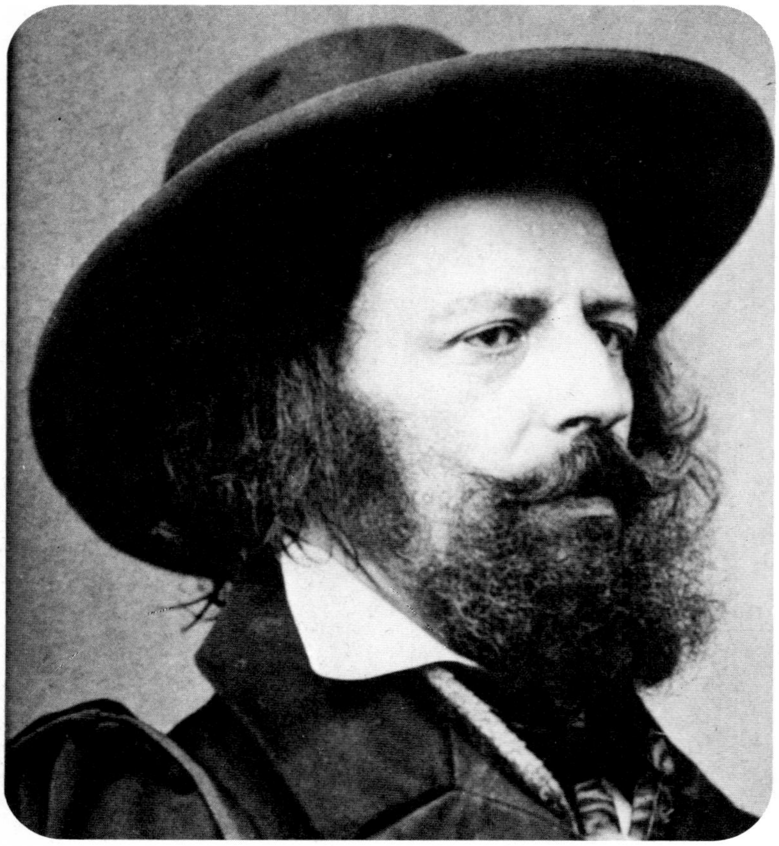

Alfred, Lord Tennyson (1809–1892), the most famous poet of his day, succeeding another giant, Wordsworth, as Poet Laureate. *In Memoriam* is his masterwork

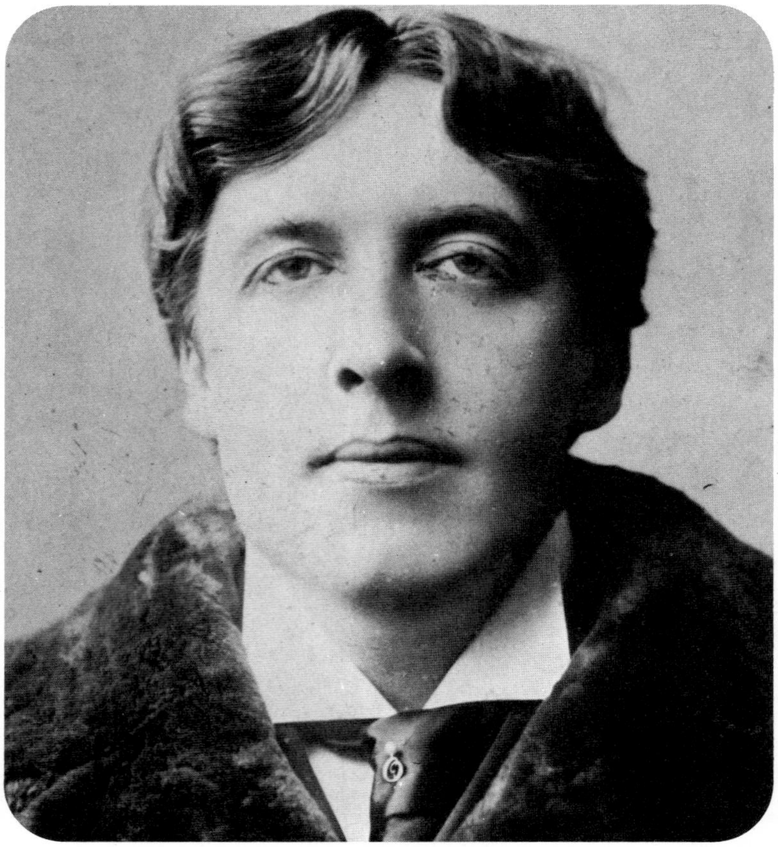

Oscar Wilde (1854–1900), the most notorious name in the puritanical calendar, created an incomparable theatrical masterpiece, *The Importance of Being Earnest*

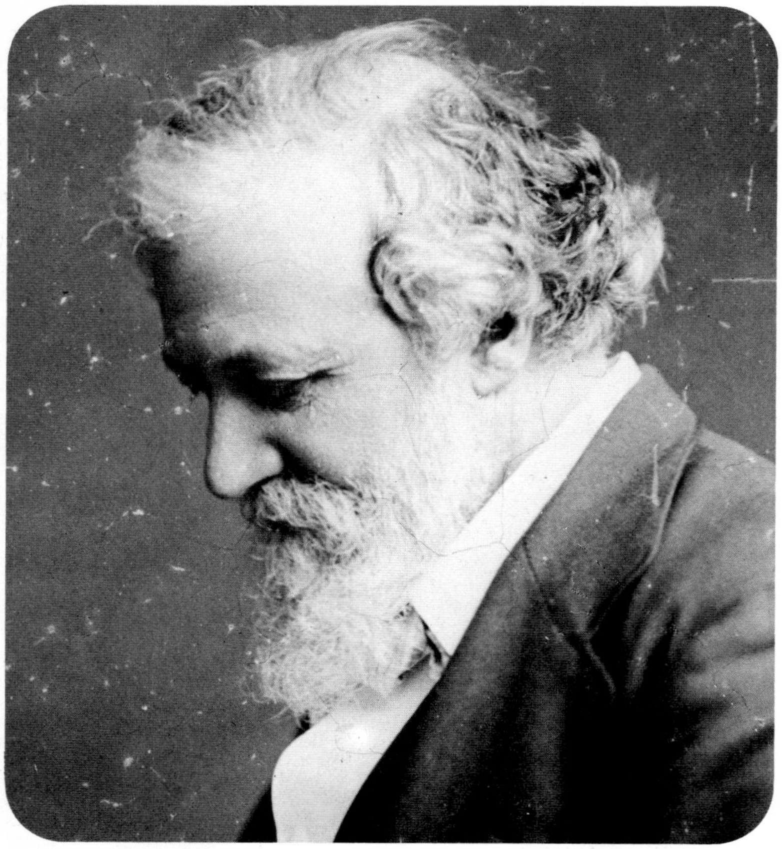

Robert Browning (1812–1899), an inventive poet of dashing style and apt imagery; he married Elizabeth Barrett, the greatest English woman poet

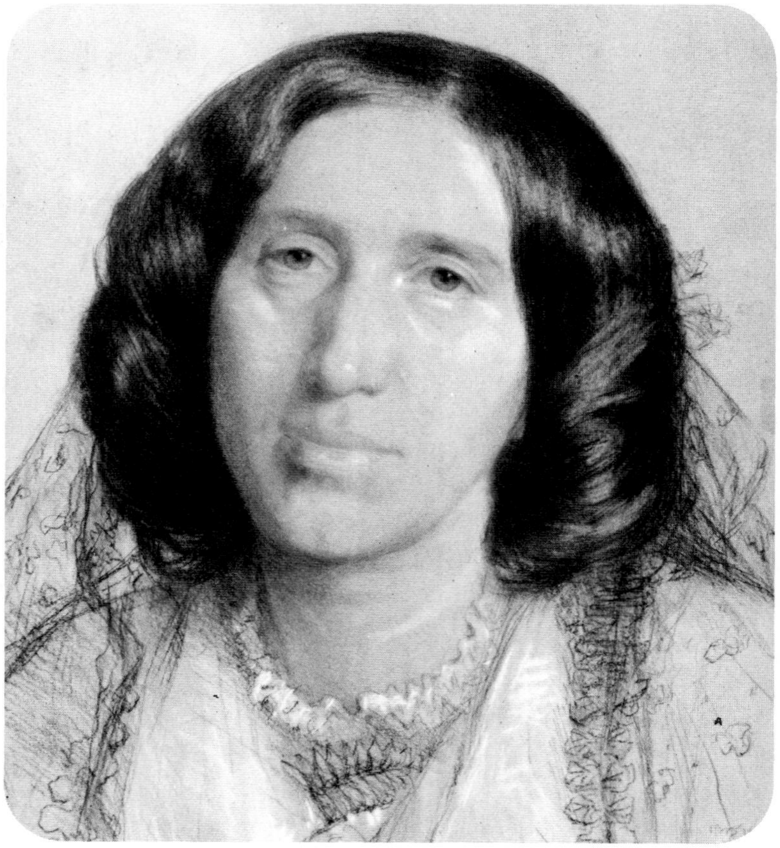

George Eliot (1819–1880) – the nom-de-plume of Mary Ann Evans. Her novels displayed a drive and intensity quite alien to contemporary women novelists

to be recognised for their talents, the majority happily forgotten beneath a detritus of turgid prose. It was an age of popularisation – for the first time authors found themselves writing for a lower-middle-class audience with money to buy books and leisure to read them. As in most things, the Victorian literary legacy was solid, inventive and built to last

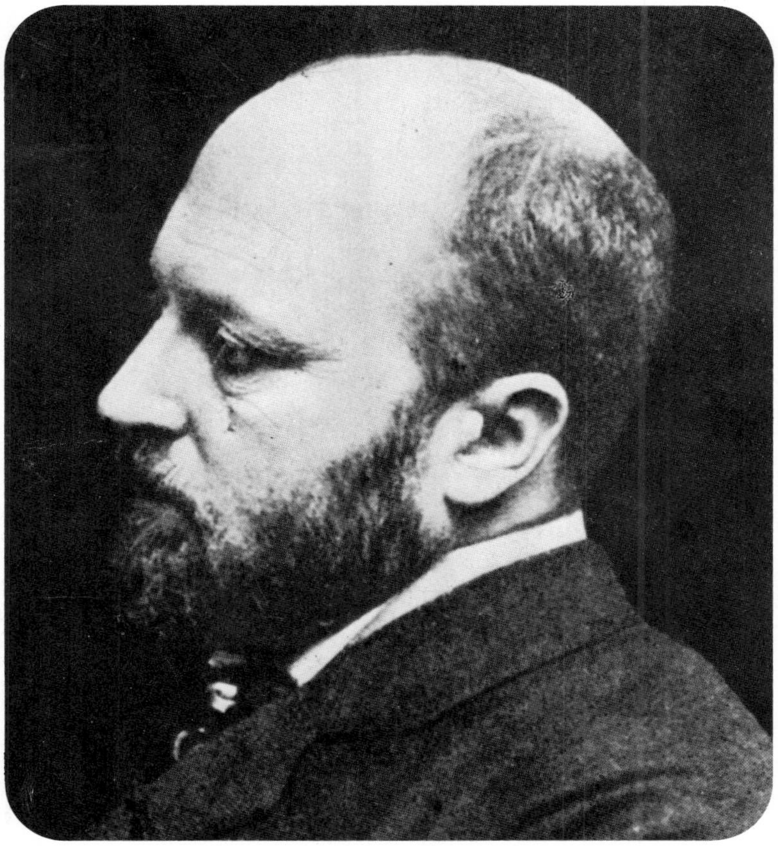

Henry James (1843–1916), born in New York. His subtle, urbane, prose-ridden novels dealt mostly with the clash of European and American cultures

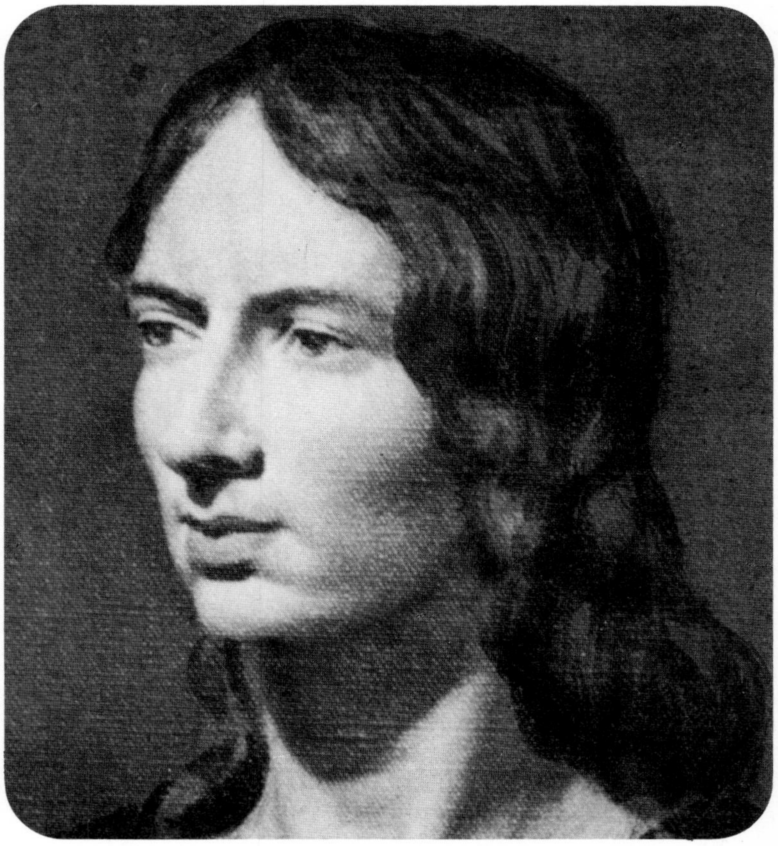

Emily Bronte (1818–1848), author of but one novel, *Wuthering Heights*, but an undoubted literary genius, living in circumstances too arduous to sustain her

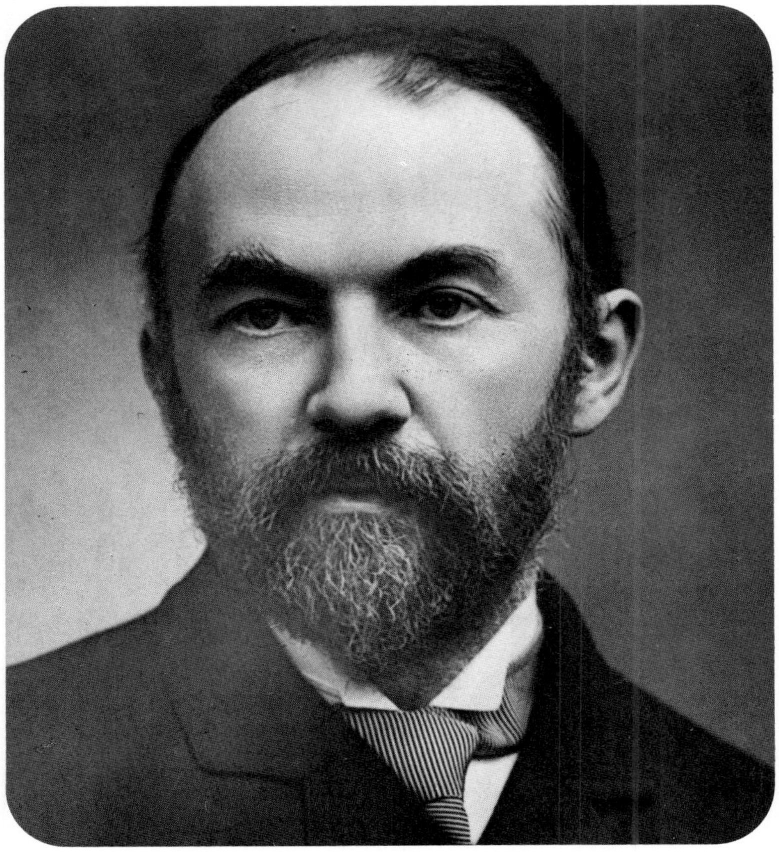

Thomas Hardy (1840–1928), writer of forceful novels of man's struggle against an implacable destiny, using as his background 'Wessex' – the rural West Country

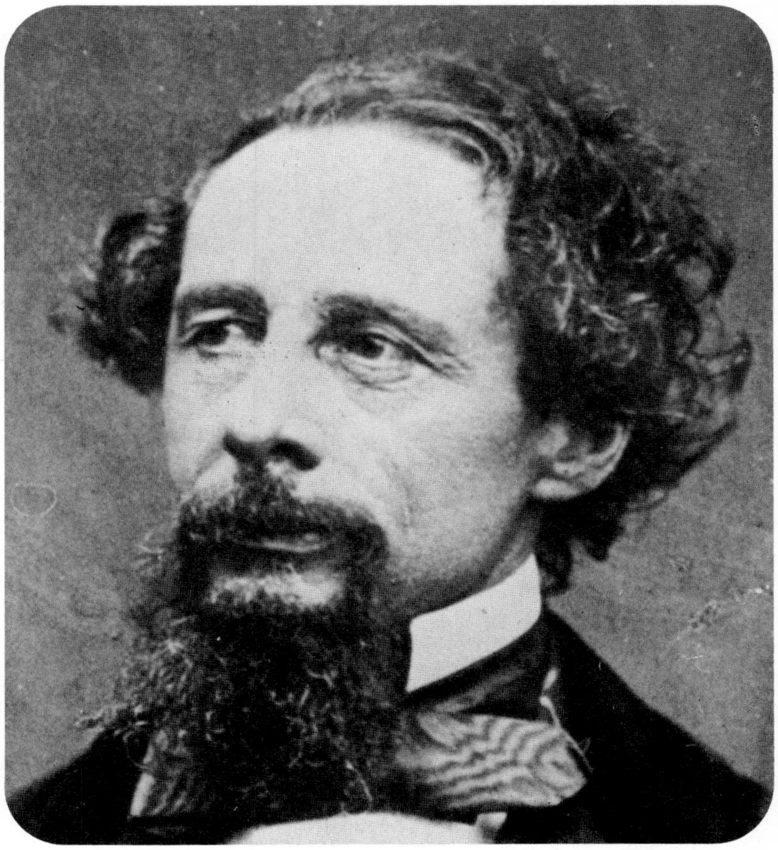

Charles Dickens (1812–1870), pre-eminent among English novelists, a chronicler of early Victorian life without equal, a masterly campaigner against social injustice

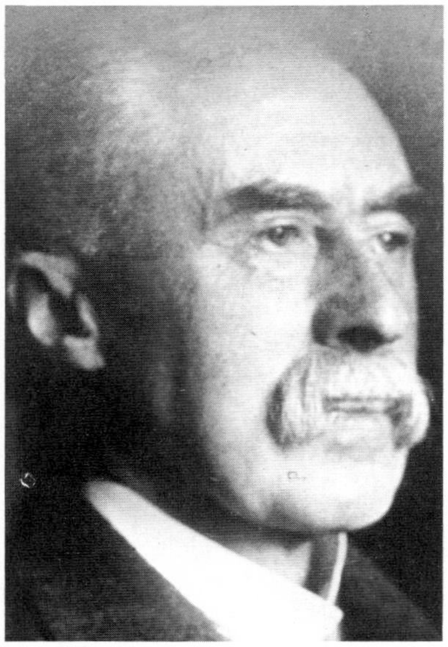

A. E. Housman, scholar in classics, author of the remarkable *A Shropshire Lad*

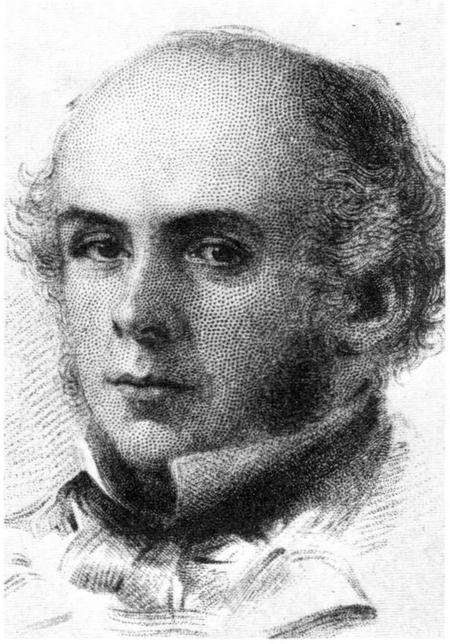

A. H. Clough, educationist and poet, his work influenced by his conflict with religion

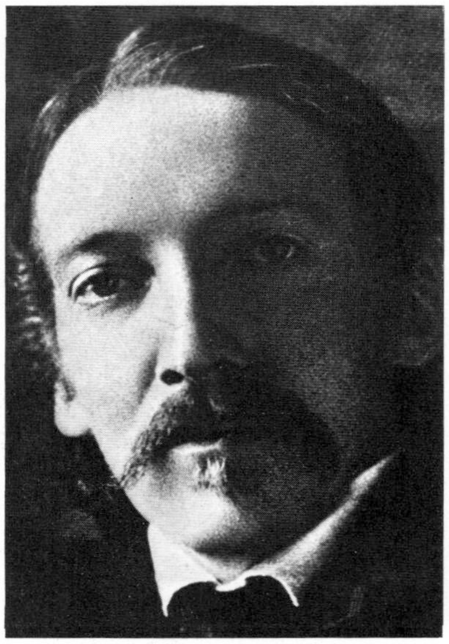

Robert Louis Stevenson, Scottish traveller and novelist, author of *Treasure Island*

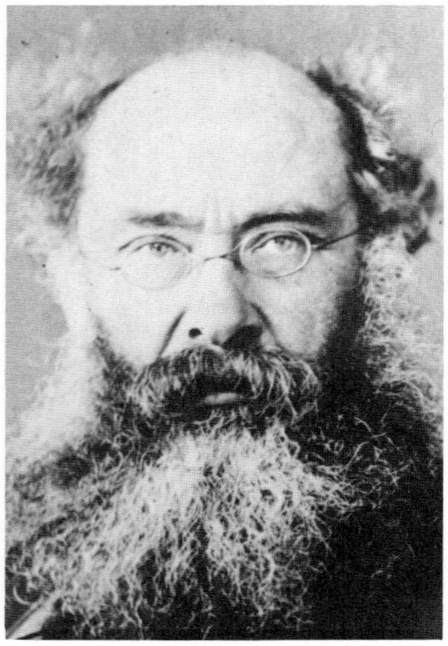

Anthony Trollope, prolific novelist, full-time civil servant, son of best-selling mother

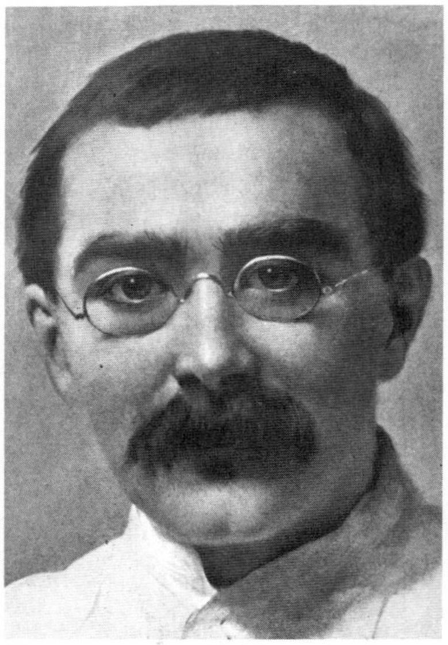

Rudyard Kipling, journalist globe-trotter, the popular poet of Empire and Army

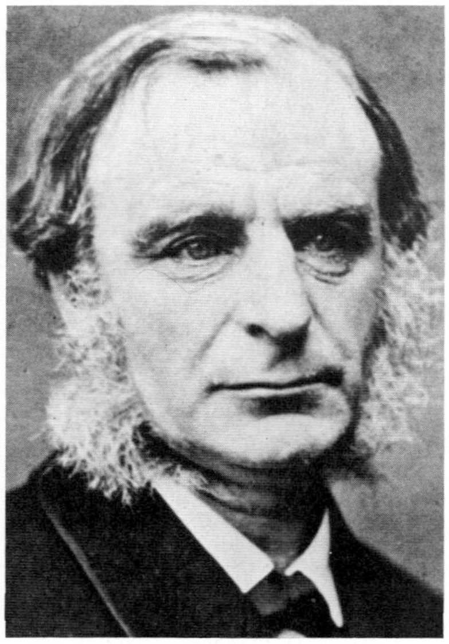

Charles Kingsley, social reformer, proselytiser with *The Water Babies* and *Hereward*

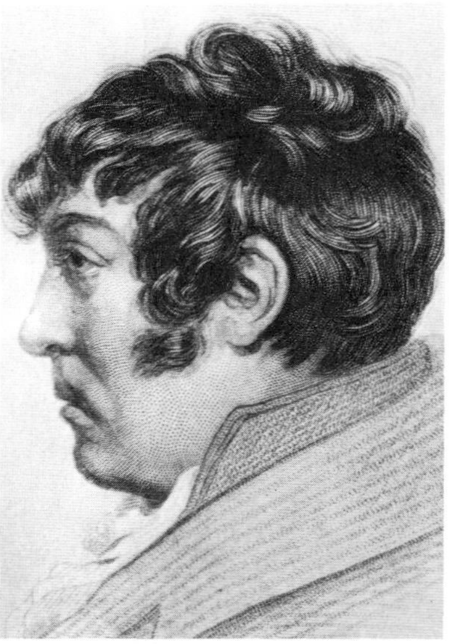

Walter Savage Landor, long-lived poet and essayist, domiciled mostly in Italy

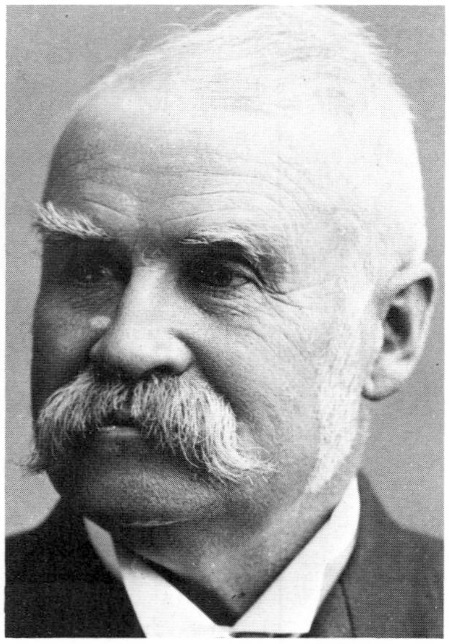

W. S. Gilbert, satirical poet, humorist, most famous for comic operas with Sullivan

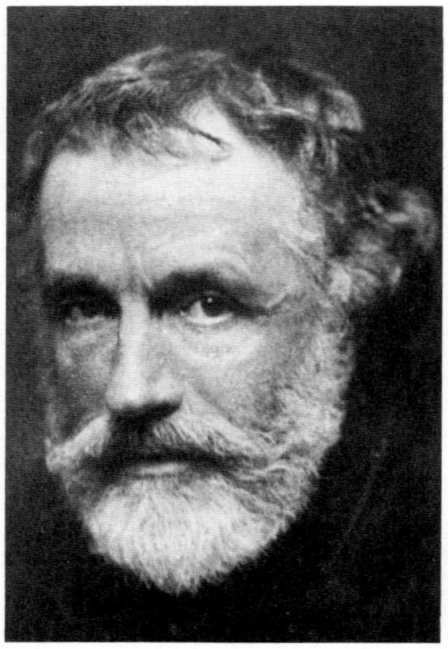

George Meredith, novelist linked with the Pre-Raphaelites, and accomplished poet

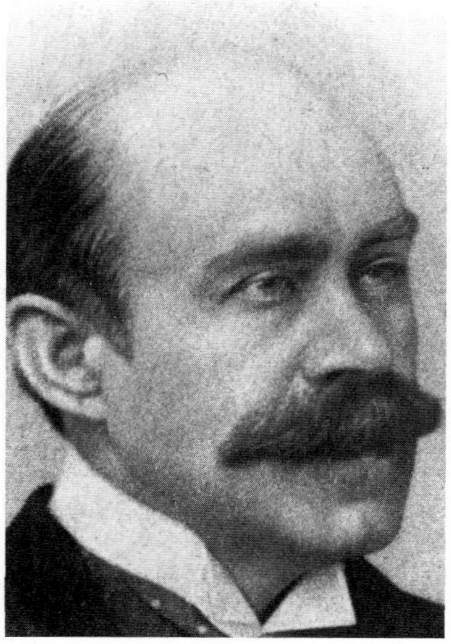

Walter Pater, Oxford romantic historian, associated with the Pre-Raphaelite Brotherhood

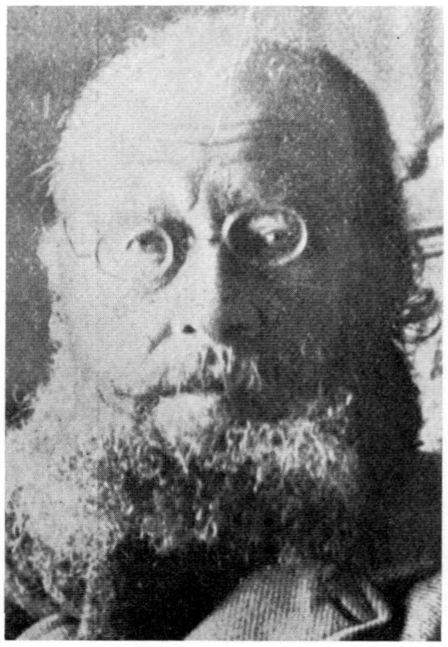

Edward Lear, nonsense versifier of monumental imagination and a minor painter of skill

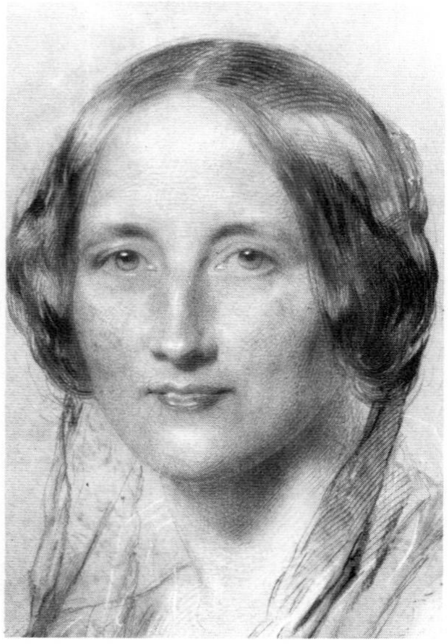

Mrs Gaskell, chronicler of life in early Victorian Cheshire, and the clash of industry

Literature flourished in Victorian England. The English novel, originating only in the previous century, came to full flower. Dickens and the Brontes, Thackeray and Hardy, George Eliot and Trollope – there was never such an age of giants. Reading around the hearth was a popular pastime in that pre-television era, and the latest instalment of a popular novelist's work in weekly parts was eagerly awaited across the land. Charles Dickens consolidated his vast

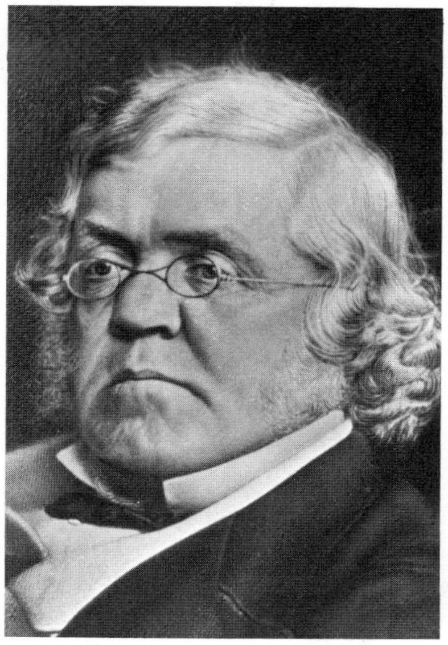

W. M. Thackeray, prolific novelist and essayist, journalist, humorist – *Vanity Fair*

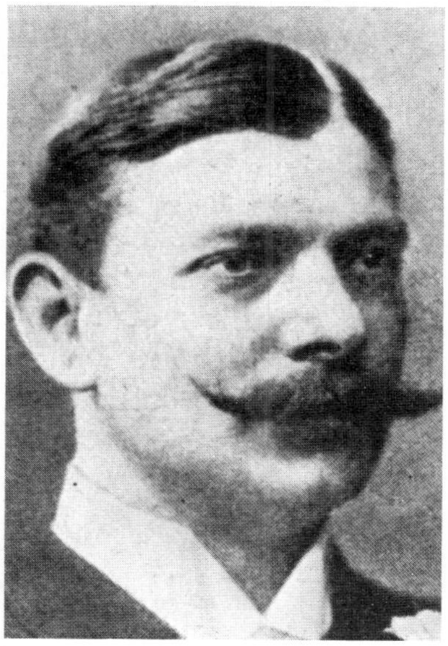

Frank Harris, journalist and literary catalyst as editor of *The Fortnightly Review*

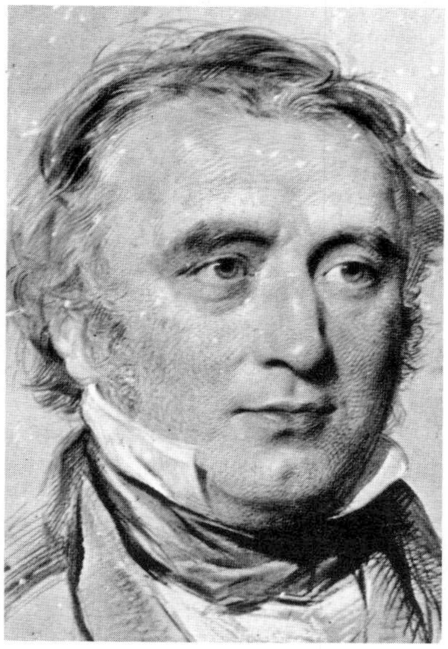

Lord Macaulay, politician, historian, essayist and polymath with literary potency

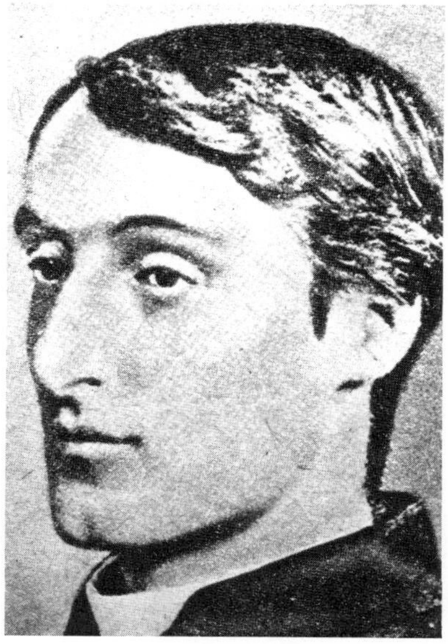

Gerard Manley Hopkins, innovator in rhythms and metre, later became a Jesuit

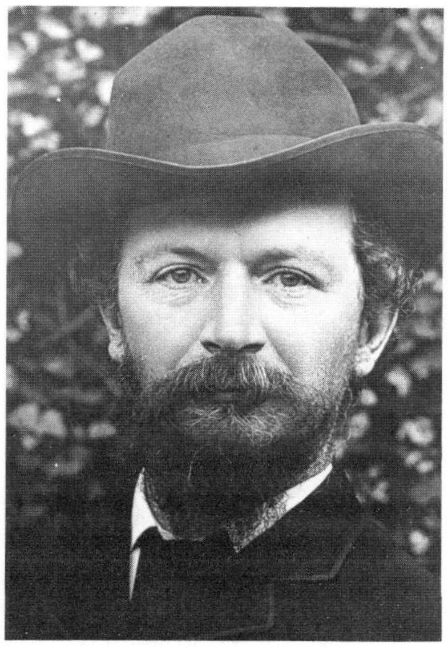

Algernon Swinburne, poet connected with the Rossetti circle, and acute literary critic

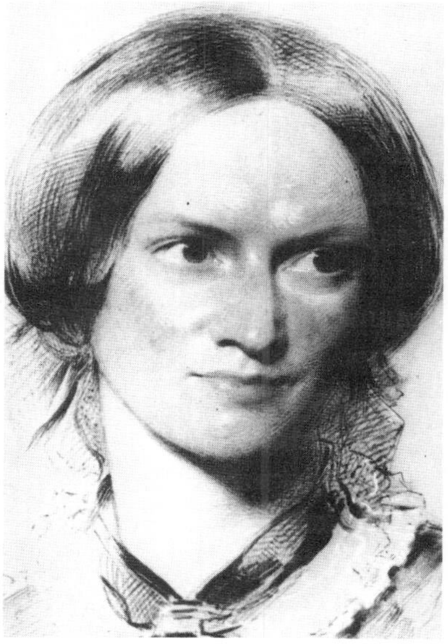

Charlotte Bronte, survived her sisters and her brother, wrote *Jane Eyre* and *Villette*

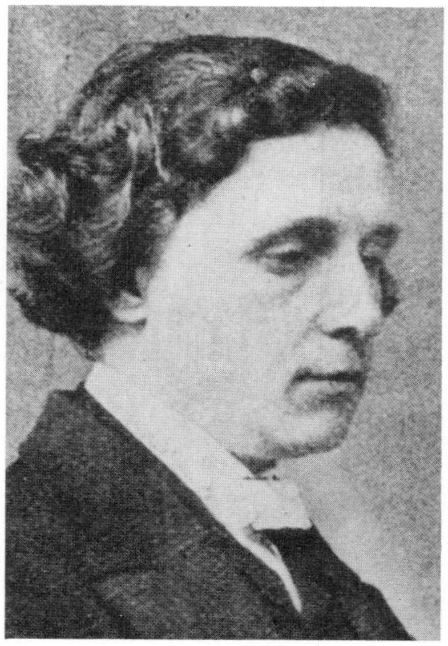

Lewis Carroll, Oxford don and creator of *Alice* books, unique in their conception

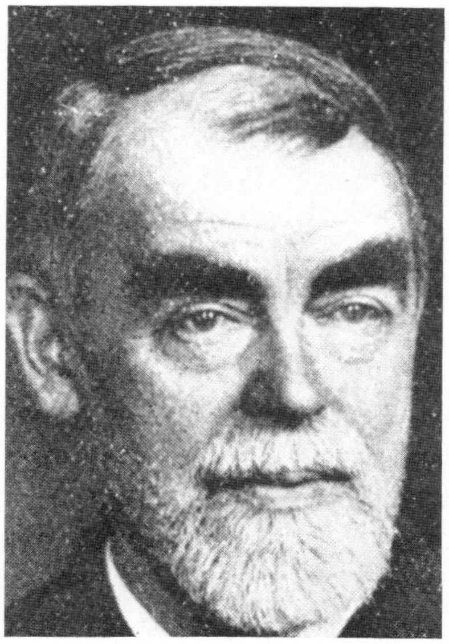

Samuel Butler, anti-clerical and satirical novelist, author of *The Way of All Flesh*

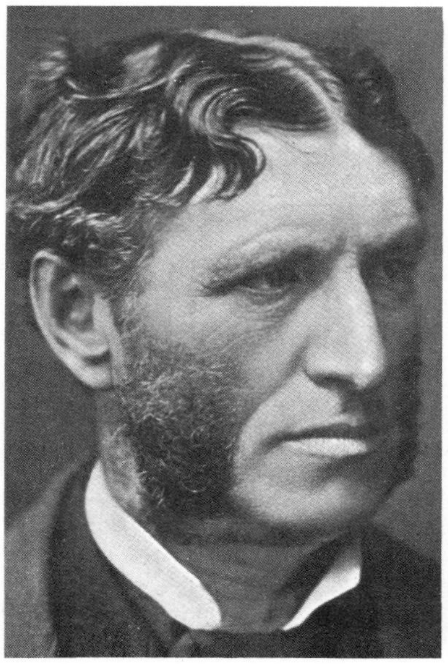

Matthew Arnold, school-inspector turned poet, famous for *The Scholar Gypsy*

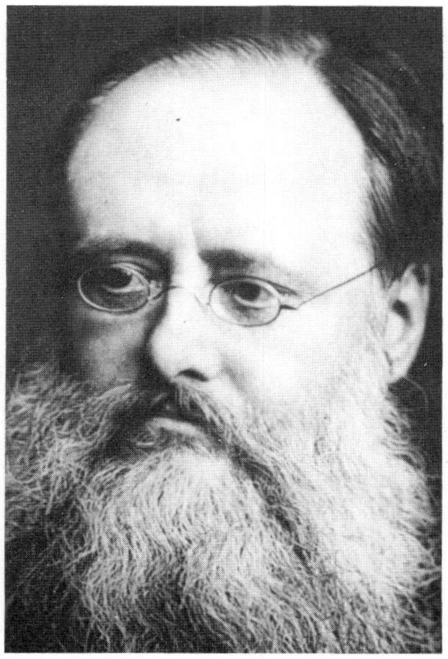

Wilkie Collins, probably the inventor of detective fiction with *The Moonstone*

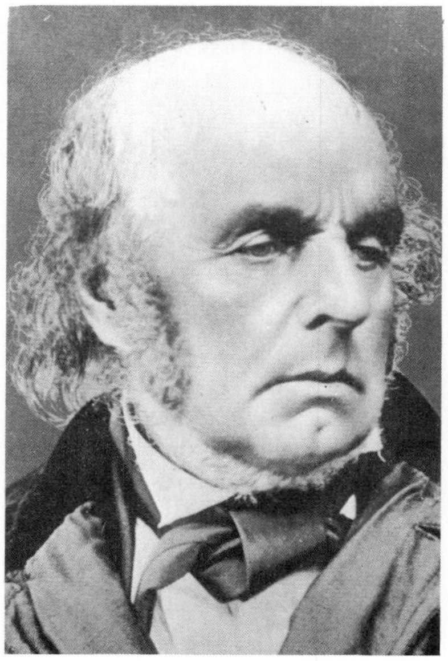

Edward Fitzgerald, translator of Omar Khayyam, distinguished Cambridge classicist

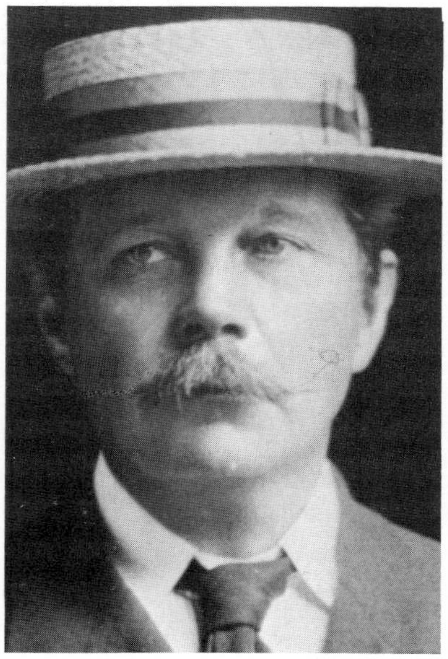

Arthur Conan Doyle, historical novelist, and creator of Sherlock Holmes

reputation with public readings from his books in large halls on both sides of the Atlantic. Poetry recitals could also command large audiences, and most Victorians could quote extensively from the corpus of English literature. The Laureate was truly a national figure, and the office was not devalued until Alfred Austin succeeded Tennyson. By the end of the century the popular presses of Harmsworth and Newnes had garnered an enormous new reading public

OUTRAGEOUS OUIDA

By Terry Coleman

The 'best-seller' was a phenomenon unknown before the Victorian age; and it
was a woman who was to become the most celebrated best-seller
writer of the era. Despite the claim that no decent woman would read her
novels, Ouida was world-famous by the time she was 28

Maria Louisa Ramé – Ouida – £200 a week on hothouse flowers

Max Beerbohm described Ouida in an appreciatory essay as "one of the miracles of modern literature". Her output was immense – "A man might as well preach Malthusianism in a rabbit-warren, as counsel Ouida to write less." She published in all 47 books, some of great length, besides innumerable magazine articles on social and literary subjects. Her supreme virtue was her readability; everyone read her from Samuel Smiles to Lord Rosebery. G. K. Chesterton was right: "Though it is impossible not to smile at Ouida, it is equally impossible not to read her." In her vitality and imaginative resources she approached genius. Syntax, like spelling, did not bother her; she wrote at a gallop in a large flowing hand. Her unconventionality shocked some, as the lush pictures of High Society which she painted in her novels shocked even more. Indeed, 'shocking' was the epithet usually applied to her, and her books were forbidden fruit in 'decent' houses. Yet she was a liberal-minded,

warm-hearted woman, and the enemy of any form of cant. Though she antagonised many by her rudeness, she had numbers of admirers, among them being Bulwer-Lytton and his son, the Viceroy of India, Ruskin, Lord Curzon, Wilfrid Scawen Blunt, Max Beerbohm, Sydney Cockerell and Norman Douglas.

Maria Louisa Ramé was born on January 1, 1839, at Bury St Edmunds. Her father Louis Ramé was French. A mysterious figure, perhaps an agent of Louis Napoleon, he would disappear for months on end, finally being lost sight of in the troubles of the Commune. Her mother, whose maiden name was Susan Sutton, was from a middle-class Bury family. 'Ouida' was the child's early attempt to pronounce 'Louisa'. From her father Ouida derived some knowledge of French, a love of literature, and a fierce belief in liberal principles. When she was 11, she accompanied her mother on a trip to Boulogne, where her father introduced her to members of the emancipated circle around Princess Laetitia Bonaparte. Already Ouida was precociously well read, given to dreaming, but determined in her resolve to improve herself. At 14 she wrote a history of England.

In 1857, finding Bury lacking in 'spirit', Ouida persuaded her grandmother and mother to move to London, where they set up house at Ravenscourt Park, Hammersmith. There she astonished the staid neighbours by walking about alone except for her great dog Beausire, a habit she considered Byronic. She was now hard at work on her romances, and her family doctor introduced her to his cousin W. Ainsworth Harrison, the editor of *Bentley's Miscellany*, who immediately saw the popular appeal of her subjects and style. The first of these novelettes, *Drag: or The Derby and What Came of It*, appeared in April and May, 1859. Within three years Ouida had published 17 stories, with such titles as *Deadly Dash, The Beauty of Vicq D'Azyr, Belles and Blackcock, Fleur-de-lys and the Two Viscounts*. Their popularity was unprecedented.

In 1861 she published her first novel, *Held in Bondage*, the story of Granville de Vigne of The Dashers, who "hunted with the Pytchley, stalked royals in the Highlands, flirted with maids of honour, supped in the Bréda Quartier, had dinners fit for princes at the Star and Garter, and pleasant hours in *cabinets particuliers* at Venours and Maison Dorée". *Strathmore* followed in 1865 and *Chandos* the next year, both highly successful; but it was the publication in 1866 of *Under Two Flags*, perhaps her most popular novel, that established Ouida at 28 as a writer of international reputation.

On the death of her grandmother in this year Ouida

and Mme Ramé moved first to 'fine apartments' in Welbeck Street, and in 1867, as a consequence of the fame and money derived from *Under Two Flags*, they took a suite in the new Langham Hotel – opposite the present headquarters of the BBC. Here in rooms with drawn curtains, lit by candles in sconces, amid great quantities of expensive exotic flowers, Ouida, a diminutive figure in gowns by Worth, held her receptions. With her mother as chaperon, she gave dinners to officers of 'the Brigades', who were encouraged to talk over their port as if in their mess. Ouida shocked female society by not withdrawing, preferring to smoke and drink with her guests.

Under Two Flags is compulsive reading, and satisfies so many of our unconscious fantasies that criticism of inaccuracy of detail is beside the point. Bertie Cecil, "one of the cracks of the Household", lived in the "delicious confusion" of bachelor luxury. 'Beauty', as Bertie was known in the Brigades, appears after his bath, "On the softest of sofas, half-dressed". His face, with its "wonderful love-me look", showed "as much delicacy and brilliancy as a woman's, handsome, thoro'bred, languid, nonchalant, with a certain latent recklessness under the impassive calm of habit . . ."

Bertie, to save others' reputations, joins the Foreign Legion, and there he encounters Cigarette, the Legion's mascot. Ouida shows, in the character of Cigarette, that thoro'bredness eclipses class distinctions. "Her mother a camp follower, her father nobody knew who, a spoilt child of the army from her birth, with a heart as bronzed as her cheek, and her respect for the laws of meum and tuum nil. Yet with odd stray, nature-sown instincts here and there of a devil-may-care nobility . . .' Ouida's descriptive sketches of Africa were uncommonly accurate and vivid. But it was the gamin figure of Cigarette, equivocal in point of sex, which touched Victorian sentiment. Her ultimate self-sacrifice saves Beauty from the firing squad. He returns to England and marriage with the fragrant Princess Corona.

Sophisticated conventional critics thought this stuff ludicrous, but Ouida and her faithful public knew better. Like George Sand, she understood the movements of the human heart and could express its unconscious desires with a very conscious power. She was now earning more than any contemporary English writer, but her expenditure on entertaining and dress was lavish. Hot-house flowers alone cost her up to £200 a week. Ambition was becoming megalomania.

In her own love affairs life dealt harshly with Ouida. At 32 she had fallen in love with the handsome Italian tenor Mario de Candia. At his triumphant farewell performance at Covent Garden in *La Favorita*, in the presence of royalty, Ouida flung from her box a bouquet which struck the stage heavily. Among the flowers was an ivory cigar-case inscribed with a quotation adapted from Dante. Though Mario was married to Guilia Grisi, the equally famous soprano, Ouida showed here her contempt for conjugal fidelity – "hearth-bound monogamy". Mario, however, did not respond to her advances. The object of her next, and greatest, passion, the

Marchese Lotteria Lotharingo della Stufa, was unmarried. A handsome courtier in attendance on the Italian royal family, he was already (unknown to Ouida when she arrived in Florence in 1871) the acknowledged *cavalier servente* of the imperious expatriate Mrs Janet Ross. Open warfare soon broke out for the possession of the Marchese, and Ouida's antics in Florence and in Rome, where she pursued him, were the talk of society.

When after ten years of procrastination he finally cut her, she was broken-hearted. In 1878 the publication of *Friendship*, a thinly disguised account of Mrs Ross's machinations to hold the Marchese, split Florence into pro- and anti-Ouida factions. Her last love was for Robert 2nd Earl of Lytton. Visiting England in 1886, Ouida was invited to stay at Knebworth. Here she proposed to Lytton that he leave his family and join her in Italy. Ultimately however, to escape her, he barricaded himself in his study.

Abroad Ouida insisted on being addressed as Mme Ouida or Mme de la Ramée. From 1874, until she was evicted in 1888, she lived in style in the Villa Farinola at Scandici outside Florence with her mother and a collection of dogs, which she refused to house-train and fed extravagantly. She took a villa in the mountains for one dog that disliked the heat. In the garden was the dogs' cemetery. Her victoria upholstered in oyster-grey and drawn by two Maremma ponies was a familiar sight in Florence. She was received at court and in the drawing-rooms of the aristocracy.

In her humanitarian zeal she wrote *A Village Commune* (1881), in support of the Italian peasantry against the abuses of bureaucracy, a book praised by Ruskin. Her evocations of Garibaldian Italy are some of her best work. Vernon Lee recognised this quality, as did Henry James, who was otherwise antipathetic both to her person and her writing – "She was *curious*, in a common, little way." Ouida was volubly opposed to vivisection and all cruelty to animals, jingoism, socialism, conscription, reporters ("the vilest spawn of the most ill-bred age"), cads, 'the new woman', Queen Victoria, and (mildly) Jews. In 1882 she produced a children's book, *Bimbi*, which she dedicated to the Prince of Naples. She considered *Bimbi* the best child's book since *Alice in Wonderland*. In the Eighties and Nineties she brought out 26 books. But she was always short of money.

After her mother's death in 1893 Ouida became increasingly misanthropic and quarrelsome, the latter trait taking the form of persistent litigation. Early this century the splendour of her former living had changed into actual poverty. She lived only for her dogs, moving from town to town to avoid the orders for muzzling them. Refusing proudly to admit her distress, she was with difficulty prevailed on to receive a Civil List pension in 1907. On January 25, 1908, Ouida died in a small house in Viareggio, and was buried in the beautiful Protestant Cemetery at Bagni di Lucca, where an unknown admirer raised a monument 'To the Writer of Incomparable Novels'. In Bury St Edmunds her friends erected a memorial, a drinking-trough for horses and dogs, with an inscription by Lord Curzon.

TELLING THE CHILDREN

By Marion Giordan

Grasping the new opportunities offered by the advent of mass publishing, the
Victorians educated, cajoled and proselytised their children through
the medium of popular literature. The sentimental illustration opposite is from a
forgotten book, *Queen of the Meadow* by Robert Ellice Mack

The Cock House at Fellsgarth by Talbot Baines Reed – one of the
increasingly popular genre of stories set in boys' public schools

The books written for Victorian children reflected a
change in direction from books of earlier years – written
in stiff, formal language, intended to educate and instruct,
and to exhort the child to lead a God-fearing life. Those
themes were still apparent in many of the children's
books published during Victoria's reign, but the presentation changed. Writers became more aware of a new, large
and profitable audience, with their own fantasies and
outlook, leading a separate life from the world of adults.

The stories were written and illustrated to be attractive
and interesting to children, and this is what makes them
different from the books which had gone before. But all
the time it was an adult's view of life they read about – a
conventional view of Victorian middle-class life. Writers
of the time were conscious that the child was potentially
an adult, and that early influences would mould him into
either the conforming or the trouble-making Victorian
adult. The books imposed on the child middle-class
patterns of hard work, endeavour, religious conformity,
submissive stay-at-home girls and 'manly' boys. It was
an orderly society where people knew their place, where
the upper classes were naturally superior, and where
the working classes were respectful and humble.

A world of a more remote kind appeared in the fables
of Aesop and La Fontaine, in the classical legends of
Greece and Rome, in the fairy stories of the brothers
Grimm, and in the Arthurian legends: brave fighters,
terrible giants, wicked old women, good and bad spirits,
people returning from long journeys, magical beasts, and
beautiful princesses. But even here there was good and
bad: wickedness was eventually punished and upright
courageous behaviour was rewarded.

It was all rather solemn. Humour was not very common, and the type of fantasy seen in Edward Lear's
Nonsense Verses was something of an exception.

Even Lewis Carroll's *Alice* stories, apparent dream
fantasies of a small girl, were firmly fixed in the setting
of a well-to-do family, with all the accoutrements of a
staff of gardeners, large well-kept grounds, croquet
parties, servants to fetch and carry, to answer the door,
and to cook and serve. Throughout both books Alice is
aware of the social differences between herself and other
classes, like the Sheep, the Mock Turtle, and Billy the
Lizard, and equally aware of her social parity with the
Red and White Queens, and with the bachelors of independent means like the White Knight, the White
Rabbit, and the Caterpillar.

For Victorian boys the fantasies were about adventure:
Mr Midshipman Easy and *Masterman Ready* by Captain
Marryat, *Coral Island* and many others by R. M.
Ballantyne, *Treasure Island* and *Kidnapped* by R. L.
Stevenson, and a great many other books of that type.
A brave boy entered a life of adventure, often on board
ship, travelling hundreds of miles to see sights no other
boy of his age had seen, enduring hardship and danger,
but emerging safe and sound and highly regarded for his
bravery and resource. He was seldom anything less than

"The enraged animal hugging him close in its huge paws" – illustrating an adventure in *Chatterbox*, the popular children's annual

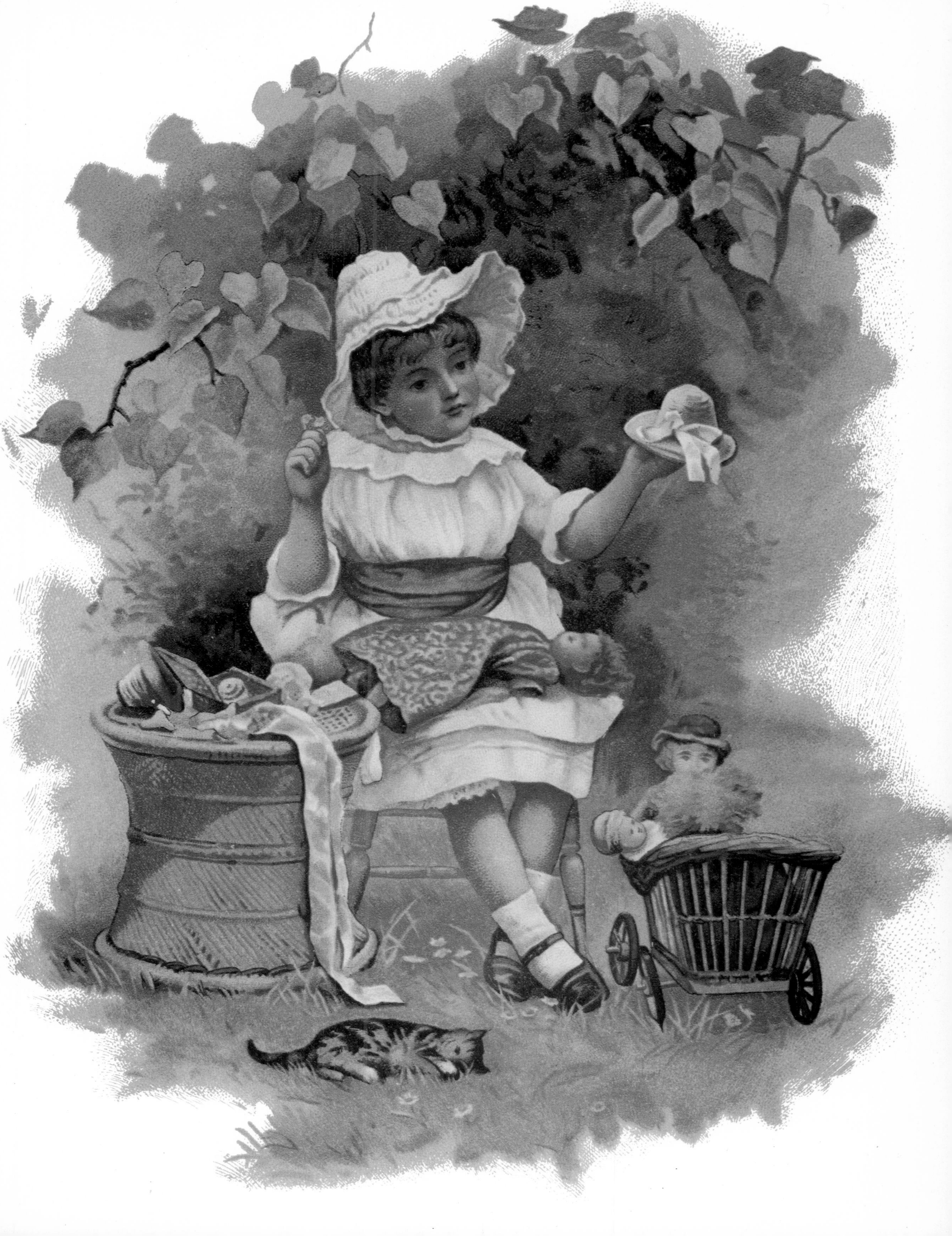

Here are two bunches of cherries. — How many are there in the first? How many in the second? How many are 3 & 2? Of what colour are these cherries? What shape are they? What is inside a cherry? Of what use are cherries? Are they good? (5 = 3 + 2.)

If 2 out of 5 cups are broken how many remain? Tell me some other easily broken vessel? What is the use of cups? Who makes them? From what are they made? (describe to the child how they are made.) (2 from 5 = 3, 5 times 1 = 5 = 5 times 1.)

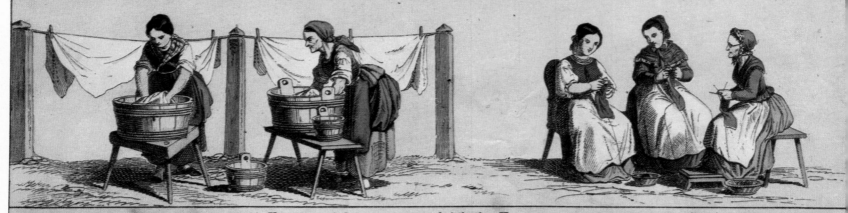

How many women are 2 women & 3 women? How many of these 5 women are knitting? How many are not knitting? What are they doing? What are they washing? How is washing done? Why is washing necessary? Point out the clothes drying? 5 = 2 & 3, 1 times 2 women 1 times 3 women = 5 women.)

honest, straightforward, fearless and popular. In the end he returned home to his family, who were impressed by his adventures, welcomed him back and granted him a status he did not have before.

This pattern of boy behaviour – boy-life, as it was called – was developed in another genre of writing for adolescents: the books of sterling example. Books like *Brave Boys Who Have Become Illustrious Men* by J. M. Darton, or *Clever Boys Who Have Become Famous Men* by Joseph Johnson, set standards of behaviour based on notable lives – missionaries, explorers, inventors, philanthropists, even politicians. The picture that emerged was that of the fine upright boy with a frank, fearless gaze. He was truly British, with blue or grey eyes and fair curly hair (or at least nothing darker than brown). He was a church-going Christian, humbly devout, dutiful to his parents, helpful to his sisters, strong in the face of temptation from the evils of drink and bad companionship. He was a hard worker gaining the respect of employers and fellow workers to win through to some degree of commercial or worldly success. *John Halifax, Gentleman* by Mrs Craik, and *Little Lord Fauntleroy*

The ability to read provided the means for making progress. Above and opposite: an early primer teaching how to read and count. A type of fantasy was represented (opposite) by the fables (*The Fable of the Fox*, by Walter Crane) and by Edward Lear's *Nonsense Verses*

by Mrs F. M. Burnett, are well-known examples; for the Victorian parent these books described the ideal Victorian son while giving the young boy a set of ambitions and achievements widely accepted at the time.

For girls the picture of life is less active and more firmly based on the home. Popular stories were lives of members of the Royal Family, particularly Queen Victoria as a young girl, and her daughter Princess Alice of Hesse, who, after having seven children in 11 years and a number of family tragedies, died nursing her family through diphtheria. Other books of exemplary lives, like *Twelve Notable Good Women* by Rosa N. Carey, and *Famous Girls* by J. M. Darton, drew on the Bible, English history, and philanthropic contemporary ladies like Florence Nightingale for their stories of lives to be emulated. The ideal girl was submissive, devoted to her mother, and accepting the authority of her father and the natural superiority of her brothers. She stayed at home,

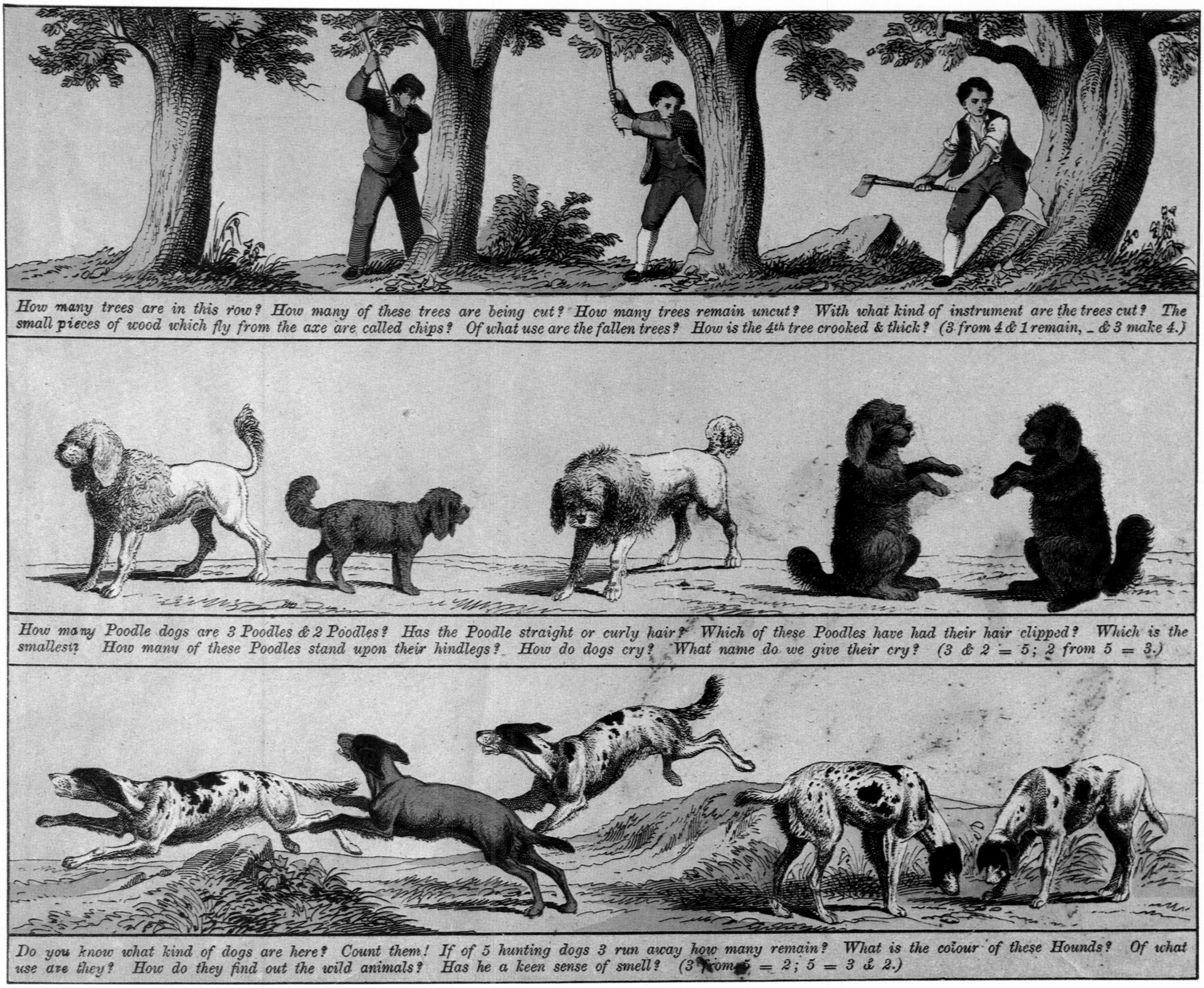
How many trees are in this row? How many of these trees are being cut? How many trees remain uncut? With what kind of instrument are the trees cut? The small pieces of wood which fly from the axe are called chips? Of what use are the fallen trees? How is the 4th tree crooked & thick? (3 from 4 & 1 remain, _ & 3 make 4.)
How many Poodle dogs are 3 Poodles & 2 Poodles? Has the Poodle straight or curly hair? Which of these Poodles have had their hair clipped? Which is the smallest? How many of these Poodles stand upon their hindlegs? How do dogs cry? What name do we give their cry? (3 & 2 = 5; 2 from 5 = 3.)
Do you know what kind of dogs are here? Count them! If of 5 hunting dogs 3 run away how many remain? What is the colour of these Hounds? Of what use are they? How do they find out the wild animals? Has he a keen sense of smell? (3 from 5 = 2; 5 = 3 & 2.)

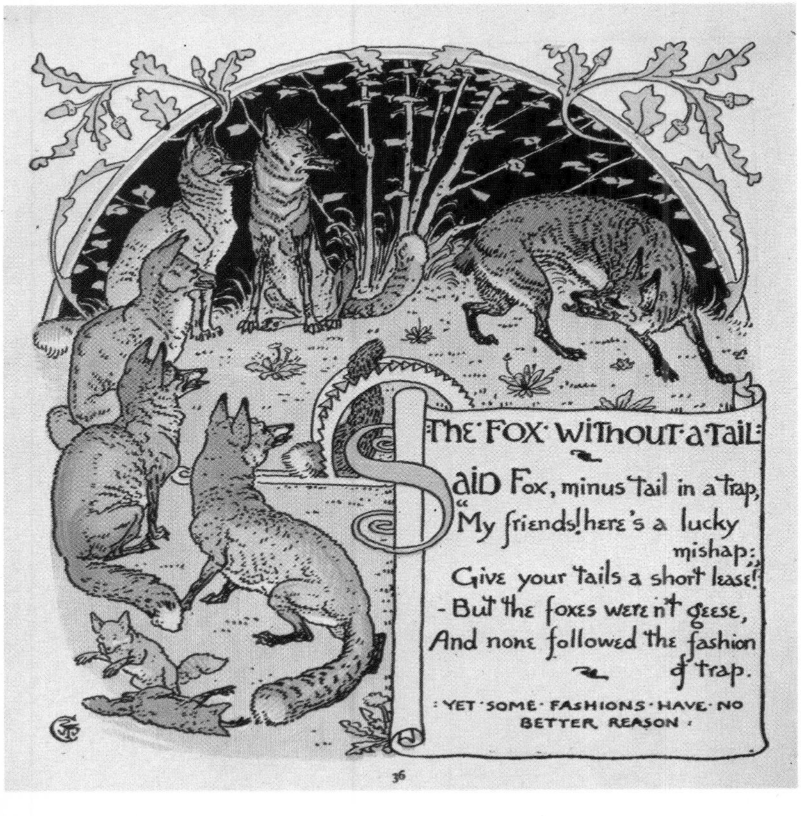
THE FOX WITHOUT A TAIL
SAID Fox, minus tail in a trap,
"My friends! here's a lucky mishap:
Give your tails a short lease!"
- But the foxes weren't geese,
And none followed the fashion of trap.
YET SOME FASHIONS HAVE NO BETTER REASON
36

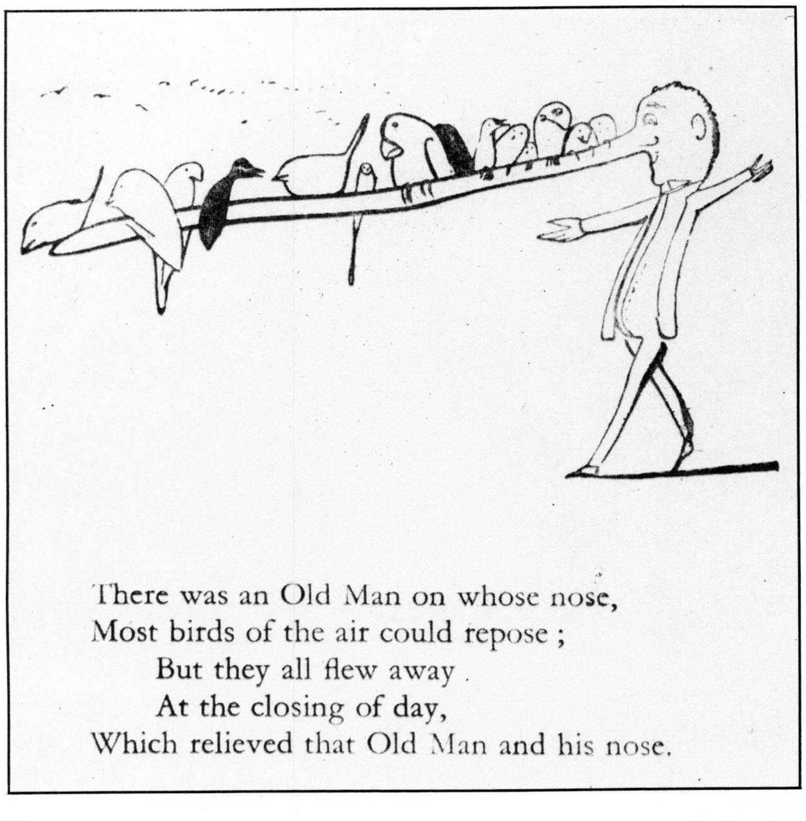
There was an Old Man on whose nose,
Most birds of the air could repose;
But they all flew away
At the closing of day,
Which relieved that Old Man and his nose.

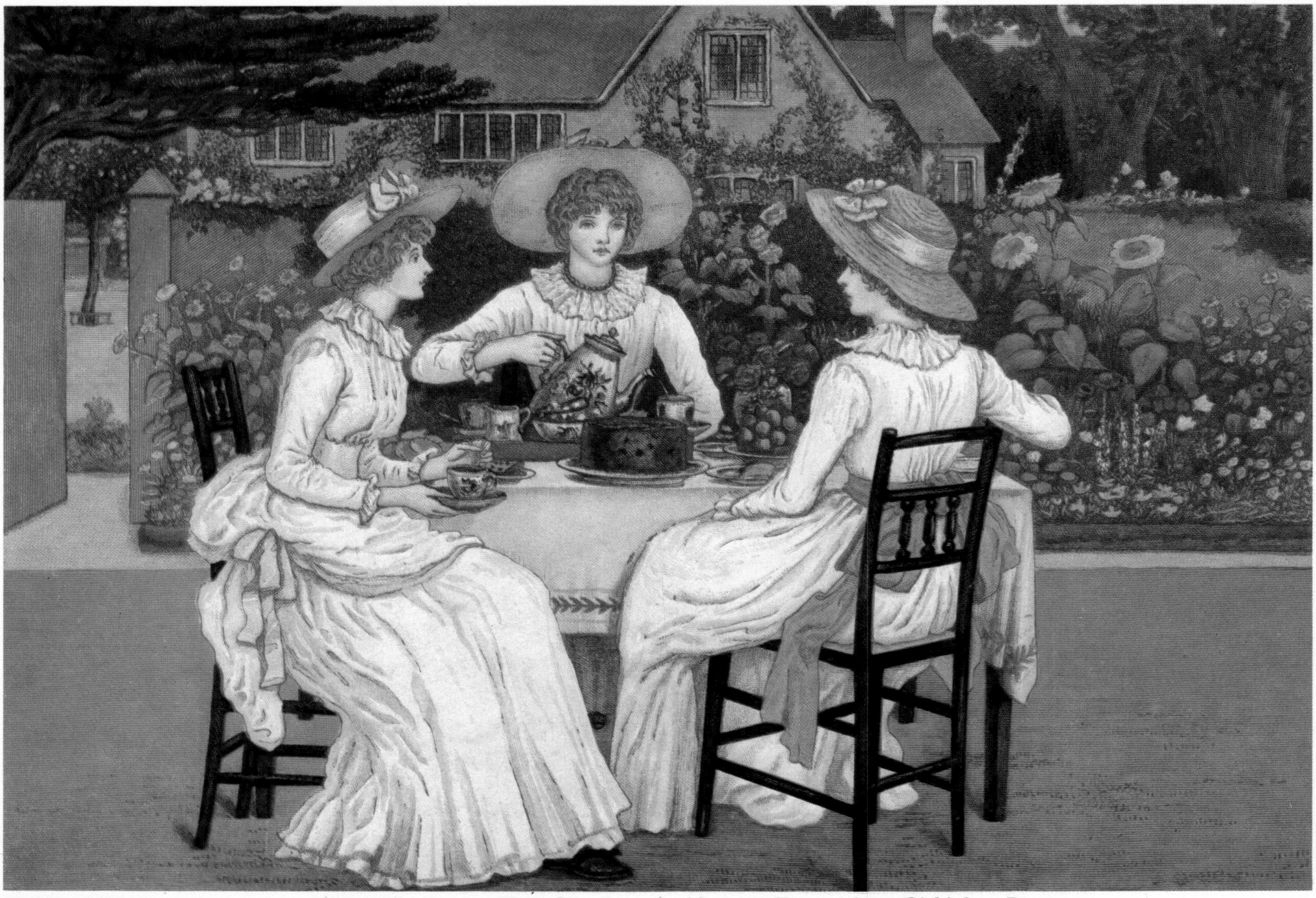

Children's books made the name of many illustrators: Kate Greenaway's *Afternoon Tea* was from *Girls' Own Paper*

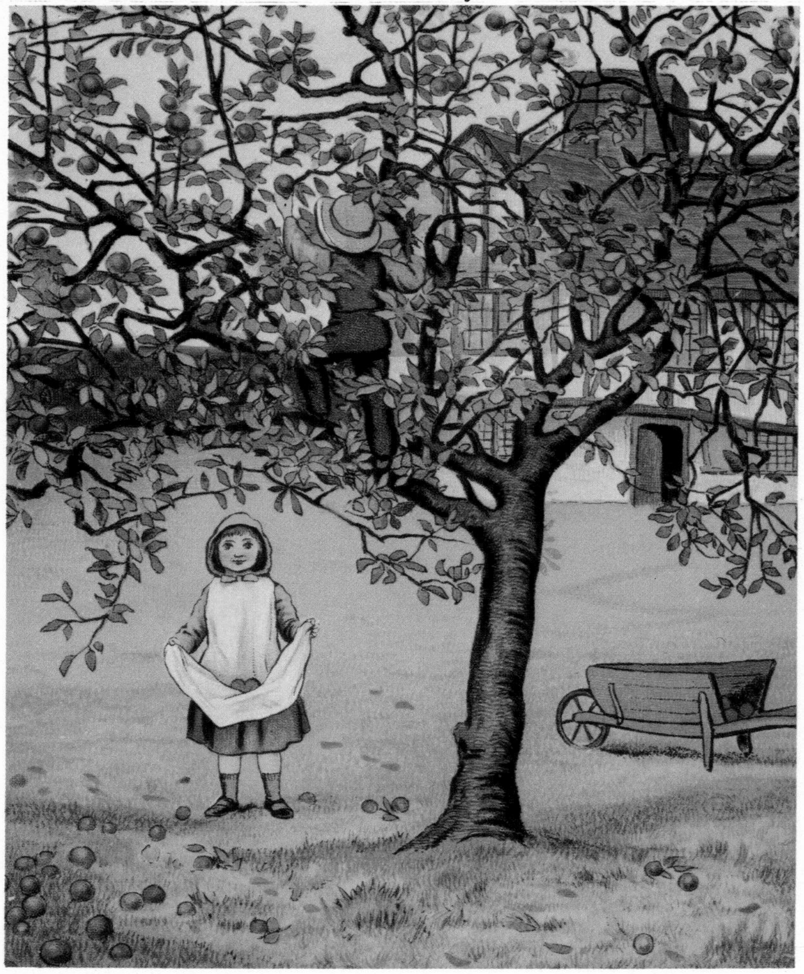

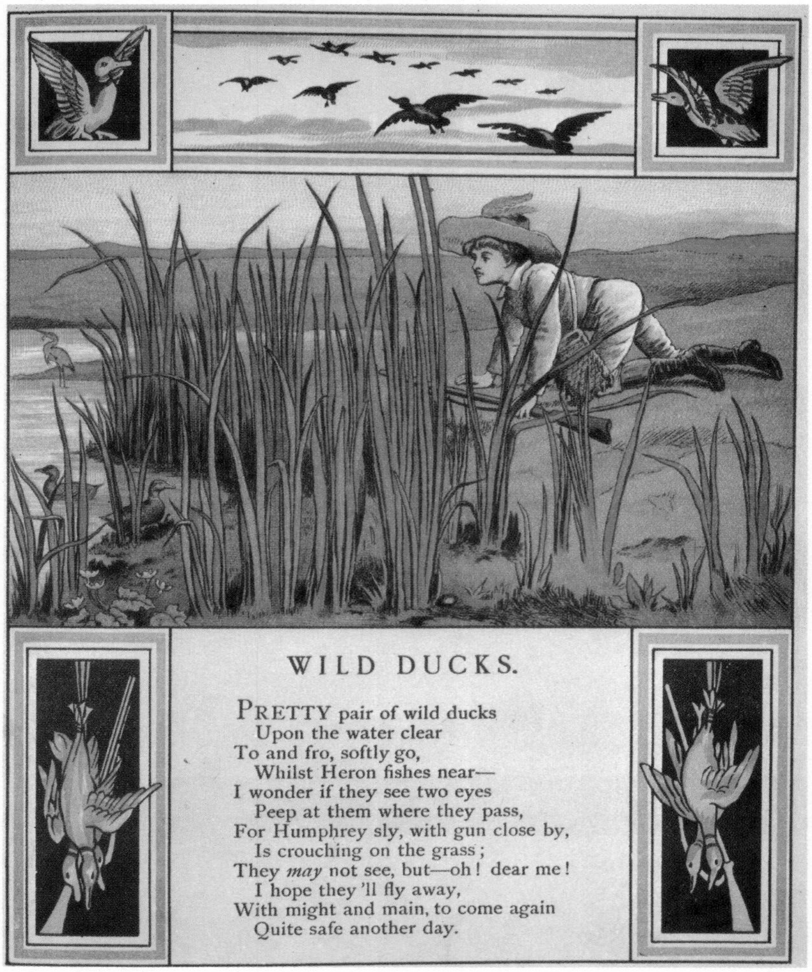
WILD DUCKS.
PRETTY pair of wild ducks
Upon the water clear
To and fro, softly go,
Whilst Heron fishes near—
I wonder if they see two eyes
Peep at them where they pass,
For Humphrey sly, with gun close by,
Is crouching on the grass;
They *may* not see, but—oh! dear me!
I hope they'll fly away,
With might and main, to come again
Quite safe another day.

'The Cottage Child' by J. G. Sowerby, and a poem decorated by Thomas Crane, both from the magazine *At Home*

often in a very restricted social setting, seeing few people and those only on a comparable social level. With luck she married within her own class, age and income group. If she had to work to help the family, it was only for a short time.

Much of this was reflected at length in *The Daisy Chain* and its sequel, *The Trial*, by Charlotte M. Yonge. Two of the elder girls in the May family of 11 children supervised the younger children, taught in Sunday school, raised money to build a church in a poor area, and looked after their father after their mother's death. The boys had less restricted lives – they went to sea, became missionaries or doctors. The girls stayed at home and it was made plain to one of them, Ethel, that she had to give up all idea of marriage to look after their father.

Illness and death, especially of children and mothers, were commonplace, and indeed children were regarded as expendable. To die of some sudden afflicting disease, to be orphaned, to be left to the care of hostile people, or to be turned out on to the streets, were real fears, as were the fears of accidents involving horses. Carriages overturned, horses bolted, someone was picked up from the ground as if lifeless and indeed might never recover. Margaret May in *The Daisy Chain* was crippled for life in an accident in which her father was severely disabled and her mother killed – a typical piling on of detail which revealed the insecurity of an apparently secure life.

The working classes in this ideal world of children's books were respectful, often with a simple religious faith. Sometimes they were drunkards, violent, neglecting their children (*His Father* by Silas Hocking). A child's death might redeem them, or perhaps a few words of prayer from a child.

The upper classes had a natural nobility of bearing, appearance, and behaviour. A popular subject was the long-lost heir, as in *The Little Duke*, by Charlotte M. Yonge. A child of apparently humble birth impresses onlookers by his natural nobility: the movement is always upwards. He is found to be the son of a noble family, unlike Pip in Dickens's *Great Expectations*, who suffered a severe emotional shock on finding that his benefactor was not a lady of good family but an escaped convict.

Whether these fantasies accurately reflected children's lives, other views of history might tell. In big towns gangs of boys lived on the streets from the age of about nine, children worked in coal mines and in factories; the books reflect very little of this. The deaths of children did not reform the working classes to religion or spur them on to work hard in order to improve their lives. As Charles Booth discovered, the very poor stayed poor. The orphan was more likely to go into the workhouse than to find himself the lost son of a wealthy man.

Children's books sold in great quantities: it was a profitable line at a time when capacity to get some kind of education meant the difference between remaining in a life of poverty or moving on. Most of the books were probably bought by parents for their children, and they favoured those stories which represented the well-ordered Victorian world. They wanted the child growing up in it to become the conforming Victorian adult.

A Tenniel illustration for Alice's Adventures in Wonderland – the fantasy is disappearing as the characters return to their places and Alice nears the end of her dream. Below: *The Farmer's Boy* by R. Caldecott – the idyllic but imaginary peace of life on the farm

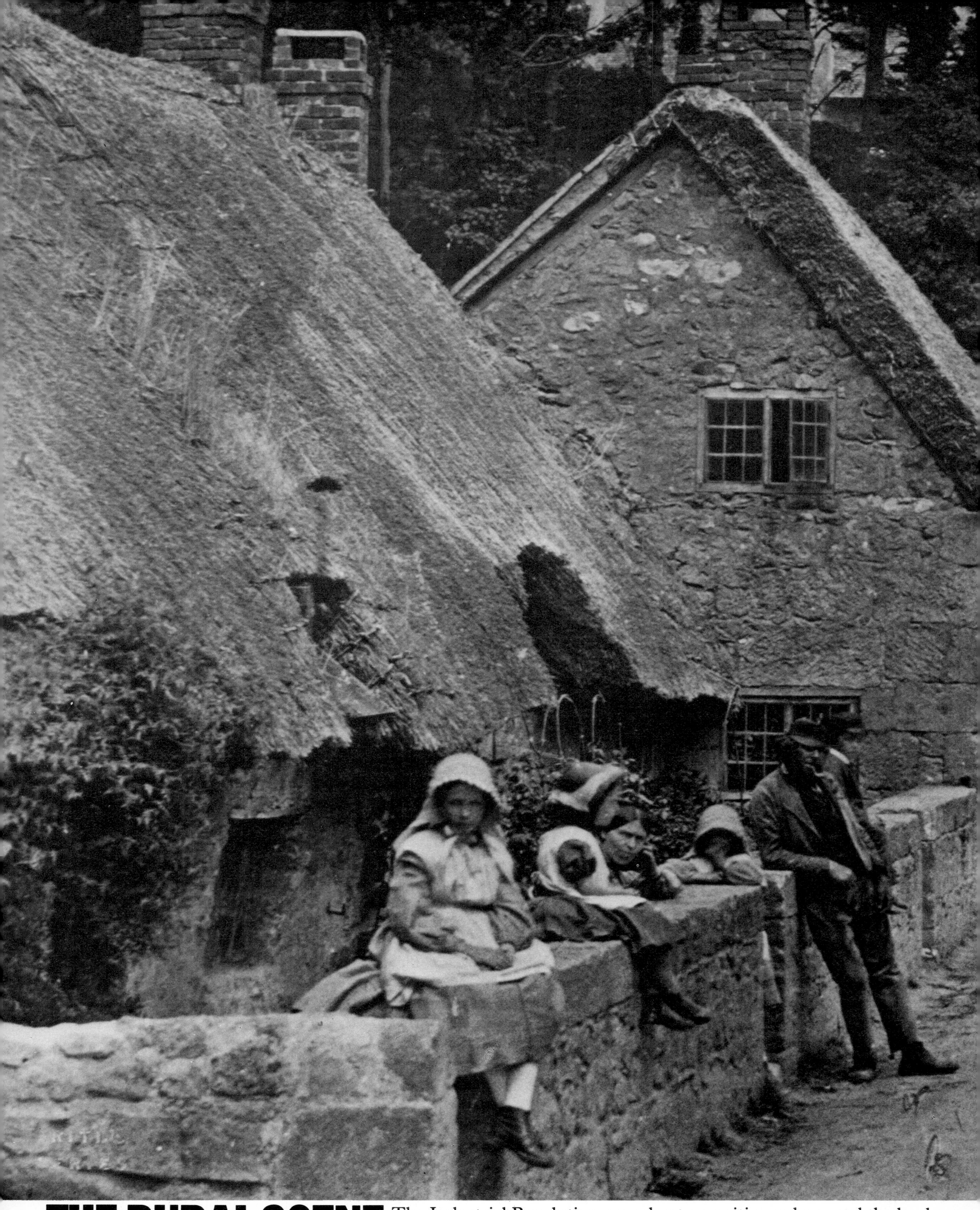

THE RURAL SCENE

The Industrial Revolution carved out new cities and ravaged the landscape
been for centuries. The Victorian period saw the passing of Britain's long a

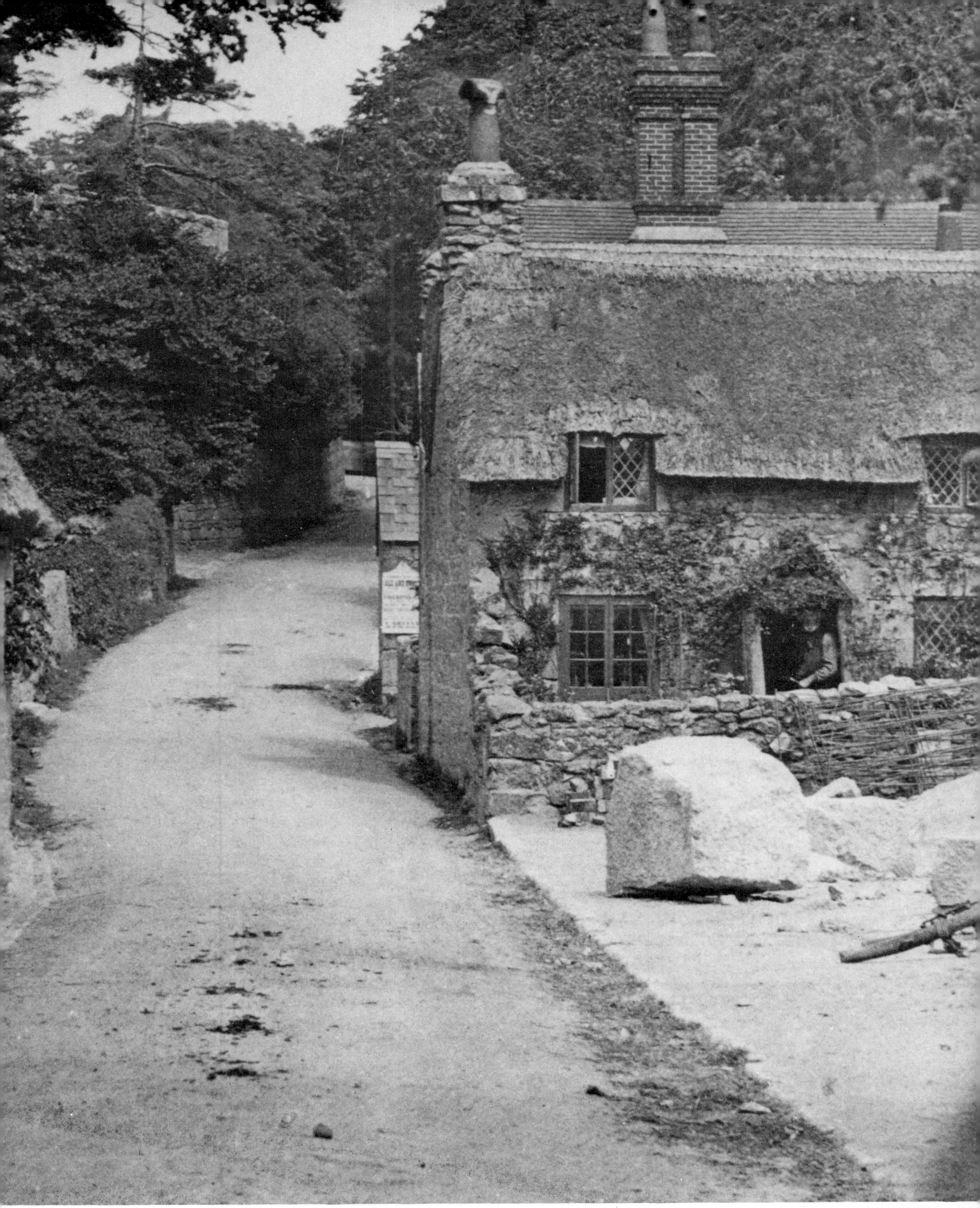

spoil heaps and factories. But away from the new industrial centres life was as placid, secure and unthreatened as it had
ian tradition – these pictures (overleaf: the town of Lewes in 1870) are the last glimpse of an all but forgotten rural past

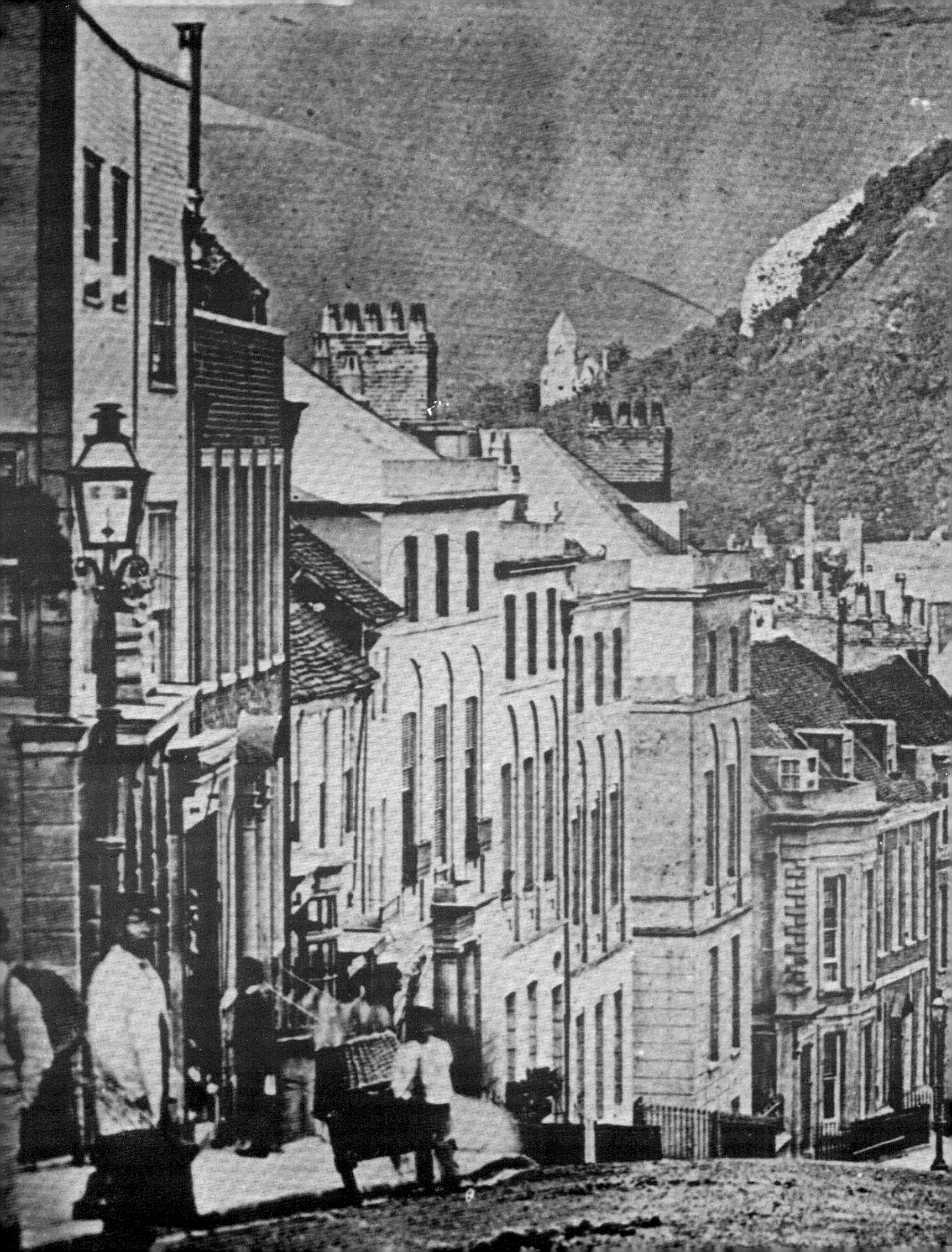

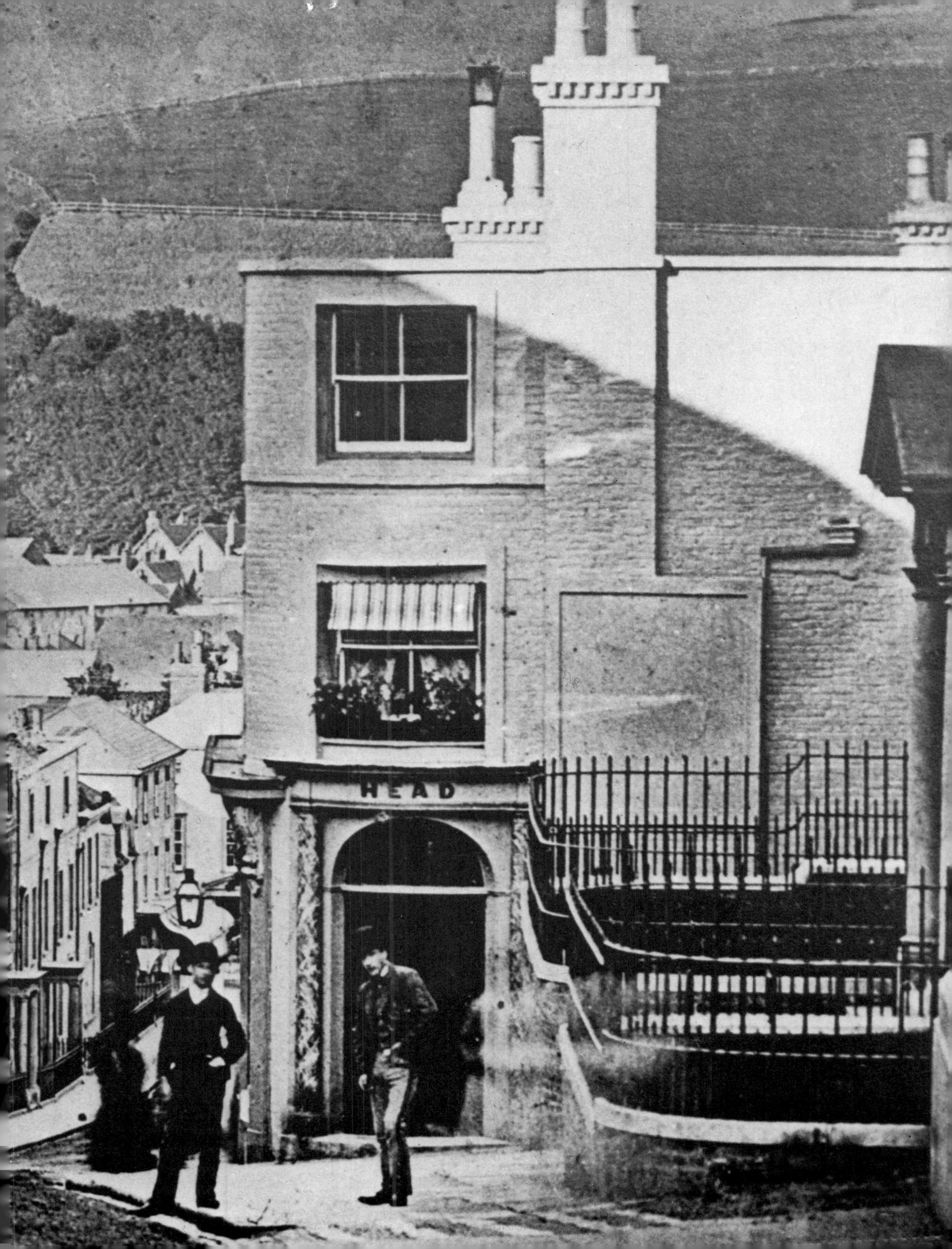
HEAD

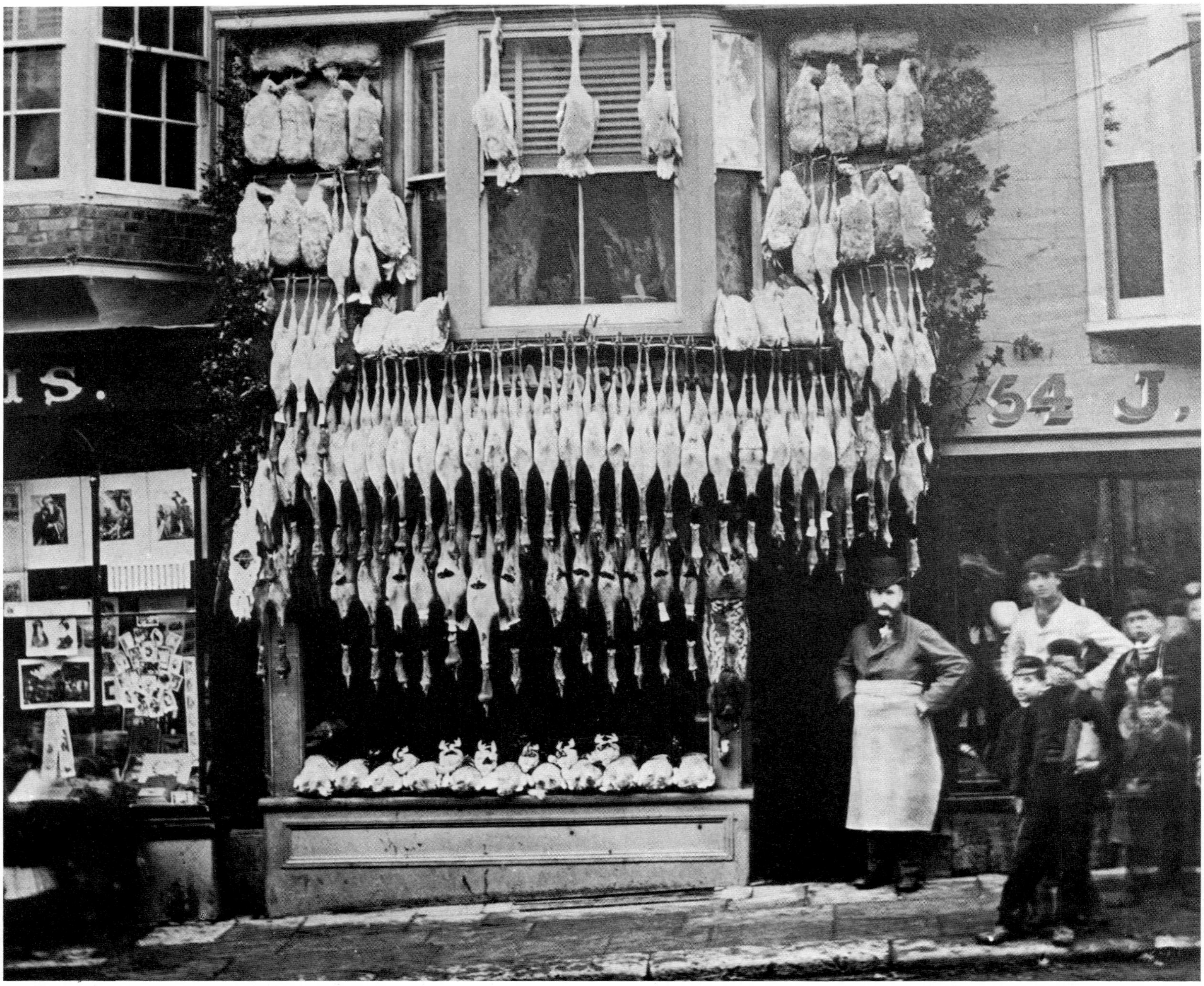
US.
54 J.

Above: the High Street butcher and poulterer made much of the Christmas season, with more than a hundred turkeys adorning the façade of his shop, even jammed up under the eaves. Opposite top: donkeys were still used as beasts of burden in the 19th century; today Ireland is the only part of the British Isles where they are still in regular employment. Here a milkmaid is bringing in the morning yield

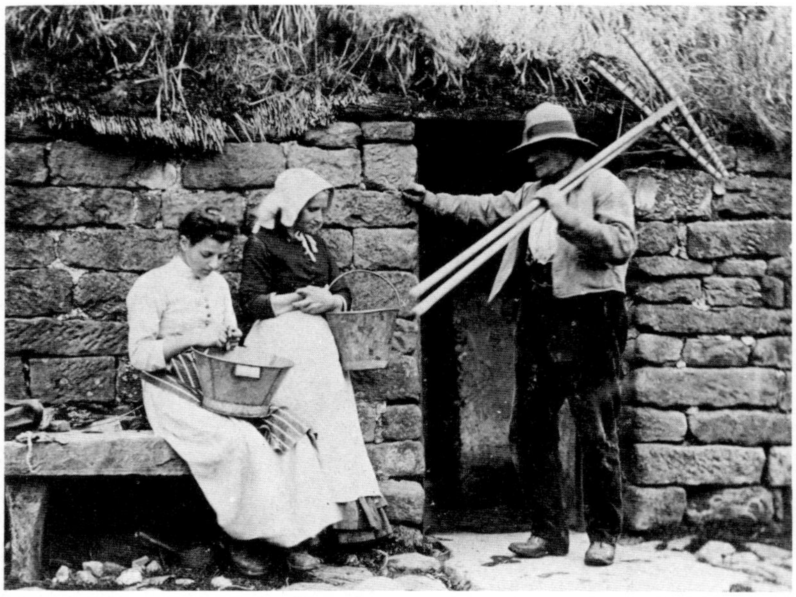

For the farmworker life followed a simple, industrious pattern of early-rising and manual toil. The cottage in the above picture is primitive and the man's wooden tools unchanged in centuries. Right: workers in the fields take a midday respite. There was an honest simplicity about the farm labourer, untainted by the exploitation and misery of the towns, and the repose and contentment that showed in the peasant faces provided an inspiration for several Victorian painters

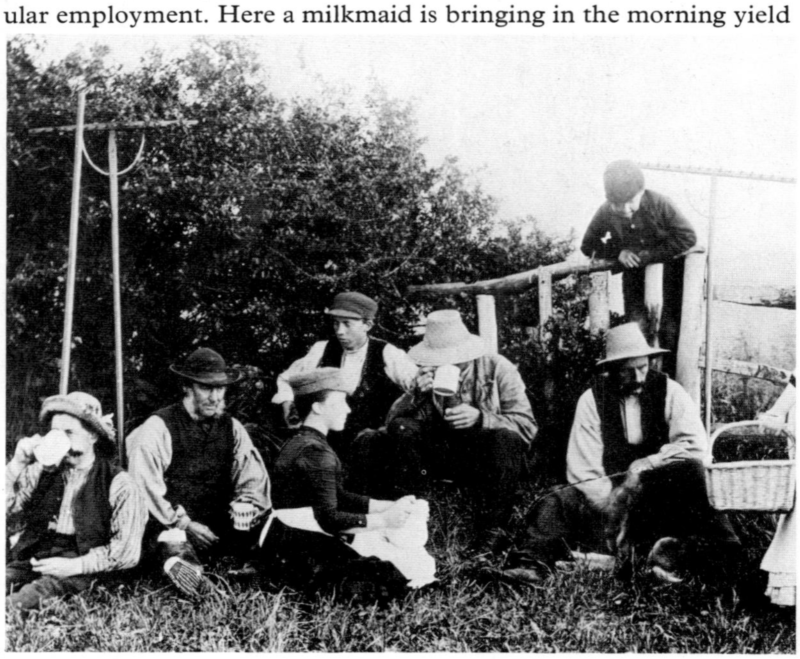

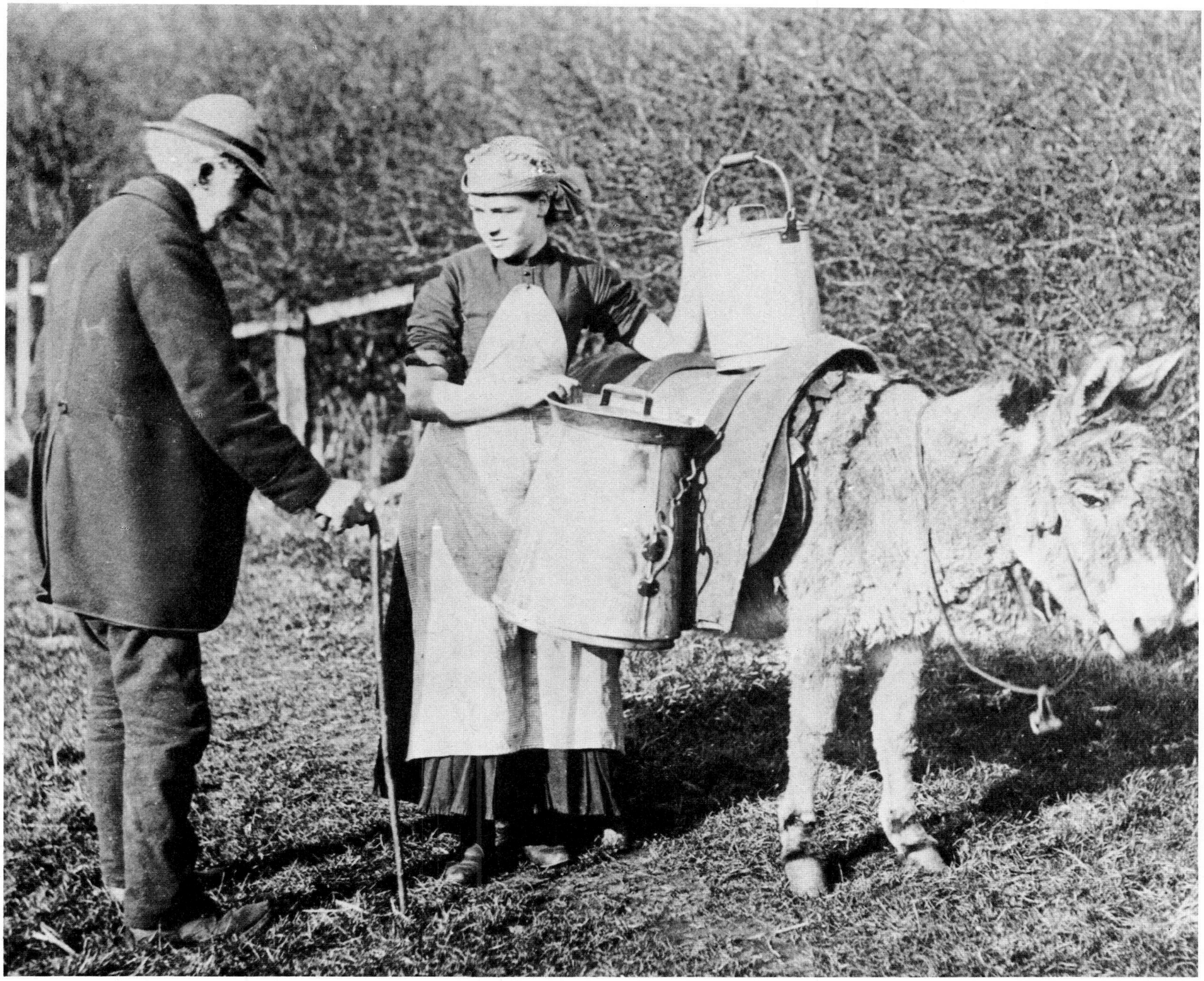

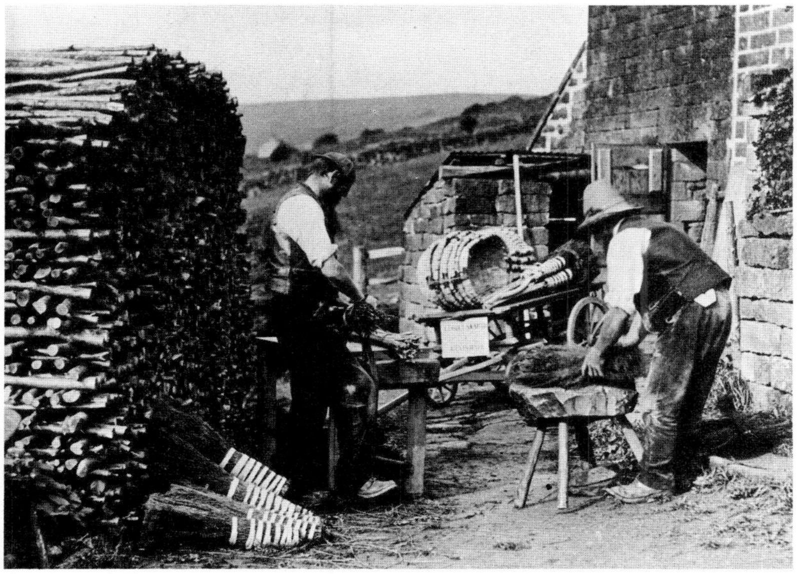

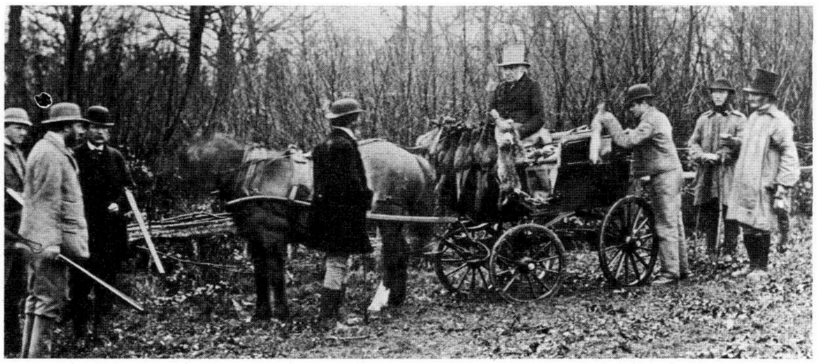

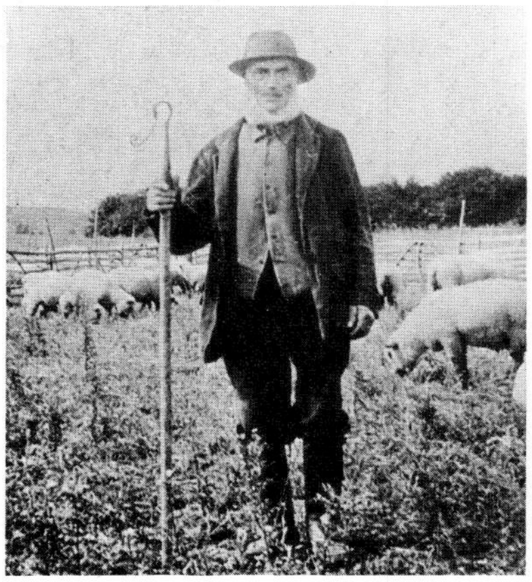

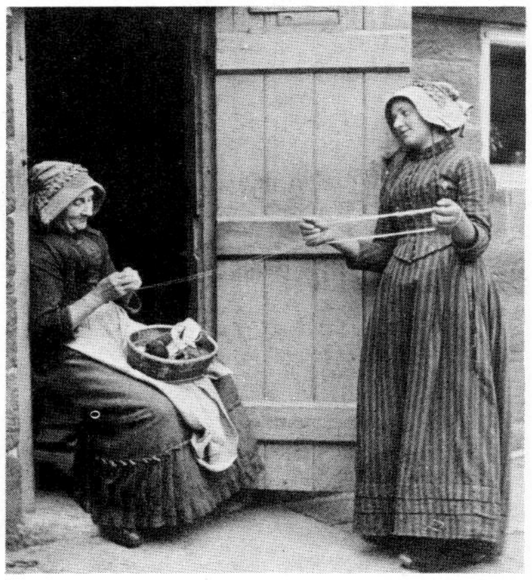

Above: broom-maker at work in Yorkshire, binding together bundles of twigs in a traditional manner. Centre right: a country squire enjoying a day out with the guns. His modest retinue includes a coachman, a groom, three gamekeepers and a couple of other servants. Right and far right: the grassroots of Yorkshire's prosperous wool trade. A shepherd with his flock, and women winding wool by a farm door; though posed, the women convey a feeling of rural domesticity

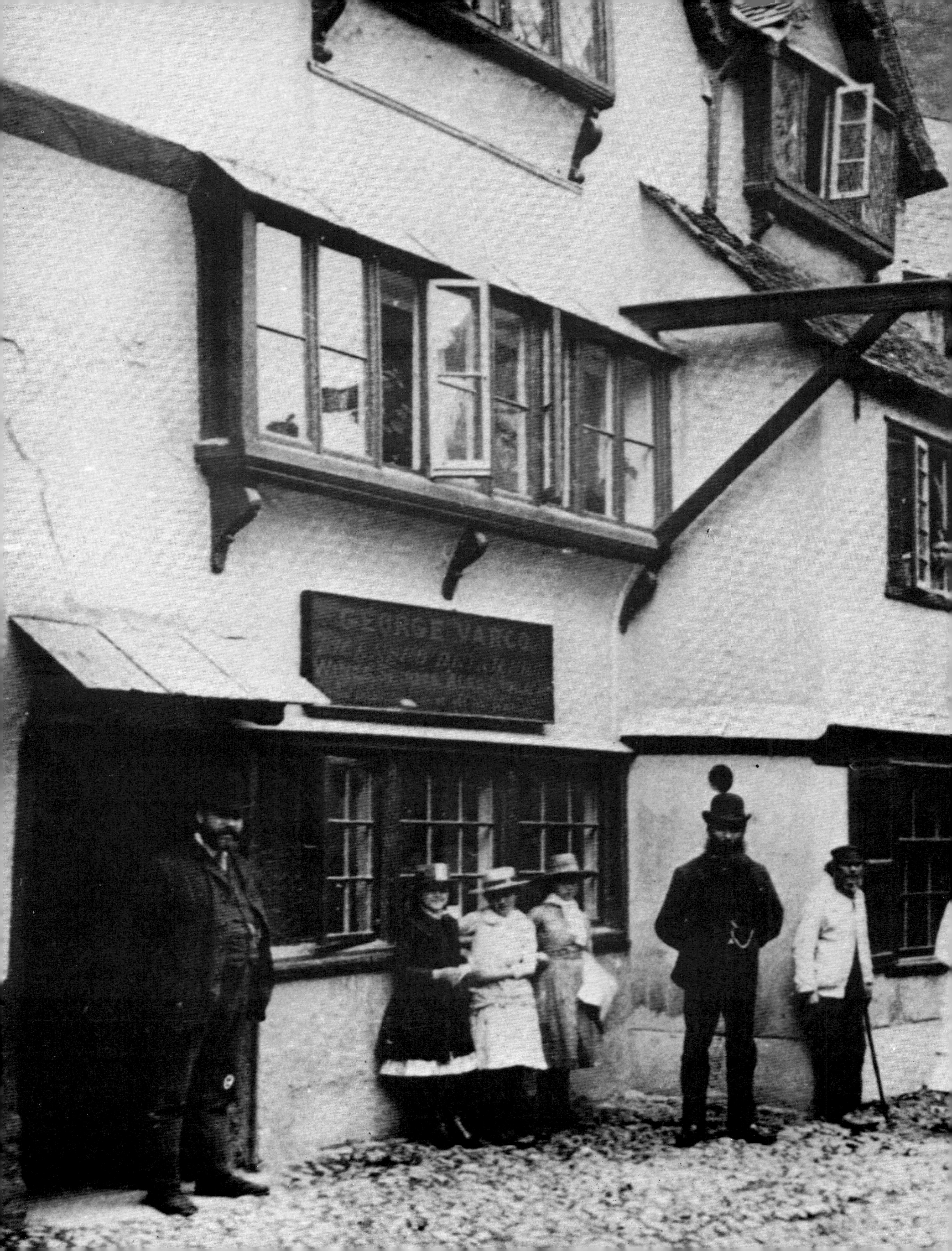
GEORGE VARCO

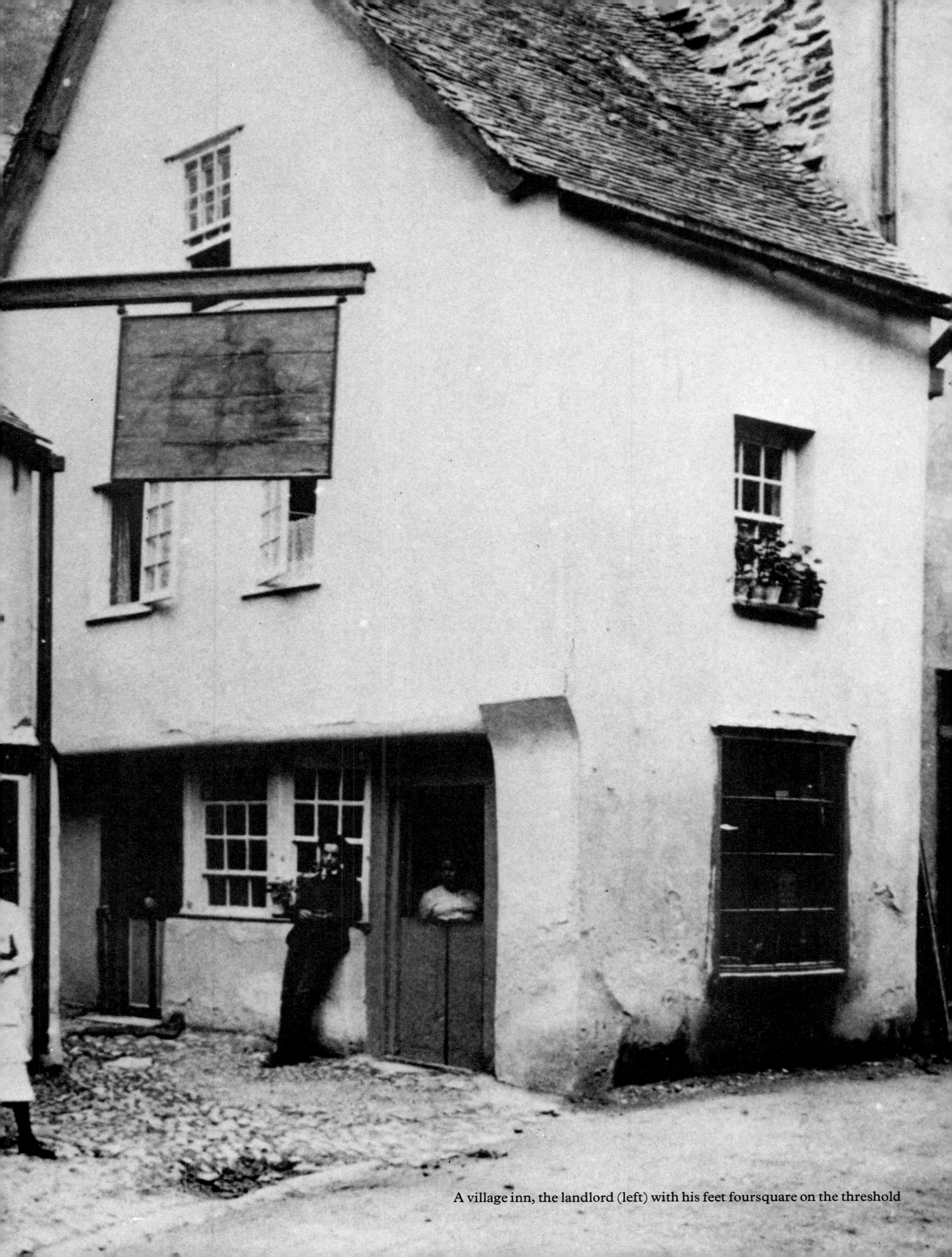

A village inn, the landlord (left) with his feet foursquare on the threshold

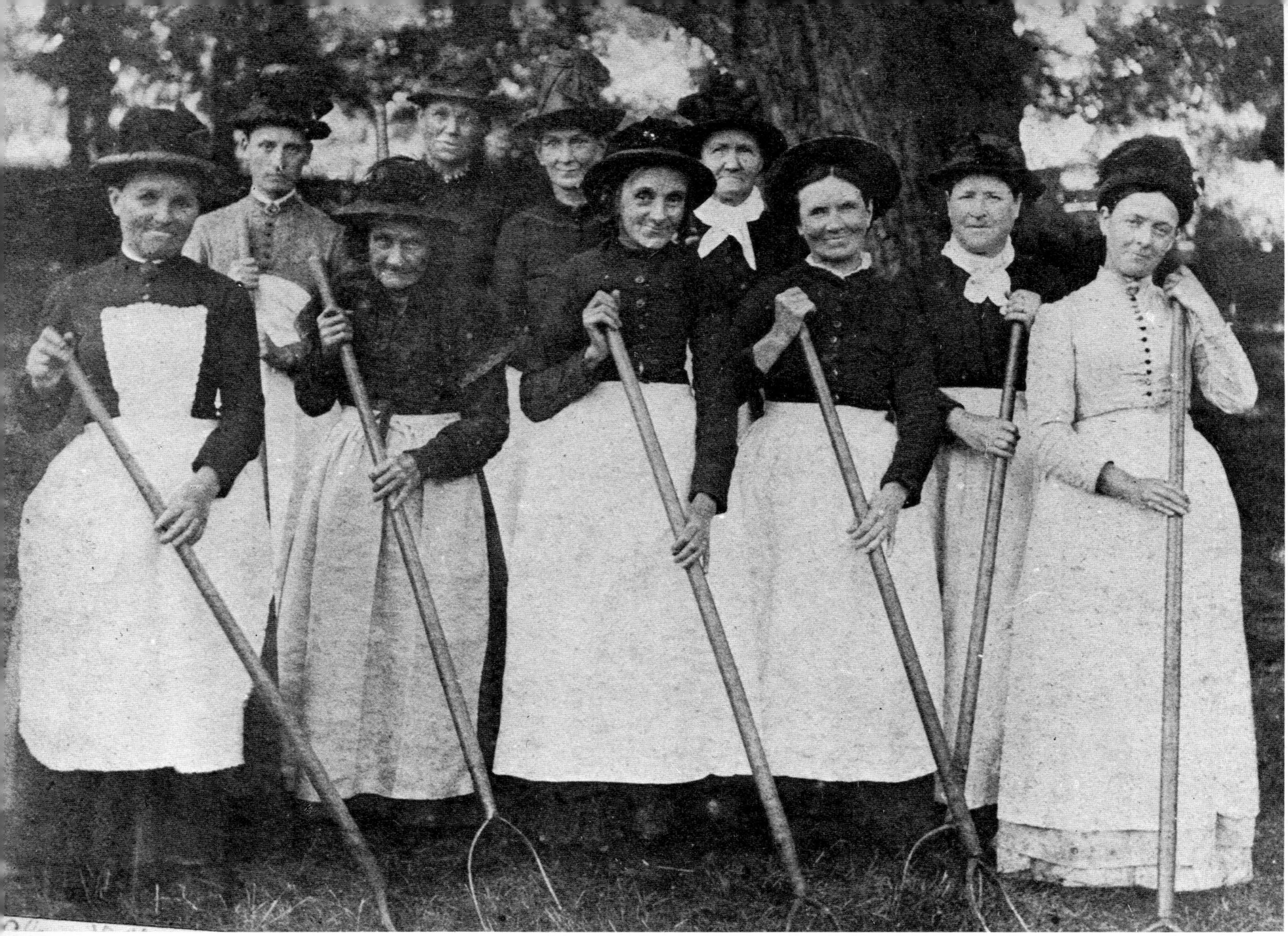

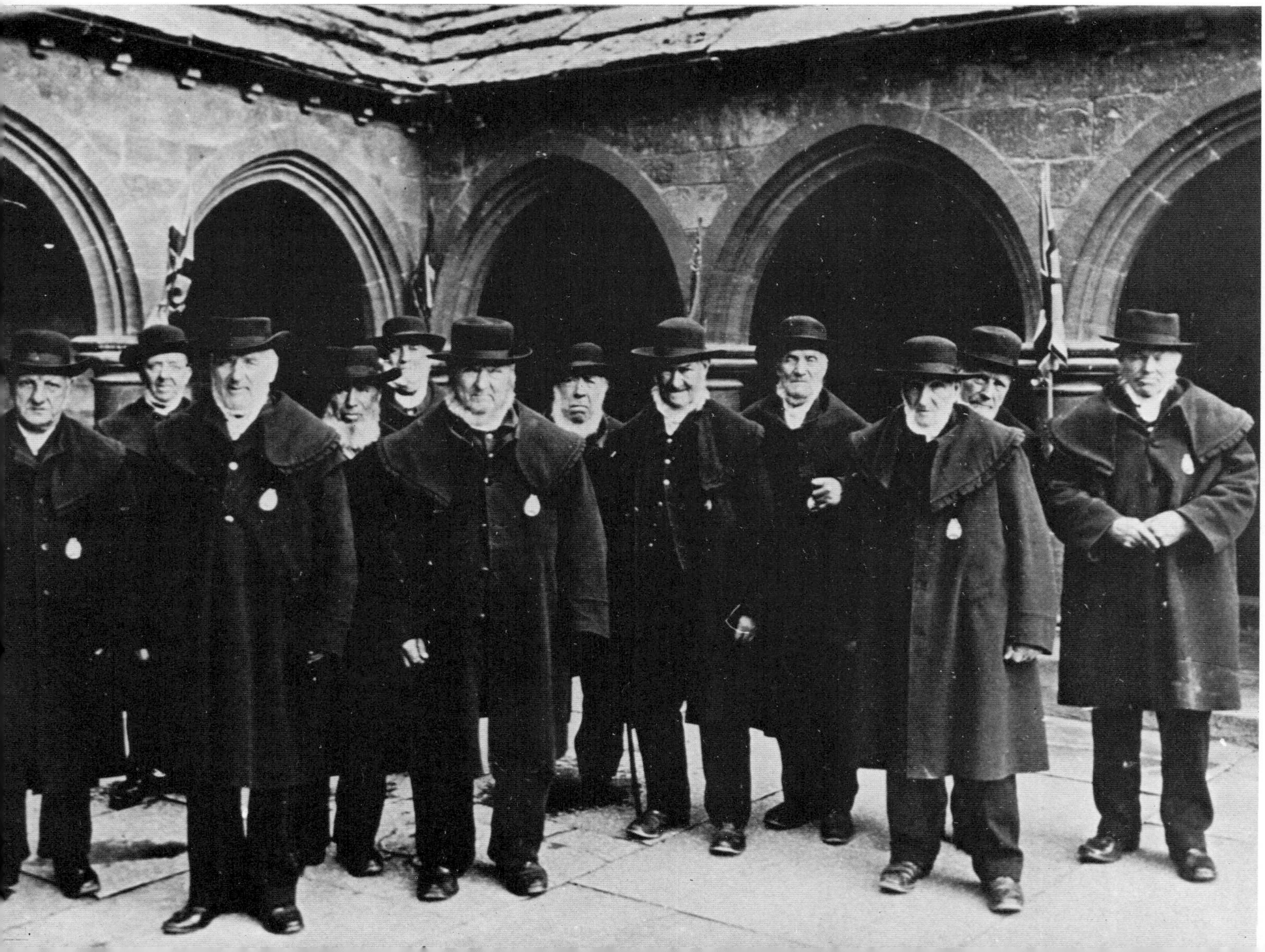

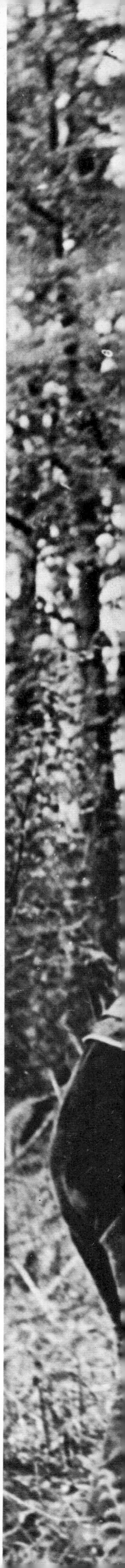

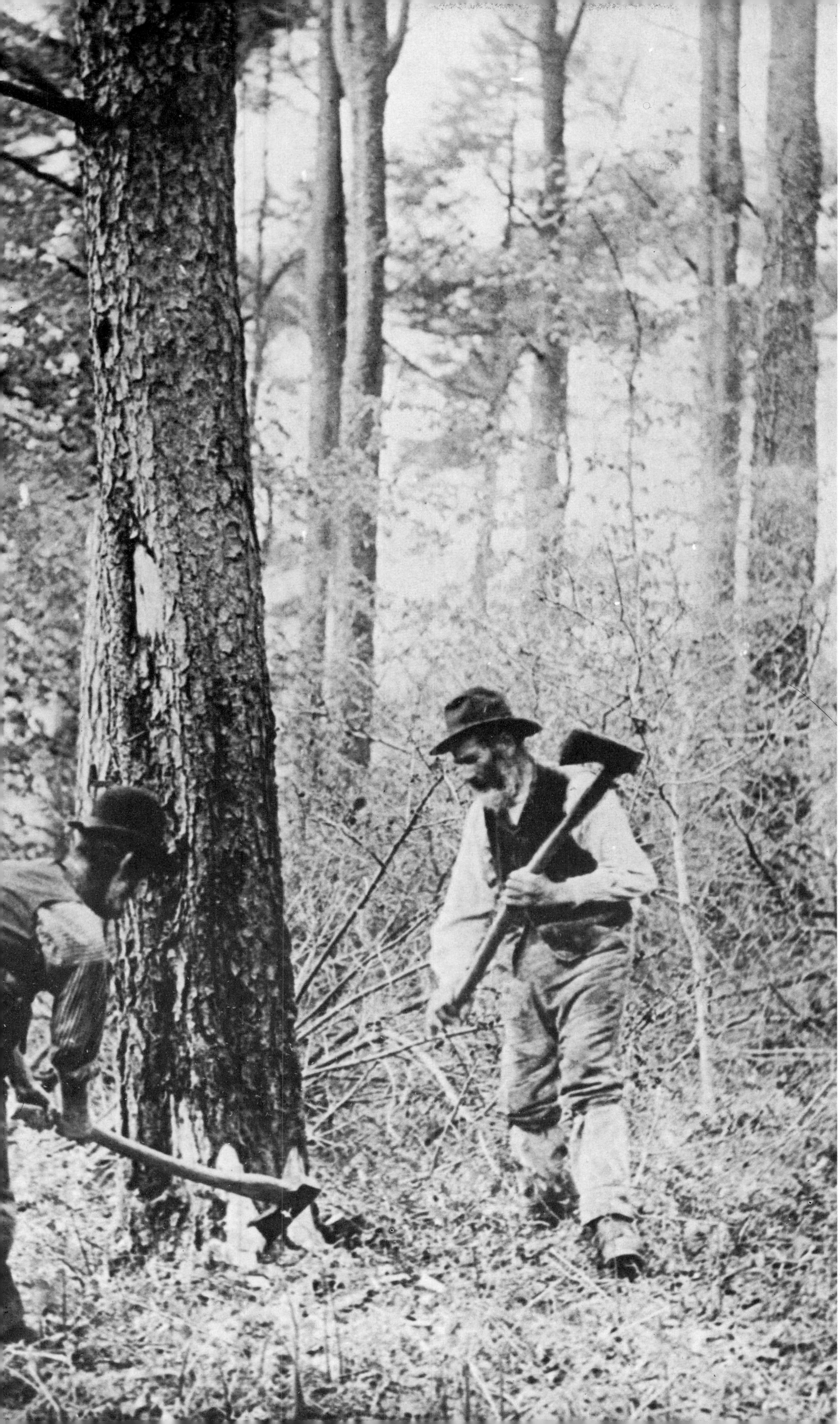

Women toiled in the fields as much as men, as the parade of aproned ladies armed with pitchforks testifies (opposite top). Below, a group of country coachmen pose in the uniform of their trade. Left: two woodmen, in the days before the invention of bandsaws, attack a diseased tree with axes

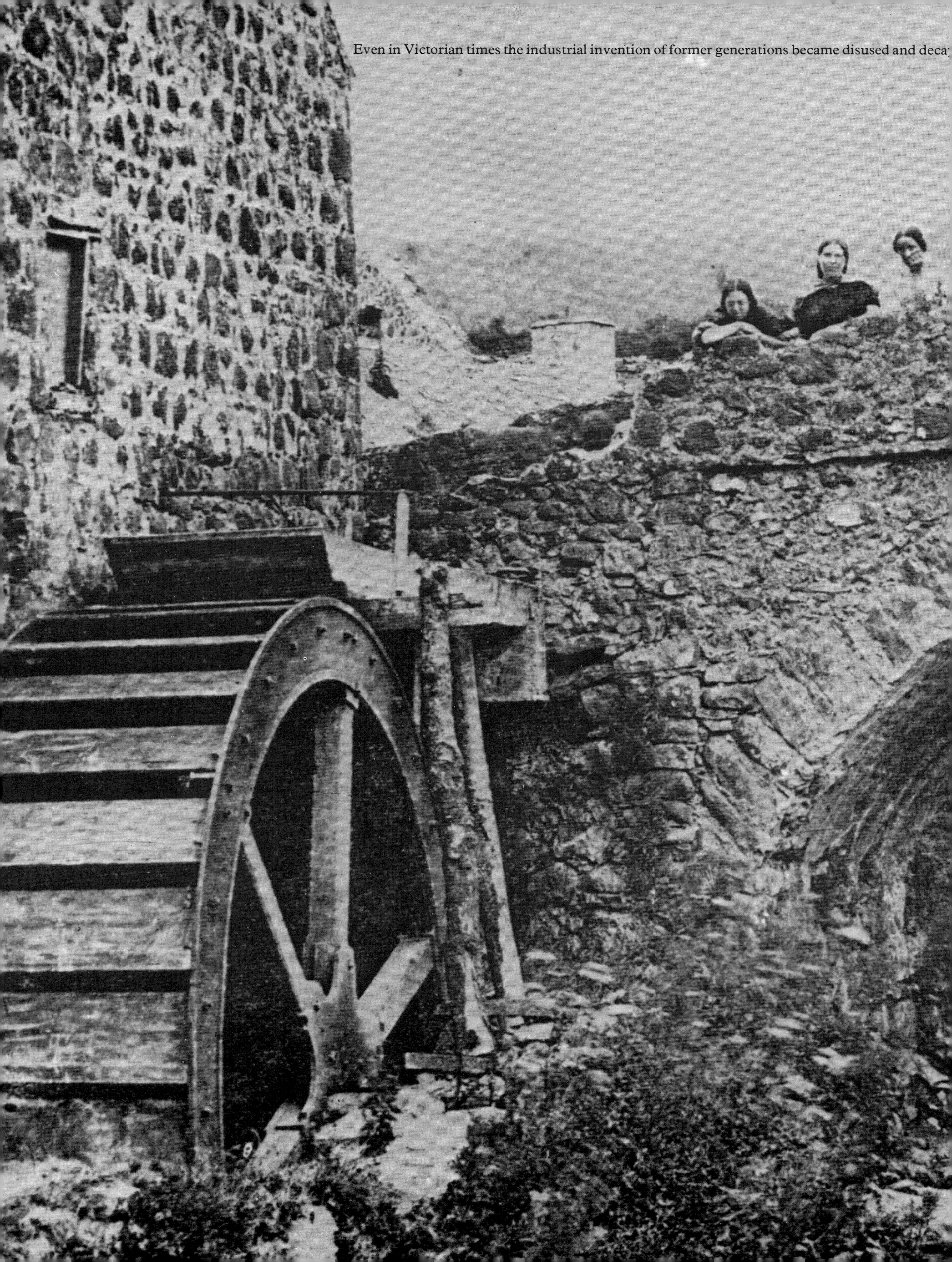

Even in Victorian times the industrial invention of former generations became disused and deca

.is derelict waterwheel stood by a northern stream

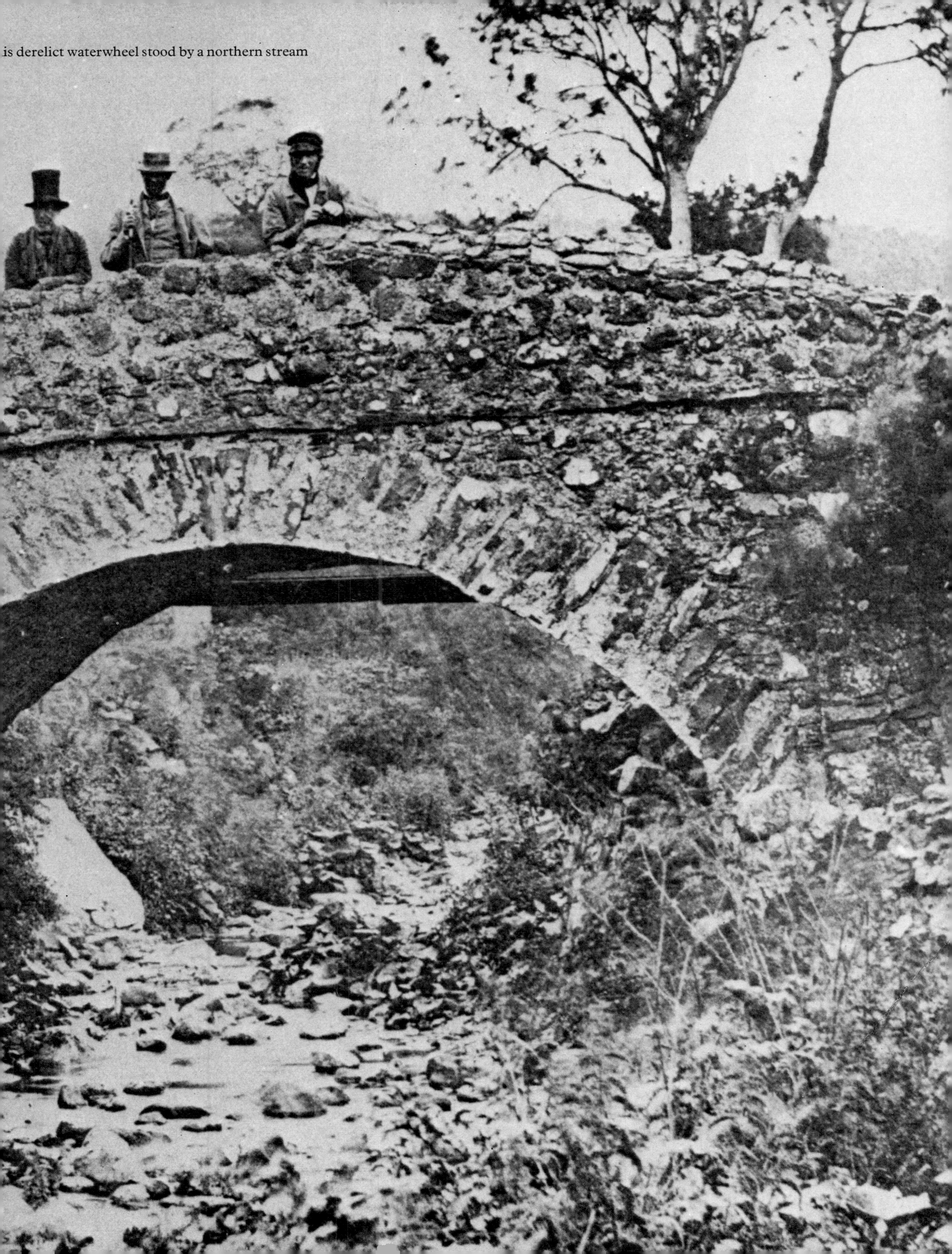

THE VICTORIAN CHRISTMAS

By John Pudney

The Victorians did not invent Christmas; but with the help of the Prince Consort,
Charles Dickens, and a growing breed of enterprising tradesmen, they
succeeded in converting the winter solstice into the year's most important family festival

Did Dickens invent Christmas? Did the Prince Consort? Such suspicions are bandied about during the annual debunking season, the opening of which is marked by those self-righteous Personal ads in *The Times* by non-senders of cards.

The debunking is not new in itself, though it has had to swell up to meet the prodigious and sometimes grotesque manifestations of the times. After all, Dickens was referring to the Christmas tree in 1850 as "the new German Toy". Disillusionment starts with the suspension of belief in Father Christmas, which for the tiniest tots means merely an autumnal pram ride to the nearest shopping centre, and goes on from there.

Yet no amount of commercialisation on the one hand, or of exposure and rationalisation on the other, can destroy a mystique which has infected so many civilisations of mankind for thousands of generations at the time of the winter solstice. Christmas is always being modified by such people as Charles Dickens or the Prince Consort, but basically it is instinctive in Western Man, its spirit rooted in pre-Christian history. Cromwell or Lenin may spike this instinct: yet it survives and flourishes. It is surely a Good Thing. Enemy armies have

'Three Generations' – church on Christmas morning, 1883

fraternised on Christmas Day. People even hesitate to bomb one another. However disenchanting the plastic trees, the chemical snow, the mini-skirted Father Christmasettes, there is the fundamental comfort that we are all trying to love, not to kill, one another.

The overall image is benign. It is in the application of it spiritually, mentally, physically that one can get adrift. Fitting facts, circumstances, people, personality to the image: breaking the image down to human needs: selecting. Too often Christmas is regarded as a static image. Yet even with its unvarying ingredients and atmospheric adornments, and the chorus of "we always do this and that", no two Christmases are ever exactly alike. Age alone is a potent variant; one only has to think of one's attitude to Christmas age ten, 20, 30 and so on, and of the groupings and regroupings of family and domestic life, to realise how personally this is a variable feast. It demands flexibility. It thrives on novelty and surprise as well as revival and tradition. You don't really want that Christmas of your childhood.

No wonder then that there has been so much change over the years in this continuing festival. Changes in attitude, customs, observances, habits, equipment, magic and myth. Though the commonest ingredient of all is a longing for the "good old days", the present offers an abundance and diversity of festival element which can never have been approached in the past. There is indeed surfeit. Discrimination is a necessity. Yet everything basic has its roots in the tradition of good will and owes only its promotion and slant to the convivial Dickens and the home-loving great-great-grandfather of our present Queen.

The Prince Consort's promotion of the Christmas tree was not a conscious effort to improve the festivities of the nation he had married into. Nor was he the first with it, though his introduction of it to the royal family circle at Windsor in 1841 was to lead to widespread popularity. There were already merchants settled in Manchester who had transplanted the tree custom from Northern Europe where it had been popular for centuries.

Prince Albert's trees, and his family, proliferated during the following years, a trend soon reflected in the trade. By the early 1850s Christmas trees in their hundreds were changing hands in Covent Garden market.

These novelties were in fact but a variation of a most ancient theme, the symbolic display of evergreens at the time of the winter solstice. Throughout Europe and Western Asia people have traditionally held festival in mid-winter with fire and light and with green boughs and tree branches.

In Britain in mediaeval times there were the 12 days of holiday for Christmas with holly, ivy, bay, rosemary and

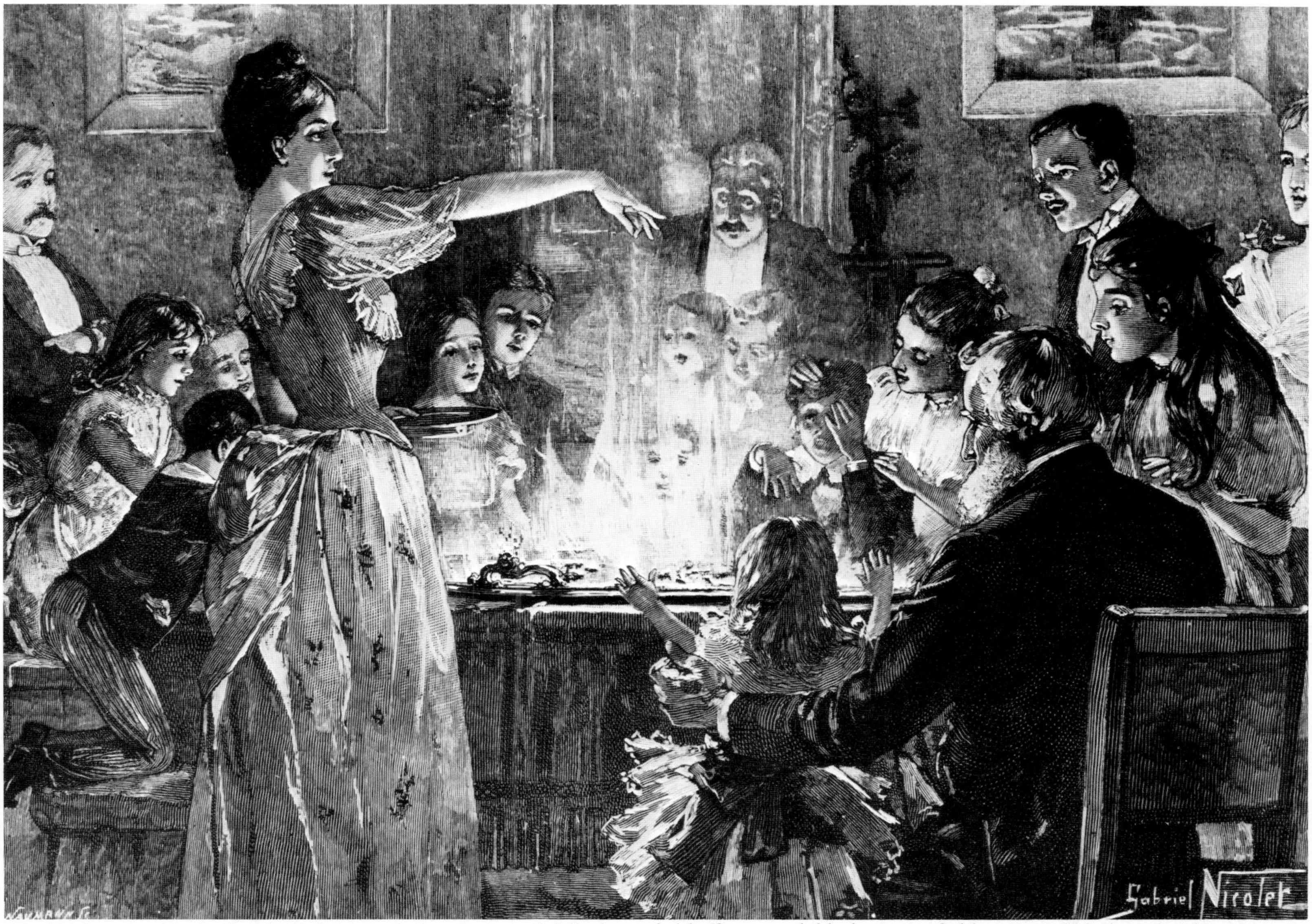
Gabriel Nicolet
The Dickensian ideal – "such dinings, such dancings, such blind-man's bluffings, such kissing-out of old years and kissings-in of new ones"

mistletoe in profusion. Mistletoe was for kissing but never for church decoration. John Stow in his *Survey of London* written in the 16th century leaves no doubt about the traditional evergreens. ". . . against the feast of Christmas every man's house, also their parish churches, were decked with holme, ivy, bayes and whatsoever the season afforded to be green."

There is abundant proof of the potency of the evergreens for our ancestors in the form of the carol. Defined originally as a ring dance with vocal accompaniment the carol has suffered its ups and downs. Chaucer associated "karolying" with an invitation "to dauncen". As a popular form of self-expression they waxed with the ballads in the 15th century and flourished throughout the 16th.

"The truth is that carols are a national creation," writes Percy Dearmer. ". . . The carol arose with the ballad in the 15th century, because people wanted something less severe than the old Latin office hymns, something more vivacious than the plainsong melodies."

So we in this century are the beneficiaries of the treasure of pop poetry, often garlanded with traditional greenery.

"The holly and the ivy,
When they are both full grown,
Of all the trees that are in the wood,
The holly bears the crown."*

We all know it, though some of us may not be aware of its pagan origins and the delightful symbolism of the masculine holly and the feminine ivy. But a century ago it would have been quite unfamiliar, for carols suffered such a decline during the 17th and 18th centuries that they were almost extinct at the time of the boyhood of Charles Dickens, when William Hone in *The Everyday Book* was writing: "Carols begin to be spoken of as not belonging to this century . . ."

Fortunately, about that time in the 1820s a versatile character named Gilbert Gavies came to the rescue and published a collection of traditional carols. Gavies was a president of the Royal Society, M.P. for Bodmin (many

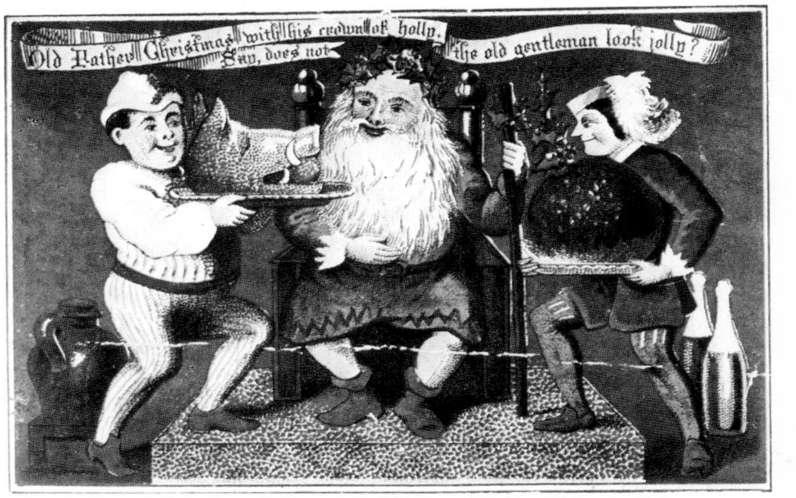
Old Father Christmas with his crown of holly.
Say, does not
the old gentleman look jolly?
Boar's head and plum pudding – the English tradition

**Oxford Book of Carols,* O.U.P.

HAPPY LITTLE FACES! WE WISH YOU ALL THE JOY THAT A NEW YEAR BRINGS, FOR EVERY GIRL AND BOY
Hand-in-hand with Christmas – the New Year festivities

carols had been preserved in Cornwall), was associated with Sir Humphrey Davy and was responsible for choosing Brunel's design for the Clifton Suspension Bridge. He wrote of carols being sung in the west of England "up to the latter end of the late century". During the Victorian age the carol gradually re-emerged, though it was not until the end of the century that Cecil Sharp rescued *The Holly and the Ivy* from oblivion. Charles Dickens's choice of *A Christmas Carol* as the title of the book which did so much to establish the Victorian Christmas had little or nothing to do with the specific promotion of the carol as a musical item. Dickens did not invent this or any other aspect of Christmas. Rather he brought together all the traditional threads of festivity, folklore, myth, custom and orchestrated them on a grand scale.

He was not just a propagandist finding good material in Christmas and writing in cold blood. He believed passionately in the season of goodwill. He identified himself with the whole event. In his study of the youth of the author, *The Making of Charles Dickens*, Christopher Hibbert writes: "There was one memorable Christmas, in particular, the one after he finished *A Christmas Carol*. He had been utterly absorbed in the theme of that book, throwing himself into the writing of it with an enthusiasm that he had scarcely ever felt before, sharing the joys and sorrows of his characters as though they were his own. He had always been liable to do this, being as moved to tears by the tragedy of Little Nell, as to laughter by the comedy of his letters – George Putnam noticed in America how, when he was writing to his friends at home, Dickens' face would be 'convulsed with laughter at his own fun'. Now, over *A Christmas Carol*, he admitted that he 'wept and laughed, and wept again, and excited himself in a most extraordinary manner in the composition; and thinking whereof he walked about the back streets of London 15 and 20 miles many a night when all sober folks had gone to bed'. He had finished it in less than two months, despite a great deal of unaccustomed rewriting, and then, again in his own words, 'broke out like a madman'.

"And so at Christmas that year there were 'such dinings, such dancings, such conjurings, such blindman's buffings, such theatregoings, such kissings-out of old years and kissings-in of new ones' as had ever taken place 'in these parts before'. And at a children's party at the Macreadys' house his excitement was feverish. He performed a country dance with Mrs Macready; he displayed his remarkable skill as a conjuror, producing a plum pudding from an empty saucepan and heating it up over a blazing fire in Clarkson Stanfield's hat ('without damage to the lining'), changing a box of bran into a live guinea-pig. Jane Carlyle, who was at the party and watched him exert himself until 'the perspiration was pouring down', thought that, although he seemed '*drunk*' with his efforts, he was 'the *best* conjuror' she had ever seen."

Charles Dickens was well launched on Christmas before the greeting cards, which subsequently so often reflected his sentiments and his characters, were under way. Indeed the date of the first publication of *A Christmas Carol* coincides with the production of the first Christmas card of all. It was designed by John Calcott Horsley (later a Royal Academician) on the initiative of Henry (later Sir Henry) Cole. It cost a shilling, sold about 1000 copies during that first Christmas of 1843, and came under attack on grounds of "encouraging drunkenness".

But the idea took. Some ten years after Dickens' death the Christmas card had proliferated to such an extent that *The Times* wrote of it: "Although the popular use of Christmas cards is no doubt condemned by stern philosophers of the unemotional school as so much worthless sentiment, it is not only . . . productive of considerable moral benefit, but it also works in operation a substantial good by the development of a new department of art."

Such was the Victorian blessing bestowed upon the entry of the card into big business. But the 'stern philo-

Topping out the Tree – Prince Albert's best-loved import

sophers' in the earliest Christian times were against anybody giving anybody anything. Present-giving, like the greenery, was a part of the Roman Saturnalia. The early Christian fathers frowned on its pagan origins and for some centuries Christians did not exchange gifts at the time of the winter solstice, though they had adopted its date for Christmas Day. Present-giving, which of course vanished with all Christmas customs under the Puritans, was well re-established before Victoria came to the throne. A German innovation which may well have stemmed from the influence of the Prince Consort was the Christmas stocking and all the fun of secrecy and concealment associated with present-giving.

That popular and, it now seems, almost deathless image of the stage coach laden with festive gifts was observed in real life by Washington Irving (1783–1859), the American writer, born of English parents, who contributed impressively to the build-up of the Victorian Christmas. "In the course of a December tour in Yorkshire, I rode a long distance in one of the public coaches, on the day preceding Christmas (he wrote); the coach was crowded both inside and out, with passengers, who, by their talk, seemed principally bound to the mansions of relations or friends, to eat the Christmas dinner. It was loaded also with hampers of game, and baskets and boxes of delicacies; and hares hung dangling their long ears about the coachman's box, presents from distant friends for the impending feast."

Irving's relish is a reminder that the feast really was a feast by long tradition – long before Tiny Tim rounded off *A Christmas Carol* by observing "God Bless Us Every One". Toward the end of the 18th century nearly 1000 Christmas turkeys arrived in London in a single day from the Norwich area, and this was but one source of supply. From the Middle Ages onward the royal, the noble and the wealthy favoured exotic birds such as roasted swans or peacocks at Christmas. The goose was for everybody. The turkey which arrived in this country in the 1540s only gradually took over the Christmas table and has never entirely superseded the goose. "In great houses," writes Laurence Whistler, in *The English Festivals*, "the main dish was the boar's head, once eaten in honour of the 'golden-bristled sun-boar', still garnished with rosemary and bays for the summer returning, and still with its mouth propped open on a solar apple or orange."

Christmas puddings first appeared about 1670 superseding an earlier dish of stiffened plum porridge. Mince pies were known to Shakespeare, and in the 16th century they contained mutton, tongue, chicken and egg as well as fruit and spice. A tradition we seem to have lost is that of Christmas pie. In 1770 Sir Henry Grey's housekeeper in the country made one for her master and sent it to him for his Christmas dinner in London. "It contained four geese, two turkeys, four wild ducks, two rabbits, two curlews, seven blackbirds, six pigeons, four partridges, six snipe, two woodcock, and two neats' tongues. The pastry was made with two bushels of flour and 20 pounds of butter."

The sense of togetherness, of all ages and all classes mingling for the feast, was a tradition which Dickens re-

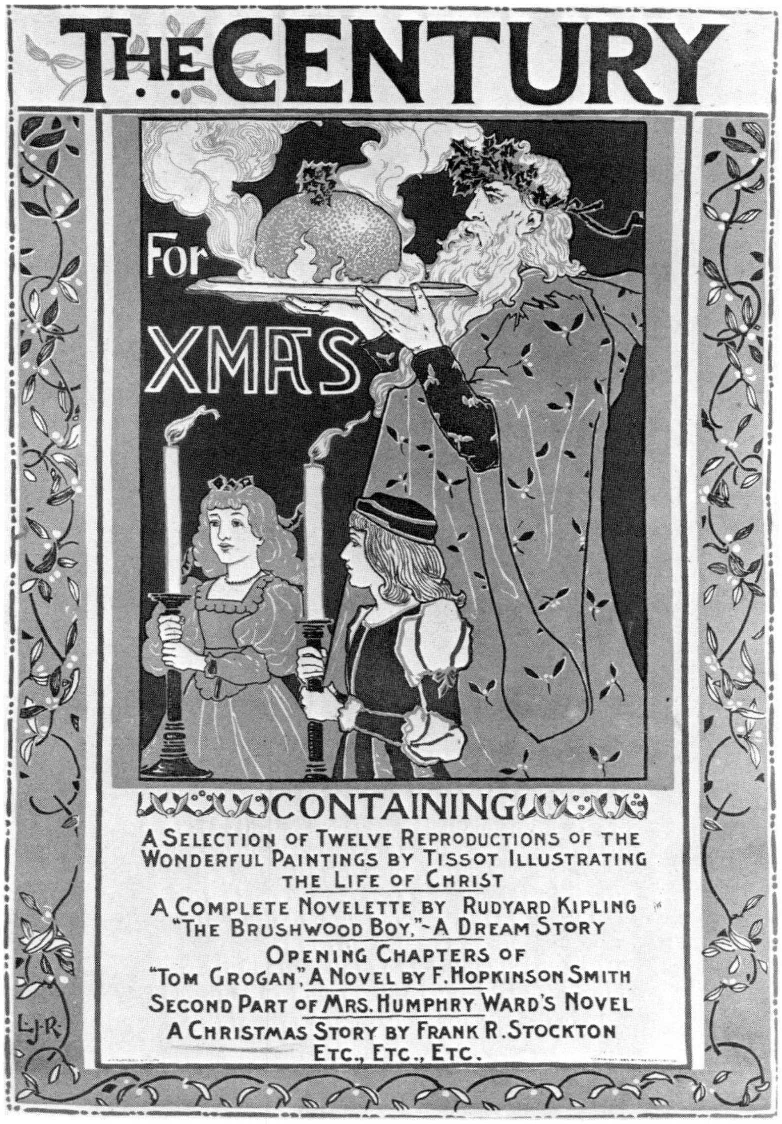
THE CENTURY
For
XMAS
CONTAINING
A Selection of Twelve Reproductions of the Wonderful Paintings by Tissot Illustrating the Life of Christ
A Complete Novelette by Rudyard Kipling "The Brushwood Boy."–A Dream Story
Opening Chapters of "Tom Grogan," A Novel by F. Hopkinson Smith
Second Part of Mrs. Humphry Ward's Novel
A Christmas Story by Frank R. Stockton
Etc., Etc., Etc.
L.J.R.
Seasonal reading – a magazine advertisement, 1895

focused in *A Christmas Carol*, and this is still the basis of our contemporary Christmas though we have improved it by opening it up with a wider sense of community. There is a feeling now that everyone should participate and the institutional Christmas is something we do very well. Television and radio, street decoration, community carol singing are manifestations of the universality of Christmas which would have delighted Dickens – and what a TV show he would have put up. On the debit side there is much hysteria, gross surfeit, vulgarity, waste and commercialisation. These are the elements that must be freely admitted.

There have always been just complaints about the feast of the winter solstice. Few have been more self-righteous than that of the Puritan Hezekiah Woodward in a tract in 1656. "The old Heathen's Feasting Day, in honour to Saturn their Idol-God, the Papist's Massing Day, the Profane Man's Ranting Day, the Superstitious Man's Idol Day, the Multitude's Idle Day, Satan's – that Adversary's Working Day, the True Christian Man's Fasting Day . . . We are persuaded, no one thing more hindereth the Gospel work all the year long, than doth the observation of that Idol Day once in a year, having so many days of cursed observation with it."

Modern extremists tend to be less vocal and indeed are more likely to take a pill during Christmas week and wake up when it is over.

Index

Page references in bold type refer to illustrations. Titles of books, plays, poems, songs, paintings and drawings, etc, are listed in italic. The names of ships are listed in quotation marks.

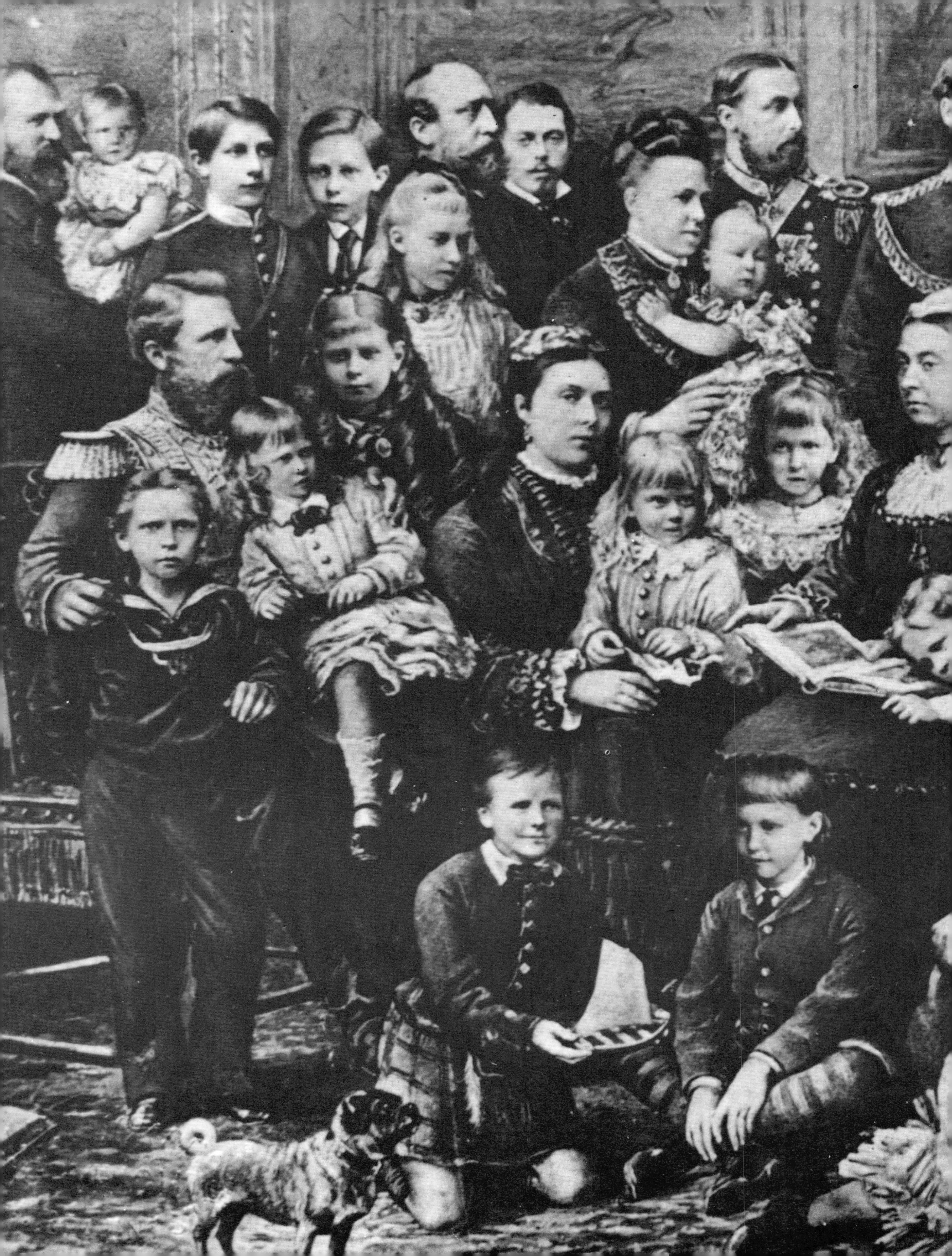